Scripting a New Gender Politic

Scripting a New Gender Politic

Telugu Women's Journals, 1883–1960

Shaik Mahaboob Basha

With a Foreword by

Mrinalini Sinha

Orient BlackSwan

SCRIPTING A NEW GENDER POLITIC: TELUGU WOMEN'S JOURNALS, 1883–1960

ORIENT BLACKSWAN PRIVATE LIMITED

Registered Office
3-6-752 Himayatnagar, Hyderabad 500 029 (Telangana), India
e-mail: centraloffice@orientblackswan.com

Other Offices
Bengaluru, Chennai, Guwahati, Hyderabad, Kolkata,
Mumbai, New Delhi, Noida, Patna

First published 2025

ISBN 978-93-5442-984-2

040842

Typeset in
Minion Pro 10.5/12.75
by Le Studio Graphique, Gurgaon 122 007

Printed in India at
Avantika Printers Private Limited, New Delhi 110 020

Published by
Orient Blackswan Private Limited
3-6-752, Himayatnagar, Hyderabad 500 029 (Telangana), India
e-mail: info@orientblackswan.com

Dedicated to the memory of Seema Tabassum,
my daughter

Contents

Tables and Images

Tables

Images

Abbreviations

AIWC	All India Women's Conference
AMMS	Andhra Mahila Mahasabha
ARMS	Andhra Rashtra Mahila Mahasabha
INC	Indian National Congress
IPC	Indian Penal Code
NCWI	National Council of Women in India
WIA	Women's Indian Association

Acknowledgments

This book is an outcome of my PhD thesis, submitted to the Jawaharlal Nehru University (JNU), New Delhi, in 2015. A number of people have helped me in giving shape to this project. It is with a profound sense of gratitude that I place on record their invaluable contributions. First and foremost, I shall forever be indebted to my teachers, Professor Indivar Kamtekar and Professor Mahalakshmi Ramakrishnan, who patiently guided me through the overwhelming ocean of historical research. Their affectionate and scholarly supervision and unrelenting support were unparalleled. They have been extraordinarily generous with me, often going beyond the call of duty and boosting my morale whenever I found myself questioning my abilities. But for their constant encouragement, neither my PhD, nor this book would ever have been possible. I count them among the blessings of my life.

I simply cannot express in words my deep sense of gratitude to Professor Mrinalini Sinha for writing the Foreword to the book: I deem it a great privilege. I am extremely thankful to Professor Vasudha Dalmia for her encouraging words as an examiner of my PhD thesis, and also for suggesting that I work with Orient BlackSwan for the publication of this book.

The teachers at the Centre for Historical Studies, JNU, have always been very supportive. I profusely thank all the teachers who taught me at the MA level. I take this opportunity to especially thank Professor K. N. Panikkar for introducing me to intellectual history and Professor Neeladri Bhattacharya for his wonderful encouragement. The suggestions of Dr Rakesh Batabyal and the late Dr Vishalakshi Menon proved very helpful. Special thanks are due to Professor Avijit Pathak, who taught me many beautiful things of life, apart from showing deep interest in my academic pursuits. I am greatly indebted to the late Professor P. Ramalakshmi *garu* of the Acharya Nagarjuna University, Guntur, Andhra Pradesh, for sparking my interest in the Telugu women's journals of the colonial period. A chance meeting with her at the Andhra Pradesh History Congress in 2001 at Osmania University, Hyderabad, changed the course of my research. From Gudipati Venkata Chalam, I permanently shifted focus to women's journals.

I visited a number of libraries to collect the materials used in this book. Among them are Sri Gautami Prantiya Granthalayamu, Rajahmundry; Saraswata Niketanam, Vetapalem; Andhra Pradesh State Archives and Research Institute, Hyderabad; Sri Krishnadevaraya Andhra Bhasha Nilayam, Hyderabad; Ram Mohan Library, Vijayawada; Sundaraiah Vignana Kendram, Hyderabad; C. P. Brown Library, Kadapa; Town Library, Kurnool; Anveshi Research Centre for Women, Hyderabad; Nehru Memorial Museum and Library, New Delhi; and the Tamil Nadu State Archives, Chennai. I thank the officers and all the staff members of these extraordinary libraries (some of these institutions are over 120 years old!) for allowing me to consult primary source materials. The archives of the Press Academy of Andhra Pradesh, unfortunately now shut, were especially useful in terms of cross-verifying information gathered from primary sources.

I am beholden to Professor Vakulabharanam Ramakrishna for his great love, affection and scholarly suggestions. His gentle approach really helped me overcome many of my personal problems and concentrate on academics. I thank the late Professor V. Lalitha for always being deeply interested in my research and encouraging me. I am particularly thankful to Dr B. R. Prasad Reddy and Sri Chinta Srinivasa Reddy for their keen interest in my academic work and consistently encouraging me to do better. From the bottom of my heart, I say my *salaams* to Sri Kopparthy Venkata Ramana Moorthy for patiently hearing many of my questions and offering his candid suggestions. Sri Ramineni Bhaskarendra Rao, a walking encyclopedia on the sources of modern Andhra history, helped me locate a number of sources. The word 'thanks' can scarcely do justice to his generous help. Discussions with Dr Vakulabharanam Rajagopal proved very fruitful in sharpening my ideas and for this I am deeply grateful. I thank Professor Inukonda Lakshmi for her constant encouragement and Dr Inukonda Thirumali for his comments and suggestions. Special thanks to Professor Shaik Mastan, Professor Rekha Pande, Professor K. S. S. Sheshan, Professor Mushtaq Ahmad Kaw, Professor S. M. Azizuddin Husain, Professor Deepak Kumar, Mr Rajen Habib Khwaja, Professor Perwez Nazir, Professor Danish Moin, Professor Farida Siddiqui, and Professor Chandni Bi *aapa* for showing deep interest in my academic as well as personal well-being.

I sincerely thank Professor Syed Ainul Hasan, Vice-Chancellor of Maulana Azad National Urdu University (MANUU), Hyderabad, and

Professor S. K. Ishtiaque Ahmed, Registrar of MANUU, for their help. I am very grateful to Professor Vishwanathappa, Professor Salma Ahmed Farooqui, Professor P. F. Rahaman and Professor Razaulla Khan, Director of the Centre for Distance and Online Education, MANUU, for their constant encouragement with my academic work. I am deeply grateful to Sri Ghattamaraju Ashwaththanarayana *garu* and Sri Bangaru Ramachari *garu* for encouraging me in numerous ways.

During my fieldwork in Rajahmundry, I gained two wonderful friends, the late Tadimalla Ravi Prakash, and Krishnamoorthy, whose help I fondly recall and register. I would like to thank my friends V. Samba Siva, Sheelam Subba Rao, Jan Nisar Moin, M. Jeevan, Pravin Donthi, Dusi Srinivas, Mohammad Mohsin, Fayaz Kotay, Vinod Singh and Puja Mishra for coming forward to help me whenever I needed it. Further, friends like Karim *bhai*, Reyaz *bhai*, Meer Abul Hussain, A. Subash, Mohd Aasim, Pervaiz Khanday, Sister Samana Zafar, Khursheed Ahmad Bhat, Khalid Ponmulathodi, Abdul Majid, Ikramul Haque, Daud Ibrahim and Mohd Haris have always been very supportive and I thank all of them.

I am very grateful to Nilanjana Majumdar and Roopa Sharma of Orient BlackSwan not only for their generosity but also for competently handling the publication of the book, and for taking personal interest in its timely and efficient publication. Words fail to express my gratitude to Sanna Jain, who edited the manuscript. She meticulously looked into all the details that go into the publication of a book; in fact, conversations with her during the entire process of editing proved to be a rich learning experience for me.

My heartfelt gratitude to our family friends for their constant support: Gaffar *bhai* and Rabbani *aapa*; Gurrappanna and Sujata *akka*; Hidayathulla *Hazrath* and Yasmeen *aapa*; Abdul Sattar Khan *Hazrath* and Naseem Athhar *aapa*; G. Srinivas and Nagamani *akka*; Venkatesanna, Rattaiah, and Ramachandra and their families; David Edwin *anna*; Bijendra Singh and Vishalakshi; Urmila *didi* and her family; Kamala aunty and Colonel Tarachand uncle; Elizabeth aunty and her family; Sitaiah uncle and Rama aunty.

But for the strength provided by my family members, I could not have completed this work. My younger brother, Dr Shaik Mahaboob Sharief, stood by me like a mountain and helped me rise up. I thank all the members of my sister Mahboob Chand's family. My parents, Shaik Mahaboob Saheb and Fatima Bibi, and my parents-in-law, Khaja Hussain and Noor Jahan, have been my perennial source of strength. My wife, Haseena—the spring of my life—sacrificed a lot to facilitate my academic pursuit. Without her unflinching support, this book would have remained a mere dream. The sweet smiles of my sons, Tipu and Moin, infused me with newfound enthusiasm. Last but not the least, I thank Khadar Basha *dadabhai*, my maternal uncle Khadar Mohiuddin, and Samad *mamu* for their wonderful encouragement. And, finally, I thank my *maatru bhoomi*—motherland—Porumamilla, in YSR Kadapa District, Andhra Pradesh, for the beautiful childhood memories, including of its rich library.

Foreword

I am pleased to have this opportunity to write a foreword for Shaik Mahaboob Basha's book. I served as an external examiner for Basha's doctoral thesis, which is the basis for this book; however, I can take no credit for it. That properly belongs to him and to his teachers and mentors. My pleasure is that of a scholar of modern India. I am indeed delighted that Basha's valuable research has seen the light of day and become readily available to scholars and readers.

It would be a truism to say that mainstream historical narratives of India, or for that matter of most parts of the world, have not yet caught up with women's contributions to history, especially those of ordinary women. Despite many advances over the years, there is still much more work to be done towards 'restoring women to history'.[1] One crucial arena of this struggle is the rearticulation of a still masculinist mainstream history. Another is to be found at the level of basic information. To be sure, the women's and gender historians, as well as other critical and feminist scholars today are concerned with a lot more than simply retrieving women from the past.[2] Yet their goal of transforming and producing new historical knowledge cannot be realised without basic information—more than what

[1]This was the subtitle for an ambitious publishing project by the Organization of American Historians (OAH), launched in the 1980s, to integrate women's history with the histories of different regions of the world. See *Restoring Women to History: Teaching Packets for Integrating Women's History into Courses on Africa, Asia, Latin America, the Caribbean, and the Middle East* (Bloomington, 1988).

[2]For a critique of an old-time women's history that was content largely with the work of recovering women, and an argument for a more ambitious agenda for feminist historiography, see Joan Scott, 'Gender: A Useful Category of Historical Analysis', *American Historical Review* 91 (5), 1986, pp. 1053–1075. In the Indian context, see Kumkum Sangari and Sudesh Vaid, 'Recasting Women: An Introduction', in Kumkum Sangari and Sudesh Vaid, ed., *Recasting Women: Essays in Colonial History* (New Delhi, 1989), pp. 1–26.

we currently have—about a group who make up at least half of the human population. There is still much critical work to be done through a focus on the ever-vexed but still necessary category of 'women'.[3]

As is also well known, English has never been—and will probably never be—the primary medium of communication for most women across India. That is why historical scholarship about women's writing and reading practices in the many regional and local languages of India is crucial. Basha's book does for nineteenth- and twentieth-century women's print culture in Telugu what others have done for Bangla, Hindi, Tamil, Urdu, Marathi, Oriya and English. The book, complete with appendices that provide detailed information about women's periodicals in the Andhra region and English translations of some important interventions by women authors, provides an invaluable resource for building feminist scholarship about India. To create a fuller picture of women in modern India we need precisely to learn more about the many linguistic communities of India. The book, which is based on an extraordinarily rich archival base of Telugu-language material, is part of a broader turn in the scholarship toward a broad-based recognition of the distinct regional histories of India.[4] The proliferation of scholarship on different regional and local language communities in India is needed to challenge unfounded pan-India generalisations based on a few limited studies.

The book's twin emphases on women's print culture and on a regional, linguistic community are especially apposite in relation to the many twists and turns in the historiography of social reform. The subject of social reform in colonial India, central to Basha's book, has long interested scholars of modern India. At one time, social reform was primarily associated with the modern, progressive ideas brought about because of colonial influence and with the initiatives for improvement undertaken largely by a handful of pioneering Indian men and their organisations. The heyday for social reform was acknowledged to be in the early nineteenth century and was thought to have peaked in the decades just preceding the advent of

---

[3] I have made this argument elsewhere; see 'Gendered Nationalism: From Women to Gender and Back Again?', in *Routledge Handbook of Gender in South Asia*, ed. Leela Fernandes (London, 2014), pp. 13–27.

[4] For the recognition that social reform developed distinct trajectories depending upon the customs and practices in the different regions concerned, see G. Arunima, *There Comes Papa: Colonialism and the Transformation of Matriliny in Kerala, Malabar, c. 1840–1950* (New Delhi, 2003).

anticolonial nationalism in the late nineteenth century.[5] By the 1980s and 1990s, many of these assumptions were being seriously reconsidered. This was in large part because of the work of feminist historiography which, along with the parallel historiographical interventions associated with subaltern studies, the early modernists and Dalit studies, was changing the face of Indian historiography.

The most remarkable contributions of feminist historiography were to challenge the binary opposition between tradition and modernity and to question the meaning of progress, especially when seen from the perspective of women of different classes, castes, regions and faiths. By so doing, this feminist scholarship not only challenged many of the assumptions of the earlier historiography about social reform, but also recognised that nineteenth-century social reform—especially as it came to be centred on the 'woman's question'—was in fact critical to the project of political nationalism. This was the context for Partha Chatterjee's influential reframing of the earlier consensus about the periodisation of social reform: the supposed disappearance of social reform from the late nineteenth century onwards with the advent of political nationalism. In his now famous argument about the 'nationalist resolution of the woman's question', which both built on and departed from the concerns that had motivated feminist historiography, he argued that social reform did not exactly disappear in the era of late-nineteenth century political nationalism. Rather, it came to be articulated in a different register: no longer as a subject to be debated with the colonial state in the effort to secure reform legislations, but as an internal community matter to be debated within the community according to the dictates of its own norms and interests.[6]

The subsequent mainstreaming of this revised paradigm for understanding the relationship between anticolonial nationalism and social reform has produced its own ambivalent outcomes. On the one hand, such a mainstreaming paved the way for a new and welcome gender-sensitive scholarship that recognised the 'woman's question' as crucial to—rather than as apart from—the contours of anticolonial political nationalism. But, on the other hand, it continued to marginalise or underestimate women as subjects in themselves—rather than mere ideological objects—of a reform

[5]For two classic studies of social reform that helped in setting up aspects of this paradigm, see S. Natarajan, *A Century of Social Reform in India* (Bombay, 1959); and Charles H. Heimsath, *Indian Nationalism and Hindu Social Reform* (Princeton, 1964).

[6]Partha Chatterjee, 'The Nationalist Resolution of the Women's Question', in Sangari and Vaid, ed., *Recasting Women*, pp. 233–253.

agenda still seen largely as the preserve of men.[7] By the same token, this expanded understanding of anticolonial nationalism absorbed the project of social reform exclusively within its own terms. Hence the conflict between colonialism and nationalism, more than conflicts around gender, caste, class, religion or region, became the dominant lens through which scholars perceived even the long history of social reform.

These blind spots provided fodder for critics who took up the challenge once again of recentring women as subjects in their own cause and of rescuing social reform from a fixation with the singular contradiction of colonialism versus nationalism. Their agenda has reanimated the study of social reform—that had all but disappeared into the folds of anticolonial nationalism—and given rise to different sets of questions. One is the making of the respective domains of the social and the political; another is the changing contours of their relationship.[8] These are some of the layers of the historiography of social reform that foster a new appreciation for the twin emphases of the book.

Scripting a New Gender Politic invites us to revise our understanding of the vitality of the social reform movement in India long past the period that, as per older assumptions, witnessed an eclipsing of social for political reform. His focus on women as subjects/agents of social reform does not demonstrate the shift away from the state and legislative intervention that had supposedly occurred by the late colonial period. As we know from other studies, women, through their writings, organisations and direct interventions, carried forward the torch of the social reform movement with incredible zeal and efficacy, not always biding the call to make social reform a matter of internal community reform.[9] The chronological span of Basha's study from 1883 to 1960, especially by extending into the early post-independence decades in India, also contributes to the effort to bring social reform out of the shadow of the anticolonial struggle. The wealth of material that Basha has uncovered from just one region—the Telugu-speaking areas of the erstwhile Madras Presidency—has provided an

[7] This is the burden of the critique in my book *Specters of Mother India: The Global Restructuring of an Empire* (Durham, 2006).

[8] For some examples, see Indrani Chatterjee, ed., *Unfamiliar Relations: Family and History in South Asia* (New Brunswick, 2004); Sinha, *Specters of Mother India*; and Rachel Sturman, *The Government of Social Life in Colonial India: Liberalism, Religious Law, and Women's Rights* (New York, 2012).

[9] For a review of some of this scholarship, see Sumit Sarkar and Tanika Sarkar, *Women and Social Reform in Modern India: A Reader*, 2 vols (Ranikhet, 2007–2008).

opportunity for engaging with the long history and historiography of social reform anew.

The implications of this study, moreover, point existing historiography in several new directions. One direction that emerges from the renewed focus on 'women's voices' is the possibility of exploring women as architects of robust political and intellectual visions of their own. By uncovering the extent and depth of women's engagement with the hot-button issues of social reform, such as child marriage, widow remarriage and domesticity, Basha refutes simplistic accounts of women as merely the victims or proponents of a 'new' or improved patriarchy. Here we see extensive debates among 'women intellectuals' that cover a range of positions on these topics: some opposed the 'reformist' contributions of a liberal patriarchy in defence of orthodoxy; others supported it; and still others, who constitute most of the voices examined here, challenged the contours of this patriarchy to make more radical demands for women. We thus see substantial arguments being made by women about such things as women's rights to their own sexuality; about the rights of women to an identity independent of that of their husbands; or about the right of women to be paid for housework. This is a far cry from the tendency in most scholarship to overemphasise either the constraints of the limited visions for women prescribed by men, or the self-constraints adopted by women who, it is too quickly assumed, failed to carve out an independent position for themselves. The grounds from which women articulated their positions on the various topics of reform provide another opportunity from which to re-examine arguments around tradition and modernity. Basha's book offers a glimpse of what it might mean to see these women as intellectuals in no small part because he tracks the arc of their thinking across a variety of archival sources: women's journals, autobiographies, fictions, private letters and visual sources. We begin to see here the outlines of a possible intellectual history of the reformist ideas of Telugu-speaking women intellectuals. There is still an ingrained tendency in scholarship to focus more on women's actions than on their ideas: a kind of reluctance, in effect, to recognise women as intellectuals and political thinkers.[10] An intellectual history of women's ideas about social reform waits to be written.

---

[10]For some efforts at giving women activists their due as intellectuals, see Mrinalini Sinha, 'Historically Speaking: Gender and Citizenship in Colonial India', in *The Question of Gender: Joan Scott's Critical Feminism*, ed. Judith Butler and Elizabeth Weeden (Bloomington, 2011), pp. 80–101; and Achyut Chetan, *Founding Mothers of the Indian Republic: Gender Politics of the Framing of the Constitution* (Cambridge, 2022).

Another direction that the book pushes towards is the possibility of studying the reach of social reforms beyond the exceptional and extraordinary at the levels of the everyday and the ordinary. Basha's pointed focus on the Telugu-speaking area already contributes to a widening and deepening of the scholarship on women and social reform beyond the hitherto 'advanced' regions in India. What Basha's work demonstrates is the vibrancy of the debate on the 'woman question' well beyond the regions that have typically dominated scholarship, thereby demonstrating the potential of similar studies for other regions. The book clearly establishes the wide reach of the debates on the woman's question and their impact. That reach is illustrated, for example, in the figures provided for widow remarriages performed in the Telugu speaking region, even in small towns and villages across India. This is a decidedly different picture of social reform than the typical top-down, and more metropolitan focus, of the changes that the movement is supposed to have wrought in the twentieth century. Indeed, we see in this work not just 'women intellectuals', but many an ordinary widow or her mother who took the risky initiative of saving herself or her daughter from the practices of enforced widowhood. The book reminds us how rare it remains to get fine-grained social histories of the multiple ways the woman's question was translated on the ground across different areas and communities in India.

The obstacles to writing such histories remain enormous, of which the limitations of the archives and the difficulty of working across several languages are the most obvious. One may enquire about the relative absence of Telugu-speaking women of different faiths beyond the largely Hindu women (albeit of different castes) who are encountered in the book. We can only speculate whether this reflects a silence in the archives or the fact of largely religiously segregated women's spaces in the Telugu-speaking region. The attempt to remove social reform from the preserve of only select areas and groups will always remain a challenging one. Yet, as is hinted in this book, the rewards for bringing such questions as widow remarriage to the level of the lived decisions of ordinary people are huge. They open a new frontier for the scholarship on women and social reform.

Mrinalini Sinha

Introduction

Dear readers of *Hindu Sundary*!... If we observe the development of the journal, we can confidently state that it will serve as a guide to our children much better... [than] it has so far done to us [*sic*]. In our Telugu country, we did not have journals where women published their writings. *Savithri* [another women's journal] was published from Kakinada for some time... but it extinguished. This *Sundary* also faced such problems, ceased for some time and, with the encouragement of sisters desiring education, restarted publication for the last six months... Though the journal has not yet matured enough, it has the [good] practice of publishing anything, if the writer happens to be a woman. Encouraged by this, the enthusiastic women are continuing writing and thereby becoming more educated. I and a few young women like me got habituated to writing because of this journal. Apart from this, this is the chief source of our happiness because, through this, we are getting to know the educated women located in different parts of Andhra. Therefore, let us be united to sustain this small baby.

Balantrapu Sheshamma[1]

Journals like 'our Grihalakshmi' contribute to women's development. You may ask, how? It is imparting to us knowledge in household management, cooking, child-rearing and gardening; improving the skills of poetry and logic; providing information on devotion, health and hygiene, handicrafts and music; giving us knowledge of the world and all such information essential to women. By this, it is making us strong with knowledge, opening our eyes, giving us self-esteem, improving our morality, and earning us fame. That is why I am saying that such writings help us

[1] Balantrapu Sheshamma, 'Ayikamatyamu' (Unity [among Women]), *Hindu Sundary*, January 1910, pp. 13–14. 'What a staff/supporting stick was to a blind man, the journal was to women', she declared.

progress. As the month begins, we eagerly await its arrival. Hardly would it have arrived, when women snatch it from one other's hands just the same way an eagle rushes down to catch its prey. This very fact establishes the popularity of writings in *Grihalakshmi* and its contribution. It houses the information useful to all—from children to the elderly.

Achanta Satyavatamma[2]

There is no doubt that welfare of a nation depends on noble women. It is highly appreciable that women not only produce children but also become their teachers and carefully nurture them. To do that, it is indispensable that women have noble ideals, broad-mindedness, and are skillful in the art of teaching.... However, it is rare that all mothers in [India] are educated. It can be said that, even if they wish, they may not get to receive education... Therefore, it is essential that such women are given education in an easy way in secular, moral, economic and political matters, to the extent desirable, by women themselves. Given the current conditions in the country, there is no other way other than the journals to properly achieve [the objective of educating women]. These journals provide us with the opportunity to simultaneously communicate the same thing to all women located in far-off places. Therefore, women alone have to assume charge as editors of journals and get educated women to contribute to them on various matters.... Journals alone are the chief sources, which easily communicate to the world of women the various matters useful in the journey of family life. It is no exaggeration to say that only the educated women are capable of discharging such duties.

Pasupuleti Lalita Devi[3]

---

[2] Achanta Satyavatamma, 'Abhyudayaniki Avasaramyna Rachana Vidhanam' (Writings Useful to the Progress [of Women]), *Grihalakshmi*, October 1938, p. 515.

[3] Pasupuleti Lalita Devi, 'Streelu Patrika Sampadakuluga Vunte...' (If Women are Editors of Journals...), *Grihalakshmi*, October 1938, pp. 510–511. The power of the women's journals in terms of offering what Himani Bannerji called 'a wide communicative space' to women was well recognised and appreciated by Andhra women intellectuals as far back as 1903. See Bannerji, 'Fashioning a Self: Educational Proposals for and by Women in Popular Magazines in Colonial Bengal', *Economic and Political Weekly* 26 (43), 1991, pp. WS50–WS62. Kotikalapudi Sitamma, one of the celebrated activist-intellectuals in colonial Andhra, termed *Hindu Sundary* an 'ambassador' (*dutika*) of women. The 'ambassador' brought even those women 'living in far off places' closer, and the exchange of ideas made possible with the 'help' of the *Hindu Sundary* gave them 'immense happiness'. Kotikalapudi Sitamma, 'Patrika Sahapathinulakoka Vignapanamu' (An Appeal to the Co-Readers of *Hindu Sundary*), *Hindu Sundary*, April 1903, pp. 4–5.

These epigraphs demonstrate many extraordinarily significant aspects of the relationship between women and print culture in colonial India/Andhra.[4] The first epigraph illustrates the transformative role print culture played in the lives of women. Print culture—in this context, women's journals—provided a space that was previously unavailable, where the educated women of Andhra could publish their writings and exchange ideas with other women and men. It was also a place where women experimented in the art of writing. And, surely, many of them became familiar with writing because of this space. What is equally significant is that these journals provided visibility to many educated women who, although distantly located, became aware of each other's existence. This knowledge about each other was not just a source of 'happiness', but also an important source of encouragement: Women intellectuals felt that they were not alone and there were in fact a number of other 'sisters' like them, who thought similarly and reflected on issues concerning women. This discovery was made possible by a burgeoning print culture that became available to the women of Andhra in the last two decades of the nineteenth century, bolstering the perception of an intellectual-activist community of women working for the common cause of women's development. Women clearly understood the multiple advantages that accrued to them from print culture and therefore they stressed on 'sustaining' women's journals. That was why Balantrapu Sheshamma invoked the image of a nurturing 'mother'[5] and appealed for them to together raise the 'small baby' called *Hindu Sundary*, the first women's journal in Telugu to be edited by

---

[4]Colonial Andhra consisted of the districts of Northern Circars, i.e., Ganjam, Visakhapatnam, Godavari, Krishna, Guntur and Nellore (coastal Andhra), and the Ceded Districts of Bellary, Cuddapah, Kurnool, Anantapur and Chittoor (Rayalaseema region). They formed a part of the erstwhile Madras Presidency. The area broadly corresponds to the state of Andhra Pradesh today. The districts of Ganjam and Bellary fall within Odisha and Karnataka, respectively.

[5]Along with the 'mother' image, women also invoked the image of mother-in-law. Appealing to the 'co-readers' of *Hindu Sundary*, Kotikalapudi Sitamma wrote that Sattiraju Sitaramaiah, the founder of the journal, gave it away as a 'daughter-in-law' to 'all of us women' and 'placed the entire burden of raising her on us'. Women were not to ill-treat 'her' as mothers-in-law normally would do. Instead, as per the saying, '*anna bidda kanna bidda samamannattu*' (the brother's daughter is like a woman's own daughter) they were to raise her 'with care and affection'. See Kotikalapudi Sitamma, 'Patrika Sahapathinulakoka Vignapanamu' (An Appeal to the Co-Readers of *Hindu Sundary*), *Hindu Sundary*, April 1903, pp. 4–10; for this reference, pp. 4–5.

women.[6] The fact that the journal, which had earlier ceased publication, was restarted by 'the encouragement' provided by 'sisters desiring education' speaks volumes of women's commitment to save and sustain the spaces that allowed them to 'break out of invisibility'[7] and build bonds of sisterhood among an emerging intellectual community.

Print brought before women a wide variety of information that they believed was useful to their 'development'. They were enthralled by this new medium that made women 'sound in knowledge' and 'opened their eyes'. The imagery used by Achanta Satyavatamma, of an eagle snatching its prey, aptly describes women's eagerness to 'consume' the contents of the print journal and their enthusiasm about its arrival. The journal also honed their ability to keenly observe and reflect on the larger world around them.

As the third epigraph suggests, women's journals were a crucial medium for educating women. The quote also demonstrates the journals' reach across wider audiences and great distances, and the simultaneous and easier communication of information and knowledge they facilitated. Further, it reminded women of their *agency*. As members of the community of women, it was not only their responsibility to educate their sisters; it was understood that *only they* could properly communicate with fellow women. The exhortation to work as editors and contributors implied that women understood their own requirements better, that they were better equipped to communicate with each other and that they must therefore take charge of social change. It also tells us about the bonding that was expected to exist between women editors of these journals, educated women and those women in need of education. Print culture had a significant positive impact on the lives of women in colonial Andhra and therefore they held it in high esteem.

Academic interest in print culture is of recent origin, barely over half a century old. In the European context, a number of scholars have studied the role print played in important social transformations. E. L. Eisenstein

---

[6]Kotikalapudi Sitamma emphasised that it was better that a particular race (in this case, the 'race of women') discussed its problems from within rather than these being pointed out by others. Women would not be so 'deeply hurt' if a woman, a member of 'our race', highlighted the demerits in women. But they were sure to be hurt if men, the 'other race', did the same. Therefore, she suggested, it was better that women made use of the space provided by *Hindu Sundary* to discuss and solve their problems. And the 'right time' for doing it came in the form of *Hindu Sundary*. Ibid., p. 6.

[7]I have borrowed the phrase from the title of a book: Aparna Basu and Anup Taneja, ed., *Breaking out of Invisibility: Women in Indian History* (New Delhi, 2002).

termed it as 'the unacknowledged revolution'.[8] Print brought 'uniformity' and 'standardisation' and played an extraordinary role in the 'diffusion of classical literature', aided in the 'propagation of Reformation ideas' and in spreading the message of Enlightenment. It also helped vernacular languages and encouraged the development of national literatures.[9] Print led to an expansion of the reading public as the number of books published increased manifold, which 'reached wider and wider audiences with increasing ease'.[10] L. Febvre and Jean-Henri Martin, however, cautioned against being overenthusiastic about the impact of printing. They would not like to term it a 'revolution'[11] and do not credit it as having caused the Reformation, for 'it was perhaps the case that a book on its own had never been sufficient to change anybody's mind'. However, print had the capacity 'to serve the interests of those who wished to influence thought and mould public opinion'.[12] Roger Chartier studied 'plurality' in terms of multiple appropriations of the printed material, that is, how the same books were differently read and used by different social groups, and contested the notion of the existence of 'pure and homogeneous cultures' in society.[13]

Print proved extraordinarily powerful in forging national, regional and community identities in India.[14] Scholars have recently begun to study the history of Indian print cultures and the complex roles they played in the social, cultural, and political definitions and redefinitions of colonial Indians' life-spaces. The print-public spheres that emerged in various parts of colonial India have been studied by several scholars, including Francesca

---

[8]Elizabeth L. Eisenstein, *The Printing Press as an Agent of Change: Communications and Cultural Transformations in Early-Modern Europe*, 2 vols (Cambridge, 1979).

[9]Ibid. See also L. Febvre and Jean-Henri Martin, *The Coming of the Book: The Impact of Printing, 1450–1900* (London, 1990 [1976]).

[10]Ibid., p. 252.

[11]Ibid., p. 9.

[12]Ibid.

[13]Roger Chartier, *The Cultural Uses of Print in Early Modern France* (Princeton, 1987).

[14]Benedict Anderson's brilliant study demonstrated the power of print in forging national identities in the context of Asia and Africa. See *Imagined Communities: Reflections on the Origin and Spread of Nationalism* (London, 1983). For the way print forged social identities in colonial Bengal, see Anindita Ghosh, *Power in Print: Popular Publishing and the Politics of Language and Culture in a Colonial Society, 1778–1905* (New Delhi, 2006).

Orsini,[15] Veena Naregal,[16] Anindita Ghosh[17] and A. R. Venkatachalapathy.[18] Recently, Indian historiography has moved away from its earlier focus on elite and male-centric print cultures towards a more inclusive perspective that pays attention to 'low' or 'insignificant' print cultures of the non-elite sections of society, including women's print cultures. This rigorous academic exercise has enabled recognition and appreciation of the 'other' universe in which print culture proliferated.

Against this background, this book adds to the existing body of literature on print cultures in colonial India. With a focus on women's print culture, particularly women's journals in Telugu that began publication during the colonial period, it enhances our understanding of women's engagement with the public sphere through the mediation of print. The study covers a period of about 80 years, covering both the colonial and post-independence periods. *Sathihitha Bodhini*, the first journal published for women in 1883, is taken as the starting point of the study. The year 1960 is taken as the closing year. However, it should be noted that some journals like *Grihalakshmi* and *Andhra Mahila* continued publication beyond 1960. The period of study helps us to identify and examine how women's collective consciousness evolved and the diverse issues they took up over time. Studying the first decade of post-independence India is significant because it enables an understanding of whether the concerns of women after independence remained consistent with issues raised in the colonial period, and to what extent.

Although women engaged with a wide range of themes during this period, I have confined my study to three critical issues of the social reform movement: (i) child marriage; (ii) widowhood and widow remarriage; and (iii) domesticity and women's education. Intellectual-activist groups from colonial Andhra felt that these were the most important issues of the day, meriting serious attention. Unless especially mentioned, all translations presented in the book are by me. As the focus is on recovering the voices of women, somewhat lengthy quotes from their writings and speeches became inevitable.

---

[15] Francesca Orsini, *The Hindi Public Sphere, 1920–1940: Language and Literature in the Age of Nationalism* (New Delhi, 2002).

[16] Veena Naregal, *Language Politics, Elites, and the Public Sphere: Western India under Colonialism* (Ranikhet, 2001).

[17] Ghosh, *Power in Print*.

[18] A. R. Venkatachalapathy, *The Province of the Book: Scholars, Scribes, and Scribblers in Colonial Tamilnadu* (Ranikhet, 2012).

The core argument of the book is that social reform did not decline in Andhra with the emergence of the national movement. Women marched ahead with the torch of social reform throughout the first half of the twentieth century. This book posits that women were active *agents* of sociocultural change. I term these women intellectuals *feminist* as they clearly understood their dismal conditions and the reasons behind them, criticised the various agents of their subordination (including religion) and worked for bettering their conditions. They refused to accept that they were 'inferior' to men and asserted their equal capacity in terms of physical and intellectual strength. At a later stage, they questioned male power and domination in all spheres of life and desired the establishment of a democratic relationship between women and men.

Women's Print Cultures in India: An Overview

A number of scholars have begun using women's journals as historical source material to explore various aspects of women's development in colonial India. Such work recognises that woman-centred sources are crucial for constructing historical discourses from their point of view. This welcome academic enterprise has thrown light on multiple ideas about and of women, resulting in a gendered understanding of modern Indian history. Studies of vernacular women's journals have ushered in a pan-India understanding of women's engagement with the public sphere, and further, the ways in which women's involvement has shaped and re-shaped the same. It is therefore necessary to revisit some of the existing scholarship on women's participation in Indian print cultures, both at the national and regional levels.

Sonal Shukla has studied *Stree Bodh*, the first ever women's journal published in colonial India.[19] Started in January 1857, the Gujarati monthly surprisingly survived for about a century. Meant specifically to supply leisure-time reading material to upper-middle– and middle-class urban Parsi women, but also read by Hindu and Muslim women, the journal encouraged an enlightened subordination of women to their anglicised husbands. Although it made a sincere effort to provide 'as much general knowledge' to women as possible by carrying lucid and well-illustrated

[19]Sonal Shukla, 'Cultivating Minds: 19th Century Gujarati Women's Journals', *Economic and Political Weekly* 26 (43), 1991, pp. WS63–WS66.

articles on topics ranging from scientific inventions, geographical regions and the animal world to important periods in history, the thrust of the journal remained on the transformation of women into efficient homemakers and enlightened companions to their husbands. It aimed at the production of a 'native' version of the idealised Victorian womanhood. Therefore, the journal extolled virtues such as honesty, hard work, thrift, softness, etc., and instructed women about various dos and don'ts to follow in their everyday family lives so as to keep their husbands happy and relaxed. Shukla's contention is that *Stree Bodh* could not really be called a journal for social reform—it clearly and carefully avoided discussing issues of ongoing reforms (such as the Age of Consent Act, 1891) because it wanted to keep women out of the public sphere and did not really want to empower them. However, the proliferation of patriarchal views under the guise of reform was questioned by women contributors like 'Aunt Kolli' from Navsari, Gujarat.[20] The journal, according to Aunt Kolli, unfairly blamed women for domestic turmoil and the 'unhappiness of men' in marital life. Despite such internal critique, limitations persisted. The journal had the motto, 'The greatness of the country depends upon the education the mothers receive'.[21] And the education it imparted to women abetted their subjection in sophisticated ways. Rather than empowering women, it empowered men by carefully tailoring women's desires, aspirations and conduct and by largely manufacturing women's consent to the male project of women's reform.

Beginning with *Balabodhini* (1874–1878), a number of women's journals were published in Hindi in the colonial period. Scholars like Vasudha Dalmia, Vir Bharat Talwar, Francesca Orsini, Kamlesh Mohan and Shobna Nijhawan have studied these journals, drawing attention to a large number of unsung heroines who contributed to the formation of the pre-independence Indian women's movement. The journals opened up a varied universe to women in colonial India.

Vasudha Dalmia has discussed the way the woman's question was addressed in Bharatendu Harishchandra's works across three different literary traditions—*Balabodhini*, the first women's journal in Hindi, *Chandravali*, a religio-erotic play, and *Kulin Kanya athva Chandraprabha aur Purnaprakash*, a novel advocating social reform.[22] Dalmia observed that *Balabodhini*, being a didactic journal, advocated a strict regimentation in

[20] Ibid., p. 66.

[21] Ibid., p. 63.

[22] See Chapter 11, 'Generic Questions: Bharatendu Harishchandra and Women's Issues' in her *Hindu Pasts: Women, Religion, Histories* (Ranikhet, 2015), pp. 251–285.

the spheres of activities of women and men—the private and the public. Even as the journal carried a few articles that rhetorically discussed the 'equality'[23] of women and men, which it claimed had once existed in ancient India, it established men's authority and women's subservience. The journal emphasised Victorian notions of domesticity and elaborated on 'desirable' and 'undesirable' behaviours of women. They were instructed on good wifely and motherly behaviour, and the husband was depicted as a god-like figure in their lives. Women were told to find their happiness in the happiness of their husbands. Articles in the journal closed off outside spaces such as fairs and markets to women. Even religious congregations of women on river banks were discouraged because such things, the journal threatened, led to 'shameless conduct'.[24] They were not to observe fasts, except those that ensured a longer life for their husbands, because in such situations the burden of domestic work would fall on mothers-in-law, which was not at all desirable. Women were not to visit their natal homes against the wishes of their husbands.

Dalmia observed that almost all the contributions to *Balabodhini* were by men. Therefore, they supplied only 'useful' material and there was no scope for women's entertainment. The editor of the journal and its contributors felt that it was enough to train women in the 'newly emerging middle-class social code'.[25] Significantly, 'this male editorship probably accounted for the extremely controlled, even censored, nature of the subject matter' offered by *Balabodhini*.[26] Just as Sonal Shukla observed in the case of *Stree Bodh*, the hotly-debated issues of social reform did not figure in the columns of *Balabodini* either (except for the issue of educating women in 'useful' matters), presumably because male patriarchs did not want women 'to participate in the debate'.[27]

While *Balabodhini* treated women as mute objects who should faithfully follow the sermons delivered by liberal patriarchs, two other works by Harishchandra, published in the same period, depicted women as having agency and an independent voice. Themes such as women's expressions of erotic love, and their questioning of the husbands and patriarchal barbarity, which were forbidden in the journal, found profound expression in these writings. As Dalmia notes, *Chandravali*, the play written

[23] Ibid., pp. 257–258.
[24] Ibid., p. 262.
[25] Ibid., p. 264.
[26] Ibid., p. 260.
[27] Ibid., p. 265.

in 1876, 'clearly refused' the binary of spheres and celebrated women's expression of *sringara*.[28] Its expression through the medium of religion granted it 'legitimacy'.[29] In *Kulin Kanya*,[30] 'a daring social reform novel' written in 1880,[31] women characters exhibited unconventional behaviour and attempted to 'topple patriarchy'.[32] The 'daring and impertinent' women in the novel 'mercilessly expose the wiles' of men and establish themselves as agentic figures. By highlighting such mutually opposing streams of thought—one oppressive and the other emancipatory—produced at the same time by the same author, Dalmia offers fresh historiographical insight on how such dissimilar and diametrically opposed views could coexist as they did in Harishchandra's writings across different mediums.

In his study of Hindi women's journals published during 1910–1920,[33] Vir Bharat Talwar locates the emergence of a 'feminist consciousness' in women's writings of the period, as reflected in women-edited journals such as the *Grihalakshmi* and *Stree Darpan*, and observes that some 'special features' of today's feminist movement can be traced back to the women's movement that developed across the Hindi belt in the World War I period.[34] This was a time when a number of women's organisations sprang up in different parts of colonial India, including the United Provinces. In the space provided by these journals, women discussed issues such as women's education, *purdah*, women's health, child marriage, the problems of widows and double standards vis-à-vis widow and widower remarriage, etc. Even though some feminists lambasted widowers for remarrying any number of times, they did not openly advocate widow remarriage, but proposed solutions such as establishing *ashrams* 'to keep the widows busy'.[35] The women's movement of the period, according to Talwar, drew inspiration from three sources: Indian history and the *Puranas*; the Western women's movement; and the Indian national movement. Notwithstanding the influence of the nationalist movement, Talwar maintains that Indian feminism has pre-Gandhian roots and women began their own movement through the space

[28] Sringara is the *rasa* denoting romantic and erotic love.

[29] Ibid., p. 274.

[30] It was authored by Mallika, Harishchandra's partner in literary enterprise, but appeared in his name.

[31] Ibid., p. 255.

[32] Ibid., p. 274.

[33] 'Feminist Consciousness in Women's Journals in Hindi, 1910–20', in Sangari and Vaid, ed., *Recasting Women*, pp. 204–232.

[34] Ibid., p. 206.

[35] Ibid., pp. 213–220.

provided by the women's journals and women's organisations. Thus, while the Gandhian movement did increase the public and political participation of women, it should be noted that since Gandhi himself was 'much less of a feminist',[36] feminists during this period had to be more cautious about the philosophical limitations of an otherwise 'magical' Gandhism. In other words, women created their own spaces and launched their own *feminist* movement.

Francesca Orsini has analysed the three most important Hindi women's journals—*Grihalakshmi*, *Stree Darpan* and *Chand*, all published from Allahabad.[37] They were important because they exemplified a 'shift in women's journals from a reformist to a radical-critical stage'.[38] Disagreeing elsewhere with Talwar's characterisation of Hindi women's journals as 'feminist',[39] Orsini suggests going beyond studying these journals in terms of women's political participation and the discourse of women's rights, to focus instead on 'the emotional and imaginative dimensions' and 'the redefinition of gender roles' demonstrated in them.[40] She considers the journals 'as an institution in their own right, which evolved in many unexpected directions'.[41] While discussing *Grihalakshmi*, the first Hindi women's journal to be edited by a woman, Orsini states that it encouraged role-based education for women, was almost entirely focused on the household, and pursued a reformist path firmly rooted in the image of the 'ideal' Hindu woman. Information about the 'outside world' was, therefore, very rarely found in its pages. Despite this limitation, the space provided by the journal helped women 'gain unprecedented confidence'[42] and a public voice. Orsini

---

[36] Ibid., p. 231.

[37] Francesa Orsini, 'Domesticity and Beyond: Hindi Women's Journals in the Early Twentieth Century', *South Asia Research* 19 (2), 1999, pp. 137–160.

[38] Ibid., p. 138.

[39] She writes: 'It is difficult, and in most cases misleading, to call these journals 'feminist', for... the strategies and idioms used in championing women's voices and issues differed explicitly from the confrontational attitude of suffragettes in Europe and America. Besides, as with education and literature for women, journals too were primarily meant to instruct girls on their roles within the household and only gradually widened their concerns. In the process, the boundaries of what was "useful for women" (*Stri-upyogi*) were dramatically redefined.' Orsini, *The Hindi Public Sphere, 1920–1940*, pp. 260–261.

[40] Orsini, 'Domesticity and Beyond', *South Asia Research*, p. 139.

[41] Ibid.

[42] Ibid., p. 142.

sees 'great strategic value'[43] in the journal's emphasis on domesticity at the core of women's *dharma* because the emphasis on women's ideals and duties provided a strong base to speak in favour of women's worth. However, at a later stage in its circulation, *Grihalakshmi* moved beyond the boundaries of domesticity and included new discourses about gender identity.

Stree Darpan, 'the most recognisably feminist of Hindi women's journals',[44] was founded by Rameshwari Nehru, who remained its editor from 1909 to 1924. It 'went a big step further' and functioned as a vehicle of social and cultural criticism and spread political and rights consciousness among middle-class women. Unlike *Grihalakshmi*, its canvas covered wide-ranging issues and carried articles against role-based education. It was novel in terms of its 'combativeness' and advocacy of women's rights and gender equality. By the end of the 1920s, like many other Indian-language women's journals in colonial India, *Stree Darpan* acquired a sharp 'nationalist' edge, and simultaneously grew bolder on the home front as well, posing many uncomfortable questions to liberal patriarchs and patriarchal orthodoxy alike. Kamlesh Mohan too concurs that the journal gave visibility and voice to the 'mute group'—women—and fashioned their minds and images.[45] A 'social-action journal', it functioned with the twin goals of making women suitable wives of their husbands and fighters for gender justice and Indian independence. The burgeoning women's movement, national movement, economic independence, and political rights of women were discussed in later volumes of the journal.

The issue of women's education was treated seriously. While what constituted 'suitable education' for women was initially a matter of much debate, the need for an education that would foster independence emerged at a later stage among a section of radical women. Some, like Bhagyawati, condemned purdah as the 'inveterate enemy' of women's health and education. One interesting aspect of *Stree Darpan* is that it accommodated mutually opposing views on women's issues, particularly the highly contentious issue of widow remarriage, and thus became 'a forum for creative dialogue'. On this particular question, the journal itself maintained an ambivalent position. However, there were a number of radically questioning women who stridently criticised the social sanction accorded to widowers' remarriage and the discrimination against widow remarriage.

---

[43] Ibid., p. 143.

[44] Ibid., p. 145.

[45] See Chapter 3, Kamlesh Mohan, *Towards Gender History: Images, Identities and Roles of North Indian Women with special reference to Panjab* (Delhi, 2007), pp. 106–147.

The acute sense of devaluation of women, including widows, was expressed by women intellectuals using emphatic phrasing: Hukma Devi's article in March 1918, for example, was titled 'Ardhangini Ya Paon Ki Jooti', (The Better Half, or Slippers under the [Husband's] Feet?). While Rameshwari Nehru was cautious in attacking men's prejudices, Uma Nehru, who held 'ultra-progressive views', ruthlessly attacked men's hypocrisy and selfish mentality, as well as the patriarchal glorification of women's beauty as a hallmark of femininity, in articles like 'Hamare Samajik Dhaanche', 'Hamari Soortein', etc.

Stree Darpan mobilised a number of women into the women's and the nationalist movements. It played a significant role in developing a positive self-concept among north Indian middle-class women, who developed a new sense of self-worth, self-respect and pride in their identity as women. The columns of the journal are witness to the fact that the process of reformulation of ideas touched even 'ordinary' housewives with very little education. Despite limitations such as the inability of contributors and the editor to break away from tradition, their failure to recognise the 'heterogeneity of women's oppression', and the omission of Muslim women's issues, the journal is significant for it provided a space for women intellectual-activists in colonial north India.

Another journal, *Chand*, brought women's journals closer to the 'mainstream' Hindi press. It broke the mould of *stri-upyogi* literature by pushing the boundaries of social criticism and locating the woman's question at the heart of the nationalist project. This journal extended the boundaries of 'what women should know' and 'what women should say'. The long and topical editorials, infused with a strong sense of mission, posed a powerful challenge to various strands of orthodoxy and firmly advocated gender equality. By housing a variety of information—local, national, and international; political, social, economic and cultural—and with a thrust on women's activities across the globe, *Chand* provided a wider political education to women, fostered civic and political consciousness and stimulated a critical attitude. Breaking the boundaries of 'what women should say', it allowed the whole range of women's experiences to flow into the public sphere. With *Chand*'s intervention, women's consciousness about their rights radically changed and the 'emotional' aspects of women received greater focus. The deployment of the idiom of 'service' (*seva*) provided respectability to women's engagement with the public sphere.

Hindi women's journals such as *Stree Darpan* and *Chand* enabled women to question dominant definitions of gender identity and redefine gender roles. They 'widened' women's concerns and established them as political subjects. 'This process of expansion and radical criticism produced a redefinition of women's roles both within the family and household and in the public domain', writes Orsini.[46] However, in tracing their later trajectories, she concludes that the mainstream women's journals in post-independent India lost the 'radical' edge.[47]

Shobna Nijhawan's book-length study examines women's and girls' periodicals in Hindi that were edited by women, such as *Stree Darpan*, *Grihalakshmi*, *Arya Mahila*, *Chand*, *Kumari Darpan* and *Kanya Manoranjan*.[48] The book discusses the format and structure of the periodicals as a 'genre' and the various themes dealt within, and also provides a refreshing set of full-text translations for representative writings published in these journals. Nijhawan analysed the many roles that the journals played in north Indian women's lives. They served as 'disseminators of ideologies' pertaining to women's roles in public and private, forged bonds among a 'newly imagined yet heterogeneous' community of women, helped create a network of female activists and, most importantly, helped women gain access to the public space. She defines these journals as 'social feminist documents' that put the nation first and women's interest second.[49] Unlike Orsini, she rightly describes the contributors to the women's periodicals as 'feminist'.[50] She demonstrates, like Talwar, that Indian feminism had 'pre-Gandhian roots'. By discussing supposedly private matters in the public, women's journals and their female contributors broke the binary between the two so-called separate spaces. Thus, Nijhawan's study clearly negates the thesis of the separation between the inner and outer domains that was proposed by Partha Chatterjee. The journals, according to Nijhawan, not

[46] Orsini, 'Domesticity and Beyond', *South Asia Research*, p. 159.

[47] Ibid., p. 160.

[48] Shobna Nijhawan, *Women and Girls in the Hindi Public Sphere: Periodical Literature in Colonial North India* (New Delhi, 2012).

[49] Ibid., p. 14.

[50] The journals developed among women 'a feeling of self-worth, a process that can be labeled "feminist" to the extent that it was couched in an overall perception of women as political subjects', Nijhawan remarked. She rightly argues that 'the refusal to adopt western feminist concepts from movements for equality and enfranchisement did not make the periodicals less feminist than their western counterparts. The writers, male and female, exhibited a deep understanding of women's subjugation and articulated their opinions in women's periodicals. They investigated the causes for women's oppression and sought answers on how to remediate social ills. Women's periodicals are thus excellent sources to display this feminist consciousness in the Hindi vernacular.' Ibid., pp. 13–15.

only redefined the meaning of politics but also 'contested the "successive" approach of the Indian National Congress (INC), arguing that social reform… was a precondition for political independence, not a logical consequence thereof'.[51]

It is this network of female activists created by women's journals, in combination with women's organisations, that facilitated the large-scale participation of north Indian women in the freedom movement. Women's journals such as *Stree Darpan* 'resolved the tension between self-sacrifice and self-interest by addressing nationalist *and* feminist issues simultaneously'.[52] Nijhawan's argument that women's periodicals in Hindi not only 'initiated' the women's movement but also kept the woman's question alive during the heyday of the Indian national movement is well corroborated. The intention of her work 'to further open the field to scholarship on periodicals on an all-India basis out of which there might emerge an even larger, supra-regional study of *Indian* women's periodicals'[53] must be taken very seriously, and I hope that my work adds to the larger 'supra-regional' picture of Indian women's periodicals in the colonial period.

Gail Minault studied three Urdu women's journals—*Tahzib un-Niswan* (1898–1950s), *Khatun* (1904–1914) and *Ismat* (founded in 1908), published from Lahore, Aligarh and Delhi, respectively.[54] While the first was a weekly, the other two were monthlies. All three were started by men. Sayyid Mumtaz Ali and Shaikh Abdullah, the founders of the first two journals, were actively assisted by their wives, Muhammadi Begam and Waheed Jahan Begam, respectively, in editing the journals. Issues such as women's education, domestic management, personal conduct of women with other members in the family and reforming popular customs were discussed in the columns of *Tahzib un-Niswan*. Further, the journal advocated women's rights from the point of view of Islam. By the end of the second decade of the twentieth century, political issues like non-cooperation and the *swadeshi* movement started appearing in its pages. A number of younger Muslim women writers used its space to criticise practices like purdah, polygamy and unilateral divorce. Thus, *Tahzib un-Niswan* helped 'reorient' the thought process of Muslim women to a larger extent. *Khatun* concentrated primarily on the promotion of women's education and advocated the establishment of girls'

[51] Ibid., p. 19.

[52] Ibid., 44.

[53] Ibid., p. 18.

[54] Gail Minault, 'Urdu Women's Magazines in the Early Twentieth Century', *Manushi*, no. 48, (September–October) 1988, pp. 2–9.

schools and, therefore, 'provides important documentation for the history of Muslim women's education'.[55] *Ismat* was founded by Rashidul Khairi to encourage 'creative writing' by women and, therefore, it consciously avoided political discussions. In the early days of its print run, there was no discussion of women's rights in Islam. Its didactic contents informed women about the ways of keeping their husbands happy and turning the home into a haven. The traditional attitude of the journal, unsurprisingly, was criticised by a few contemporary Muslim women intellectuals.

Despite the fact that there were certain differences among these journals in terms of the treatment of women's issues, all three, by and large, agreed on the question of women's role and place in society. They championed women's education and 'defined greater enlightenment for women in terms of competent domesticity rather than individual autonomy'.[56] What is remarkable about these journals, however, is that they provided space for women to air their views and register their voices. Minault rightly contends that in terms of Muslim women's development, 'examined in their historical context... these women's magazines were brave pioneers, expanding the frontiers of women's roles and consciousness at a time when those frontiers were severely limited'.[57]

Mytheli Sreenivas, drawing on Francesca Orsini's periodisation of Hindi women's journals, has categorised Tamil women's journals—some edited by women, and others by men—in two phases.[58] In the first phase, from the 1890s to the year 1920, Sreenivas observed that journals aimed at training women to become 'efficient and capable wives and mothers'. Women were expected to become companionate wives, sharing in their husband's emotional life. Thus, they were trained in what Sreenivas termed 'appropriate domesticity'.[59] In this phase, the focus of the journals was on reforming women, rather than the social conditions that caused the subordinate situation of women—the journals did not make 'marriage itself

[55] Ibid., p. 5.

[56] Ibid., p. 9.

[57] Ibid., p. 2.

[58] See Chapter 4 in Mytheli Sreenivas, 'Marrying for Love: Emotion and Desire in Women's Print Culture' in her *Wives, Widows and Concubines: The Conjugal Family Ideal in Colonial India* (New Delhi, 2009), pp. 94–119. Apart from the journals published in Tamil, she examined two journals—*Indian Ladies Magazine* and *Stri Dharma*—published in English.

[59] Ibid., p. 98.

an object of reform'.[60] Family and conjugality were treated as 'private' affairs that could not be publicly scrutinised and questioned.

In the second phase that began in 1920—the 'radical-critical phase'—though the model of 'appropriate domesticity' continued to find a place in the journals, the focus was on reforming oppressive socio-economic practices rather than women. Sreenivas remarked that this 'new focus... emerged around the question of dowry'. The journals represented dowry 'as the quintessence of an inappropriate commercialisation of family relationships'.[61] They emphasised that, in marriage, except the 'emotional bond' between the couple, nothing else should matter. Some of the authors invoked the 'emotional paradigm of marriage in order to challenge women's subordination in family and society'.[62] According to them, gender equality was a precondition for a conjugal/emotional companionship.

Sreenivas studied *Matar Marumanam*, a journal that took a radically critical stand on gender relations, making the institution of marriage, particularly widow remarriage, central to its critical engagement with society. At first glance, the journal appeared to present widows as passive objects of reform through the contradictory visual representations it featured. In reality, as Sreenivas demonstrated, the writings within the journal established widows as 'desiring subjects' and agents of social change. Through the use of 'affective terminologies' such as *kathal* (romantic love), *inpam* (joy or pleasure, including sensual pleasure) and *anpu* (affection/bond between husband and wife), the journal explored the 'interior emotional aspects' of women in general and widows in particular. These writings portrayed the 'emotional' experiences and desires of widows, treating this inner self as the real self of widows. Pushing the inner desires of widows to the exterior of public debate necessarily challenged the social conventions of widowhood which mandated against its expression. 'By validating a widow's desire, the narratives in *Matar Marumanam* complicate the portrayal of widows as passive objects of reform.'[63]

Michelle Elizabeth Tusan has analysed mainly the English section of the *Stri Dharma*,[64] a multilingual monthly journal (published in English,

---

[60] Ibid., p. 101.

[61] Ibid., p. 102.

[62] Ibid.

[63] Ibid., p. 116.

[64] Michelle Elizabeth Tusan, 'Writing *Stri Dharma*: International Feminism, Nationalist Politics, and Women's Press Advocacy in Late Colonial India', *Women's History Review* 12 (4), 2003, pp. 623–649.

Tamil, Telugu and later Hindi) of the Women's Indian Association (WIA). Unlike other scholars who studied *Stri Dharma* 'either as the propaganda arm of the WIA or a tool of feminist imperialist ambition', Tusan examined it as an 'advocacy medium' for and by women. She observed that

> unlike British women's advocacy journals of the late nineteenth century... *Stri Dharma* did not appropriate 'the cause' of Indian women to bolster the British feminist imperial project. Rather, the journal criticised and debated colonialism as a source of women's oppression.[65]

Thus, *Stri Dharma* combined both feminism and nationalism in its pages: Indian women associated with it stuck to feminist ideals, necessitating collaboration with the colonial state by pushing for legislative reform; but at the same time, they popularised the cause of nationalism, which required criticising and confronting colonialism. Contesting Partha Chatterjee's thesis about the relationship between social reform and Indian nationalism, Tusan argues that

> *Stri Dharma*'s strong legislative reform agenda suggested that liberal feminist ideology helped inform women's participation in the nationalist project and thus complicated Chatterjee's analysis that the women question had been 'resolved' wholly from within an early nationalist model that posited a passive female subject'.[66]

Tusan examined *Stri Dharma*'s feminist-nationalist role during the Salt Satyagraha of 1930 to establish how nationalism could be 'enlisted in the service of feminism in order to challenge traditional gendered hierarchies'.[67] The nationalism of Indian feminists associated with the journal was clear from the fact that despite collaborating with Western women such as Margaret Cousins, they 'incorporated only select elements of the liberalism advocated by international feminists' and rejected 'those ideas outside of the dominant nationalist discourse'.[68] Further, they drew inspiration from India's past in their search for solutions to urgent problems faced by Indian women, and many, like Sarojini Naidu, emphasised that the Indian women's movement would be led by Indian women alone, not by foreigners, even as the latter were welcome to make 'special contributions'.[69] The addition of a Hindi-language section in the journal and its advocacy of Hindi as

---

[65] Ibid., p. 624.
[66] Ibid., p. 635.
[67] Ibid., p. 636.
[68] Ibid.
[69] Ibid., p. 631.

the future language of bonding in the independent nation is seen by Tusan as proof of the journal's commitment to Indian nationalism.[70] With these and other examples, she concluded that 'rather than subsume the feminist movement, as Chatterjee has claimed, nationalism provided a vehicle for the brief manifestation of a woman-directed nationalist reform agenda spearheaded by interwar Indian feminists'.[71]

A considerable number of works have addressed the articulation of the 'woman's question' in the colonial period in India. Geraldine Forbes' *Women in Modern India* is a vital account of the women's movement, largely focusing on the colonial period.[72] The book charts the journey of Indian women's movement in both colonial and independent India. Beginning with the period of nineteenth-century social reform, the book analyses the educational project proposed for women and the emergence of women educators; the creation of national women's organisations that established women as *actors* with organisational capabilities; and the movements undertaken by women for asserting their civil and political rights, which demonstrate their potential of mobilising and lobbying to ameliorate their conditions. She discusses their involvement in the nationalist movement by citing a multiplicity of experiences (both positive and negative), their participation and contribution to the workforce, their involvement in diverse movements that coincided with a shift from their earlier ideology of 'social feminism'[73] to more 'radical ideologies' as well as their position in independent India.

The significance of the book lies in the innovative use of a number of non-conventional sources such as women's magazines, diaries and letters, songs, pamphlets, literature and photographs. This has allowed Forbes to go beyond the 'elite' women—though they still occupy a major part of the book—in presenting the story of the Indian women's movement in modern India. That the author herself was involved in the project of 'uncovering' a variety of historical source materials produced by women added to the richness of the narrative. The book successfully dispels both colonialist and nationalist 'essentialist' histories of Indian women where they were presented

[70] Ibid., p. 633.

[71] Ibid., p. 642.

[72] Geraldine Forbes, *Women in Modern India* (New Delhi, 1998).

[73] Forbes wrote: 'The women involved in the women's movement justified their new roles within the ideology of social feminism, that is, they tied their arguments about women's rights to women's obligation to perform traditional roles and serve the needs of the family.' Ibid., p. 7.

as mute objects and as being very 'low' or 'high' in status. The book presents women as *actors* in modern Indian history, both shaping and being shaped by it. More significantly, the reader witnesses the history of Indian women through their own eyes and voices; in other words, the book privileges women's 'own accounts'. With solid and irrefutable examples, Forbes has demonstrated that Indian women were already present in public life well before Gandhi entered the picture, and that 'if the [male] nationalists solved the woman's question, it was in terms of their own discourse; the women's discourse about women's problems was alive and well'.[74]

Padma Anagol's *The Emergence of Feminism in India, 1850–1920* tells us the story of the genesis and growth of feminism in India by focusing on Maharashtrian women.[75] She made use of a number of primary source materials, including women's journals edited by the '*kartris* or "women-editors"',[76] thereby 'tracing the development of feminist consciousness before the rise of Gandhi and mass nationalism'.[77] Anagol uncovered 'a long but hidden tradition of feminist thought and politics' of late nineteenth and early twentieth-century Maharashtrian women, whose 'advances and achievements… were lost by the peculiar alignments made between feminism and nationalism during the 1930s and 1940s'.[78] With this, she tells us that 'historical processes could not always be studied as unilinear trajectories. The search for continuities from the colonial past to the present in the case of women's history could prove a futile one'.[79] Shifting women to the centre, Anagol presents them as agents and feminist activist-intellectuals who confronted various structures and institutions of patriarchy, though they did not always succeed in thoroughly subverting them. She has no reservations in terming the late nineteenth- and early twentieth-century Indian women intellectuals as 'feminists' and defines 'Indian feminism' as 'a theory and practice based on presenting a challenge to the subordination of women in society and attempting to redress the balance of power between the sexes'.[80] With this, she urges scholars to stop seeing Indian women from the lens of Western women's history, which

[74] Ibid., p. 7.

[75] Padma Anagol, *The Emergence of Feminism in India, 1850–1920* (Ashgate, England, 2005).

[76] Ibid., p. 72.

[77] Ibid., p. 13.

[78] Ibid., pp. 219–220.

[79] Ibid.

[80] Ibid., p. 13.

skews our vision. Through an interwoven story composed of women's thoughts, words and deeds, Anagol establishes them as *agents* in history, rather than silent spectators to important developments. They had views which they aired; they spoke their minds, acted on the field and shaped their destinies. Thus, methodologically, Anagol moved beyond established historiographical traditions, forcing scholars to rethink our assumptions.

Women-edited journals were an important primary source for Anagol. She identified 10 Marathi journals which 'allowed for the development of the notion of *bhaginivarg* [sisterhood] within the larger women's collective'. The journals provided a space to women to reflect on a range of issues. However, not all were in favour of reform; such ideas were opposed by many traditional and conservative women. Much like other scholars of print culture, Anagol observed that there was a difference in the nature of journals edited by men and by women. While the former were 'didactic' and 'usually intolerant of discussion and dialogue', the latter, that is, 'the journals produced by women for women created an environment that allowed them to express their views unmediated by men who retained control over many other aspects of their lives'.[81] The observations she made in the context of Marathi women's journals are particularly helpful in gaining a perspective while examining women's journals in Telugu. With a fresh methodology and unconventional woman-centred primary source materials, Anagol's book shattered the image of the passive Indian woman waiting to be saved by external agents, whether Indian men or British colonialism, and argued for a fresh approach to historiography with a focus on women's consciousness, agency and active involvement in sociocultural reform, shaping their own destiny and that of society and nation.

In an influential article, Partha Chatterjee has discussed how Indian nationalists resolved the woman's question.[82] Indian nationalism was as much a cultural movement as it was political. According to him, nationalist ideology was premised on a separation between the material and the spiritual, which were represented by the British and Indians, respectively. These domains corresponded with the 'outer' and the 'inner'. Women were assigned the task of safeguarding the spiritual sovereignty of the 'inner' and ensuring the true identity of India. Nationalist men strongly felt that while they could make some compromises with colonialism with regard to the 'outer' domain, no compromise could be made with regard to the 'inner'.

---

[81] Ibid., pp. 72–73.

[82] Partha Chatterjee, 'The Nationalist Resolution of the Women's Question', in Sangari and Vaid, ed., *Recasting Women*, pp. 232–253.

Thus, the domains of operation of women and men were clearly defined and corresponded with the inner/outer dichotomy.

However, given the conditions of colonialism, it was impossible to keep the 'home'/ women from outside influence and 'serious threat' of Westernisation. Therefore, certain concessions had to be made to grant limited 'freedoms' to women—to receive education and go out into the public—so long as this 'freedom' did not threaten and jeopardise the 'spiritual essence and sovereignty' of India, which women were seen to embody. Indian women were not to imitate the Western women. This resulted in the creation of a 'new patriarchy' and a 'new woman', the latter completely subordinated within the former. Rather than being constantly regulated by male authority figures, women were required to willingly recognise the significance of this newly *granted* freedom; the educational project suggested for women aimed to promote acceptance of this social order. This 'new woman', in Chatterjee's reading, was to mark her difference from three segments of women: the Western woman, the traditional purdah-bound Indian woman and the 'coarse' common woman of the lower class/caste groups. Male nationalists deployed both coercion and persuasion to accomplish this task. Thus, controlling women—and their domains of operation—was an essential characteristic of the Bengali masculinist, nationalist project. This control over women 'compensated' for men's loss of power in the 'outer' domain. In this way, nationalist men resolved the woman's question according to their 'own agenda and preferred goals'. Despite its influential status as an important historiographical intervention, Chatterjee's position has been critiqued for its simplistic understanding of the problem and the 'resolution'. His analysis may hold true for the Bengal context; however, as we shall see, it definitely does not apply in the Andhra region.

Judith Walsh has studied the various changes that occurred in nineteenth-century Indian domesticity owing to the influence of English colonial culture. Focusing on Bengali domestic manuals written for women during 1860–1900, she analysed how the force of colonial modernity was contested and negotiated by English-educated and reform-minded men in nineteenth-century Calcutta specifically, and Bengal as a whole.[83] Contextualising the production of Bengali domestic manuals in the discourse of nineteenth century 'global domesticity', she said that they were all 'hybrid' in nature. She focused on 'the politicisation of daily and domestic life combined with the changing structures of life in British India to prompt

[83] Judith E. Walsh, *Domesticity in Colonial India: What Women Learned When Men Gave Them Advice* (New Delhi, 2004).

Indian men and women to rewrite an older patriarchy and to write new homes, families and national identities as well'.[84] Male reformers felt that Indian domestic life indicated its low civilisational status and, therefore, needed corrections. Reforming the domestic life of middle-class Indians and adjusting it to the changing demands of British rule was at the heart of the social reform project initiated by Indian men. In a way, social reform manifested as reforming the relationship between husband and wife and the conditions of their domestic life.

Walsh observed that during this period, everything had to move from the unconscious and casual to conscious and careful. Bengali domestic manuals advised women on a range of issues—how to sweep the floor, mend socks, arrange the kitchen, maintain proper conduct with husband and other elders of the home, etc. Walsh emphasised that the manuals attempted to remove young wives from the grips of 'old patriarchy', which mandated them to be illiterate as well as subservient to all in the family, especially the mother-in-law and older women. Though domestic manuals implanted a 'new patriarchy' with the husband assuming the central place in a woman's life, they did acquire some freedom—freedom to receive education, a newfound closeness with their husbands as companionate wives and leeway to attend public gatherings along with their 'modern' husbands.

Drawing from primary source materials including women's journals, autobiographies, biographies and didactic manuals, Meredith Borthwick has studied the gradual emergence of the *bhadramahila*, the 'mothers, wives and daughters' of the Bengali *bhadralok*, from the secluded space of purdah to a wider domain between 1849 and 1905. [85] The period is marked by heightened reformist activities, particularly for the education of women and marriage reform. Influenced by British culture and affected by the stressful economic circumstances under colonial rule, the Bengali bhadralok—a set of English-educated professional classes who worked in colonial offices as lawyers, teachers, doctors, etc.—undertook the project of reforming the conditions of women. Western-influenced men considered the traditionalist purdah-bound women unsuitable for their modern requirements and idealised the Victorian model of womanhood. Women were expected to inculcate virtues like regularity, punctuality, thrift, orderliness, industriousness and become nurturing mothers who could train

---

[84] Ibid., p. 2.

[85] Meredith Borthwick, *The Changing Role of Women in Bengal, 1849–1905* (Princeton, 1984).

children in matters such as good habits and thereby secure their future. The bhadramahila enthusiastically responded to the new opportunities made available to her. She received education, participated in public life through women's associations and shared an intimate conjugal relationship with her husband in the new environment of nuclear family. That third aspect was in sharp contrast to the traditional joint family set-up where spouses could hardly interact with each other during the day. Borthwick noted that though the bhadramahila gained access to education, relatively widened public spaces and drew closer to husband; at the same time, she lost some control over the household, which she had enjoyed when purdah-bound, its management now being dictated by her husband. The guardianship of men ensured the 'controlled emancipation of women'. However, as Borthwick observes, it is noteworthy that the new roles and ideals of womanhood adopted by the Bengali bhadralok and echoed by the bhadramahila in the nineteenth century became common in Hindu households in the twentieth century.

In *Hindu Wife, Hindu Nation*,[86] Tanika Sarkar discussed the relationship between the woman's question and the emergence of Hindu cultural nationalism in Bengal. Drawing on wide-ranging primary source materials, including women's writings, Sarkar discussed the central role the woman's question played in political discourses of the nineteenth-century Bengali public sphere, as well as its instrumentality in forging a community identity among middle-class Bengali Hindus. Significantly, she locates issues of nationalism in the domain of the family, the supposed 'private' sphere; in other words, she demonstrates the politicisation of the institution of family and conjugal relationships in colonial Bengal.

Of particular significance to my work is her discussion about nineteenth-century writer Rashsundari Debi's powerful desire to receive education, which led her to make a 'deeply transgressive departure' from the 'good wifely behavour'.[87] Recognising Rashsundari's sense of agency in her rebellious actions, expressed through religiosity, Sarkar shows how Debi's autobiography upset traditional patriarchy and asserted women's right to spirituality. Sarkar pertinently remarked that Rashsundari's sources of inspiration were neither Indian male reformers nor Christian missionaries and British colonialists. Colonial Indian women like Rashsundari were motivated by their 'inner desire' to receive education and made use of

---

[86] Tanika Sarkar, *Hindu Wife, Hindu Nation: Community, Religion and Cultural Nationalism* (Ranikhet, 2001).

[87] Ibid., p. 96.

indigenous resources like the Vaishnavite religion. In expressing uneasiness at patriarchal control, Rashsundari was not alone:

> All varieties of women's writings unanimously identified and condemned two problem spots within the Hindu woman's existence—the pain of patri-locality and the longing for knowledge. Whatever the format and whatever the basic political stance towards patriarchy, women's writings at this time agreed on these points of criticism.[88]

Sarkar established that Indian women were not mute spectators and mere objects of reform. Though there were strenuous efforts by reformers and orthodox intellectuals, Indian women refused to be passive and voiced their own preferences. The book focuses on the seemingly apolitical aspects of the nineteenth- and twentieth-century Hindu family and reads political meanings into this domain. Sarkar reveals how vital the Hindu family and intimate relations between man and a woman were in the formation of community and communal identities. 'The Hindu woman's body became a deeply politicised matter—it alone could signify past freedom and future autonomy,' Sarkar emphasised.[89]

In her work on colonial Bengal, Anandita Ghosh rightly identifies a significant gap in modern Indian historiography regarding the status of print and literature as sites of contestation for power by various social groups.[90] The novelty of Ghosh's approach lies in the attention she pays to the print cultures and cultural preferences of the 'lesser bhadralok' or 'petty bhadralok'—the educated but 'not prosperous' urban middle class, which 'resisted the moves by its more successful upper rungs to sanitise its cultural domain'.[91] The other two groups that she focused on were women and poor Muslims. She meticulously examined the way the 'low-life "popular" print cultures' of these groups, largely produced in the Battala print market, 'ran counter' to elite literary discourse. Ghosh successfully demonstrated that the elite culture of the bhadralok could neither provide a universally accepted standard nor succeed in wiping out the lesser print cultures of the 'lesser' people. Despite being branded as 'vulgar' by the bhadralok, who clandestinely read the 'cheap' Battala products, these cultures survived with 'vigour' as Battala market's brisk business attests. Ghosh made a pertinent remark about the power and function of print: contrary to the general

---

[88] Ibid., pp. 47–48.
[89] Ibid., p. 228.
[90] Ghosh, *Power in Print.*
[91] Ibid., p. 21.

understanding, it did not perpetuate dominant cultural norms, but rather opened up avenues for more democratic writing, with a wider section of people actively participating in it and leaving behind their own mark.

Ghosh devotes a chapter exclusively to women's print cultures, which existed despite women being 'doubly subjected' to colonialism and indigenous patriarchy. Ghosh argues that 'a closer look' at women's print cultures certainly helps us identify their own voices. Women did not simply mimic male agendas but charted their own paths, both covertly and overtly. *Basar* or wedding songs, which were a source of excitement and delight for women, and which were treated by the bhadralok as 'a societal disease', writes Ghosh, 'in reality, redefined women's sexuality in positive and celebratory terms rather than posing it as dangerous to males'.[92] Recovering the 'reluctant voices' of women and their writings on 'forbidden themes', Ghosh showed how women refused to conform. Even seemingly non-rebellious women like Rassundari Debi were in fact engaging in a 'conscious rebellion': she refused to conform to patriarchal prescription that women must not read and write. Ghosh summarised women's responses, as evidenced in their writings, in the following words:

> Contrary to prevalent understandings... women were *active* users and appropriators of print literature, and not condemned to a life of passive reception and endless mimicry of the hegemonic discourse. They manipulated print and used it intelligently to meet their own agendas and express their non-conformist world views—sometimes modestly, sometimes combatively.... [I]n patronizing Battala brand novels and dramas, women were expressing their cultural position in unequivocally dissident terms. The active denigration or suppression of some of these expressive forms by the educated bhadralok might be viewed as an index of the threat they posed to contemporary dominant representations of gender.[93]

Women's Print Culture in Telugu

In tandem with the overall academic engagement with India's print cultures, a few scholars have studied women's journals published in Telugu. Dantu Padmavati's book,[94] although primarily examining women's journals

[92] Ibid., p. 233.

[93] Ibid., p. 258.

[94] Dantu Padmavati, *Aspashta Pratibimbalu: Telugulo Streela Patrikalu—Oka Parisheelana* (*1883–1947*) (Hyderabad, 1989).

published till 1920, also included some broad observations about the journals published till 1947, the year India became independent. Padmavati is concerned with two important questions: (i) to 'what extent' the journals discussed the problems of women, and (ii) why their 'nature' was so. She observed that there was a difference between the journals edited by women and men: the later were didactic in nature and most of the contributors were men; the former accommodated a number of women's writings and treated women's issues in a 'positive' way. Journals edited by men sought to cast women in a mould that was convenient for them and were therefore deliberately selective about the information they published. Despite noting some differences, Padmavati found that journals edited by women were not too different and appeared to be dancing to the tune set by reformist men.

This analysis holds true only to a limited extent. As Padmavati herself remarked, though cursorily, women's consciousness had undergone a change by the 1940s (in fact, the process had started much earlier). The scope of the study did not allow for a full engagement with a number of dissenting voices of women, say on the issue of widow remarriage, which began to surface in the 1910s itself. The scheme of the study—studying each journal separately, its nature and its treatment of women's issues, rather than a thematic analysis—also placed certain constraints on its capacity to focus on women exclusively. Therefore, one does not find women writers in large numbers, as one may otherwise expect from such scholarship. Despite these limitations, Padmavati's work remains significant.

In his article, V. Ramakrishna analysed Telugu women's journals published during the nineteenth and early-twentieth centuries.[95] His chief concern is to examine how far the journals 'reflected' the contemporary reform concerns. Dividing them into two phases—the first from 1883–1919 and the second from 1920–1947—he observed that while early journals like *Sathihitha Bodhini*, *Telugu Zenana*, *Savithri* and *Anasuya* were concerned primarily with women's education, social reform and women's needs in general, later journals like *Grihalakshmi* and *Andhra Mahila* discussed issues like women's freedom and their political participation. He noted that there was a 'subtle distinction' between the journals edited by women and men: while the male-edited journals had 'instructional and sermonising tone', the women-edited journals had a 'positive' tone. While authors were predominantly men in the former, women authors were prominent in the

[95]V. Ramakrishna 'Women's Journals in Andhra during the Nineteenth Century', *Social Scientist*, 19 (5–6), May–June 1991, pp. 80–87.

latter. He found that 'the intentions of the editors were the true reflection of the views of the contemporary reformers, who wished to make women cultivate elements of culture and modern living and wean them away from ignorance and gossip'. He observed a 'positive impact' of these journals on the consciousness of women. However, his agreement with Atlury Murali without verification, that women's consciousness 'remained within the contours of bourgeois ideology articulated by the petty-bourgeois male reformers in the nineteenth and early twentieth centuries', cannot be accepted given the extensive evidence available to the contrary.

V. Ramakrishna's *Social Reform in Andhra (1848–1919)*[96] is by far the most comprehensive account of the social reform movement in the Telugu districts of Madras Presidency. Corresponding with the lifespan of Veeresalingam, the tallest of Andhra's social reformers, Ramakrishna discusses the social and political ideas of Veeresalingam, his movement for spreading education among women, and the widow remarriage movement initiated by him. Apart from this, it also discusses the Social Purity and Brahmo Samaj movements in Andhra. Using wide-ranging primary sources, Ramakrishna offers important insights on the ideas and activities of male social reformers like Veeresalingam, Raghupati Venkataratnam Naidu, Desiraju Pedabapaiah and Unnava Lakshminarayana, etc. Given the nature and scope of the work, naturally, not many women figure in it and those mentioned appear as the objects of 'upliftment'. In other words, women and their activism is presented to examine the 'extent' to which the movement initiated by Veeresalingam 'spread' and succeeded.[97] Therefore, women's own involvement in a social reform movement that largely concerned their issues received only negligible attention, and women's perception of the social reform movement is, naturally, conspicuous by its absence. Thus, the book is a commendable but male-centred account of the social reform movement. A closer examination of other sources—particularly journals published by a number of caste associations and the activities of the caste-specific reform leaders and, most significantly, the women's journals edited and published by women—challenges Ramakrishna's conclusion that 'after 1907 [the time when the intense Swadeshi Movement emerged in Andhra]... social reform gradually receded into the background giving place to the nationalist movement'.[98] The book, however, provides a crucial foundation for further research on the social history of Andhra region.

---

[96] V. Ramakrishna, *Social Reform in Andhra (1848–1919)* (New Delhi, 1983).

[97] Ibid., pp. 97–103.

[98] Ibid., p. 189.

This period was followed by the social reform movement in Andhra during 1920–1947, which has been studied by S. Inna Reddy.[99] Exploring otherwise neglected primary sources such as the journals published by caste associations and women-edited and published journals, Inna Reddy has rightly observed that 'the presence of a strong hegemonic national movement' could not devour the social reform movement.[100] His remark that 'an important aspect of post-Veeresalingam period was that women members in the society began to organise themselves in order to fight for the rights of their own,'[101] and recognition that there arose a 'women's movement' during the period of his study are well substantiated by historical evidence. Despite the heartening fact that Inna Reddy's work made use of new sources, particularly women's journals, and recognised women as active players in the social reform movement, it did not bring women to the centre-stage of discussion. Therefore, there are few detailed accounts of women's voices.

Vakulabharanam Rajagopal argues that social reform in Andhra was sustained during the nationalist period due to compelling critiques of crippling native practices, including those associated with women; some of these critiques were posed by colonialists.[102] He disagrees with Partha Chatterjee's influential proposition and instead argues that in the Andhra region, anticolonial nationalism successfully 'accommodated' colonial critiques of Indian society, including those concerning the so-called inner/ spiritual domain. He makes his point by analysing the ideas of Veeresalingam as embodied in his novel *Rajasekara Caritramu* (1878) and his autobiography *Sviya Caritramu* (the first part published in 1911 and the second part in 1915). He observes that with the rise of a nationalist spirit after 1907, even though the English-educated youth dissociated themselves from Veeresalingam's ideas and plunged into nationalist activity and some nationalists wished to abandon social reform altogether, there emerged another 'model' of nationalism in Andhra which combined political nationalism with a programme of radical social reform. The nationalist non-Brahmin leaders, who combated Brahmanical ideology and supremacy in the public sphere, appropriated the 'legacy' of Veeresalingam.

---

[99]'Social Reform Movements in Andhra (1920–1947)', PhD thesis submitted to the University of Hyderabad, 1998.

[100]Ibid., p. 63 and 58.

[101]Ibid., p. 64.

[102]Vakulabharanam Rajagopal, 'Fashioning Modernity in Telugu: Viresalingam and His Interventionist Strategy', *Studies in History* 21 (1), n. s., 2005, pp. 45–77.

With regard to Veeresalingam's ideas and activities, Atlury Murali states that Veeresalingam's reform efforts concerning women were a part of the 'national regeneration mission'.[103] Though women were removed from the clutches of traditional patriarchy, they were still asked to remain subservient to men/husbands. Murali found that literary figure Gurajada Appa Rao went beyond Veeresalingam, treating women as independent human beings with self-agency. He also argued that though the nationalist movement did lead to the slowing down of the social reform movement, it could not halt it, for a number of nationalist leaders persisted with the project of reform. Various caste associations that emerged in the early twentieth century carried this forward. The kind of broader reform sought by non-Brahmin caste associations was 'qualitatively' different from the nineteenth-century reform movement, posing questions and challenges to Brahmanical hegemony; however, Murali notes that this did not add any other dimensions to the project of women's reform. In terms of their ideology concerning women, non-Brahmin caste associations were no different. To substantiate his claim that social reform movement progressed even during the peak of the nationalist movement, Murali's analysis rightly focused on the activities of Darishi Chenchaiah. He asserts that there was 'some positive shift' in women's consciousness, for they began to realise their degraded conditions, worked toward their amelioration and demanded equal rights compared to men in civil and political matters. However, he hastily concluded that 'the overall perspective of women remained within the contours of bourgeois ideology articulated by the petty-bourgeois male reformers'.[104] It is difficult to agree with his conclusion about women's consciousness because a number of women's writings in journals, some of which Murali in fact based his conclusion on, actually prove the contrary: The sources untapped by Murali show women tirelessly working to erase the *lakshmana rekha* drawn by reformist and nationalist liberal patriarchs.

Vakulabharanam Rajagopal, in his study of a hitherto forgotten woman's autobiography in Telugu, writes that the account 'contains a radical critique of religion and society'.[105] Authored by a widow, Edidamu Satyavati, and published in 1934, the autobiography strategically made use

[103] Atlury Murali, 'Perspectives on Women's Liberation: Andhra in the Nineteenth and Early Twentieth Centuries', *Studies in History* 3 (1), n. s., 1987, pp. 97–120.

[104] Ibid., p. 119.

[105] Vakulabharanam Rajagopal, 'The Rhetorical Strategy of an Autobiography: Reading Satyavati's *Atmacaritamu*', *The Indian Economic and Social History Review* 40 (4), 2003, pp. 377–402.

of the ideal of *pativrata* to launch a critique of the oppression of women in Indian society; she also questioned 'contradictions' in the creation of god and questioned the latter's very existence. Stating that categories like 'new woman' and 'bhadramahila' are inadequate to explain the radical pronouncements of women like Satyavati, Rajagopal placed her in a spectrum of indigenous resistance along with women like Tarigonda Vengamamba.[106] 'Such resistance predated the impact of Western ideas and social reform endeavours', he emphasised. While his identification of the 'agency' of Satyavati is acceptable to a limited extent, his conclusion that Satyavati was the only woman to have gone beyond the dominant stream of thought about women,[107] and that 'women's journals edited by women themselves did not make any serious departure from the existing mould' can be contested, given that there were a number of women whose writings were arguably better articulated and more radical than those of Satyavati.

Relying on the conclusions drawn by Murali, Rajagopal and others, Inukonda Thirumali downplays the critical consciousness of Andhra women. According to Thirumali, 'the gender movement in Andhra remained confined to the male prescribed agenda'[108] and women 'worked in active cooperation of their men [*sic*] and sincerely implemented the male agenda for women. The gender issues raised and discussed were not in the interest of women at all, not even from the point of view of women.'[109] However, quoting my work,[110] he admits that 'elementary level opposition to patriarchal practices was found in the voices of' some of the Andhra women intellectuals.[111] He proposes that women's consciousness and

[106]Upon her husband's death, 'poet-saint' Vengamamba (1800–1866), then a child widow, refused to let her hair be shaved off as was mandated by Brahmanical tradition. Her resistance shocked her contemporaries, particularly religious heads in her society. For more details, see Susie Tharu and K. Lalitha, ed., *Women Writing in India: 600 B.C. to the Early Twentieth Century*, vol. 1 (USA, 1994), pp. 122–142.

[107]To arrive at this conclusion, he compares Satyavati's thoughts with those of Kanuparti Varalaksmamma, a contemporary of Satyavati. However, Varalaksmamma's *Sarada Lekhalu*, which he examined, is far from representative of the whole stream of women's thought in the 1930s. One needs to look at other women's writings as well.

[108]Inukonda Thirumali, *Marriage, Love and Caste: Perceptions on Telugu Women during the Colonial Period* (New Delhi, 2005), p. 134.

[109]Ibid., p. 140.

[110]S. Mahaboob Basha, 'Challenges to Patriarchy in Colonial Andhra: A Study of Women's Writings (1928–1942)', in Inukonda Thirumali ed., *South India: Regions, Cultures and Sagas* (New Delhi, 2004), pp. 195–226.

[111]Inukonda Thirumali, *Marriage, Love and Caste*, p. 141.

their movement in Telangana was qualitatively different from that of the largely Brahmin and other upper-caste women's movement in Andhra.[112] While we may agree with Thirumali's thesis that the lower caste/class or working women's consciousness in Telangana emerged from their everyday experience, we certainly cannot afford to underplay Andhra women's consciousness—there is plenty of evidence to suggest that Andhra women moved far beyond the 'male prescribed agenda' and pursued new modes of thinking to liberate themselves from the clutches of patriarchy.

A Note on Sources

I have used a variety of primary sources for this book. This includes editorials, articles, poems, short stories, plays and novels, readers' letters to the editor, advertisements, reviews and obituaries published in women's journals; proceedings of conferences organised by women's organisations and texts of speeches by women on these occasions; a few personal papers such as women's letters addressed to their husbands and friends; autobiographies of women and men; creative literature (short story, novels, playlets, songs, poetry, etc.) produced by women; women's memoirs recounting their involvement in the social reform, nationalist and communist movements; domestic manuals authored by women and men; and a number of women's photographs. These largely untapped sources in the Telugu vernacular, which constitute the 'women's archive', allow us to go beyond the elite, official and male-centered archives that have obscured our image of history and rendered women's words and deeds nearly invisible.

The most important of my sources are the journals edited by women. Women's engagement with journalism, a reflection of their concern and commitment to the cause of women and social change, continued rather than fading away through the heyday of the Indian national movement. Women's journals open to us an entirely new world of information about feminist (and a few anti-feminist) foremothers who are otherwise completely forgotten and who heralded and consolidated the women's

---

[112] About women in Telangana, he writes: 'The Telangana working-women negated the Andhra women's movement in terms of objectives, militancy and sectional or class participation… The Telangana women understood gender equality from the folk, tribal and peasant point of view'. Ibid., p. 151. He concludes that the Telangana women's consciousness was not only qualitatively different but also superior to that of Andhra women.

movement in colonial Andhra. The journals bring to light a wide variety of unheard but extraordinarily significant voices from the region. Apart from women's journals, I have also used a number of other journals, including caste-exclusive journals and nationalist journals and newspapers, which not only helped in cross-referencing but also in locating the echoes of women's concerns elsewhere in the print culture of this period.

The personal letters written by women, particularly to their husbands, reveal their *inner* lives: their relationship with and expectations regarding husbands, the affective aspects of their lives, their adjustments and maladjustments within particular family arrangements (whether joint or nuclear), family pressures and curtailed aspirations, etc.

Women's autobiographies enable us to understand how women viewed themselves and others. They furnish a number of details, including about the domestic lives of women and men. This proves enormously helpful in analysing the world from the women's point of view.

The photographs that I have used, most of them from women's journals, add life to the writings of women. It is not just the words and deeds of the actors that acquire new life but also the actors themselves. The very fact that women allowed themselves to be *known* and *seen* in the 'public' cuts at the roots of patriarchal culture, which stubbornly disallowed women from being publicly seen, talked about and commented upon. Women's pictures published in these women's journals erase the patriarchal stigma of confining women to the *inner* quarters of the home.

The Structure of the Book

The book has five chapters, excluding the introduction and the conclusion. In Chapter 1, I situate the emergence of the woman's question in colonial Andhra in the context of British colonial critique of Indian culture and civilisation. The first three sections of the chapter discuss the ideas and activities of male social reformers and intellectuals. By examining the emergence of female social reformers and their activities, particularly the formation of women's organisations and the acceleration of women's movement, Chapter 1 challenges the common assumption that social reform receded with the emergence of national movement. To substantiate my stand that social reform did not decline in Andhra, I discuss the reform activities undertaken by various caste associations as well as some nationalist leaders. I demonstrate how a few women intellectuals questioned male nationalists who suggested that social reform/the woman's question could wait until political freedom was achieved. It is crucial to note how print culture helped sustain the woman's question and powerfully contributed to the making, consolidation and acceleration of the women's movement in colonial Andhra.

Chapter 2 provides biographical and historical detail about the women's journals, the chief source of this study, through a discussion of women's journals edited by both women and men. Details such as periodicity, editors, place of publication, duration of publication, circulation, subscribers, contributors and the issues discussed in the journals, etc., are provided. As I shall argue, while the first two male-edited women's journals were didactic in nature, with almost all contributors being men; the women-edited journals dealt with women's issues in a more sympathetic and positive fashion. The most significant aspect of the latter was that most of the contributors were women. This chapter makes it evident that women's print culture helped them to create a strong gender identity and thereby keep the woman's question alive throughout the period of my study. By encompassing an astonishing variety of their thoughts and deeds, the journals establish the women of colonial Andhra as intellectuals, activists and *agents* of self and social change. It was these journals that strongly advocated for women's perspectives and without them, women writers could not have found a collective space to articulate their individual and collective aspirations. As rightly observed by a contemporary woman intellectual, women's journals functioned as 'ambassadors' of the women's cause. More importantly, the journals turned a number of women into accomplished writers and beginners received training in the art of writing. The fact that the women's journals were managed by women themselves encouraged many a woman to correspond with other 'sisters' without any hesitation. Women's print media thus aided the emergence of a constituency of intellectual-activist women in colonial Andhra. It was on the basis of these platforms that women intellectuals were able to fire volleys at patriarchal society and culture.

Women intellectuals' discourses on the problem of child marriage form the focus of Chapter 3. Women extensively wrote about the limitations that child marriage imposed on girls. Initially, they argued against child marriage by invoking the *shastra*s. However, they later went beyond the shastra-based argument and wanted an end to the practice because it inhibited the natural growth of girls/women. Their sustained campaign against the practice, in combination with a few other factors, led to the passage of the

Child Marriage Restraint Act, popularly known as the Sarda Act, which was passed in 1929 and came into effect in April 1930. The 'progressive' section of women celebrated the passage of the Act. However, they were worried about violations of the law by conservative sections who exploited various loopholes in the Act. Therefore, they consistently argued for its stringent implementation and demanded amendments to make it more effective. While they were appreciative of the colonial government for the passage of the Act, they were resolute in criticising its indifference towards strict implementation. Women demanded a further increase in girls' age of consent so that the latter could fully enjoy the various opportunities of life. They condemned mismatched marriages with large differences in the spouses' age. I also analyse the stance of 'conservative' women who supported the practice of child marriage because, according to them, it ensured the conjugal fidelity of Indian women and the 'honour' of the Indian nation. The juxtaposition of the voices of 'conservative' and 'progressive' women makes the contemporary picture clear.

Chapter 4 deals with women's perspectives on widowhood and their involvement in the widow remarriage movement. Women intellectuals undertook a sustained campaign against the many atrocities perpetrated against widows. Initially confining themselves to merely describing the sufferings of widows, they later advocated for widow remarriage. Even after this shift, at first they only advocated remarriage for widows who had not engaged in sexual relations; roughly from the 1920s, they began to advocate remarriage for adult widows, including those with children. The chapter demonstrates how, from the 1910s onwards, women intellectuals moved away from shastra-based arguments in favour of widow remarriage and emphasised that widows had a *right* to remarriage and a sexual life. Widows were unequivocally established as *active agents*, casting their own destiny and effecting sociocultural change. The chapter also discusses the 'conservative' perspective of a section of women who bitterly opposed widow remarriage and vehemently attacked its proponents and representatives.

Chapter 5 examines domestic ideology as it emerged in the late-nineteenth and early-twentieth centuries in the Andhra region as well as multiple perspectives on women's education. It is important to understand how 'native intellectuals', both women and men, responded to colonial critique of Indian domestic arrangements—material as well as interpersonal. It was men who first expressed their desire for a thorough reordering of the domestic domain, particularly demanding changes in the ways women ran the family, conducted themselves with their husbands and other members, etc. Men demanded that women learn the 'art' of domestic management and become educated in order to provide enlightened company to their husbands and better training to their children. The intellectuals saw the home as a microcosm of the nation. 'Civilising' the home, according to them, was a precondition to 'civilising' the nation and thereby countering the colonial state. Although British domesticity provided them with a model, they did not copy it wholesale but rather made modifications on indigenous and 'nationalist' lines. We will see how, in the beginning, women intellectuals positively responded to such demands, since liberal patriarchy provided them with relative freedom unavailable in the strictures of 'old patriarchy'. However, as they strategically made use of the freedom newly granted to them and gained a voice, they began to question male domination in the family and society, as also discrimination against women, and demanded equality with men in all aspects of life. They questioned patriarchal culture and structure, including religious injunctions and institutions that stifled their natural growth and demanded radical changes in society based on gender equality. This was an unintended consequence of the male-centred project of social reform. Women intellectuals demanded an education that would enable them to realise their fullest potential as human beings. They refused to be confined to the domestic domain and demanded an expanded public space. They firmly believed that half the sky was theirs and they needed to capture it.

The conclusion of the book brings together the findings on all the themes outlined here, presenting analyses and evidence from Chapters 1 to 5.

I have translated four articles penned by women intellectuals and one article by the male editor of a women's journal in the appendices. The former, published during the late colonial period, demonstrate the radically changing consciousness of the women of colonial Andhra. The latter not only indicates the unease of liberal patriarchs in the face of increasingly outspoken women, but also brings to the fore that though the lakshmana rekha was redrawn by men time and again, women intellectuals repeatedly attempted to cross it.

1

The Woman's Question

Intellectual Currents and New Modes of Collective Action

> Let us glance at the condition of our women. Deprived of all education, confined within the four walls of the house, seeing little of the world and knowing little of it, immersed in superstitions and oppressed by custom, our women—to our shame, be it said—are really no better than slaves! Whether from a feeling of jealousy, or from a desire to shield them against the ravages of our Mahomedan conquerors, [*sic*], we imposed on our women restrictions and customs which have degraded them to their present low condition. And now, unable to protect themselves and unfit to assert their rights and elevate their condition, our women—permit me to say it—are no better than our cattle, and verily have we become cattle-dealers and cattle-owners. We have degraded our women and they have degraded us and our society.[1]

This emphatic description alerts us to the alarming condition of women in the Andhra region at the dawn of the twentieth century. Nineteenth-century Hindu society in Andhra was plagued by numerous social evils. Most alarming among them were those associated with the maltreatment of women. Women, and upper-caste Hindu women in particular, suffered from the consequences of illiteracy, child marriage and enforced widowhood. The practice of 'selling' away young girls to 'old vampires' out of 'greed' for a bride price (*kanyasulkam*) was so rampant, particularly among Brahmins, that a prominent contemporary literary figure observed in shock that 'strange, as it may sound, bargains were sometimes struck for children in the womb. Such a scandalous state of

[1] R. Venkata Subba Rau, ed., *Kamala's Letters to Her Husband* (Madras, 1904), p. 191.

things was a disgrace to society'.[2] Child marriages often culminated in early widowhood. Since remarriage was made a taboo, widows were seen as having no value in the patriarchal order and had to undergo untold suffering: they were mercilessly disfigured, chronically starved and forced to undertake back-breaking domestic chores from dawn to dusk. Their own kith and kin scorned them. Left without any legitimate mode of romantic or sexual partnership, any such relationships were deemed 'illicit', resulting in 'illegitimate' pregnancies, foeticide, infanticide, and social disgrace.[3] Some preferred death to such a torturous existence.[4] However, among lower caste communities in the countryside, widow remarriage (*maru manuvu*) was not unknown.[5]

This 'scandalous' condition of women provided a golden opportunity to the colonial masters to condemn 'native' culture as barbarous, assert their civilisational superiority, and hence their moral right to rule over the 'uncivilised' natives and impart culture and civilisation.[6] By pointing at the deplorable state of gender relations among the colonised, the imperial

[2]Gurajada Appa Rao, 'Preface' to the first edition of *Kanyasulkam* (1897). Setty Eswara Rao, ed., *Gurajada Rachanalu: Kanyasulkam (Mali Koorpu, 1909)* (Hyderabad, 2007 [1986]).

[3]In the play *Kanyasulkam*, the head constable says: 'In these days, do not you see small girls being sold to older men, and the widows getting pregnant everywhere?… What to talk of the number of widows getting pregnant in all the taluqs where I served. If you ask me, I say that it is better widows remarry.' *Kanyasulkam*, pp. 123–124.

[4]Oka Andhra Stree, 'Hindu Vitantuvu' (Hindu Widow), *Vivekavathi*, January 1914, pp. 108–109. In Adurti Bhaskaramma's short story, 'Prabhavati', the central character thinks that 'in this society, which is full of evil practices, death is better than life'. *Bharati*, August 1926.

[5]For a detailed account of the social, economic and cultural conditions in the Andhra region during the nineteenth century, see V. Ramakrishna, *Social Reform in Andhra (1848–1919)* (New Delhi, 1983), pp. 1–36.

[6]For example, berating Hindu civilisation for according a low position to women, James Mill wrote: '[Hindu women were in] a state of dependence more strict and humiliating than that which is ordained for the weaker sex…. Nothing can exceed the habitual contempt which Hindus entertain for their women…. They are held in extreme degradation, excluded from the sacred books, deprived of education and (of a share) in the paternal property…. That remarkable barbarity, the wife held unworthy to eat with her husband, is prevalent in Hindustan'. James Mill, *The History of British India*, with notes by H. H. Wilson, 5th edn, (London, 1840) pp. 312–313, cited in Uma Chakravarti, 'Whatever Happened to the Vedic *Dasi*? Orientalism, Nationalism, and a Script for the Past', in Kumkum Sangari and Sudesh Vaid, ed., *Recasting Women: Essays in Colonial History* (New Delhi, 1989), p. 35.

masters simultaneously established their 'higher morality' and the 'moral inferiority' of the subject population, securing a 'psychological advantage' over them. Thus, the British legitimised their intervention in 'saving' native women from the barbarity of men.[7] This, in turn, injected a deep-rooted inferiority complex among the native intelligentsia. In their urge for a 'national cultural defence', intellectuals and reformers in Andhra, like their counterparts in other parts of colonial India, sought to 'correct' the conditions of women and return them to the 'original' status they had supposedly enjoyed 'in the ancient past' by undertaking the project of social reform. Hence, they advocated women's education, condemned 'devilish' practices like child marriage and *kanyasulkam*, and campaigned for widow remarriage. Though Kandukuri Veeresalingam (hereafter Veeresalingam) is credited with pioneering the social reform movement in Andhra, notions of reform were certainly present in the region long before his arrival on the scene.

Intellectual Currents before Veeresalingam (Early Nineteenth Century)

Before Veeresalingam, who is hailed as the *Yuga Karta* (harbinger of a new era), a few intellectuals had already articulated an emerging consciousness for reform with a special focus on women's problems. Enugula Veeraswamaiah (1780–1836), a Brahmin and a *dubashee* in the *Sadr Diwani Adalat* (Supreme Court) of Madras, discussed and criticised various social problems that afflicted Andhra society in his travelogue *Kasiyatra Charitra* (1838). A strident critic of traditional practices, he condemned the ill-treatment of women and so-called untouchables. He attacked the practice of sati and advocated women's education as well as widow remarriage. One of the founders of the 'Hindu Literary Society' in Madras in the 1830s, he made remarkable contributions to the spread of English education and creation of an enlightened consciousness.[8]

[7] See Uma Chakravarti and Kumkum Roy, 'Breaking Out of Invisibility: Rewriting the History of Women in Ancient India', in S. Jay Kleinberg ed., *Retrieving Women's History: Changing Perceptions of the Role of Women in Politics and Society* (Paris, 1992 [1988]), pp. 319–337.

[8] For details, see V. Ramakrishna, *Social Reform in Andhra*, pp. 57–58.

Samineni Muttoonarasimmah Naidoo of Rajahmundry, a district Munsiff, made some of the most important contributions in this direction. He authored *Hitasoochanee* (Moral Instructor in Prose) around the year 1850, keeping in mind the 'special needs of women'. The book contained eight essays, each dealing with a different topic such as education, marriage and medicine. He was far ahead of his contemporaries on the issue of marriage. It is remarkable that he emphasised 'mutual love' and 'consent' between the marrying parties about 170 years ago, and was highly critical of the ostentatious celebration of marriages involving 'wasteful expenditure'. Citing the *shloka*s recited during marriage, he successfully proved that marriages in the past were performed only after girls had attained proper age and maturity of mind. Condemning the practice of child marriage that was then in vogue, he proposed 12 and 16 years, respectively, as the right marriageable age for girls and boys. He stated that child marriages frequently caused widowhood, which in turn often led to debauchery and infanticide.[9]

Jiyyar Suri's *Stree Kalakallolini* (1875) was a valuable addition in this regard. Chiefly meant for girls, the Telugu text contains short essays, with titles in English, too. A few of these titles were: 'Female Education is not Contrary to Ancient Usage', 'Un-educated Females are Enemies to Children', 'The Beauty of Knowledge', 'The Earth and Other Elements Serve Mankind', and 'The Whole World Forms One Family'. These titles are self-explanatory.[10]

G. Vedantachari, Deputy Inspector of Schools, Visakhapatnam, made a significant move to promote marriage reform. He submitted a memorandum to the Government of Madras in 1870 in which he reviled 'the present style of Hindoo marriages' as 'very ignominious and absurd'. He held early marriages, the disproportionate age gap between husband and wife, their lack of knowledge about each other before the wedlock and the practice of kanyasulkam as the chief problems connected with the institution of marriage. According to him, such practices resulted in widowhood and concomitant 'scandalous' behaviours. Proposing remedial measures, he recommended that early marriages and kanyasulkam be

[9] Ibid., pp. 58–59.
[10] Ibid., p. 59.

banned, a minimum age limit for marriage fixed (nine years for girls, and sixteen for boys), and the consent of the couples be sought.[11]

Dampuru Narasaiah, editor of *People's Friend*, published in Madras, campaigned against child marriages through letters carried in the *Madras Times* in 1865. Citing scriptural sources, he argued that the practice of child marriage was 'contrary to the very sentiments and doctrines expressly promulgated in the sacred formula pronounced on the celebration of the marriage itself; and in the sacred books, on which, our marriage rites are founded'.[12] He emphasised that girls should be free to select their grooms.

In addition, several others such as Vennelacunty Soobrow (1784–1839) and Chadaluvada Anantarama Shastry (the latter proposed 16 years as the age of consent for girls) worked to inculcate a new kind of consciousness about reform.[13] Thus, by the time Veeresalingam entered the scene of social reform, these intellectuals had already laid the foundations of a favourable intellectual atmosphere conducive to social action. Their ideas were to become more prominent and pronounced, and translated into action in the 1870s.

Practising Reform and Casting a Perfect Companion: Kandukuri Veeresalingam (1848-1919)

Although reformist ideas were present in Andhra society long before Veeresalingam, they acquired concrete shape as a movement under his leadership. He undertook a comprehensive programme of reform, his efforts ranging from writing, publishing and public speeches to direct action—establishing institutions to carry forward the mission of reform—and encouraging others to follow in his path taking 'huge and painful social risks'.[14]

[11] He drafted a questionnaire on these issues and requested the government to circulate it among leading scholars and public men of all districts in Andhra, and elicit their opinions before making favourable laws on them. Ibid., pp. 59–60.

[12] Ibid., pp. 103–104.

[13] Ibid., pp. 58–60.

[14] Comparing reformers with nationalists, Sumit Sarkar and Tanika Sarkar observed that 'if they [social reformers] took no political risks, as later nationalists would, they took huge and painful social risks'. See 'Introduction', *Women and Social Reform in Modern India*, vol. 1 (Ranikhet, 2007), p. 9.

Alarmed at the cultural 'degradation' of upper-caste Hindus, particularly Brahmins, and the dismal status of women, Veeresalingam sought to correct the system and regain the 'glorious past' of 'our country'. Ameliorating the condition of women was a fundamental feature of this process of 'regeneration' and cultural defence.[15] For instance, in September 1879, Veeresalingam addressed a gathering on behalf of the Rajahmundry Widow Remarriage Association:

> O my countrymen! Recall for a minute that ancient time when people of the other countries learnt civilisation from the Hindus. Do not you feel happy that your country was the centre of all knowledge and arts then?… Did not the women of our country, having received education, enjoy equal respect to men in such noble times? To establish that they enjoyed a high status in the ancient times, I am recalling the names of the virtuous women such as Sita, Shakuntala, Anasuya and Avva… Countrymen! Keenly observe the present conditions…. The same Hindu country, which had embellished the whole world in the past, has become an object of ridicule to all [today]… Countrymen! Think a bit about your country's ancient glory and its worst, most heinous condition in the present. Should we sit silently rubbing our hands when the same people [the Europeans], who had gained knowledge [and learnt culture and civilisation] from our predecessors, are pointing their accusing finger at us saying that we have degenerated?[16]

Despite recognising the connection between cultural regeneration and the emergence of a national consciousness and pleading for simultaneous liberation in both sociocultural and political matters, he believed sociocultural reform held greater value: the 'country could not be developed unless the home was developed'.[17] And the home could not be developed without improving the conditions of women.

---

[15] See Kandukuri Veeresalingam, 'Stree Punarvivaha Pravartaka Samajamuvaaru Hindudesha Mahajanulaku Cheyu Vignapanamu' (Appeal of the Widow Remarriage Society to the Gentlemen of India), in Akkiraju Ramapati Rao ed., *Veeresalingam Rachanalu: Upanyasalu, Vyasalu, Jivita Charitralu*, vol. 5 (Hyderabad, 1986), p. 24.

[16] Ibid., pp. 17–26.

[17] For Veeresalingam's views on this, see his speeches—one delivered at the third Godavari District Social Conference held at Eluru in June 1897, and the other on the 'National Congress' delivered at Rajahmundry. 'Elurulo Jarigina Moodava Godavari Mandala Sanghika Sabhalo Sabhanayakatvamu Vahinchinappudu Cheyabadina Prasangamu', and 'Deshiya Mahasabha' in Akkiraju Ramapati Rao ed., *Veeresalingam Rachanalu*, vol. 5, pp. 26–42 and 105–138.

Holding the degraded position of women as one of the most potent reasons for national cultural degeneration, Veeresalingam said that 'our development relies on women's development'.[18] So as to ensure development for women, and thereby the country, he sought to remove all the barriers that hindered women's progress: he advocated women's education, attacked the practices of child marriage, kanyasulkam, enforced widowhood and *varasulkam* (dowry).

Veeresalingam accorded supreme importance to women's education, for he thought that 'until and unless women became educated, the country could not progress'.[19] Veeresalingam firmly believed that

> it was impossible for men to achieve progress, if women were kept in a degraded position. If men were to progress, they needed to upgrade the position of women by giving them education. If men alone made progress keeping women in slavery, they could not really progress; rather it was inevitable that they would fall [and fail].[20]

He engaged in a protracted intellectual battle with the opponents of women's education. When the latter argued in contemporary journals that 'women did not deserve education,' he sarcastically replied that 'men did not deserve education'.[21] Countering conservatives who opposed women's education on the grounds that women did not have to earn a living, in his article, 'Women's Education', Veeresalingam forcefully argued:

> There are some, who think that education is for securing jobs, for making a living, and ask, 'why do women need education when they do not have to work and earn?' I wish to ask them, 'In that case, where is the need for education for rich men who do not have to earn their living?' Though uneducated, a labourer makes a living out of his toil. One can take up a number of professions for making a living; education is not necessary to eke out one's livelihood. Education is for something else; for knowledge, for wisdom and for the fulfillment of deeper and nobler urges of life. Women need education for the same purpose.[22]

However, did Veeresalingam really want women's education 'for the fulfillment of deeper and nobler urges of life'? A close scrutiny of his

---

[18] Ibid., pp. 31–32.

[19] Ibid.

[20] Kandukuri Veeresalingam, *Sweeya Charitramu* (*Autobiography*), Part 2 (Rajahmundry, 1936), pp. 203–204. The *Sweeya Charitramu* was first published in 1911.

[21] V. Ramakrishna, *Social Reform in Andhra*, p. 76.

[22] Ibid.

statements on the 'need' for educating women demonstrates the opposite. He wanted women to be educated to become good housewives, perfect companions to their husbands, and good mothers. The educated woman transformed her home into heaven. In his words:

> The wife is a queen in the house. The supreme dharma for her is to look after the chores of the house and make the family comfortable and happy. She should be helpful in all her husband's deeds and counsel him with good advice. She should impart education to her children and act as a good mother. She should be a wise person who generates enthusiasm and happiness in the family. These characteristics cannot be developed unless she is educated.[23]

Educated women, according to Veeresalingam, realised the indispensability of *pativratyam* (conjugal fidelity), turned themselves into 'virtuous' women without requiring male supervision, lessened the burden of men by managing the home themselves[24] and properly nurtured their children. It was his firm belief that 'unless women helped, no social reform would achieve complete success'.[25] Only education could ensure a 'happy conjugal life'.[26] He wanted women to become perfect companions to their husbands, much like his own wife—this was only possible if they received education.[27]

To channellise his ideas, Veeresalingam started schools for girls, one in Dowaleswaram (1874) and the other in Rajahmundry (1881).[28] In a co-educational school in Rajahmundry, founded in 1907, *panchama* (so-called 'untouchable') boys were also admitted. He advocated vocational education

---

[23] *Sathihitha Bodhini* (1888). Cited in Atlury Murali, 'Perspectives on Women's Liberation', *Studies in History* 3 (1), p. 120. See also fn. 28 in ibid.

[24] He wrote in *Vivekavardhani* (1875): 'The burden of managing all affairs at home was shouldered by women, not by men. If they were educated, how successfully and carefully could they manage these affairs? Since females at present do not possess such skills, the whole burden was passed on to men—and even after their day-long work outside, were they not forced to see the domestic affairs with disgust? Moreover, if women were educated like men, their children would become most intelligent.' Cited in Atlury Murali, 'Perspectives on Women's Libertation', p. 100.

[25] *Vivekavardhani* (1875). Ibid., p. 100.

[26] Kandukuri Veeresalingam, 'Bharyabhartala Aikamatyamu' (Unity/Compatibility between Wife and Husband), *Vivekavardhani*, 15 June 1875. In Akkiraju Ramapati Rao ed., *Veeresalingam Rachanalu*, pp. 196–198.

[27] For the description of his wife, see the epigraph at the beginning of Chapter 5, this volume.

[28] V. Ramakrishna, *Social Reform in Andhra*, pp. 93–94.

for women with the hope that it would enable them to learn useful skills so that they could earn and achieve some financial independence within the family. Under control of the Prarthana Samaj, Veeresalingam started a night school for the working classes.[29] He constantly campaigned for the establishment of girls' schools through print media. In addition, he authored a number of books keeping in mind the 'special needs' of women,[30] and published a journal, *Sathihitha Bodhini*, exclusively for women.[31] Inspired by his example, several people came forward to establish girls' schools, and several societies sprang up for the promotion of women's education throughout colonial Andhra, with the movement spreading even to remote areas.[32] Veeresalingam treated the 'cruel practices' of child marriage, kanyasulkam, enforced widowhood, disfiguring of widows and dowry as mutually interlinked and advocated complete eradication. Holding them to be a 'serious blot' on 'our world's greatest Hindu country', causing 'humiliation' before the foreigners 'who had learnt civilisation from us', he appealed to 'our noble countrymen' to act urgently to do away with all such practices.[33]

Equating the practice of child marriage with 'sale of human flesh', he mounted a scathing attack on parents—particularly Brahmins,[34] among whom the practice was most prevalent, and whom he accused of being 'more cruel than the butcher, who sold animal's flesh, including the flesh of the [holy] cow'.[35] Berating parents, particularly fathers, he said that 'possessed by the vampire of greed, they cut the throat of their innocent daughters' and 'sacrificed them by giving them in marriage to such old men, who were only

---

[29] Atlury Murali, 'Perspectives on Women's Liberation', p. 103.

[30] Kandukuri Veeresalingam, *Sweeya Charitramu*, Part 2, pp. 204–214 and 249; Part 1, p. 414.

[31] For more information about the journal, see Chapter 2, this volume.

[32] For the spread of Veeresalingam's movement and its impact, see V. Ramakrishna, *Social Reform in Andhra*, pp. 94–103.

[33] Kandukuri Veeresalingam, 'Stree Punarvivaha Pravartaka Samajamuvaaru Hindudesha Mahajanulaku Cheyu Vignapanamu', September 1879, in Akkiraju Ramapati Rao ed., *Veeresalingam Rachanalu*, vol. 5, pp. 17–19.

[34] 'The evil practice was a disgrace to the entire community of Brahmins,' said Veeresalingam. See 'Kanyasulkamu', *Vivekavardhani*, May 1880 in ibid., p. 168.

[35] 'Elurulo Jarigina Moodava Godavari Mandala Sanghika Sabhalo Sabhanayakatvamu Vahinchinappudu Cheyabadina Prasangamu' (Presidential Address deliverd in the Third Godavari District Social Reform Conference held at Eluru) in ibid., pp. 34–36. See also 'Kanyasulkamu', *Vivekavardhani*, May 1880 in ibid., pp. 167–169.

eligible to be either grandfathers or great-grandfathers of the brides'.[36] Such fathers, according to him, 'were the *rakshasas* [demons] of the *kali* age, who needed to be excommunicated'.[37] Child marriages adversely affected the educational opportunities of both boys and girls;[38] moreover, he concluded that '*Kanyasulkam* was one of the chief [wicked] results of the poisonous tree called child marriage'.[39] Child marriages were generally mismatched: they did not allow for 'friendship' to develop between husband and wife, negating the possibility of a happy conjugal life.[40] Advocating post-puberty marriages, he emphasised that 'brides should have the freedom to choose the groom'.[41] He wanted the British government to create a law banning the practice.[42]

The issue of enforced widowhood—'the most brutal consequence of child marriage'—consumed most of Veeresalingam's time and energy. He vividly described the kinds of atrocities, including the horrific practice of disfiguration, perpetrated on widows (who were often very young) at the hands of their own kin.[43] According to him, enforced widowhood, apart from causing great personal misery to the widows, resulted in social 'immorality'. Even if widows could put up with physical hardship, the prohibitions on their sexuality were severe to the point that they were nearly impossible to abide. This often led to 'illicit' and often exploitative relationships, and pregnancies that, due to social censure, resulted in foeticide, infanticide, or abandonment of the infants.[44] To avert such a sorry state of affairs, Veeresalingam, along with a few of his friends including Challapalli Bapaiah and Pyda Ramakrishnaiah, championed the widow remarriage movement. The 'Rajahmundry Widow Marriage Association' was formed in 1879 with Veeresalingam as its secretary. Apart from campaigning in favour of widow remarriages through his powerful writings and lectures, he toured important towns in Andhra to mobilise public opinion in its favour. The movement

[36] Ibid., p. 168.

[37] Veeresalingam, 'Elurulo Jarigina Moodava Godavari Mandala Sanghika Sabhalo…', p. 35.

[38] Ibid., p. 34.

[39] Ibid.

[40] Veeresalingam, 'Bharyabhartala Aikamatyamu', pp. 196–198.

[41] 'Elurulo Jarigina Moodava Godavari Mandala Sanghika Sabhalo…', p. 35.

[42] 'Kanyasulkamu', *Vivekavardhani*, May 1880, in ibid., p. 169.

[43] Veeresalingam 'Stree Punarvivaha Pravartaka Samajamuvaaru Hindudesha Mahajanulaku…', p. 21.

[44] Ibid., pp. 22–24.

yielded positive results, with the first widow remarriage being performed on 11 December 1881 in Rajahmundry. In order to widen the movement's base, he celebrated widow marriages either in person or through his friends in towns as far apart as Vijayanagaram, and Bellary, Guntur and Bangalore. To further strengthen his campaign, Veeresalingam started a 'Widows' Home' in first Madras (1898) and later Rajahmundry (16 January 1905). By 1905, as many as sixty-three widows had been married.[45]

Simplifying the marriage ceremony by avoiding 'unnecessary expenses' and 'extravaganza'; abolishing dowry; condemning *nautch* and alcoholism; fighting corruption in the officialdom—these were among the other important issues that constituted Veeresalingam's reform project.

In his campaign in favour of women's education and widow remarriage, and against child marriage and kanyasulkam, Veeresalingam extensively quoted the shastras to prove and defend his point.[46] Regressive practices, according to him, were a result of the 'cruel devil' called 'tradition', and not the shastras. Hindus had strayed from the straight path shown by the shastras and become slaves to tradition, which they had enthroned by dethroning the shastras.[47] He bluntly attacked members of the orthodoxy who misinterpreted the *shrutis*, *smritis* and shastras and themselves concocted a few, in the process becoming 'new Brahmas' [gods of creation], and attributing their dogmas 'to the ancient sages' to carry out their murky mission.[48] Though Veeresalingam himself did not believe in the scriptures,

---

[45]The marriages were not confined to the Brahmin caste alone. Fifty-seven were among Brahmins (some of which were of different sub-castes), three among Vaisyas, one among Viswabrahmins, one of Adivelama caste and another of Vellala caste. For a detailed discussion on the widow marriage movement initiated by Veeresalingam, the friends who supported his mission, the orthodox reaction, and the spread of the movement, see V. Ramakrishna, *Social Reform in Andhra*, pp. 109–133.

[46]Arguing against child marriages, he stated: 'According to Manu and Kashyapa, a purchased maiden could not be a wife but only a maid servant. Accordingly, she is not eligible to perform the religious rites intended to propitiate the Manes.... [Despite this], the self-styled upper caste people [Brahmins] continued to indulge in this devilish practice unashamedly.' Cited in V. Ramakrishna, *Social Reform in Andhra*, p. 107.

[47]'Stree Punarvivaha Pravartaka Samajamuvaaru Hindudesha Mahajanulaku Cheyu Vignapanamu', September 1879, in Akkiraju Ramapati Rao ed., *Veeresalingam Rachanalu*, p. 20.

[48]'Deshabhivruddhi Sadhanamu', *Vivekavardhani*, October 1883, in ibid., p. 189.

he had to strategically invoke the same to combat the orthodoxy and convince a wider section of people.[49]

Given the multifaceted reform efforts that he had undertaken over a period spanning about half a century, it was not surprising that Veeresalingam commanded enormous respect among his contemporaries—particularly women, the chief beneficiaries of the movement—and gained their admiration.[50] He was later hailed as the *Vegu Chukka*, or the 'Morning Star'.[51] However, his idea of reform was not without its limitations. As we have demonstrated, his project of women's education was aimed at firmly implanting a 'new patriarchy' by transforming women into mere 'shadows' of their husbands. Uma Chakravarti's observations on how nineteenth- and early-twentieth-century male social reformers reacted to the changing conditions of widows apply to Veeresalingam as well:

> It is important to recognise that the male reformist discourse [on the plight of the young widow] was essentially a humanist rhetoric which was confined to a description of the oppressive cultural practices that spelt the social death of the upper-caste widow. The analysis of men had in the main concentrated on the place of custom and the 'aberrations' of tradition, rather than the structural elements in which the upper-caste widows' social death was located. Male writing had tended also to exonerate religion, and to carefully distinguish custom from religion. Most significantly, there was a complete silence on the crucial issue of the material and ideological arrangements of Brahmanical patriarchy which underpinned the practices associated with widowhood among the upper castes.[52]

The widow remarriage campaign was restricted to child widows only, or presumably those who had not engaged in sexual relations—the issue of

---

[49] In a meeting at Madras, Veeresalingam was asked if he had faith in the sacred texts. He replied in the negative. He stated that he quoted from them for two reasons: to defend himself from the arguments of the pandits and to convince the religious-minded. See V. Ramakrishna, *Social Reform in Andhra*, p. 115.

[50] Women of the colonial period paid glowing tributes to Veeresalingam. For example, see Palaparti Sarojini Devi, 'Andhra Stree Janodhdharakudu' (Emancipator of Andhra Women), *Grihalakshmi*, October 1932, pp. 643–645; Manikonda Suryavati, 'Mahilabhyudayaniki Pantulugari Krushi' (Contribution of [Veeresalingam] Pantulu to the Progress of Women), *Andhra Mahila*, 1 June 1944, pp. 15–19.

[51] Mallampalli Somasekhara Sarma, 'Vegu Chukka' (Morning Star), *Kinnera*, Madras, n. d. Cited in V. Ramakrishna, *Social Reform*, pp. 87–88.

[52] Uma Chakravarti, *Rewriting History: The Life and Times of Pandita Ramabai* (New Delhi, 1998), p. 247.

adult widows' remarriage was not consciously included in Veeresalingam's project.[53] While mainly focused on conducting widow marriages and increasing their numbers, he rarely bothered about temperamental suitability and mutual affection between the couples in question. Such imbalances, more often than not, resulted in a fractured marital life for the new couples.[54]

Envisioning an Independent Existence for Women: Gurajada Venkata Appa Rao (1862-1915)

Gurajada Venkata Appa Rao, popularly remembered as Gurajada, was a contemporary of Veeresalingam 'and an eyewitness to the reform movements in Andhra'.[55] Employed in the service of the rajah of Vizianagaram, Ananda Gajapathi, Gurajada was a poet and a playwright. A fine intellectual endowed with finer literary taste, he was a keen observer of life and its many facets.[56] He was highly optimistic about the advancement of women in the twentieth century, to the extent that he believed 'modern woman would rewrite human history'.[57] Though he did not engage in active social reform, he produced literary masterpieces which held up a mirror to his contemporary social milieu. His progressive ideas were reflected in poems such as 'Mutyala Saramulu' (July 1910), 'Kasulu' (August 1910), 'Lavanaraju Kala' (May 1911) and 'Kanyaka' (October 1912), published in *Andhra*

[53] He said: 'though we know it for sure that our shastra approved widow marriage, presently we are, however, working for the remarriage of those who are widowed before attaining puberty.' See 'Stree Punarvivaha Pravartaka Samajamuvaaru Hindudesha Mahajanulaku Cheyu Vignapanamu', September 1879, in Akkiraju Ramapati Rao ed., *Veeresalingam Rachanalu*, p. 25.

[54] V. Ramakrishna, *Social Reform*, p. 132. The very first widow remarriage miserably failed. Details are presented in Chapter 5, this volume.

[55] V. Ramakrishna, 'Reform Literature: Gurajada's Kanyasulkam', *Proceedings of the Andhra Pradesh History Congress* (Tirupati, 1993a), p. 166.

[56] Ibid., pp. 164–168. For an analysis of Gurajada's works and place in modern Andhra history, see V. Ramakrishna's two articles 'Kanyasulkam: Parichayam' and 'Kanyasulkam: Jaatiyodyamam' in his *Charitra, Samskruthi: Vyasavali* (Hyderabad, 2008b), pp. 99–102 and 103–108, respectively. For a through and brilliant study of Gurajada, see K. V. Ramana Reddy, *Mahodayam: Jaatiya Punarujjivanamlo Gurajada Sthanam* (Vijayawada, 1969).

[57] See Gurajada's letter (dated 21 May 1909) to Ongolu Muni Subramanyam Pantulu. Setty Eswara Rao ed., *Gurajada Rachanalu: Jabulu—Javabulu, Dinacharyalu* (*Gurajada's Writings—Letters and Diaries*) (Hyderabad, 2000), p. 8.

Bharati, and 'Desha Bhakhi' (1910), 'Manishi' (1912) and 'Poornamma' in *Krishna Patrika*. 'Kanyaka' and 'Poornamma' shed light on the pathetic conditions of women in the Hindu religious and social system.[58]

While each of his works was remarkable for its novel themes and techniques, his magnum opus was the play *Kanyasulkam*. First staged in Vizianagaram in 1892 to resounding success, it was published five years later in 1897.[59] Though the play was mainly concerned with the practice of kanyasulkam, it highlights intricately woven themes such as widow remarriage and the anti-*nautch* movements. The play depicts the 'sale' of a young Brahmin girl to a man old enough to be her grandfather. The marriage obviously ends in a fiasco.

Gurajada vividly portrayed the disastrous consequences of kanyasulkam. Characters like Buchchamma, Pootakoollamma and Minakshi—all widowed at a young age—represented the worst victims of the practice. Most importantly, Gurajada identified the material dimensions of kanyasulkam and enforced widowhood.[60] He successfully brought to light the ill effects of the suppressed sexuality of young widows.[61] While reformers like Veeresalingam focused on the problems of women and wanted to reform their conditions, Gurajada, apart from throwing light on the constraints imposed on women, highlighted the limitations of reform efforts in effecting any qualitative change in the position of women.

With searing sarcasm, the play ridiculed wicked persons like Gireesam—a character representing 'pseudo-reformers'—who, under the

---

[58] Setty Eswara Rao ed., *Gurajada Rachanalu: Kavitala Samputam* (*Gurajada's Writings: Collection of Poetry*) (Hyderabad, 1995 [1984]).

[59] A revised edition came out in 1909. In the 'Preface to the Second Edition', Gurajada wrote: 'It was my original intention to reprint the play with slight alterations, but… I recast it. In the process, it has gained considerably in size. In its present shape it is almost a new work. … When I wrote the play, I had no idea of publication. I wrote it to advance the cause of Social Reform.' Setty Eswara Rao, ed., *Gurajada Rachanalu: Kanyasulkam* (*Mali Koorpu*) (Hyderabad, 2007[1986]).

[60] When girls were married to old men, many of them became widows soon. Parents, particularly fathers, became happy that their widowed daughters 'inherited' the dead husbands' property. This was portrayed by the character Agnihotravadhanlu. Gurajada made the point clear through a dialogue between Agnihotravadhanlu and Gireesam. Ibid., p. 38.

[61] Through the creation of characters like Pootakoollamma, Buchchamma and Minakshi, Gurajada conveyed the message that the 'un-harnessed sexuality' of young widows led to 'immorality'. Girisam maintains illicit relationship with Pootakoollamma, and exploits her even financially; Buchchamma, a child widow, elopes with Girisam; Ramappa Pantulu exploits Minakshi sexually.

garb of being 'reformers' tried to exploit young widows, and who came forward to marry widows for material gains without any real sense of conviction. Wielding humour as a powerful weapon, Gurajada took aim at the ambiguity of contemporary social reformers. In his short story 'Samskarta Hridayam' (Heart of a Reformer), he exposed the contemporary social reformers' lack of social experience, their moral ambiguity, and their inability to comprehend the problems of marginalised women. More importantly, he transformed women from being *objects* of reform to *subjects* with a consciousness of their own. Thus, when Sarala, a *nautch*-girl in the story, is offered matrimony, she responds in a sharp tone: 'So you mean that I should be a life-long slave to some rogue'. Further, she questions, 'which respectable man will marry a nautch-girl like me?' The protagonist, Professor Ranganathaihru, is aghast. Gurajada's explanation of the professor's silence was an indictment of the reformers' utopian approach to women's issues:

> The question posed by Sarala never occurred before to [Professor] Ranganathaihru. Never was this problem thoroughly discussed. How is the eradication of prostitution possible and how it is not possible: he had never thought about these things. Except for reciting theories from the books, he never knew how to translate those ideas into life. Nautch-girls mean only one definition! They were defeated women in life.[62]

In *Saudamini*, an unfinished novel written in English,[63] Gurajada dealt in-depth with the various problems of women and visualised their 'independent' existence. It was his conviction that women should enjoy 'equal opportunities'. Holding that a 'real life was only that which gave her an identity of her own', he emphasised a woman's need for space. Far ahead of his times, Gurajada differentiated between a woman's 'own life', and that of her 'family life'. He was saddened that 'women were denied the opportunity to take part in all the activities undertaken by men outside the home.'[64] To him the epithet of '*abala*' (weak), used contemptuously and also to pity the 'second sex', was patriarchal and 'a meaningless word'. He wanted women 'to

[62] Atlury Murali, 'Perspectives on Women's Liberation', p. 107. Such ambiguity and humiliating puritanism was represented by the character Saujanya Rao Pantulu, a reform-minded 'gentleman', in *Kanyasulkam*. Setty Eswara Rao, ed., *Kanyasulkam*, pp. 175–176.

[63] Gurajada prepared in English a sketch for the novel. The title was given by the editor. Setty Eswara Rao, ed., *Gurajada Rachanalu—Kathanikalu* (*Gurajada's Writings—Short Stories*) (Hyderabad, 1984), pp. 55–67.

[64] Ibid., p. 62.

stand up and rebel'.[65] Gurajada felt that women should be trained in martial arts and possess weapons like firearms and knives for their protection.[66]

The institution of marriage and its instrumentality in ensuring women's subordination could not escape Gurajada's notice. In a letter to a friend, he wrote,

> Don't think that I am belittling the importance of the institution of marriage in the history of social evolution.... If the institution of marriage has been conducive to progress, it must not be forgotten that the idea of the inviolability of marriage tie was the cause of untold tragedies.[67]

In *Saudamini*, the hero exhorts the heroine: 'There is the tradition of freedom in you by birth. By marrying, why should you sell yourselves to the other?'[68] According to Gurajada, women should marry such men 'who found beauty in their eyes and lives more than in their bodies, for the beauty of the body perished [with time].'[69] In his view, domestic work, including cooking, sapped all the 'energies' of women.[70] He visualised the position of women beyond the kitchen and appealed to them to free themselves from domestic drudgery. He suggested that women should step out of the home 'to walk in open air, ride a bicycle and a horse, and live like a philosopher'.[71]

Fundamentally a humanist and universalist, Gurajada presciently declared that 'caste and religion would perish and knowledge alone would stand'.[72] Gurajada, whose ideas hold continued relevance even today, was among a set of influential intellectuals who introduced new ideas to Andhra

[65]The poet in *Saudamini* replies to another character thus: 'Woman should rebel... You say that she is weak. [It is] a meaningless word. In our country the peasant woman is stronger than the man, and has [enormous] patience [to bear anything]. Who sows crops? Tell, idiot, who beats cotton? Who takes out the seeds from tamarinds? Who is carrying out all sorts of other work? Who husks rice?' Ibid., p. 64. Gurajada draws a distinction between women of 'upper' and 'peasant' castes. The 'upper caste' woman carried water and performed all domestic work, including cooking.

[66]Ibid., p. 64.

[67]Cited in V. R. Narla, *Gurajada* (New Delhi, 1968), p. 56.

[68]Setty Eswara Rao, ed., *Kathanikalu*, p. 66.

[69]Ibid., p. 67.

[70]In *Saudamini*, the Poet argues: 'Cooking [at home] should be abolished. Food should be purchased from the market... There should be a market in every street corner. Families will go there and eat. Then there will be no botheration of cooking and other things. How much energy [and time] will be saved then.' Ibid., p. 64.

[71]Ibid., p. 66.

[72]See 'Mutyala Saramulu' in Setty Eswara Rao, ed., *Gurajada Rachanalu—Kavitala Samputam*, pp. 5–6.

society. Both Chalam, who advocated women's liberation, and Sri Sri, who propagated socialist ideas (from the 1930s and 1940s onward) were greatly influenced by him.[73]

Gurajada certainly went a step ahead of Veeresalingam: by treating women as 'subjects' and not as 'objects'; by articulating the material dimensions behind the practices of kanyasulkam and enforced widowhood; and by visualising an independent existence of women. Nevertheless, his work was limited since, unlike Veeresalingam, he never directly participated in the social reform movement and instead remained a critical outsider.

Did the Woman's Question Decline in Early-Twentieth-Century Andhra?

It has been observed by scholars that discourses about social reform began to decline 'from the first decade' of the twentieth century. Explaining 'the slow process of decline of the reform activity in Andhra', V. Ramakrishna attributes it to the 'growth of the nationalist movement from the first decade' of the twentieth century, the rise of 'Hindu revivalism' under the Theosophical movement led by Annie Besant, 'the formation of caste associations' and 'certain personal factors… [regarding] Veeresalingam' to account for the decline of the reform movement.[74] This proposition is true only to a limited extent: Nationalism did shift many *men* of the *Brahmin* caste, their committed followers and lesser-known leaders from social to political activity. However, this shift was *not complete* (as we shall discuss in detail). Nor could the 'Hindu revivalism' stem the tide of social reform despite its enduring appeal to the orthodoxy.[75]

[73]V. Ramakrishna, 'Kanyasulkamlo Samskarana Bhavalu' in *Noorella Kanyasulkam* (1892–1992), special edition (Vijayanagaram, 1992), p. 11.

[74]V. Ramakrishna, *Social Reform in Andhra*, pp. 189–204.

[75]The *Telugu Zenana* published a summary of an article by Besant along with the two rejoinders against it. Annie Besant eulogised the *pativratya* dharma of Indian women. She held an extremely conservative attitude towards widow remarriages, suggesting that widows should 'strictly practice celibacy' and 'serve others'. One rejoinder from Bombay criticised and ridiculed her views. While agreeing with her argument that discouraging child marriages would naturally and gradually bring down the number of widows, the writer asked: 'what about the fate of present widows?' The other rejoinder, a speech by Kolachalam Venkata Rao Pantulu, expressed similar views. See 'Hindu Vitantuvulanu Gurinchi Beasant Dorasanigari Abhiprayamu' (Mrs. Besant on the Hindu Widow [translation as in original]), *Telugu Zenana*, February 1904, pp. 230–233.

V. Ramakrishna marked the year 1907 as the turning point in the 'decline' of the reform movement: Bipin Chandra Pal visited towns such as Rajahmundry, Kakinada and others in 1907 spreading the message of nationalism, attracting 'many local students and others who were hitherto followers of Veeresalingam'.[76] Nevertheless, the vibrancy of the reform movement may also be assessed by the 'vigour' of campaigning undertaken in favour of reform—the number of lectures delivered and books and journals published; establishment of reform institutions such as girls' schools and widow homes; the number of widow remarriages performed; the extent to which it involved people; and, crucially, its geographical reach. If we compare pre- and post-1907 reform activities on the basis of these parameters, we do not really observe a decline of the social reform movement.

Evidence available from the beginning of the twentieth century to 1947 and beyond shows an entirely different picture. What actually declined was the centralised leadership rooted in one or two individuals. Consequently, what we observe is an emergence of pluralistic leadership coming from various social segments and a replacement of old players with new ones. Most important in this shift is the entry of women on the stage of social reform. A close examination of print media of this period, particularly the journals published/edited by various caste associations and by women, points to the fact that social reform continued with the same enthusiasm, if not more, in the early twentieth century. It brought new players into its fold, spreading to newer and farther places and in some measure acquiring new dimensions, though the core ideology of the nineteenth-century reform did not change much other than being under the leadership of women. In other words, the most significant aspect of early-twentieth-century reform was that women, thus far the mere *objects* of reform, gained the status of *subjects* advocating *self-agency*.

Nationalist Leadership and the Woman's Question

As noted earlier, nationalist politics pushed much of the male youth from social reform to political reform/nationalism. However, they were not completely divorced from social reform and still evinced an interest in it despite giving precedence to political reform.[77] Nationalist men like Konda

[76] V. Ramakrishna, *Social Reform in Andhra*, p. 198.

[77] V. Ramakrishna writes: 'During the post-1907 period, when social reform activity continued, people who were politically active gained upper hand over the reformers.

Venkatappaiah, Chennapragada Bhanu Murthi, Mutnuri Krishna Rao, Bhogaraju Pattabhi Sitaramaiah, Ayyadevara Kaleswara Rao, Gadicherla Harisarvottama Rao[78] and Darishi Chenchaiah (once a member of the Gadar Party) continued the social reform movement, albeit with less intensity (with the exception of Chenchaiah, who later emerged as a vibrant social reformer). It was the practice of the Congress to hold a social conference after its political one. Likewise, the nationalists in Andhra regularly organised district and *taluq* level social conferences after the political conferences in the first two decades of the twentieth century. At these social conferences, all the issues of social reform were regularly discussed and resolutions passed, with a special emphasis on the women's issues.[79] The continued investment of nationalist leaders in these issues can be gauged by the fact that leaders like Konda Venkatappaiah, Chennapragada Bhanu Murthi, Mutnuri Krishna Rao and others conducted a widow remarriage at Bandar (Machilipatnam) in 1906—the heyday of the Vandemataram Movement—despite severe opposition from the orthodox sections of society.[80]

If the nineteenth-century male reformers wanted to cast wives as perfect educated *grihalakshmi*s, merely 'shadows' helping their husbands fulfil their social mission and personal ambition, the male nationalist leaders of the twentieth century went a bit further. To the burden of *pati bhakti* (devotion to husband), which the nineteenth-century reformers comfortably and zealously put over the heads of women, the nationalists added another—the burden of *desha bhakti* (devotion to the country). If in the previous century women were expected to closely follow their reforming husbands in the social reform movement, in the twentieth century they were to follow them in the national movement. If women were earlier expected to cultivate virtuous children, now they were to groom their children to be patriots as well. In the nineteenth century, they were to become pativratas; in the twentieth they were to additionally become *deshavrata*s (devoted to country) and *viramata*s (mothers of valourous children).

This was clearly demonstrated by the resolutions passed during the conferences. A resolution was regularly passed underlying the significance of achieving political reform first as it was considered the bedrock upon which all other reforms would rest and these conferences would eventually conclude with slogans of Vandemataram.' Ibid., pp. 198–197.

[78] Ibid., pp. 199.

[79] Ibid., pp. 189–204.

[80] *Bharata Swatantra Sangrama Charitra*, Part III (Vijayawada, 1984), pp. 9–10. Cited in Atlury Murali, 'Perspectives on Women's Liberation', p. 108.

The type of education advocated for women during the nationalist period was in consonance with this perspective. For example, here are the views of a nationalist writer:

> As long as women, who are Mother Goddesses, are not free and are steeped in ignorance, the nation cannot progress. When Mother Deity is in a mean position, her son cannot become a great soul. When the Mother is not free, her son cannot be free.[81]

Women's education was sought with the expectation that they would groom children in line with nationalist objectives. Advocating women's education, another male nationalist wrote:

> Why should women be educated? To make children brave and enthusiastic; to recognise their tastes and talents; and [to] thus encourage them. Each and every mother should desire that her sons must become the pillars of society. Mothers should teach them patriotism, and infuse in them independent ideas. That is their duty.[82]

Nationalist women, too, held similar views.[83]

Caste Associations and the Woman's Question

Due to changing dynamics in the 1900s–1910s, a new set of players entered the arena of social reform. These were the various non-Brahmin social segments. Under their leadership, the movement acquired a new dimension and widened its social and geographical reach. Owing to economic and other shifts in the nineteenth century, non-Brahmins in Andhra had begun to develop a new consciousness from the late nineteenth century,[84] and this

[81] *Satyagrahi*, 16 April 1928. Cited in Atlury Murali, 'Perspectives on Women's Liberation', p. 114.

[82] Punugupati Ramakrishna Rao, 'Vidyavatula Kartavyam' (The Duty of Educated Women), *Grihalakshmi*, July 1941, p. 296.

[83] At the Bejawada Andhra Mahila Sabha in 1929, Turlapati Rajeshwaramma said: 'Women do not need all those elements of education which men need. Men learn to earn a living. Women should learn just for the sake of knowledge. Women generally do not need jobs. Therefore, they need only that kind of education which inculcates in them morality, patriotism, devotion to God and husband and prepares them as good mothers, better housewives and *Veeramatas*.' Turlapati Rajeshwaramma, 'Andhra Mahila Sabha–Bejawarda', *Grihalakshmi*, 1929, p. 902.

[84] For details, see 'Change and Conflict: Emergence of Non-Brahmin Consciousness in Andhra during 19th Century' in S. Inna Reddy, 'Social Reform Movements in Andhra (1920–1947)', PhD thesis submitted to the University of Hyderabad, 1998, pp. 132–159.

was organised into a movement in the twentieth century.[85] Non-Brahmin caste groups such as the Vaishyas, Kammas, Kapus, Reddys, Velamas, Vishwa Brahmins, Balijas, Padmashalis, and also a few other 'lower' non-Brahmin castes began to organise themselves, questioning the ritual superiority of the Brahmins, their monopoly over public spaces including educational institutions and public employment, and challenging their worldview. In their push for vertical social mobility and a 'respectable' place in society, they formed various caste associations. Reforming the condition of women was one of the central concerns/programmes of caste associations.

The 'Arya Vaishya Mahasabha' (established in 1907),[86] 'Vishwakarma Kuloddharana Sangham' (1903),[87] 'Kamma Mahajana Sabha' (1910),[88] 'Reddy Mahajana Sangham' (1913),[89] 'Gouda Sangham' (1907),[90] 'Naidu

[85]For a detailed analysis, see 'Growth and Consolidation: Endeavours of Reform among Non-Brahmins in Early 20th Century' in ibid., pp. 160–224.

[86]Atmuri Lakshminarasimham (1845–1901) was instrumental in organising the Vaishyas. An acclaimed scholar, he contested the ritual superiority of the Brahmins and challenged Hindu religious heads; he was actively involved in social reform and raising women's issues and was very close to Veeresalingam for some time. For a study of the life and letters of Lakshminarasimham, see Grandhi Venkata Subbaraya Gupta, *Sri Atmuri Lakshminarasimha Somayaji Jeevita Charitramu, Upanyasamulu* (Bezawada, 1922).

[87]The Vishwa Brahmins were one of the most serious contenders to ritual status and even superiority over Brahmins. Their journal, *Prabodhini*, apart from voicing with vehemence their ritual superiority, pleaded for social reform with a special focus on the development of women's education. Vakulabharanam Ramakrishna and K. H. S. S. Sundar, *Legacy and Continuity: Social Reforms in Andhra Pradesh, 1850–2000* (Varni, 2007), p. 75.

[88]Mainly concentrated in Krishna, Godavari and Guntur districts, the Kammas were one of the chief beneficiaries of the construction of the Krishna and Godavari anicuts. With economic prosperity, they turned their attention to social status, and contested the ritual as well as secular monopoly of Brahmins. For more details, see S. Inna Reddy, 'Social Reform Movements in Andhra (1920–1947)', PhD thesis submitted to the University of Hyderabad, 1998, pp. 182–200.

[89]The first conference of the 'Reddy Jana Sangham' was held in 1913 at Cuddalore. The Sangham regularly organised conferences across the region and emphasised the need for social reform with a special focus on women's issues; they also developed a youth wing. However, unlike the Vaishyas, Vishwabrahmins and Kammas, the Reddys did not directly challenge the supremacy of the Brahmins. See Vakulabharanam Ramakrishna and K. H. S. S. Sundar, *Legacy and Continuity*, p. 76.

[90]Koppala Hanumantha Rao organised it at Challapalli, Krishna District, in 1907. Ibid., p. 76.

Sangham' (1910),[91] as well as associations of the Agnikula Kshatriyas,[92] Andhra Kshatriyas,[93] Devangas,[94] Telagas,[95] Setty Balijas,[96] Padmashalis and Mangalis (traditionally employed as barbers)[97] were formed in this period. A few sub-caste associations also came into existence.[98] With the realisation that 'a journal could achieve what a thousand men could not by visiting village after village', and 'journals were at the root of the development of any country or society',[99] several caste associations began to publish their own journals. Apart from consolidating caste identities, these journals spread the message of reform and mobilised public opinion in its favour: For example, see *Chowdari*, *Kammakula Pradeepika* and *Kamma Maharaju* of the Kammas; *Vasavi* of the Vaishyas; *Reddy Rani* of the Reddys; *Kshatriya Patrika* of the Kshatriyas; *Telaga Sanghabhivardhani* of

[91] It was set up in Madras. Ibid.

[92] Associations of the Agnikula Kshatriyas were active in the Krishna and Godavari districts. Associations were formed in places such as Korangi (1901), Bandar (1915) and Vijayawada (1927). A night school was started in Vijayawada to educate young boys, and the association maintained an education fund for scholarships. S. Inna Reddy, 'Social Reform Movements in Andhra (1920–1947)', PhD thesis submitted to the University of Hyderabad, 1998, pp. 214–215.

[93] The association of the Andhra Kshatriyas was active in the Godavari delta region. It was established with the objective of 'social, moral, intellectual, economic, industrial, agricultural and physical improvement among the members'. Ibid.

[94] The Devangas formed an association in 1925 under the leadership of Dr Sajja Suryanarayana Rao. In the same year, an All India Devanga Conference was held at Madras under the lead of P. T. Kumaraswamy Chetty. In his welcome address, among other things, he touched upon the issue of improving the conditions of women. Ibid., pp. 211–213.

[95] For details, see ibid., 218–220.

[96] The Setti Balijas formed their association in 1920 at Bodasakuru under the leadership of Dommeti Venkata Reddy. Mainly concentrated in the Godavari region, it was perhaps the most active and successful organisation among the non-Brahmin caste associations. That the Setti Balijas were more reform-oriented in terms of inter-caste relations was best demonstrated by the fact that Madras-based Dalit leader C. Basudev inaugurated their 15th annual conference in 1935. Ibid., pp. 216–218.

[97] Ibid., pp. 215–216.

[98] For example, the 'Niyogi Mahasabha', an association of the Niyogi Brahmins, was formed to fight against the Vaidiki Brahmins over questions of superiority and government patronage. They started a journal, *Niyogi Patrika*, to ventilate and propogate their concerns. Vakulabharanam Ramakrishna and K. H. S. S. Sundar, *Legacy and Continuity*, p. 75.

[99] Addepalli Satyanarayana, 'Vaishyulara Melkonudu' (O Vaishya Breathren, Awake!), *Vasavi*, October 1931, pp. 245–246.

the Kapus; *Devangaseva* of the Devangas; *Padmashali* of the Padmashalis; *Padmanayaka* of the Velamas; *Yadava* of the Gollas/Kurumas; *Agnikula Kshatriya* of the Agnikula Kshatriyas; *Adi Kshatriya* of the Adi Kshatriyas; *Prabodhini* and *Panchanana* of the Vishwa Brahmins. While a few, such as the *Vasavi*, enjoyed a fairly large circulation of about 3,000 and survived for about two decades, journals like the *Prabodhini* had a limited circulation of about 300 and could not survive for more than a decade. The journals contain a wealth of information on the activities of the various caste associations and apprise us of their dynamics. They offer firsthand accounts of the reform movement. One must note that these caste journals were all edited by men; women played a role only as contributors.

Almost all caste associations adopted the programme of the nineteenth-century reformers. They prioritised the spread of education in their respective caste groups, with a special emphasis on the promotion of women's education. They campaigned for the eradication of child marriage, enforced widowhood and dowry. Further, these associations appealed for the establishment of caste-specific schools, particularly for girls, and the simplification of marriage rituals and expenses. They organised conferences regularly in various towns and villages and developed branches even in smaller towns. Some associations expanded their movement by forming separate wings, with concrete programmes, for youth and women. Caste conferences mobilised people in large numbers for annual conferences and other meetings, discussed issues of social reform, and passed resolutions. Their reform activities were obviously restricted to a particular caste. Nonetheless, these reform efforts were qualitatively different from the nineteenth-century reform movement in the sense that they attempted to liberate non-Brahmins from the hegemonic influence of the Brahmins. A few non-Brahmin leaders treated 'social evils' from a different perspective: Practices like child marriage, dowry and enforced widowhood, which victimised women, were seen primarily as Brahmanical, and hence as something to be abandoned by non-Brahmins.[100]

An examination of the resolutions passed by various caste associations and the programmes they undertook reveals that social reform got accelerated under their leadership rather than 'slowing down', as claimed

[100]Delivering the presidential address at the Reddy Conference held at Nambur in 1916, Koti Reddy of Cuddapah district argued from this angle. *Andhra Patrika*, 19 June 1922, pp. 2–3.

by some.[101] The caste associations were, indeed, more interested in social reform than in the struggle for political freedom. These associations also led to the democratisation of the movement as well as its leadership.

The most vibrant among the caste associations was the 'Arya Vaishya Mahajana Sabha'. Under the able leadership of Darishi Chenchaiah, Shikharam Kotishwara Gupta, Tumpudi Bhagavantam Gupta, Mote Narayana Rao, K. S. Gupta, Atyam Narasimha Moorthy, Majeti Ramachandra Rao, Lingamallu Jagannatham, Shikhakollu Pattabhiramulu Gupta, Grandhi Subbaraya Gupta Sharma, Kotta Achchaiah Setty, Eturi Venkata Subbaiah, C. S. Gupta, Kopparapu Subbaiah and others, the organisation prospered. In its annual conferences held in different parts of Andhra, it emphasised the need for rapid development of the Vaishya community. The conferences especially focused on women's issues such as promotion of education, performing post-puberty and widow remarriages, banning the practices of kanyasulkam and *varasulkam* (dowry), etc. It developed a women's wing, 'Arya Vaishya Mahila Mahasabha', and also a youth wing, the 'Arya Vaishya Yuvajana Mahasabha', which also regularly conducted conferences and passed resolutions in favour of social reform. Vaishyas of the Nizam state also began to organise themselves. Their first conference was held on 12 and 13 February 1938 in Hyderabad.[102]

The journal *Vasavi*, as discussed earlier, was published by the Arya Vaishya Yuvajana Mahasabha and played a crucial role in communicating the message of reform. *Vasavi* began publication in March 1926 from Madras, with Tumpudi Bhagavantam Gupta as its editor. Barely a year into its publication, it already enjoyed a circulation of 2,150 copies. It was stated that the journal would 'publish every thing except political issues that will help promote the welfare of the Vaishyas'. Further, the journal promised to 'accommodate the arguments of pro and anti reform groups of people'.[103] Overall a pro-reform journal that provided a counter to conservative publications like the *Vaishya Patrika*, the journal undertook a rigorous campaign in favour of post-puberty marriages, widow remarriage, promotion of women's education and the overall development of the

[101] V. Ramakrishna, *Social Reform in Andhra*, p. 202.

[102] For the resolutions passed in the conference, see 'Nizam Rashtra Prathamarya Vaishya Mahasabha (The First Conference of the Arya Vaishyas of Hyderabad State), *Vasavi*, May 1938, pp. 58–62.

[103] See 'Swa Vishayamu', (Ourselves), *Vasavi*, March 1926, pp. 1–2. The annual subscription rate initially was Re. 1, which was later increased to Rs. 2.

Vaishyas.[104] As a result of rigorous campaigning and sustained efforts, more widow remarriages were performed among Vaishyas, and they encouraged even those from other castes, for example Kammas and Vishwa Brahmins, by providing a model to emulate.

Not surprisingly, Darishi Chenchaiah, the most prominent among the caste-specific social reform leaders in the post-Veeresalingam era, came from the Vaishya community. Born in Kanigiri village, a draught-prone area in Nellore district in 1890, Chenchaiah studied at Kanigiri, Ongole, Madras, and the University of California, Berkeley, from where he obtained a BSc. in Agriculture Engineering. During his student days in India, he was influenced by Veeresalingam, Brahmo Samaj and to some extent Buddhist ideas of rationalism.[105] As a founding member of the Gadar Party, he took part in dynamic revolutionary activities and was consequently jailed.[106] After his release in December 1919,[107] he wanted to participate in the freedom struggle. Since he 'disliked the politics, objectives and methods of Congress under the leadership of Gandhi,' he remained aloof from the Congress.[108] But the fiery zeal that he had acquired during his stint in the

[104] See 'Swa Vishayamu,' (Ourselves), *Vasavi*, February 1928, pp. 465–469. Of these, its enthusiastic campaign in favour of child widow remarriages is the most significant. It extensively carried details of those seeking remarriages; once a marriage was performed, it published a photograph of the couple.

[105] Darishi Chenchaiah, *Nenoo-Naa Desham* (Autobiography) (Vijayawada, 1985 [1952]), pp. 31, 35, 212, 224, 352–353.

[106] In his 384-page autobiography, he devoted 112 pages to narrating his experiences in the Gadar Party and his contributions to it. See ibid., pp. 44–156.

[107] In about 36 years of his public life, he was jailed four times—twice by the colonial government, and twice by the independent Indian government. He spent for about eight years in eight different jails in Bangkok, Singapore, Calcutta, Lahore, Delhi, Cannanore, Coimbatore and Vellore. In Singapore, he served a six-month term of solitary imprisonment. For his involvement in the Communist Party, he served a jail term of about ten months in independent India. Ibid., pp. 369–370.

[108] He attended during the 1920s a few sessions of the INC held in places such as Ahmedabad, Kakinada and Madras. He especially disliked how the Congress defined freedom and its inclinations towards dominion status. To him freedom meant 'guaranteeing stomach full of food, clothes, house, education and medical facilities to every Indian.' Ibid., p. 154. For his views on Congress, see ibid., pp. 157–159, 169–171. His disillusionment with Congress led him to join the Socialists and finally the Communists. For details, see ibid., pp. 269–384.

Gadar Party did not allow him to remain idle and he decided to concentrate on social reform.[109]

His first initiative was to ameliorate the deplorable condition of sex workers. Along with Yamini Poornatilakamma, who belonged to the kalavantulu community, a lineage of hereditary singer-dancers, he started the *Kalavantula Samskarana Sangham* in 1921, which conducted the marriages of many kalavantulu women. After this, he turned his attention to 'awaken' and enlighten people belonging to his caste. Through fiery writings published in the *Vasavi*[110] and the platforms afforded by various Vaishya conferences, he made fervent appeals for the 'all round development' of the caste group. Apart from emphasising education, particularly women's education and condemning practices such as child marriage and enforced widowhood, he advocated the 'establishment of gymnasiums for cultivating strong physical bodies', 'annihilation of the tyranny of the Vaidiki Brahmins and the arrogance of the *Mathadhipatis*',[111] establishment of *Gurukulams* where Vaishya boys would be taught the Vedas and other scriptures and developing a Vaishya priestly class.[112] He presided over the first conference of the 'Arya Vaishya Yuvajana Mahasabha' and appealed to the youth to work for social reform.[113]

Under Chenchaiah's leadership, the widow remarriage movement got a new lease of life: until this point, only three widow marriages had been

---

[109]He listed 12 issues undertaken as part of his activism and reform efforts. Ibid., pp. 159–160.

[110]To shake the Vaishyas from their slumber he gave a loud 'wake up' call. Several of his essays published in *Vasavi* had the title, 'Melkonudu—Vaishya Sodarulara!' (O Vaishya Brethren! Wake Up). For example, see *Vasavi*, March 1926, pp. 4–6; April 1926, pp. 14–19; May 1926, pp. 5–9. He urged the Vaishyas to educate themselves, abandon their inferiority complex, do away with retrograde social practices in order to be perceived as 'civilised' and thus work for the betterment of their caste, community and country.

[111]He got Pakayaji, disciple of Sri Shankaracharya Kalyananda Bharati, beaten up. Darishi Chenchaiah, *Nenoo-Naa Desham*, pp. 190–193.

[112]Darishi Chenchaiah, 'Rabovu Yuvajana Mahasabha' (The Forthcoming Youth Conference), *Vasavi*, December 1926, pp. 17–19.

[113]The conference was attended by about 500 persons who came from various parts of Andhra. Several resolutions were passed on issues such as widow remarriages, post-puberty marriages, and establishment of libraries, reading rooms, gymnasiums, hostels and the institution of scholarships for poor Vaishya children. It was also decided to start a journal. A reform lunch/dinner had been arranged to refute excommunication being imposed on the couple of widow remarriage. Darishi Chenchaiah, *Nenoo—Naa Desham*, pp. 196–197.

performed among the Vaishyas[114] owing to orthodox elements within the community and particularly in Guntur.[115] In terms of conducting such marriages, Chenchaiah did not believe in 'individual heroic acts' of 'secretly' performing marriages; he strove for 'public acceptability'.[116] The first widow remarriage under his leadership was conducted in Guntur amid intense opposition. A grand procession was taken out in the evening which ended in violence between the pro- and anti-reform groups, with 32 persons being injured.[117] Subsequently, Chenchaiah displayed great personal interest in conducting widow remarriages in many other places such as Eluru, Bandaru (Machilipatnam) and Visakhapatnam,[118] and also conducted such marriages among the Kammas and Vishwa Brahmins.[119] Together with friends like Tumpudi Bhagavantam Gupta and Mutta Venkata Subbarao, he established a 'Widows' Rescue Home' (*Vitantu Sharanalayam*) in Madras in 1930 for widows belonging to different castes.[120] He encouraged many others to set up similar institutions.[121] Branded by 'a few Brahmins as castiest', he remarked that his detractors 'lacked foresight and failed to see the progressive aspect of his movement'.[122]

Agents of Social Change: Emergence of Women Activists

Social reform was not the exclusive preserve of men. With the spread of education and the resultant reform consciousness, women gradually

---

[114] Ibid., pp. 194–195.

[115] Ibid., pp. 196–205.

[116] Ibid., p. 224.

[117] Ibid., pp. 198–205.

[118] Ibid., pp. 205–215.

[119] For details, see ibid., pp. 217–229.

[120] Ibid., p. 215. With his inspiration, one of his friends, Addepalli Sarva Setty, started a Shelter Home at Narasapuram, which became a major centre of widow remarriage movement during the 1930s and 1940s. Ibid. Also see *Vasavi*, April 1938, p. 32; July 1938, p. 137; January 1939, p. 328.

[121] He encouraged Turlapati Rajeshwaramma, and his first wife, Annapoornamma, towards establishing a women's organisation (Bharata Mahila Sangham) and an orphanage to provide shelter to orphaned children and 'fallen' women. Both the organisations were set up in Vijayawada. See 'Turlapati Rajeshwaramma' in Darishi Chenchaiah, *Naa Divya Smrutulu* (Vijayawada, 1961), pp. 84–93.

[122] He said that his movement was not against the national movement. 'In fact, my work is to help the national movement'. Darishi Chenchaiah, *Nenoo-Naa Desham*, pp. 187–188.

developed an interest in social issues, particularly with an aim to enhance their position in society. Initially, they remained mere 'shadows' of their male relatives. With the encouragement provided by reform-minded fathers, brothers, and husbands, women began to take part in reform activities undertaken by their male relatives. Later, they developed an independent voice of their own and successfully moved out of the overarching shadow of men. In their analysis of social issues that adversely affected them, a section of women found men to be responsible for their dismal position and condemned male domination in every walk of life. They took various discriminatory social and religious institutions to task. Even during the heyday of nationalism, when many nationalist men chose to relegate the issue of social reform to the margins, women steadfastly sustained the movement in their own terms. At times, women gave greater importance to social reform than to the national movement.

Kandukuri Rajyalakshmamma (1851–1910) was 'undoubtedly the first woman in Andhra Pradesh to plunge into the work of social reform'.[123] Married to Veeresalingam, she contributed significantly to his mission; he fondly and gratefully acknowledged her work, stating that: 'she supported him in all his good deeds and stood by him... [through] thick and thin'. She even boldly brushed aside the objections of close relatives who wanted her to dissuade Veeresalingam from his 'adventurous activities'. The committed Rajyalakshmamma 'neither stepped back, nor did she ever pull him back'.[124] Without her active involvement and tireless support—she even braved social boycott—the widow remarriage movement initiated by her husband would never have registered the success it did.[125] Apart from arranging

---

[123] Volga, Vasant Kannabiran et. al, *Mahilavaranam*: *Womanscape* (Secunderabad, 2001), p. 37.

[124] Veeresalingam, *Sweeya Charitramu*, Part 2, pp. 425–438.

[125] She was a source of immense support and courage to the young widows who rushed to the rescue home she was looking after in her house. She taught the uneducated widows and readily came forward to attend to them whenever they needed her help even dropping her personal work. When the domestic aids refused to cooperate with her for her involvement in the movement she walked to the Godavari to fetch water and cooked herself. She started the 'Patita Yuvati Rakshanashala' (Rescue Home for the Fallen Young Women) and helped seven 'fallen' or outcast women. She got three of them married, and carefully nursed the children when the remaing widows delivered babies and returned to their homes. She moved freely with people of all castes and was deeply concerned about improving the lives of women in 'prostitution'. She set up the Victoria Girls' School in her home. For more details, see ibid. Also see Volga, Vasanta Kannabiran et al., *Mahilavaranam*, p. 37.

for the celebration of widow marriages performed in Rajahmundry, she accompanied her husband to far-off places to conduct such marriages. Further, Rajyalakshmamma gladly donated her wealth worth Rs. 40,000 (imagine its worth in 1906!) to the 'Hitakarini Samajam' founded by her husband; she also set up a Prarthana Samaj for women, arranged women's meetings, and composed hymns. Additionally, she contributed a few pieces to the contemporary women's journals. She was a source of such great strength to Veeresalingam that, after her death, he became utterly helpless. Unsurprisingly, one chapter in the second part of his autobiography (dealing with the years 1910–1913) was titled '*asahaya dasha*' (phase of helplessness).

As we shall see in subsequent chapters, the twentieth century saw the emergence of a large number of unknown or lesser-known women on the stage of social reform. Women established schools, widow homes, and widow marriage associations throughout the first half of the twentieth century. Like the Veeresalingam couple in the late-nineteenth and early-twentieth century, reformer 'couples' emerged. The Unnava couple (Lakshminarayana and Lakshmibayamma) was united in standing up to the orthodoxy.[126] The Darishi couple (Chenchaiah and Annapoornamma) was lauded in an article published in *The Hindu* (Madras edition) on 1 December 1931:

> The great advance made by the reform movement in Andhradesa in recent years is in no small measure due to the courage with which Srimati Annapurna Devi stood by her husband in the early stages of the movement and the cheerfulness with which she faced persecution and social ostracism which it then involved. She did splendid social service, silently though, and was responsible for reclaiming a large number of innocent girls from a life of shame and degradation. It can be said that the reform movement in Andhradesa has suffered not a little by the premature death of an able and sincere social worker.'[127]

Annapoornamma was one of the most prominent women intellectual-activists of Andhra. Born in Bellary, then a part of the Ceded Districts (in present-day Karnataka), she attended school and college with the encouragement of her widowed mother and was married to Chenchaiah at the age of fifteen. In keeping with the companionate model, she closely followed and actively assisted her husband in his social reform programmes.

---

[126] See Kanuparti Varalakshmamma, *Unnava Dampatulu* (Vijayawada, 1963).

[127] For more details on her, see Darishi Chenchaiah (compiled), *Marapurani Annapoorna* (*Unforgettable Annapoorna*), n. d. (preserved at Gautami Library, Rajahmundry).

An activist in the widow remarriage movement, she and her husband performed 18 marriages across different castes. Annapoornamma was additionally part of a three-woman delegation representing women from the Andhra region in the 1929 AIWC (All India Women's Conference) session held in Bombay and served as secretary of the women's organisation at Vijayawada. She worked with Yamini Poornatilakamma, participated in the Civil Disobedience Movement, and was a prolific writer, regularly contributing to the *Vasavi*.

After Annapoornamma's death, Chenchaiah married Subhadramma, a reformer in her own right.[128] A founder-member of the WIA when she was just 18 years old, she took active part in all the campaigns undertaken by the WIA. Later, part of the Executive Committee of the Madras branch of the AIWC, she was also the first secretary of the 'Harijana Seva Sangham'. Subhadramma later became a socialist. Several others too emerged as reformers from the 1910s.

Non-Brahmin women shouldered the responsibility of reform. As noted earlier, the Chenchaiahs were Vaishyas. So were Battula Kamakshamma,[129] Kalangi Sheshamamba,[130] Atyam Satyavati Devi,[131] Pulavarti Kamalavati

[128] Chenchaiah and Subhadramma's was an intercaste marriage as the latter was from a Brahmin family. An extremely sensitive child, she opposed the forcible tonsuring of her widowed aunt. She trained in the Montessori system of education and worked as a teacher for five years. For further details, see Darishi Chenchaiah, *Nenoo–Naa Desham*, pp. 240–241, 256–259 and 373–378. A prolific writer, she regularly contributed to contemporary women's journals such as *Grihalakshmi* and *Andhra Mahila*. For the latter, she managed the column '*Pillala Shikshana: Shastriya Drukpatham*' (Scientific Approach to Child-Rearing). She was a radical advocate of the civil and political rights of women.

[129] See Chapter 5, this volume.

[130] She established a school for Vaishya girls in Guntur in the year 1926; by January 1929, about 140 girls were on the rolls of the school. For details, see Kalangi Sheshamamba, 'Vaishya Yuvati Vidyalayamu, Gunturu', *Vasavi*, July 1929, pp. 153–154. Also see *Vasavi*, June 1928, pp. 95–99; *Vasavi*, January 1929, pp. 399–400.

[131] President of the 'Widow Remarriage Association', Narasapur, she co-conducted several widow remarriages. The Association provided shelter to many widows. See 'Vaishya Vanitaratnamulu', *Vasavi*, July 1938, p. 127. For the Widow Remarriages performed by the association, see 'Stree Punarvivaha Sahayaka Sanghamu, Narasapuramu', *Vasavi*, April 1938, p. 32.

Devi,[132] Shikharam Kamalamba,[133] Tumpudi Satyavati Bhagavatamma,[134] Salla Soundaryavalli Amma,[135] Samarthi Swarnamma,[136] Kolla Kanakavalli Tayaramma,[137] and many others. Kadapa Ramasubbamma[138] was a Reddy;

[132] A scholar of great calibre, she not only contributed to the contemporary women's journals reflecting on women's issues, but also authored books such as the *Victoria Cross*. For her scholarship, she was honoured with the title 'Kavi Tilaka'. Kamalavati Devi presided over the eighth 'Arya Vaishya Mahila Mahasabha'; for her presidential address, see *Vasavi*, June 1929. For more details on her public participation, see *Vasavi*, June 1928, pp. 97–99. For examples of her writings, see 'Arya Vaishya Mahilamanula Kartavyamu' (The Responsibility of Arya Vaishya Women), *Vasavi*, July 1929, p. 124; 'Prema Vivahamulu' (Love Marriages), *Vasavi*, March 1935, pp. 378–384; 'Vunnata Vidyala Agachatlu', *Vasavi*, August 1933, pp. 143–144; 'Pashchatyulananukarinchuta' (On Imitating the Western People), *Vasavi*, November 1931, p. 271; 'Pushkaramu Baala Vydhavyamunu Maanpinadi', *Vasavi*, September 1932, pp. 194–198; 'Streelu—Naatakaranga Praveshamu' (On the Entry of Women in Theatre), *Vasavi*, June 1929, pp. 83–89. The last one was a prize-winning essay that brought her a gold medal from the 'Progressive Union' at Nellore.

[133] At just 15 years of age, Kamalamba translated Bhandaru Atchamamba's *Abala Sachcharitra Ratnamala* into Kannada. The book got the distinction of being prescribed by the Mysore University as a textbook for the *Madhyama* examination. She presided over several women's conferences. See 'Vaishya Vanita Ratnamulu', *Vasavi*, September 1938, pp. 183–184. A prolific writer, she widely published in the contemporary journals. For example, see 'Streelu Abalala?' (Are Women Weak?), *Vasavi*, July 1930, pp. 168–177; and the prize-winning 'Bharata Grihiniketti Vidya Avasaramu?' (What Kind of Education Does the Woman of an Indian Household Need?), *Vasavi*, July 1928, pp. 143–147.

[134] For details of various women's conferences she presided over, see *Vasavi*, August 1928, pp. 196–200; June 1929, pp. 98–100.

[135] Salla Soundaryavalli was a member of the WIA. She was a part of the delegation which met the Secretary of State, Montague, in 1917, to demand electoral franchise for women. She presided over multiple conferences, including the 1918 session of the Andhra Mahila Sabha in Kadapa and the third Arya Vaishya Women's Conference. For more details, see *Vasavi*, June 1928, pp. 103–105.

[136] Hailed as a genius, she wrote novels such as *Indira*, *Shyamala* and *Mallika Vasantamu*. See *Vasavi*, May 1938, pp. 55–57; September 1938, p. 183.

[137] She presided over the Arya Vaishya Women's Conference held at Mahanandi. See *Vasavi*, September 1938, p. 183.

[138] Inspired by her husband, a barrister and leader of the Reddys in the non-Brahmin movement and later a prominent freedom fighter, she took active part in the Non-Cooperation and Salt Satyagrapha Movements. She was a staunch advocate of Separate Andhra State. She was President of the Cuddapah District Educational Council and later of the Cuddapah District Board. The women's journal *Grihalakshmi* wrote about her achievements: 'it was a matter of prestige not only for the Andhra women but also for all Indian women. We are congratulating Smt. Ramasubbamma for setting the role model'. See 'Sampadakiyamulu: Shrimati Ramasubbammagari Paripalana Praabhavamu',

Jaasti Sita Mahalakshmi,[139] a Kamma; and Pulavarti Eeshwaramma,[140] a Vishwa Brahmin.

Yamini Poornatilakamma undertook reform among the kalavantulu community.[141] She was an accomplished scholar, poet and orator. Though she was already working to introduce reforms among the *kalavantulu*, the idea materialised only after she came in contact with Darishi Chenchaiah. She stayed in Chenchaiah's residence as his guest in Madras for some time, whilst seeking medical treatment for her oldest daughter. It was here that her ideas acquired concrete shape. She established the Kalavantula Samskarana Sangham at Adyar, Madras, in 1921, of which she became the secretary, while M. Venkata Rao and Darishi Chenchaiah became president and treasurer, respectively.[142] She toured the Andhra region, arranging conferences and delivering lectures in favour of reform in order to generate public support. Many responded positively, including the women and men

---

Grihalakshmi, September 1940, p. 432. She was invited to preside over the eighth Krishna District Women's Conference held on 4 April 1953 at Ghantasala. *Grihalakshmi*, April 1953, pp. 228–231.

[139] She presided over the first Kamma Women's Conference held in 1934 at Tenneru. *Grihalakshmi*, June 1934, pp. 303–306.

[140] One of the very few educated women from her caste, she regularly contributed to the Vishwa Brahmin caste journal *Prabodhini* and advocated women's education. For example, see 'Stree Vidya' (Women's Education), June 1915, pp. 7–11; 'Bharyaye Mantri' (The Wife is Minister), July 1915, pp. 21–23; 'Guname Roopamu' (Virtue is Beauty), August 1915, pp. 19–22. For other women's views on her, see 'Upadeshamu', *Prabodhini*, September 1915, pp. 12–14.

[141] The *kalavantulus* were part of a lineage of hereditary singer-dancers, sometimes referred to as *devadasis* or courtesans, who were associated with the performing arts and with sex work. They were known as *bhogamvallu*, but this term fell out of use in the early twentieth century due to pejorative connotations. The social reformer M. Venkata Rao coined the present-day name *kalavantulu* (artists) to promote self-esteem and respect. Poornatilakamma, who lived for 69 years, was born to a family of *kalavantulu* but did not undertake the traditional occupation to which her community was generally confined. She was influenced by Gandhi, took part in the freedom struggle and was even jailed for her participation. The influence of Gandhism was so strong that once she became a 'disciple' of Gandhi in 1919, she began to wear *khaddar* clothes and operate the *charkha* (spinning wheel). For details, see Darishi Chenchaiah, *Nenoo–Naa Desham*, pp. 175–182. Also see 'Srimati Yamini Poornatilaka', in Darishi Chenchaiah, *Naa Divya Smrutulu*, pp. 78–83.

[142] Before starting the association, Chenchaiah arranged her lectures in the National University, Adyar, and the Theosophical Society, to popularise Poornatilakamma and mobilise public opinion and sympathy for her mission. Darishi Chenchaiah, *Nenoo–Naa Desham*, p. 178.

belonging to her caste. At a conference held in Narasapuram, a *kalavanthin*, along with her sister, declared that she had decided to renounce her profession, expressed her desire to be trained as a teacher and appealed for help. In response, the 'Hindu Yuvati Sharanalayamu' was established to arrange for the rehabilitation of such women. To sustain the movement, Poornatilakamma published a fortnightly journal, *Hindu Yuvati*, which she herself edited.[143] Within three years of the launching of the movement, as many as 350 kalavantulu women were married. By 1930, the movement had spread far and wide with three more centres of reform being set up across the Andhra region.[144]

Women were so deeply concerned about the social reform movement that they came forward to financially assist in the ventures of reformers. About one such contribution, Veeresalingam wrote in the May 1897 issue of *Satya Samvardhani*:

> With regard to donations, another aspect has to be significantly mentioned. Learning that we are going to get prayer hall constructed, without our asking, three women heartily came forward, one contributing three rupees and the other two, rupees five each, thus a total of thirteen rupees were sent to me. I could have gratefully mentioned their names here. But I feel sorry for being unable to do that because of their request for anonymity. I feel that God likes more the threes and fives devotedly donated by the dependent women than the hundreds, two hundreds and three hundreds donated by the rich and earning men. [145]

Women's serious involvement in the social reform movement was a result of the realisation that their *agency* was a must in their development. Women gradually lost faith in the altruism of men's involvement in these efforts. This aspect manifested clearly from the 1930s: For instance, in a speech

[143]This important journal, unfortunately, is not available today. For a few details, see Chapter 2.

[144]For details, see Darishi Chenchaiah, *Nenoo-Naa Desham*, pp. 175–182. See also 'Srimati Yamini Poornatilaka', in Darishi Chenchaiah, *Naa Divya Smrutulu*, pp. 78–83.

[145]Kandukuri Veeresalingam, *Sweeya Charitramu*, Part 2, pp. 69–70. Similarly, when Veeresalingam proposed the establishment of a shelter home for widows in Madras, several women, including Europeans, made financial contributions. Fortunately, he recorded their names: Ms (Dr) McFeyil (Rs. 50), Ms Manning (Rs. 20), Bhaskarabhatla Lakshmamma (Re. 1), Kotikalapudi Sitamma (Rs. 5), Racharla Ratnamma (Rs. 4), Damaraju Sundaramma (Rs. 4), Sattiraju Sheshamanikyamba (Rs. 2) and Kandukuri Rajyalakshmamma (Rs. 5). Ibid., p. 106.

at the Godavari District Women's Conference held on 23 September 1933, Sarangu Sitadevi forcefully advocated women's self-agency.[146]

Women combined intellectualism with activism right from the start of the twentieth century. A pioneering role was played in this regard by the young Bhandaru Atchamamba.[147] A scholar-activist who only lived for about 30 years, Atchamamba (1874–1905) significantly contributed to the women's movement in colonial Andhra. She has the distinction of being the first woman short story writer, and also the first women's historian in Telugu. Her book, *Abala Sachcharitra Ratnamala* (*Lives of Noble Women*) dealt with 'heroines' in different periods of history, such as the queens Durgavati, Chand Bibi and Lakshmibai of Jhansi, as well as modern women such as Dr Anandibai Joshee, to prove the 'self-worth of women by dispelling the various deep-rooted prejudices against them'.[148] An ardent advocate of the cause of women, she travelled widely throughout the country and particularly encouraged the women of Andhra to come together by forming their own organisations. She emphasised women's education and unity in her lectures at several women's organisations as well as widely published articles in contemporary women's journals such as the *Hindu Sundary*. By the dawn of the twentieth century she had so firmly established herself as an accomplished scholar that Sattiraju Sitaramaiah, the founder of *Hindu Sundary*, requested her to become its editor, which she declined since she resided far away from Andhra.[149] Women from colonial Andhra treated her as a role model. She died of the bubonic plague on 18 January 1905, presumably contracted while serving plague-stricken children in Bilaspur. Her contemporaries paid glowing tributes to her contributions to the women's movement.[150]

---

[146] See 'Mahila Sabhalu', *Grihalakshmi*, November 1933, p. 755. Palagummi Satyanandam expressed similar views in her article, 'Streelu—Swatantryam' (Women and Independence), published in the 16 October 1945 issue of *Andhra Mahila*. She suggested to women that 'it was women who had to solve their problems. Men found neither the need nor the opportunity/time to solve women's problems. Hence, women should have adequate representation in the legislative bodies to reflect upon, identify and solve their specific problems.' Several such voices could be found in the succeeding chapters.

[147] For a few details on her life and achievements, see Volga et al, *Mahilavaranam*, p. 41.

[148] The book was published in 1901.

[149] Thus, she just missed the credit of being the first woman editor in Telugu. Sattiraju Sitaramaiah, *Sweeya Charitra*, pp. 81–82.

[150] When she passed away, the December 1904–January 1905 issue of the *Hindu Sundary* published an article appreciating her commendable services. Veeresalingam

While individual women were deeply interested in reforming their conditions and willing to do so in association with men and through organisations founded by male reformers, their collective journey for social reform really began with women starting their own independent organisations. A number of women's organisations were set up in the early twentieth century. As the organisations attest women's initiative and agency, it is necessary to dwell on them at some length.

Women Cross Domestic Thresholds: Formation of Women's Organisations[151]

The efforts of male social reformers in nineteenth-century India resulted in a new consciousness among a section of women who, by the close of the nineteenth century, took the issue of reform into their hands. They started several journals and established a number of organisations. Apart from regional organisations,[152] there emerged three major national organisations: the WIA in 1917, the National Council of Women in India (NCWI) in 1925, and the AIWC in 1927.[153]

---

published an article in the *Telugu Zenana* appraising her contribution to the women's movement in Andhra. See 'Srimati Bhandaru Atchamambagaru' (The Late Mrs B. Atchamamba), *Telugu Zenana Patrika & Sathihitha Bodhini*, February 1905, pp. 225–229. Atchamamba's photograph decorated the cover page of the June 1914 issue of the *Hindu Sundary*. For her short stories, see Sangisetty Srinivas, ed., *Bhandaru Atchamamba Toli Telugu Kathalu* (Hyderabad, 2010).

[151] I have borrowed the phrase 'crossing thresholds' from Meera Kosambi's *Crossing Thresholds: Feminist Essays in Social History* (Ranikhet, 2007).

[152] For women's organisations founded in Bengal, see Geraldine Forbes, *Women in Modern India* (New Delhi, 1988), pp. 70–71; and Bharati Ray, 'The Freedom Movement and Feminist Consciousness in Bengal, 1905–1929' in Bharati Ray ed., *From the Seams of History: Essays on Indian Women* (New Delhi, 2001 [1995]), pp. 204–205. For women's organisations in Maharashtra, see Padma Anagol, *The Emergence of Feminism in India, 1850–1920* (London and New York, 2017 [2005]), pp. 64–72. For organisations founded in the Hindi belt, see Suruchi Thapar-Bjorkert, *Women in the Indian National Movement: Unseen Faces and Unheard Voices, 1930–42* (New Delhi, 2006), pp. 218–222.

[153] For details, see Geraldine Forbes, *Women in Modern India*, pp. 72–83. For an in-depth study of the AIWC, see Aparna Basu and Bharati Ray, *Women's Struggle: A History of the All India Women's Conference 1927–2002*, 2nd ed. (New Delhi, 2003 [1990]).

Colonial Andhra too witnessed the emergence of women's organisations from the beginning of the twentieth century, fuelled by these new modes of thinking:

> There are a number of problems specific to women, which need to be resolved by women themselves. In such matters, whatever the amount of effort men put, without our help, they cannot shoulder that burden all alone and succeed. More importantly, they do not know about our problems in such a greater detail as we do. To discuss such problems and find solutions, we need women's organisations.[154]

The Aska Stree Samajamu, the first known important women's organisation in Andhra, was established at Aska (in present-day Odisha) on 18 September 1902. Burra Buchchi Bangaramma (hereafter Bangaramma) was its founder-secretary. Monthly meetings were conducted regularly and the organisation emphasised the promotion of girls' education.[155] Women met regularly and discussed and delivered lectures—these were on a range of issues such as the dismal position of Hindu women, promotion of women's education, devotion to husband and god, loyalty to the British Raj, friendship and unity among women and the need for women's organisations. Initially, there was so much opposition to the organisation that 'it was criticised in and around the village'. Gradually, 'the clouds of criticism scattered, and even the old ladies started attending its meetings'. The organisation maintained close ties with British women.[156]

[154]See Tumpudi Satyavati Bhagavatamma's presidential speech delivered at the seventh Arya Vaishya Women's Conference held at Vayalpadu on 14 July 1928. 'Adhyakshopanyasamu', *Vasavi*, August 1928, pp. 196–200; for this reference, p. 196. In her welcome address to the same conference, Polepalli Ranganayakamma said that 'the problems faced by the society of women had to be discussed and resolved in women's conferences themselves'. Further, she remarked that 'she treated it to be her fortune to seeing women gathered in the conference hall to discuss such matters and put them into practice.' Ibid., p. 195.

[155]Bangaramma found that many girls of Aska were unable to attend the girls' school as it was away from the village. Hence, she proposed that a bullock cart be hired for conveyance, and its maintenance cost raised through voluntary contributions. Women happily agreed to the proposal and the girls started attending the school.

[156]Burra Buchchi Bangaramma, 'Aska Hindu Stree Samajamu Prathama Samvatsarika Reportu' (The First Annual Report of the Aska Hindu Women's Association), *Hindu Sundary*, December 1903; 'Stree Vidyabhimani' (pseudonym), 'Aska Stree Samajapu Samvatsarotsavamu', *Telugu Zenana*, October 1903, pp. 115–17.

The Brundavanapura Stree Samajamu was founded in Machilipatnam by Oruganti Sundari Ratnamba,[157] an MA, in November 1902. It soon became defunct, but was revived on 17 September 1904 with the efforts of Prabhala Satyavatamma, Nadhavazhzhala Saraswatamma, Valluru Parvatamma, C. Pankajamma and others. Motupalli Rajabayamma managed it single-handedly, discharging the duties of secretary, treasurer and librarian. Meeting once or twice a month 'according to convenience', its main objectives were discussing issues such as household management, women's health, natural science and history; delivering lectures; and reading good books (*sadgranthamulu*). Twenty-four meetings in total were conducted in 1905; in 1906, approximately 50 women attended the meetings. The organisation had a library with a good number of books and a few journals. Most significantly, it established a girls' school which eventually grew into a girls' high school, later taken up by the government. It appears to have continued well beyond the 1960s.[158]

The Bharati Samajamu was begun by Bangaramma in 1904, based in Visakhapatnam. Buddhavarapu Veeralakshmamma and Bulusu Sooramma were its president and secretary, respectively. Its seventh anniversary, celebrated on 16–17 May 1912, was attended by 300 women, including a few English women. Kandukuri Venkayamma Rao, the woman zamindar of Urlam, presided over the assembly and delivered a lecture focusing on issues such as the low position of women and the need for their education, particularly higher education. She also addressed a number of other issues, inclusing child marriage, kanyasulkam, *varasulkam*, women's freedom and independence, particularly economic independence, pativratyam (conjugal fidelity), prostitution, etc. Rao strongly advised women to pursue careers in medicine as this would enable women patients to consult woman

---

[157] An Indian Christian woman, she was also known as Hyenna Ratnam. Having studied at Noble College, Machilipatnam, she became the disciple of Sir Raghupati Venkataratnam Naidu, a well-respected reform leader. After the death of her husband, a barrister, she served as the principal of the Vani Vilas Girls' College in Bangalore. Her older sister Kamala Sattianathan was the editor of *The Indian Ladies' Magazine* and their father was a famous public personality. See Ayyadevara Kaleswara Rao, *Navyandhramu: Naa Jeevita Katha* (Hyderabad, 2006 [1959]), p. 38.

[158] Dronamraju Durgamma, 'Brundavanapura Stree Samajamu', *Hindu Sundary*, December 1906, pp. 7–10; 'Brundavanapura Stree Samajamu—Gata Samvatsara Charitramu—Secretary Riportu' (The Women's Organisation of Brundavan—Last Year's History–Secretary's Report), *Hindu Sundary*, December 1906, pp. 10–17; 'Brundavana Stree Samajamu', *Hindu Sundary*, May 1905, pp. 41–46.

doctors without hesitation. As their presence in the assembly suggests, the organisation maintained close contact with English women.[159]

Another body, the Stree Sanatana Dharma Mandali, was established in Guntur (Arandal Peta) probably in 1906.[160] Along with Eka Venkata Ratnamma, president of the organisation, and Ippagunta Venkamamba, its secretary, Patri Sheshagiramma, Govindaraju Adilakshmamma and Poluri Manikyamba were among its important functionaries. By March 1910, there were 200 members. The organisation established a school for Hindu girls in 1908 with an all-women faculty.[161] The organisation owned its own building and employed a woman attender. An important constituent in the history of the women's reform in Andhra, it was active for many years and deserves recognition for hosting the first all-Andhra Women's Conference in 1910 and inaugurating the pan-Andhra women's movement.

The idea of establishing the Andhra Mahila Samajamu at Barampuram (Brahmapur, now in Ganjam District, Odisha) was first articulated by Mosalikanti Ramabayamma, editor of *Hindu Sundary*, but did not materialise until 1906, when the idea took concrete shape with the efforts of the local women.[162] The by-laws of the organisation were prepared in 1912,[163] with Gade Chudikudutamma as president, Meenakshamma as vice-president and Varahagiri Venkata Subbamma (whose son, V. V. Giri, would later become President of independent India) as secretary. Women met weekly at the homes of members to discuss various issues concerning women. Gade Chudikudutamma had a building constructed for the organisation near Victoria market, while other women contributed furniture, etc. Though its name suggested that it was an organisation of 'Andhra women', membership was open to other linguistic communities as well, including Europeans. The organisation maintained a library, the Vijayalakshmi Pustaka

[159] *Vivekavathi*, July 1912, pp. 301–302.

[160] 'Stree Sanatana Dharma Mandali', *Hindu Sundary*, February–March 1910, pp. 41–43.

[161] See the observations made by Varanasi Annapoornamma, President of the Reception Committee of the first Andhra Mahila Mahasabha (AMMS) in *Upanyasa Manjari* (Kakinada, 1910), pp. I–II. She was 'very happy' to note that the management of the school was planning to appoint a 'trained female teacher'. Ibid., p. II.

[162] The following information about the organisation is from its Diamond Jubilee Souvenir. *Andhra Mahila Samajamu, Barampuram (Ganjam): Vajrotsava Sanchika—1972.* Other details not available.

[163] Creating scientific, social and moral consciousness among women; encouraging fine arts and handicrafts useful to women; and spreading of valuable knowledge, were some of the objectives of the organisation.

Bhandagaram, which prospered under the care of Konda Vijayalakshmi, a polyglot who had translated Premchand's *Sevasadan* into Telugu. The organisation remained active through the years and regularly sent their representatives to important women's meetings and organisations. Sitabai attended national women's forums like the AIWC; Bodapati Alivelamma participated in conferences by AIWC's regional branch, the Andhra Rashtra Mahila Mahasabha conferences held in Kakinada, Eluru, Bezawada, etc. The organisation supported the Child Marriage Bill (popularly known as the Sarda Bill, eventually enacted in 1929) and sent resolutions to the colonial government. In her reminiscences, Mulavisala Rajeshwari writes that her 'burlesque on the evil consequences of child marriage' was staged in collaboration with the organisation. Her one-act play on alcoholism, titled *Surapaanam*, was also staged around 1936. She wrote that the women of the organisation 'always thought about making progress. Like this, we served the nation indirectly.'[164] The Andhra Mahila Samajamu was later active during calamities such as the Bengal famine in 1943, a devastating cyclone in Odisha in 1968, etc. What is important about this organisation is that unlike many of the early women's organisations that were active only briefly, or did not do well despite their years, it actively sustained itself as an organisation and even brought out a volume in 1972 to celebrate its 'diamond jubilee'.

The Hindu Stree Vidyabhivardhani Samajamu was established in 1910 at Kurnool again at the initiative of Bangaramma.[165] Janamma and S. Sundaramma were its president and secretary. It conducted weekly meetings where 30 to 40 women assembled, and a total of 35 meetings were conducted in 1911. Women discussed issues such as women's education, devotion to god and husband, morality, compassion, cleanliness, chastity and household management. An event to commemorate its first anniversary on 9 November 1911 was attended by about 200 women, including a few Europeans (like many other organisations in this period, the Samajamu maintained close ties with European women). Delivering the inaugural address, Bangaramma stressed the significance of women's education.[166]

The Satya Samvardhani Samajamu was established on 6 January 1911 in Vijayanagaram. P. Lakshmikantamma was unanimously elected its

[164] Mulavisala Rajeshwari, 'Naa Anubhavalu' in ibid., pp. 25–26.

[165] See 'Hindu Stree Vidyabhivardhani Samajamu', *Vivekavathi*, May 1912, p. 254.

[166] S. Sundaramma, 'Kurnoolu Stree Vidyarthini Samajapu Reportu', *Hindu Sundary*, March 1912, pp. 16–19; S. Sundaramma, 'Kurnoolu Stree Vidyarthini Samaja Dwitiya Samvatsara Reportu', *Hindu Sundary*, December 1912, pp. 14–17.

permanent president. Gundala Subhadramma and P. Tripura Sundaramma were its secretaries. The organisation listed 15 topics for regular discussion, including women's education, position of women, unity among women, advantages of women's organisations, child marriage, etc. The organisation possessed a large number of books. Its second anniversary, celebrated in 'grandeur' on 4 January 1913, was presided over by Kallepalle Venkata Ramanamma. It was attended by 300 women on the first day, and 500 on the second. The issue of enforced widowhood received greater attention.[167]

The Shri Vidyarthini Samajamu (established on 30 January 1903 in Kakinada), also known as Kakinada Vidyarthini Samajamu, was perhaps the most vibrant of all the organisations established before the 1920s. Pulugurta Lakshmi Narasamamba (henceforth Narasamamba) was its founder-secretary.[168] About 30 women regularly assembled on Fridays at her residence and by the end of 1903, as many as 60 meetings had been held. After a few years, it went through a period of inactivity and was revived on 8 April 1910 with Narasamamba as president. Balantrapu Sheshamma and Damerla Sitamma became its secretaries. 'Promoting education among all the Telugu [Hindu] women', 'raising their moral standards' and thus 'making them useful to society and country' were its chief objectives. To achieve this, a five-fold strategy was designed: Enrolling all the 'respectable' and caste Hindu women (*Hindu kulastreelanellara*) as members, and conducting weekly meetings; mobilising funds for the organisation; maintaining a library; establishing a Girls' School, where widows (*vitantu sodarimanulu*), girls (*kanyamanulu*) and women of the *zenana* would be enrolled; establishing girls' schools and women's organisations in the neighbouring towns and villages and encouraging others towards the same.[169] Its work proceeded smoothly for a year after revival.

---

[167] See 'Satya Samvardhani Samajamuyokka Dwiteeya Samvatsara Reportu' (Second Annual Report of the Satya Samvardhani Samajamu), *Hindu Sundary*, January-February 1913, pp. 9–15.

[168] She provided a detailed account regarding the founding of the organisation. Bhandaru Atchamamba, a scholar, activist and the author of *Abala Sachcharitra Ratnamala*, provided the inspiration. For more details, see Pulugurta Lakshmi Narasamamba, 'Shri Kakinada Vidyarthini Sanghamuyokka Praprathamavatsara Vishayagnapanamu' (The First Annual Report of the Kakinada Vidyarthini Samajamu), *Savithri*, March 1904.

[169] See 'Sri Vidyarthini Samajamu, Kakinada', *Savithri*, March 1911, pp. 17–21.

Image 1.1: The Shri Vidyarthini Samajamu, Kakinada

Source: *Grihalakshmi*, June 1934.

Soon the organisation became a site of a heated and protracted controversy. Controversy raged about the presence of remarried women (*punarvivahitalu*, that is, widows who remarried) in the regular meetings of the organisation, and also in its first anniversary celebrations held on 30 April 1911 along with the second Andhra Mahila Mahasabha. Narasamamba opposed the presence of the *punarvivahita*s who, according to her, were not '*kulanganas*' (chaste women). The conservative group—headed by her—expelled the secretaries on the charge that they had 'transgressed the rules of the organisation' by bringing remarried women to its meetings. The 'expelled' secretaries fought back intensely and their claim was supported by many. Narasamamba was ultimately replaced by Kallepalle Venkata Ramanamma, who served as president till 1916. The organisation headed by Ramanamma and the secretaries who had earlier been expelled was recognised as the 'authentic' organisation. It was registered in their name on 27 September 1911 with clearly outlined rules and regulations regarding the conduct of the organisation.[170] New office-bearers were also elected. By 30 March 1913, it had 37 members. Nalam Raghavamma succeeded Venkata Ramanamma as president. From the 1940s onwards Koka Krishnavenamma and Vemuganti Papayamma headed the organisation.

[170]See 'Sri Vidyarthini Samajamu, Kakinada', *Hindu Sundary*, October 1914, pp. 1–6.

The Samajamu is remarkable for several reasons and contributed immensely to the regional women's movement. It published the famous women's monthly *Hindu Sundary* for more than half a century; took the initiative in convening state-level women's conferences like the Andhra Mahila Mahasabhas; and it started a girls' school, the Shri Mahila Vidyalayamu, as well as a library, the Rajyalakshmi Pustaka Bhandagaramu. The organisation seems to have been active till the 1960s.

The Sharada Niketanamu was established in 1922 in Guntur by Unnava Lakshmibayamma and her husband, the famous nationalist and social reformer, Unnava Lakshminarayana. It is important to note that this was a residential institution where girls lived and studied, several of whom were educated free of cost. For instance, the institution is recorded to have provided for a young girl, Pichchamma, who was from an oppressed caste. Since the organisation was headed by nationalists, its students played an important role in the freedom movement. Sharada Niketanamu was actively engaged in social reform and conducted 30 widow remarriages. The Niketanamu was active for at least a quarter-century: its 'silver jubilee' celebrations were presided over by Sangam Lakshmibayamma, an alumnus.[171]

The Bharata Mahila Mandali was founded by Komarraju Atchamamba in 1928 at Vijayawada. Turlapati Raja Rajeshwaramma served as its president. Initially, its membership was very low with just five to six members, but it rose to 50 by 1940. Women regularly assembled in the organisation's spacious grounds and played various sports like tennis, carrom and badminton. It also played an important role in the propagation of Hindi.[172]

The Stree Hitaishini Mandali was established in 1931 at Bapatla. Velagapudi Saraswatamma and Kanuparti Varalakshmamma were its president and secretary, respectively. Women regularly assembled here twice a week to read newspapers and magazines and discuss literary and social issues. Varalakshmamma invited many learned women and men from various places to deliver lectures and educate its members[173] and the

---

[171] Kanuparti Varalakshmamma, *Unnava Dampatulu* (*The Unnava Couple*) (Vullipalem, 1963).

[172] 'Bharata Mahila Mandali, Bezawada', *Grihalakshmi*, May 1940, p. 193.

[173] On the occasion of its fourth anniversary, lectures were delivered on issues such as the need for women's organisations, women's education, right to property, domestic management, etc. A few women read their poems and girls performed plays on social issues like dowry. A large number of women attended it. See 'Sabhalu-Nivedikalu: Stree Hitaishini Mandali, Bapatla', *Grihalakshmi*, September 1935, pp. 569–572.

Image 1.2: Sharada Niketanamu, Guntur

Source: *Grihalakshmi*, October 1929.

Mandali organised a unique programme of 'summer classes' for women in Andhra in 1941.[174] It remained active even after independence. Malladi Subbamma, a well-known activist, served as its secretary for five years.[175]

The Stree Vidyabhivardhani Samajamu was established in 1938 at Narasaraopeta with the encouragement of Unnava Lakshmibayamma and Rayasam Ratnamma. Meetings were conducted once a month, structured around enlightening lectures on women's issues. It had a library; books were sent to members' homes, catering to the needs of the otherwise busy

[174]Kanuparti Varalakshmamma, 'Streela Vesangi Pathashala, Bapatla' (Women's Summer School, Bapatla), *Grihalakshmi*, September 1941, pp. 427–428.

[175]*Stree Swechcha,* August 2001, p. 50.

housewives, and thus inculcating a taste for reading. About 25 girls attended its stitching and music classes.[176] The Sri Bala Saraswati Samajamu was established at Tanuku (West Godavari district) in 1932 in the memory of Bala Saraswati, daughter of Inturi Premavatamma. Devulapalli Satyavatamma acted as its president. The organisation got a building constructed and was registered in 1941.[177]

The Andhra Mahila Sabha was the most prominent women's organisation in the period, and remains influential to the present day. Established under the able leadership of Gummadidala Durgabayamma, better known as Durgabai Deshmukh, it had its genesis in a small children's club named 'The Little Ladies of Brindavan', which was formed in June 1938 at Mylapur, Madras.[178] The organisation with its present name came into existence on 4 February 1942. Lakshmi Venkayyamma Rao, the Rani of Mirzapuram, was its president. Rani Rao Rajyalakshmi (Rani of Jayapuram) and Vijayalakshmana Rao (Rani of Vuyyuru) served as vice-presidents. Durgabai Deshmukh was secretary and Nirmala Devi the joint secretary. It had 13 lifetime members.[179]

The organisation was extremely involved in promoting women's education. Knowledge of Hindi was emphasised. Subjects like English, history, mathematics, science, etc. were also taught. Many girls attended their classes, passed various examinations conducted by different boards and universities, obtained degrees and took to professions, particularly

---

[176] *Andhra Mahila*, February 1946, p. 43.

[177] It had many wings dealing with education, industry, health, music, drawing, etc. Sanskrit, Hindi, Telugu, History, Geography, Mathematics, music, drawing and primary health were the subjects taught in the school attached to it. Girls were trained to take up examinations such as 'Bhasha Praveena' in Sansktrit, and 'Bhasha Visharada' in Hindi. Training was provided both in vocal and instrumental music. By 1946, 53 girl students had enrolled there. The organisation had a rich library with a collection of about 3,000 books on various subjects, and many journals. *Andhra Mahila*, 15 May 1944, pp. 25–26; *Andhra Mahila*, March 1946, p. 40.

[178] See 'Andhra Mahila Sabha Sankshipta Charitra' (Brief History of Andhra Mahila Sabha), *Andhra Mahila*, February 1944.

[179] The objectives read as the following: 'Our aim is the upliftment of Andhra women; progress of the Andhra [region] is our ideal. We are committed to the promotion of education, knowledge and the arts [among women]. We would like to bring all women of Andhra on a single platform. We carry forward with this mission and work for the victory of the women's movement. Thus, we ensure the well-being of the country'. Ibid.

teaching.[180] Along with the improvement of knowledge, emphasis was laid on inculcating a taste for fine arts. Training was provided in theatre, arts and literature. Its industry wing promoted the *Swadeshi* principles of using home-spun cloth. The Sabha had a 'debating club', where women discussed issues that concerned them. Further, it published a women's journal, the *Andhra Mahila*, for the promotion of women's writings. The Sabha maintained a hostel to accommodate poor and orphan girls from different parts of Andhra and enable their education.[181]

There were several other organisations, such as the Balika Vidyabhivardhani Samajamu (established in March 1905, Bellary, now in Karnataka),[182] Helapura Zenana Prarthana Samajamu (24 November 1910, Eluru),[183] Bharata Mahila Sharada Samajam (Anantapur), Mahila Samajamu (Nandyala) and Mahila Samajamu (1942, Madanapalli).[184] Apart from organisations established in towns, several also sprang up at the village level. The Tadikonda Grama Mahila Sanghamu was established in 1942 at Tadikonda with the efforts of a few women of the village.[185] The Mahila Sanghamu established in Gudivada, Krishna District, in September 1945 remained a vibrant space well into the late 1960s.[186] The Grama Mahila Sanghamu, Panditavillooru, was established in February 1942. Several district and *taluq* level women's organisations too came up. As caste consciousness entered new phase in Andhra from the early twentieth century, many more caste associations emerged which undertook social

[180] See 'Maa Vidya Shakha' (Our Education Wing), *Andhra Mahila*, 5 June 1945, pp. 2–6.

[181] *Profile of Andhra Mahila Sabha*, other details not available.

[182] 'The Hindu Girls' Education Society, Bellary', *Telugu Zenana*, April and May 1905, p. 342.

[183] Sattiraju Shyamalamba, 'Helapura Prarthana Samajamu', *Hindu Sundary*, April 1912, pp. 28–31.

[184] Malladi Subbamma, *Women's Movement and Associations: Regional Perspective (1860–1993)* (Hyderabad, 1994), 1994, p. 59.

[185] By 1946, it had 215 members. No caste discrimination was allowed while enrolling members. Women from all castes, including the 'untouchable' women, were present in it. See 'Tadikonda Grama Mahila Sanghamu', *Andhra Mahila*, February 1946, p. 42.

[186] For its history and achievements, see the essay titled 'Mahila Sanghamu—Gudivada', in S. Manorama Devi et al., ed., *Mahila Sanghamu: Gudivada-Bhavana Prarambhotsava Sanchika, 28 April 1966*, other details not available, pp. 1–5.

reform activities. Gradually, caste-based women's organisations too came into existence.[187]

Image 1.3: Bharata Mahila Sharada Samajamu, Anantapur

Source: *Grihalakshmi*, September 1936.

Separate women's organisations associated with the Communist Party of India (CPI) were established in the early 1940s. Differences between the Communist and the pro-Congress women came to a head at the annual session of the AIWC held at Kakinada in December 1941.[188] Despite this,

---

[187] For example, the Vaishya Streela Sanghamu (Vaishya Women's Association) was established in Chennapuri (Madras) probably in 1911. It convened a conference in 1911, chaired by Kamalamba and attended by 500 Vaishya women. See 'Vaishya Streela Sanghamu', *Savithri*, 1911, p. 13. The Vaishya Seva Sadanamu was founded by Nalam Ramalingaiah in Rajahmundry (1920). The Akhila Bharata Arya Vaishya Mahila Sabha (All India Arya Vaishya Women's Conference) was held on 7 June 1944 in Kurichedu. It was presided over by Chunduri Ratnamma. *Andhra Mahila*, 1 August 1944, p. 9. The Kammas—an affluent peasant caste—rigorously pursued reform activities in their caste group and gradually separate women's associations came into being. The first Kamma Women's Conference was held on 27 March 1934 at Tenneru. It was presided over by Jaasti Sita Mahalakshmi. *Grihalakshmi*, June 1934, pp. 303–306.

[188] AIWC membership fees became the bone of contention. AIWC leaders turned down a proposal by Communist leader Manikonda Suryavati to lower the fees to 4 *anna*s from the existing Rs. 3. Goparaju Sitadevi, another prominent Communist, observed in her autobiography that Congress women leaders such as Konda Parvatidevi maintained

the former continued to carry out their work on the AIWC platform till 1947. Over January and February 1943, the CPI conducted a month-long training camp for women in Vijayawada that proved deeply impactful and accelerated the Communist women's movement.[189] Donning khakhi shirts and shorts and holding sticks, women communists marched through the streets of Vijayawada during the camp.[190] Several district-level conferences were held before the launch of the state-level Sangham. Thousands of women thronged these meetings.[191] The Krishna District Women's Sangham organised its seventh conference at Katuru on 29–30 April 1945.[192]

Although the women communists had been planning to float a state-level organisation since 1941, their plan did not materialise till 1947.[193] The state-level ARMS was organised on 15–16 February 1947 at Chivuluru in Guntur district. The conference clearly stated their reasons for breaking away

---

a hostile attitude towards their Communist counterparts and were not ready to work with them. She complained that women of the AIWC restricted the membership only to urban, educated women and did not allow the women's movement to expand to rural areas. This has led to the formation of alternative women's organisations, where rural peasant and labouring women were represented. Goparaju Sitadevi, *Janani, Janma Bhoomischa: Goparaju Sitadevi Sweeya Charitra*, (Vijayawada, n. d.), pp. 41–42.

[189] Ibid., pp. 42–45.

[190] Sitadevi wrote in excitement that the 'women's march-past surprised the people of Bezawada'. Further, she remarked that 'the Communist movement created great consciousness, self-confidence and courage among women'. Ibid., p. 47.

[191] Ibid., pp. 52–55.

[192] Founded in 1937, by 1945 it was the largest such association with branches in 220 villages and a membership of 11,000. It undertook a campaign in 200 villages, and among 20,000 women, in favour of proposed amendments to the Hindu Law to ensure equal rights to women. In this regard, it collected signatures of 8,000 women and men and submitted a memorandum to the government. Ibid., pp. 62–63.

[193] As we have noted earlier, although there were differences on the issue of membership fee and the non-recognition of the members enrolled by them, communist women did not completely break away from the ARMS. The 17th conference of the ARMS (Rajahmundry, 1945) dealt a harsh blow to the Communists. Here the by-laws of the organisation were changed. One such change debarred any woman whose husband was already married from becoming members. Evidently this was aimed at excluding Dr Komarraju Atchamamba, an important Communist leader, since she was the second wife of her husband. See Malladi Subbamma, *Women's Movement and Associations*, pp. 81–82. A few women criticised the rule: B. Kameshwaramma, for instance, termed it as 'disgusting' and stated that 'inserting such rules in the constitution to settle personal scores was gross injustice'. See 'Andhra Rashtra Mahila Sabha Kartavyamu' (Duty of the Andhra Rashtra Mahila Sabha), *Andhra Mahila*, January 1946, p. 5.

from the ARMS/AIWC and the need for a more radical organisation.[194] The Sangham's inauguration was preceded by a huge procession of some 2,000 women; the public meeting held during this time was attended by 10,000 people, of whom 6,000 were women. The cultural programme was attended by 15,000 people. The objectives of the Sangham were clearly laid down and office-bearers elected.[195] The second conference of the Andhra Rashtra Mahila Sangham was held at Vijayawada in May 1948. The government of independent India banned the conference and imposed Section 144 of the Indian Penal Code (IPC) on the area, prohibiting any gatherings. Defying the ban, a thousand women took out a procession. The police used tear gas on the procession and arrested 75 women. The Sangham published a monthly, *Andhra Vanita*, which too was banned.[196]

The communist women's organisations marked a sharp departure from the other women's organisations. They fostered a new consciousness among women and emphasised a new value system in the women's movement, thereby freeing it from the confines of the middle class and ensuring that it reached the grassroots. In other words, they democratised the women's movement. Goparaju Sitadevi, a prominent communist leader and activist in the contemporary women's movement, proudly claimed that 'unlike the AIWC, which was confined to the urban centres [and the middle class], the specialty of the ARMS was that it expanded the women's movement by taking it to rural areas'.[197] An editorial in *Andhra Mahila* substantiated her claim.[198] These organisations were so vibrant—and therefore such a threat

---

[194] The report submitted at the conference claimed that there were 100 women's organisations (associated with the Communist Party) spread in seven districts. They had 25,000 members, and 725 trained cadres. Goparaju Sitadevi, *Janani, Janma Bhoomischa*, p. 65.

[195] The detailed by-laws were prepared and approved by the conference. A few notable goals were: working to achieve equal civil, political and economic rights of women; promoting scientific temper among women and encouraging them towards social service and reform; working with other democratic organisations and the national movement for achieving complete independence for the country; and establishing a democratic government. Ibid., p. 66.

[196] Ibid., p. 69.

[197] Ibid., p. 66.

[198] The editorial commented that women's organisations associated with the Communist Party exhibited political consciousness, and 'began a new chapter in the women's movement in Andhra'. See *Andhra Mahila*, 20 September, 1945, p. 3. This remark is important because it comes from a journal, whose founder is a staunch Congressite.

to other groups—that a few Congress leaders, including prominent peasant leader N. G. Ranga and Ayyadevara Kaleswara Rao, made sexually charged comments and spread canards against women communists.[199] There were several others, including women, who made absurd remarks and leveled baseless allegations about the communist women's associations,[200] which were vehemently countered by them.[201]

Thus, a large number of women's organisations, established throughout the first half of the twentieth century, sustained the social reform movement in Andhra. It was not surprising that Ayyadevara Kaleswara Rao, a prominent nationalist leader, expressed his admiration for this period: 'those had been the days of women's organisations. They created among women consciousness and an urge for education and individuality.'[202]

In Pursuit of an Expanded Public Space: The Andhra Mahila Mahasabha

Even as there were consistent efforts to establish women's organisations in various towns and villages, attempts were also made to bring all women of the Andhra region on a single platform. As a result, the Andhra Mahila Mahasabha (AMMS), formally known as the All-Andhra Women's

[199] Goparaju Sitadevi brought to light the meanness of such leaders. She said that rather than appreciating and encouraging women who came forward, the Congress leaders issued derogatory statements that such women were 'butterflies'. Goparaju Sitadevi, *Janani, Janma Bhoomischa*, pp. 63–64. Dr Komarraju Atchamamba lashed out at such people in her presidential address, delivered at the Krishna District Conference of communist women. Ibid.

[200] Kilaru Tripuramba attacked communist women, writing that their programme was simply communist propaganda and not a women's movement. She also alleged that they did not work for women's right to inheritance, which the ARMS did. She sought to exclude communist women from the larger movement. See *Andhra Mahila*, January 1946, p. 44.

[201] Bhupatiraju Venkamma sharply reacted to the charges made by Tripuramba. Stating that they were 'far from the truth', she detailed various programmes undertaken by communist women's organisations and emphasised that only they could truly work for the progress of women. Also she attacked ARMS' decision to exclude communists from its ranks. See Bhupatiraju Venkamma's rejoinder to Kilaru Tripuramba, 'Stree Sanghalu–Communistulu' (Women's Organisations and the Communists), *Andhra Mahila*, March 1946, p. 13.

[202] Ayyadevara Kaleswara Rao, *Navyandhramu*: *Naa Jeevita Katha*, p. 64.

Organisation, came into existence. Its first conference was held on 2 June 1910 in Guntur under the auspices of the Stree Sanatana Dharma Mandali. Pulugarta Lakshmi Narasamamba presided over it. Although the exact number of women who attended the conference is not known, sources mention that women in 'big numbers', and 'from all over Andhra', attended the conference, and that it was 'successful'.[203] AMMS conferences thereafter convened annually in different parts of Andhra.

The second AMMS was held on 28–29 April 1911 at Kakinada under the aegis of the Kakinada Vidyarthini Samajamu, with Narasamamba as its convener. Details regarding the issues to be discussed, arrangements for the conference and other relevant information were notified in the March 1911 issue of *Savithri*. Quite surprisingly, widow remarriage was not included among the proposed discussion; instead, the meet chose to discuss 'how widows could make themselves useful!'[204] The third AMMS conference, (23–24 May 1912, Nidudavolu) was presided over by Bangaramma and its agenda included some 20 topics.[205]

The fourth conference was held on 23–24 March 1913 at Machilipatnam. It is noteworthy that the nature of the issues discussed at this Mahasabha was markedly different from earlier AMMS conferences. A few among them were: the need for, and the means of, promoting women's higher education throughout the country; appealing to the government for the establishment of girls' schools in every village and town; establishing shelter homes for 'victimised women' and educating them; appointing female teachers, particularly widows, in girls' schools; appealing to the government to establish a training school for girls who received higher education in

[203] Women's education was emphasised, including vocational education for girls. The AMMS expressed happiness at the emergence of 'numerous' women's organisations at local level. It urged that these organisations meet every week or month, discuss women's issues and thus work for greater progress. 'Andhra Mahila Mahasabha, Kakinada', *Savithri*, March 1911, p. 6.

[204] Several women delivered speeches on issues like women's education, health, spiritual knowledge, devotion to god, unity among women, pativratyam, child marriages, etc. See ibid., pp. 1–8.

[205] A few among the listed issues were: women's education, characteristics of educated women, characteristics of women who were proud of being educated, service that women could render to the nation, marriage dharmas hindering women's education and the ways to eradicate them, were widow remarriages helpful to women's education? What was essential for the progress of the nation–widow remarriages or celibacy, duties of widows, domestic management, pativratya, etc. See 'Andhra Mahila Sabha, Nidudavolu', *Hindu Sundary*, April 1912, pp. 22–25.

Telugu medium; appealing also to award scholarships to widows and enhance salaries for women teachers; discouraging the marriage of girls below the age of 16 years; abolishing the practices of kanyasulkam and varasulkam; opposing marriages between men above 40 years of age and girls younger than 16; bringing unity among the four *varna*s and various sub-castes; appealing to the rich and those without children to donate part of their wealth to educational institutions or establish schools themselves; and encouraging the establishment of women's associations in various parts of the country. It is interesting to note that the issue of widow remarriage was not included in this extensive list, suggesting that orthodox opinion against widow remarriages in the AMMS remained dominant.[206]

The fifth AMMS meeting (11–12 May 1914, Vijayawada) was presided over by Kotikalapudi Sitamma; about 200 delegates from various parts of Andhra attended the conference, apart from 400–500 local women.[207] The sixth meeting was held in 1915 at Visakhapatnam[208] and the seventh in May 1916 at Kakinada.[209] The eighth AMMS conference was held on 1–2 June 1917 at Vikramapuri (Nellore) with Kashinathuni Ramabayamma as general president. About 500 delegates from various parts of Andhra attended the conference and a total of seventeen issues were raised. Women's education was emphasised and it was felt that educated women should maintain 'good conduct'. Addressing the conference, Kanchanapalli Kanakamma focused on the limited educational opportunities available to women and the lack of schools for girls. Most importantly, she proposed establishment of a women's university.[210] The ninth AMMS was held at Cuddapah in June 1918.[211] Many more conferences of the AMMS may have been conducted, details of which are no longer available.

[206] 'Andhra Mahila Sabha', *Hindu Sundary*, January-February 1913, pp. 22–24.

[207] Motupalli Rajabayamma, who reported the proceedings, felt happy at the 'large turnout of women' and held it to be a 'sign of women's likely progress in future'. See 'Aidava Andhra Mahila Mahajana Sabha', *Hindu Sundary*, May 1914, pp. 13–14.

[208] 'Saptama Andhra Mahila Mahasabha', *Hindu Sundary*, April, 1916, p. 48.

[209] Ibid., p. 48.

[210] 'Enimidava Andhra Mahila Sabha', *Hindu Sundary*, June 1917, pp. 2 & 6.

[211] *Soundaryavalli*, July 1918, pp. 31–32. It was presided over by Salla Soundaryavalli Amma, who spoke on issues like compulsory education, regional languages, nationalist education, child rearing and the evil effects of western culture on Indians, particularly women. Resolutions were passed demanding a women's college in the ceded districts (Rayalaseema), and a women's university in Andhra.

Integrating with the Pan-India Women's Movement: The Andhra Rashtra Mahila Mahasabha

Image 1.4: Saptama Andhra Rashtra Mahila Mahasabha, Eluru

Source: *Grihalakshmi*, 1934.

The Andhra Rashtra Mahila Mahasabha (ARMS) came into existence in 1927 as a regional branch of the AIWC. It regularly conducted annual conferences in different parts of Andhra, integrating the Andhra women's movement with pan-India activism. The first ARMS conference was held in 1927 at Kakinada. The third conference, which was held in 1929 at Vijayawada and presided by Muthulakshmi Reddy, passed 12 resolutions regarding women's right to property, the Sarda Act, abolition of the devadasi system, Hindu–Muslim unity, ban on liquor, etc.[212]

The fifth conference (21–22 November 1931, Guntur) was held at Rayasam Ratnamma's initiative. Adipudi Vasundhara Devi, who had both an MA and a BSc., presided over it and Dr Danamma, a Christian woman, headed the reception committee. Apart from the 60 delegates who came from all over Andhra, a large number of women from Guntur and neighbouring areas too attended the conference. According to Kanuparti Varalakshmamma, the conference was 'distinctly different' from many other women's conferences held there because it attracted women of all

[212] 'Andhra Mahila Sabha–Bejawada', *Grihalakshmi*, December 1929, pp. 901–908.

religions and castes. The discussions held over a number of women's issues generated great 'enthusiasm and heat'.[213] The sixth conference was held in November 1932 at Rajahmundry.[214] The seventh conference, held on 4–5 November 1933 at Eluru in West Godavari district, was presided over by Muthulakshmi Reddy.[215] Resolutions adopted in the conference included proposals for registered marriages, women's right to inheritance, abolition of prostitution, establishment of orphanages, co-educational spaces, and higher education for girls (particularly medical education), and a separate college for Andhra women. However, a resolution proposing the use of contraceptive measures was defeated. Another resolution proposing women's right to divorce was opposed and subsequently withdrawn.[216] The eighth conference, held on 18 November 1934 at Madanapalli, was presided over by Durgabai Deshmukh.[217]

The fourteenth conference was held on 16–17 December 1939 at Kadapa. A total of 200 delegates travelled to attend the conference from all over Andhra; around 1,000 women from the area attended the conference on its opening day and nearly double this number on the second. Among the participants, many were Muslim and some Christian. A total of

---

[213] Resolutions included: establishment of a separate medical college for women; co-education at the primary stage, where exclusively women would be appointed as teachers; the mother tongue (Telugu) as a medium of instruction in high schools; establishment of high schools in every important town of Andhra, and a separate girls' college in the Andhra region; women's entry in Government jobs; right to inheritance and divorce; ban on polygamy; abolition of purdah and untouchability; and a ban on liquor. Varalakshmamma, who reported the proceedings, remarked that the absence of discussions and resolutions on political issues was a 'serious lacuna' in the conference. Kanuparti Varalakshmamma, 'Gunturu Mahilasabha Visheshamulu' (Highlights of the Women's Conference held in Guntur), *Grihalakshmi*, February 1932, pp. 1049–1055.

[214] Achanta Lakshmi Devi presided over it. In her presidential address, she touched upon issues such as women's education, child marriages, purdah, abolition of untouchability, the need for funding to support pregnant women and women's health. See Malladi Subbamma, *Women's Movement and Associations*, p. 52.

[215] In her presidential address, she touched upon issues such as need for social reform, women's participation in freedom struggle, role of women's associations in the improvement of the conditions of women, and women's rights.

[216] The resolution demanding separate Andhra State was rejected to be placed before the Executive Committee. Muthulakshmi Reddy was reviled for being responsible for its rejection. 'Sampaadakiyamulu' (Editorials), *Grihalakshmi*, December 1933, pp. 851–853.

[217] 'Sampaadakiyamulu: Andhra Mahila Sabha', *Grihalakshmi*, December 1934, p. 767; 'Vaartalu–Visheshamulu: Andhra Desha Mahila Sabha Tirmanamulu'. Ibid., pp. 754–755.

40 resolutions were adopted.[218] The fifteenth conference, held on 24 November 1940 at Nandyala, was presided over by Kameshwaramma.[219]

As a result of a growing impetus to forge 'bonds of sisterhood', women thus established organisations throughout the early twentieth century. Geographically, these organisations were spread from Aska in Ganjam—the northern-most coastal district—to Bellary, Anantapur and Kurnool in Rayalaseema. While early women's organisations were established in towns that were centres of the social reform movement, others soon took root not only in smaller towns but also in villages. Most organiations were established by those women whose families had a reform background. Later, some organisations, particularly in small towns and villages, came into existence independently with the collective efforts of local women, many of whom belonged to 'upper' and middle caste and class backgrounds.

As mentioned earlier, some organisations were able to sustain their momentum, while other smaller bodies were unable to survive. Among the former was Shri Vidyarthini Samajamu which, following its revival in 1910, had a clear impact on the trajectory of women's organisations as a whole. The Samajamu was the first full-fledged and registered women's organisation with clearly laid-down objectives, proper office-bearers and an efficient division of labour. Its revival marked a significant change in the activities, attitude and direction of the organisations in general. The Samajamu did not limit itself to the convening of meetings and conferences: it undertook multiple concrete functions such as running a women's journal, starting a school for girls, maintaining a library and taking initiative and leadership in organising the All-Andhra Women's Conference meetings. By the time the Sharada Niketanamu came into existence (1922), there was a marked change in women's consciousness. With the experience gained through participation in the freedom movement, which had expanded their access to public space, many women began taking an active part in the local women's organisations. The Sharada Niketanamu and others took to active social reform by performing as many as 30 widow remarriages. Gradually, large organisations such as the Andhra Mahila Sabha emerged.

In due course of time, a few *mandal* and district level organisations sprang up, covering a wider area. Some, like the West Godavari District Women's Organisation, developed several branches in different places and could rise to the level of staging protests to resolve women's everyday

[218] *Grihalakshmi*, January 1940, pp. 750–763.

[219] 'Sampaadakiyamulu', *Grihalakshmi*, December 1940, pp. 666–667.

concerns. Communist women's organisations began a new chapter in the women's movement in colonial Andhra. By reaching out to the rural poor and raising new issues, they further democratised the women's movement. The AMMS brought all women from the region on a single platform. As we have seen, the early organisations focused mainly on women's education, need for 'unity among women' and the establishment of more associations. Gradually, they became more vocal on women's issues, and by the late 1930s and early 40s, women's organisations like the West Godavari District Women's Association took to grassroots activism addressing the day-to-day problems of women.

Political issues were conspicuously absent from the programme of early women's organisations. Although the Sharada Niketanamu in the 1920s discussed the issue of the freedom movement and women's role in it and even participated in it, this period saw only a few resolutions supporting the nationalist struggle. Organisations influenced by 'nationalist' leaders, were relatively few prior to this period. A close scrutiny of the programmes of women's organisations, speeches by prominent women reformers and various resolutions passed in meetings would give the impression that they were almost obsessively involved with women's issues; the freedom movement did not attract them much, particularly in the initial phase. Before the 1920s, women's organisations largely felt that the arena of politics was not their forte and only men need concern themselves with it. It is surprising that even the ARMS remained more or less indifferent, much to the dissatisfaction of nationalist women like Kanuparti Varalakshmamma.[220] It may, therefore, be concluded that the issue of freedom movement was subordinated to women's own issues.

Women's organisations played a transformative role in women's lives. Initiated, organised and exclusively attended by women, they opened up a new public space, however limited it may have been, for women to come together, share their views and find solutions to their problems. The AMMS, organised since 1910, enlarged the public space for women.[221] Transforming

---

[220]While reflecting on the proceedings of the fifth ARMS, she felt that the non-inclusion of political matters was a 'serious lacuna' in it. She was also 'pained' at the reluctance of women to express any gratitude towards Gandhi and Sarojini Devi. See Kanuparti Varalakshmamma, 'Gunturu Mahilasabha Visheshamulu', *Grihalakshmi*, February 1932, pp. 1049–1055.

[221]Women from far-off places attended these conferences, covering long distances to do so, at times all alone. To women who were secluded and confined to the four walls of their homes, travelling such long distances, attending the conferences and staying away from homes for a week or so was of great significance; it opened up a new world.

women into public speakers was another significant contribution of the women's organisations.[222] Additionally, they served as training grounds imparting organisational skills to women.[223] Assessing the impact of women's organisations/conferences, Tumpudi Satyavati Bhagavatamma stated that

> though not everybody could understand the advantage of women's conferences, we could not say that it was not there. Earlier, we did not at all know how to conduct meetings. We did not know what to do in them. We could not find anybody who could speak in the conferences. But, now [by 1928], we have a number of scholars, organisers and orators.[224]

The women's organisations suffered from certain difficulties and limitations, the most pressing of them being financial. As a result, several organisations could not sustain themselves. Low membership too was a big hurdle, at least in the initial stages. Though membership increased gradually, prevailing orthodoxies discouraged many women from joining the movement for a fairly long period.[225] There was a general opinion that at least a few of the

---

[222] All the organisations conducted meetings where women spoke and delivered speeches. Initially only a few women were prepared to participate, but gradually a good number of women became enthusiastic about delivering speeches. The transformation of women into public speakers/orators was interesting in itself. Initially, women's speeches were marked with a sense of inferiority. However, the practice of public speaking (before women, and at times before mixed-gender audiences) made them confident. Gradually, changes occurred in the *tone* of women's speeches: they not only exhibited confidence but also proved to be persuasive orators. At times, they addressed meetings/conferences attended by not less than a thousand people. Their passion for public speaking was so great that 'they even forgot the time limit', and 'became angry when reminded of the shortage of time'! This shows the degree to which Andhra women became confident and zealous about public speaking, particularly into the late 1920s and after. Kanuparti Varalakshmamma vividly portrayed women's transformation into public speakers and orators. See 'Gunturu Mahilasabha Visheshamulu', *Grihalakshmi*, February 1932, pp. 1049–1055.

[223] Women received training in organisational skills—conducting meetings, reflecting on their own and other issues, passing resolutions, negotiating with government through appeals, signature campaigns, and demonstrations and agitations. Certainly a few women, such as Durgabai Deshmukh, emerged as leaders with amazing potential. Such training prepared them for future leadership roles in post independent Andhra/India.

[224] 'Adhyakshopanyasamu' (Presidential Address), *Vasavi*, August 1928, pp. 196–200, for this reference, p. 197.

[225] Looking at the kind of programmes these organisations undertook, some developed 'negative attitude and denied any financial assistance'. A few women also shared this negative view. The orthodox men were alarmed with the presence and

women's associations were 'not doing well'. The common complaint was that they 'did not have a definite programme and were active only during the celebration of anniversaries'.[226] Some of them seemed to have degenerated into being mere 'recreation clubs' unconcerned with the plight of women.[227]

Most of the organisations were overtly upper caste in character, with membership restricted to women of the four varnas only. Further, while in principle they were open to all 'caste Hindu women', Brahmin women's domination was conspicuous. Women from Dalit castes were barred. For example, the very first rule of the Shri Vidyarthini Samajamu barred Mala and Madiga women from becoming members.[228] Confined to the upper castes, the sisterhood these organisations wished to create inevitably remained a fractured one.

Despite this shortcoming, the most remarkable achievement of these organisations remains the creation of gender consciousness and a sense of shared identity among women. Some of them established schools for girls, while others took up a sensitisation campaign in favour of women's education, appealing to parents to let their daughters to attend schools. Organisations like the Shri Vidyarthini Samajamu and the Andhra Mahila Sabha published women's journals and encouraged women's writings.[229]

---

programmes of these associations, and took all measures to ensure that their women did not attend the meetings. See 'Gunturu Mahilasabha Visheshamulu', *Grihalakshmi*, February 1932, p. 1051.

[226] 'Stree Sanghalu' (Women's Organisations), *Andhra Mahila*, January 1946, p. 5; *Grihalakshmi*, 1930, pp. 820–821; *Andhra Mahila*, May 1947.

[227] Kanuparti Varalakshmamma came down very heavily upon such organisations. In her playlet, 'Ladies Clubbu', a burlesque, she ridiculed their practices. See *Grihalakshmi*, April 1942, pp. 87–95.

[228] The rule reads: 'except women of the low castes such as the *Mala* and *Madiga*, all other respectable and household women would be eligible for enrolling'. See 'Shri Vidyarthini Samajamu, Kakinada', *Hindu Sundary*, October 1914, p. 2. However, the upper caste bias did not go unquestioned. A few women like Sattiraju Shyamalamba and Kalagara Pichchamma questioned the upper caste bias. Sattiraju Shyamalamba and Kalagara Pichchamma, 'Kakinada Vidyarthini Samajamuvarikoka Vinnapamu' (An Appeal to the Kakinada Vidyarthini Samajamu), *Hindu Sundary*, April 1912, pp. 31–33. There were not many organisations which did not follow any caste bar, and admitted women of all castes.

[229] It should be interesting to note that it is the women's organisations which published the two most important women's journals of the time, the *Hindu Sundary* and the *Andhra Mahila*, which had long runs, respectively. These journals moulded the ideas of women, transformed at least a few of them in to accomplished writers, and helped in spreading the message of sisterhood and consolidating it.

It is noteworthy that these very organisations later became instrumental in reaching out to people, particularly women, with the welfare schemes and programmes of the independent Indian State through its Central Welfare Board, which was instituted to promote the welfare of women and children. Assessed individually, many women's organisations—with their low membership, limited areas of operation (at least initially) and with little improvement in later years—may not give the impression of a grand success. But if seen collectively, they were certainly successful not only in terms of creating awareness and consciousness-raising, but also in terms of certain concrete actions. In tandem with the women's journals, they formed the bedrock of the women's movement in colonial Andhra.

'Do Not Abandon Our Issues': Women in/and the Indian National Movement

> I am really vexed living in Chataparru and wasting my life. I feel that I will be spoiling my life, if I live at home [for long]. I am seriously thinking of joining Gandhi's ashram.... Once I decide, I pray to my parents to leave me to dedicate myself to the motherland. My love! You please help me in this. I just do not want my life to be wasted; yes, I will not allow it to happen. Please help me.... Please do not reveal my plans of joining the ashram to anybody. I am very much worried about it. May God bless me! My beloved! Help me; help me, please.
>
> Annapoorna Devi's letter to her husband, dated 16 November 1919[230]

[230] Maganti Bapineedu ed., *Annapoorna Devi Lekhalu* (*Letters of Annapoorna Devi*), n. d. pp. 19–21. The letter was posted from Arogyavaramu (Madanapalli, Chittoor District). The book is preserved at Saraswata Niketanam, Vetapalem. It may have been published in the year 1931 for Unnava Lakshminarayana, who wrote an 'afterword' (*kada maata*) to the book, signed the text on 3 January 1931. This invaluable source contains 77 letters written by Annapoorna Devi. Seventy-five of them were addressed to her husband Maganti Bapineedu. The book is particularly significant for it represents the companionate model of conjugality that was gaining strength in Andhra in the backdrop of the national movement. The way she addressed her husband was really very remarkable and novel for her times: 'Naa Priyamyna Needu' (My Dear Needu), 'Priyuda' (My Beloved), 'Priyatama' (My Love), 'Priyatama Needu' (Dear Needu) and 'Mee Priyamyna Anna' (Your Beloved Anna), etc. Second, it tells us the story of women's physical and emotional involvement in the national movement and the various pressures, including familial, that operated on them. When Annapoorna Devi passed away, Gandhi wrote to her husband and offered condolences, stating that 'if the latter lost his dear wife, the former lost a dear daughter.' See Gandhi's letter, in his own handwriting, in the

> Nobody is above the nation, including me. Motherland first, all others are next.
>
> –Annapoorna Devi's letter to her husband, dated 17 November 1920.[231]

> Do not forget the nation, even if you happen to forget me.
>
> –Annapoorna Devi's letter to her husband, dated 9 November 1920.[232]

The letters of Maganti Annapoorna Devi, a prominent nationalist and feminist intellectual activist, amply demonstrate the strong appeal of the Indian national movement for women in the Andhra region, how deeply it influenced them and the ways in which they engaged with it.

Annapoorna Devi (1900–1927) was the only child of Kalagara Ramaswamy and Pichchamma and was born in Chataparru. Unlike many others, her reform-minded parents decided to educate her. She received her elementary education in Eluru and later joined a Mission School in Guntur. Although her parents were not wealthy, they sent her to Calcutta, where she studied in a Brahmo Girls' School and lived in the home of the famous Brahmo leader Hemachandra Sarkar. She passed the matriculation examination in Madras, appearing as a private candidate. In 1920, at the age of twenty, she married Maganti Bapineedu. The letters excerpted here are all addressed to her husband, Bapineedu. In one of them, she states:

> I feel sorry for not being able to write to you for two to three weeks. I could not write for one week because I had been to Bezawada [Vijayawada]. Two lakh people came to see Mahatmaji [Gandhi]. I had the fortune of seeing Sarala Debi. In Bezawada and Eluru, I welcomed the Mahatma on behalf of women. Initially, I was scared to approach the Mahatma. Because the responsibility of inviting fell on me, I discharged the duty.... In Bezawada, when Mahatma Gandhi asked me as to what I would offer to the nation, I had offered two pairs of [gold] bangles. When he came to Eluru, I offered all my remaining [gold] ornaments to the nation. Now, I have no ornaments except a bangle each in the hands and the ornament you tied

---

volume. A number of women published obituaries, acknowledging her contribution to the national movement in glowing terms. See Dronamraju Lakshmibayamma, '"Nannu Marachinanu Deshamunu Marava Vaddu": Kee. She. Annapoorna Devi Charitra', *Bharati*, October 1929, pp. 627–631; 'Shrimati Kee. She. Maganti Annapoorna Devigaru', *Hindu Sundary*, October 1928, pp. 9–12. Her life became a subject of textbook lessons and Maganti Annapoorna Devi is perhaps the most famous name that school students in the region remember today.

[231] Ibid., pp. 42–46; for this reference, p. 45. The letter was posted from Chataparru.

[232] Ibid., pp. 49–52; for this reference, p. 52. The letter was posted from 'Swarna Niketanamu', Hyderabad.

Image 1.5: Maganti Annapoorna Devi

Source: *Grihalakshmi*, November 1929.

in my neck as a mark of our marriage. You will be surprised to see the clothes I am wearing. I will use only the handwoven cotton cloth until the achievement of Swarajyam.... Both of us will have to boycott the foreign cloth till our death.... Wherever you see, you will find the charkhas. The charkha is not an ordinary thing. That is the wheel of Vishnu. The sound it generates is nothing but the majestic sound of the Vedas.... If we conduct according to the Mahatama, we can achieve Swarajyam in just six days.... Ours is a non-violent sacred movement.... Is the Mahatma an ordinary

> mortal? No. He is not. There seems to be some magical power in him.... I am ready to sacrifice even my life and follow his orders.
>
> –Annapoorna Devi's letter to her husband, dated 12 April 1921[233]

Annapoorna Devi and Maganti Bapineedu's match may be termed a 'reform marriage' on several counts. The marriage chants were recited in Telugu, rather than the usual Sanskrit and the priest was a non-Brahmin. In 1920, the year of their marriage, Bapineedu left for the USA to pursue higher education in agriculture. Annapoorna, too, had planned to study in the US, but the call of nationalism stopped her; when confronted with these contrary pulls, she embraced nationalism happily.

Annapoorna Devi always wore *khaddar* clothes and moved from village to village selling swadeshi clothes and propagating nationalist ideology, incurring the displeasure of her in-laws. Women of that era remembered her fiery speeches. She disliked foreign clothes to the extent that she burnt all her wedding sarees, each worth Rs. 500, a large sum at the time. In Vijayawada, when Gandhi asked women to make donations for the national movement, she immediately donated her gold bangles. When a surprised Gandhi asked 'if she had the permission of her parents', she promptly replied that 'they would not object [to] her decision'. A staunch follower of the swadeshi movement, when her husband returned to India, she went to see him at the port itself, flung his foreign clothes into the ocean, and gave him khaddar clothes. She established the 'Sri Mohanadasu Khaddaru Parishramalayamu' at Eluru to popularise Khaddar and attended the Ahmedabad session of the INC in 1921.

> Everybody is surprised that I gave away my silk clothes for burning. I heard that Gandhiji showed them to many in Bombay... Since 1 August, there is not even a single foreign cloth in our home. My heart's suffering is beyond descrption when I see foreign made clothes... Sixty crore rupees are drained from this country. Because of this, six crore Indians are suffering from abject hunger. Use of Swadeshi clothes gives life to many [of our Indians]. Is it strange to burn such clothes? How does it matter, even if it is a wedding saree? That, too, is equal to poison. Out of ignorance, we had committed a number of sins. Do we need to continue with them still? Without asking you, I offered your wrist watch and [gold] ring to Tilak Swaraj Fund. I did that assuming that you would agree to that. Do those, who are ready to offer their life to the nation, care for wedding clothes and ornaments? I am not doing all these things for earning people's appreciation. Though I am doing it secretly, information is leaking out. I

[233] Ibid., pp. 90–97. The letter was posted from Chataparru.

am very much embarrassed. I am worried that I am unable to serve the nation more and more. I think how much more I would have offered to the nation, had I been a millionaire and feel sorry for not being that.

–Annapoorna Devi's letter to her husband, dated 23 November 1921.[234]

Given the strong nationalist feelings they possessed, it is no wonder that women like Annapoorna Devi were prepared to sacrifice everything, including their lives, for the sake of the nation, questioned husbands and were even prepared to 'abandon' them (even if rhetorically) to enable service to the 'motherland':

> You have escaped immediately after marriage. I do not know how much more time I will have to await you? You do not love me. May be you got a number of educated and beautiful women there! Am I of any more use to you? Perhaps you treat me like a cheap animal after your arrival here! The attitude of the foreign returned people is like this. My sadness is equal to my happiness with regard to your arrival. Happiness is natural. But why am I sad? It is because I am afraid that you may enter government service. I am scared that you may not put on the Swadeshi clothes and burn the foreign clothes and that you may not take part in the Non-Cooperation Movement and thereby earn me accusations. When I am suggesting other women to serve the nation even by abandoning their husbands and if you conduct against my wishes, I may have to commit suicide. For that I am preparing myself right from now. … You use the foreign clothes you have with you there. Take a photograph on nationalist lines by putting on the wedding clothes, i.e., *panche, chokkayi* and *kandua*. … Do not get new pants stitched. You do not need them here in India. We should burn all your foreign clothes the moment you deboard the steamer.
>
> –Annapoorna Devi's letter to her husband, dated 22 February 1922.[235]

> When women, who do not know what politics is, are going to jail how can you step back? Is your life more precious than the lives of women? Are you weaker than women? Are you ignorant? If new people do not join the movement to sustain it, how can Swaraj be achieved? … I believe that, if at all you have any love for your wife, you come to India soon after the examinations. Will you not come to serve India even when you hear that I am jailed? You are not so stone-hearted. I am thrice certain. You will certainly come. If you treat that your wife's life is your own life, come immediately after the exams. If you do not come, you will reap its fruit.

[234] Ibid., pp. 119–120. The letter was posted from Egaramu.

[235] Ibid., pp. 131–132. The letter was posted from Chataparru.

> Do as you like. But you will suffer all your life. Coercing somebody into serving the nation is of no use at all. Is not your heart melting even after learning that the Mahatma is jailed? For whose sake Swaraj is? Is not it for the sake of Indians? Are you not an Indian? How long will you forget your mother land and be there in a foreign country?
>
> –Annapoorna Devi's letter to her husband, dated 6 March 1922.[236]

Apart from her activism as a nationalist, she was a scholar, polyglot and translator with exceptional oratory skills. A girls' nationalist school named Annapoorna Devi Jaatiya Paathashala was established in Eluru to keep her memory alive after her death.

Women from the Andhra region played a significant role in India's freedom movement.[237] While identifying a precise starting point is difficult, we have already noted that women from the region were politically active and participating in the public sphere through women's organisations and by running women's journals, well before M. K. Gandhi entered the stage of Indian national movement. The Gandhian movement further expanded their arena of activity, diversifying and intensifying them. Many women from Andhra attended the Calcutta Session of the INC in 1917. When Annie Besant, an important Home Rule leader, was arrested in 1917 in Ootacamund, a large number of women participated in protest meetings organised in places such as Guntur, Vijayawada, Kakinada, Machilipatnam, Madanapalli, Bellary, Cuddappah, Chandragiri, Eluru and Tenali.

Large-scale participation of women from colonial Andhra can be seen from the launch of the Non-Cooperation Movement in 1920. The Chirala Perala Movement and the Pullari Satyagraha in Palnadu in 1921 provided a fillip to women's direct resistance to colonial dominance. The people of Chirala and Perala protested against municipal authorities in 1919 for a tenfold increase in taxation, from Rs. 4,000 to Rs. 40,000. This resulted in massive protests, memoranda submitted to the government and a no-tax campaign by the people. The colonial government arrested 12 protesters for

---

[236] Ibid., pp. 141–142. The letter was posted from Chataparru.

[237] The information on Andhra women's role in the Indian National Movement is culled from Volga et al., *Mahilavaranam*; K. Janaki, *Role of Women in Freedom Struggle in Andhra Pradesh* (Hyderabad, 1999); Vasa Prabhavati, *Bharata Swatantryodyamamlo Telugu Mahilala Patra* (*Role of Telugu Women in India's Struggle for Independence*) (Hyderabad, 2003); V. Kotishwaramma, *Bharata Swatantrya Samaram—Andhra Mahilala Mahojwala Patra* (2001); Sarojini Regani, *Highlights of the Freedom Struggle in Andhra Pradesh* (Hyderabad, 1998 [1972]).

refusing to pay the tax. One of them was an elderly woman named Ravuri Alivelu Mangatayaramma, perhaps one of the first women to be put behind the bars for a political offence. The magistrate's court in Bapatla awarded her a seven-day jail sentence.

Gandhi advised a mass exodus to nullify the imposed municipality. At midnight, 25 April 1921, under the leadership of Duggirala Gopalakrishnaiah, 13,573 villagers (out of a total population of 15,326) evacuated Chirala Perala and moved to makeshift set of improvised shelter named Ramnagar. D. S. R. Rao, a correspondent of *The Hindu* who visited the place, remarked that 'it was a sight to watch them and their furniture move from their old homes to their new parnasalas'.[238] They experimented with the idea of a parallel government, establishing panchayat representatives of all communities, passing necessary legislative enactments, and issuing administrative orders. They spent 11 months in this manner, until Gandhi called off the Non-Cooperation Movement following the violent Chauri Chaura incident in 1922. As of now, no historical records are available to assess the impact of the event on the lives of women involved in the movement.

Defiance of colonial forest laws was a significant aspect of the Non-Cooperation Movement in Andhra and depended on women's active involvement. The people of Palanadu had to pay an exorbitantly high tax called 'Pullari' for letting their cattle grazing on forest land. They suffered constant persecution at the hands of the subordinate staff of the forest administration. As the colonial administration paid no heed to their demands, the people organised a social boycott of forest and revenue departments. Amid drumrolls they announced that no washerwoman or barber would serve the officials and the boycott grew to a complete suspension of essential services to all government officials. Unnava Lakshminarayana and Madabhushi Vedantam Narasimhachari, who were deputed by the Andhra Pradesh Congress Committee (APCC) to lead a peaceful protest in Palnadu, were arrested in Macherla. Protesting the arrest, the former's wife, Unnava Lakshmibayamma led a massive protest in Guntur and a no-tax campaign in Palnadu. The *Andhra Patrika* issue of 17 August 1921 reported that 'when Unnava's wife hailed her husband on his arrest in Guntur, hundreds of women steered the chariot of Swaraj with their gentle hands.... In this, you can see the outpouring of people's power.' The situation escalated in February 1922, when Swaraj was proclaimed in

[238] K. Janaki, *Role of Women in Freedom Struggle in Andhra Pradesh*, p. 41.

several villages. On 26 February, on the outskirts of Minchalapadu, when the police seized 50 goats and 120 buffaloes that had been sent to graze in defiance of forest rules, the posse was attacked by a crowd of 200–300 men and women. In the firing that followed, Kanneganti Hanumantu, one of the leaders of the Palnadu struggle, was among the people killed. In the aftermath, 9 women and 28 men were arrested.

The AICC sesssion held in Kakinada in 1923 acquired greater significance due to these events. A number of women came forward to render their services as office-bearers and volunteers. Duvvuri Subbamma was one of the chairpersons of the Reception Committee. A 15-year-old Durgabai (later known as Durgabai Deshmukh) recruited many women as volunteers but could not work herself because she was too young. For women, the experience of leaving their homes, their villages and their families was enormously liberating. This was a period when Duvvuri Subbamma, Ponaka Kanakamma and Unnava Lakshmibayamma 'exceeded the men propagandists in their ability to sway large masses of people'.

The Salt Satyagraha Movement further intensified women's nationalist activism. In March 1930, the APCC decided to launch the Salt Satyagraha simultaneously at several places. The centres were: Mypadu (Nellore District), Machilipatnam (Krishna District), the beach opposite the town Hall in Visakhapatnam, Mettapalem and Chollangi villages in Kakinada (East Godavari District), residence of Konda Venkatappayya in Guntur and Berhampore and Naupada in Srikakulam District. The movement was inaugurated on 6 April 1930 in the East Godavari District where a large mass of people broke the Salt Law at Chollangi.

Women in Andhra began to make salt in Guntur near the home of Konda Parvatamma, wife of Konda Venkatappayya, inviting lathicharge and arrest in Mypadu of Nellore District, near Chinnapuram in Bandar, near Vadarevu in Chirala, etc. In Guntur, as the girls of Sharada Niketanam, a nationalist girls' school established by Unnava Lakshmibayamma, applied vermilion marks to the foreheads of the satyagrahis, singing nationalist songs, the satyagrahis broke the Salt Law and courted arrest. A total of 200 people, women and men, walked five miles to the camp at Vadarevu, made salt and returned home.

The Satyagraha camps in Devarampadu, Nellore, Komaravolu ashram and Angaluru ashram worked tirelessly during the Salt Satyagraha. Women assumed leadership everywhere. Unnava Lakshmibayamma went to the Devarampadu camp. The batches of Satyagrahis, who came to the camp, would halt at every village they passed through holding meetings.

If police occupied one camp, then another batch of volunteers would enter the fray. The Devarampadu camp was attacked by the police thrice and a hundred women faced the police and took part in the Satyagraha boldly. More than ten women were arrested on 3 and 4 April 1930 in the Nalluru camp. Gaddapati Pichchamma led a procession of women carrying national flags on 8 April 1930 in Repalle. When six women from the camp were arrested, the situation grew tense. With Pichchamma leading them, the women took over the camp and set fire to foreign goods. After arresting them, the police made them walk to the sub-jail of Repalle.

Near the Komaravolu ashram, women fought fiercely to protect the national flag from the police and took over the Bhatlapenumarru Library. In the early stages, the police would throw dirty water mixed with chilli powder at them instead of arresting them. They would abuse them and transport them far from home, forcing the women to walk back for miles. The colonial government hired hooligans to harass these women emotionally and physically and thus attempted to break their will. In the second phase, as the government realised that it was difficult to deter the women satyagrahis, arrests became inevitable. Katragadda Hanumayamma was sentensed to a year's imprisonment and fined Rs. 400 for feeding women satyagrahis. Women avoided the police and travelled from village to village propagating patriotic ideas. An 11-year old girl, Sugunamani, was awarded a two-year jail sentence after she manufactured salt in Angaluru. She was sent to the Borstal School. In Siddapuram, West Godavari District, Tallapragada Vishwasundaramma conducted a camp. The Reserve Police wrought havoc on a camp set up in the Gandhi National School. Many women were arrested, including Duggirala Kamalamma, Dasari Krishnaveni, Sringavarapu Lakshminarasamma, Kommuri Veera Venkatamma and Sattiraju Shyamalamba. Many Congress meetings were held all over Andhra defying prohibitory orders and Section 144. Women presided over these meetings. Rudraraju Bangaramma presided over a district conference held in Palakollu. Tallapragada Vishwasundaramma presided over a meeting in Guntur Taluq. Kambhampati Manikyamba presided over the Tenali Taluq meeting. Vedantam Kamala Devi presided over the Andhra State Political Conference. The *Andhra Patrika* of 1932 showered praises on Gummadidala Durgabayamma, Unnava Lakshmibayamma and Achanta Rukminamma for breaking Salt Law in Madras, Guntur and Vedaranyam, respectively, and for their acts of bravery. On the arrest of Achanta Rukminamma, *The Hindu* commented that 'the imprisonment of women of the cultural calibre like Mrs. Lakshmipati and others, who have joined the movement, must inevitably move popular imagination powerfully.'[239] In connection with women's participation in the movement, the General Secretary of the Andhra Provincial Congress Committee reported to the All India Congress Committee that 'it was a happy feature that women even of purdah and pregnant ladies were pouring in large numbers in the cause of their motherland. The untiring zeal with which the lady Satyagrahis worked shoulder to shoulder with the male volunteers and made the cause a great success could not be underestimated.'[240]

After the Salt Satyagraha, many women went to jail for individual Satyagraha. In her *Naa Jailu Gnapakalu*, Sangam Lakshmibayamma described in glowing terms the tranformative role the freedom movement played in women's lives. The jail brought to them an entirely new world, making the bonding of jailmates stronger. Even there, they continued with their nationalist activities and worked for jail reforms.[241] Many women were jailed for taking part in the Quit India Movement also.

Apart from Gandhian non-violent movement, women participated in other forms of nationalist action as well, including violent resistance. When Mudtivarthi Satyanarayana and Vemuri Venkatasubbaiah, the convicts in Ongole Bomb case, escaped from the police, Ravipati Lakshmi Devi and Subbamma gave them shelter. The police took Subbamma into custody and tortured her in the Kurichedu police station to tap information. Yakasiri Chellamma in Venkatagiri, Duggempudi Veeramma in Durgasamudram and Gunamma in Parlakimidi fought with the officials of the forest department and won the right to graze their cattle. Sasumanu Gunamma assumed leadership over the struggle in the Mandasa estate in Sompeta in 1940. She was pregnant when she confronted the police in Rajimanipuram and died in a firing. The village was named after her as Veeragunamapuram. Gorla Punnamma was also wounded in the firing and was sent to jail. There were women who were pregnant and delivered children in jail, like Koneru Bharatamma and women who went to jail with suckling infants like Saraswati Gora. Women associated with the Communist Party used to march through the streets of Vijayawada wearing Khaki shorts and weilding sticks. Students and labourers were urged to go on strike. Lawyers and government servants were persuaded to resign and no-tax

---

[239] K. Janaki, *Role of Women in Freedom Struggle in Andhra Pradesh*, p. 67.

[240] P. Sivasankar Reddy, 'Civil Disobedience Movement in Andhra, 1930–1934', memiographed paper.

[241] Sangam Lakshmibai, *Naa Jailu Gnapakalu–Anubhavalu* (*My Jail Experiences and Reminiscences*), Neti Seetadevi, comp. (Hyderabad, 1980).

campaigns intensified throughout Andhra. On 15 September 1942, eleven Congressmen, led by Melly Zollinger, a Swiss woman who married Uppala Lakshmana Rao, visited the houses of lawyers in Vijayawada and requested them to suspend practice. On 2 October 1942, Melly Zollinger was arrested, when she hoisted a Congress flag, distributed leaflets, shouted slogans and attempted to hold a meeting in Vijayawada.

Most of the women who enriched the Indian national movement with their participation were also active in the field of social reform and women's development. They used the rich experience they gained from their involvement in political activities to futher the agenda of the women's movement. Women held both nationalism and feminism to be equally important. They wanted simultaneous liberation for themselves and the nation. It is this thinking that made them question men as the latter appeared to be abandoning the women's issues. Holding men responsible for the 'unsatisfactory' and slow pace of the women's movement, Gadicharla Ramabayi, editor of the journal *Soundaryavalli*, remarked in its June 1918 issue,

> The secretary presented the Secretary's Report in the recently held all-Andhra Women's Conference.[242] In that, it was indicated that progress [of the women's movement] is unsatisfactory. Men are independent. At a time when their work itself is not really very satisfactory, how can the work of women, who are dependent and are overburdened with domestic work, be satisfactory? However, we should not keep quite. As far as I know, today the onus lies more with men. They have drowned themselves in the freedom struggle. They are not providing encouragement to the women's movement the way they have done till recently. In fact, there are some who are arguing that freedom movement has to be accorded priority and other movements should wait. Thinking this way is incorrect [*idiyantayu bhrama*]. Movement for Swaraj can become real freedom movement only when all the movements take place simutaneously. Mere shouting will not help achieve all the tasks. Therefore, I request our brothers to show the same interest in the women's movement and help it march ahead.[243]

While most Andhra women intellectuals wanted a simultaneous liberation of women and the nation, there were a few like Komarraju Atchamamba who urged women (in 1937) to challenge and overthrow male domination, and

---

[242] She was refering to the ninth Andhra Mahila Mahasabha held at Cuddapah in June 1918.

[243] See 'Andhra Mahila Sabha', *Soundaryavalli*, 1 (1), Kalayukti–Shravanamu, July 1918, p. 32.

emphasised that women's liberation from the clutches of male domination was much more important than the political liberation of the country from foreign domination. In other words, for her women's liberation preceded national liberation.[244]

Maganti Annapoorna Devi questioned the 'unjust' underrepresentation of women in the INC. Referring to the Congress session to be held in December 1921, she wrote to her husband that, of the 24 Andhra members elected to the All India Congress Committee, there was only one woman (Ponaka Kanakamma) to 'represent women'. 'If we go by statistics, number of women is more than that of men. I fail to understand as to how only one woman is sufficient to represent women when there are these many to represent men. How unfair men are! I have decided to discuss the matter with Sarojini Devi and Sarala Devi', she complained.[245]

If the founding of the women's organisations marked women's activism at the grassroots, their collective intellectual marathon was flagged off by their editing and publishing of the women's journals from the turn of the twentieth century. By 1947, Andhra women edited as many as 21 journals through which they campaigned for women's development and social reform. A study of these journals helps us understand women's perspectives, otherwise marginalised in historical writing. By mapping the intellectual journey of women, these journals tell us the story of women's ideas and ideals, reflect their desires and aspirations and attest to their perception of the world around them. By establishing women as *active agents* casting their future with their own hands, the journals dispel the deep-rooted notion that women remained mere passive recipients and 'objects' of reform. In other words, through these journals, the *self-representation* and *agency* of women becomes crystal clear. Before we turn our attention towards narrating the accounts of various women's journals, an overview of nineteenth-century Telugu journalism is necessary.

An Overview of Telugu Journalism

Vrittantini, the first known Telugu journal, was published from Madras from 1838 to 1842. Before Veeresalingam started *Vivekavardhani*,

[244] Komarraju Atchamamba, 'Neti Rajakeeyalu-Streelu' (Today's Politics and Women), *Grihalakshmi*, June 1937, p. 295.

[245] Maganti Bapineedu ed., *Annapoorna Devi Lekhalu*, pp. 118–119. The letter, numbered 36, was dated 23 November 1921 and was written from Egaramu.

there were a few journals such as *Vartamanatarangini* (started in 1842, Madras), *Hitavadi* (1862), *Dinavarthamani* (1862), *Sriyakshni* (1863), *Tatwabodhini* (1864), *Sujanaranjani* (1864), *Andhra Bhasha Sanjivani* (1871) and *Purusharthapradayini* (1872). Religious and literary issues and also occasional articles on matters of public and political interest found a place in the columns of these journals.[246] The *Purusharthapradayini* 'was a full-fledged journal which levelled powerful criticism of social problems such as caste system, idolatry, prohibition of widow remarriages and the like. It was a forward looking journal in more than one respect and served as a model for Veeresalingam's journals', and thus 'made a mark in Telugu journalism'.[247] With Veeresalingam's *Vivekavardhani* (started in October 1874, Rajahmundry),[248] 'Telugu journalism attained maturity and respectability.'[249] Several other journals like *Andhra Prakashika* (1885), *Hindujana Samskarini* (1885), *Satya Samvardhani* (1891), *Shashilekha* (1894) and *Deshabhimani* (1896) came to be published by the close of the nineteenth century. Most of these journals carried on a crusade against social evils and championed the cause of women in particular by focusing attention on their problems.[250]

However, there were a few anti-reform journals. The most notable among them was the *Andhra Bhasha Sanjivani*. Edited by Mahamahopadhyaya Kokkonda Venkata Ratnam Pantulu (hereafter Kokkonda), a quintessential orthodox who fought against social reform all through his life, the journal provided platform to conservatives. An arch-rival of Veeresalingam in matters of social reform, Kokkonda started the *Hasyavardhani* and appended it to his *Andhra Bhasha Sanjivani*. To pay him back in the same coin, Veeresalingam started the *Hasyasanjivini*. Kokkonda's journals opposed reforms such as women's education and widow remarriage. For example, *Hasyavardhani* carried an article titled, 'Women do not Deserve Education'.[251] Other anti-reform journals like the *Swadharma Prakashini* (1872, Madras, edited by Kotishwara Sharma), *Analpajalpita Kalpavalli* (1880, Bandar,

---

[246] V. Ramakrishna, 'Women's Journals in Andhra during the Nineteenth Century', pp. 80–81.

[247] Ibid., p. 81.

[248] For a discussion on the journal, see Potturi Venkateswara Rao, *Andhra Jaati Akshara Sampada*, pp. 121–128.

[249] V. Ramakrishna, 'Women's Journals in Andhra during the Nineteenth Century', p. 81.

[250] Ibid.

[251] For a few details of the *Andhra Bhasha Sanjivani*, see Potturi Venkateswara Rao, *Andhra Jaati Akshara Sampada*, pp. 113–119.

that is, Machilipatnam, Dasu Sriramulu), *Mandara Manjari* (1897, Kakinada, Ogirala Jagannatha Rao), *Rajayogi* (1893, Kakinada, Gurajada Sriramamoorthy), *Shruti Dharma Sanjivani* (1917, Bejawada, Veerabhadra Pakayaji), *Varnashrama* (1929, Bejawada, Mopidevi Venugopala Rao), *Varnashramadharma Samsthapanamu* (1926, Kavali, Pinnamraju Venkata Subramanya Sharma), too, tried to stem the tides of social reform.[252]

As women's issues constituted the nucleus of social reform movement, as a part of the all-India phenomenon, journals meant exclusively for women began to be published in Andhra from the last two decades of the nineteenth century. The *Sathihitha Bodhini* (1883–1905) was the first women's journal in Telugu, the *Telugu Zenana* (1893–1907) being the second. Women began publishing and editing the women's journals right from the start of the twentieth century. *Hindu Sundary* was the first women's journal edited by women. *Grihalakshmi*, *Savithri*, *Vivekavathi*, *Sundari*, *Anasuya*, *Stri Dharma*, *Soundaryavalli*, *Andhra Lakshmi*, *Hindu Yuvati*, *Bharata Mahila*, *Grihalakshmi*, *Andhra Mahila* and *Vanita* were some of the important women's journals. Before examining how the women's journals discussed women's issues, I will present their various details in the next chapter.

[252] Ibid., p. 495.

2

The New Print-Public Landscape

A Survey of the Journals

In this chapter, I outline the circumstances in which various Telugu women's journals were published in the late nineteenth and early twentieth centuries. I shall discuss each journal separately; the broader issues discussed within these journals allow us to gauge possible shifts in content as well as the contexts that shaped them.

Sathihitha Bodhini (1883-1904/1905)

Sathihitha Bodhini was the first women's journal in Telugu. Founded and edited by Veeresalingam, it began publication in April 1883 as a monthly journal from Rajahmundry, the nucleus of the social reform movement. After three years, the journal ceased to publish for about two years, until 1888 when it was revived.[1] In September 1904, it merged with *Telugu Zenana*, another women's journal. Its cover page stated in Telugu that 'it would be published every month for women'.[2] Below the masthead, an announcement in English stated that it was 'an illustrated monthly magazine for the use of the females'. A *sloka* (verse) printed on the first page reads: 'Women forcibly confined to homes by their men were not well protected: women who took care of themselves had better protection and safety'.[3] The annual subscription rate, inclusive of postage, was Rs. 2, half-yearly Re. 1, and

[1] See 'Prakatana' (Announcement), *Sathihitha Bodhini* 3 (1), 1888 (Jyestha Masa).

[2] See the cover pages of the issues of 1888.

[3] V. Ramakrishna, 'Women's Journals in Andhra during the Nineteenth Century', *Social Scientist* 19 (5–6), 1991, p. 82.

a single copy made available at 0.4 annas.[4] Each issue had around 15 pages in early 1888, which increased to 20 and then to 24 over the course of the year. The journal was illustrated with pictures and printed at the Vivekavardhani Press. While we do not know the actual circulation of the journal, it is clear that Veeresalingam made effective use of it, particularly among the literate women of the Andhra region. Veeresalingam, in his autobiography, clearly mentioned that because 'there were no good books for women in Telugu' he published *Sathihitha Bodhini* to ensure their 'progress'.[5]

As its name indicated, the journal was instructional in nature. It instructed women on the dos and don'ts of everyday life and attached supreme importance to the promotion of women's education. Explaining the importance of education to women, the very first issue stated that 'if a mother was uneducated... she spoilt her children. If she was educated, she took all necessary care in training them at home, and thus made them learned and wise.'[6] Another essay was provocatively titled *Chaduverugani Streelu Tama Biddalaku Shatruvulu* (Uneducated Women are Enemies of Their Children).[7] The journal emphasised the indispensability of pativratyam (conjugal fidelity) for women and appealed to them to inculcate and protect their sense of fidelity. It held that education alone could ensure and enhance this. The June 1883 issue, for instance, stated that

> men had been trying hard since ancient times to guard the pativratyam of women. Women's chastity could not be protected by the vigilance and supervision of men. It was possible only through the character women acquired by receiving education, and not by the force men employed.[8]

Apart from these two dominant themes, articles appeared on several other themes, including virtues like compassion, helpfulness, patience, courage and pride, as well as more specific topics: women's responsibilities at home (*grihini dharmamu*) and household management, child-rearing (*balashikshanamu* and *biddalanaagnalonunchuta*), frugality (*mita vyayamu*), money (*dhanamu*), jewellery (*aabharanamulu*), extravagance (*amitatvamu*), elementary science with a special emphasis on women's health (*deharogyamu*), quarrelsomeness (*taguvulamaritanamu*), back-biting (*kondemulu chepputa*), the relationship between mothers-in-law

---

[4]See the cover pages of the issues of 1888.

[5]Kandukuri Veeresalingam, *Sweeya Charitramu* (Rajamundry, 1911), pp. 203–204.

[6]Potturi Venkateswara Rao, *Andhra Jaati Akshara Sampada* (Hyderabad, 2003 [2000]), p. 107.

[7]*Sathihitha Bodhini*, May 1883.

[8]Potturi Venkateswara Rao, *Andhra Jaati Akshara Sampada*, pp. 107–108.

and daughters-in-law and atrocities perpetrated by the former against the latter (*attagari kodandrikamu*), current conditions of Hindu women (*Hindu sundarula prastuta sthiti*), on Queen Victoria (*Sri Victoria Maharagnigaru*), omens, superstitions and belief in astrology (*shakunamulu* and *jyotishshastramu*), and topics of natural science such as the microscope (*sookshma vastudarshaka yantramu*), volcanoes (*agni parvatamulu*) and snakes (*paamulu*). Almost all these articles were authoured by men, the chief contributor being Veeresalingam. Most of his writings intended for women were first published in *Sathihitha Bodhini*. He consciously adopted a 'simple' and lucid style, often presenting content in the form of moral tales and stories. The *Deharogyadharma Bodhini*, Veeresalingam's book of which some parts appeared in the journal, deserves special mention for it was perhaps the first in Telugu to discuss women's health issues in some detail.

The journal represents men's curiosity and their anxiety to 'educate' and 'reform' women. It is very clear that its aim was not to make women independent but instead to transform them into skillful managers of the home, enlightened companions to their husbands and good mothers who raised their children on 'scientific' principles. Veeresalingam wanted women to 'transform' themselves into ideal and companionate homemakers, much like his own wife who followed him like his 'shadow'.[9]

Telugu Zenana (1893-1907)

The *Telugu Zenana Patrika* (popularly called *Telugu Zenana*) was the second women's journal.[10] Generally associated with Rayasam Venkata Sivudu (1870–1954; hereafter Venkata Sivudu), one of the leading figures in the social reform movement in colonial Andhra,[11] it was, in fact, founded

[9] Kandukuri Veeresalingam, *Sweeya Charitramu*, Part 2, pp. 425–438.

[10] It explicitly stated on its front cover (sub-title) that it was 'a monthly published for women and girls'. However, in the early issues, the subtitle appeared as 'A monthly journal for Zenana Reading'. See *Telugu Zenana*, front cover, February 1899. Unless otherwise especially mentioned, all references in this section are from *Telugu Zenana*.

[11] Born in Velivennu village in an Aarvela Niyogi Brahmin family, Venkata Sivudu served as a teacher in several regions including Guntur and Parlakimidi and was the principal of the Venkatagiri Raja's College, Nellore. He was a close follower and associate of Veeresalingam and a staunch advocate of women's education. Apart from editing *Telugu Zenana*, he ran another journal, *Satya Samvardhani* (1891–1899). He published a number of books, including an autobiography *Atma Charitramu*. *Atma Charitramu* merits special mention as it is a mine of information on Andhra society in

by Malladi Venakata Ratnam in July 1893 in Guntur. A year later, in June or July 1894, the journal changed hands and was owned, edited and published by Venkata Sivudu.[12] It was published in several places including Madras, Bezawada (Vijayawada) and Rajahmundry as Venkata Sivudu did not own a printing press.[13]

Initially, *Telugu Zenana* had only 16 pages making it 'difficult to publish sufficient number of articles'. Venkata Sivudu increased the number of pages and doubled the rate of annual subscription from Re. 1 to Rs. 2.[14] By 1900, the journal's pages and subscription rate had doubled.[15] All the girls' schools under the control of the British government received it.[16] However, it did not have more than 300 subscribers all through its publication run of about 15 years.[17] When Veeresalingam became its joint editor in September 1904, on his suggestion, the subscription rate was decreased to Re. 1. This measure must have earned it a few more subscribers.

At times *Telugu Zenana* had two editors. In 1902, it was co-edited by brothers Venkata Sivudu and Venkata Ramayya. In September 1904, when Veeresalingam's *Sathihitha Bodhini* merged with *Telugu Zenana*, Venkata Sivudu and Veeresalingam worked jointly as editors. Venkata Sivudu was greatly excited and jubilant about this collaboration:

> I am glad to announce that hereafter the Telugu Zenana Magazine will be under the joint editorship of Mr. Pantulu [Veeresalingam] and myself.... The work for a good cause in the company and guidance of such scholar and patriot—to whom already the present editor has been bound by many a sacred tie—is no small privilege. It is very confidently hoped that the magazine will prosper under his fostering care.[18]

Veeresalingam's association certainly enhanced the image of the journal. Moreover, the journal became a site of heated debates. Veeresalingam's burlesque, 'Savithri Satyavati Sambhashanamu—Stree Vidya' (Dialogue

---

the 1880s–1930s. For more details, see Tekumalla Kameshwara Rao, *Naa Vaangmaya Mitrulu* (*My Literary Friends*), (Hyderabad, 1996), pp. 88–90.

[12] Rayasam Venkata Sivudu, *Atma Charitramu* (Autobiography; Madras, 1933), pp. 228–229; '*Swa Vishayamu*' (Ourselves), August 1904, back page.

[13] *Atma Charitramu*, p. 412.

[14] Ibid., p. 323.

[15] Ibid., p. 395.

[16] Ibid., p. 323.

[17] Sattiraju Sitaramaiah, *Sweeya Charitra* (Autobiography; Eluru, 2002), p. 97. Sitaramaiah was the founder of *Hindu Sundary*.

[18] 'Ourselves', August 1904, back cover.

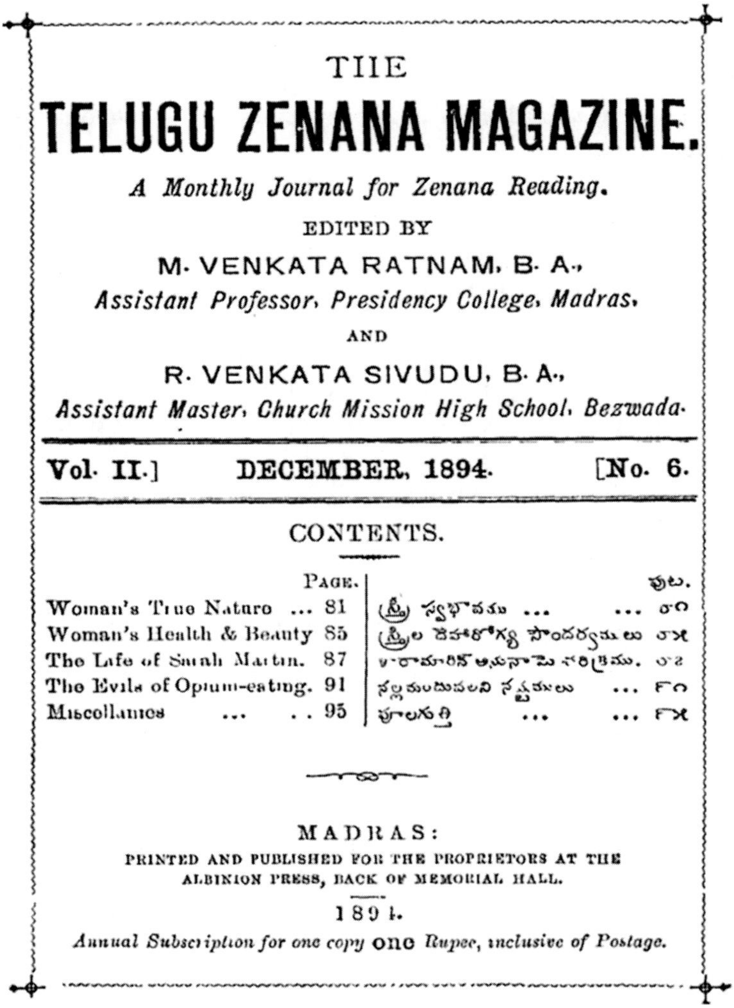

THE

TELUGU ZENANA MAGAZINE.

A Monthly Journal for Zenana Reading.

EDITED BY

M. VENKATA RATNAM, B. A.,

Assistant Professor, Presidency College, Madras,

AND

R. VENKATA SIVUDU, B. A.,

Assistant Master, Church Mission High School, Bezwada.

Vol. II.] DECEMBER, 1894. [No. 6.

CONTENTS.

	PAGE.		పుట.
Woman's True Nature ...	81	స్త్రీ స్వభావము	౮౧
Woman's Health & Beauty	85	స్త్రీల దేహారోగ్య సౌందర్యములు	౮౫
The Life of Sarah Martin.	87	సారామార్టిన్ అనునామె చరిత్రము.	౮౭
The Evils of Opium-eating.	91	నల్లమందుతినుటవలని నష్టములు ...	౯౧
Miscellanies	95	పూలగుత్తి	౯౫

MADRAS:

PRINTED AND PUBLISHED FOR THE PROPRIETORS AT THE ALBINION PRESS, BACK OF MEMORIAL HALL.

1894.

Annual Subscription for one copy ONE *Rupee, inclusive of Postage.*

Image 2.1: The *Telugu Zenana*

Source: *Telugu Zenana*, December 1894.

between Savithri and Satyavati on Women's Education), published in the October 1904 issue, generated such a fiery controversy that it was a talking point for nearly a year.[19] With this, the initial excitement of Venkata Sivudu

[19] The controversy is addressed later in the chapter, in the section on *Savithri*.

faded, and he feared that such prolonged controversies may affect the growth of the journal.[20]

By 1904, Venkata Sivudu had developed 'grave doubts regarding the necessity for continuing the Zenana Magazine' for 'two more journals edited for and by Telugu ladies had been published in Telugu'.[21] When he 'consulted some of his friends [including Veeresalingam] regarding this matter', they expressed their 'sincere opinion, that, in spite of the advent of [the] two journals… the necessity for a Telugu Journal devoted to Female Education and conducted by Hindu Gentlemen, did not and for any long time to come would not, cease'.[22] The recognition of the continued relevance of the journal run by 'Hindu Gentlemen' convinced him to continue publication.

Telugu Zenana was published with the purpose of educating women. In its first issue (July 1893), the objectives were clearly stated:

> Though there are many Telugu women who can read, it appears that no journal is published for them to enable them to make proper use of their leisure time. Our women generally attend schools only until they are ten–twelve years old.… Then on, they do not get to study at home [and]… forget all that is learnt.… The more knowledgeable they become, the better they can manage the home. If they learn good things during their leisure time, rather than indulging in useless gossip, it brings them pleasure. Hence, we are publishing this Zenana Magazine.[23]

The mission statement of the journal promised that it would 'publish articles on the improvement of women and on all those aspects useful to them', as well as moral tales that would 'improve women's wisdom'.[24] 'All the things that ensure their well being—Science, various news items—etc. will be written in a simple style,' Venkata Sivudu clarified.[25] Initially, Venkata Sivudu wrote most of the articles. Apart from independent pieces, he translated several items from English and serialised them.

The dominant theme in *Telugu Zenana* was '*griha nirvahakatvamu*' (household management). It is not an exaggeration to say that there was not a single issue without an item on or related to this theme.[26] Adhering to

---

[20] *Atma Charitramu*, p. 456.

[21] He was obviously referring to the women's journals *Hindu Sundary* and *Savithri*.

[22] See 'Ourselves', August 1904, back cover.

[23] Cited in Potturi Venkateswara Rao, *Andhra Jaati Akshara Sampada*, p. 157.

[24] Ibid.

[25] Ibid.

[26] Venkata Sivudu began writing a book titled *Griha Nirvahakatvamu* in August 1895. This was first serialised in *Telugu Zenana*. See *Atma Charitramu*, pp. 263–264. It was

nineteenth-century reformers' perception that women's proper space was the home and the hearth, articles and stories in *Telugu Zenana* emphasised the need for women to master the intricate details of household management. Emphasising housekeeping as the primary responsibility of women, an article opined that 'setting the house right was the duty of women, not men'. Women were asked to master it so as 'not to get ostracised' at their in-laws' home. The journal prefigured women as embodiments of patience, a quality that men naturally lacked, and so it found women to be more 'suitable' and 'qualified' to manage the household.[27] Cooking was seen as an 'instinctive quality' that rich and poor women alike should master.[28] Thus, *Telugu Zenana* undertook a rigorous campaign exhorting women to master the art of housekeeping for their future career as wives and mothers. It sought an educational paradigm that provided them training and enhanced their skills in this domain.

Telugu Zenana steadfastly promoted women's education. Articles encouraged women to receive education and published statistical details of girl students, reports about girls' schools, verses hailing women's education, etc. An article written in the form of a dialogue between two girls discussed the 'benefits' of women's education. When Kamalamba asked about the advantages of women's education, Ratnamba replied:

> If girls are educated, they gain knowledge and turn moral. It would be useful for their children. They [educated women] will not remain the

---

eventually published as a book. The theme was so popular during the colonial period that 300 copies were quickly sold and he published a revised edition. Ibid., p. 335. Sivudu was 'extremely happy' that even the second edition sold well. Ibid., p. 362.

[27] It further said that if men took to this job, homes would turn 'disgusting like a poultry farm'. It exhorted women to learn the intricacies of household management right from childhood so as to make their future roles as wives 'a heaven on the earth'. See V. Narayana Murthi, 'Griha Nirvahakatvamu' (Management of the House: translation as in original), December 1902, pp. 161–164. Also see Stree Hitabhilashi (pseudonym), 'Ramudu-Sita: Griha Nirvahakamunu Bodhinchunoka Katha' (Rama and Sita: A Story on the Management of the House: translation as in original), January 1903, pp. 217–223. One short story compared the family lives of two women—one who mastered the skills of household management, and the other who was ignorant of it. The first one's life was shown in a bright light. But the latter's family life was highly disordered. See 'Sita—Savithri': Griha Nirvahakatvamunu gurinchina yoka Paathamu' (Sita and Savithri: A Lesson on Household Management: translation as in original), April & May 1905, pp. 318–322.

[28] R. Venkayya, 'Griha Nirvahakatvamu' (Hints on Domestic Economy: translation as in original), March 1903, pp. 273–277.

> mere slaves of husbands. They become their friends. They learn pativrata *dharma* [by themselves without requiring special training] and become humble companions to their husbands.[29]

All articles on the subject held similar views. Reports with statistical details on the status of women's education unanimously supported increasing the number of girls' schools.[30] A few articles focused on the 'defects' of girls' schools and criticised parents' indifference or complacency towards girls' education.[31] It was emphasised that 'only when women became educated like men, and moulded themselves according to the desires of men that the reform efforts became fruitful without causing much strain' (to men!)[32] Hence, fervent appeals were made to all the 'lovers of female education' to establish schools where there were none, and encourage existing ones.

Telugu Zenana condemned child marriage. Publishing statistics of widowhood in the Bengal Presidency, the May 1903 issue held child marriages to be responsible for creating an 'alarming situation'.[33] The June 1903 issue published a detailed article on 'The Baroda Child-Marriage Prevention Bill'.[34] Another article, authored by Lingam Sundaramma, a Class 6 student at the Government Girls' School in Srikakulam, mounted a scathing attack on child marriages. In this, she blamed parents for 'spoiling their innocent [girls]', and stressed that girls should marry only when they came of age.[35]

It is quite surprising that despite its 'progressive' stand on women's issues (however limited it was), the *Telugu Zenana* did not overtly advocate widow remarriages. Fewer articles were published on this issue compared with issues such as household management and women's education, and even these were related to statistical details on widows published in other

---

[29] Y. Ganganna, a teacher in Kakinada, authored it. 'Iddaru Balikala Sambhashana' (A Dialogue between Two Girls: translation as in original), February 1899, pp. 250–252.

[30] 'Some Figures from the Recent Census Report—Female Education in the Madras Presidency', May 1904, pp. 339–340.

[31] 'Some Defects in Indian Girls' Schools', April 1903, pp. 314–316.

[32] R. Krishnamurthi, 'Stree Vidya Yokka Prasthuta Sthiti (The Present State of Female Education: translation as in original), January 1901, pp. 214–216.

[33] 'Hindu Deshamloni Yatibalya Vivahamulu' (Infant Marriages in India), May 1903, pp. 347–348.

[34] June 1903, pp. 365–368.

[35] 'Balya Vivaha Sambhashana' (A Dialogue on Early Marriages), April & May 1905, pp. 348–349.

journals,[36] news of widow remarriages,[37] or the establishment of widow homes.[38] The February 1904 issue published a summary of an article by Annie Besant on Hindu widows,[39] and the two rejoinders against it.[40]

This is not to suggest that *Telugu Zenana* was against widow remarriage. Venkata Sivudu was a staunch advocate of widow remarriage and actively participated in the widow remarriage movement. Veeresalingam's role as a pioneer of the widow remarriage movement has already been discussed in Chapter 1. *Telugu Zenana*'s silence or passivity was due to enormous pressure from the British government and their censorship rules. Venkata Sivudu discussed this strict supervision and scrutiny in his autobiography, *Atma Charitramu* (1933).

While considering an increase in the size and subscription rate of the journal in 1898, Venkata Sivudu wrote to Mrs Brander, the Government Examination Officer (*prabhutva pareekshadhipuralu*) asking for her opinion. She in turn asked for the opinion of P. Ramanujacharyulu, an Assistant Examination Officer at Bellary, who 'fully consented' Venkata Sivudu. However, Swamy Rao, a local-level officer at Rajahmundry, disagreed stating that while the subscription rate could be increased, the magazine could not publish matters related to social reform (and widow remarriage in particular). Holding his comments to be 'absurd and irrelevant', Venkata Sivudu wrote in a perturbed tone:

---

[36] For instance, the May 1903 issue, which carried details about widows in Bengal Presidency, was very passive in its commentary. Identifying child marriages as the underlying problem, it lamented that they were widespread but, quite surprisingly, did not explicitly state that widows be remarried, as one would naturally expect from a 'reform' journal! See 'Hindu Desamuloni Yatibalya Vivahamulu' (Infant Marriages in India), May 1903, pp. 347–348.

[37] The January 1903 issue published a news item on a widow remarriage performed in Guntur. 'Vrittantamulu', p. 223. Also see December 1903, back page.

[38] An announcement in the December 1904 issue informed widows about the proposed establishment of a Widow Home at Rajahmundry. 'Prakatana: Vitantu Sharanalayamu' (An Announcement Regarding Widows' Home), December 1904, back cover. After the Widow Home was established, another news item was published in the January 1905 issue. 'Vrittantamulu', p. 221. The news item overtly appealed to the public to send widows there.

[39] 'Hindu Vitantuvulanugoorchi Beasant Dorasanigari Yabhiprayamu' (Mrs. Besant on the Hindu Widow), pp. 230–233.

[40] The article and rejoinders have been discussed in Chapter 1, this volume. What is more important for us is that *Telugu Zenana* abstained from commenting at all on the debate. It just left the matter to the readers!

> Though I am an admirer of social reform, I am not campaigning in favour of widow remarriages in the journal. I am publishing only very brief news items on reform now and then. I wondered, and got angry, at the short-sightedness of Swamy Rao. While replying to Mrs. Brander's letter, I requested her not to get misled by the misinformation regarding reform a few narrow minded educated people were spreading! Then the British accepted the proposed changes in the journal.[41]

Thus, one may conclude that the silence of the journal on the issue of widow remarriage was indeed a forced silence. However, by way of publishing news items and other details regarding the condition of widows, *Telugu Zenana* tried to sensitise the public. That the journal published a few items on 'social reform' despite such proscriptions speaks of its commitment to the cause.

Telugu Zenana reflects a keen interest in the bourgeoning women's movement in colonial Andhra. By publishing the reports of various women's organisations, and also the full-length speeches of women delivered at several conferences, the journal helped spread the message of the women's movement to different corners of the region.[42] Another significant practice of the journal was that it prominently carried readers' responses. One letter to the editor focused on domestic violence against women.[43] Another letter, written by a woman named Sitamma, brought to light the travails of her friend 'Sushila' (a pseudonym), who was maltreated and subsequently

---

[41] Rayasam Venkata Sivudu, *Atma Charitramu*, pp. 323–324.

[42] For example, see 'Mrs. D. W. Kamalakar on Female Education', February 1904, pp. 229–234. The same issue published Burra Buchchi Bangaramma's speech delivered at the 'Aska Women's Association'. See 'Mrs. Bangaramma's Address', pp. 244–247. The January 1905 issue published the speech of Kotikalapudi Sitamma delivered on 21 January at the women's association in Rajahmundry. See 'Hindu Sundarula Vidyabhivruddhi' (Development of Education among Hindu Women), pp. 213–220.

[43] This letter was significant because it was perhaps the first to shed light on violence, particularly domestic violence vis-à-vis women. It was remarkable for it used the word '*himsa*' (violence). Many aspects of domestic violence, particularly wife-beating, were brought to light. The letter mentioned several incidents of physical abuse against the wife that the writer had witnessed and suicides resulting from extreme cruelty. The writer argued for government intervention and urged that the editor of *Telugu Zenana* feature writings on the subject occasionally to bring about a 'change of heart' in cruel men and give confidence to survivors of abuse. See 'Mithyapura Nivasi', 'Streelanu Himsinchuta: Oka Jaabu' (Maltreatment of Women: A Letter: translation as in original), June 1903, pp. 353–357.

abandoned by her husband.[44] Yet another woman, Vemuluri Ammiraju, in her letter, cursed her sister's child marriage and lamented her early demise during childbirth.[45]

Telugu Zenana carried a few regular columns. Under the column '*Vrittantamulu*' (New and Notes), it reported important news items and events of significance, generally related to the reform efforts. Under the head '*Grandha Vimarsanamu*' (Notice on Books), the journal published book reviews. Kotikalapudi Sitamma's *Upanyasa Manjari* (Collection of Essays) was reviewed in the October 1903 issue. When Bhandaru Atchamamba passed away, a lengthy obituary authored by Veeresalingam was published along with her full-size photograph.[46] A few articles and verses were published on themes such as 'Devotion to Husband',[47] 'Advice to Nursing Mothers,'[48] etc. *Telugu Zenana* emphasised that knowledge of music was an essential ingredient to cast oneself as a Grihalakshmi.[49] The journal is especially important for modern Telugu literature because it was the first to publish the short stories of Bhandaru Atchamamba, an early Telugu feminist. Her earliest short stories 'Prema Parikshanamu' (The Test of Love: translation as in original), and 'Eruvula Sommu Baruvula Chetu' (Story of a Golden Nose-Ring: translation as in original) were first published in the *Telugu Zenana*.[50] Atchamamba is the first Telugu woman to have published short stories and four out of 11 of these were published in *Telugu Zenana*.

The *Telugu Zenana* best demonstrates the motives behind the project of social reform initiated by male social reformers. By visualising women primarily as wives, housewives and mothers, emphasising their place and role at home, and by informing and asking them to master the intricacies of household management, *Telugu Zenana* neatly put forth the patriarchal sexual division of labour. The journal wanted women to be educated, not for their own sake as individuals who could realise their own potential, but to encourage them to fit perfectly into the designs of men. The journal, in fact, reflected the images of ideal companions in the dreams of 'progressive'

---

[44] 'Sitamma' (probably pseudonym), 'Sadhava Vydhavyam' (An Unhappy Marriage: A Letter; translation as in original), July 1903, pp. 35–37.

[45] See 'Oka Uttaramu' (A Letter), May 1903, p. 348.

[46] 'Srimati Bhandaru Atchamambagaru' (The Late Mrs. B. Atchamamba), February 1905, pp. 225–229.

[47] 'Pati Bhakti' (Devotion to Husband), October 1903, pp. 112–114.

[48] 'Pillala Tallulako Salaha' (Advice to Nursing Mothers), June 1903, pp. 369–370.

[49] K. R. S., 'Sangeetamu' (Music), December 1904, pp. 161–167.

[50] See July 1898, pp. 193–198; September 1898, pp. 89–96.

men of British Andhra. The *Telugu Zenana* sculpted a 'new woman' who could come up to the expectation of her English-educated and reform minded 'modern' husband by casting herself as his 'shadow'.

Hindu Sundary (1902-beyond 1960)

Hindu Sundary, literally meaning 'Hindu Beauty', was the first women's journal in Telugu to be edited by women.[51] It began publication in April 1902 and, surprisingly, enjoyed such a long career that it went on to be published beyond 1960. It was started, printed, published and initially edited by a man—prolific writer, researcher, and journalist Sattiraju Sitaramaiah (1864–1945).[52] Initially published from Ellore (Eluru), Godavari District, in April–May 1905 it shifted to Kanteru, a nondescript village where Sitaramaiah chose to settle permanently. Sitaramaiah wanted a woman to take charge of editing the journal from the very beginning, but the women he reached out to were reluctant to accept the offer.[53] Even his attempt to

[51] Unless otherwise mentioned, all references in this section are from *Hindu Sundary*.

[52] Sitaramaiah, a Niyogi Brahmin, was from Kanteru village in West Godavari District. He began his career as a teacher in the Mission School, Rajahmundry; later, he became a successful private lawyer and also occupied important public positions. His journalistic career began as a correspondent to the *Andhra Prakashika*, a weekly published from Madras. Later, he acquired a printing press and published a few journals such as the *Telugu Law Vartamani* and the *Deshopakari*. Sitaramaiah was interested in women's development; he functioned as a link between the literate women of Andhra, passing on the address of one woman to the other and encouraging them to correspond and cultivate friendships. He treated the act of introducing one woman to the other as 'a movement' and was thus seen as an 'ambassador' of women's friendship. Women fondly addressed Sitaramaiah as *annayya/annagaru* (elder brother). Sitaramaiah had an uneasy relationship with Veeresalingam. His autobiography *Sweeya Charitra* is remarkable in that it provides interesting details about the earliest women's movement—the way literate women came to know one another, the story of how women came to edit journals, their tensions, jealousies and competition, etc. For more details, see Sattiraju Sitaramaiah, *Sweeya Charitra* (Autobiography; Eluru, 2002). See also Tekumalla Kameswara Rao, *Naa Vaangmaya Mitrulu*, pp. 44–50.

[53] He requested well-known women who had established themselves as learned and scholastic women, including Bhandaru Atchamamba, Pulugurta Lakshmi Narasamamba and Mosalikanti Ramabayamma. All of them declined, stating that they could not 'bear the burden'. Atchamamba was willing to accept the role but expressed her inability to do so since she resided in Maharashtra. Sattiraju Sitaramaiah, *Sweeya Charitra*, pp. 81–82.

source an article by a Hindu woman for the first issue failed and finally he approached Mandapaka Johanamma, a native Christian woman, who 'dared' to publish a piece.[54] However, soon many women began to contribute to the journal. In December 1903, two women editors took over—Mosalikanti Ramabayamma and Vempali Shantabayamma. Shantabayamma passed away soon after, in April or May 1904; Mosalikanti Ramabayamma remained its sole editor till January 1908, after which the journal ceased publication for a while.

It was with the encouragement of women like Tumu Venkata Narasaiahmma, Venna Mangatayamma and particularly Balantrapu Sheshamma and Madabhooshi Choodamma that Sitaramaiah could 'venture' to restart the journal in June 1909.[55] After its revival, Mosalikanti Ramabayamma once again assumed the charge as editor while Tumu Venkata Narasaiahmma, her childhood friend and classmate, and Venna Mangatayamma, her sister, assisted her as joint editors.[56] In March 1913, about four years after its revival, *Hindu Sundary* came under the management of the Shri Vidyarthini Samajamu, the most vibrant women's organisation of the time.[57] From June 1913, Madabhooshi Choodamma and Kallepalle Venkata Ramanamma, important office-bearers of the *Samajamu*, became its editors. Balantrapu Sheshamma, another important functionary of the *Samajamu*, became its manager. The name of the press was changed to *Vidyarthini Samaja Mudrakshara Shala* and the venue of publication shifted to Kakinada, where the organisation was located.[58] During the 1940s, the journal was edited by Balantrapu Sheshamma and Vemuganti Papayamma became the honorary Secretary. Thus, the journal saw a succession of women editors.

Hindu Sundary clearly stated that it was 'conducted in the interests of the Telugu women'. Initially it had around 25 pages, and the annual subscription rate was Re. 1, inclusive of postage. After its revival, the

---

[54] Sattiraju Sitaramaiah, 'Swa Vishayamu' (Ourselves), June 1909, p. 2.

[55] Ibid., pp. 4–5.

[56] Ibid., p. 6. See also Tumu Venkata Narasaihamma, 'Vignapanamu' (An Appeal), June 1909, pp. 33–35.

[57] Kellapalle Venkata Ramanamma, Balantrapu Sheshamma, Madabhooshi Choodamma and Damerla Sitamma of the *Samajamu* requested Sitaramaiah to hand it over to the *Samajamu*, which he readily and happily obliged. 'Swa Vishayamu' (Ourselves), March 1913, pp. 1–4. He hoped that *Hindu Sundary*, being a women's journal, would 'prosper' under the exclusive management of women without any male association.

[58] 'Swa Vishayamu' (Ourselves), June 1913, pp. 1–3.

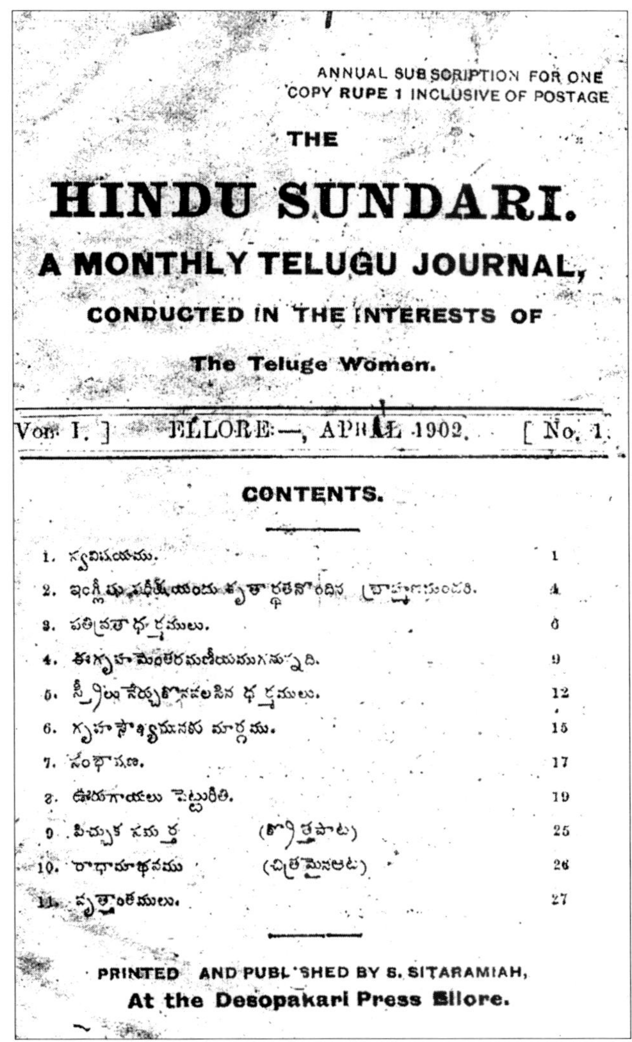

ANNUAL SUBSCRIPTION FOR ONE COPY RUPE 1 INCLUSIVE OF POSTAGE

THE

HINDU SUNDARI.

A MONTHLY TELUGU JOURNAL,

CONDUCTED IN THE INTERESTS OF

The Teluge Women.

Vol. I.] ELLORE:—, APRIL 1902. [No. 1.

CONTENTS.

PRINTED AND PUBLISHED BY S. SITARAMIAH,
At the Desopakari Press Ellore.

Image 2.2: Cover page of *Hindu Sundary*

Source: *Hindu Sundary*, April 1902.

annual subscription rate was increased to Rs. 2 (inclusive of postage); the half-yearly subscription was Rs. 1.40, and a single copy was available at 0.4 paisa. The subscription rate remained the same all through the remaining period of its publication. Unlike many other women's journals, *Hindu Sundary* soon became very popular, amassing as many as 800 subscribers

Image 2.3: Mosalikanti Ramabayamma, first Hindu editor of a Telugu journal and the first woman editor of *Hindu Sundary*

Source: Sattiraju Sitaramaiah, *Sweeya Charitra* (Eluru, 2002).

within just two years.[59] In the next 10 years, however, the increase in subscribers slowed down.[60] Eventually, the sum collected from subscriptions was barely sufficient to meet the expenditure incurred and it was only with the generous contributions of 'patrons' and 'sympathisers' that the journal

[59]This was a remarkable achievement. *Telugu Zenana*, despite a publication period of about 15 years, had 300 subscribers. Sattiraju Sitaramaiah, *Sweeya Charitra*, p. 97. Sitaramaiah happily wrote that the journal had attracted many women within six months of publication. Impressed by the journal, the School Inspectress issued an order that the journal be sent to all the government-run schools. Ibid., p. 72.

[60]'Shri Vidyarthini Samajamu, Kakinada', October 1914, p. 32. See also 'Swa Vishayamu' (Ourselves), June 1913, p. 3.

could sustain itself.[61] Financial constraints often delayed publication, and some times two to three issues were combined. The editors lamented that 'though there were thousands in favour of women's education, it was a matter to be regretted that *Hindu Sundary*, the only journal published by and for women, had to face financial hardships'.[62] That despite such pressing difficulties the *Hindu Sundary* managed to survive for more than half a century was truly noteworthy. The journal was particularly popular in the coastal districts.

The most significant aspect of *Hindu Sundary* was that it transformed many women into accomplished writers, marking a shift from a scenario where women 'hesitated even to publish their names in journals'. Women fondly recalled and acknowledged this shift.[63] Between 1903 and 1909, the number of women who had contributed to the journal increased steadily to around 100. Sitaramaiah was extremely happy about this heartening development.[64] Articles published in *Hindu Sundary*, particularly during the first two decades, were almost exclusively written by women: this enhanced its image as a 'true women's journal'. The journal provided a platform for women's public self-expression. Through its columns, they communicated with their 'sisters' located in far-flung areas and built intellectual bonds among themselves.

Hindu Sundary was an eloquent advocate of the women's cause. The journal was sensitive to the complex issues faced by widows, and nearly every issue contained articles about them. Forcible tonsuring of widows was seen as 'the most brutal crime' and article after article condemned it vehemently. Mosalikanti Ramabayamma, the first woman editor of *Hindu Sundary*, launched a signature campaign against this 'horrendous barbaric practice'.[65] *Hindu Sundary* published several articles that advocated widow

---

[61] 'Shri Vidyarthini Samajamu, Kakinada', October 1914, p. 32.

[62] 'Vignapanamu' (An Appeal), August 1909, pp. 1–2.

[63] Balantrapu Sheshamma wrote that 'though it was not a full-fledged journal, it published everything that women wrote' to encourage them. 'As they kept on writing', they became well versed with the art of writing. She further said that 'she, along with a few others, became habituated to writing' and gradually transformed into good writers. 'Aikamatyamu' (Unity [among Women]), January 1910, pp. 13–17.

[64] 'Swa Vishayamu' (Ourselves), June 1909, pp. 1–6.

[65] 'Vitantu Shiromundanamunu goorchina Mahajaru' (Petition Regarding the Tonsuring of Widows), July 1904, pp. 146–153. Also see 'Hindu Vitantuvula Shiromundanamu' (Tonsuring of Hindu Widows), October–November 1905, pp. 198–201.

remarriage.[66] They also emphasised that the Dharmashastras approved of widow remarriages. While many articles similarly cited the shastras, a few, like those of Uppuluri Nagaratnamma, stated that since a law had been enacted (the Widow Remarriage Act of 1856) legalising widow remarriages, one need not bother about the sanction or ban of the shastras.[67] The journal's positive attitude towards the widow question is best represented by a controversy that broke out in the Shri Vidyarthini Samajamu.[68] It launched a sustained campaign against the practice of child marriage, blaming the practice for the high incidence of widowhood and terming it a 'major obstacle' to women's educational advancement.[69] *Hindu Sundary* advocated post-puberty marriages. However, there was a difference of opinion among the writers regarding the 'right marriageable age'.[70]

The issue of women's education was very dear to *Hindu Sundary*. Among the various deep-rooted prejudices against women's education the journal tried to dispel was that women, if educated, became immoral and turned disobedient. Condemning those who propagated such views as 'hate mongers',[71] *Hindu Sundary* emphasised the advantages of women's education.[72] Though a few articles had titles like 'Streela Unnata Vidya'

---

[66] These writings were characterised by vivid descriptions of the conditions of, and multiple atrocities inflicted on, widows. For example, Varanasi Kameshwari, 'Mana Hindu Vitantuvula Dusthiti' (Miserable Plight of Our Hindu Widows), April 1905, pp. 1–5.

[67] 'Stree Punarvivahamulu' (Widow Remarriages), October–November 1911, pp. 26–30.

[68] See Chapter 4, this volume.

[69] 'Andhra Mahila Sabha: Sabhathipurali Upanyasamu' (Presidential Address delivered at the Andhra Mahila Mahasabha), March 1913, pp. 23–40.

[70] Kalagara Pichchamma proposed 16 years for girls and 25 years for boys. 'Balya Vivahamulavalana Kalugu Nashtamulu' (The Evil Effects of Child Marriages), April 1912, p. 8. Mosalikanti Ramabayamma held 16 years to be the right age for girls to get married. 'Rajaswalananatara Vivahamulu' (Post-Puberty Marriages), March 1912, p. 30. Women like Kallepalle Venkata Ramanamma felt that the British government should intervene and ban the practice of child marriage. 'Stree Vidyaku Bhangakaramulagu Vyvahika Dharmamulu: Vanini Tolaginchu Upayamulu' (Marriage *Dharma*s Harmful to Female Education: Remedies), May 1912, pp. 19–22.

[71] Mosalikanti Ramabai, 'Aikamatyamu' (Unity [among Women]), November 1903, pp. 16–18.

[72] For example, see Lakshmikantamma, 'Stree Vidya' (Women's Education), November 1902, pp. 19–22; Bhandaru Atchamamba, 'Bharya Bhartala Samvadamu: Stree Vidya' (Dialogue between Wife and Husband on Women's Education), December 1902, pp. 1–10; Gunadala Subhadramma, 'Stree Vidya' (Women's Education), December 1903, pp. 23–24; Suryanarayana Moorthy, 'Stree Vidya' (Women's Education'), July 1905, pp. 141–148.

(Women's Higher Education), by this term they only meant the capacity to read 'big *grandhas*' and understand them.[73] The journal also published articles by women like Unnava Lakshmibayamma which emphasised that women could and should take up examinations for higher degrees like the BA.[74]

Uppuluri Nagaratnamma wrote that 'education was equally beneficial' to women and men.[75] Others held the view that 'without the progress of women's education, women could not afford to get freedom' and thus established a link between education and freedom.[76] Articles focused on the discouragingly low levels of literacy among women. By providing statistical details, they questioned the discrimination against girls' education. Parents 'preferred' the education of boys; they even 'sold off their property to give them education', even as they mercilessly sold off their daughters to 'old vampires'.[77] It was suggested that girls 'should not be married off until they completed their education' and that their choice in marriage should be given due consideration.[78] It is significant to note that women were emphasising 'choice' in marriage as early as the beginning of the twentieth century. A

---

[73] Pulugurta Laskhmi Narasamamba, 'Streela Unnata Vidya' (Higher Education of Women), May 1903, pp. 5–15.

[74] 'Stree Vidya' (Women's Education), November 1903, pp. 14–16.

[75] According to her, an educated woman could 'earn her livelihood' as a teacher in case her husband passed away. 'Stree Vidya' (Women's Education), April 1912, pp. 19–22. She was so radical that she pointed out the 'conspiracy' of men behind the creation of various Dharmashastras that denied women education and freedom by sanctioning a secondary status. She emphasised that, had women written the shastras, they must have ensured that women enjoyed a higher, or at least equal, status and freedom to men. One could easily sense the emerging feminist radicalism in her pronouncements.

[76] It was emphasised that 'women should have freedom to be educated', and education to enjoy freedom. Writers appealed to women to actively take up their cause on their own rather than depend on men. See 'Oka Stree' (A Woman), 'Stree Vidyabhyudayametulanagunu' (The Road to Women's Educational Advancement), May 1912, pp. 11–16. Damerla Sitamma wrote that 'one could never understand the problems of the other perfectly', and hence, she suggested women to 'take up their own agency to solve their [own] problems' for men—the other—could never understand the problems of women. 'Stree Vidya Vishayamu' (Regarding Women's Education), January 1912, pp. 1–4.

[77] 'Andhra Mahila Sabha: Sabhadhipurali Upanyasamu', March 1913, pp. 23–40. See also July 1917, p. 10; September 1917, p. 13.

[78] Achanta Rukminamma, 'Stree Vidya, Vivahamunaku Tagina Vayassu' (Suitable Age for Women's Education and Marriage), February 1912, pp. 20–25.

few women like Subhadra stressed that women 'definitely needed English education'.[79]

Hindu Sundary paid great attention to publishing the details of various women's organisations and conferences. Such rich details—which together comprise the women's archive—are of enormous help to a social historian and offer evidence of women's activism in colonial Andhra. These details help us understand the women's movement from women's point of view. The journal's pages were inundated with full-length speeches delivered at various women's conferences. Reports of the presidential addresses and other speeches delivered at the All-Andhra Women's Conferences (or the Andhra Mahila Mahasabhas), the number in attendance, etc., provide a wealth of information and emerge as a lively picture of the women's movement.

The journal also published brief biographical accounts of prominent contemporary women like Pandita Ramabai Saraswati[80] and Swarnakumari Devi.[81] The September–October 1903 issue published an account of Bhandaru Atchamamba along with her photograph.[82] Biographical sketches of other leading activist-intellectuals like Kotikalapudi Sitamma, Uppuluri Nagaratnamma, Burra Buchchi Bangaramma, Achanta Rukmini Devi and Kanchanapalli Kanakamma were written with great care. Such presentations projected these accomplished women as role models and inspired other women. The March 1913 issue published the family photograph of Sitaramaiah. A few articles were published on Veeresalingam on his birth anniversary.[83]

Several other items also found a place in the columns of *Hindu Sundary*. Many articles were on the usual themes of domestic management, marital life and social reform, fashioning an image of woman only as home-maker, devout and submissive wife and 'upholder of Hindu tradition'. Women were

---

[79] Subhadra, 'Streelaku Englishu Vidya Avasarama?' (Do Women Need English Education?), February 1912, pp. 5–7.

[80] 'Pandita Ramabai Saraswati', January 1910, pp. 1–7.

[81] 'Srimati Swarnakumari Devi', February–March 1910, p. 9. Her photograph was also published in the same issue, p. 7.

[82] 'Srimati Bhandaru Atchamamba', pp. 1–7. Again, an essay paying tribute was published in the December–January 1905 issue after Atchamamba passed away. 'Kirtisheshuralagu Srimati Bhandaru Atchamamba', pp. 300–304.

[83] For example, see Kotikalapudi Sitamma, 'Rai Bahadur Kandukuri Veeresalingam Pantuluvari Janmadina Smaranamu' (Remembering Veeresalingam on his Birth Anniversary), May 1904, pp. 46–50. See also 'Rai Bahadur Kandukuri Veeresalingam Pantuluvari Janmadinotsavamu' (Birth Anniversary of Veeresalingam), May 1904, pp. 50–53.

expected and encouraged to mould themselves to fit neatly into the structure of the 'new patriarchy'. Apart from these, articles on '*aikamatyamu*' (unity [among women]) stressed the need for women to forge bonds of sisterhood; unless women achieved unity, they would never be able to launch or sustain their movement. Under the head '*Vartamanamulu*' ('News'), later changed as '*Vaartavali*' ('Chain of News'), *Hindu Sundary* published several news items on local, national and international issues. The most significant among them were those related to reform efforts.[84]

Hindu Sundary experienced tremendous decline in and after the 1940s. Financial difficulties compelled it to reduce the size to 24 pages. The number of women authors declined drastically in the same period.[85] Among the 12 items in the September 1942 issue, eight were authored by men. The genre, nature and contents of the writings also witnessed a change, with more short stories and fewer essays. Though women's issues were still raised, they lost the earlier focus and verve. New issues, particularly those related to the 'national' movement, like promotion of Khaddar, communal amity, the question of untouchability, constructive work, etc., began to appear. They informed women about the role they were required to play in such 'national' programmes. Accordingly, the cover pages featured nationalist symbols such as the picture of *Bharata Mata* (Mother India).

---

[84] For example, the August 1909 issue published the shocking news of a young widow who 'ran away from home to get remarried', and the way she was brutalised by her father. The news item said that her late husband had permitted her to adopt a boy to inherit his property as they had no children. But after his death, the girl wanted to remarry, ran away from her home and took shelter in a widows' home. Her father made allegations of theft and forcibly brought her back. Afraid that she may remarry, he forcibly shaved her head. She filed a case against her father and the hearing was ongoing when the article about it was published. 'Vartamanamulu', August 1909, p. 30. A news item published the statistics of widows in the Bengal Presidency. It condemned child marriages and proposed widow remarriage. 'Vartamanamulu', May 1903, back page. Another news item was about the conference of the Andhra Mahila Mahasabha that was scheduled for 12–13 May 1915 at Visakhapatnam. 'Vaartavali', May 1915, p. 2.

[85] Vemuganti Papayamma, editor and honourary secretary, was greatly aggrieved and complained that women writers 'gradually lost interest' in the journal and shifted to other journals: 'they lacked the commitment and imagination to improve *Hindu Sundary*.' Further, she sarcastically remarked that 'to boast of themselves as editors of journals', a few women brought out 'a [new] journal everyday', the fate of which was 'like the sunlight for three days [i.e. very short-lived]'. She lamented that '*Hindu Sundary* would not have so declined had there been "aikamatyamu" [unity] among women.' See 'Swa Vishayamu' (Ourselves), February 1945, p. 2. Also see 'Swa Vishayamu' (Ourselves), July 1941, p. 2.

That the *Hindu Sundary* was the first women's journal to be edited by women has its own significance, and it was additionally one managed by a women's organisation, the first of its kind in Andhra. The journal created an enlarged public space, thus far hardly available to women, for collectively channelling their aspirations. It laid a firm foundation for women's journalism in Telugu at the beginning of the twentieth century and groomed many women journalists, granting them the tools to represent themselves and write their own future. Though women have had a long tradition of writing in Telugu, dating to the early fourteenth century, it was with *Hindu Sundary* that women's collective intellectual journey began, gathering momentum in the 1930s and 1940s and registering heartening success. The success of *Grihalakshmi* and *Andhra Mahila* in the late 1920s and after owes, in part, to the pioneering work of *Hindu Sundary.* The seed of women's consciousness, which *Hindu Sundary* so painstakingly planted in the first two decades of the twentieth century, eventually branched out in multiple directions. This was the journal that inaugurated an extremely dynamic phase of women's intellectual work in colonial Andhra.

Savithri (1904-1917)

The *Sri Savithri* (popular as *Savithri*), published monthly, was the second women's journal to be edited by women.[86] Edited by Pulugurta Lakshmi Narasamamba,[87] it began publication in January 1904 from Cocanada

[86] Unless otherwise especially mentioned, all references in this section are from *Savithri.*

[87] Born in 1878 to a family of scholars, Narasamamba was the disciple and follower of Kashibhatta Bramhaiah Shastri, a conservative and rival of Veeresalingam. Though she did not receive any formal education, her scholarship was remarkable: at the age of 15, she authored a *Kavya*—the *Mahilakalabodhini*. The book was intended to highlight the 'advantages of women's education', and was deliberately written 'in an easy style so that the school-going girls could understand it'. A polyglot, she had good command of Hindi and Bangla: she translated a few works from those languages into Telugu. She authored several books and was frequently published in contemporary journals as well. Narasamamba was the founder of the 'Shri Vidyarthini Samajamu', Kakinada, and was instrumental in convening the first All-Andhra Women's Conference (Andhra Mahila Mahasabha) in 1910. See Utukuri Lakshmikanthamma, *Andhra Kavayitrulu*, other details N.A., pp. 141–143. For a brief biography, see 'Srimati Pulugurta Lakshmi Narasamambagaru', *Andhra Mahila*, January 1950, pp. 43–44. The sketch was published on the occasion of her being honoured with the award, "Kaavya Kalaa Visharada", on 15.11.1949, by the Sri Tirupati Trilinga Vidya Pithamu.

(Kakinada) and appears to have continued till 1917. Its publisher was Pulugurta Venkata Ratnam, Narasamamba's husband. Due to financial constraints and other reasons, its publication was paused for a few years in between.

Image 2.4: Cover page of *Savithri*

Source: February–March 1907.

Narasamamba was motivated by a desire to start a women's journal that was 'entirely managed' by women. She recognised that educated women, despite having the capacity to write, had certain 'inhibitions' in communicating with the editors of the contemporary women's journals, who were typically men. Therefore, to 'encourage women' to write freely and exchange their views with other women, she thought it her 'due responsibility' to start a journal and 'work for the progress of women'. She remarked that she 'dared to shoulder the burden of managing the journal'.[88] Many women and men came forward to help her in this venture.[89]

Each issue of *Savithri* had 35–40 pages. The annual subscription rate, inclusive of postage, was Re. 1, and the price of a single copy was 2 paisa. It appears that *Savithri* had about 1,500 subscribers.[90] The journal enjoyed a fairly wide reach that extended to Bellary, Kadapa, Dharmavaram, Chandragiri, Rayachoti, Vayalpadu (in the Ceded Districts/Rayalaseema), Kanigiri, Nellore, Bangalore, Bombay, Madras, Hyderabad, etc.[91] Despite its otherwise smooth run, difficulties surfaced in the later years of its publication—the February, March and April issues of 1912 had to be published together due to financial pressures.[92]

---

[88] See 'Vignapanamu' (An Appeal), December 1904, p. 1. Balantrapu Sheshamma made the point clear. According to her, Narasamamba recognised that women were reluctant to publish in journals like *Telugu Zenana* and *Hindu Sundary* that were managed by men. Thus, the journal would 'encourage and benefit the world of women'. 'Telugudeshamandali Streela Vidya' (Women's Education in the Telugu Country), March 1904, p. 12.

[89] *Savithri* had a few 'chief patrons' who paid Rs. 10 per annum; 'patrons' and '*sahayulu*' (donors/helpers) paid Rs. 5 and Rs. 3, respectively. See 'Adanika', February 1904. A few women 'patrons' were: Chintalapudi Venkata Ramanamma, Nalam Subhadramma, Muchcharla Bhramaramba, Bhupatiraju Appala Narasayyamma, Kolluri Satyanarayanamba, Valluri Venkateshwaramma, Choragudi Sitamma, Gundu Atchamamba, Gade Chudikudutamma, Davuluri Dameshwaramma and Mantripragada Kamarajamma. See 'Vignapanamu' (An Appeal), December 1904, pp. 1–2.

[90] See 'Srimati Pulugurta Lakshmi Narasamambagaru', *Andhra Mahila*, January 1950, p. 43.

[91] November 1904, pp. 12–15.

[92] Dwelling on this, Narasamamba wrote that annual subscription revenue did not meet the expenditure of publication and she herself had to bear the expenditure of postage and *gumasta kharchu* (salary for the peon). Subscribers became indifferent: Despite accepting the copies, they did not bother to pay the subscription fee! Some did not even bother to inform whether they needed the journal or not, and a few returned it via value payable post, causing loss to the editor. This also resulted in delayed publication. See 'Vignapanamu' (An Appeal), February, March and April 1912, p. 1. See also 'Vignapanamu' (An Appeal), September 1910, p. 1.

Savithri lived up to its stated objective of promoting women's writings. Most of the writings published in it were by, for and about women. Balantrapu Sheshamma, Damerla Sundaramma, Burra Buchchi Bangaramma, Gundu Atchamamba, Manyam Venkata Subbamma, Demerla Sitamma, Uppala Narasamamba, Atmuri Annapoornamma, K. Kanakamma and Kallepalle Venkata Ramanamma were a few among its women contributers. Narasamamba, the editor, was the most frequent contributor; most of her works were serialised in the journal. The journal also had contributions from men, among who were Sunkara Rangaiah, Pulugurta Venkata Ratnam, Mangipudi Venkaiah, Devaguptapu Sanyasi Raju, Vemuganti Ramakrishna Rao, and Nandagiri Trayambaka Rao.

Speeches by women, delivered at various women's organisations/ conferences, and particularly those delivered at the Shri Vidyarthini Samajamu (which was founded and initially headed by the editor of *Savithri*) were published by the journal, as well programmes and annual reports of various women's associations, and announcements regarding women's conferences.[93] Details about a few girls' schools were also published.[94] The column '*Stree Rogamulu*' (Diseases That Affect Women), by Nandagiri Trayambaka Rao, discussed women's health.

Savithri was obsessed with inculcating morality and pativratya dharma (conjugal fidelity) among women. Writings—mostly in the form of verse—emphasising mortality and pativratya as the quintessence of *sati* dharma were regularly published. It is remarkable that though most of these writings were by men, it was a favourite theme of women writers also. Titles are indicative of the journal's thrust: 'Niti Padamulu' (Verses on Mortality),[95] 'Sati Dharmamulu' (Duties of a Virtuous Woman),[96] 'Stree Niti Dipika' (A Guide to Women's Morality),[97] 'Stree Niti Ratnavali' (A String of Gems on

93 For example, see 'Kakinada Vidyarthini Sanghamuyokka Praprathamavatsara Vishaya Vignapanamu' (The First Annual Report of the Kakinada Vidyarthini Samajamu), March 1904, pp. 1–7. The October 1904 issue published the second annual report of the 'Aska Stree Samajamu', pp. 1–4.

94 Damerla Sitamma, 'Rajamahendravarapu Mission Balika Pathashala' (The Girls' Mission School at Rajahmundry), March 1911, pp. 22–24.

95 See January, March and April 1904 issues.

96 It was serialised. See the January, February and April 1904 issues.

97 It was written by Kolagnati Kotaiah, and serialised. It had several parts like 'Gurujana Priti' (How to Please Elders), 'Pativratya Padhdhati' (Methods of Maintaining Conjugal Fidelity), 'Griha Karya Nirvahakata' (Domestic Management), 'Shishu Poshana' (Child-Rearing), etc. See August 1904.

Women's Morality),[98] 'Stree Niti Gitamulu' (Verses on Women's Morality),[99] 'Niti Padamulu' (Verses on Morality),[100] 'Sadvartanamu' (Good Conduct)[101] and 'Pativratyamu', the last two appearing in prose form.

All these writings had a single-point agenda of casting women in the mould of pativratas by inculcating in them morality, good conduct, devotion to husband, submission, and self-sacrifice. Women's education was sought as a potential instrument to train women in marital and domestic conduct, in keeping with the reformist ideas of the time. Since a woman's duty was to serve her husband like a *dasi* (slave), she could provide him enlightened company and service. Education inculcated good conduct, kept her involved, and saved her from indulging in 'unnecessary' and 'cheap' gossip.[102]

Savithri took an extremely conservative stand on the issues of child marriage and widow remarriage. Narasamamba was a staunch advocate of child marriage and even the practice of sati, and a bitter critic of the very idea of widow remarriage. While recognising that the practice of child marriage was against the Dharmashastras, she still held it to be a 'noble' practice that 'saved the noble virtue of pativratya, the source of India's [*Hindu Deshamu*] honour and reputation'. She felt that it was good to marry off girls 'before [the evil idea of] love sprouted in them', to prevent their thoughts from flowing in the 'wrong directions' and causing damage to their chastity. She quoted a few English scholars who praised such marriages. Narasamamba sarcastically remarked that the modern social reformers 'who were hell-bent on spoiling the world acclaimed *Hindu dharma*' should accept that marriage reform was unnecessary and 'stop creating nuisance'.[103]

Savithri maintained an even more conservative and pernicious stand on the question of widow remarriage. Narasamamba was bitterly opposed to widow remarriage. According to her, marriage for the Hindu woman was only once: remarriage amounted to 'prostitution'. Remarried women

[98] It was authored by Sunkara Rangaiah, and serialised since October 1904.

[99] Pulugurta Lakshmi Narasamamba wrote these verses. See the February, March and April 1912 issues.

[100] Ibid.

[101] Damerla Sundaramma wrote this essay. See October 1904.

[102] 'Stree Niti Deepika'. See also Devaguptapu Sanyasi Raju, 'Satimani' (A Jewel-like Wife), June 1911; Ryali Janaki Ramayamma, 'Stree Vidya' (Women's Education), October, November and December 1911, pp. 13–14; Uppala Narasamamba, 'Stree Vidya Pancharatnamulu' (Verses on Women's Education), September 1910.

[103] Pulugurta Lakshmi Narasamamba, 'Pativratyamu' (Conjugal Fidelity), July 1911, pp. 2–17.

(punarvivahitalu) were not to be accorded the status of 'kulanganas' or 'respectable women'. Widow remarriage was seen as a serious affront to the pativrata dharma of Hindu women; it tarnished the glorious Hindu dharma as a whole. She stressed that 'a widow's duty was to observe strict celibacy'. When social reformers like Veeresalingam cited the approval of the Dharmashastras, she paid them in the same coin to defend her arguments against widow remarriage. As discussed in Chapter 1, at the height of her conservatism, she expelled Damerla Sitamma and Balantrapu Sheshamma, the secretaries of the Shri Vidyarthini Samaju, for the 'sin' of bringing punarvivahitalu to the meetings of the organisation.[104]

The Manyam Subbamma—Veeresalingam Controversy

What made *Savithri*'s run remarkable was that it was involved in a protracted intellectual battle with Veeresalingam. It became a site of heated debate by providing a platform to conservative women who were engaged in a war of words with social reformers.

In its August and September 1904 issues, *Savithri* carried an article titled 'Sati Dharma Prakashika' (Illuminator of the Sati Dharmas), by Manyam Venkata Subbamma, a Vaishya woman, hailing the *Manusmriti* and justifying the servile position of women. To substantiate her stand, she extensively quoted from the *Manusmriti*, *Veda*s, various shlokas and a few English works. In the October 1904 issue of *Telugu Zenana*, Veeresalingam published a sharply critical burlesque in response to this article, titled 'Savithri Satyavati Sambhashanamu—Stree Vidya'. He ridiculed Manyam Subbama by adding the suffix 'Shastri', an honorific generally used only for Brahmin men, to her name. The dialogue contained many other derisive remarks.[105] Veeresalingam, stunned by Subbamma's display of Sanskritic prowess, was convinced that the piece was authored by a man. Beyond the prejudiced idea that a *woman* could not have produced such scholarship, what really alarmed Veeresalingam was the extreme conservatism of the article. He thought it would have 'disastrous effects on women's development'.

[104]See Pulugurta Lakshmi Narasamamba, 'Andhra Mahila Mahasabha', June 1911, pp. 2–20. See also another of her article, 'Kulanganalu', (Respectable/Chaste Women), October 1911, pp. 1–9. Her ideas on widow remarriages are discussed in detail in Chapter 4, this volume.

[105]Kandukuri Veeresalingam, 'Savithri Satyavati Sambhashanamu—Stree Vidya', *Telugu Zenana*, October 1904, pp. 121–126.

Narasamamba soon published a scathing rejoinder, the 'Kamala Vimala Samvadamu—Stree Vidya' (Dialogue between Kamala and Vimala on Women's Education). Of the two characters, Kamala voiced the views of Narasamamba: 'out of sheer jealousy', she wrote, the 'self proclaimed favourites of women's education' in fact 'worked against it'. To Vimala's question as to why they were jealous of women, Kamala replied that the male reformers 'were jealous because women did not hold the same views as theirs; did not praise them; did not follow their guidelines, and charted their own way by using their own brains'. They discouraged women by 'unleashing vile criticism' to counter women's writings. In addition, she said that as women moved forward, these 'jealous' men 'ridiculed' them. Further, she implicated Venkata Sivudu for publishing Veeresalingam's article in his journal. Addressing him, she sarcastically remarked, 'how great is your love for women's education! Well! Well!'[106]

Manyam Subbamma, whose piece was the nucleus of the controversy, also published a rejoinder. In a lengthy article titled 'Oka Prakatanamu—Oka Manavi' (An Announcement and an Appeal),[107] she accussed Veersalingam of making 'baseless allegations'. Subbamma warned that such writings 'humiliated not only her, but also all educated women who had been writing in the journals', and remarked that believing in such 'self-styled advocates of women's education' was like 'swimming the Godavari holding the tail of a dog'. She expressed her readiness to 'face any test to establish her scholarship'. Finally, Subbamma appealed to women 'to treat it as an [insulting] issue concerning all of them' and act accordingly.[108]

An enraged Veeresalingam replied that he had initially 'thought it below his dignity to react to such rebukes of the unwise', but his 'opponents took it to be his incompetence' and ridiculed him in the journal *Aryamatabodhini*.

---

[106] November 1904, pp. 1–8. Narasamamba continued to take on Veeresalingam. Addressing women in the December 1904 issue, she alleged that the self-styled social reformers were impeding women's progress. She appealed to women not to be discouraged by such vile criticisms, which were 'far from truth'. See 'Vignapanamu' (An Appeal), December 1904, pp. 1–6.

[107] An infuriated Subbamma said that she had considered it to be 'ignoble to react to such vile criticism' aimed only at 'defaming' her. A few of her friends suggested her to 'ignore' such a 'mean criticism' as one ignored a monkey, which ridiculed others being ignorant of its own beauty, and a dog which simply barked at those who went on a royal path. However, a few others suggested her 'to do something about it to expose the meanness' in the writer [i.e. Veeresalingam]. Hence, she became ready to publish the rejoinder.

[108] Manyam Subbamma, 'Oka Prakatanamu–Oka Manavi', December 1904, pp. 1–9.

'The rejoinder written in the name of Manyam Subbamma', in his view, had 'no substance other than rebukes and allegations' and was befitting 'the stories narrated by a buffoon in street dramas'. He claimed that he knew the 'real author', who was based in Kakinada, and was 'notorious' for such things (writing under women's names), and said that 'he did not want to desecrate his journal [*Telugu Zenana*] by mentioning that sinner's name'. Claiming that Narasamamba's husband Pulugurta Venkataratnam had confided to his sources, Veeresalingam reiterated his allegations, contending that no 'self-respecting woman' could write in such a 'nasty way'. Reflecting on Narasamamba's criticism of his reformist perspective, he wrote that 'he had begun working for the cause of women long before she was born' and that 'she was a damn conservative who was averse to any progress'. Taking Subbamma at her word, he asked the editor of *Savithri* to arrange for a 'test' to ascertain authorship.[109] We do not know what happened later.

The foregoing discussion is indicative of the bitter fights between reformers and conservatives in this period. In addition, it establishes quite unequivocally that not all women supported the reform efforts. Some, in fact, bitterly opposed them. The *Savithri* proved to be a conservative journal with a clear agenda of casting women in the traditional pativrata mould. Even its name, which invokes the memory of the self-effacing ancient pativrata, Sati Savithri, is emblematic of the journal's stand on women's issues. The formal *grandhika* (bookish) register of its writings complemented its conservatism. When the tides of social reform were surging, *Savithri* was vehement in its resistance. Indeed, her problematic views aside, the episode also brings out Narasamamba's sense of conviction in her own views and her willingness to publicly debate a figure of Veeresalingam's stature.

Vivekavathi (1909-1934)

The Christian Literature Society (*Krystava Vidyabhivardhani Samajamu*), Madras, founded the journal *Vivekavathi*, literally 'wise woman', in October 1909.[110] It ran for a quarter-century without any breaks. Sources suggest that

---

[109] He announced that he would go there wherever the test was conducted, and if Subbamma proved her scholarship, he would change his views and tender a public apology through an announcement in the journal. See 'Zenana Patrika—Savithri', *Telugu Zenana*, April and May 1905, pp. 322–329.

[110] Unless otherwise especially mentioned, all references in this section are from *Vivekavathi*.

it was printed at the SPCK Press, Vepery, Madras, till November 1910[111] and later at the Christian Literature Society Press. *Vivekavathi* stated in English that it was intended 'for the home'. In Telugu, it stated that '*Vivekavathi* was a monthly which published several items that women could read'.[112] The name of the journal was unique among its contemporaries: While *Savithri* and *Anasuya* invoked the memory of the Hindu pativratas and *Andhra Lakshmi* and *Andhra Mahila* emphasised regional identity, here was a secular name.

The cover page of each issue featured a woman standing in a dignified posture, with an open book in her left hand, perhaps a figuration of *Vivekavathi*. This innovative measure no doubt would have appealed to many a woman. A verse in *utpalamala* metre published in every issue, just below the masthead, stated the aims and objectives of the journal. Below it appeared the Biblical maxim: 'a virtuous woman was more precious than a pearl' (*gunavatiyayina stree mutyamukante namoolyamynadi*). It was a visually pleasing journal and the paper used was of very high quality (especially compared to other women's journals). Moreover, *Vivekavathi* contained a large number of fascinating illustrations, which added to its visual appeal.

Vivekavathi saw several editors—all of them Christian women—over its publication history. A 'Miss McLaurin' was its founding editor.[113] The second editor was Ms Archibald, MA, who lived in Chicacole (Srikakulam, the northern part of the Telugu-speaking districts of the erstwhile Madras Presidency). She edited *Vivekavathi* between October 1910 and August 1913.[114] The third editor was Mrs Mc Cauley, a BA. She lived in Guntur and continued as editor for a longer time.[115] Mrs Shreenivassa BA, LT, was the fourth editor.[116] A 15-member committee called the 'Vivekavathi Committee' managed *Vivekavathi*—impressively well-coordinated, it consisted mostly of foreign Christians and one or two Indian Christians.[117]

Vivekavathi had 32 pages, although the number decreased to 24 in the 1920s. Its annual subscription rate, which remained the same throughout its period of publication, was 12 *anna*s, and the cost of a single copy was 1 anna.

---

[111] The second issue (November 1909) indicated this. See p. 64.

[112] See the October 1912 issue.

[113] She lived in Vuyyuru, Krishna District.

[114] Ms Archibald was affectionately called 'the mother of *Vivekavathi*.' October 1913, pp. 1–2.

[115] September 1913, inside back page.

[116] She lived in Tirupattur, North Arcot District.

[117] October 1915, inside back cover.

Image 2.5: Cover page of *Vivekavathi*

Source: *Vivekavathi*, December 1913.

It enjoyed a relatively wide circulation. From only 300 subscribers at the end of its first year (October 1910),[118] its numbers increased phenomenally to 1,400 by February 1913[119] and to around 1,500 by October 1913. The editor was happy to state that *Vivekavathi* 'developed much during the four years

[118]'Patrika Sampadakurali Vyasamu' (Editorials), October 1913, p. 2.
[119]'Patrika Sampadakurali Vyasamu' (Editorials), February 1913, p. 132.

[of its publication]'.[120] The fact that the journal reached Burma (present-day Myanmar), drawing in both subscribers and article submissions from the region, indicates its widespread popularity.[121] A few women's organisations requested the editor to send *Vivekavathi* free of cost; this request was gently rejected since the journal was 'already available at a subsidised price' and thus it was not very difficult for the women's organisations to subscribe to *Vivekavathi*.[122] It was very likely that a substantial number of its subscribers were Telugu Christians. Many Hindus were also on the list of its subscribers.

The editors undertook a rigorous campaign to promote its circulation.[123] On the completion of three years of its publication, the editor urged the readers to help increase its circulation to 4,000.[124] At the height of the campaign, articles and stories in the form of a dialogue hailed the qualities of the journal. In a dialogue, '*Vivekavathi Sambhashana*' (Dialogue on *Vivekavathi*), it was presented as a 'friend' and a leisure-time companion to women.[125] Another dialogue between a mother and daughter showered

---

[120]'Patrika Sampadakurali Vyasamu' (Editorials), October 1913, pp. 1–2.

[121]'Ayachotla Jarigina Sangatulu' (News Items on Several Events from Various Places), September 1912, p. 383. *Vivekavathi* seems to have impressed many and they wrote letters to the editor expressing their admiration for it. 'An active Hindu BA' was reported to have promised that 'he would try to contribute a few articles to *Vivekavathi* to demonstrate how much he loved the small but beautiful journal'. 'Patrika Sampadakurali Vyasamu' (Editorials), October 1912, pp. 1–2. 'A Brahmin from a small village' was reported to have written that 'he was happy to see *Vivekavathi*.' He showed the illustrations to his wife and explained to her the contents in it. The woman immediately expressed her desire to be educated so that she could read *Vivekavathi*. He started teaching her despite her parents' opposition. Ibid., p. 2. For people's appreciation for *Vivekavathi*, see also the December 1912 issue, inside back cover.

[122]'Patrika Sampadakurali Vyasamu' (Editorials), February 1913, p. 132.

[123]'Patrika Sampadakurali Vyasamu' (Editorials), March 1912, pp. 161–162.

[124]'Patrika Sampadakurali Vyasamu' (Editorials), October 1912, p. 4.

[125]The dialogue is between Kamala, an uneducated widow, and Shyamala, an educated one. Kamala complained that she was being bored up and asked Shyamala whether she did not face the same problem. The latter said that she did not because she read a book [*Vivekavathi*], if she felt so. She further said that she had been getting a book by spending 12 annas a year, and it was 'her friend in those difficult times.' Also she said to Kamala that the latter 'would not leave it if she started reading; and one would feel like reading it always, and it lived up to its name.' Finally, she suggested Kamala to get a copy for herself. Chaganti Kantamma, '*Vivekavathi* Sambhashana' (Dialogue on *Vivekavathi*), October 1912, pp. 22–24.

praises on *Vivekavathi*.[126] The editors also offered incentives for promoting its circulation.[127]

Compared with other women's journals like the *Savithri*, where the grandhika style dominated, *Vivekavathi*'s style was very simple, lucid and appealing. This was a deliberate editorial choice. The *shudda* grandhika or *gramya* style was consciously avoided and a 'middle path' adopted in order to reach out to the common people.[128] It is also apparent that the linguistic register corresponded with that of the Telugu edition of the Bible. The journal maintained regular interaction with its readers and elicited their feedback.[129] This was a first in Telugu-language women's journalism.

Vivekavathi's policy prioritised women's writings. Men who sent contributions remained on the wait list and were requested to 'excuse' the delayed publication of their pieces.[130] The journal's contributors—women and men—were mostly Christians although many Hindu women and men also published in it. Articles appeared in the journal on the themes of social reform, women's education, child marriage, health, alcoholism, religious matters (particularly those pertaining to Christianity), household management, childcare and a few political issues. It carried regular columns like '*Ayachotla Jarigina Sangatulu*' (News and Notes), '*Dyvabhakti Vishayamulu*' (Religious [Matters]), '*Stree Paraspara Kshemartha Vishayamulu*' (Mutual Welfare [of Women]), '*Griha Vishayamulu*' (Matters Concerning Home Management) and '*Vydya Vishayamulu*' ([Matters Concerning] Medical [Knowledge]). Some pieces like *Hemalata* (a novel) and '*Englanduloni Yarunodayamu*', etc. were serialised. Interestingly, *Vivekavathi* also carried an 'index' (*Vivekavathi Vishaya Suchika*) of back issues at the end of each volume.

Each issue of the journal published an editorial, which dealt in brief with several issues under different heads. Alhough the editorials touched

---

[126]'Balika Vishayamulu' (Children's Stories: translation as in original), October 1913, pp. 15–17.

[127]For example, a complimentary annual subscription of *Vivekavathi* was promised to those who could bring in 12 subscribers. See 'Patrika Sampadakurali Vyasamu' (Editorials), June 1912, p. 258.

[128]'Patrika Sampadakurali Vyasamu' (Editorials), October 1912, pp. 3–4; 'Patrika Sampadakurali Vyasamu' (Editorials), October 1913, p. 3.

[129]The journal asked whether the items it carried were of any use to them in real-life situations, and requested readers' responses. Such feedback, it was felt, would allow for a better understanding of how different readers made use of the journal. 'Patrika Sampadakurali Vyasamu' (Editorials), August 1915, p. 323.

[130]'Patrika Sampadakurali Vyasamu' (Editorials), October 1912, p. 2.

upon a variety of issues, they paid more attention to social reform, particularly women's education and development. An editorial remarked that it was 'sorrowful and shameful' that the wives of even educated men remained uneducated.[131] Some editorials hailed British rule. The 'editorials' of 'the Royal Number' (that is, December 1913) had subtitles like 'Our King', 'Our Queen', 'How Indian Women may be Loyal [to the King/Queen]', 'The Influence of the King's Picture', 'A Teacher's Share in Teaching Loyalty [to the British Crown]'. In the end, the 'editorials' hailed Jesus as 'Our King of Kings'.[132] This clearly demonstrated the *colonising* and *imperial* objectives of *Viveḳavathi*.

The journal accorded supreme importance to women's education. It sought to make its readers 'wise mothers', for an unwise mother's children would eventually get 'spoilt'.[133] One article was titled, 'Uneducated Mothers are Enemies of Their Children'.[134] Some articles advocated the self-agency of women in furthering the cause of women's education[135] and remarked that there was nothing wrong if educated women chose to take up jobs.[136] Some

---

[131] The journal's editorials appreciated educated women, who excelled in various examinations and exhorted other women to follow their example. For example, the June 1912 editorial mentioned Ms Hilda Lazarus, who completed her BA and was studying at the Medical College in Madras, one among 34 female students. The editorial commented that it was 'heartening to learn that women were becoming ready to purse Medicine, which was an important profession.' In addition, it published the news of a Brahmin widow, Subbulakshmamma, being awarded a gold medal for her proficiency in English language. See 'Patrika Sampadakurali Vyasamu' (Editorials), April 1912, pp. 193–195; June 1912, pp. 257–258. The editorial in the September 1913 issue applauded Kanchanapalli Kanakamma, who excelled all in the *Parishad* examination conducted by the Vignana Chandrika Mandali. It suggested women to educate themselves by giving such examinations. Further, it promised that names of women who passed such examinations would be published in *Vivekavathi*. See 'Patrika Sampadakurali Vyasamu' (Editorials), September 1913, pp. 353–356.

[132] 'Patrika Sampadakurali Vyasamu' (Editorials), December 1913, pp. 65–68.

[133] 'Patrika Sampadakurali Vyasamu' (Editorials), April 1912.

[134] Kattirasetty Keshavamma, 'Chaduverugani Streelu Tama Biddalaku Shatruvulu' (Uneducated Women are Enemies of their Children), August 1913, pp. 333–335. She read this essay at the women's organisation in Srikakulum. Interestingly, while advocating women's education, she also argued that there should be a law, which prosecuted the parents, if they did not educate their daughters. See ibid., p. 335.

[135] Damerla Sitamma, 'Stree Vidya Etlunnadi? Daninabhivruddhi Cheyuta Etlu?' (How is the Condition of Women's Education and How to Improve It?), April 1912, pp. 197–200.

[136] Vadrevu Sundaramma, 'Sangha Samskarana Vishayamulu' (Matters Concerning Social Reform), November 1912, pp. 39–40.

articles stressed the need for English education for girls.[137] A few others advised women not to read 'bad books' like the *Tara Shashanka Vijayamu* and *Radhika Santvanamu* (which had erotic content) for they made them 'morally corrupt'.[138] This advocacy of women's education contained an imperialist streak. Since children spent most of their time with mothers and were to be trained to be loyal to the British government, mothers had an important role to play and therefore required special instruction.[139] Women's education could ensure unflinching loyalty of their sons and daughters to the colonial power. This aspect of *Vivekavathi* distinguishes it from other women's journals of the time.

Vivekavathi launched a crusade against the practice of child marriage and enforced widowhood. Writings criticising child marriage normally took the form of dialogue and stories.[140] The journal encouraged post-puberty marriages because child marriage and the consequent early pregnancy risked the health and life of 'child wives' as many of them died during delivery.[141] *Vivekavathi* was an ardent advocate of widow remarriage. Several articles were published in favour of them. 'Oka Andhra Stree' (a pseudonym that literally translates to 'an Andhra Woman') wrote that the widows were subjected to 'untold suffering' and that 'one could write any number of pages' on their 'miserable conditions'; it was better that the widows died committing *sahagamana* (sati) rather than suffer routine ignominy.[142] *Vivekavathi* published a novel—*Hemalata*—advocating widow remarriage. The protagonist of the novel became a child widow because

---

[137]Burra Buchchi Bangaramma, 'Sangha Samskarana Vishayamulu' (Matters Concerning Social Reform), February 1913, pp. 149–150; April 1913, pp. 197–199 and May 1913, pp. 231–234.

[138]'Dushta Grandha Pathanamu' (Reading Bad Books), February 1913, pp. 133–134. See also K. Agnes Daniyelu, 'Chedda Grandhamulu Chaduvutavalani Keedulu' (Evil Effects of Reading Bad Books), February 1913, pp. 141–144.

[139]'Patrika Sampadakurali Vyasamu' (Editorials), December 1913, pp. 65–68.

[140]A dialogue titled 'Balya Vivahamu' (Child Marriage) ridiculed old men who married 'small [young] girls'. It compared the *tali* (sacred thread) with a 'hangman's rope'. Condemning 'greedy parents' who sold off their daughters to men as old as 'grandpas', it cursed that such parents would be 'ruined'. July 1915, pp. 302. Another story brought to light such greed in parents. However, here the child, being educated, resisted being 'sold' off to an 'old grandpa'. See Vadrevu Sundaramma, 'Vrudhdha Bharta, Bala Bharya', (Old Husband and Child Wife), December 1912, pp. 85–87. The purpose of the story was to demonstrate that educated girls/women could change their destiny.

[141]'Patrika Sampadakurali Vyasamu' (Editorials), March 1915, pp. 161–163. Also see 'Patrika Sampadakurali Vyasamu' (Editorials), August 1912, pp. 321–322 and 324.

[142]'Hindu Vitantuvu' (Hindu Widow), January 1914, pp. 108–109.

she was married to an old man. Later, Prabhakar Rao, a reform-minded young man, married her. The novel stressed that *enlightened women* were a *must* to ensure the success of the widow remarriage movement and that Christian missionary women were the ones who brought enlightenment to their Indian sisters.[143]

The editorials took a lot of interest in publishing news items and other matters related to widows.[144] Providing statistical data on widowhood in India, *Vivekavathi* questioned whether it was not 'our duty' to raise the marriageable age of 'our daughters' to 'relieve' them from the 'frightful slavery of widowhood'.[145] The journal published the news of widow remarriages performed in different places[146] and carried brief accounts of widow homes.[147]

Vivekavathi encouraged women's organisations and regularly published brief accounts about them.[148] Speeches of women delivered at the women's

---

[143] *Hemalata* was authored by a certain 'Navavidhani' (a pseudonym that translates to 'modern person'), and was serialised in *Vivekavathi* from November 1911 to June 1913. It dealt with several interwoven themes such as women's education, bride price, missionary work, the deep-rooted prejudice against Christian Missionaries and the way they overcame them and served Hindu women. It tried and succeeded in establishing the benevolence of Christian missionaries: the latter *gave* knowledge to the *ignorant* Indian women and cared for them in their difficult times. The civilising mission of the British and the 'White woman's burden' were clearly established.

[144] The March 1915 issue published data on widows under the head 'some startling facts concerning child widows' and idenitfied child marriages as the chief cause of the problem. 'Were they to undergo sufferings until they breathed their last', asked the writer, rueing the stigma against remarriage, and commented that 'it would be a great injustice, if they had to [suffer].' March 1915, pp. 161–163.

[145] 'Ayachotla Jarigina Sangatulu', July 1913, p. 319.

[146] For example, the November 1909 issue published details of a widow remarriage performed in Kurnool (Rayalaseema) perhaps in October 1909. Interestingly, the news item claimed that it was the 'knowledge of the Christ' (*Kreestu gnanamu*) that made the marriage possible! See 'Nanachotla Jarigedi Vishayamulu', November 1909, p. 34.

[147] 'Ayachotla Jarigina Sangatulu', September 1913, p. 384. See also 'Patrika Sampadakurali Vyasamu' (Editorials), May 1915, p. 227.

[148] For example, the May 1912 issue published an account of the 'Hindu Stree Vidyabhivardhani Samajamu' at Kurnool (Rayalaseema), p. 254. The September 1912 issue furnished a few more details of the same organisation; pp. 353–354. An account of the 'Bharati Samajamu' (Visakhapatnam) was published in the July 1912 issue; pp. 301–302. The July 1912 issue published the news of the third conference of the 'Andhra Mahila Sabha' held at Nidudavolu, Krishna District, where 150 women assembled. 'Ayachotla Jarigina Sangatulu', p. 318.

conferences, too, were given due importance.[149] Women were told that attending meetings of women's organisations was a 'noble deed'.[150] Educated men who were reluctant to send their wives/sisters/daughters to such meetings were criticised and ridiculed.[151]

Vivekavathi aimed to raise Indian health standards, particularly for women. From the colonisers' perspective, Indians were stereotyped as 'unclean' and 'uncivilised', lacking proper knowledge of health and hygiene. They believed in 'silly but dangerous superstitions', consulted country doctors and untrained midwives, spoilt their health and easily succumbed to illness. They did not know who the 'true god' was and therefore wandered in wilderness. It was thus the responsibility of the already 'protected' and 'civilised' Christians to 'save' the foolish Indians.[152] Hence the journal undertook the mission of 'saving' and 'uplifting' them by imparting 'scientific' knowledge about everyday journey in life and especially medical knowledge. 'Scientific' columns like 'Prakruti Pathamulu' (Lessons on Biology) and 'Vydya Vihayamulu' ([Matters Concerning] Medical [Knowledge]) were serialised.[153] *Vivekavathi* launched a serious campaign against alcoholism

---

[149] For example, the July 1911 issue published the speech of Uppuluri Nagaratnamma delivered at the Kakinada Vidyarthini Samajamu. She spoke on 'Aikamatyamu' (Unity [among Women]). See pp. 299–300. S. Adinarayana Rao's speech on 'Raja Bhakti' (Devotion to the King) delivered at the women's meeting in Srikakulam to celebrate the king's coronation was published in the March 1912 issue, pp. 168–169. The May 1912 issue published the speech of Uppuluri Nagaratnamma delivered at the women's meeting in Kakinada on the occasion of the coronation ceremony of the King; it had the title 'Angleya Paripalanamuvalani Labhamulu' (Benefits of British Rule), pp. 234–237.

[150] 'Patrika Sampadakurali Vyasamu' (Editorials), September 1912, p. 354. See also 'Patrika Sampadakurali Vyasamu' (Editorials), August 1912, p. 322.

[151] Ibid., pp. 322–323. See also 'Patrika Sampadakurali Vyasamu' (Editorials), September 1912, p. 354.

[152] H. S. Hensman, 'India Deshasthulaku Avashyakamainavi' (Certain Essential Things Required for Indians), November 1909, pp. 58–61. H. S. Hensman, 'Hindu Desha Streela Sthitini Gurinchi' (About the Condition of Indian Women), December 1909, pp. 83–86.

[153] *Prakruti Pathamulu* featured illustrated guides on human physiology. For example, see the issues of June 1912, pp. 267–269; August 1912, pp. 335–336. *Vydya Vishayamulu* discussed the causes of various diseases and suggested remedies. In addition, it emphasised the necessity of cleanliness, proper nutritious food, proper care for the sick, etc. Commenting on the high magnitude of child/infant deaths, it suggested women should shun all superstition and consult qualified (that is, colonial) doctors.

and smoking because they thoroughly spoilt health and made one morally corrupt and financially ruined.[154]

As discussed earlier, the journal also aimed to preach Christianity and making Indians loyal to the British Crown. The column '*Dyvabhakti Vishayamulu*' (Religious Matters) was geared towards the former, as were articles, stories, dialogues, etc., that emphasised the superiority of the Christian faith and projected Jesus as the only 'true god'. Criticising practices like idolatry, these writings by turns persuaded and intimidated people towards Christianity. They were generally written in a dialogic form.[155] In a dialogue between a Christian and a Hindu, the latter was pushed into accepting that 'the entire Hindu religious system was false' (*Hindu mata siddhantamulanniyu bootakamulu*) and that the Hindus could not attain *moksha*. When their *Trimurthi*s—Brahma, Vishnu and Maheshwara—themselves could not attain moksha, how could they ensure that for their followers? Finally, the Christian intimidates the Hindu to speed up to take the 'protection' of Jesus, the 'true saviour' saying that '*Aalasyam Amritam Visham*', i.e., delay turns nectar into poison. And, without delaying, the Hindu gets 'protected'![156]

Several editorials, articles and verses eulogised British rule and showered praises on Queen Victoria.[157] S. Adinarayana Rao remarked that the British

---

[154] See 'Madyapaana Visarjana' (Quitting Alcohol), November 1909, pp. 38–40. See also 'Durvaadukalu' (Bad Habits), February 1920, pp. 110–112; 'Madyapaana Nishedhamau' (Banning Alcohol), December 1915, pp. 84–85; D. Daaveedu [David], 'Madyapaana Mahatmyamu' (The Evil Effects of Alcoholism), July 1912, p. 313; 'Cigaretlu' (Cigarettes), December 1915, p. 85.

[155] See Lusie Ammal, 'Nijamyna Devudevaru?' (Who is The Real God?; translation as in original), November 1915, pp. 213–214. For an example of dialogic writing, see Adapaka Polaiah, 'Christmas Dinamuna Christavalayamulo Hindu Christava Vidyarthulakugaligina Sambhashana' (A Christmas Dialogue [between a Christian and a Hindu Student]: translation as in original), December 1913, pp. 88–92.

[156] M. Augustine Narasimhulaiah, 'Dyvabhakti Vishayamulu: Kreestu Swamy Punaruththanamu' (Religious Matters: The Resurrection of Jesus Christ), April 1920, pp. 161–164.

[157] The editorial of December 1913 suggested how Indian women might express loyalty to the British Crown and teach the same to their children. It advised them to hang pictures of the King and Queen and the British flag in their homes and discuss them daily with the children. Similarly, teachers were reminded of the 'great task' of inculcating love and loyalty among students. They were expected to teach 'true love for the country' and warned against 'throwing bombs on the British officials and killing them [*sic*]'. It also said that 'our King was not only a benevolent ruler but also a good husband and father,' and that he possessed 'unstained character'. 'Patrika Sampadakurali

had rendered an 'enormous service' especially to women.[158] For Uppuluri Nagaratnamma, British rule was 'more benevolent and beneficent' than the rule of 'divine incarnations' like Rama, Sri Krishna and Yudhistara (the eldest of the Pandavas of the epic *Mahabharata*). Never before had Indians experienced and enjoyed such a 'just rule'.[159] Madiraju Janaki Ramaiah held that 'the God on the earth was none else but the British government itself, which saved [Indian/Hindu] women by abolishing the practice of sati.'[160] For Tallapudi Venkataswami Naidu, British rule meant liberation; its Indian subjects felt as happy as convicts who had just been 'released from the prison'.[161] Several verses in the journal praised colonial rule.[162]

Vivekavathi was not the only journal to praise colonial rule; in fact, other early women's journals also took a similar stance, for example *Hindu Sundary*. An enthralled Veeresalingam was all praise of colonial rule. In his opinion, it was 'God's grace' that Indians got the British government, which was 'heaven' compared to pre-colonial India, a kind of 'hell'.[163] Writer-intellectual Mosalikanti Ramabayamma, the first woman editor of *Hindu Sundary*, was so deeply impressed by British rule that in her opinion, had the British not banned practices like sati, not a single woman would still be alive in India. For her, the British government was 'exalted' (*Maha Ghanata vahinchina British Prabhutvamu*) and 'virtue personified' (*Sarva Dharma Swaroopulagu... Doratanamu vaaru*).[164] How, then, was *Vivekavathi* different? Unlike other publications, it explicitly articulated a position against burgeoning nationalism, advancing the credo that the sun

---

Vyasamu' (Editorials), December 1913, pp. 65–68. The December 1912 issue published a 'National Anthem', part of which read: 'God save our gracious King/ Long live our noble King/ ... Long may he reign/ ...', p. 69.

158 'Raja Bhakti' (Devotion to the King/Queen), March 1912, pp. 168–170.

159 'Angleya Paripalanamuvalani Labhamulu' (Benefits of British Rule), May 1912, pp. 234–237.

160 'Angleya Paripalana Labhamulu' (Benefits of British Rule), December 1913, pp. 69–71.

161 'Britishuvari Paripalana Melulu' (Benefits of British Rule), December 1915, pp. 68–69.

162 A. Tavitanna, 'Pattabhisheka Padyamulu' (Verses on Coronation), January 1912, p. 104; Balakavi Malladi Venkata Vishweshwara Sharma, 'Navaratnamulu: Angleya Prabhutva Prashamsa' (Nine Jewels: In Praise of the British Government), ibid., pp. 119–120; Benguluri Nagaratnamu, 'Darbaru Padyamulu' (Verses on Durbar), March 1912, pp. 170–171.

163 Akkiraju Ramapati Rao ed., *Veeresalingam Rachanalu*, pp. 105–115.

164 'Vitantu Shiromundanamunu goorchina Mahazaru', *Hindu Sundary*, July 1904, p. 152.

must never set on the British Empire, and that colonial rule must continue in India without any interruptions. It was only because of British rule that 'justice' prevailed in India. It expressed dismay that Indian 'nationalism is [suddenly] emerging' despite this positive atmosphere. While *Vivekavathi* admitted that nationalism in itself was not a bad idea, it argued that a few Indians were 'trying to grab' power from the British. *Vivekavathi* warned that it does not at all 'accept forcible capture' of power from the British.[165] Perhaps the journal wanted its readers to think that the British did not employ any 'force' and had not themselves 'captured' power: they had simply persuaded erstwhile kings and queens to surrender rule!

Other columns that *Vivekavathi* published included 'Uttara Pratyuttaramula Shakha' (Question and Answer Wing),[166] 'Balika Vishayamulu' ([Girl] Children's Stories)[167] and 'Stree Paraspara Kshemartha Vishayamulu' (Mutual Welfare)[168]. Overall, *Vivekavathi* represented the 'maternal imperialism'[169] of Christian missionary women.

Anasuya (1917-1924)

Edited by Vinjamuri Venkata Ratnamma,[170] *Anasuya*, a monthly journal, began publication from Cocanada (Kakinada) in July 1917, and continued

[165] Vol. I, No. 1, October 1909, p. 4.

[166] March 1912, p. 161; May 1912, p. 244 and July 1912, p. 309.

[167] The 'Balika Vishayamulu' published free verse in an easy and attractive style and encouraged girls to get educated, maintain cleanliness, adopt good conduct and manners, etc. It also featured short stories. For example, see November 1912, p. 49; December 1912, pp. 82–83; February 1912, pp. 146–147; September 1913, pp. 368–370.

[168] The column 'Mutual Welfare' was related to women: it informed them about how to keep the home clean, take care of children, the need for their being educated, etc. See June 1912, pp. 260–265; April 1913, pp. 213–215.

[169] I have borrowed the concept from Barbara N. Ramusack, 'Cultural Missionaries, Maternal Imperialists, Feminist Allies: British Women Activists in India, 1865–1945', in Nupur Chaudhuri and Margaret Noble, ed., *Western Women and Imperialism: Complicity and Resistance* (Bloomington and Indianapolis, 1992), pp. 119–136. For works of similar nature, see Antoinette M. Burton, 'The White Woman's Burden: British Feminists and "The Indian Woman," 1865–1915' in ibid., pp. 137–157.

[170] Vinjamuri Ratnamma (1889–1950) was born in 1889 in Pithapuram. She was the daughter of Devulapalli Tammanna Shastri, the Court Poet at the Pithapuram Princely State, and the sister of Devulapalli Krishna Shastri, the most famous modern romantic poet in Telugu. Born into a learned and reform-oriented family, she became a prolific writer and widely published in journals. She played a prominent role in the various

probably until the end of 1924.[171] The publisher was Vinjamuri Ratnamma's husband, Vinjamuri Venkata Lakshmi Narasimham. The cover page depicted a woman standing in a beautiful garden, holding what looked like flowers in one hand, with the auspicious 'Om' inscribed on the top of the picture. A poem at the bottom read: 'Jewel-like sisters! May you gain reputation as Anasuyas by learning the histories of the *Saadhvi* mothers, become wise and inculcate virtues with education.'[172]

Each issue of *Anasuya* had about 45 pages—remarkable compared to other women's journals, particularly those that appeared before 1920. The annual subscription rate, inclusive of postage, was Rs. 1.50 and a single copy was available at 3 annas. There is scarcely any information regarding the number of subscribers and extent of circulation. It was popular in the towns of coastal Andhra, including Kakinada, Vijayanagaram, Rajahmundry, Peddapuram, Guntur, Angalur and Nellore. The journal was not published regularly: this is evident from a few combined issues available for the journal, for example for September–October 1919, and November–December in the same year.

The editor stated in the very first issue that 'she would get experienced female writers to contribute to the journal', and that '*Anasuya* would publish articles on issues such as domestic management, histories of *Puranic* women, biographical sketches of modern accomplished women,' etc.[173] Though women's writings were preferred,[174] men's writings were also published.[175] Articles, verses and novelettes appeared on issues such as conditions of women, their education, child marriage, conjugal fidelity, the need for women teachers, unity among women, women's independence and health and hygiene.

The journal paid great attention to the promotion of women's education. Dispelling misconceptions arising from anti-reform rhetoric, Gopisetty

---

women's organisations. For details, see Utukuri Lakshmikantamma, *Andhra Kavayitrulu*, pp. 137–139.

[171] Unless otherwise especially mentioned, all references in this section are from *Anasuya*.

[172] For example, see the cover page of the September 1918 issue.

[173] Potturi Venkateswara Rao, *Andhra Jaati Akshara Sampada*, p. 229.

[174] Kanuparti Varalakshmamma, Chintapenta Venkata Narasamamba, Gudupudi Indumatidevi, Atkuri Venkata Ramanamamba, Gopisetty Suryanarayanamma, N. K. Meenakshi Sundaramma, Chedalapaka Varalakshmidevi, etc. were a few among the women contributors. Vinjamuri Ratnamma, the editor, contributed a few pieces.

[175] Male authors included Venkata Parvatishwara Kavulu, Vanguri Subba Rao and T. Venkaji.

Suryanarayanamma argued that education of women 'ensured the progress of the country'. Educated women performed 'domestic duties' skilfully, educated their children and contributed to the development of the country. She emphasised that pativratyam and other 'virtues' in women would be inculcated through a 'good education'. She suggested that women be taught in their mother tongue.[176] Vinjamuri Ratnamma, the editor, emphasised that it would be an 'enormous help to female education,' if women became teachers. According to her, only women should teach in girls' schools because 'women understood the feelings, tastes and expectations of women better than men.' She gave examples of other countries like England and America, where women teachers predominated, and called upon 'Hindu women' to come forward to take up the profession.[177]

Anasuya was a bitter critic of the practices of child marriage and dowry. Bramhandam Kanakasundaramma contributed a verse to the journal stating that 'it was better to tie a boulder to the neck [of a girl] and throw her into a well than force her into child marriage'. The verse went on to state, 'it was better to hang a boy than get him married for the greed of dowry; it was better to slit the throat of a girl than marry her off without her consent; it was better to poison a five-year-old girl than marry her off to a man of sixty years'. It emphasised that marriages performed with 'mutual consent brought greater happiness.'[178]

Gudipudi Indumati Devi, in an article titled 'Are Women Inferior to Men?', questioned the patriarchal ideology that rendered women physically weak and intellectually inferior. She held men responsible for women's vulnerability and advocated 'women's freedom', which helped them realise their full potential. However, in an apparent contradiction, she also saw women as 'soft natured' and 'physically as delicate as flowers'! [179]

Anasuya published the novel '*Premalata—Sweeya Charitramu*' (*Autobiography of Premalata*). This fictitious autobiography shed light on the patriarchal power relations in the family, with a special focus on the barbarous treatment meted out to young wives at their marital home, particularly at the hands of cruel mothers-in-law. The 'autobiography' described domestic drudgery that fatigued child wives and their anxieties

---

[176]'Stree Vidya' (Women's Education), November–December 1919, pp. 17–19.

[177]'Streelupadhyayinuluga Undutavalani Labhamulu' (Advantages of Having Female Teachers), September–October 1919, pp. 2–8.

[178]'Abala Vilapamu' (Lamentation of Women), September–October 1919, pp. 43–44.

[179]'Streelu Purushulakante Dakkuva?' (Are Women Inferior to Men?), September 1918, pp. 41–44.

and sufferings in the joint family system. Authored by famous writer Kanuparti Varalakshmamma, it reflected on the routine forms of violence perpetrated on girl-wives in the domestic sphere and mounted a scathing attack on the figure of the merciless mother-in-law.[180]

A unique feature of *Anasuya* was its *Anasuya Bahumati Pariksha*, or examination, for which women were awarded certificates and medals. The syllabus included history, natural science, the Puranas, etc. The examination was conducted at several centres including Kakinada, Brahmapur (in present-day Odisha), Dhavaleshwaram (near Rajahmundry), Peddapuram, Guntur, Vijayanagaram and Angalur. 'Highly educated people' set the question papers and evaluated the answer scripts. The examination was held in high esteem. The fact that some of the examinees were from such far-flung places as Nellore speaks for its popularity. The examinees' best essays were subsequently published in *Anasuya*. Names of the qualified candidates were forwarded to the British government for admission to teacher-training colleges.[181] Women were enthusiastic about taking up the examination, for those who cleared it commanded enormous respect in society.

The editor encouraged women to contribute their writings to the contemporary journals without hesitation. Addressing those who had certain inhibitions regarding the publication of their names in the journals, she persuasively said that 'there was no harm' in it. Asking them whether they did not 'put their signatures' (write their names) in the letters they wrote to their brothers, she tried to convince that 'it [writing for journals] was just like that.'[182] Like other journals, *Anasuya* published the accounts and reports of women's organisations.[183] Under the column, '*Muchchatalu*' (Tidings), news items related to women were published.

The journal had a very brief career but its impact was significant. Although the name *Anasuya* invokes the memory of the ancient pativrata Sati Anasuya, the journal reflected the emerging progressive perspective among Telugu women.

---

[180] Kanuparti Varalakshmamma, 'Premalata—Sweeya Charitramu', July–August, pp. 13–29 and September–October 1919, pp. 9–30.

[181] One such examination was conducted on 12 July 1919. 'Anasuya Bahumati Pariksha', November–December 1919, pp. 81–83.

[182] Vinjamuri Venkata Ratnamma, 'Vaarta Patrikalu, Vaanivalana Labhamulu' (Advantages of Journals and News Papers), January 1920, p. 9.

[183] See 'Shri Sharada Samajamu—Aidava Varshika Nivedika' (Fifth Annual Report of the Shri Sharada Samajamu), May 1924, p. 42. The 'Sharada Samajamu' was a women's organisation established at Anantapur (Rayalaseema).

Andhra Lakshmi (1921-1924)

The *Andhra Lakshmi*, another monthly journal, began publication in December 1921 and likely continued till the end of 1924.[184] Edited by Kallepalle Venkata Ramanamma[185] (1864–1935; hereafter Venkata Ramanamma) and published by Kallepalle Shivaramaiah, it was published from Barampuram, Ganjam District (in present-day Odisha), the northernmost Telugu-speaking district of the erstwhile Madras Presidency.

Venkata Ramanamma delineated the journal's objectives in its first issue. Since women's journals like the *Telugu Zenana*, *Hindu Sundary* and *Anasuya* had by then ceased publication, she thought of 'filling the gap by publishing a journal, which would be useful to women.'[186] While journals like *Savithri*, *Anasuya*, *Hindu Sundary*, and *Hindu Yuvati* stressed religious identity, *Andhra Lakshmi* emphasised a regional as well as religious identity.

Each issue of *Andhra Lakshmi* had around 50 pages. The annual subscription rate, inclusive of postage, was Rs. 2; price of a single copy was 4 annas.[187] It appears that the number of subscribers was small, and earnings from subscriptions did not meet expenditure. A story in 1922 highlighted the financial difficulties of the journal.[188]

The cover page featured Lakshmi, the Hindu goddess of wealth, with coins rolling forth from her right hand; a verse in *shardula* metre below the masthead stated the objectives of the journal. The editor said that *Andhra Lakshmi* 'was a monthly published for the benefit of women. It would

---

[184] Unless otherwise especially mentioned, all references in this section are from *Andhra Lakshmi*.

[185] An activist-intellectual who played a prominent role in the contemporary women's movement, she served as the president of the Shri Vidyarthini Samajamu, Kakinada, for 1911–1916. She took a leading role in convening the Andhra Mahila Mahasabhas, the state level women's conferences. She was instrumental in reviving the *Hindu Sundary* and edited the same for some time. A prolific writer, she published widely on women's issues in the contemporary journals.

[186] Potturi Venkateswara Rao, *Andhra Jaati Akshara Sampada*, pp. 262–263.

[187] Patrons and '*Sahayulu*' (Helpers) paid Rs. 10 and Rs. 5, respectively. *Andhra Lakshmi* had a few chief patrons. Vadrevu Padmanabhamma, the Maharani of Tuni, and Varada Kameshwara Naidu, etc. were a few among them. It had about 30 patrons. Choragudi Kailasamma, Duggirala Ramanamma, Kommuri Lakshminarasamma, Gade Choodikudutamma, Gajavilli Subhadramma, Digumarti Rajyalakshmamma, Kondapalli Venkata Ramanamma, Unnava Mahalakshmamma and Perla Annapoornamma were a few among the women patrons.

[188] 'Kamala Vimala Samvadamu' (Dialogue between Kamala and Vimala), October 1922.

publish the histories of ancient *Sadhvimanis* and accounts of educated and accomplished modern women; novelettes, short stories, playlets, songs, verses and all those things useful to women.'[189]

Andhra Lakshmi is remarkable for being the publisher of Kanuparti Varalakshmamma's famous *Sharada Lekhalu* (*Letters of Sharada*), although the letters had initially begun serialisation in *Anasuya*.[190] A prominent intellectual and an organiser for the women's movement in the Andhra region, Varalakshmamma discussed several women's issues, the national movement and social reform, offering incisive social commentary. One of the letters urged women to subscribe to *Andhra Lakshmi*. Commenting on women's indifference towards journals aimed at them, it sarcastically remarked that 'our urban women were more interested in theatre than journals; they had a taste for *pakodis*, not journals. They could subscribe [to *Andhra Lakshmi*] for one year, if they avoided spending on sweetmeats.'[191] Other women contributors included Gudupudi Indumatidevi[192] and Vadrevu Padmanabhamma (Pithapuram).[193] A historical novel, *Rukmini*,

[189] Ibid.

[190] Written using the pseudonym 'Sharada', the letters are addressed to a fictitious female friend, Kalpalatha. Written over the 1920s and 1930s, the *Sharada Lekhalu* was a significant literary text. K. N. Kesari, the founder of *Grihalakshmi*, got them published at his Lodhra Press in 1934. Varalakshmamma remained an important public figure after independence; she was the first woman writer from Andhra Pradesh to receive the Andhra Pradesh Sahitya Academy Award. For more details, see Dasari Sharada, 'Jeevana Rekhalu' in *Srimati Kanuparti Varalakshmamma Shatajayanti Sanchika* (Hyderabad, 1996). See also Polapragada Rajyalakshmi, *Kanuparti Varalakshmamma* (New Delhi, 2000).

[191] Potturi Venkateswara Rao, *Andhra Jaati Akshara Sampada*, p. 263.

[192] 'Molla Kulataya?' (Is the Poetess Molla a Fallen Woman?), October 1922, pp. 22–24. Indumati Devi condemned the bizarre allegation that Molla was a '*jaarini*' (fallen woman) because Molla's *Ramayana* contained certain stanzas depicting *sringara* (romance/erotica). She defended Molla, calling her a '*maanavati*' (respectable woman), not a '*kulata*'. This argument, while important, would be problematic by today's standards, since it reinforces a binary between women who are deemed respectable, and those who deviate from social norms and are therefore disreputable. Atukuri Molla, who belonged to potter caste, was a medieval female poet who authored the *Ramayana* in Telugu. The work is famous as *Molla Ramayanamu*. For a few details on Molla, see Susie Tharu and K. Lalita, ed., *Women Writing in India: 600 B.C. to the Early 20th Century*, vol. 1 (London, 1991), pp. 94–98. See also Andra Sheshagiri Rao, *Andhra Vidusheemanulu* (*Women Scholars of Andhra*) (Visakhapatnam, 1995), pp. 98–154

[193] 'Streelakalankarameddi?' (Which is the [True] Ornament of Women?), October 1922, pp. 13–15. The author stressed that jewellery did not really enhance the beauty of women. What really embellished them were the virtues of education, humility and

authored by Akundi Venkata Shastri, was serialised in the *Andhra Lakshmi*.[194] Under the column '*Vividha Vishayamulu*' ('Various Matters'), it published several general matters of interest. It published advertisements of *Ayurvedic* medicines[195] and books.[196]

Grihalakshmi (1928-1961)

Edited by K. N. Kesari,[197] *Grihalakshmi* began publication as a monthly journal from Madras on 1 March 1928, and continued beyond 1960, with a break between 1942 and 1947.[198] As the title suggests, it was meant for the 'goddess of the home', or the housewife. The journal ran for about 30 years.[199]

---

devotion to husband, the last being the 'most important decoration'. She held it to be 'wrong to trouble husband for jewellery' and exhorted women to cultivate the 'beauty of heart and mind' rather than physical beauty.

[194] Interestingly, the novelist dedicated the novel to women who wanted to fashion themselves on the pattern of the great *saadhvis* such as Sita, Savithri, Damayanti, etc. and *veera vanitas* (valorous women) such as Rani Samyukta and Durgavati. These were ideal women, ever memorable to the 'Hindu race' and the 'Indian Aryan religion'.

[195] Ayurvedic pharmaceutical companies such as Messers Ratnam Brothers (Maruteru, Krishna District), T. N. Murthy and Co. (Barampuram, Ganjam District) and Messers B. S. Rao and Brothers (Barampuram, Ganjam District) advertised their products. The Ayurvedic products included 'Amruta Manjari', 'Ashantakavati', 'Rutushulahari', 'Amrutoushadhi', 'Taamara Naashani' and 'Parimalananda Pogaku Masala'. Most advertisements were for products that claimed to resolve women's health problems such as menstrual disturbances. For example, see October 1922 issue, pp. 45–47.

[196] Books such as *Kamala*, *Sri Varalakshmi Shatakamu*, *Sri Mahalakshmi Puja Paatalu*, *Ekanta Seva Keertanalu* and *Kanchanamala* were advertised. For example, see October 1922 issue, pp. 48–49.

[197] Kota Narasimham, popularly known as Dr K. N. Kesari (1875–1953), did various jobs in Madras before becoming an extremely successful Ayurveda practitioner, with his own dispensary and line of medicines. He was a philanthropist who donated to various women's organisations, 'Women's Homes' and schools, and helped girls and women who were pursuing an education. He founded the 'Kesari Vidyalayam' to promote women's education. His autobiography, *Naa Chinnanati Muchchatlu*, published in 1953, reflects on various contemporary issues in some detail. For a brief biographical sketch of Kesari, see Tekumalla Kameshwara Rao, *Naa Vaangmaya Mitrulu*, pp. 112–114. At a later stage, Chivula Chenchu Punnaiah (C. C. Punnaiah) edited *Grihalakshmi*.

[198] 'Grihalakshmi Tapalu Pette', January 1950, p. 5. Unless otherwise especially mentioned, all references in this section are from *Grihalakshmi*.

[199] In this regard, *Grihalakshmi* stands next only to *Hindu Sundary*, which enjoyed the longest career of publication among all the colonial women's journals in Telugu.

Each issue had around 64–70 pages, which enabled *Grihalakshmi* to cover a wide variety of topics. In the year 1940, it had 2,000 subscribers. The annual subscription rate, inclusive of postage, was Rs. 3; half yearly was Rs. 1.80, and a single copy was sold at 0.40 annas. For Burma, the rates were different.[200] By 1950, the annual subscription rate was increased to Rs. 4.80, the half-yearly rate to Rs. 2.80, and a single copy priced at 6 annas.[201] The journal had its agents in a large number of big and small towns in Andhra. With agents even in small towns like Kambham, Giddaluru, Markapur, and Proddatur, and reaching as far as Rangoon (Burma), the journal clearly had an extensive network of circulation. *Grihalakshmi* aimed at the 'over-all well-being of women': It regularly informed them about their rights and duties, emphasised the need for 'development' and attempted to mobilise them for social and political activity. While it invited contributions from both women and men, the number of women writers was clearly much higher, and as the editor once clarified, the journal was primarily meant for women.[202] Instructions to writers clearly stated that they 'should aim at the amelioration of women' and the language could be either spoken (*vyavaharika*) or bookish (grandhika), but not a mixture of both.[203]

Many prominent women of the period contributed to *Grihalakshmi*. The journal's range of themes included women's education, freedom, and independence; patriarchy and discrimination; child marriage, enforced widowhood, and divorce; conflicts and tensions among women in the family, the man-woman relationship, and domestic labour; women's civil and political rights and women's participation in social and political movements, especially the national movement. The editorials in *Grihalakshmi* discussed not only the issues concerning women but also national and international political issues. By May 1933, the journal had an eight member advisory committee (*Grihalakshmi Salaha Sanghamu*), of whom five were women. All the members were well known and committed to the development of women.[204]

---

[200] May 1940.

[201] January 1950.

[202] 'Grihalakshmi Tapalu Pette', January 1950, p. 7.

[203] May 1940.

[204] May 1933, pp. 263–264. Its women members included: Kanuparti Varalakshmamma (reputable intellectual-activist whose commitment to the cause of women was 'unparallelled', from Bapatla, Guntur District), Vinjamoori Venkata Ratnamma (editor of the women's monthly, *Anasuya*; from Kakinada), Chilakapati Sitamba (noted literary figure from Adorupalli, Nellore District), Telikicharla Vasundhra Devi (a

Image 2.6: Cover page of *Grihalakshmi*

Source: *Grihalakshmi*, March 1940.

The issue of women's education was a favourite of *Grihalakshmi*'s editors. By the time the journal came into existence, women's education had acquired wider acceptance. The focus of the debate now shifted to the

BSc from London; also an MA., LT, and lecturer at Queen Mary College, Madras), Gampa Shivakantamma (member of Municipality, Barampuram, Ganjam District; founder-member of the Barampuram Women's Organisation). Men also participated, including Rayasam Venkata Sivudu, Ongolu Venkata Rangaiah and V. Venkata Subbaiah. K. N. Kesari was hopeful that 'with their suggestions and help, the journal would prosper acquiring more beauty and receiving wider appreciation.'

'kind of education' women needed to receive. In *Grihalakshmi*, we find both 'traditional' and 'modern' voices. The traditional voices remarked that since women's 'main sphere of activity' was the home, a 'separate curriculum' suitable to the nature of their work was necessary. This would comprise cooking, housekeeping, stitching, music, childcare, primary health, etc. They emphasised the 'natural differences' between women and men: while the man was a bread-winner, the woman was a bread maker; the former needed to go out while the latter was to remain at home. Thus, they emphasised a patriarchal, sexual division of labour.[205] The editor K. N. Kesari also held similar views, though he wanted women to enter the 'public space'. However, a number of radical voices resisted this view. According to them, education should not be designed along the lines of gender differentiation; the learner should be able to choose the kind of education she wishes to pursue.[206]

Grihalakshmi launched a crusade against the practice of child marriage and strongly advocated widow remarriage. We find a large number of articles on these issues. Writings on child marriage unanimously demanded total eradication of the 'evil practice'. They vividly described various adverse effects it had on girls/women.[207] Various writers eagerly welcomed the Child Marriage Restraint Act, popularly known as the Sarda Act. However, Deshiraju Bharati Devi identified loopholes in the Sarda Act and, along with other women, demanded amendments to prevent their misuse.[208] *Grihalakshmi* published a large number of articles advocating post-puberty marriages and insisted on the 'consent of girls' in marriage.[209] Marking a shift from earlier discourses, several writings in *Grihalakshmi* eschewed any dependence on the Dharmashastras for their arguments against child

[205] N. Rajyalakshmamma, 'Steelaketti Vidya Avasaramu?' (What Kind of Education Do Women Need?), August 1930, pp. 430–431; Vedula Minakshi, 'Streejanochitamagu Vidya' (Education that Suits Women), January 1939, pp. 793–796; Kodali Sitaramadevi, 'Griha Kritya Vignanamu' (Scientific Knowledge of Household Management), November 1929, pp. 746–747; Muppalaneni Pushkaramba, 'Stree Vidya–Daani Aavashyakata' (The Need for Women's Education), July 1932, pp. 356–357.

[206] Nandagiri Indiradevi, 'Vanitaloka Samskaranamu' (Reforming the World of Women), 1938, p. 908.

[207] Maddali Sitaramamma, 'Baalya Vivahamulu' (Child Marriages), November 1929, pp. 695–697; Atluri Venkata Sitamma, 'Baalya Vivaha Nishedhamu' (Abolition of Child Marriages), October 1929, pp. 641–644.

[208] Deshiraju Bharati Devi, 'Abhivrudhdhi Kavalenanna' (If At All We Want to Make Any Progress), October 1941, pp. 433–434.

[209] D. Anasuyamma, 'Patananiki Karanamu Veru' (The Reason for the Degeneration [of Women] is Different), March 1938, pp. 31–32.

marriage. They asserted that even if they approved of such marriages, such practices should not be allowed considering women's well-being, particularly their health and educational opportunities. The Dharmashastras were to be discarded if they supported such marriages.[210]

Grihalakshmi treated the widow question very seriously. Like elsewhere, writings on widows held child marriage primarily responsible for the high incidence of widowhood. Expressing alarm at the outrageous tonsuring of widows and condemning multiple atrocities inflicted on them, article after article caustically attacked opponents of widow remarriage. Contirbutors questioned the 'double standards' maintained in Indian society that allowed a man to remarry 'the very next day' after his wife passed away, but banned the remarriage of a widow and uneqvivocally supported widow remarriage.[211]

Grihalakshmi paid serious attention to the problem of dowry. Analysing its 'evil effects', writings on dowry remarked that 'it adversely affected the educational opportunities of women'.[212] These ridiculed boys who studied not to gain knowledge, but to extract maximum dowry. Writers for the journal agreed that a sustained campaign was needed to sensitise people, particularly mothers of bridegrooms, on this issue.[213] *Grihalakshmi* also undertook a rigorous campaign in favour of women's civil and political rights. It regularly published articles about various measures undertaken by the government for women. These articles analysed various proposed bills, new legislation, and their possible effects on women. Interestingly, *Grihalakshmi* conducted debates among women on various issues, for instance whether women required a right to divorce.[214] Such outreach facilitated democratic discussion and a diversity of opinions. To encourage women in their pursuit of knowledge, *Grihalakshmi* instituted an annual award, the highly esteemed

[210]Maddali Sitaramamma, 'Baalya Vivahamulu' (Child Marriages), November 1929, pp. 695–697.

[211]Kuditipudi Atchamamba, 'Vydhavyamu–Dharmashastralu' (Widowhood and the Dharmashastras), February 1939, pp. 820–822.

[212]Kongara Annapoornamma, 'Varashulkamu' (Dowry), December 1929, pp. 805–807; K. Sarojini Devi, 'Katnalu Techchina Kotta Anarthamu' (The New Evil Effects brought by Dowry), December 1940, pp. 623–624; Pulipaka Baalaa Tripura Sundaramma, 'Yem Cheyyadam…?' (What to Do…?), June 1940, pp. 221–224.

[213]Ibid.

[214]Under the head, 'Vidakula Chattamu' (Divorce Act) *Grihalakshmi* published the opinions of 40 women in the year 1930, bringing to light the multiple perspectives of women on this issue. See March, pp. 41–47; April, pp. 130–131; May, pp. 172–173; July, pp. 362–366; August, pp. 426–429; September, pp. 519–527.

'Grihalakshmi Swarnakankanam' (Grihalakshmi Golden Bracelet), which honoured a woman scholar with the *swarnakankanam* as a mark of her scholarship.[215] The Award exists even today.

Image 2.7: Kanuparti Varalakshmamma honoured with the Grihalakshmi Swarnakankanam

Source: *Grihalakshmi*, April 1934.

Grihalakshmi additionally focused on writings about women's health, for which they elicited contributions from both women and men. Problems related to menstruation and pregnancy were discussed in detail, and women were given advice on the latter.[216] These articles advocated 'special medical

[215]Kanuparti Varalakshmamma (1934), Kanchanapalli Kanakamba (1936), Pulavarti Kamalavati Devi (1937), Balantrapu Sheshamma (1939) and Ratnala Kamala Bai (1939) were a few among the recipients of the award.

[216]Vavikolanu Padmasanamma, 'Garbhini Stree Poshana' (Taking Care of Pregnant Women), August 1929, pp. 404–405; Aluru Ramachandraiah, 'Garbhavatula Niyamamulu' (Certain Essential Things to be Observed by Pregnant Women), October 1930, pp. 669–671; 'Garbhadharana Chihnamulu', September 1930, pp. 541–542; and Satyamvada, 'Garbhini Streela Jagratta' (Precautions to be Taken by Pregnant Women), January 1941, pp. 699–670.

facilities' for women and children. Information on various medicines available in the market was disseminated through advertisements.[217] 'Cleanliness' was emphasised for maintaining good health. Women were asked to 'bathe regularly, keep the surroundings clean, drink boiled water, and sleep in properly ventilated places'.[218] Articles emphasising the need for 'physical exercises to ensure good health and avoid early ageing' also appeared.[219] Articles on the 'scientific methods' of childcare were prominently featured.[220]

Grihalakshmi carried a variety of columns. The column 'Soundarya Poshana' (On Beautification) offered beauty tips, as the name suggests, and included advertisements for cosmetics.[221] Many women enthusiastically contributed to the column on 'Paka Kala' (The Art of Cooking), sharing their expertise on a wide variety of cuisines, albeit all-vegetarian fare (reflecting the upper-caste slant of many such periodicals). This column indirectly stressed that it was the 'duty' of women to master the 'art of cooking'.

Under the column 'Mahila Sabhalu' (Women's Conferences), *Grihalakshmi* published about a large number of regional and national women's organisations, and extensively covered activities undertaken by them.[222] It also carried photographs of a number of women scholars and activists as well as from women's conferences. Under the column 'Pushpachchayamu' (literally 'Bunch of Flowers', a column for miscellaneous writings), the journal published excerpts from contemporary magazines, particularly the opinions of famous personalities on different issues, including important national and international issues, India's freedom

---

[217] Advertisements for '*Lodhra*', a tonic for 'menstrual problems' appeared regularly. The tonic was prepared at 'Kesari Kutiramu', an establishment of Dr Kesari, the founder of the journal and thus promoted his commercial ventures.

[218] Mogasati Appala Narasamma, 'Parishubhrata' (Cleanliness), July 1930, p. 355.

[219] B. Rajamma, 'Streelu—Vyayama Viharasthalamulu' (The Need for Physical Exercise and Picnic Spots for Women), September 1935, pp. 532–533; Kamalakshamma, 'Vidyarthinulu–Vyayamamulu', November 1930, pp. 741–742.

[220] Guttavarapu Lakshmi Narasaiah, 'Shishu Samrakshana ' (Protection of Children), April 1934, pp. 140–144; Burra Venkata Nancharaiah, 'Shishu Shikshanamu' (Training of Children), September 1935, pp. 582–584, and March 1946, pp. 1022–1024.

[221] For instance, advertisements for Lux soap, detergents, jewellery, Pond's cream, hair oil, hotels, and diamonds. As women's health received greater attention, medicines aimed at women were extensively advertised, including 'Lodhra Tonic' for menstrual issues, 'Dongre Balamrutamu' for fertility, and 'Radzo' for pregnant women.

[222] For example, see 'Andhra Mahila Sabhalu', November 1933, pp. 753–755; 'Mahila Sabhalu', December 1933, pp. 830–838; 'Sabhalu-Prathama Kamma Mahila Sabha', June 1934, pp. 303–308.

movement, women's health, sociopolitical problems, etc. Articles on women from other countries like USA, France, Russia, Tibet, China and Poland focused on their advancement and the rights they enjoyed.[223] Translations of articles by prominent public figures like Gandhi and Vivekananda, scholars like A. S. Altekar, and short stories by Premchand were published.[224] Several pieces from *Chand*—a women's journal in Hindi[225]—too were published in translation. There was a children's column, 'Bala Vignana Shakha', which published small stories and poems. Other columns included 'Patrika Parichayamu' to introduce readers to various newspapers and magazines, 'Alochana' (Thoughts), and 'Kathalu–Kaburlu' (Stories and Gossip).

There was some tension between the editor's ideology and the aspirations of women intellectuals. Though the editor was fairly 'progressive', he wanted women to adhere to a male-prescribed agenda for women's development. In his view, men and women had 'different roles to perform'.

However, several women's writings in *Grihalakshmi* questioned the new, liberal patriarchal prescriptions with their *radical* pronouncements. From asserting that women were not weak and possessed physical and intellectual strength equal to men, to rejecting the sanctity of Hindu scriptures, to scathing attacks on patriarchal domination, they held men 'responsible for the dismal condition of women'. One author, V. Saraswati, wrote that 'Indian men or, for that matter, all men in the world were selfish'. According to her, 'men were solely responsible for the superstitions present among women. Just as the Brahmins suppressed the non-Brahmins, men suppressed women.'[226] Women's consciousness underwent such a

---

[223] These articles provided insights into relations between the sexes in these countries, the position of women, their education and employment status, and government policies related to women's development. Writers compared the conditions of Indian women with those of women from other countries. Articles on women in other Indian states were also published. For example, see Chatti Rama Rao, 'Tibettu Streelu' (Women in Tibet), April 1934, pp. 127–130; Vadlamudi Venkataratnam, 'Russia–Streelu' (Women in Russia), March 1932, pp. 41–42; Bulusu Lakshmanamoorthy, 'Angla Streelu–Parliament' (Women in the British Parliament), August 1929, pp. 446–450; Allada Rama Ahalya Devi, 'Panjabu Yavatula Samsara Padhdhatulu' (Domestic Life of the Punjabi Women), March 1936, pp. 124–125.

[224] For example, see Premchand, 'Shanti', September 1936, pp. 512–521.

[225] For a discussion on Chand, see Francesca Orsini, *The Hindi Public Sphere, 1920–1940: Language and Literature in the Age of Nationalism* (New Delhi, 2010[2002]), pp. 267–289.

[226] V. Saraswati, 'Srimati Vidyasundari Benguluru Nagaratnamu Gariki, V. Saraswati', December 1929, pp. 917–919. Several other women shared this view. See Cherukuru Nagabhooshanamma, 'Inkennallu Manakee Banisatvamu?' (Slavery of Women: How

tremendous transformation that they held the 'double standards' and 'opportunism' of men to be responsible for the 'failure' of the social reform movement.[227] Recognising that both women and men suffered under colonial rule, Darishi Subhadramma remarked that 'she felt sorry to say that women were more suppressed than men'; they suffered multiple disabilities 'though they were equal to men in number'.[228] Women mounted a blistering attack on Hindu religious texts and Puranic heroes for engendering the dismal condition of women. They did not hold them sacrosanct and in fact repudiated them for granting subordinate status to women. Women thus identified a gender bias in Hindu religious texts.[229]

Writing for the journal in 1937, Komarraju Atchamamba urged women to challenge and overthrow male domination, and emphasised that women's liberation was much more important than the political liberation of the country from foreign domination. In other words, women's liberation must precede the national liberation. According to her, women needed 'unrestrained freedom' to realise their potential.[230]

This vociferous condemnation of men alarmed Kesari. Perturbed by the pointed attacks on men, the editor warned that 'women should avoid the mindless condemnation of men, be friendly with them instead, and work for their own improvement by taking men into confidence'.[231] Lamenting the erosion of men's power, Kesari wrote elsewhere (in true liberal-patriarch fashion!) that women and men enjoyed different rights as per 'nature' and women were the 'queens of [the] homes', and that women were not to

---

Long Must it Last?), October 1941, p. 449. Also see her 'Mana Patananiki Maname Karanamu', (We Alone are Responsible for Our Degeneration), 1938, pp. 686–689.

[227] See 'Mahila Sabhalu', November 1933, p. 755.

[228] Darishi Subhadramma, 'Bharata Streela Prastuta Sthiti' (The Present Condition of Indian Women), May 1938, p. 146.

[229] V. Saraswati, 'Smt. Vidyasundari Benguluru Nagaratnamu Gariki', December 1929, pp. 917–919; Dharmavaram Lakshmi Devi, 'Sharadaku Pratyuttaramu' (A Reply to Sharda), October 1929, pp. 651–656.

[230] Komarraju Atchamamba, 'Neti Rajakeeyalu-Streelu' (Today's Politics and Women), June 1937, p. 295. There were several other women, who expressed similar views. See Darishi Subhadramma, 'Bharata Streela Prastuta Sthiti' (The Present Condition of Indian Women), May 1938, p. 146.

[231] 'Sampadakiyamu: Vudyamabhivrudhdhiki Ninda Yeduru Chukka' (Editorial: Accusation is an Obstacle to the Advancement of the Women's Movement), March 1938, pp. 70–71.

demand 'unnatural rights aping Western values'. If they did, 'society would be destroyed'.[232]

Such warnings, persuasions, and intimidation from the (male) editor only bolstered the radical consciousness that developed among a section of women writing for and reading *Grihalakshmi*. The growing apprehensions of men, particularly the 'reforming' new patriarchs, indicated how far men thought women should go. It demonstrated men's anxiety that a section of women had crossed these boundaries. *Grihalakshmi* became an unintentional catalyst for women's *radical* endeavours.

Andhra Mahila (1944-beyond 1964)

Andhra Mahila began publication in Madras on 15 May 1944 and continued for about twenty years.[233] Founded, edited, and published by Gummadidala Durgabayamma, later famous as Durgabai Deshmukh, it was printed at the 'Andhra Mahila Press'.

The Andhra Mahila Sabha 'recognised the necessity of a journal that could be beneficial especially to women', and to 'channelise the aspirations of the women's movement in Andhra'.[234] It enjoyed the services of several editors, associate editors and co-editors for different periods.[235] Channaghantamma, a co-editor of the journal in 1952, became its editor in 1953. Subsequently, Durgabai's name appeared only as 'founder' of *Andhra Mahila*. After Channaghantamma, Lakshmi Raghuram (also known as Lakshmi Raghuramaiah) served as editor for eight months. Between mid-1955 and 1959, Adurti Bhaskaramma served as editor,[236] after which Lakshmi Raghuram returned to the post. Ramalakshmi Arudra was a joint editor with Raghuram.[237]

---

[232] See 'Sampadakiyamu' (Editorial), January 1939, pp. 809–810.

[233] Unless otherwise especially mentioned, all references in this section are from *Andhra Mahila*.

[234] 'Sampadakiyamu' (Editorial), 15 May 1944, pp. 5–6.

[235] Mallavarapu Vishweswara Rao was its associate editor initially. 'Vignapti' (An Appeal), 15 May 1944. Achyutuni Girija (1945–1946), Kancharla Sugunamani (1947), and Mamidipudi Vaidehi (1948) served as assistant and co-editors, respectively, before 1950.

[236] See the editorial note dealing with the change of editors over a period of time. July 1955, p. 3.

[237] March 1959.

Image 2.8: Cover page of *Andhra Mahila*

Source: *Andhra Mahila*, September 1956.

Andhra Mahila began its run as a fortnightly journal with 20 pages. The unavailability of newsprint quota forced the journal to become a monthly, probably from January 1946.[238] After 1947, there was a tremendous increase in the page extent of the journal, with each issue containing over 50 pages and the annual number exceeding 150 pages. Initially, each copy was priced at 8 annas, but this was reduced to 4 annas from 15 July 1944. The annual subscription rate was Rs. 5; a half-yearly subscription was Rs. 2.80.[239] In May 1951, the annual subscription rate increased to Rs. 6, and a single

[238] May 1948, p. 9.

[239] 'Manavi' (An Appeal), 15 July 1944, p. 2; 'Gamanika' (Notice), 1 August 1944, p. 6.

copy was for Re. 0.8; this rate remained static till the end of its publication. However, welfare organisations and libraries could subscribe to *Andhra Mahila* for just Rs. 3.[240] We do not know the exact number of its subscribers and the extent of its circulation. Given the popularity of the Andhra Mahila Sabha, Durgabai Deshmukh's stature, and the absence of any other women's journal when *Andhra Mahila* began publication (*Grihalakshmi* had temporarily ceased publication at the time), it must have enjoyed a wide area of circulation. According to Durgabai, *Andhra Mahila* was 'in great demand'.[241] It advertised for agents 'in each town of the Telugu districts'.[242]

Andhra Mahila attracted a large number of writers and had a waitlist before long. The editor repeatedly appealed to the writers not to be 'disappointed' if their writings were published late or not at all. Writings on 'social and political matters' were given priority. Though it was not a policy of the journal to prefer women's writings, it did publish a large number of women authors.

The journal reflects a radical change in women's consciousness. A staunch advocate of women's rights, it featured numerous articles on women's civil and political rights. It undertook a rigorous campaign for women's right to inherit and to obtain divorce, and advocated a more political representation of women. Articles and short stories appeared on issues like women's education, child marriage, and dowry. Of the last two, the problem of dowry received greater attention.

Andhra Mahila published a variety of columns. The most remarkable among them was 'Mahilalalo Jagruti' (Women's Awakening), which carried accounts of a large number of women's organisations located in different parts of Andhra.[243] Being the mouthpiece of the Andhra Mahila Sabha, it regularly published details of its various programmes.[244] The proceedings of the conferences of the Andhra Rastra Mahila Mahasabha (ARMS),

[240] April 1960, p. 26.

[241] Durgabai Deshmukh, *The Stone That Speaketh*, vol. I (two volumes) (Hyderabad, 1980b), p. 42.

[242] 'Agentlu Kavalenu' (Agents Required), November 1948, p. 37.

[243] Achyutuni Girija, the assistant editor, made announcements appealing to the women's organisations 'to help their mission' by sending their reports. December 1945, p. 4; See also January 1946, p. 42; March 1946, p. 40; April 1946, p. 46. *Andhra Mahila* got a very good response because of which the accounts of a large number of women's organisations came to be published.

[244] For example, see the November 1948 issue, which published the full details of the Andhra Mahila Sabha. They included its rules and regulations, details of the Executive Committee, its aims and objectives, etc. See also the May 1948 issue.

the Andhra branch of the All India Women's Conference, were also published regularly. The journal exhorted women associated with various organisations, particularly the ARMS, to 'shed their differences, be united and work for the progress of women'.[245]

The column 'Dooraseemala Nari Prapancham' (Women of Other Countries) covered the condition of women in other countries, including USA, China, Japan and the Soviet Union.[246] Darishi Subhadramma handled the column 'Pillala Shikshana—Shastriya Drukpatham' (Scientific Approach to Childcare) for over five years, discussing in detail the various 'scientific methods' of raising children.[247] 'Satya's' column,[248] 'Streela Pradhana Samasyalu' (Main Problems Faced by Women), discussed various problems faced by women including marriage, economic dependence, lack of education, ill-health, children, sex work, religion, politics, etc.[249] Satya's writings were very radical. Achyutuni Girija's column 'Prastuta Paristhitulu' (Present Conditions) reflected on the social and political problems of the time. The entry in the May 1951 issue discussed the problem of dowry at length.[250]

Gandhi's views on issues like women's education, non-violence and women, dowry, widowhood, service to the nation, etc., were published

---

[245]'Andhrabhyudayame Ashayamugaagala Andhra Nareemanulaku O Chinna Manavi' (A Small Appeal to the Andhra Women Whose Sole Aim is the Progress of Andhra), January 1949, p. 48.

[246]M. S. Padmavatamma wrote on American women. See April 1948, pp. 33–35. J. V. Radha Krishnaiah discussed the lifestyle of Japanese women. See 5 September 1945, pp. 29–31. Devulapalli Achyutam wrote on the domestic life of women in Socialist Russia. See 'Socialist Russialo Samsarika Jivanamu', June 1948, pp. 17–18. Darisi Subhadramma wrote on the progress made by Chinese women. See November 1952, pp. 14–15.

[247]For example, see May 1949, pp. 79–80; June 1949, pp. 9–11 and 14.

[248]We do not know whether the columnist was a man or woman. 'Satya' was perhaps a pseudonym. I searched for the writer's identity over 20 years, but in vain.

[249]See 'Vivahamu' (Marriage), 3 November 1945, pp. 36–40; 'Arthika Daasyamu' (Economic Slavery/ Dependence), 1 December 1945, pp. 33–34; 'Biddalu' (Children), January 1946, pp. 17–19; 'Anarogyamu' (Ill-Health), March 1946, pp. 7–8; 'Vidya' (Education), April 1946, pp. 11–12; 'Padupu Vrutti' (Prostitution), May 1946, pp. 21–23; 'Matamu' (Religion), July 1946, pp. 23–24; 'Rajakiyamulu' (Politics), August 1946, pp. 17–19.

[250]Achyutumi Giriija, 'Katnalu–Black Markettu' (Dowry and Black Market), May 1951, p. 16. Interestingly, dowry is treated as a 'black market' transaction.

under the column 'Gandhiji Emantaru?' (What Does Gandhiji Say?).[251] Another column, 'Rajakeeyalu' (Politics), which dealt with regional, national and international politics, was first handled by Gollamudi Ramachandra Rao and later by Jonnalagadda Radhakrishna. 'Grandha Sameeksha' (Book Review) introduced readers to importantl books.[252] 'Maa Vidyarthinula Ishtagoshti' (Debates Among our Girl Students) carried the proceedings of the Telugu and the Hindi debating clubs of the Andhra Mahila Sabha, usually organised on topics like co-education and English education for women.[253] Gradually, senior women began to participate in the debate clubs too, leading to the creation of a new column, 'Sabhyurandra Charcha' (Debates among the Women Members). Women debated whether they could be politically active, their right to property, the problem of dowry, etc.[254]

K. Ramalakshmi's column, 'Jeevita Charitra', published biographies of prominent women like Pandita Ramabai, Maharani Setu Parvatibai, and Abala Bose.[255] Many articles were published on Veeresalingam hailing him as a 'revolutionary' who worked 'for the progress of women'.[256] Writings of

---

[251] For example, see 'Purushulakante Stree Jaati Hinama?' (Are Women Inferior to Men?), 15 May 1944, pp. 7–8; 'Stree Vidya Vidhanam' (Systerm of Women's Education), 15 June 1944, pp. 7–8; 'Abalalu–Ahimsa' (Women and Non-Violence), 1 July 1944, pp. 5–6. The 20 April 1945 issue published his views on dowry and widowhood, pp. 17–18.

[252] Komarraju Atchmamaba's *Prasuti–Shishu Poshana*, 20 December 1944, pp. 17–18; Utukuri Lakshmikantamma's *Andhra Kavayitrulu*, December 1952, pp. 27–28; K. N. Kesari's autobiography, *Na Chinnanati Muchchatlu*, November 1953, p. 119, and P. Sridevi's novel, *Kalatita Vyaktulu*, January 1959, pp. 17–19, were a few among the important books reviewed.

[253] For example, see 20 July 1945, pp. 25–26; 05 September 1945, pp. 63–64.

[254] For example, see 'Streelu-Rajakeeyalu' (Women and Politics), February 1946, pp. 7–19; 'Asti Hakku leni Gruhaadhikaram Budbudaprayam' (Control over Home is Useless without the Right to Property), December 1946, pp. 9–10; 'Vidakula Chattamu–Bharatiya Samajaniki Hanikaramynadi' (Right to Divorce is Harmful to Indian Society), February 1947, pp. 33–34; 'Bahubharyatvam, Vidakula Billu' (On Polygamy and Divorce Bill), June 1947, pp. 9–11; 'Hindu-Muslim Anykyata' (Disunity between Hindus and Muslims), March 1946, pp. 18–19.

[255] See November 1954, pp. 14–16; December 1954, pp. 53–55, and January 1955, pp. 13–15, respectively.

[256] For example, see S. Muthulakshmi Reddy, 'Krutagnatanjali' (A Thanks-giving Salutation), 1 June 1944, p. 14; Manikonda Suryavati, 'Mahilabhyudayaniki Pantulugari Krushi' (Contribution of Veeresalingam to Women's Progress), 1 June 1944, pp. 15–19; 'Viplavakarudu Veeresalingam' (Veeresalingam, the Revolutionary), June 1947, p. 6;

prominent women of the time like Kamala Devi Chattopadhyaya, Renuka Ray, Padmini Sengupta, Janaki Menon and Rajkumari Amrit Kaur were published in translation. *Andhra Mahila* published several special issues, including a 'Gandhi Memorial Issue' (February–March 1948). After the 'Central Social Welfare Board' was established, *Andhra Mahila* published special supplements under the title *Sanghika Sankshemam*.[257] In her column, 'Soundarya Poshana' (Beautification), Suveni Kashyap offered tips to women on various techniques of beautification. *Andhra Mahila* published a large number of advertisements. Films were advertised, and a few of them reviewed.

The editorials in *Andhra Mahila* were remarkable not only for their radical content, but also for their critical insights. With their incisive analysis of various issues, particularly those concerning women, they forcefully represented the woman's point of view. Editorials discussed issues such as women's education, right to divorce, inheritance, elections, political parties, family planning, sexual harassment, etc. Criticising the proponents of a 'separate curriculum' for women, an editorial commented that women were 'equally eligible' for receiving 'any kind of knowledge', and questioned 'why at all there should be any difference in the curriculum of men and women when they had to perform the same roles in society'. In addition, it questioned the separation of domains into public and private.[258]

In a biting editorial in February 1947, *Andhra Mahila* held men to be chiefly responsible for the 'dismal position of women'. It particularly criticised 'Congress men' for 'not recognising women as equal partners in the freedom movement', and for failing to see the 'significance of women in social service'. It questioned this group of men on their unilateral decisions regarding domestic laws, since they disproportionately impacted women. It suggested that Congressmen should 'take appropriate measures for upgrading the status of women rather than treating their wives as mere

---

Adurti Bhaskaramma, 'Mahapurushudu Sri Veeresalingam' (Veeresalingam, the Great Man), May 1948, pp. 25–26.

[257]These supplements published the details of the various social welfare schemes undertaken by the Government of India. In addition, they informed the activities carried out by several State Boards. For example, see '*Sanghika Sankshemam*', supplement, November 1954; see also December 1954; January 1955.

[258]'Streelaku Pratyeka Vidya Vidhanam' (Separate System of Education for Women), 15 August 1944, pp. 4–5.

possessions'. This defiant piece challenged the patriarchal outlook held by a large number of Congressmen.[259]

An editorial in March 1947 criticised the Madras government, headed by Tanguturi Prakasham, for lacking gender sensitivity in its development programmes.[260] The August 1951 editorial demanded equal pay to women employed in government service.[261] The editorial of December 1951 reflected on the negligible representation of women in politics,[262] and another in January 1952 exhorted women to exercise their right to vote.[263] Reviewing the country's status seven years after attaining independence, the editorial of September 1954 expressed satisfaction at India's progress, even as it commented: 'still there was much to achieve, particularly with regard to the progress of women'.[264] The editorial of March 1956 was on sexual harassment faced by women and girls, particularly in educational

---

[259]'Stree Jati Abhyunnati' (Progress of the Race of Women), p. 4.

[260]The editorial essay remarked that the government 'neglected' the women's issues. It suggested that 'there should be a well defined programme for the improvement of women', and reminded that the women's issues were 'no less significant' than the programme of uplifting of the *harijans* (the term popularised by Gandhi to refer to oppressed castes) and the promotion of khadi. Further, it emphasised that 'progress of women was crucial to the progress of the country.' It suggested for the creation of a separate cell [ministry] for women's welfare and advancement. See 'Mana Prabhutvamu–Mahilabhyudayamu' (Progress of Women and Our Government), pp. 5–8.

[261]It exhibited enormous faith in women's capability in discharging their public functions equal to that of men. It questioned whether it was not 'injustice' (*adharmam*) to discriminate against women in terms of payment for their equal work to men. It ridiculed the Indian representative at the UN, who abstained on the question of equal payment to women. See 'Samana Vetanalu' (Equal Wages), pp. 9–10.

[262]'Ennikalu–Streelu' (Elections and Women), pp. 7–9.

[263]'Ennikalu–Streela Badhyatalu' (Elections and the Responsibilities of Women), p. 8.

[264]'Yedella Swatantryam' (Seven Years of Independence), pp. 3–4.

institutions.[265] The issue of family planning was discussed in the editorial of March 1959.[266]

Andhra Mahila rigorously campaigned for women's civil and political rights, with several articles seeking the redressal of legal disabilities suffered by women under the existing Hindu Law. They welcomed the Hindu Law Committee headed by Sir B. N. Rao, appointed in 1940. Tikkavarapu Shakuntala Devi expressed confidence that the Bill proposed by the Rao Committee 'would do justice to women by cremating the outdated [moth-eaten] Hindu Law'.[267] Chandra Savithri Devi published a powerful rejoinder to an article critiquing the Rao Committee Bill.[268] Women increasingly advocated an equal right to property and divorce. They desired a radical change in existing laws that discriminated against women and envisioned a gender just society.

As mentioned earlier, the practice of dowry received serious attention in *Andhra Mahila*. Many short stories and articles condemned the practice

---

[265] Reflecting on a piece about sexual harassment published in various newspapers, it commented that 'eve teasing and sexual harassment were rampant near the gates of girls' colleges, bus stops, beaches,' etc. The problem of sexual harassment multiplied in co-educational institutions. Boys made derogatory remarks and sang filthy songs, scribbled uncivilised words and pictures on desks and walls. They spread rumours if a girl spoke to boys and took to 'character assassination'. As one may expect, the article suggested that boys should 'remember their sisters and mothers' in such moments and reminded them that even their sisters might become the victims of sexual harassment. The editorial concluded by stating that if boys did not abstain from harassing girls, the whole system of education, educational institutions and the various plans of education would turn 'as useless as the scent poured into ash.' See 'Boodidalo Posina Panniru' (Scent Poured into Ash), pp. 3–4.

[266] Commenting that the family planning programme undertaken by the Government of India did not register much success, it suggested that proper efforts should be made to spread the message with great rigor and enthusiasm. People were to be sensitised regarding the advantages of small families. It observed that 'men did not show required interest' in it. If the family planning programme was to be successful, men should also take equal interest in it rather than putting the entire burden on women. See 'Kutumba Niyantrana' (Family Planning), pp. 3–4.

[267] 'Chedalu Pattina Hindu Lawku Antyakriyalu: Rao Committee Billu Stree Lokaniki Sabhyata Chekurustundi' (Funerals to the Moth Eaten Hindu Law: Rao Committee Bill will do Justice to the World of Women), 5 January 1945, pp. 21–22.

[268] 'Streelu Shakti Lenivaruganuka Rao Committee Pratipadinchina Hakkulu Nirakarinchala?' (Should We Oppose the Rights Proposed by Rao Committee because Women are [Allegedly] Powerless?), 15 February 1945, pp. 19–21.

and discussed measures that could contain the 'vampire of dowry'.[269] The journal also brought to light incidents of dowry deaths, for instance a report about an 18-year-old girl who died by suicide in 1950 due to dowry-related pressures.[270] The issues of child marriage and widow remarriage received comparatively little attention. M. Varalakshmi of Srikakulam, in a letter to the editor, opined that the debating clubs of the Andhra Mahila Sabha should concentrate on 'more progressive [and important] issues' rather than the 'routine' topics like child marriage and women's education.[271]

With its unwavering commitment to the cause of women, *Andhra Mahila* created a radical rights' consciousness among women, moulded public opinion in favour of women's civil and political rights, and successfully mobilised them. Through its campaigns, it courageously questioned and criticised the patriarchal outlook of both government and society at large. Given the wide range of issues it addressed, the journal emerged as a radical advocate of women's issues. No doubt, this was also driven partly by Durgabai Deshmukh, whose reputation as an activist was well-established at the time.

Vanita (April-December 1956)

Vanita began publication on a monthly basis in April 1956 and continued until the end of the year.[272] A mouthpiece of the Andhra Yuvati Mandali,[273] an important women's organisation in Hyderabad, it was edited by Abburi Chaya Devi, a renowned writer who later worked as a librarian at the

---

[269] For example, see Mallavarapu Vijayalakshmi, 'Katnam Leni Pelli' (Marriage without Dowry), June 1948, pp. 7–10. See also Lakshmi Raghuramaiah, 'Inka Katnalenduku? Antaa Cheppedivare, Chesedivarevaru?' (Why Does Dowry Persist? Everyone Preaches, But No One Practises), April 1949, pp. 20–21; G. S. Rajeshwari Patnaik, 'Varakatnalanu Nishedhinchandi' (Ban Dowry), March 1950, pp. 13–14.

[270] 'Baadhyulevaru?' (Who is Responsible?), December 1950, p. 54.

[271] See 'Paathakula Lekhalu' (Letters to the Editor), April 1947, p. 12.

[272] Unless otherwise especially mentioned, all references in this section are from *Vanita*.

[273] Yallapragada Sita Kumari and Illindala Saraswati Devi established the organisation in 1935. For details, see 'Andhra Yuvati Mandali', 15 April 1956, pp. 53–57. See also 'Andhra Yuvati Mandali Karyakalapalu' (Activities of the Andhra Yuvati Mandali), December 1956, pp. 3–4.

Jawaharlalal Nehru University, New Delhi.[274] The annual subscription was Rs. 3 and each issue ran into around 64 pages. Prominent women writers of the time like Nandagiri Indira Devi, Tenneti Hemalatha, Vallabhaneni Rangadevi, Unnava Vijayalakshmi and S. Sridevi contributed to *Vanita*.

The editorial of the inaugural issue itself clarified its feminist stand on women's issues:

> Women's journals are essential to remove women from dark boundaries called kitchen and the obstcles haunting them, to tell them what is happening outside under the sky... to inform [them about]... the role they need to play in... [the] wider world... Today, women have the responsibility of setting right not just the home, but also the nation. However, the question is to what extent our women are able to recognise this dual responsibility... 'Vanita' is taking birth to build a wider platform for making our dormant women to recognise this need, for awakening them.[275]

The editor was clear that although 'women today constituted half of the nation's population', they were 'economically dependent' and the 'continuous burden of family weakened them in multiple ways'. In a fast-changing world where new ideas were rapidly emerging, it was 'inevitable' that they too would be affected by social transformations and would have to adapt to the same.[276]

In accordance with its stated objectives, the journal carried articles, short stories and poems on women's education and employment,[277] equal representation in politics,[278] the problem of dowry,[279] health, childcare, gardening and beautification. The editorials were varied: the August 1956 editorial appealed to readers to 'remember the forgotten heroines, who struggled for women's development';[280] the following month featured an

---

[274] Issues of the journal were obtained with permission from Chaya Devi, whom I met at her residence in January 2012.

[275] See 'Sampadakiyam' (Editorial), 15 April 1956, pp. 5–6.

[276] Ibid.

[277] S. Rajyalakshmi, 'Upadhyaya Vruttilo Stree' (Women in the Teaching Profession), 15 April 1956, pp. 9–13. 'Streelu-Udyogalu' (Women and Employment), 15 May 1956, pp. 24–27.

[278] S. Rajyalakshmi, 'Samana Pratinithyam' (Equal Representation in Political Bodies), 15 August 1956, pp. 52–54. See also Gnana Kumari Heda, 'Congresu Partilo Mahilalu' (Women in the Congress Party), November 1956, pp. 30–32.

[279] Nandagiri Indira Devi, 'Varakatnalu-Madhya Taragati Kutumbalu' (Dowry and Middle Class Families), 15 July 1956, pp. 5–9.

[280] 'Eerojuna' (Today), p. 1.

editorial arguing for 'girls' freedom and independence'.[281] Other editorials dealt with issues like women's representation in local political bodies[282] and the importance of women's organisations.[283]

Soundaryavalli

Another monthly journal *Soundaryavalli* was founded in 1918. Edited by Gadicharla Ramabai,[284] it was published from Madras. Each issue had around 35 pages, and the annual subscription cost Rs. 3. An analysis of the journal's contents shows that despite having a woman editor, the focus was not on women's issues. Unlike other women's journals, nowhere did the journal state that it aimed for a female readership. While the journal had more contributions from men than women, prominent women writers of the time, including Salla Soundaryavalli Amma, Achanta Rukminamma, Kanchanapalli Kanakamma, and Ponaka Kanakamma were associated with the journal and listed as *vilekhakulu* (journalists/contributors). Women's issues comprised only one among several themes that the journal

[281] 'Aadapillanu Adupulo Unchadam!' (Keeping Girls under Control!), pp. 3–4.

[282] 'Panchayitilu-Streelu', 15 June 1956, p. 3.

[283] 'Samaajaalu' ([Women's] Organisations), 15 May 1956, pp. 3–4.

[284] In the journal, her name was accompanied by the phrase 'Harisarvottamaraya Sati' in brackets, identifying her as the wife of Harisarvottama Rao, a prominent freedom fighter and leader of the movement for a separate Andhra province. This was probably the first journal where the woman editor identified herself by her husband's name. This may have been to gain credibility—Sarvottama Rao was a well-respected public figure, the first political prisoner from the region.

discussed.[285] It paid more attention to the creation of a strong regional identity among the Andhra people.[286]

Other Women's Journals

Many other women's journals appeared in this period. For some of these, only a few copies remain, while others are completely absent from archives. One journal, *Stree Hita Bodhini*, began publication in 1893 from Kakinada, under the editorship of Rapaka Kaustubham.[287] Remarkably, it was available free of cost.[288] A 'monthly Telugu magazine for women', *Balika*, began publication in March 1896 from Chicacole (Srikakulam). Sangitarao Baupiraju, a First Grade Pleader, was its editor. Most of its contributors were men, and it focused on the development of women's education.[289] *The Maharani*, a monthly 'pictorial magazine for girls' schools and home reading' began publication in January 1889 and continued perhaps until the end of 1892. The *Grihalakshmi*,[290] with Raja Mantripragada Bhujanga Rao and Nandiraju Chalapati Rao as its publisher and editor, respectively, was published from Eluru in 1903.[291] The *Sundari* was published from Komari Palem in Godavari District in 1909, with B. Narayana as its editor.[292]

---

[285] For a few examples of articles that specifically discuss women's experiences and organisations, see 'Shishu Poshana: Mana Vidhayaka Krityamu' (Child Rearing: Our Responsibility), Kalayukti–Shravanamu (July) 1918, pp. 19–20. The same issue published the detailed account of the ninth 'Andhra Mahila Sabha' held at Cuddapah in June 1918. See 'Andhra Mahila Sabha', pp. 31–32. The issue also included a group photograph of women at the conference, and another of Soundaryavalli Amma. The Maharani of Baroda wrote a three-part article on Japanese Women ('Japanu Streelu'), serialised in the first three issues of the journal. Kanchanapalli Kanakamma's 'Hindu Dharmashastramulu' was published in the third issue, pp. 14–15. Salla Soundaryavalli Amma's article, 'Stree Vidyabhivriddhi: Ati Baalya Vivahamulu' (Child Marriages and the Development of Women's Education) was published in the fourth issue. See, pp. 7–8.

[286] For some more details of the journal, see Potturi Venkateswara Rao, *Andhra Jaati Akshara Sampada*, pp. 231–233.

[287] Dantu Padmavati, *Aspashta Pratibimbalu*, p. 42.

[288] Potturi Venkateswara Rao, *Andhra Jaati Akshara Sampada*, p. 164.

[289] Initially, it had 15 pages; later the number increased to 30. The contents page was published in both Telugu and English. Dantu Padmavati, *Aspashta Pratibimbalu*, pp. 42–43. See also Potturi Venkateswara Rao, *Telugu Jaati Akshra Sampada*, pp. 148–149.

[290] This journal is not be mistaken for the *Grihalakshmi* of K. N. Kesari.

[291] Dantu Padmavati, *Aspashta Pratibimbalu*, p. 44.

[292] Ibid., p. 46.

Streelakoraku Vartamanamulu (Messages for Women) was founded in Guntur in 1898. Edited by E. S. McCauley (E. S. Mecauli Dorasanigaru), this journal primarily propagated Christianity among women.[293] The Telugu section of the multilingual (English, Telugu, Tamil and later Hindi) *Stri Dharma*, a mouthpiece of the Women's Indian Association which began in 1918 from Madras, was edited by Malati Patwardhan.[294] *Bala Bharati*, a journal devoted to training women and children in music and edited by Jagannatha Sharma, appeared in 1918.[295]

Yamini Poornatilakamma started the *Hindu Yuvati*, the first women's fortnightly, in 1923: it was published from Madras. The chief aim of the journal was to reform the *kalavantulu* (see Chapter 1).[296] It is very unfortunate that copies of such an important journal are not available today. Poornatilakamma edited another journal, *Vishwagnani*, also published from Madras.[297]

The *Bharata Mahila* was started in 1925. Published from Anantapur, it was edited by U. Sundaramma.[298] The *Yashoda*, edited by T. K. Yashoda Devi, came out from Rajahmundry in 1930.[299] The *Shri Sharada Niketanamu*, an illustrated monthly published by the Sharada Niketanamu at Guntur, was intended to spread awareness among women (*streelalo prabodhamu galiginchutakugaanu*). It began publication from Guntur perhaps in July 1937. Three women were on the editorial board of the journal. The annual subscription was Re. 1 for general subscribers and Rs. 5 for the patrons.[300] The *Soubhagya*, a monthly published by the women's welfare department of the Government of Madras, was founded in 1945.[301] The ARMS, an organisation of the Communist women of Andhra, published *Andhra Vanita*, a monthly, around March/April 1948. Hardly two issues of the journal were out when the Congress government banned its publication.[302]

---

[293] Ibid., p. 46.

[294] For more details on the journal, see Michelle Elizabeth Tusan, 'Writing *stri dharma*', discussed in the Introduction, this volume.

[295] Dantu Padmavati, *Aspashta Pratibimbalu*, p. 47.

[296] Ibid., p. 48.

[297] Ibid., p. 50.

[298] Ibid., p. 49.

[299] Ibid., p. 50.

[300] 'Shri Sharada Niketanamu, Gunturu', *Grihalakshmi*, May 1937, p. 183.

[301] See Devulapalli Ramanuja Rao et al., ed., *Telugulo Parishodhana: Rajatotsava Sanchika*, (Hyderabad, 1983), p. 453.

[302] Goparaju Sitadevi, *Janani, Janma Bhoomischa: Goparaju Sitadevi Sweeya Charitra*, p. 69.

Darishi Subhadramma edited it.[303] *Vanita Vihar* began publication in early 1949 from Rajahmundry and was edited by three women—Satyavati Devi, Rajyalakshmi and Mahalakshmi. K. Rangamma Reddy edited the *Narilokam*, a monthly, which was published from Vijayawada.[304]

Rivalry among Women's Journals

Another important dimension of this print culture is the rivalry that developed among some popular women's journals. Aggravated by personal competition among their founders, the journals competed for fame and material benefits, and feared each other's success.

The first instance of such competition was between *Hindu Sundary* and *Savithri*, the earliest journals edited by women. Sitaramaiah, the founder of *Hindu Sundary*, provided a candid account of the conflict in his autobiography. Here, the problem began with Sitaramaiah's search for a woman editor. *Hindu Sundary*'s competitors believed that the presence of a woman editor would directly affect the fortunes of a women's journal and the profits of its founders.[305]

As mentioned earlier, Sitaramaiah found it difficult to hire a woman editor for the journal as many candidates refused the position. One of them was Pulugurta Lakshmi Narasamamba, who later became the editor of *Savithri*. Narasamamba's public announcement of her intention to edit a women's journal, after having rejected *Hindu Sundary*, caught Sitaramaiah unaware. His autobiography details how hurt he felt when she sought his advice and 'blessings' and began using all his 'connections' to mobilise potential women contributors and supporters.

---

303 Kondapalli Koteshwaramma, *Nirjana Varadhi* (Autobiography) (Hyderabad, 2012), pp. 134–135.

304 The information was provided in the 'Received' column in the December 1956 issue of *Vanita*, p. 39.

305 Until Sitaramaiah employed a woman editor, women's journals such as *Sathihitha Bodhini* and *Telugu Zenana* had only male editors. This 'inhibited' women from 'freely corresponding' with the editors of such journals for corresponding with men was not treated an 'honourable' behaviour. This gave rise to the feeling that women should edit women's journals for such an arrangement would 'encourage' women allowing for 'communication without any hesitation'. This also meant that the entire literate female constituency would shift there resulting in the increased circulation of a women's journal, and the consequent possible profit of the proprietor.

Several women expressed their enthusiasm about Narasamamba's forthcoming journal and some associated with Sitaramaiah promised to support her venture. Fearing a 'natural gender solidarity' ('*sahajamagu swajatyabhimanamu*')[306] that could threaten the prospects of *Hindu Sundary*, Sitaramaiah hastily roped in women to edit his journal just ten days before *Savithri* was launched![307] Thereafter, the editors of these two journals never got along well with each other.[308]

Women's development apart, the circulation of women's journals involved many other considerations, including material wealth and fame. Almost all women's journals carried advertisements of various kinds. Products like medicines or cosmetics that were 'useful' to women figured prominently. Through such practices, journals also promoted commercial ventures of their founders. K. N. Kesari is a classic example in this regard. A successful Ayurvedic medical practitioner, Kesari manufactured several medicines, particularly those useful to women and children, in his Kesari Kutiramu. These products were regularly advertised in *Grihalakshmi*. If not for his journal, Kesari would have had to spend heavily on advertising his products. Such arrangements, while highly beneficial to the publishers, could also shape interpersonal dynamics. In the *Hindu Sundary–Savithri* rivalry, one factor was that while Sitaramaiah wanted Narasamamba to edit *Hindu Sundary*, her husband, Pulugurta Venkataratnam, wanted an independent journal of his own. Infuriated, Sitaramaiah contemptuously wrote that 'by publishing the journal [*Savithri*] Venkataratnam, perhaps, intended to supplement the meagre income that he earned as a school teacher'.[309] Of course, if the publication of *Savithri* helped Venkataratnam make some money, the same could be said of Sitaramaiah, and many others like him.

In the 1920s, new women's journals such as the *Anasuya* and *Andhra Lakshmi* arrived on the scene. By now, women editors had over the reigns

---

[306] Sattiraju Sitaramaiah, *Sweeya Charitra*, p. 76.

[307] The announcement that Veeresalingam would jointly edit *Telugu Zenana* with Venkata Sivudu further increased his anxiety about the future of his journal. Ibid., p. 76. The story of women becoming editors of women's journals in Telugu was not as simple as one might assume. For this fascinating story, see Sitaramaiah's *Sweeya Charitra*, pp. 75–83. One would witness anthills of jealousy and contempt the competing women harboured for one another. They exchanged letters making sarcastic remarks at one another.

[308] A contemporary named Kallakuri Narasimham also observed this unhealthy atmosphere. See ibid., p. 86.

[309] Ibid., p. 76.

of *Hindu Sundary*, and they did not like the arrival of these new journals. Their resentment intensified as *Hindu Sundary* began to show signs of decline. A sense of anger and anguish that women writers 'gradually lost interest' in *Hindu Sundary* and shifted to other women's journals is palpable in editorial remarks that lament a lack of women's solidarity. This lack of commitment and imagination to improve *Hindu Sundary* was attributed to the writers' ambition to become editors. Vemuganti Papayamma, an honorary secretary, sarcastically remarked that 'to boast of themselves as editors of journals', some women brought out 'a journal everyday', whose fate was 'like the sunlight for three days', that is very short-lived. '*Hindu Sundary* would not have suffered such a fate had there been *aikamatyamu* [unity] among women', she lamented.[310]

Assessing the Impact of Women's Journals

The social reform movement initiated by liberal men positively affected women. The new literate women readily recognised the need for their *agency* rather than being passive *objects* of reform. In their war against patriarchal cultural norms that subordinated and subjugated them, they wielded the weapons of words. The emergence of women's journalism was a direct result of the change-oriented outlook of the emerging female intelligentsia. Budding women intellectuals weaponised print culture to fight and fell the banyan tree of patriarchal culture. Not surprisingly, the dawn of the twentieth century witnessed a proliferation of women's journals edited and managed by women.

Liberal men started and edited the first two women's journals. Within two decades, women began to publish and edit their own journals. What was more significant was that women were clearly aware of the continued relevance of their journals. If one journal ceased publication, a new journal was born. Women did not want any break or interruption in their mission; they did not want, it appears, any rest in their combat.[311]

Apart from being powerful distance educators of women on a regular basis, the women's journals provided them with an expansive textual

---

[310] 'Swa Vishayamu' (Ourselves), *Hindu Sundary*, February 1945, p. 2.

[311] It is very surprising that journals like *Hindu Sundary* sustained themselves, amid pressing difficulties like severe financial constraints and social apathy, for more than half a century. This speaks volumes of the commitment and perseverance of women to march ahead with their agenda and continue their movement.

territory where they moved freely, frankly speaking their minds in public. Through their columns, women launched a crusade against the social evils that adversely affected them and discussed all the issues that concerned them. If the early journals exhibited considerable ambivalence and wanted women to be reformed within the boundaries of a liberal patriarchy, the later journals gradually brought about a paradigmatic change, redrawing the contours and asserting women's individuality and independence. The early journals focused on limited issues such as women's education, child marriage, condition of widows and women's reformed domesticity. The later journals like *Grihalakshmi* and *Andhra Mahila* expanded the concerns of women. They discussed their freedom and independence, amelioration of legal disabilities, demanded civil and political rights, representation in politics, condemned male domination and advocated a society that ensured gender equality and justice. With a continued discussion of women's issues, the journals created favourable public opinion and transformed women's consciousness. More importantly, they saved the woman's question from being overshadowed and swallowed by the other contemporary struggles such as the national movement.

By, for, and about women, the journals give us tremendous insights into the minds of a cross-section of the second sex in the first half of the twentieth century in Andhra. The pages of the journals unveil how women spoke for themselves and for others, grappled with the wide gap between their aspirations and the unfavourable ground realities and fought against internalised patriarchal mindsets as well as the larger patriarchal world, which condemned them to slavery and misery. They spread before us the map of women's consciousness and the agenda they set for themselves and the larger nation. Across these journals, one finds a variety of visions and voices.

These journals, with the direct or indirect support of women's organisations, formed the backbone of the women's movement in colonial Andhra.[312] In the chapters that follow, we shall see how women made use of the print culture, marching ahead on a programme of collective emancipation.

[312] One would be surprised to know that the region does not have as many women's journals after independence as those found during the colonial period.

3

Autonomy and Legal Reform

Debates on Child Marriage and *Kanyasulkam*

Under the orders of His Highness the Maharajah of Vizianagaram, a list was prepared ten years ago, of Brahmin *sulka* marriages [child marriages], celebrated in the ordinary tracts of the Vizagapatam [Visakhapatnam] during three years. The list is by no means exhaustive as the parties concerned were naturally averse to admitting acceptance of bride-money; but such as it is, it forms a document of great value and interest. The number of marriages recorded reached one thousand and thirty four, giving an average of three hundred and forty four for the year. Ninety nine girls were married at the age of five years, forty four at four, thirty six at three, six at two, and three at the age of one!—the babies in the last instance carrying a price of from three and fifty to four hundred rupees a head. Strange, it may sound, bargains are sometimes struck for children in the womb. Such a scandalous state of things is a disgrace to society, and literature cannot have a higher function than to show up such practices and give currency to a high standard of moral ideas.[1]

Better tie a boulder [to her neck] and drop her into a well,
Than marry her off in infancy.
Better kill a boy by hanging,
Than marry him off in the greed of dowry.
Better slit the throat of a girl
Than marry her off without her consent.
Better kill a girl by poisoning
Than marry her off to an old man of sixty years.

---

[1] Gurajada Appa Rao, 'Preface' to the first edition of *Kanyasulkam* (1897). Setty Eswara Rao, ed., *Gurajada Rachanalu*: *Kanyasulkam* (*Mali Koorpu*) (Hyderabad, 2007 [1986]). The 'preface' was written in English.

Marriages with the mutual consent of bride and groom
Will fetch more happiness and pleasure,
And last [long] causing feast to our eyes
Than such marriages [as mentioned above].
O Andhra brothers! Please understand.[2]

The magnitude of the problem of child marriage and kanyasulkam (bride-price) in the Telugu-speaking districts of the Madras Presidency prompted a wide-ranging discourse among both women and men. Gurajada Appa Rao was one of several influential men who condemned these practices in their literary expressions; Bramhandam Kanakasundaramma's poem articulates women's resentment against them, and reflects the sustained campaigns that women undertook for marriage reform.

Tables 3.1–3.3 demonstrate the problem of child marriage in India, Madras Presidency, and the Telugu-speaking districts within the Presidency.

Table 3.1: Number of child marriages and child widows in India (0–15 years of age), as per 1931 Census

Age (Years)	Child Marriages		Child Widows	
	1921	1931	1921	1931
0–1	2,144	21,330	197	594
1–5	82,860	3,77,983	6,536	13,196
5–10	8,26,483	20,19,675	46,275	54,475
10–15	27,69,585	33,33,957	1,36,509	98,326
Total 0–15	36,81,072	57,52,945	1,89,517	1,66,591

Source: *Grihalakshmi*, December 1933, p. 833.[3]

Census figures revealed that in Madras presidency, the number of married girls under the age of 15 increased between 1901 and 1931. It increased from 92 to 108 among Hindus, 44 to 55 among Muslims and 25

[2]Bramhandam Kanakasundaramma, 'Abala Vilapamu' (Lamentation of Women), *Anasuya*, September–October 1919, pp. 38–44; for this reference, p. 44. Unless especially mentioned, all translations are by me.

[3]Statistics furnished by Muthulakshmi Reddy in her presidential address to the seventh ARMS held at Eluru on 4 November 1933. Data relates to population in Madras, Bengal, Bihar, Orissa and Assam. See 'Saptamandhra Rashtriya Mahilasabha, Eluru, 4 November 1933 lo Srimati Doctoru Muthulakshmi Reddygari Adhyakshopanyasamuloni Pradhana Bhagamulu', *Grihalakshmi*, December 1933, pp. 832–834.

to 35 among Christians per every 1000 girls married.[4] Between 1921–1931, 'infant marriages', that is, marriages of girls below the age of five, increased from 21 to 47 among Hindus.[5] The problem of child marriage was acute in coastal Andhra; in the Ceded Districts (the last five districts in Table 3.2), it was less prevalent.[6] Table 3.2 shows the proportion of marriages with girls under the age of 15 per 1,000 marriages.

In terms of a caste-wise analysis of infant marriages, over 1921–1931, they increased from 6 to 20 among Telugu Brahmins, from 8 to 15 among Odhras, 160 to 353 among Kalingas, 35 to 55 among Telagas, and 5 to 26 among Malas; the incidence decreased from 15 to 2 among Tamil Brahmins and from 2 to 1 among Tamil Vishwa Brahmins. The number of such marriages increased by 30 times among the Telugu Malas (a so-called Untouchable caste) compared to Tamil Malas. Between 1921 and 1931, while infant marriages among the Telugu Brahmins increased by more than three times, among the Telugu Malas, the increase was by more than five times. As per the 1931 Census, among the Karanams, for every 1,000 marriages, 142 were infant marriages. While there were 31 widowers aged below one year, there were 47 widows. Excepting one, who belonged to South Canara, all others were Telugus. Of them, 14 were from Ganjam, 34 from Visakhapatnam and the remaining are from other districts.[7]

---

[4] Garimella Satyanarayana, 'Andhrulu–Atibalya Vivahamulu' (Infant Marriages among the Andhra People), *Grihalakshmi*, May 1933, pp. 194–197, for this reference, p. 194.

[5] Ibid., pp. 194–195. It was Satyanarayana's definition.

[6] Garimella Satyanarayana concurs with the reading that child marriages were more prevalent in the coastal districts of Andhra. He sarcastically remarked that the 'more modern/civilised' districts such as East Godavari (plains), West Godavari (plains), Krishna and Guntur occupied top positions. The practice of child marriage was more prevalent among people living in the plains than among the 'superstitious' people living in the agencies (forest regions). He observed that in Ganjam district, child marriage was more common among the Kalingas and the Karanams than people of other castes. Interestingly, Satyanarayana also noted that as the Telugu districts moved northwards, closer to the Odhra districts (present-day Odisha), the number of child marriages increased, with Visakhapatnam ranking first. Ibid., p. 195.

[7] Ibid., p. 196. Explaining the reason as to why the problem was acute in the coastal Andhra region, Satyanarayana opined that it cannot be explained by the criterion of educational backwardness because Salem, the most educationally backward district in Madras Presidency, had less than one such marriage per every 1000. 'There does not appear to be any kind of relationship between higher state of education and the prevalence of such evil practices.' Though the Krishna, West Godavari and East Godavari districts ranked 4th, 5th and 7th in terms of educational status, they had a big number

Table 3.2: Girls aged 0–15 years who were married, per 1,000 marriages, as per 1931 Census

District	Number of Child Marriages (per 1,000 Marriages)	
	0–5 Years	5–10 Years
Visakhapatnam (plains)	111	442
East Godavari (plains)	104	193
Guntur	103	167
Ganjam (plains)	98	416
West Godavari	87	177
Krishna	57	145
Nellore	24	86
Visakhapatnam (agency)	13	77
Ganjam (agency)	08	416
East Godavari (agency)	04	96
Bellary	6.60	–
Kurnool	4.80	–
Cuddapah	3.35	–
Anantapur	2.00	–
Chittoor	1.87	–

Source: Garimella Satyanarayana, 'Andhrulu–Atibalya Vivahamulu' (Infant Marriages among the Andhra People), *Grihalakshmi*, May 1933, p. 195.

The percentage of girls married in infancy or childhood (out of the total population of girls) is shown in Table 3.3.[8]

Given the situation, marriage reform, particularly the eradication of child marriage and enforced widowhood, was a pressing concern for most educated women in Andhra in the late nineteenth and early twentieth

of infant marriages. 'I cannot say anything other than that it is a characteristic of the Andhras. This being so, they will have to try in every way to remove it,' Satyanarayana stressed.

[8]This estimate is based on the contemporary articles and calculations which heavily depended on census figures. For details, see Garimella Satyanarayana, 'Andhrulu-Atibalya Vivahamulu', *Grihalakshmi*, May 1933, p. 194. Cited in S. Inna Reddy, 'Social Reforms Movement in Andhra' (1998), PhD thesis submitted to the University of Hyderabad, p. 71. Inna Reddy mistook the month to be October; in fact, it is May.

Table 3.3: Married girls in the age group of 0–13 (in per cent)

Age Group	Percentage of Girls Married
Below 1 Year	0.8
1–2	1.2
2–3	2.0
3–4	4.2
4–5	6.6
5–10	19.3
10–13	38.1

Source: S. Inna Reddy, 'Social Reforms Movement in Andhra', p. 71.

centuries. As discussed in Chapters 1 and 2, women registered their disapproval through women's journals, voicing their anger at such practices and their harmful consequences. Convinced that child marriage was the root cause of the multiple difficulties faced by women, they launched a sustained campaign against it. Women intellectuals criticised child marriage on several grounds. They pointed out the adverse effects on the health of 'child-wives' because of early sexual intercourse, pregnancies and motherhood at very young ages, and the consequent high incidence of maternal and infant mortality.[9] Such marriages deprived girls of the 'bliss of childhood' and

[9] Vemuluri Ammiraju of Rajahmundry published a letter in *Telugu Zenana* about the postpartum death of her 20-year-old sister. A bereaved Ammiraju wrote that her sister delivered a baby on 14 March 1903, got sick seven days later, and died on 27 March. Blaming child marriage for her sister's 'premature death', she appealed to the 'elderly to work for eradicating such an evil practice, which caused such a grief to the country'. See 'Oka Uttaramu' (A Letter), *Telugu Zenana*, May 1903, p. 348.

Kashinathuni Ramabayamma provided data for Madras Presidency: In 1910, 1,26,088 boys and 1,09,097 girls died before reaching the age of 1 year. Further, she observed that though the number of maternal deaths could not be precisely calculated, women who died between the ages of 15–30 should be taken as maternal deaths. See 'Andhra Mahila Sabha: Sabhathipurali Upanyasamu' (Presidential Address delivered at the Andhra Mahila Mahasabha), *Hindu Sundary*, March 1913, p. 35. In India, out of the 100 live births, 19.4 and 18.7 died in 1921 and 1929, respectively. For every 1,000 deliveries in Madras Presidency, there were 17.5 maternal deaths out of 100 (source did not mention for which year this applied). See B. Venkatasubbaiah, 'Maatru, Shishu Samrakshanamu–Germany, Russia Deshamulaloni Padhdhatulu', (Protection of Mother and Child–Methods followed in Germany and Russia), *Grihalakshmi*, April 1936, pp. 99–106. In 1929, in Madras city alone, 3,000 maternal deaths occurred. See Kanuparti Varalakshmamma, *Sharada Lekhalu*, part 2, p. 31.

severely curtailed their educational opportunities. The early wifehood of girls led to acute anxiety, for they often could not stand up to unreasonable demands at their marital homes. Besides this were numerous issues: that the child-wife and her often older husband were often incompatible; that it resulted in the very high incidence of child widows; that they 'weakened' the 'Indian race'; that Europeans looked down on Indian culture due to such practices; and that they were against the 'original' religion of the Aryan Hindus. Briefly put, child marriage stifled the 'natural growth' of women's personality and individuality.

Therefore, women campaigned for an increase in the age of consent of girls, the postponement of consummation of marriages where the age could not be raised, and desired post-puberty marriages, particularly emphasising the 'consent' of girls. They adopted several methods to discourage child marriage. Through poignant descriptions of the hardships suffered by girl-wives, they sought to evoke sympathy among the larger public and condemned parents by subjecting them to social shame. The strategy of shaming was a particularly powerful means to discourage older men from marrying very young girls. This campaign worked through various literary genres, most commonly prose (essays), but also poetry, short stories, dialogues, polemics and novelettes. The most important aspect of women's essays was that they frequently made their case based on statistical evidence from decennial censuses conducted by the colonial government, which strengthened their stand. Words and phrases such as '*pillalu*' (small children), '*pasi koona*' (little infant), '*kasugayalu*' (literally, 'unripe fruit'; a mere child), '*kandlu teravani pasi paapalu*' (little infants, which have not yet opened their eyes), '*norerugani pasi pillalu*' (small children who have no mouth/voice, that is, extremely innocent children), '*mukku pachchalarani pasikoonalu*', '*bommala pendli*' (marriage of dolls), '*shishu vivaha mahopadravam*' (the great calamity of infant marriage), etc. were frequently used to move the hearts of readers. While the phrase '*baalya vivahamu*' is the Telugu equivalent for child marriage, '*atibalya vivahamu*' (literally 'very child marriage') may be translated as infant marriage.

Child Marriage is against the 'Original' Hindu Religion?

A recurring theme in arguments rejecting child marriage was their recourse to Hindu scriptures. They argued that child marriages were never a practice in India, for the Hindu scriptures emphasised choice-based adult marriages only. In an essay read out at the annual conference of the Sri Vidyarthini Samajamu at Kakinada, Damerla Sitamma observed that there was a 'lot of difference' between the past and present practices regarding marriage dharma, and the present 'tradition' of child marriage 'transgressed the [original] dharma'.[10] According to Sitamma, 'in the ancient times, men and women married, if they so desired, after they were grown up, and after the completion of education; if they did not like marriage, they observed *brahmacharya* (celibacy) all life'. [11] 'Marriage was optional then', she continued, 'But today, parents are getting their infant children, who have not yet opened their eyes [*kandlu teravani pasi paapalu*], married as if the world existed only for marriage'. Sitamma argued that 'we had evidence from the Vedas [and other scriptures] that marriage had to be decided by men and women independently with a man desiring a wife, and a woman desiring a husband'.[12] Gargi and Sulabha, the legendary Vedic women, remained eternal *brahmacharinis* (spinsters) because of the 'optional' nature of marriage in the past.

Criticising the practice of 'selling and purchasing of brides', Damerla Sitamma pointed to the prescription of Bodhayana, according to whom, a girl purchased by offering money (kanyasulkamu) could not become a wife and was therefore ineligible to participate in *yagna*s and *yaga*s. 'Kashyapa termed her to be a slave', she reminded her audience. She was worried that despite kanyasulkam being abhorred by the shastras as a 'horrible sin' (*ghora paatakamu*), it was still on the rise. Emphasising that 'our shastras and Puranas did not know what child marriage was', she remarked that 'all actions performed those days were all abhorred by the shastras' (*shastra dooshyamule*). According to her, it was because of 'ignorance' of the prescription of the shastras that kanyasulka marriages and dowry had increased. Hence, she appealed for the 'revival' of the original practice:

> Child marriages are the root-destroying insects [*verupurugulu*], which completely uproot the [original] religion of the *rishi*s [sages]. Kanyasulka [bride-price] and varashulka [dowry] are factors of great sins. We are feeling happy by indulging in such bad practices, boasting ourselves of being great people, [but, in fact] destroying all glory, and just like the blind

[10] Damerla Sitamma, 'Vyvahika Dharmamulu' (Marriage Dharmas), *Hindu Sundary*, July 1911, pp. 12–18.

[11] Citing a *shloka* from the *Atharvaveda*, she said that 'marriage should be by choice and after men and women completed their education'. Ibid.

[12] Ibid.

> man thinks that all the world is dark, we think that the present practices are exquisite, and fling our shastras to a corner. There are so many reasons for the extinction of all the [glorious] past practices. As and when time warranted, the wise have changed the shastras. It is now necessary to change the tradition according to the needs of the present time. What we need are good men and women who will revive the already existing provisions in the shastras rather than inventing new ones.[13]

Providing age-wise statistics of child marriages[14] and child widows,[15] Damerla Sitamma urged listeners to look at 'the magnitude of the problem', emphasising that the figures showed them 'how many widows were there even among the infants (*mukkupachchalarani pasikoonalu*)'. Stressing that 'they were in lakhs', she questioned 'if it was not the monstrous practice of child marriage, which was responsible for the [high incidence] of widows [even among] infants below the age of one year'.[16]

According to Kanchanapalli Kanakamma, though accepting gold and ornaments for the adornment of girls had been an accepted practice in the past, it was 'unacceptable' according to the shastras. She sought to prove her point by referring to certain shlokas and the commentary of Gulluka Bhattu. 'Receiving petty amount during *kanyadan* itself became a sale deed. When people were taking heavy amount and giving virgin girls, what else was it, if not selling virgin girls?'[17]

Referencing the Grihyasutras such as Sankhyayana, Khadira, Hiranyakeshi, Apasthambha and Gobhila, Damerla Sitamma stressed that post-puberty marriages were the 'real' ancient tradition. Citing the Gautama Sutra (Chapter–I, Sutra–I), according to which, only an adult woman who was not sexually active ('*yukta vayasugala kanya*') was eligible for marriage, and that the man had to independently see the prospective bride and arrange the marriage, she commented: 'When we had these many examples, it was deeply saddening to marry off such infants who had not even opened

---

[13] Ibid. pp. 15–16.

[14] She provided the following data. Child marriages performed below 1 year: 10,507; below 4 years: 2,58,760; below 9 years: 22,01,404; and below 14 years: 60,16,759. Total: 84,86,430. Ibid., p. 17.

[15] Child widows below the age of 1: 859; between 2–4: 1,886; between 3–4: 3,732; between 4–5: 8,189; between 5–10: 78,407; and between 10–15: 2,27,367. Total: 3,20,431. Ibid.

[16] Ibid.

[17] Kanchanapalli Kanakamma, 'Kanyasulka Nishedhamu' (Abolition of Bride-Price), *Hindu Sundary*, October 1914, pp. 3–4.

their eyes (*kandlu teravani kasugaayalu*)'.[18] She used the analogy that 'when we offered *daan* [alms], we gave ripened fruit, not the raw one, and everyone knew that'. Referring to Devayani and Mytreyi, 'who married as per their choice', she emphasised women's choice in marriage, not parents' coercion, and argued that, 'only then [when choice-based marriages became the norm], our country would develop'.[19]

Apart from being against the injunctions of the shastras, child marriages injured the physical health of the children married. Damerla Sitamma reflected on the 'indescribable' evil effects of child marriages thus:

> It is impossible to describe the evil effects of child marriages. If people are getting weaker, fickle-minded and insane day-by-day, child marriages are responsible for it. How can the brain of a boy of hardly 15-years-old and a girl of 12-years-old be mature? How can the children born to such couples, whose mental faculties as well as physical organs have not matured enough, become intelligent [*dhimantulu*]? This [child marriage] alone is responsible for untimely deaths. There is no reason other than this.[20]

Child Marriage Affects the Educational Opportunities of Girls

Achanta Rukminamma focused on how the practice of child marriage blocked educational opportunities of girls.[21] Comparing the dismal educational attainments of Indian children (out of 100 children of school-going age, hardly four attended school) with those of Japan, another Asian nation (where the corresponding figure was 47.5), she wrote that 'there was no doubt that child marriages were responsible for the removal of women's education [in India]'.

The practice of child marriage destroyed the educational opportunities of girls because 'hardly before the completion of 10 or 12 years, and much before they gained some knowledge of the world around them', they were removed from schools. 'What could they learn in this short span of 3–4 years? Their [lack of] knowledge was revealed in [their poor performance

[18] Damerla Sitamma, 'Vyvahika Dharmamulu' (Marriage Dharmas), *Hindu Sundary*, July 1911, pp. 12–18.

[19] Ibid.

[20] Ibid., p. 16.

[21] 'Stree Vidya, Vivahamunaku Tagina Vayassu' (Suitable Age for Women's Education and Marriage), *Hindu Sundary*, February 1912, pp. 20–25.

Image 3.1: Achanta Rukminamma

Source: *Grihalakshmi*, May 1935.

in] additions and subtractions alone. Their handwriting was illegible. They did not know even alphabets properly,' she elaborated.[22] Echoing a common refrain among upper caste reformers, she was dismayed that the 'Brahmin girls', and 'girls of reputable [Hindu] families', despite being 'more intelligent' than the native Christian women—who attained higher education, and even MA degrees—could not attain even minimum education because of child marriage.[23]

---

[22] Ibid., p. 21.

[23] This kind of comparison between the upper-caste and Shudra and Christian women's development can be found in several other women's writings. It perhaps helped whip up feeling of innate superiority among the upper castes. These comparisons were often worded as a 'threat' that their social 'inferiors' were superseding them by allowing women's education, and that 'upper castes' were in danger of lagging behind. The fear

Addressing a Hindu women's conference on 12 February 1912 in Barampuram (Brahmapur), Cary A. Tennent,[24] an American missionary, reflected on how the practice of child marriage stifled the educational opportunities and aspirations of women.[25] Recounting her experiences with native women, she compared the status of women in India with that of America. Informing Indians that 'women's education alone was responsible for the development of England and America', where women had the opportunities for education, employment and self-fulfillment, she promised them that 'if we improved [Hindu] women's education, the evils in society would disappear soon'. About the way child marriages obstructed women's educational advancement, she observed:

> I have visited several primary schools [in India]... [Among the students], I have seen many being married at 5 and 10 years old. Most importantly, the Komatis [Vaishyas] marry off [girls] in early childhood. A five-year-old girl told me that her twenty one-year-old husband was studying in a college. Out of the 80 students in the school, 12 are already married. The eldest among them is [just] 9 years old. The number of child widows is also large. If the situation is like this, how can they [girls] receive higher education? [Given the current practice] girls are bound to become wives by the time they are 11 or 12-years-old, and, at times, mothers even. The physical health of the child being delicate, children born to her are becoming feeble. In America, girls not only receive higher education

---

finds explicit articulation in an article for *Hindu Sundary*: 'If our Brahmin girls do not have proper education like our boys, they lag behind the Christian and Sudra castes' girls by 2 to 3 generations, and will be eligible only for cooking and carrying water because the Christians and Sudras are educating their girls'. See 'Vinnapamu' (An Appeal), *Hindu Sundary*, March 1912, pp. 32–33.

[24]She established the Hindu Marriage Reform Society, which by 1913 had 350 branches all over India. Contemporary Hindu women held her in high regard and expressed their gratitude for her contributions to the women of India. Christian missionary women such as Tennent appeared to Hindu women 'like God's angels' who 'remained unmarried to help others'. For one example of such appreciation, see Sattiraju Shyamalamba, 'Upanyasamu' (Lecture), *Hindu Sundary*, March 1912, p. 34. Shyamalamba felt that assembling with Tennent indicated Hindu women's 'new development' and 'an auspicious day in our life'. For Kalagara Pichchamma, she was a '*mahopakari*' (great benefactor), who was 'incarnated to uplift our India'. Kalagara Pichchamma, 'Balya Vivahamulavalanagalugu Nashtamulu' (Damages Caused by Child Marriages), *Hindu Sundary*, April 1912, pp. 7–10.

[25]Cary A. Tennent, 'Balya Vivahamu [Streela] Vunnata Vidyaku Aatankamu' (Child Marriage is an Obstacle to [Women's] Higher Education), *Hindu Sundary*, April 1912, pp. 11–14.

> but also are taught household management despite the presence of any number of domestic aids in their homes. There is no compulsion of marriage there. More significantly, if someone decides not to marry, and dedicates her life to help the orphans, such a woman is greatly honoured. They become lawyers, inspectors, journalists, doctors, etc. A few engage themselves in social service. Some work for people without expecting any salaries. We encourage women to take up such work.... In America, widows are treated compassionately.... We must give sufficient education to the Indian widows so that they become teachers in girls' schools.... Hindu women's social and educational advancement is my purpose. That is my happiness. It is none other than the [bad practice of] child marriage, which is obstructing [my purpose and dream].[26]

Mosalikanti Ramabayamma commented that the popular saying '*Vivaho Vidya Naashaya*' (With marriage is destroyed education), applied to women also.[27] Terming the performance of child marriage a 'horrible act', Kalagara Pichchamma held it responsible for the 'deteriorated condition of our country'. She observed that 'there was a complete lack of education, and women's education was further lower than that of men'; child marriage aggravated the problem of women's education.[28] The educational deprivation of women due to child marriage created multiple problems in one's domestic life, turning it into a territory of 'perennial strife' between wife and husband, thus sapping any sense of marital bliss.[29] Referring to Samyukta, Manjari, Vimala and Indira, who were said to have received education, exhibited courage entering the battlefield and in killing their enemies, Kalagara Pichchamma said that all of them married as adults and according to their wish and choice. Following their example, boys and girls should marry as per their wish. She proposed the right marriageable age to be at least 16 years for girls and 25 years for boys.[30]

However, women like Gade Chudikudutamma doubted the efficacy of appeals for post-puberty marriages, and of parents' capacity to educate girls till that age, given practical constraints.[31] Unequivocally stating that

[26] Ibid.

[27] Mosalikanti Ramabayamma, 'Rajaswalanantara Vivahamulu' (Post-Puberty Marriages), *Hindu Sundary*, March 1912, pp. 22–32.

[28] Kalagara Pichchamma, 'Balya Vivahamulavalanagalugu Nashtamulu' (Damages Caused by Child Marriages), *Hindu Sundary*, April 1912, pp. 7–10.

[29] Ibid., p. 10. For a detailed discussion, see Chapter 5, this volume.

[30] Ibid., p. 8.

[31] Gade Chudikudutamma, 'Barampuram Streela Sabha' (The Barampuram Women's Conference), *Hindu Sundary*, April 1912, pp. 14–16.

'marrying off girls in childhood' was an 'unjust and injurious' practice that caused the 'degeneration of our society', she hoped that 'we could abolish this practice now' because of the presence of 'benevolent' British rule.[32] Pointing to the problem of unavailability of suitable grooms for adult women and, most importantly, the lack of adequate higher educational institutions for girls (compounded with the economic status of parents), she settled at suggesting that parents should not marry off their daughters before the age of 10–12 years. However, those who could afford to keep their daughters unmarried until after puberty may do so. Analysing the entire issue, she said:

> To arrange post-puberty marriage of girls, it is becoming difficult to find suitable grooms in various castes. Suppose we keep girls unmarried until after their puberty, what is the use?... Why because, we do not have sufficient number of colleges to educate adolescent girls. Such colleges are in [far away] big towns such as Madras and Calcutta, not in small towns. [Moreover], not all parents have the means to send their daughters to such big towns. Because such schools imparting higher education are not in small towns, of what use is it to keep our girls unmarried until they attain puberty? Given the reasons explained above, it is very difficult to keep girls unmarried even after they attain puberty. Therefore, I feel that we can arrange the marriage of our girls between 10–12 years old, and until then, we can educate them by sending to schools. Hence, I am emphasising that, today, all must decide that we will not arrange the marriage of our girls before they are 10-years-old. If it is possible for someone to keep their daughters unmarried beyond 10-years-old, they may do so.[33]

[32] Ibid., p. 15.

[33] She is quite practical in assessing the contemporary situation. What is remarkable is the direct relationship she has established between the availability of adequate girls' higher educational institutions and increasing their age of marriage. Was she indirectly urging for the establishment of higher educational institutions for girls in small towns, and blaming the lack of the same? If there were more such institutions, girls' parents may be persuaded into keeping their daughters unmarried even after puberty. Establishment of girls-only higher educational institutions was a pre-condition to proposing and practicing post-puberty marriages. One wishes she had expanded on this argument. Ibid. However, at a later stage, she clearly spoke in favour of post-puberty marriages of girls. In her presidential address to the sixth annual function of the Barampuram Women's Conference (1920), she stated: 'Times have changed. The idea [is] that nation cannot attain independence unless women enjoy independence. The good time of treating women equal to men has come.' Therefore, 'a few more reforms [apart from educating women] were to be effected in society. We must remove the deep rooted practice of child

Child Marriage Deprives Girls of their Childhood

Women held child marriage responsible for depriving Indian girls of the 'blissful' experience of childhood. According to Achanta Rukminamma, child marriage was not only alarming but also cruel and shameful.[34] Her article in *Hindu Sundary* was published under an emotive sub-heading: 'Hindu girls do not experience childhood at all'. Explaining this further, she wrote:

> A teacher keeps telling me that Hindu girls are not at all experiencing childhood. This is very true with regard to our Brahmin girls. Till the age of 7 or 8, they are treated like children. [Thereafter], thinking marriageable age has arrived the moment girls enter the eighth year, parents marry them off without taking into consideration their likes or dislikes. By 11–12 years of age, the girls are forced to lift the burden of family life over their heads. Perhaps, by the time this child completes 12 years of age, she becomes the mother of a child. In such a situation, where does she get the opportunity to enjoy childhood? In the European country [*sic*], people really treat a 12-year-old girl as a child. There, girls [of that age] concentrate on their books, plays, toys, songs, etc.[35]

Achanta Rukminamma emphasised that girls should not be married off until they finish their 'complete education' and acquired the capacity and skills to run her family. 'It is not merely age that should determine when girls married. We ought to take into account the wish/will of girls. This meant, each girl should marry only after ascertaining whether she had the capacity and desire to manage the new job [of wifehood] accruing to her upon marriage'.[36]

Several others joined her in mourning the loss of girls' childhood. Mosalikanti Ramabayamma wrote that 'when a girl was to enjoy playing with toys and singing songs, the big boulder called *mangalasutra* [sacred thread] was tied' around her neck, and therefore she 'lost all happiness of childhood', and faced the troubles in the in-laws' home'.[37] 'The little girl' was

---

marriage and perform post-puberty marriages.' See 'Vividha Vishayamulu' (Various Matters), *Anasuya* 3, 8–9, February and March, 1920, pp. 4–5.

[34] Achanta Rukminamma, 'Stree Vidya, Vivahamunaku Tagina Vayassu' (Suitable Age for Women's Education and Marriage), *Hindu Sundary*, February 1912, pp. 20–25.

[35] Ibid., pp. 22–23.

[36] Ibid., p. 25.

[37] Mosalikanti Ramabayamma, 'Rajaswalanantara Vivahamulu' (Post-Puberty Marriages), *Hindu Sundary*, March 1912, pp. 22–32.

forced to think that 'it was her life's mission to swim the [dangerous ocean of] family life'.[38] Apart from in-laws, particularly the mother-in-law who had a reputation for turning young girls' lives into 'hell', the situation worsened if the child-wife was unskilled in various aspects of domestic management, which indeed was most often the case. Kanuparti Varalakshmamma's fictional autobiography—*Premalata*: *Sweeya Charitramu* (Autobiography of Premalata) explores in great detail the taunts and torments that child-wives often suffered at the hands of their mothers-in-law.[39]

'Nirbandha Dampatyamu': Child Marriage Leads to Enforced Conjugality

That child marriage led to 'enforced conjugality' (*nirbandha dampatyamu*) and the consequent bitterness in domestic life, culminating in emotional estrangement of the married couple, ran one argument in the *Hindu Sundary*.[40] Arguing particularly from the point of view of men and mothers-in-law, the author (presumably a man) observed that child marriages frustrated the desire for compatibility between the conjugal couple. 'If their attitudes and tastes did not match as they grew up, quarrels became

[38] Ibid., p. 28.

[39] This fictional autobiography is remarkable for it shed light not only on the patriarchal power relations in the family but also put the same to ruthless criticism. It reflected on domestic violence against child-wives and raised a serious challenge to merciless mothers-in-law. The heroine, Premalata, was wedded off at an early age and neglected by her ailing husband. She became a victim of domestic drudgery. Her mother-in-law always tortured her with barbs and insults. The magnitude of torture was so great that she could not get proper food or taste the coffee she had prepared and had to be content with being 'half-hungry' all the time. While her natal home was a haven, where everyone attended to her, the marital home was a kind of hell where she had to attend to everybody. The most interesting part of the 'autobiography' was Premalata's appeal for the humane treatment of daughters-in-law. Most importantly, she earnestly appealed to parents to train their daughters well in the art of domestic management right from childhood so that 'they would not face the same murderous difficulties she had to suffer at the in-laws' place'. See Kanuparti Varalakshmamma, *Premalata: Sweeya Charitramu* (*Autobiography of Premalata*), *Anasuya*, July–August, pp. 13–29, and September–October 1919, pp. 9–30.

[40] 'Rajaswalanantara Vivahamulu Sarva Saukhyamulaku Hetuvulu' (Post-Puberty Marriages are always Beneficial for they bring Happiness), *Hindu Sundary*, July 1909, pp. 29–32. A man perhaps wrote the essay. He used a new phrase 'enforced conjugality'.

inevitable, but it was not possible to break the marriage. The result was enforced conjugality causing perennial misery'.[41] Linking this frustration to the deeply-contested issue of sex work, he was certain that it was this maladjustment that compelled men to seek sex outside the marital domain. 'Many [unfortunate] men pretended to have a smooth family life partly because of the fear of elders, partly because of the modesty they acquired through education, and partly because of social fear: under compulsion and against their conscience, they produced children', he argued. Such husbands feared that 'mutual quarrels between wife and husband affected the healthy growth of their children' and therefore 'surrendered to foolish wives pretending as if they were companionate conjugal couple.' Abstaining from 'elaborating' on this issue for it was 'not good [shameful/insulting] to the race of men', he pitied that 'only their hearts understood the misery caused to them by their [child] wives.' He concluded that 'companionate couples, who really enjoyed their family lives, were very few'.[42]

The child daughters-in-law proved to be a big headache to mothers-in-law for the former 'reached the in-law's homes in an uncivilised state and the burden of training and righting their behavior fell over the heads of the latter, and the ensuing frictions in the process were termed as the travails of *kodandrikam*'. This resulted in 'misunderstanding[s] between the parents of the boy and the girl'. Men, according to him, suffered the most in the entire process:

> As the young husband is dependent on his parents, he cannot stand by his wife [in domestic conflict] resulting in the wife losing affection for him. He too cannot develop love for such a wife, who is not affectionate towards him, and who is worthless in the opinion of his people. Even when the couples are compatible, the husband cannot remove the difficulties of his wife because of his dependence, and the wife is worried because of the difficulties caused to the husband because of her. Whatever it may be, they produce children at a very young age. We can easily imagine how strong, knowledgeable, patriotic, and courageous the children born of such couples, who did not have physical maturity, proper knowledge, mutual love, happiness, and fearlessness, will be. Only the experienced know the fate of such children nourished by such a mother, who is married while being a child herself.... Women are the lifeline of a society. A society where their conditions are not good is either stagnant or dead. Whatever efforts we may put, so far as child marriages exist, women cannot receive

[41] Ibid., p. 30.

[42] Ibid., p. 31–32.

education. Unless women's education is improved, they cannot become independent. Unless women enjoy independence, society cannot attain higher status.[43]

Parents of Girls are Culpable

Women held 'stone-hearted' parents of girls culpable for the dismal state of affairs. Varanasi Kameshwari remarked that it was a girl's misfortune to be born to Hindu parents, since they 'treated the birth of girls as a jail (*chera*) [sentence], and to release themselves soon, they married them off to some old man or a weak fellow, without bothering about the couple's happiness', thereby absolving themselves of any responsibility. 'If they [parents] were really concerned about their happiness', she reasoned, 'why were they so enthusiastic about performing such marriages'? 'Being unkind, only our Hindus performed such marriages, not people of other religions,' Kameshwari claimed.[44] Mosalikanti Ramabayamma complained that parents 'started searching for a groom the very moment a girl was born and arranged her marriage without thinking whether the girl was eligible for the post of best housewife'.[45]

A dialogic piece written by Lingam Sundaramma, a student of Standard VI at the Government Girls' School in Srikakulam, forthrightly attacked child marriage. Sundaramma blamed parents for 'spoiling their innocent daughters' by arranging their marriages with 'some old man or a sick fellow'. In doing so, they 'became responsible for uprooting the *kalpavriksha* [the wish-fulfilling tree in Hindu mythology] of a happy family life'. Imposing familial duties onto these girls right from childhood, according to her, was the same as hanging a clog below the neck of a bull to prevent it from straying (*aabotuku gudikarranu kattinatlu*). It was better that parents performed the marriages of dolls than child marriages. Ensuring the ruin of innocent children by performing child marriages, simply for the happiness of elders, was a 'sinful act' which was like 'sport to the cat, death to the rat' (*pilliki chelagatamu, yelukaku praana sankatamu annatlu*). She stressed that girls should marry 'only after they gained the

[43] Ibid.

[44] Varanasi Kameshwari, 'Mana Hindu Vitantuvula Dusthiti' (Miserable Condition of our Hindu Widows), *Hindu Sundary*, April 1905, pp. 1–5, for this reference, pp. 2–3.

[45] Mosalikanti Ramabayamma, 'Rajaswalanantara Vivahamulu' (Post-Puberty Marriages), *Hindu Sundary*, March 1912, p. 23.

knowledge of good and bad' and prayed to elders to abstain from and 'eradicate such sinful acts'.[46]

Kashinathuni Ramabayamma criticised families where 'ever since a girl was born, bargains for marriage started taking place', and 'the sacred tie was tied in her neck at the earliest possible time'.[47] In a blistering attack on the recklessness of parents in the wellbeing of girls, another writer, Kalagara Pichchamma, remarked that 'they [parents] arranged the marriage of infants just the same way one arranged the marriage of dolls' (*bommala pendli*). While the 'married infants did not comprehend what marriage was', parents 'enjoyed watching the rituals… least bothered about the damages' and 'subjected them [girls] to innumerable difficulties'. Parents, she noted, 'anxiously awaited' the time of girls' exit from their homes.[48] 'What for marriage? For the happiness of the girl or, in the greed of the property of the groom', she angrily questioned. Such families had no sympathies for the suffering of girl widows: following sexist double standards, they did not conduct remarriages for women even as widower remarriages were widely accepted.[49]

Kanchanapalli Kanakamma was deeply critical of the 'commodification' of girls in transactions of the marriage market. Kanakamma maintained that '[the] natural love of parents for the girls was destroyed' when they treated their daughters as 'commodities to sell'. Such parents did not wish for their daughters' welfare and development—arranging a girl's marriage with a virtuous man did not yield much in terms of material wealth. 'As greed increased, so did the harm to girls', she noted:

> If we think a little bit how harmful it proves to the girl, our hearts burst [*gundelaviyunu*]. One man is sick and old-aged, but wealthy; the other is young [and healthy but not wealthy and, hence, cannot offer kanyasulkam]. Parents, who want to become rich by filling their stomachs with the money of kanyasulkam, offer their daughter to the first, [not the latter]. Therefore, harm is certain for the girl. Though selling of girls is prohibited in the smritis and in fact treated as a sin, and the hells it will

---

[46] However, she did not specify the right marriageable age. Lingam Sundaramma, 'Balya Vivaha Sambhashana' (A Dialogue on Early Marriages), *Telugu Zenana*, April and May 1905, pp. 348–349.

[47] See 'Andhra Mahila Sabha: Sabhathipurali Upanyasamu' (All-Andhra Women's Conference: Presidential Address), *Hindu Sundary*, March 1913, p. 34.

[48] Kalagara Pichchamma, 'Balya Vivahamulavalanagalugu Nashtamulu' (Damages Caused by Child Marriages), *Hindu Sundary*, April 1912, pp. 7–10.

[49] Ibid.

lead to are clearly explained, to those people, who do not care and have fallen prey to the vampire of the greed of money, there is no such thing as discretion! Their hearts are like a hard stone.[50]

'O You the Old Grooms! Do not Slit the Throats of Virgin Girls': Against Old Men Marrying Small Girls

Older men who were eager to marry young girls,[51] and parents who readily arranged such matches in greed of money,[52] were severely lampooned. A piece published in *Vivekavathi* ridiculed old men who married 'small girls'. It compared the 'tali' (sacred marriage thread) with the hangman's noose. Accusing 'greedy parents' who sold off their daughters to men as old as 'grandpas', it cursed them and declared that 'such parents would be ruined'. Though short, this dialogic piece was a powerful burlesque. When the first character, Kamalamba, asked whether the bridegroom was good-looking, the second character Neelamaba quipped: '[It is] not necessary to talk about his beauty. He is as tall as the barb tree. He is bent probably because he is crooked or old. Bald headed, white bearded, and cannot say about his eyesight. But one thing is certain that he does not have teeth; if he speaks, we will get wet [from a shower of spit].'[53]

---

[50] Kanchanapalli Kanakamma, 'Kanyasulka Nishedhamu' (Abolition of Bride-Price), *Hindu Sundary*, October 1914, pp. 3–4.

[51] *Vasavi* published the news of 60-year-old man who married an 11-year-old girl in Machilipatnam under the title, 'A Strange Marriage'. See 'Vaartalu: Vichitra Vivahamu' (News: A Strange Marriage), *Vasavi*, July 1926, p. 34. Such old men were variously criticised and ridiculed as '*musali bhallookamulu*' (old bears). See Ayitaraju Jeedikanti Rama Rao, 'Hyndava Yuvati Duravastha' (Miserable State of Hindu Women), *Hindu Sundary*, March 1912, p. 9.

[52] An octogenarian married a 13-year-old girl in Tirupati (perhaps in July 1887) by offering Rs. 10,000 to the girl's father. Commenting on the 'sorrowful act', the *Hindujana Samskarini* appealed to the government to ban such marriages. See *Hindujana Samskarini*, August 1887, p. 18. A writer, 'Oka Sanghikudu' (a pseudonym), wrote to one journal about the kanyasulka marriage of a certain Rattaiah (age not mentioned) with a 6-year-old girl named Minamma, the fifth daughter of Chodavarapu Brahmaiah, in which Rs. 450 was paid as kanyasulkam. See 'Oka Sanghikudu', 'Vivaha Vaartalu' (News of Marriages), *Prabodhini*, June 1915, p. 24. The *Prabodhini* was a caste-specific, pro-reform monthly published by the Vishwabrahmins. The marriage was most likely within that caste.

[53] See 'Balya Vivahamu' (Child Marriage), *Vivekavathi*, July 1915, p. 302.

In a short story titled 'Vrudhdha Bharta, Bala Bharya' (Old Husband and Child Wife), Vadrevu Sundaramma brought to light such greed in parents.[54] The Brahmin parents in the story married off their 13-year-old educated girl to an old widower aged 70 years, who had already married thrice and had a son and a widowed daughter, by accepting Rs. 1,400 and some gold as kanyasulkam. While the parents were settling the bargain, the girl resisted the marriage arguing that 'she liked neither the groom nor the gold'. Wondering how the 'old grandfather could desire marriage', she prayed to parents to give her in marriage to 'an English educated young man'. But the greedy parents forcibly married her off. Appalled by this, the enraged girl thought, '*Chhee Chhee*! Are they my parents anymore? They will eat up the money and gold. This old man will die soon and I will have to suffer in his home all life turning into a domestic drudge.'

Having made up her mind to accompany her old husband, she said:

> Grandfather [*tatagaru*], I go with you. If you do not take me along with you now, I will die plunging into a well. Then you will lose both money and wife. Because they have sold me off, I should not continue in their home any longer. Shall we keep an animal in the sellers' home after we have purchased it? I will go with you [at this very moment].

After reaching the 'grandfather's home,' one day, she pleaded with him:

> Grandfather, you are not at the suitable age to marry me. You give me in marriage to your [young] son. You do not have to give me the measure of a gram of gold. I will serve you more than your daughter will. Why talk so many things? Is it not [true] that in the greed of money you married off your daughter to an old man? Your son-in-law died within one month of the marriage. Similarly, I will also meet the same fate of your daughter. You are an elderly person. Therefore, think well, and marry me to your son.

Having mulled it over, the old man arranged the marriage of his son and 'wife', and the author concluded that the wedded young couple lived amicably. Sundaramma's clever parody brought out the inherent contradictions of such an episode. Interestingly, throughout the story the girl 'wife' addressed her old 'husband' as 'grandfather'. The story certainly was outrageous since it ended with the marriage of stepmother and stepson. 'But was the practice of child marriage less outrageous?' is perhaps the question that the author wanted to evoke.

[54] *Vivekavathi*, December 1912, pp. 85–87.

Kanuparti Varalakshmamma's short story, 'Kanakavalli', published in two installments in *Anasuya*, comprehensively exposed the disastrous consequences of getting young girls married to old men.[55] The protagonist, 9-year-old Kanakavalli, 'an intelligent and beautiful girl studying in the fifth standard and a darling lass of her parents', was given in marriage to a 50-year-old man named Bhairavamoorthy, who lived in the faraway Nizam state. He already had a 10-year-old son from his first marriage. Bhairavamoorthy offered a huge bride price—jewellery worth Rs. 2,000 and valuable sarees to both the bride and her mother. The greedy mother felt happy thinking it to be a 'good match'. However, 'Kanakam [Kanakavalli] did not like the match at all. She was upset looking at the [grandfather-like] groom. But, who was there to bother about her consent?' Varalakshmamma complained that in matters concerning marriages, parents enjoyed 'excessive power' and the 'consent of the girls was least thought about'.

Varalakshmamma's description of Bhairavamoorthy was primed to spark revulsion towards such grooms:[56]

> He is about 50-years-old.... There are wrinkles on his face. His eyes have gone deep inside. There are no more than two to three teeth in his mouth. May be for fashion or may be because he cannot walk properly, he walks with the help of a stick. Perhaps he is suffering from vision deficiency, he reads books, holding them at some distance and with the help of spectacles.

No sooner did Kanakavalli's menarche appear than her husband arrived demanding consummation of the marriage, 'just the same way an eagle rushed down to catch a mouse'.[57] Soon after, he took her away to his place. At his home, his widowed sister Gauramma 'ruled the country of home most autocratically', placing the burden of managing the home on Kanakavalli and causing great suffering. Used to the bad habit of backbiting, she frequently complained against Kanakavalli, resulting in the latter's being brutally beaten by her irate husband. The authour pitied that 'like a Donda fruit in a crow's beak, our dear Kanakam fell into the hands of this old husband' (*kaaki mukkuku donda pandu gattinatlu*).[58]

---

[55] *Anasuya*, April 1924, pp. 34–44 and May 1924, pp. 13–24.

[56] *Anasuya*, April 1924, p. 39.

[57] Ibid., p. 43.

[58] Donda is a bright red fruit. The proverb is used to convey the absurdity of 'a beautiful thing possessed by a person who is unworthy of it.' Captain M. W. Carr, *A Selection of Telugu Proverbs Translated and Explained* (New Delhi, 1986 [1868]), p. 44.

One day, when her neighbour Sundaramma enquired about her wellbeing, Kanakavalli replied with tears welling in her eyes:

> What happiness? My happiness ended in my natal home itself. I came here with two things accompanying me—grief and sufferings… I know quite well that I will no longer have happy days. What can I do? This is the good thing done to me by my mother. Had my mother, who raised me so affectionately because I am her only child, not married me to this old fellow out of her greed for jewellery, I would have been very happy.… Without heeding the words of my good father, she at once broke the creeper of my fortune. Because of her deed, I am forced to swim the ocean of grief all through my life like this.… How can I be happy when my husband, who is under the influence of the wicked Gauramma [her sister-in-law], is treating me cruelly like the saying 'for an old man, a young wife is like poison'? I am not worried because my husband is old. As you said, I will treat it to be God's wish. But I am worried for the reason that he does not know my heart and ill treats me.… In the name of tradition [*achara*], I am not allowed to eat three times a day. How-many-ever times my father requested him to send me to my natal home for these last three years, he refused and, furthermore, hurled any number of abuses at my father. He got the compound walls of home raised the same way the walls of a jail are raised. They say that, otherwise, I may tread the wrong paths.… Elder sister! No more I will have happiness in this family life. Only Gangabhavani [water in some lake, well or river] has the capacity to provide me comfort. Day by day, I am getting more dejected. I do not know when God will pity me [by bringing death].

Unable to tolerate the routine torture, Kanakavalli committed suicide. Her suicide note, published in a Telugu newspaper under the title 'Letter of a Girl Who Committed Suicide', stated:[59]

> O parents of girls! A word to you—
> Please do not give your loving daughters over to old fellows either in the greed of money or jewellery and do not tread the path of unrighteousness.… Have you really understood what girls mean? They are such virtuous beings [*punya sheelalu*], who always desire the wellbeing of their natal home even if they are undergoing intense suffering. Therefore, it is your due responsibility to desire their welfare more and arrange suitable marriages for them. It is not at all just on the part of parents to apply butter in one eye and lime in the other [i.e. treat sons and daughters differently]. Daughters are the same as sons. Moreover, the daughters go

[59] *Anasuya*, May 1924, pp. 20–22.

to others' homes [in-laws' homes] much before they are twelve-years-old. Therefore, O you the parents! Marry your daughters to suitable grooms and relieve yourselves from sin and them from suffering. This is my humble prayer to you.

And you, the old grooms! A word to you! Do not trouble yourselves and the small virgin girls by marrying them. You may marry them hoping that they will relieve you from the difficulties of old age; however, your wish will be a short-lived one. Just the same way a kingdom will turn averse to a wicked king, the young and beautiful girls will always have aversion for you, and not love and affection. Alas! Why are you so mad? Can the East and the West ever meet? Can darkness and light ever be friendly? Can love and affection exist between an old husband and a young wife? No, never. It is three times certain. Therefore, O you the old grooms! Do not slit the throats of virgin girls with your foolishness. This is all I have to pray to you.

Yours,
Dear daughter appeals, with folded hands,
to the great people of Andhra, Kanakavalli.

Varalakshmamma brilliantly wove several related aspects into the story. Like many of her contemporaries,[60] she blamed the practice on 'uneducated, rough and foolishly stubborn' women who had immeasurable 'greed of jewellery'. They pressurised their 'good' husbands into marrying off their daughters quite early. She exposed how the emerging demand for heavy dowries forced parents of moderate means to 'sell' their daughters to old men.[61]

[60] In another short story, this one by S. Annapoorna Devi, the author blamed the mother, Shantamma, and grandmother for the miserable end of 7-year-old Kamala. Despite reservations expressed by Kamala's father, Shantamma insisted on arranging Kamala's marriage with the 30-year-old Rama Rao, who 'did not have proper health' and died soon, leaving the 7-year-old Kamala widowed. At the age of 14, 'when she gained the capacity to think', Kamala asked her mother when she would be married. Shantamma replied that Kamala had already been married and widowed. Unable to come to terms with the truth, a shocked Kamala died within a week. The devastated mother, beating her breast, realized that 'she only [had] slit the throat of her daughter' by getting her married so young. See S. Annapoorna Devi, 'Nene Nee Gontu Kositini' (I Only Have Slit Your Throat), *Grihalakshmi*, May 1928, pp. 56–58.

[61] In the story, prospective grooms demanded a dowry of Rs. 500–1,000 to marry Kanakavalli. Varalakshmamma commented that 'these days when dowry demands are high, how could the daughters of Subbarayadu, who had moderate means, get good matches.' She succintly demonstrated how excessive dowry demands forced parents to take recourse to selling of brides. *Anasuya*, April 1924, p. 35.

Varalakshmamma's treatment of the burgeoning profession of marriage brokers and shrewd professional matchmakers is equally instructive. She exposed the heinousness of the marriage broker Peraiah Shastry, indicting the 'business' of matchmaking, wherein the businessmen habitually told a bundle of lies and lured greedy parents, particularly mothers, into accepting older grooms for their daughters:

> Ah! My heart shivers, if I think of that trade and the trader. The pen is not moving ahead. Tear-filled eyes are unable to see the pages properly. However, with the grand expectation that, if the heinous deeds [*duragatamulu*] of this Shastry are explained, our readers may not fall prey to the magic of such wicked Brahmins and avoid offering their daughters, I am briefly narrating his evil work. By getting the beautiful, virtuous and educated and innocent girls married to old monkeys, who cannot stand up from the places they are seated… the treachery this Shastry has done to the innocent girls is simply beyond description. I do not know how the proverb, 'you must get a marriage conducted even if it involves telling a hundred lies', came into existence; but, following this, this Shastry has slit the throats of uncountable number of girls. Because of his blessings… many old men became bridegrooms. This wicked Brahmin lured the greedy and foolish parents and spoilt the lives of a number of girls. He turned their lives into perennial misery.… Like this, he amassed huge wealth. He proved to be a cruel hunter to the girls. No, no. The hunter causes pain to the bird only at the time of squeezing its throat. Because he [Peraiah Shastry] causes perennial misery to girls all through their lives, we cannot compare him to a hunter. Then, how to call him? Shall we call him the messenger of Yama [*yama bhatudu*], the God of death? No, this also does not suit because the yama bhatudu punishes the guilty only. Because he is a malefactor to the extremely innocent and powerless infants, he is an extremely cruel fellow. He proved so ferocious to girls, the same way a tiger was to a lamb.

In a truly remarkable set of developments, Varalakshmamma got the guilty punished by the colonial state.[62] Demanding a law banning men aged 40 years and above from marrying young women,[63] Varalakshmamma concluded the story with the following remarks.

---

[62] Both Bhairavamoorthy and his sister Gauramma were imprisoned. Experiencing the result of his 'sin', he died eighteen months after the death of his wife. The termagant Gauramma was punished with a rigorous jail sentence of 12 years. *Anasuya*, May 1924, p. 23.

[63] Kanuparti Varalakshmamma, *Sharda Lekhalu*, September 1930, pp. 186–191.

> At last, the lives of our Kanakavalli, her parents, and Bhairavamoorthy, who married her, ended up so miserably like this. The reading world of sisters may read the story fully and carefully, understand the moral it intends to convey, and be [wise and] vigilant, while arranging the marriages of their daughters.[64]

The story was illustrated with the following pictures:

Image 3.2A: Mahalakshmamma, the mother, requesting the *purohit* to arrange a 'good match' for her daughter

[64] Ibid., p. 24.

Image 3.2B: The bridegroom Bhairavamoorthy, who is like a skeleton and cannot walk without the aid of a stick

Source: *Anasuya*, April 1924.

Another critic of the practice of child marriage was Achanta Satyavatamma, who advocated companionate marriages. She stressed that girls must be married to young men so as to ensure 'companionate conjugal life'. She was extremely unhappy that girls who remained unmarried till 14 years of age, in accordance with the Sarda Act, often ended up marrying older men rather than young men. Invoking the proverb, 'he watched [the field] until the harvest, and then let it go to the jackals' [*eenagachi nakkala palynatlundi*],[65] she appealed to young men to realise the 'objective' of the

[65] Captain M. W. Carr, *A Selection of Telugu Proverbs Translated and Explained* (New Delhi, 1986 [1868]), p. 23.

Sarda Act and shun making dowry demands that were scuttling marriages between evenly-matched couples. They would thereby 'teach a lesson to the prospective older grooms, who were eagerly waiting to devour at once the jewel-like girls'.[66]

In a one-act play published in *Andhra Mahila*, Kamala, the 16-year-old prospective bride addressed her 55-year-old widower-groom as 'grandfather' (*tatagaru*), much like the protagonist of Sundaramma's story.[67] The widower, Panakala Rao, offered a bride-price to orphaned Kamala's uncle and aunt. Kamala was made to believe that the match was with Panakala Rao's 20-year-old nephew and agreed to the match. On the wedding day, seeing Panakala Rao dressed like a bridegroom, she laughed and told her aunt to see the strange thing that 'the grandfather… looked like a co-groom ('*toda pelli kodukulaaga*')'.

Upon learning that he was the actual groom, Kamala refused to marry Panakala Rao and told her aunt that 'she would rather agree for death, but not that marriage'. Questioning her uncle (*maamaiah*), she pointed out 'how horrible it was that they showed her the young man but arranged her marriage with the old man in the greed of money'. Turning to Panakala Rao, she said:

> *Tathaguru*!… I am saying by taking an oath on God. Ever since you [and your nephew] came to see me, I thought him to be the groom…. People assume the young men to be grooms. Who will assume the accompanying old men to be grooms!… Had I known the truth, I would have refused then itself.

When Panakala Rao, 'possessed by the devil of lust', sought to 'forcibly marry her', Kamala cried out:

> *Tathaguru*, I salute you. You are my only hope. You are an elderly person. To me you are like a father. Tell me, if you had a daughter like me, would you have arranged such a marriage? Please pardon me for asking like this. Who will listen to my grief? If you really have any sympathy for me, marry me to that boy. I am telling the truth. I built many mansions of hope thinking that he is the groom. You are educated. You have a heart. Do not you know well about the fate of people who have such marriages? Look, I am falling at your feet. I will not leave them unless you give me the boon. Fulfill the wish of your daughter.

---

[66] Achanta Satyavatamma, 'Sarda Chattamu – Yuvakula Badhyata' (Sarda Act and the Responsibility of Young Men), *Grihalakshmi*, August 1940, pp. 328–329.

[67] Samayamantri Rajyalakshmi Devi, 'Katha Addamga Tirigindi' (The Story has taken a Wrong Turn), *Andhra Mahila*, 19 February 1944, pp. 29–34.

Kamala's appeals sparked a change of heart and Panakala Rao, grateful that 'she taught him a lesson' and saved him from 'sinning', arranged her marriage with his nephew, as per her wish.[68]

Endorsing the views of Christian missionary women that Hindus 'sold off' their children, Gade Chudikudutamma lashed out at girls' parents for 'looting the grooms' families to the extent of pushing them to poverty by selling their daughters'. Writing that the practice of kanyasulkam and *varasulkam* should be stopped, she reiterated that such practices represented two kinds of 'sin': 'Firstly, they almost ruined the grooms' families. Secondly, they spoilt their daughters.'[69]

Demanding Post-puberty, Choice-based Adult Marriages

Mosalikanti Ramabayamma, the editor of *Hindu Sundary*, launched a comprehensive programme against child marriage and advocated post-puberty marriages.[70] Holding the practice of child marriage as 'the most important reason' for the 'degenerate conditions of women', she emphasised that it 'transgressed two principles—one that of shastras, the other that of nature'. Most child marriages 'ended up either in incompatibility or in producing unhealthy children,' she said.[71] Citing *mantra*s chanted during marriage, certain shlokas in the *Rigveda*, and the histories of a few women, she tried to prove that in ancient India, child marriages did not exist at all, and the 'virgin bride' and groom married as per their choice as adults.[72]

Deeply worried about the disastrous effects of early initiation into sex (*baalya samagamamu*), Ramabayamma laboured hard to prove that it was deeply 'unnatural' and cruel.[73] 'Do you think that these marriages, which

---

[68] For another example of such writing that mocked old men's attempts to remarry, see 'Aa ...!', *Grihalakshmi*, December 1936, pp. 747–754.

[69] 'Barampuram Streela Sabha' (The Barampuram Women's Conference), *Hindu Sundary*, April 1912, pp. 14–16.

[70] Mosalikanti Ramabayamma, 'Rajaswalanantara Vivahamulu' (Post-Puberty Marriages), *Hindu Sundary*, March 1912, pp. 22–32.

[71] Ibid., pp. 24–25.

[72] Ibid., pp. 25–27 and 23.

[73] Early consummation proved a nightmare to child-wives. In his autobiography, Gudipati Venkatachalam, the front ranking male feminist intellectual in Andhra, vividly described how his sister, Ammanni, was scared of it and how inconsolably she cried after knowing that the ritual of her consummation was fixed, and that her husband was coming. Chalam even wrote a letter to his brother-in-law that 'Ammanni did not

Image 3.3: Kashinathuni Ramabayamma

Source: *Telugu Samachar*, n. d.

are against the Vedas, are in accordance with the principles of nature?' she reasoned.[74] Citing the *Vivaha Nisheka Dharma Dipika*, she argued that child marriages caused an 'untimely' sprouting of sexual desire because husband

like it.' *Chalam* (1972), (Vijayawada, 1986), pp. 18–19. Women brilliantly depicted the traumatic experience of girl-wives' early and, most often, forced consummation. In her short story, Tumpudi Sushila Bhagavati portrayed how the 12-year-old Sundari was terrified by early consummation. After her horrible experience in the first night, she continuously refused to go to bed with her 30-year-old husband until the sex-hungry husband burnt her to death. See 'Ghantaiah Chesina Ghorakrityamu' (The Horrible Crime that Ghantaiah Committed), *Vasavi*, October 1926, pp. 28–30.

[74]Mosalikanti Ramabayamma, 'Rajaswalanantara Vivahamulu' (Post-Puberty Marriages), *Hindu Sundary*, March 1912, p. 28.

and wife frequently saw each other. Questioning whether 'a ten-year-old girl was suitable for sexual consummation', she criticised parents who allowed the consummation of marriage as soon as the girl (*pasi koona*) began her menses. She observed that even in the few cases where parents sought to delay consummation, the girl's in-laws would demand to take her to the marital home. 'Even the small boys, who were normally afraid of going out for urinating after sunset', Ramabayamma wrote, 'craved for their wives [*bharya, bharya ani*] and if their in-laws did not send their wives, got angry with them and eventually became an object of laughter. All this was not news for us because it was very common.'[75]

Rubbishing arguments that approved of child marriages but proposed the postponement of consummation, she wrote:

> But, will the boy, who has got complete freedom after marriage, and who is habituated to sexual [feelings] given our bad practice of arranging marriage consummation with the very onset of menarche, allow his wife to stay at natal home the very next minute after her menstruation? By mustering courage, even if parents of girls stubbornly refuse to arrange for marriage consummation, they have not been successful. They are facing accusations [*nishthuroktulu*] of groom's parents, threats of sons-in-law that the latter will drag them to law courts, and the ridicule [*parihasalu*] of people, who are devoid of any discretion of good and bad, and succumbing [to social pressure], and, by turning their hearts into stones, are agreeing to it against their conscience.[76]

Reflecting on the view that the age of consent should be fixed at 12 years for girls, Ramabayamma felt that this was scarcely any better and would lead to only slight improvements in women's education and the number of child widows.[77] Therefore, she proposed that the age of consent be raised to 16 years and appealed particularly to mothers to sympathise with their daughters, relieve them from the hellish 'living graveyard' of child marriage. Mothers were requested to encourage their daughters to receive higher education. Addressing the fear that 'adult girls might not get grooms', she stressed that it was better to remain a *brahmacharini* (spinster) for ever than suffer the miseries caused by child marriage. It was her conviction that 'it was always better to undertake socially useful work by receiving higher education [like the single Christian missionary women] and marry

[75] Ibid., pp. 23–25.
[76] Ibid., p. 25.
[77] Ibid., p. 24.

a suitable man when available' or remain single than suffer the ignominious life guaranteed by child marriage.[78]

Ramabayamma was intensely pained that people 'did not feel even an ant's bite' despite witnessing the suffering borne by child brides and continued the practice. Invoking a sense of gender solidarity, she appealed to women to 'hurry up to demonstrate their love for the race of women' (*jaatyabhimanamu*) rather than 'give an opportunity to men to blame women for being obstacles' to reform. Emphasising women's agency in solving the problems afflicting them, she reminded women that men could not solve them, and only women's resolve and concrete actions could make a difference. Addressing 'upper-caste sisters', she stated:

> The time for delivering lengthy lectures is over now. For the welfare of our own daughters, whom we produced, unless we ourselves wield the sword in our hands to slay the demon of the evil practice, our men's efforts will not achieve any success, even if they speak against it for ten thousand years.... O my respected sisters! It is impossible to make marriage reform with the efforts of men. The key is in our hands. Let us all determine once that we will not marry off our daughters until they are adults and see how our resolve will not materialise. Do you think that mothers are mere leather bags for carrying babies for nine months? *Chhee, Chhee!* No.... If all women are resolved, these two noble tasks [eradication of child marriage and development of women's education] will be achieved easily and the country will develop.[79]

Informing her readers that 'in the civilised countries, marriage was a voluntary affair and according to one's sweet will, and that there was no compulsion, and not at all as per the desire of others', Kashinathuni Ramabayamma defended post-pubertal marriages on the ground of 'everyday experience'.[80] Intelligently avoiding a discussion on whether post-puberty marriages were sanctioned or banned by the shastras,[81] she sarcastically remarked that 'we witnessed with our eyes the damages caused by the supposedly shastra-sanctioned (*shastriyamulaina*) marriages [child

[78] Ibid., p. 30.

[79] Ibid., pp. 29–30.

[80] See 'Andhra Mahila Sabha: Sabhathipurali Upanyasamu' (All Andhra Women's Conference: Presidential Address), *Hindu Sundary*, March 1913, pp. 23–40.

[81] She stated that 'she did not have the capacity to delve into the issue.' This statement was perhaps a strategic evasion of a discussion of the shastras; maybe she thought that it was no use discussing it.

marriages][82] and the benefits of *ashastriya* marriages [adult marriages]'. Stressing that 'our mother country would not develop unless child marriages disappeared and adult marriages of girls increased', she persuaded her audience:

> You have already heard of the [choice-based adult] marriages of Smt. Minakshamma and Rukminmma in Andhra.[83] In Bombay, I have seen [several] unmarried Brahmin girls, who did not marry until they were 16-years-old. One will be pleased to see those girls, who are studying freely and happily rather than drowning in the ocean of family life in childhood itself. When will our mother Andhra [*Andhramata*] get this fortune! Given our social condition, though there is no chance to stop child marriages, it is beneficial to postpone marriage consummation [*punassandhanamu*] until girls are 16-years-old. A good example is the Parsi women, who can be said to be an embellishment to the Hindu race.... They have freedom, which women need. Well dressed, they are seen in all parts of Bombay, and appear to be the crop of women's education and independence.[84]

Post-pubertal adult marriage, according to her, was very much an Indian practice. 'We had evidences from the histories of noble women [*saadhvimatallulu*] such as Sita, Savitri, Shakuntala, Damayanti, Rani Samyukta, etc. to establish that, in our country, too, in the ancient past,

[82] According to her, there were 10,000 married girls below the age of ten in Krishna District alone; their number was 1,24,000 for the Telugu-speaking districts of Madras Presidency as a whole. Ibid., p. 35. Citing the 1911 Census, she showed that there were 440,000 child widows in India. There were 2,358 child widows below the age of 16 in Krishna District alone. Ibid., p. 37.

[83] Most women who spoke and wrote in favour of post-pubertal marriage of girls treated these two women as role models. For example, Sattiraju Shyamalamaba observed that the fact of their adult marriages 'indicated that society started discarding child marriages.' 'This was indicating the progress the country was making', she said. Minakshamma married Sri Dasu Madhava Rao, a B.A., B.L., from Eluru, and Rukminamma married Dr Achanta Lakshmipati: she was 20 years old at the time of her marriage. See Sattiraju Shyamalamba, 'Upanyasamu' (Lecture), *Hindu Sundary*, March 1912, pp. 34–38. Minakshamma was the second daughter of Parameshwaraiah, an advocate. Her elder sister's was also an adult marriage, who married Barrister Ramachandra Rao of Bellari. These were the first post-pubertal adult marriages among the Brahmins in Andhra. See Kola Appala Narasimham, 'Atibaalya Vivahamulu' (Infant Marriages), *Hindu Sundary*, December 1912, pp. 17–18.

[84] See 'Andhra Mahila Sabha: Sabhathipurali Upanyasamu', *Hindu Sundary*, March 1913, pp. 35–36.

marriages were held by choice [*swayamvaramulu*].' They could choose their spouses because they were adults.[85]

Sattiraju Shyamalamaba advocated that 'our people be persuaded to note that, in the past, marriages had never been so debased as they are this day', and that there were 'uncountable number of evidence in the shrutis and smritis that, in our country, in the ancient days, girls and boys married only when they got suitable brides and grooms.' Her rhetoric was persuasive: 'How were the marriages of Sita and Rama, Rukmini and Sri Krishna, Savitri and Satyavanta, Chandramati and Harishchandra, Nala and Damayanti, Shakuntala and Dushyanta described in our Puranas?' Not only that, such examples abound in the 'historical time, too', and the marriages of Vimala and Durgavati demonstrated (*chati cheppuchunnavi*) that women of the past enjoyed freedom in marriage. However, mere 'recounting of the past glories' did not help correct 'present maladies': practice was more important than preaching. Otherwise, one would risk the hypocrisy of being as 'one who travelled on foot, but proudly boasted that his grandfather travelled in palanquin' (*tanu kalinadakanu prayanamu cheyuchu maa tata pallakinekkunani cheppukonu vaani valane*).[86]

Women's Organisations and Child Marriage

The issue of child marriage figured prominently on the agenda of women's organisations and conferences, where women stridently spoke against it and passed resolutions condemning the practice. For example, of the 15 issues women discussed in the 'regular' and 'special' meetings of the Satya Samvardhani Samajamu at Vijayanagaram, the issue of 'infant marriages' (*ati baalya vivahamulu*) was one.[87] The All-Andhra Women's Conference (or AMMS) regularly discussed the issue of child marriage. At the fourth All Andhra Women's Conference, held at Bandar (Machilipatnam), 23–24 March 1913, four out of 19 topics were about child marriage: (*a*) 'treating child marriages as reprehensible'; (*b*) 'deciding not to arrange the marriage of girls unless they are adults or, completed 16-years-old'; (*c*) 'abolishing

[85] Ibid., p. 34.

[86] Sattiraju Shyamalamba, 'Upanyasamu' (Lecture), *Hindu Sundary*, March 1912, pp. 34–38.

[87] See 'Satya Samvardhani Samajamuyokka Dwiteeya Samvatsara Reportu' (Second Annual Report of the Satya Samvardhani Samajam), *Hindu Sundary*, January–February 1913, pp. 9–15.

bride-price and dowry', and; (*d*) 'not arranging the marriage of a girl below 16 years of age with a man over 40 years'.[88] The Andhra Rashtra Mahila Mahasabhas (ARMS) extensively discussed the issue as well, and in its fifth conference, Kanuparti Varalakshmamma highlighted their enthusiastic celebration of the passage of the Sarda Act.[89]

Condemning child marriages at the All-Andhra Women's Educational Reform Conference held at Kakinada on 16–17 January 1928, women passed the following resolutions:

a. Child marriages are chiefly responsible for the lack of education, presence of ignorance, shorter life span, physical and mental weakness among Indian women.
b. This practice of infant marriage is against nature, shastra and tradition, and is harmful in every way. Therefore, this conference prays to the government to ban by law the marriages of girls and boys under the ages of 16 and 21, respectively, and punish parents for non-compliance, and thereby protect and uplift Indian Hindu women.
c. This conference is of the opinion that the All India Women's Conference must undertake propaganda in this regard in all the states, and also submit a *mahzar*, signed by one to two lakhs of women and men, to the Viceroy.[90]

Women's wings associated with various caste associations were equally quick to condemn the practice of child marriage. The Arya Vaishya Mahila Mahasabha was at the forefront of social reform. In one of its conferences in Salem (2 July 1927), women 'unanimously resolved' that 'bride-price and dowry were reprehensible'. They further resolved that Arya Vaishya girls be married only after they attained puberty and their consummation be postponed until they completed 16 years. Men over 30 years of age were to marry girls of 16 only, and it was to be ensured that the age gap did not exceed

[88] See 'Andhra Mahila Sabha', *Hindu Sundary*, January-February 1913, pp. 22–24.

[89] She said that the first item that came up for discussion on the second day of the conference (22 November 1931) was the Sarda Act. 'It was resolved that no amendment was required in the Sarda Act. Many showed enthusiasm to speak on this issue. Those who saw women lecturing in the conference against decreasing the marriageable age of girls understood well the extent to which women were in favour of the Sarda Act,' she noted in jubilation. See Kanuparti Varalakshmamma, 'Gunturu Mahilasabha Visheshamulu' (Highlights of the Women's Conference at Guntur), *Grihalakshmi*, February 1932, p. 1051.

[90] See 'Vivaha Samskaranamunu goorchina Tirmanamu' (Resolutions Regarding Marriage Reform), *Hindu Sundary*, January 1928, p. 16.

10 to 15 years.[91] At the seventh Arya Vaishya Women's Conference, held on 14 July 1928 at Vayalpadu, women resolved 'to support the Bill introduced by Harbilas Sarda in the Imperial Legislative Assembly proposing a ban on the marriages of girls and boys below the age of 14 and 18, respectively'. Proposed by Makam Kamakshamamma, the resolution was seconded by Battula Kamakshamma and was 'approved by a majority'.[92]

Speaking at the women's conferences, women vividly described the disastrous consequences of child marriages and the overwhelming burden placed on girls in particular.[93] In her presidential address to the fourth AMMS, Kashinathuni Ramabayamma persuasively summarised the adverse effects of the practice:

> Because of child marriages, [girl wives'] health will be affected. Physical strength [of mother as well as children] will deteriorate. Untimely pregnancies will take place. Weaklings will be born. Maternal ('*baalinta*') mortality will increase. Educational opportunities [of women] will go down. Number of child widows will increase. The [poisonous] trees of kanyasulkam and varasulkam will thrive. The race, which has weaklings, will decline day by day.[94]

Lecturing at the Barampuram women's conference, Sattiraju Shyamalamba narrated how both boys and girls became a casualty of child marriage. She complained that parents of boys hung the 'heavy boulder called wife'

---

[91] See 'Arya Vaishya Mahila Mahasabha–Charyakramamu' (Proceedings of the Arya Vaishya Women's Conference), *Vasavi*, August 1927, p. 197. At the first Vaishya Women's Conference of the Nizam State, women resolved that 'child marriages had to be completely abolished, if women were to have good health'. It was proposed by Battula Kamakshamma and seconded by Kanakavalli Tayaramma. The resolution appealing to the Vaishyas to stop selling brides and grooms was proposed and seconded by Singidamu Venkata Lakshmamma and Nalam Sushila Devi, respectively. The resolution that girls should not be consummated unless they attained 16 years was proposed by Nalam Sushila Devi, and seconded by Kalangi Sheshamamba. See 'Nizam Rashtra Prathama Vaishya Mahila Mahasabha: Teermanamulu' (Resolutions of the First Vaishya Women's Conference of the Nizam State), *Vasavi*, April 1938, pp. 14–15.

[92] See 'Saptama Arya Vaishya Mahila Mahasabha: Charya Kramamu', *Vasavi*, August 1928, p. 204. It was also resolved not to offer unmarried girls to widowers who were over 40 years old. Proposed and seconded by Polepalli Mangamma and Vootattooru Amritavalli Tayaramma, respectively, the resolution was 'unanimously approved'. Ibid.

[93] See the speeches of Polepalli Ranganayakamma and Tumpudi Satyavati Bhagavatamma delivered at the seventh Arya Vaishya Women's Conference held at Vayalpadu on 14 July 1928. *Vasavi*, August 1928, pp. 193–200.

[94] See 'Andhra Mahila Sabha: Sabhadhipurali Upanyasamu', *Hindu Sundary*, March 1913, p. 35.

(*gudibanda*) around the necks of boys thinking that they may not get brides once they turned older. This interfered with their education. Forced to face the difficulties of family life, they became physically weak and sick. She informed readers that there were girl-wives, all of 12 years, who died of early pregnancies: they conceived long before they had acquired any knowledge of the world. If by some chance they escaped death during labour, they struggled to raise their children. 'Is not child marriage responsible for all these travails?'[95]

In her presidential address, delivered at the seventh anniversary celebration (16–17 May 1912) of the Bharati Samajamu at Visakhapatnam, Kandukuri Venkayamma Rao, the zamindar of Urlam, opined that conducting 'child marriage implied the same forcible act of giving away cattle and goats to others' and that 'it was not a proper marriage at all'. 'Conducting child marriage for the joy [of parents] was like fulfilling a vow to the stone-made-God in the temple' (*gudilo raati devuniki mokku teerchukonuta vantidi*). She even went on to say that 'those who sold away girls for kanyasulakam were of a demon's birth'. Remarking that even though India was 'liberated from the sin of slave trade', it was still 'selling virgin girls', she wished that the 'British government relieved girls [*sic*] from the bad state of being sold away through a suitable law.'[96]

Campaign in the 1920s and After

Over the 1920s, 1930s and 1940s, women forcefully opposed child marriage and demanded that the British government intervene to eradicate it completely.[97] K. Venkata Lakshmamma found the argument of 'repairing

[95] See 'Upanyasamu' (Lecture), *Hindu Sundary*, March 1912, pp. 34–38.

[96] She advised parents to certainly examine the 'suitability' of the groom, and not to arrange marriages in haste and wait until the girl was sufficiently grown up to form an idea of her would-be-husband. 'If the true purpose of the marriage dharma was to be achieved, the match should be fixed by obtaining the consent of the girl also.' For the full text of her lecture, see 'Upanyasamu' (Lecture), August (pp. 343–345), September (pp. 355–357) and October (pp. 19–21) 1912 issues of *Vivekavathi*; pp. 20–21 for this reference.

[97] By this, we do not mean that women's demand for a ban on the practice started only during the 1920s. What we mean is that the demand was intensified now. In fact, Telugu women demanded British intervention in abolishing child marriages right from the dawn of the twentieth century. For example, women like Kallepalle Venkata Ramanamma demanded the British government to intervene and ban the practice. In

the nation' without removing child marriage to be 'very absurd'. 'Was not one to set the home front right first, before setting the outside world right?', she wondered (*Inta gelichi rachcha geluvavale gada*?). Lakshmamma exhorted the 'admirers of [the] nation' to get rid of child marriage, provide higher education to girls and thereby 'uplift the world of women'. Social development, in this view, was to precede political development.[98]

In her presidential address to the women's conference organised at Vetapalem in October 1927, on the occasion of the annual function of the Saraswata Niketanam, Shikharam Kamalamba supported raising the age of consent for girls to 16 years. Observing that many women and infants died during delivery in India, she cited both physiologists and M. K. Gandhi to argue that early motherhood was responsible for high rates of maternal and infant mortality. Referring to the bill placed in the Imperial Legislative Assembly to consider restraining the marriage of girls below the age of 12, she stressed that 'such an act was indispensable'. 'For the benefit of the country, there seemed no other alternative than passage of such a Governmental Act,' she concluded with firmness.[99]

In her speech at the All Andhra Women's Educational Reform Conference held at Kakinada on 16–17 January 1928, D. Sooryakantamma powerfully argued against child marriage on the ground particularly of its negative consequences to women's health.[100]

> Among the various tasks that we need to undertake for our development, the work concerning our health and longevity is very important. The health and life expectancy of Indian women are deteriorating day by day.... It is learnt from government's data that, compared to world standards, Indians' average life expectancy is very low. It is learnt that, while in the European countries like England, Russia and Germany, the

---

addition, she wrote that there should be a law banning the consummation ceremony until girls became major; if that was 'forced' upon them, girls should have the right to dissolve the marriage. See Kallepalle Venkata Ramanamma, 'Stree Vidyaku Bhangakaramulagu Vaivahika Dharmamulu: Vanini Tolaginchu Upayamulu' (Marriage Practices Harmful to Female Education: Some Remedies), *Hindu Sundary*, May 1912, pp. 19–22.

[98] K. Venkata Lakshmamma, 'Swayamvara Vivahamulu' (Girls' Self-Choice Marriages), *Andhra Patrika Samvatsaradi Sanchika*, 1921, pp. 156–157.

[99] See 'Stree Hitopadeshamu' (A Friendly Advice to Women), *Vasavi*, January 1928, pp. 425–429, pp. 427–429 for this reference.

[100] See 'Andhra Rashtra Mahila Vidya Samskarana Sabhalo Doo. Sooryakantamma gaariche Chaduvabadina Upanyasamu' (Speech Read out by D. Sooryakantamma at the All-Andhra Women's Educational Reform Conference), *Hindu Sundary*, January 1928, pp. 12–16.

> average life expectancy is 45 to 50 years, in India, it is merely 23 to 25. Also it is learnt that, while infant mortality... in those countries is 30 to 40 per 1000, in India, it is 200 to 300. The others [those who escaped death] are suffering from either extreme weakness or diseases. Women are more feeble and unhealthy than men. Many girls appear like old women by the time they are hardly 20 to 25-years-old.... In the other countries, young girls of 16-years-old spend their time in merriment—dancing and singing, laughing and jumping, and studying in schools. Our girls of that age would be seen being drowned in grief. They will be found in hospitals, getting operated on. Such bad conditions are more prevalent among the Brahmins than among people of other varnas. What is the reason for this? It is not necessary to reiterate that child marriage is responsible for this sad state of affairs.... Arranging for the sexual consummation of girls lacking in physical and mental maturity is as improper as eating a raw fruit by getting it artificially ripened. This practice is against nature. It is against the Dharmashastras. It is against the opinion of the majority. It is harmful. This evil practice [*dushtacharamu*], which is not found anywhere else in the world, is present in our country and is sapping our energies. Here also, it was not there earlier.... It is our duty to agitate in every way to get it abolished. In this regard, we have to pass resolutions in the state level and national level women's conferences and take the help of the [benevolent British] government.

Sooryakantamma emphasised the indispensability of legislation, since 'mere propaganda' could not produce desired results. She stressed that 'it was impossible for us to remove social evils without the help of government. Whatever amount of movement we undertook and whatever number of resolutions we passed, common people would not put a reform into practice.' Reminding the government of its responsibility, she wished that 'they should think of the welfare of people, who were their children' and abolish the practice 'the same way they introduced compulsory vaccination and primary education'. Citing another example, she wondered 'whether it could ever have been possible for Indian social reformers to remove sati, if the government did not ban it through legislation'. Sooryakantamma urged the government to introduce legislation banning marriages of girls under the age of 16 and boys under the age of 21, warning that unless parents were threatened with punishment for non-compliance, the practice would continue. She also urged the AIWC to pass a resolution and submit 'a big mahzar, signed by one or two lakh women, to our Governor General, the same way Raja Rammohun Roy did in the past'. In her presidential address to the seventh Arya Vaishya Women's Conference held on 14 July 1928 at Vayalpadu, Tumpudi Satyavati Bhagavatamma observed:

> Socially, we are subjected to innumerable number of difficulties. We are witnessing girls becoming mothers at the age of 12. Describing the health and the physical fitness of their children is not possible for women like me; it has to be imagined only. The trauma of child widows is well understood by their parents. Old age marriages [of men] have increased among us, and they are slitting the throats of the innocent infants. If we ensure that the age gap between the bride and the groom does not exceed 15 years, such evils will extinguish. It is better not arrange for the consummation of marriage until girls are 16 years old. It is madness on the part of parents to say that they cannot protect married girls until that age because they are already protecting the child widows for a lifetime.[101]

Atluri Venkata Sitamma emphasised that the Indian nation and 'race' could not be brought back to their 'original glory' without safeguarding the health of women, 'the mothers of the nation'. Weak and unhealthy mothers produced weak and sickly children who could neither protect themselves nor the nation. This was the reason that India had lost its independence to 'foreigners'. Holding child marriage to be 'chiefly responsible' for the 'utterly dismal state' of Indian society, race and nation, she analysed the vicious cycle as under, particularly bashing male arrogance.

> India, the Indian race and Indian society, which, in the past, had enjoyed an exalted position in the entire world… are so thoroughly degenerate today, they have become an object of laughter for the people of the world…. The elders are holding women's lack of knowledge and health and the consequent weakness to be chiefly responsible for such a bad state of affairs…. The day Indian men stopped respecting women and took to treating them as slaves and maids of the kitchen and assumed that [women] did not need education and knowledge, that very day their race, society and country started declining, only to [eventually] lose independence and undergo the resultant suffering. From that day onwards, the country became a house of ignorance and child marriages gained ground. In the eyes of Indian men, women became luxury items…. Because women became sickly and weak and were devoid of education, the entire Indian race became such…. We can state unequivocally that child marriages are responsible for such a bad state of things…. At that age of 10 or 12 years… the girl who cannot look after her own health, will have to take care of the health of the children! How strange! How

[101] See 'Adhyakshopanyasamu', *Vasavi*, August 1928, p. 200.

> healthy, strong and able-bodied the infants born to such tender children will be!... All know the fact of babies being stillborn in the seventh or the eighth month as the child mothers are not able to hold pregnancies and deliver safely. It is not unknown to our country's people that 50% of the pregnant girls are dying because of the labour pains. At least 10% of those with safe delivery are spoiling their health. As a result of this, though a few infants somehow survive, they are either ill-taken or perennially weak. As their mothers themselves are uneducated and sickly, they cannot provide good training to their children. The weak children have no enthusiasm for education as they have no physical and mental strength. In their youth, they do not have the strength and courage one needs to possess in that age; they are somehow able to manage the household affairs only. Such young men are becoming householders at about 16 or 17-years-of-age and are contributing weaklings to the world. It is because of this reason that the same Indians, who were strong, brave and chivalrous and had a life span of about 200 years during the time of the Mahabharata war, have become short [and ugly], weak and have a short lifespan. Can there be a more heinous state for the country than this?[102]

Sitamma supported the Sarda Act and appealed to parents to 'give good education to their daughters until they were 14-years-of-age and make the boys receive education until they were 20-years-of-age'. In an essay that won first prize in *Grihalakshmi*'s annual contest, M. Vedavalli Tayaramma strongly criticised child marriage,[103] highlighting issues of educational deprivation, the burden of domestic management at a young age, early pregnancy and related issues, incompatibility between spouses, and the risk of early widowhood. She observed that three kinds of marriage practices were prevalent in India at the time: 'infant marriages' (*shishu vivahamulu*), child marriages, adult marriages (*yuvati vivahamulu*). The first two kinds of marriage were 'performed by parents, when the children (*pasi papalu*) were in a state of ignorance'. Adult marriages, in contrast, would not take place unless the bride and the groom loved each other.

Observing that most girls were married off before the age of 10 and that only a few married at or after 12 years, she said such young couples could not understand the meaning of wife and husband and often failed to perform even the marriage-related rituals. In such a situation, 'how could the girl receive education useful to carry out her duties as a homemaker

[102] Atluri Venkata Sitamma, 'Balyavivaha Nishedhamu' (Abolition of Child Marriages), *Grihalakshmi*, October 1929, pp. 641–644.

[103] M. Vedavalli Tayaramma, 'Balya Vivahamulu' (Child Marriages), *Grihalakshmi*, December 1933, pp. 774–778.

(grihini dharmamu)?' Reflecting on the danger of early pregnancies and the high probability of maternal and infant mortality, she said:

> Because our country has hot weather, girls are attaining puberty by 11 or 12 years of age. After some time, they go to [their] in-laws' home. If such a girl becomes pregnant and begets children, it may harm her very life or, the newborn's life may be in danger. If the infant survives by the grace of God, it will be either weak, short-lived or suffer from deadly diseases for all life. While the medical doctors have opined that women will not have the physical fitness to conceive and produce children unless they are 20 years old, is it not very saddening that our girls are becoming mothers, when they have no physical fitness! It is because of this reason that in our country, as we have learnt, out of every 100 births, 75 die in infancy.[104]

Concurring with other women reformers, Tayaramma identified marriages with large age gaps as a major reason, blaming parents for giving in to their greed. The 'more saddening' aspect of child marriage, for her, was the high incidence of early widowhood, whose 'chain of sufferings' was 'impossible to describe':

> Even that [small] girl, who was married off at that state of ignorance, when she failed to even understand what [the word] husband meant, has to swim the ocean of sorrow all her life if she is widowed. Only the experienced will understand how unbearable it is to spend childhood and youth, the most enthusiastic and blissful part of human life, as one leads the middle age and old age. Caught in the fire of the misery of enforced widowhood, how many of them are not dying? Are not so many losing the honour of pativratya (fidelity), the invaluable ornament to women, [by indulging in clandestine sex?] It is just impossible to describe the chain of difficulties suffered by the girl widows in our country. Even to her parents, she [widow] appears to be a heinous creature. At last, her life's destiny is nothing but slavery (*dasyame*)![105]

Tayaramma perceptively remarked that the girl widow had the right to suffer the grief of widowhood, but no right over the property of her late husband in the set-up of a joint family. The only solace was the meagre maintenance the legal heirs gave her, which was itself often a pretext for further harassment (*mupputippalu petti vaarasulichchu bharaname gati*).[106] Reflecting on the Sarda Act, Tayaramma said that 'Sri Harbilas Sarda and

[104] Ibid., p. 776.
[105] Ibid., pp. 776–777.
[106] Ibid., p. 777.

Muthulakshmi Reddy, etc., were praiseworthy because they worked hard to get the Child Marriage Restraint Act passed in the hope that it would decrease the number of child widows and increase the educational opportunities of girls and boys in the country'.

> Because of the Act, except the Brahmins and the Vaishyas, whose numbers are very less, others will not suffer any loss. If the non-Brahmins show due interest in this regard, boys and girls will receive education, will enjoy compatible conjugal life and will be useful to the country. [If what I have said is followed], it will not be an exaggeration to state that an intelligent girl [*praagna*] of the likes of Sita, Savitri and Damayanti will go to the in-laws' home. She will make her in-laws, husband and relatives happy and will fetch reputation both to her natal home and the in-laws' home.

A staunch proponent of adult marriages, Tayaramma questioned a popular notion at the time that adult men and women would 'transgress the limits' set by the elders and, driven by 'lust', would lose their sense of judgement and agree to marry outside their caste. Allaying such fears, she said that if we provided such an education to our boys and girls, which gave them virtuous knowledge, until they attained proper age of marriage, no such bad things would ever take place. Moreover, with adult marriages, women would have the opportunity to acquire proper skills to undertake housework and men the opportunity to acquire education and wealth. The children they produced would be lively and prospering. Their family life would be so beautiful that, it would not be an exaggeration to state that, it was beyond description, and to the onlookers, it gave the greatest joy.[107] Another first prize essay, by a female student named G. Venkamma, after meticulously considering the advantages and disadvantages of child marriages and adult marriages, firmly concluded in favour of adult marriages.[108]

Going beyond the Scriptures while Arguing against Child Marriage

An important development in women's consciousness over the 1920s and beyond was that they eschewed reliance on scriptures in making their

[107] Ibid., p. 775.

[108] G. Venkamma, 'Proudha Baalya Vivahamulavalani Labhanashtamulu' (Advantages and Disadvantages of Child Marriages and Adult Marriages), *Grihalakshmi*, July 1930, pp. 367–368.

arguments. A section of women, in this respect, were unlike the nineteenth-century male reformers. They strongly felt that even if the Dharmashastras sanctioned child marriages, they were undesirable because they were barbarous and inhuman, damaged the physical and mental health of girls, and curtailed their educational opportunities. Holding the 'desire' for banning child marriage as 'more important' than injunctions given in the shastras, and emphasising that women alone were qualified to judge the desirability or otherwise of an Act banning the practice, Maddali Sitaramamma wrote:

> At last, the Child Marriage Bill has taken the shape of an Act. Just like the practice of Sati was destroyed through governmental legislation during the time of Sri Raja Rammohun Roy, today, with this Act, child marriages are also going to be destroyed. The Hindu race is not relinquishing the age-old traditions. If the harmful traditions are prevailing and getting stronger, they cannot be smashed except by governmental legislation. That such a superstitious tradition as child marriage should require government's law to be quelled only indicated the weakness of the race. Women are the victims of the worst consequences of child marriages such as widowhood. Hence, such matters have to be particularly decided by women. Only a minuscule minority supported such marriages. The rest of India opposed them in a single voice. For the lovers of reform, time, space, suitability and independent reasoning are the yardsticks of deciding the dharma. For the lovers of tradition, it is not so. Shastra alone is their armour. Even that shastra does not unequivocally state in their favour. In this age of Kali, when the secrets of the shastras are exposed, there is none who trusts them. In whatever way we see, the birth of a governmental legislation abolishing child marriage is necessary.... The voice in favour of the abolition of child marriage is reverberating everywhere. Such voice is supremely important than the whole corpus of the shastras.[109]

In her presidential address to the sixth All-Andhra Women's Social and Educational Conference held at Rajahmundry on 12 November 1932, Achanta Lakshmi Devi, an M.B., B.S., L.R.C.P., M.R.C.S., (London), exhibited similar consciousness with regard to reliance on Shastric sanction or ban concerning child marriage. She said:

---

[109] Maddali Sitaramamma, 'Balya Vivahamulu' (Child Marriages), *Grihalakshmi*, November 1929, pp. 695–697. She questioned if it was desirable on the part of parents not to allow children any right in deciding and choosing their partners. She firmly believed that the prospective brides and grooms must have the freedom, and parents were to wait until children reached that age, when they could exercise such freedom.

> Despite the fact that law is made with the efforts of Harbilas Sarda banning the marriage of girls and boys below the age of 14 and 18, respectively, it is actually not executed. Indifference of society is chiefly responsible for this. Going by medical science, it is certain that health of the women, who become pregnant below the age of 20, will be damaged. In such a situation, there is no reason to hurry up for girls' marriage. Though there are arguments that, as per religion, post-puberty marriages are not allowed for Brahmins, it is high time to change the practice as per the changing times. Let there be anything in the shastras, I pray to you all not to subject our girls to perennial sufferings in the name of religion. Women must carefully think of their wellbeing and put every effort to ensure that our children do not fall in the mouth of the vampire of child marriage. Do I need to tell the well experienced like you about the need for rigorously campaigning about the calamities caused by child marriages?[110]

The Origins of Child Marriage: Reformist Women's Views

Most reform-minded Telugu intellectuals sought to explain what they saw as the 'degeneration' of 'ancient Indian culture', including the deteriorating position of women, through a communal perspective on medieval India.[111] According to them, 'Muslim rule' had comprehensively destroyed ancient India's 'greatness'. For example, in the beginning of his career as a public intellectual, Kandukuri Veeresalingam also articulated this understanding of history. While Veeresaligam at a later stage began to identify internal causes for the 'degeneration' of Indian civilisation,[112] many others persisted with this belief. It was a routinely accepted 'truth' in their writings and speeches.

---

[110] See *Aarava Andhra Rashtriya Mahila Sanghika Vidya Vishayika Mahasabha: Srimati Doctoru Achanta Lakshmi Devi Adhyakshopanyasamu, Rajamahendravaramu, 12-11-32* (Dr Achanta Lakshmi Devi's Presidential Address to the Sixth All-Andhra Women's Social and Educational Conference held at Rajahmundry on 12.11.1932), Vani Mudraksharashala, Bezawada.

[111] For a comprehensive understanding of the communal interpretation of Indian history, see Bipan Chandra, *Communalism in Modern India* (New Delhi, 1984), pp. 209–236.

[112] John and Karen Leonard, 'Viresalingam and the Ideology of Social Change in Andhra' in Sumit Sarkar and Tanika Sarkar ed., *Women and Social Reform in Modern India*, vol. 1 (Ranikhet, 2007), pp. 350–351.

According to B. Hanumantha Rao, 'a few had said that the practice came into existence during the "Mohammadan period" to guard the chastity of women; others were said to have stated that men created such practices to keep women under their firm control'.[113] Ayitaraju Jeedikanti Rama Rao wrote that

> our ancestors conducted post-puberty marriages and performed widow remarriages before the advent of the Mohammadans. One may doubt as to how such a massive change has occurred. But, the big change has occurred because of the cruel actions during the Mohammadan period. Not just this. It is well established in history that it is during the time of the Turks and because of their evil actions that the greatness of Hindus got destroyed and the degeneration was set in.[114]

'Reading out' his address on 15 December 1912 at the Rammohun Club at Palakollu, Kola Appala Narasimham said that 'a few shlokas [mandating child marriage] were created and inserted in a few smritis to check the troubles caused to the Hindus during the Mohammadan rule'.[115]

Reformist women, too, attributed the genesis of child marriage to the so-called 'medieval Muslim rule' or 'Muslim invasions'. This certainly casts a deep shadow on their 'progressive' pronouncements on the child marriage question. While some made only cursory remarks in this regard, others treated the same in some detail. Most women intellectuals propogated a skewed, communal understanding of medieval Indian history. A classic example is Bhandaru Atchamamba's *Abala Sachcharitra Ratnamala* (first published 1901), which narrated, among others, the life histories of a few Rajput queens like Samyukta and Padmini, and modern women like Rakhmabai Kelkar, and Anandibai Joshee, etc. The book is riddled with communal interpretations of medieval India that reduced its history to stereotypical portrayals. The book deployed tropes like invoking images of destructive Muslim rule, the 'brute Mussalman' Turk who would abduct women, his aggressive sexuality and excessive immorality—these were only a few of the communal themes that recur in her assessment of medieval

---

[113] B. Hanumantha Rao, 'Atibalya Vivahamulavalani Anarthakamulu' (Evil Effects of Infant Marriages), *Hindu Sundary*, December 1909, pp. 10–15.

[114] Ayitaraju Jeedikanti Rama Rao, 'Hyndava Yuvati Duravastha' (Miserable State of Hindu Women), *Hindu Sundary*, March 1912, p. 12. See also Chintamaneni Bhavaiah, 'Atibalya Vivahamu' (Infant Marriage), *Andhra Patrika Samvatsaradi Sanchika*, 1917, pp. 185–186.

[115] Kola Appala Narasimham, 'Atibalya Vivahamulu' (Infant Marriages), *Hindu Sundary*, December 1912, p. 20.

Indian history. In a nutshell, 'Muslim rule' was villainous and ruinous, particularly causing the degeneration of Hindu women. The Mysore State, a 'Hindu kingdom', was 'usurped' by the 'wicked' Hyder Ali, who was like 'Ravana'. Tipu Sultan was a 'Muslim demon' (*Yavana Rakshasudu*) who subjected the Hindus of Mysore to innumerable troubles.[116] Sirajuddaula was a villain who 'outraged the modesty of Hindu women'.[117] However, Atchamamba was generous towards Akbar, who was 'a repository of virtues… and, compared to other Muslim kings, was like God'. However, she regretted that such a 'virtuous' king was so 'hungry of land' that he invaded the kingdom of Durgavati 'without the slightest provocation'.[118] In the chapter on Samyukta, the daughter of the Rajput king Jayachand, she described Mahmud of Ghur thus:

> As there were mutual animosities among the kings of this country, a Muslim by name Shahabuddin Ghori invaded… and started destroying the whole country. He exhibited utmost cruelty by destroying temples, unjustly killing people, outraging the modesty of women and turning them into slaves…. Therefore, Prithviraj wanted to defeat him and protect the pativratya of women, and temples.

Samyukta, in Atchamamba's rendering, spoke to her father as a modern Indian nationalist, appealing to him not to become a 'traitor', and declared that 'it was better died than called a traitor's daughter'.[119] Several such examples in Atchamamba's book demonstrate the presence of a strong current of communal understanding of history among the early Telugu feminists. The book was widely read and celebrated by Telugu women. Because it firmly established women as *sabala* (strong, opposite of *abala*, weak), many editions of it appeared, and it continues to inspire contemporary feminists as well.

Atchamamba discussed the issue of child marriage at length and strongly advocated adult marriages.[120] Narrating the various 'great damages' the 'evil practice' of child marriage caused to women and the nation, she turned to the question of its origin. Citing examples from the Vedas and *Sutras*, she firmly stated that 'in the past, it was not there in our country'

---

[116] Bhandaru Atchamamba, *Abala Sachcharitra Ratnamala* (Madras, 1901), pp. 130–139.

[117] Ibid., pp. 159–168.

[118] Ibid., pp. 94–97.

[119] Ibid., pp. 182–183.

[120] Bhandaru Atchamamba, 'Balya Vivahamulu' (Child Marriages), *Hindu Sundary*, March 1903, pp. 1–19.

but 'invented later'. She told that while there was 'no evidence' to ascertain 'the precise time' of its origin, 'it could be said that it sprouted before the establishment of Muslim rule, but got deeply entrenched during that rule'.[121] Atchamamba's legacy was carried forward by many of her sisters.

Delivering a lecture at the women's organisation at Aska (in present-day Ganjam District, Odisha), Burra Buchchi Bangaramma, the founder-secretary of the organisation, lamented over the lack of unity among Indians (by which she meant Hindus), which provided an opportunity to the Muslims to easily conquer 'Indian' rulers 'one by one'. She lamented that 'it was impossible to count the calamities the jewel-like Hindu woman was subjected to along with her sons, other family members and friends during the reign of a few of them'. She further claimed that 'it was the opinion of a few that, as a few stone-hearted Turks used to abduct unmarried young Hindu women, the practice of child marriage came into existence'.[122] Kashinathuni Ramabayamma felt that 'though child marriages were necessary to safeguard character, virtues and the purity of society, when the country came under attacks and [fell prey to foreign Muslim rule], when the conditions changed, [we must understand that] they had no more utility'.[123] Gade Chudikudutamma, who presided over the women's conference held at Barampuram, observed that 'in the past, marrying off girls in childhood was not there. This practice had come into existence during the troubled times [of medieval Muslim rule], when our country was caught in turmoil.' Being 'under the British rule now', she was confident that 'we did not have to fear any wicked people [the Muslim abductors]' and 'could abolish this practice'.[124]

Reflecting on the 'degenerated' status of marriage practices among Hindus 'today', Sattiraju Shyamalamba said that they got 'spoilt' (*chidra dasha*) 'as the country's independence was lost' in the medieval period, purpotedly because of Muslim rule. 'At a time when our country's ancient greatness declined because of Muslim invasions, these missionaries from America and Europe came to our country like God's angels and have

[121] Ibid., p. 12.

[122] See 'Srimati Bangarammagariyupanyasamu' (Mrs B. Bangaramma's Address), *Telugu Zenana*, February 1904, pp. 244–249, for this reference, pp. 247–248.

[123] See 'Andhra Mahila Sabha: Sabhathipurali Upanyasamu' (Presidential Address delivered at Andhra Mahila Mahasabha), *Hindu Sundary*, March 1913, pp. 23–40.

[124] Gade Chudikudutamma, 'Barampuram Streela Sabha' (The Barampuram Women's Conference), *Hindu Sundary*, April 1912, pp. 14–16.

helped us', she went on to say at the Barampuram women's conference.[125] 'Reading out' her lecture on 21 January 1905, at the women's organisation at Rajahmundry, Kotikalapudi Sitamma observed that 'our country's women got habituated to the jail like *zenana* living ever since the rule of the wicked Muslims'.[126] According to Mosalikanti Ramabayamma, the practice of forcibly tonsuring Hindu widows 'started during the period of Muslim rule. It was said that, because the Muslims used to abduct unmarried girls and widows with hair over their heads, and marry them, to check that trouble, [our Hindus] started tonsuring [the widows].'[127] In an article published in the *Hindu Sundary*, the author mentioned that 'the practice of child marriages was a result of the difficulties suffered by the Hindus at the hands of the [Muslim] Turks [during the medieval period]. Child marriages might have been a useful practice then'; certainly not now.[128]

Explaining the reasons for the invention of the practice of child marriage, Konakanchi Lakshmamma wrote:[129]

> Let us examine as to why our ancestors started practicing child marriage. In the past, when our ancestors led a happy life practising religion and *Vedadhyayana*, the Muslims, being extremely cruel, were desecrating our temples, destructing the images of our Gods and thus decimating our religion. At that time, our Indians did not have the capacity to face them; so, they were afraid of them. Apart from destroying this India, they used to abduct Hindu girls and convert them into Islam. Because the Muslims were scared that they might face opposition from the husbands, if they abducted married girls, they used to abduct only the unmarried girls. Unable to tolerate the torture of the Muslims, our ancestors started arranging the child marriages of their daughters.

The communal view of Muslim invasions/rule being solely responsible for any 'social evils' among Hindus, particularly those affecting women,

---

[125] Sattiraju Shyamalamba, 'Upanyasamu' (Lecture), *Hindu Sundary,* March 1912, pp. 34–38.

[126] Kotikalapudi Sitamma, 'Hindusundarula Vidyabhivridhdhi' (On the Development of Hindu Women's Education), *Telugu Zenana*, January 1905, pp. 213–220, for this reference, p. 218.

[127] Mosalikanti Ramabai, 'Vitantu Kesha Khandanamu' (Tonsuring the Widows), *Hindu Sundary*, November 1905, pp. 210–214, for this reference, p. 212.

[128] See 'Rajaswalanantara Vivahamulu Sarva Saukhyamulaku Hetuvulu' (Post-Puberty Marriages are Beneficent in Every Respect), *Hindu Sundary*, July 1909, pp. 29–32.

[129] Konakanchi Lakshmamma, untitled essay, *Andhra Patrika Samvatsaradi Sanchika*, 1917, p. 187.

remained popular throughout the mid-twentieth century. At the All Andhra Women's Educational Reform Conference held at Kakinada on 16–17 January 1928, D. Sooryakantamma repeated the claim that 'this system of [child] marriage perhaps came into existence during Muslim rule [*turakala raajya kalamu*]' to protect girls from the Turks.[130] In her essay titled 'Stree Vidya' (Women's Education), Kongara Annapoornamma too blamed Muslim rule for the utter destruction of Hindu women's education. The fear of Hindu women being 'abducted' by the Muslims resulted in the 'seclusion' of women and attempts to 'protect' them by instituting child marriages. The cumulative effect had disastrous consequences on women's education.[131] While reflecting on the Sarda Act, A. Rajamma speculated that a few provisions mandating the practice of child marriage were inserted into the smritis. She questioned as to how 'such provisions, which came into existence during the Mohammadan rule, [could] be treated as being approved by the [original Hindu] shastras'.[132]

Delivering her presidential address to the eighth Arya Vaishya Mahila Mahasabha held on 30 June 1929 at Peddapuram, after lamenting the severe damages caused by child marriages, Pulavarti Kamalavati Devi comfortably laid the blame on 'Muslims'. She said:

> This damn unfortunate practice has come to exist among us during the Muslim rule. The Muslims did not touch the married girls. Then, the whole [Hindu] society got together, and resolved to marry off the girls by the age of eight. The practice [*samskarana*, that is, reform] came into existence very fast because of the fear of the Turks. It is since so many centuries that the Muslim rule has ended. [Now] the beneficent British rule has come [*challani Britishu paalana vachchinadi*]. However, even during this situation of peace [brought by the British], is our society coming back on the right tracks? No. Not at all![133]

The conservative sections of Andhra society, who strongly defended child marriages and vociferously opposed post-puberty marriages, presented a

[130] See 'Andhra Rashtra Mahila Vidya Samskarana Sabhalo Doo. Sooryakantamma gaariche Chaduvabadina Upanyasamu' (Speech Read by D. Sooryakantamma at the All Andhra Women's Educational Reform Conference), *Hindu Sundary*, January 1928, pp. 12–16, for this reference, p. 14. See also Atluri Venkata Sitamma, 'Balya Vivaha Nishedhamu' (Abolition of Child Marriage), *Grihalakshmi*, October 1929, p. 644.

[131] *Grihalakshmi*, September 1928, pp. 27–28.

[132] See 'Pushpachchayamu: Balya Vivaha Nirodha Chattamu', *Grihalakshmi*, April 1930, p. 143.

[133] Pulavarti Kamalavati Devi, 'Adhyakshopanyasamu' (Presidential Address), *Vasavi*, 30 June 1929, pp. 32–34. For the reference, see p. 33.

polar opposite understanding of the relationship between child marriage and 'Muslim rule'. They stubbornly maintained that child marriage was an ancient Hindu practice, and not at all an 'invention' made during 'Muslim rule' and, therefore, it could not be changed. In his book *Baalyavivaha Tatva Saramu: Laukika Tarkamu*, Achyutuni Venkatachalapati Sharma discussed the issue under the sub-section, '*Mahammadiya Prabhutvamu Baalyavivaha Kaaranamaa*?' (Is Muslim Rule Responsible for Child Marriage?). He stated that 'there was not an iota of truth' in the argument holding 'Muslim rule' responsible for the emergence of the practice of child marriage. Citing a few shlokas from the *Ramayana* of Valmiki, he discarded the argument of reformers, calling it 'useless talk':

> At the time of marriage, Rama and Sita were 16 and 8 years old, respectively. Our readers may well imagine the ages of the younger sisters of Sita, who were given in marriage to Lakshmana, Bharata and Shatrughna, the younger brothers of Rama. Sir! Are they child marriages or post-puberty marriages? Turn to me and say aloud.... Is not the logic offered by our reformers that child marriages were invented during Muslim rule merely useless talk [*kantha shosha*]?[134]

Similarly, in their book, *Rajaswala Vivaha Khandanamu* (Condemnation of Adult Marriages), Chivukula Appaiah Shastry and Shivapurapu Virabhadra Pakayazi discussed the issue at some length. In a separate chapter titled '*Baalya Vivahamulu Mahammadiya Balaatkaara Janyamula*?' (Are Child Marriages a Result of Muslim Abductions?), they rubbished the arguments of the reformers in the severest possible terms and highest degree of sarcasm. They observed that, as the argument of Muslim abduction of unmarried Hindu girls resulting in the emergence of the practice of child marriage appeared 'convincing' to those advocating post-puberty marriages, somebody from among them 'created the utterly false story' (*kattu katha*). Many dragged on the 'false story' in their writings and speeches so much so that it gained 'more credibility than the shrutis and smritis'. Complaining that 'none appeared to have questioned' the validity of the reformers' claim, Appaiah Shastry and Virabhadra Pakayazi asserted that 'only those traditionalists who had either sticky mud [*banka mannu*] or buffalo's dung instead of brain in their heads would believe that story.'

Deriding the reformers' 'story' as 'strange and absurd', they embarked on telling the 'real' story. They questioned how such 'lust-blinded' Muslims

---

[134] Achyutuni Venkatachalapati Sharma, *Baalyavivaha Tatva Saramu: Laukika Tarkamu*, other details n. a., pp. 80–84.

would have verified the marital status of Hindu girls, and on what grounds the reformers thought that they could have done so. Even if one accepted the baseless 'story' for the sake of argument, they questioned the absence of any real evidence. They further remarked that Hindu women's marital status was revealed by the mangalasutra (sacred thread) which was worn around the neck and covered. 'Then, how could the Muslims recognise that this girl was married and the other was unmarried.' Lambasting the reformers, they remarked that if this was true, it only established that the Muslims had 'more reverence for Vedic dharma than our reformist brothers'. Countering the argument of the reformers by asking several other questions, Appaiah Shastry and Virabhadra Pakayazi jubilantly proclaimed that their arguments 'completely destroyed' the arguments of the reformers.[135]

The idea of 'medieval Muslim rule' being responsible for the degeneration of Hindu women persisted in the post-independence India. Speaking at the first Andhra Women Writers' Conference held in Guntur in May 1966, women intellectuals aired this view, some subtly and others blatantly. In her presidential address, Krotta Lakshmi Raghuram said that woman had enjoyed 'great honour' in the Ancient period. However, 'because of the [changed] political conditions of medieval period, a few restrictions were imposed on her.'[136] P. Yashoda Reddy dealt with the issue at some length and in a blatant way. She said that women had enjoyed 'great freedom' during the ancient period which was totally lost in the medieval period. She elaborated:

> Generally, social customs and traditions keep changing because of the changed political circumstances. The Muslim invasion [*Turushkakramana*] of the thirteenth and fourteenth centuries and the consequent political change gave a severe jolt to Hindu society at once. The social system so carefully protected for generations together suddenly collapsed. The society which suffered from the lack of a competent ruler, the society which thought that protecting women was important thought that their women did not fall in the hands of the immoral new rulers felt it important to save them. But the [Hindu] society which could not face the powerful [and rude] *mlechchas* [Muslims] had no other way

---

[135] Chivukula Appaiah Shastry and Shivapurapu Virabhadra Pakayazi, *Rajaswala Vivaha Khandanamu*. The book was serialised in the *Abhinava Saraswati* from July 1915 to November 1916. Our references are from the July–September (pp. 119–120), October (pp. 121–128), and November (pp. 129–131) 1916 issues of the journal.

[136] Krotta Lakshmi Raghuram, 'Adhyakshopanyasamu' (Presidential Address), in Nayani Krishnakumari et al., ed., *Andhra Rachayitrula Prathama Maha Sabha Sanchika, Gunturu, May 1966*, (Hyderabad, n. d.), p. 15.

> than containing the freedom of women: it put the virgin girl in the hand of a groom in childhood itself and had a sigh of relief thinking that its responsibility was over. Perhaps, at that time, there was no other better option to stop the moral degeneration that crept into society. The virgin girl who got married as a child and entered the in-laws' home had no opportunity for receiving education and cultivating the fine arts for she got busy in household activities. Like this, the temporary arrangement necessitated by the [special] circumstances gradually became a custom, tradition and a rule and arrested [Hindu] society. Liberation is not that easy once you are arrested.[137]

Such ideologies circulate even today. Thus, many women intellectuals treated the practice as an *invention* made during the medieval 'Muslim rule'.

The Sarda Act

The Making of the Sarda Act

The sustained campaign undertaken by women, coupled with several other factors, resulted in Raisaheb Harbilas Sarda introducing the Hindu Child Marriage Bill in the Imperial Legislative Assembly in 1927.[138] The Bill was referred to a Select Committee, which altered the name of the Bill from Hindu Child Marriage Bill to Child Marriage Restraint Bill, making it applicable to all communities. Meanwhile, the Sir Moropant Visvanath Joshi Committee, appointed to consider Hari Singh Gour's Bill,[139] expanded its mandate to consider the Sarda Bill.[140] The ten-member Joshi Committee, which included two women members—Rameshwari Nehru and M. O'Brien Beadon—sent out 8,000 questionnaires and toured in different parts of the country for conducting public hearing.

In its detailed report presented to the Assembly in 1929, the Committee recommended 15 as the minimum age of marriage for girls. Not surprisingly, the Bill faced opposition from both Hindu and Muslim orthodoxy. The final Bill was amended, fixing 14 and 18 as minimum ages of marriage for girls and boys, respectively. The Bill became law in September 1929 with

[137] P. Yashoda Reddy, 'Praachinandhra Kavayitrulu' in ibid., p. 31.

[138] For more details, see Geraldine Forbes, *Women in Modern India*, pp. 83–90.

[139] The 1924 Bill was intended to amend Section 375 of the Indian Penal Code to raise the age of consent for girls in both within and outside marriage, but was defeated. Janaki Nair, *Women and Law in Colonial India: A Social History*, p. 79.

[140] Ibid., pp. 79–84, for this reference, p. 80.

surprisingly little opposition—only 14 votes against and 77 in favour—and came into effect on 1 April 1930.[141]

Conservative Reactions to Sarda Act

Although the Sarda Bill faced only muted opposition in the Assembly, the reaction of society at large was a different matter. The news of the passage of the Sarda Act struck such a deep sense of terror in the hearts of orthodoxy—both Hindu and Muslim—that they created alarmist narratives of their religion being in danger and intensely opposed the Act in the press. Journals like the *Abhinava Saraswati*[142] and *Swadharma Prakashini*[143] declared a dharma *yuddham* (a war to establish dharma) against social reformers, the legislators responsible for the passage of the Act, the INC and its leaders (particularly Gandhi), and the British government. Pulya Umamaheshwara Shastri published an extremely provocative article titled 'Sarda Smriti: "Hindumata Pariksha"' (Sarda Code: A Test to Hindu Religion).[144] His voice clearly articulates the orthodox position. The Act, according to him, presented a challenge to Hinduism, and he posed the question: 'Will you swallow poison or go to jail?' He threatened that an ignominious fall was inevitable for Hindus unless every 'Indian' (that is, Hindu) who wanted to take shelter under the *Kalpavriksha* wielded counter-weapons to kill the miasma gushing out of the 'poisonous tree' called Sarda Act. Positing women's

[141] For women's lobbying to secure passage of the Act, their responses once the law was passed and their efforts to make the law more meaningful in terms of effective implementation, see Aparna Basu and Bharati Ray, *Women's Struggle*, pp. 55–60.

[142] An extremely conservative monthly journal, it was edited by Ashtavadhani Janapati Pattabhirama Shastry and published from a small village, Janapadu in Palnadu Taluq of Guntur District (1908–1940s). The journal was stubbornly opposed to social reform, including raising the age of consent or widow remarriage as well as the Congress's programme of temple entry for Dalits. Hindu religious leaders like the Jagadguru Pushpagiri Swami and Jagadguru Viroopaksha Swami and the zamindars of Gampalagudem, Nujiveedu, Nawab Peta and Muktyala were on its list of patrons. It had subscribers even in the Hyderabad state. In the beginning, the annual subscription was Rs. 2, which was increased to Rs. 3 during the 1920s. It was printed at the Chandrika Press, Guntur.

[143] Started by Lakshminarayana Dixit, it was revived in August 1907 by Kotishwara Sharma Shastri and Kanuparti Markandeya Sharma; they were its editor and assistant editor, respectively. A monthly, it was devoted to discussing religious issues of the Hindus. The journal provided a platform for highly conservative ideologues to attack social reformers. The journal survived till the 1970s.

[144] *Abhinava Saraswati*, 21 (9, December 1929), pp. 9–18.

marriage as the 'mother root' of the *Kalpavriksha*, Umamaheshwara Shastri warned that if women's marriage dharma was destroyed, all other dharmas of Hindu religion would be corrupted instantly. Those who followed the 'pure Aryan religion' knew well that post-puberty marriage and widow remarriage were 'great evils' that corrupted and destroyed race, caste, and religion, and no scholar who studied the shastras in the traditional way would ever accept their validity. Only those who had a little knowledge of the Sanskrit language, but pretended to possess complete knowledge of the shastras, and those who 'took shelter under the morally corrupt' for filling up their stomachs, did so. It was a blunder, he stressed, to debate the shastras with those who had little knowledge of even their technical terminology. Citing a few shlokas, he argued that post-puberty marriage was unacceptable not only to the Brahmins but also Kshatriyas, Vaishyas and Shudras. Therefore, all of them must oppose the Sarda Act.

Umamaheshwara Shastri emphasised that everyone—from women (the most ignorant) to great scholars belonging to the Aryan race—knew that post-puberty marriage and widow remarriage were wrong and this made any discussion unnecesary. He wondered if such debates could ever convince reformers who had enslaved themselves to an alien language and culture. Here he quoted the *sloka*, *pittena dune rasane sitapi tiktayate* (to the one with a bile-affected tongue, sugar tastes bitter). Umamaheshwara Shastri's arguments were largely based on rhetoric and extremely mocking in tone. Referring to a pro-reform argument that 97 per cent of people conducted adult marriages, he asked what harm would befall the nation if the children born of the remaining 3 percent child marriages remained weak. He rhetorically questioned whether reformers could stop the husbands of girls married after 14-years-of-age from dying, and whether it was only the husbands of child brides who were dying. Had the mothers of all Legislative Assembly members married post-puberty, and was that why they were strong enough to make laws? Perhaps the government would make a law mandating widow remarriage! Umamaheshwara Shastri wrote that he failed to understand as to why the idea of making a law banning the very institution of marriage did not strike to those who wanted the development of the country.

Additionally, Umamaheshwara Shastri was furious with the colonial government for breaking its 'promise' of non-interference in the religious affairs of Indians, and for 'conspiring' with 'Anglicised' reformers, whom he termed 'haters of the Hindu religion and dharma'. Sentiments of those like him, who were not only the true followers of Hindu religion but loyal to the crown, had been ignored. The Joshi Committee, he rued, never sought the opinion of the common masses. According to him, a survey would have shown that most were opposed to the Act. Nor did the government take into consideration the opinions of the Hindu religious pandits and the heads of various religious establishments (*pithas*). Stating that 'the test for Hindu religion has come,' he appealed to the followers of 'Sanatana Dharma' to 'open their eyes and see the true colours of reform and also the true colours of the nation's uplifters like Gandhi', who 'could not bring any financial relief to the people… [but] were hell-bent on corrupting us with the Sarda Act.'

Such fear-mongering led to fantastic claims. Among Umamaheshwara Shastri's threats was the idea that 'such people, who made the Sarda Act' would later become rulers in independent India and put people (that is, Brahmins) behind bars for wearing the sacred thread. Traditionalists were urged to sever all connections with social reformers, organise themselves and exhibit loyalty to the British crown. Here, various other reforms such as a proposed inheritance law also became matters of contention. He asked his followers to show 'who really followed the truthful Hindu religion' and disobey the Act. The intent behind his exhortations was clear: 'May you not forsake your duties towards race and religion, until there is life in your bodies; may you establish the rule of Brahma; may you become true Aryans.'[145]

Many others joined the conservative chorus.[146] Public meetings and demonstrations were held berating the Act. In an anti-Sarda conference on 21 December 1929 in Kadiri, Anantapur district—organised at the Lord Lakshminrisimha temple—Vidwan Togarcheti Bhaskara Shastrulu

---

[145] Ibid.

[146] For example, see Chivukula Appaiah Shastri, 'Prabhutvamuvaarinta Paapakaryamunakunodigattedara?' (Can the British Government Take Recourse to Such a Sinful Deed?), *Abhinava Saraswati* 20 (4), July 1928, pp. 1–5. 'Baalika Vivaha Nishedha Shashanamu: Sanatanadharma Parayanulara! Melkonudu! Nidrinchutakidi Samayamu Kadu' (The Child Marriage Restraint Act: O Traditionalists! Awake! This is not Time for Sleeping), *Abhinava Saraswati*, June 1928, pp. 1–8. 'Baalya Vivaha Nishedha Shashanamu: Sanatanadharma Parayanulara! Melkonudu!' (The Child Marriage Restraint Act: O Traditionalists! Awake!) *Abhinava Saraswati*, March 1928, pp. 1–3, the piece was reproduced from the *Swadharma Prakashini*. Pinnamraju Venkata Subrahmanya Sharma, 'Sharada Vivaha Shasanollanghanamaa? Leka Aarsha Vivaha Shastrollanghanama? Sharada Vivaha Shasanollanghaname Kartavyamu' (Which One to Violate – The Sarda Act or the Hindu Shastra? Our Duty is to Violate the Sarda Act), *Swadharma Prakashini* 6 (7), December, 1929, pp. 9–14. 'Sharada Billu, Congresuvaru, Nijamu Bayata Padinadi' (The Sarda Bill Exposed the True Colours of the Congress People), *Swadharma Prakashini*, June 1930, pp. 7–8.

spoke against the Act. It was 'unanimously resolved to oppose the Act, which destroyed Sanatana Dharma and Hindu religion'. In a conference of the Vedamata Mahasabha in Vijayawada on 13 October 1929, presided by Brahmashri Kashi Krishnamacharyulu, members of the organisation likewise 'determined to reject' the Sarda Act and also to 'get it abolished'. To materialise their dream, they resolved to establish a Sanatana Dharma Sangha across the villages of Andhra.[147] Conferences were held condemning the Act in a number of towns and villages. In places like Guntur, Muslims also held separate conferences opposing the Act. In a conference of the Dharma Samrakshana Sabha of Pithapuram, it was resolved, among other things, 'to continue performing child marriages without submitting to the Sarda Act'. The conference was presided over by Kashibhatta Brahmaiah Shastri, who was conservatism personified. Similar resolution was passed in an anti-Sarda conference held in Kakinada.[148] Many hurriedly arranged child marriage celebrations.[149] Bolisetty Venkata Hanumantha Rao remarked that

---

[147] See 'Kadiri: Sarda Nirasana Sabha' (Anti-Sarda Conference held in Kadiri), *Andhra Patrika*, 28 December 1929, p. 15; and 'Vivaha Vayonirnaya Shasana Dhikkara Sabhalu: Bezawada' (Anti-Sarda Conferences: Vijayawada), *Swadharma Prakashini* 6 (7), December 1929, pp. 15–17. There was a virtual 'revolt' against the Sarda Act 'throughout Andhra'.

[148] See 'Nirasana Sabhalu' (Conferences Opposing the Sarda Act), *Swadharma Prakashini* 6 (7), December 1929, pp. 17–20. See also 'Sharada Shasana Nishedha Sabhalu' (Anti-Sarda Conferences), *Swadharma Prakashini*, 6 (9–10), December 1929, p. 8. The April 1930 editorial of *Grihalakshmi*, pp. 81–86, vividly narrated the activism of the conservatives all over India and particularly in Madras Presidency.

[149] In Bibi Peta village in Kamareddy Taluq of Nizamabad district, one Ganji Narayana married his 13-months-old daughter to the 26-year-old Akula Viraiah. See 'Apriyalu Okati' (1 April 1930), *Grihalakshmi*, April 1930, pp. 81–82. During the period between the passage of the Act and its coming into effect, 900 marriages were conducted in the town of Machilipatnam, which had a population of 49,000. Ibid., p. 83. Terrified by the Act, a man in a village near Nellore had fixed the child marriage of his daughter. Though the girl was infected by chicken pox just one day before the scheduled date of her marriage, 'being afraid of the Sarda Act', he got her married. See 'Kathalu, Kaburlu: Tattammavaru Posinanu Pelli Chesitirenu', *Grihalakshmi*, May 1930, p. 220. The news was reproduced from the journal, *Swatantra*. Reporting an 'infant marriage' in 1932, a news item in the August 1932 issue of *Vasavi* observed that a Vaishya man from Ongole conducted his 6-year-old daughter's marriage to escape the regulation of the Sarda Act. It reported that 'the groom passed away 2 months ago', and 'the girl was 8-years-old now.' The writer remarked that 'the Sarda Act was unable to contain its transgressors, but it caused such calamities [as mentioned in the news item].' See 'Vaartalu: Pasi Paapa Pendli' (News: an Infant Marriage), p. 182. Many others held similar views that the Sarda Act spurred on more child marriages than it checked.

the period between the passage of the Sarda Act and its coming into effect reminded him of the saying, 'by the time the Setty had adorned himself, the town was in dead silence' (*Setty singaarinchukoneloga patnam maatu maniginadi*). He mentioned that, threatened by the impending danger of the Sarda Act, many traditionalists hurried up and performed a large number of child marriages, including the girls of hardly 2- or 3-years-old, without even observing the auspiciousness or otherwise of the stars (*tithi vaara nakshatramulu*), usually a must in conducting Hindu marriages.[150]

Women's Portrayal of the Conservative Reactions to Sarda Act

In a letter dated 5 February 1930 written to her fictitious friend, Kalpalata, Kanuparti Varalakshmamma described the panicked behaviour of the orthodoxy in the six months before the Child Marriage Restraint Act came into effect:

> What strange marriages! What strange processions! What a hubbub! The prices of all commodities have gone up. The cloth stores are emptied. Vegetables in market are exhausted.... The washermen have ceased washing clothes and are rushing to carry the marriage palanquins. And, not to talk about the bustle of the music bands... No need to say about the [heavy] earnings and hurriedness of the cooks and the *purohita* Brahmins.... Attending the marriages one after the other, women invitees [*perantandru*] have no leisure at all. There is no doubt that they have forgotten their homes. Single marriage, joint marriages, marriage after marriage, one marriage within the other during the months of *Kartika* and *Margashira*, and three-fourths of the railway income came from these marriage parties. Though I received only one invitation during this deluge of marriages [*pendlindla pralayamulo*], no one would have faced the troubles and suffered sleeplessness because of the disturbance these marriages caused as I did.... Scared of cold and wearied by watching [these processions], though I sleep inside the home... how can I stop the uproar of the music bands of the incessant marriage processions from penetrating my ears? Thus, I lost peaceful sleep throughout this *Margashira* month. One night in the last week, I resolved to watch with patience every procession that passed by, but in vain. Five processions passed by in just half an hour.... I had to pass the whole of the month of *Margashira* without sleep. The no moon day [*amavasya*] came. Thinking, 'today is no moon day. The *shoonyamasa* is forthcoming. There will not be

---

[150] Bolisetty Venkata Hanumantha Rao, 'Baalya Vivaha Nirodhaka Sanghamulu' (Societies for the Abolition of Child Marriages), *Vasavi*, August 1930, p. 210.

> any disturbance of the music bands hereafter. Let me have a peaceful sleep at least today', I slept. [However, I was wrong], and there was no rest on that night even for a marriage procession suddenly descended. The bride, an innocent child, may have completed hardly three years. Sitting like a doll in the marriage of dolls, she was dusting and holding up the new frock and was keenly gazing at the new gown she wore. The ten-year-old groom was falling asleep.... After four days, another procession came by. The bride and the groom were eight-years-old.... Wrapped in a big saree, the girl was seated like *Podalakamma* [a local Goddess]. Wrapped in the big saree, she appeared like a bird trapped in a [hunter's] net. The fear of the impending Act, however, caused some sort of reform among the traditionalists [sarcastic remark]. The various taboos such as observing auspicious time and stars, *vaarapu pattimpulu*, *shoonyamu* and *moudhyamu* are not found in these marriages.... Kalpalata! Looking at the bustle of these marriages, I am surprised at the foolishness of our people. Just by performing the marriages of handy infants, how are they [parents] going to be saved from the Sarda Act? Will [pro]creation cease? Will not girls be born? Will not marriages take place? Alas! How conservative they are! ... What a pity! Out of their eagerness, they are slitting the throats of infants. Kalpalata! The problems that will arise out of these irregular marriages performed during these two-three months are going to haunt the same women, for whose welfare the Sarda Act is made, for about half-a-century.[151]

The following pictures exposed the way the Sarda Act was 'welcomed' by the conservative sections of society.

Reformist Women's Perceptions of the Sarda Act

Reformist women celebrated the passage of the Sarda Act. Reflecting on the various advantages that the Sarda Act would be accruing to Indian women, Kanuparti Varalakshmamma wrote:

> The Sarda Act, which has come because of the fortune of today's women, has removed such a great difficulty [from their lives].... by the time they complete fourteen years and enter into the fifteenth year, [they] will pass the matriculation exam, if they study in English schools, and the Vidushi exam, if they study in nationalist schools. Providing opportunity for receiving education and choice in marriage are the chief most objectives of the Sarda Act. There are many more benefits that the Act will bestow upon women. The problems of girls becoming pregnant by 12 years of

[151] Kanuparti Varalakshmamma, *Sharada Lekhalu*, Part 1, pp. 155–160.

Image 3.4: Traditionalists' responses on the eve of the commencement of the Sarda Act:

1. A lawyer aiding a pandit by providing legal points to prove that the Sarda Act was not scientific (not approved by the *shastras*).
2. A *tapaswi* performing *homa* to change the mind of the British government to withdraw the Act.
3. An astrologer engrossed in preparing *jataka*s of girls by enhancing their age.
4. A 'truthful, courageous' fellow who has declared that he would go to jail by violating the Sarda Act.
5. A man on his way to Yanam, a French colony, to conduct the marriage of his underage daughter.
6. An ultra-traditionalist praying to god to bestow the boon that girls must not be born in India.

Source: *Anandavahini*, January 1930.

> age, the consequent delivery deaths, suffering from terrible weakness and diseases all through their lives, in case they escaped delivery death, etc. are removed by the Act. And, it is certain now that the innocent girls will not be thrown to old men. Foolish parents, out of their own selfish interest, cannot sell their daughters anymore. Further, we are not going to see child widows in large numbers [as we do now]. Therefore, the Sarda Act… [is] certainly not an indicator of a state of deluge as a few are arguing…. Today, Hindu women do not have the capacity to make use of them [various rights, for example of inheritance and political representation]. Without proper education and wisdom, women cannot put these rights to good use. Therefore, I wish that our Hindu women take the advantage of education being provided by Sarda Act and gain the wisdom of fruitfully enjoying the new legislations sanctioning women a variety of rights, which are a result of the sympathy of God and humans. By doing so, I wish, they contribute to the reconstruction and development of India.[152]

If education provided the basis for gaining and enjoying various rights, Sarda Act was a catalyst ensuring the relatively delayed marriages of women. As women saw a ray of hope in the Act, they consistently opposed any amendment that would render it 'useless'.[153] For one such amendment proposed by Surpat Singh, Varalakshmamma angrily remarked that it was 'improper' and quipped that 'the Act was not made in haste…[and a result of] careful thinking of about two years'. She reminded readers that the Joshi Committee had toured all over India conducting public hearings and collecting opinions of a cross-section of people, including scholars, doctors, lawyers and, importantly, women, before making its recommendations.[154]

---

[152]Kanuparti Varalakshmamma, 'Streelaku Navina Chattamulu, Vaani Prayojanamu' (The Usefulness of New Legislations Made in Favour of Women), *Andhra Patrika Samvatsaradi Sanchika*, 1930, pp. 207–208. See also Deshiraju Bharati Devi, 'Abhivridhdhi Kavalenanna' (If We [Women] Have to Make any Progress), *Grihalakshmi*, October 1941, pp. 433–434.

[153]However, they desired amendments that made it more effective. Discussion on this follows. The WIA 'most emphatically protested against the proposed amendments of the Sarda Act'. It sent a telegram to the Viceroy, which said: 'The Women's Indian Association appeals to your Excellency to uphold the Sarda Act intact, and to disallow any amendment or change on any grounds. The proposed amendments will nullify all expectations of social reformers, especially of women, who are the chief sufferers under the present customs.' See 'Amendment to Sarda Act: Women's Protest', *The Bharata Dharma*, April 1930, pp. 11–12. *The Bharata Dharma* was an English monthly, published from Adayar, Madras. S. Raja Ram and K. V. Sesha Ayyangar were editor and joint-editor, respectively.

[154]Varalakshmamma was perhaps confused about the recommended age. In fact, the Joshi Committee recommended fifteen as the minimum age-of-marriage.

Further, she said that it was passed in the Assembly, in the presence of great leaders like Vallabhbhai Patel, Jawaharlal Nehru and Madan Mohan Malaviya. She also pointed out that since there was a five month period before it came into force, the Sarda Act was not imposed overnight. (In fact, it was six months.) Remarking that 'members had every chance to repeal the Act [but they did not],' she questioned 'whether the opponents of the Act [had] dropped asleep or had been enjoying the feasts in the uncountable number of child marriages performed all these five months [*sic*]'.[155] Varalakshmamma expressed great concern about the proposal:

> The amendment proposed by Mr. Surpat Singh provides opportunity to those, who obtain a certificate from the civil court, to marry children below the age mandated by the Sarda Act. Then, what for the Sarda Act? All those who want to conduct child marriages will obtain a certificate and conduct child marriages as usual.... The Sarda Act will in fact be [a dead letter].... If some fees are to be paid for securing a certificate, it may generate some income to the court. If there are any problems, it may provide some income to the lawyers. Kalpalata!.... There are two kinds of people, who are opposed to the Sarda Act. The group of the traditionalists argues that marriages after 14-years-of-age are against the shastras. The pragmatists' group, though wholeheartedly agrees to conduct adult marriages of girls, opposes on the ground that our right of marriage should not be surrendered to the [colonial] government.... Mr. Surpat Singh's proposed amendment will result in both the loss of the right of marriage and the loss of a benefit that is to accrue through the Sarda Act. *The situation will be like the saying, 'rentiki chedda revadi'* [incurring loss at both ends]. Therefore, my dear friend! The Sarda Act, which is made keeping in mind the development of women, either has to be implemented as it is or be wholly destroyed.... Mr. Emerson has [luckily] obstructed Mr. Surpat Singh's amendment, which is aimed at destroying the Sarda Act, with the proposal that public opinion be collected. Therefore, the nation's people must once again give their strong consent in favour of the Sarda Act.... Because the matter concerns women significantly, all women have to exhibit their strongest opposition to the amendment. It is my desire that *Grihalakshmi*, too, should cooperate in this regard. I have read in the newspapers that, having understood its dangers, our [sisters of the] Madras Women's Association conducted a conference condemning the amendment. This is a very auspicious sign. I hope that the amendment will face opposition throughout India. Kalpalata! It is true that if the

[155] Kanuparti Varalakshmamma, *Sharada Lekhalu*, part 1, pp. 186–191. The letter was dated September 1930.

> nation's people remain indifferent at this moment, we will be harming the nation rather than doing any good. Let us see how the future will be.[156]

As it turned out, the government belied any fears and did not succumb to conservatives' hue and cry and amend or repeal the Act.[157] In the Ganjam Mandal Women's Conference, held in Brahmapur on 30 October 1932, 'women unanimously resolved to congratulate the members of the Indian Legislative Assembly for refusing the proposal of amendment to the Sarda Act.'[158]

Although women celebrated the passage of the Sarda Act, their enthusiasm was short-lived because the Act contained certain loopholes[159] establishing guilt and punitive action. Women found Sub-Clause (1) of Clause 11, under which a complainant was required to execute a bond of Rs. 100, to be especially prohibitive.[160] The clause read:

> 11. (1) Power to take security from complainant: At any time after examining the complaint and before issuing process for compelling the attendance of the accused, the Court shall, except for reasons to be recorded in writing, require the complainant to execute a bond, with or without securities, for a sum not exceeding one hundred rupees, as security for the payment of any compensation which the complainant may be directed to pay under section 250 of the Code of Criminal Procedure, 1898; and if such security is not furnished within such reasonable time as the Court may fix, the complaint shall be dismissed.[161]

The Sub-Clause (2) read: 'A bond taken under this section shall be deemed to be a bond taken under the Code of Criminal Procedure, 1898, and Chapter

---

[156] Ibid., p. 187 (emphasis added).

[157] For more details, see Geraldine Forbes, *Women in Modern India*, p. 89.

[158] See 'Ganjam Mandala Mahila Sabha' (Ganjam Mandal Women's Conference), *Andhra Patrika*, 05.10.1932, p. 16. The month should be November.

[159] Because the Act's jurisdiction was confined to British India, the traditionalists easily sneaked into the territories of the adjoining princely states and also into the French and Portuguese domains to conduct child marriages. That was why women regularly demanded an amendment applying the Act to the whole of India.

[160] In the Narasarao Peta Taluq Women's Conference, organised by the Stree Vidyabhivardhani Samajamu at Narasarao Peta, on 26 October 1932, women 'unanimously resolved to appeal to the government' for scrapping the sub-clause mandating a security deposit of Rs. 100, because of which nobody was ready to lodge a complaint against the violators of the Act, and this rendered the Act ineffectual. See 'Narasarao Peta Talukaa Mahila Sabha', *Andhra Patrika*, 29 October 1932, p. 5.

[161] Radha Kumar, *The History of Doing: An Illustrated Account of Movements for Women's Rights and Feminism in India, 1800-1990* (New Delhi, 1998 [1993]), p. 70.

XLII of that Code shall apply accordingly.' Women like Deshiraju Bharati Devi[162] were unhappy with Clause 9 of the Act, which stated: 'No Court shall take cognizance of any offence under this Act save upon complaint made within one year of the solemnisation of the marriage in respect of which the offence is alleged to have been committed.'[163]

Conservatives made strategic use of the loopholes. Most importantly, they performed child marriages outside the British territories such as Yanam, a French colony, and the Nizam's territories, adjoining the British-Andhra regions. Table 3.4 amply demonstrates the magnitude of the issue.

The child marriages performed in violation of the Sarda Act, as shown in this table, are all from a single village, Errupalem, the first village in Nizam's state (Hyderabad) as one crossed the railway line straddling British Andhra (Bezawada) and Hyderabad. Paritala was another village that provided 'safe refuge' to these runaway violators. Collating these figures, the secretaries of the Andhra Mahasabha of Hyderabad observed that 'because the Nizam's government did not object to child marriages, a number of such marriages had been performed. The bordering villages of the Nizam State proved superb shelters.' Brahmins accounted for 62 per cent of the marriages while the Komatis (Vaishyas) accounted for 26 per cent, with a combined share of nearly 90 per cent of child marriages performed in the Nizam's dominions. The secretaries correlated these figures with the high proportion of child widows in the community.[164] The fact that 418 child marriages were performed in one village over just four years clearly shows how conservatives circumvented the Sarda Act.[165]

---

[162]'Abhivrudhdhi Kaavalenanna' (If At All We are to Make Any Progress), *Grihalakshmi*, October 1941, p. 434.

[163]Radha Kumar, *The History of Doing*, p. 70.

[164]They further observed that as there was no law banning child marriage in the Nizam State, there was no need to speak of the deplorable situation there. To move the hearts of traditionalists, they published the photograph of a five-year-old widowed girl of the Vaishya caste.

[165]For an example of writing published at the time about this problem, see 'Oka Mathiravasai', 'Jaabu: Baalya Vaivahikotsava Sharanya Deshamu–Mana Hydrabadu Rashtramukooda!' (A Letter: Our Hyderabad State also becomes an Asylum to Child Marriage Celebrations), *Golakonda Patrika*, 20 February 1936. This also bolstered women activists' demand that Hyderabad enact a law banning the practice of child marriage. In the women's conference held along with the Andhra Mahasabha in Sirisilla in December 1935, women of the Hyderabad State unanimously passed a resolution supporting this demand. See also M. Sarva Rao, 'Hydrabadu Rashtramuloni Balya Vivahamulu' (Child Marriages in the Hyderabad State), *Golakonda Patrika*, 17 January 1936, p. 2.

Table 3.4: Child marriages of British-Andhra subjects performed in Errupalem, a bordering village in Nizam's dominions, 1933–1936

Year (in Fasli)	Total Number of Marriages Performed	Caste	Number of Marriages	Age of Girls	Place of the Performer
1342 (1933 CE)	2	Brahmin	2	10–12	Krishna, Guntur
1343 (1934 CE)	67	Brahmin	49	10–13	Krishna, Guntur
		Vaishya	13		Krishna, Guntur
		Vishwa Brahmin	2		Krishna, Guntur
		Telaga	3		Krishna, Guntur
1344 (1935 CE)	227	Brahmin	147	9–13	Krishna, Guntur
		Vaishya	47		Krishna, Guntur
		Kamma	19		Krishna, Guntur
		Telaga	5		Krishna, Guntur
		Vishwa Brahmin	4		Krishna, Guntur
		Satani	3		Krishna, Guntur
		Reddy	1		Krishna, Guntur
		Yadava	1		Krishna, Guntur
1345 (1936 CE)	122	Brahmin	65	8–13	Nellore
		Vaishya	49		Nellore
		Vishwa Brahmin	2		Nellore
		Kamma	6		Nellore
Total	**418**				

Source: 'British India Vaasula Balya Vivahamulaku Ashrayamyna Nizam Rashtra Sarihaddulu: Andhra Mahasabha Sthayisangha Karyadarshula Prakatana' (Boundaries of the Nizam State becoming the Abodes of Child Marriage Celebrations of the Subjects of British India: Announcement of the Secretaries of the Andhra Mahasabha), *Golakonda Patrika*, 18 June 1936 (1345 Fasli, Amardad 13, Thursday), p. 9.

Note: The years in parenthesis refer to the modern (Gregorian) calendar.

While those who feared punishment conveniently sneaked into bordering villages,[166] a few daredevils openly violated the Act within British boundaries. Nadendla Ramalingaiah of Kuchipudi informed the *Trilinga*, an anti-Sarda weekly, that while he was on a tour in Krishna district in the month of May 1930, he found '5 to 6 child marriages being conducted in each village violating the Sarda Act. However, there was no news about those marriages [which would have served to encourage the conservatives].' According to him, in Ulapalli village in Ramachandrapuram Taluq of East Godavari district, three child marriages were held among the non-Brahmins and five among Dalits. In Kuchipudi village in Tenali Taluq of Guntur district, between 1 April 1930 to 15 May 1930, 50 child marriages were performed 'transgressing the Sarda Act'. About 200 marriages were held in Tenali, Pedarapuru, Pedapudi and Amrutaluru villages and 'a few more were likely to take place'. In Uttamadhanapuram of Papanashanam Taluq, two child marriages took place on 19 May 1930; the Brahmin brides were below 12 years of age. A month earlier, two Dalit men named Bangaraiah and Roshaiah of Emmiganore, Adoni Taluq of Bellary district, had performed the marriages of their daughters; both girls were younger than 12. In Bhyrapuram village, Nandikotkur Taluq of Kurnool district, a child marriage was performed in the home of Mokshagundam Shastri.[167] While a few of them received punishment,[168] many went scot-free. At

[166] 'The *Madras Mail* reported that ninety weddings were performed in Yanam on one July day in 1934, and that 'the brides and bridegrooms are the children of people whose homes are in British India territory.' Arriving on 'trains and motor buses … girls between the ages [of] five and ten were hurriedly married to boys of fifteen and eighteen.' *Madras Mail*, 3 July 1934. Cited in Mytheli Sreenivas, *Wives, Widows and Concubines: The Conjugal Family Ideal in Colonial India* (Hyderabad, 2009), pp. 80–81 and 143. Also see 'Sampadakiyamulu: Sharada Chatta Savaranalu' (Editorials: Amendments to the Sarda Act), *Grihalakshmi*, March 1938, pp. 67–68.

[167] Reproduced in the *Swadharma Prakashini*, May 1930, p. 9. A news item published in the *Grihalakshmi* reported that in Adoni (presently in Kurnool District), a man of the Kurava caste (sheep breeders) had conducted two child marriages in his home, taken out a procession and violated the Sarda Act [*sharada shasanamunu dhikkarinchenu*]. *Grihalakshmi*, May 1930, p. 234. The conservative journals were more enthusiastic about publishing the rich details of violations across British India for such details served to encourage many others to follow. For example, see *Swadharma Prakashini*, May 1930, pp. 10–13; 'Sharada Billunatikraminchi 16 vela Vivahamulu' (16,000 Marriages were Conducted Violating the Sarda Act), *Swadharma Prakashini*, June 1930, pp. 4–5.

[168] Journals widely publicised instances where punishments were meted out to those violating the Sarda Act. In one case, the priest and the *kanyadata* were fined Rs. 50 each. See 'Vivaha Visheshamulu' (Marriage Matters), *Grihalakshmi*, November 1933,

times, quite ironically, the complainants themselves landed in trouble when judgments were made in favour of the transgressors.[169]

As the Sarda Act proved ineffective in restraining child marriages, Lalchand Navalrai proposed an amendment that would apply to the whole of India, and it got the assent of the Governor General on 12 March 1938. According to this, the subjects of the British government could be punished for violating the Act anywhere in India. Another amendment was proposed by B. Das to empower judges to issue an injunction to the parties concerned prohibiting a child marriage from being arranged or solemnised, which was also accepted on 9 April 1938.[170]

This caused a commotion among conservatives and was a shot in the arm for reformers. Now that the British subjects learnt that they would be punished for violating the Act even in those safe havens that had earlier

---

p. 756. The same source discussed two similar violations in Nellore. One was among the Vaishyas and the other among Brahmins; the fathers of the brides and grooms accepted their guilt and were fined Rs. 25 each, as well as Rs. 10 as *mudara* to the complainant against the expenses he incurred. Ibid. According to a report published in *Vasavi* (reproduced from *The Hindu*), one family was fined thus: Yagnaiah, the bride's father, Rs. 700; bride's mother, Rs. 100; the groom's father, Rs. 700; the groom's mother Rs. 100; the priests, Rs. 300 each. From the fine collected, Manepalli Bapanaiah, the complainant, was given Rs. 150. The Magistrate reportedly ruled that 'the Act was known to all then. The transgressors willfully violated the law. Hence, the culprits deserved stringent punishment. However, because they had accepted their crime, he was awarding lighter punishment [only]. Hence, he was not sentencing them to jail.' See 'Sarda Actu Krinda Shikshalu' (Punishments under the Sarda Act), *Vasavi*, April 1934, p. 35.

[169] This is the sad story of one certain K. Sanyasi Rao, who made a complaint on behalf of the Sarda Vigilance Society of West Godavari District. Sanyasi Rao complained that K. Sooraiah, vice-president of Velpuru Village Panchayat, West Godavari District, had performed the marriage of his 11-year-old son with the 9-year-old daughter of Palani Chiranjivi on 22 May 1932 with V. Viraiah acting as the priest. The accused claimed that the marriage was actually conducted on 29 April 1932 and the complaint, made after one year of the marriage, stood null and void as per provisions of the Act. Rao Bahadur R. Subbaiah, the District Magistrate, held the argument of the accused to be 'true', charged the complainant with mala fide intentions, and ordered him to pay the accused a compensation of Rs. 20, Rs. 10 and Rs. 5, respectively. See 'Pendli Muchchatalu' (News of Marriages), *Grihalakshmi*, October 1933, p. 676.

[170] Bulusu Venkatramaiah, *Baalya Vivaha Nirodhana Chattamu: 1938 Sam.pu 7, 19 Savarana Chattamula Prakaramu Savarana Cheyabadina 1929va Sam.pu 19va Chattamu*, Rajolu, 20 May 1938. Also see 'Sampadakiyamulu: Sharada Chatta Savaranalu' (Editorials: Amendments to the Sarda Act), *Grihalakshmi*, March 1938, 67–68; Jaya Sagade, *Child Marriage in India: Socio-Legal and Human Rights Dimensions* (New Delhi, 2012 [2005]), pp. 52 and 68–69.

provided them shelter, they conducted child marriages 'in their very homes, in a clandestine manner.'[171]

Infuriated by the ineffectiveness of the Sarda Act in containing child marriages, and the undiminished conservatism among people, Kanuparti Varalakshmamma wrote in a fresh *Letter* that 'the throat slitting [of girls] began again. Marriages of babies of days and months of age were being performed day after day without any obstruction. We did not know when the deluge will subside.'

> The vulgarities being committed by the traditionalists, who think that their *shrotriyatva* is in danger, in such marriages are countless. [Unlike the normal procedure], no whitewashing of the walls is done. Turmeric and vermilion on the thresholds are not applied; no *torana*s [garlands made preferably of mango leaves] are hung across atop the doors; and no *pandiri* [shed made of leaves] is made in the courtyard. [They observe] nothing [of these ritual decorations essential in a marriage]. At some midnight, some four elders are surreptitiously gathering in some remotely situated dirty home [*kompa*]. By throwing the two extremely innocent infants, who are still drowsy [and unable to sit or stand properly] on the marriage seats, and by reciting some two chants, and by getting the sacred thread tied, they are somehow completing the marriage. Like this, marriages are being performed in great haste, and in an inauspicious manner.... To avoid others' attention all the marks of marriage—*paaraani* [red dye applied by women at a wedding] on the feet, sandal paste on the neck, the marriage *bottu* on the forehead, another bottu on the cheek—are erased. They are [just] content if marriage is over in some or the other way.[172]

What was worse, Varalakshmamma was shocked to learn, was that such improper marriages were covertly conducted under the guise of observing the Satyanarayana Swami *vratam* (ritual) to escape notice. Noting the irony of using a *vratam* in the name of 'Satya' (truth) as a disguise for '*asatya vivahalu*' (false marriages), she commented:

> These days, Lord Satyanarayana is helping such improper and untruthful marriages very much. Now, if anybody is asked as to what is the special occasion in their home, everyone replies that s/he is observing Satyanarayana Vratam, and none says that marriage is being performed. Everything related to the marriage, from performing marriage to inviting relatives and friends for the feast is done under the guise of

[171] Kanuparti Varalakshmamma, 'Manasulo Maatalu' (Words from the Heart), *Grihalakshmi*, June 1938, p. 224.

[172] Ibid.

> Satyanarayana Vratam. Perhaps that Lord Satyanarayana is so much a protector of falsehood, so deeply he is committed to rescuing those who sought his refuge and so strong-hearted [*sic*] that he is tolerating the... sin of this illegal infant marriage and protecting the same. To conduct such marriages, earlier, people used to go to some princely state. Now, that chance is also lost. Having learnt that they will be caught [and punished] there also, and thinking that why incur wastage by going there, people are secretly performing child marriages in their very homes.[173]

Sadly noting that non-Brahmins, who did not have to fear post-puberty marriages and who faced no religious danger in this regard, also performed infant marriages imitating the *dwija*s, Varalakshmamma pessimistically stated:

> Looking at the foolish behaviour of the irrational parents, I am overcome with sorrow. I am afraid if at all the practice [of child marriage] will ever be eradicated [*sic*]. I fail to understand who the Sarda Act will save, after all these girls, for whose welfare it is made, are married off in this mad manner of auctioning.[174]

Emphasising the importance of people's vigilance in effective implementation of the Act, she exhorted people:

> In this way, the more the Sarda Act is tightened, the more it is being loosened. If the great calamity of infant marriage is to be permanently removed, the concerned have only one way. That is to establish societies for the propagation of the Sarda Act in every village, complain to the District Collector on behalf of such Sarda Societies, if somebody is going to perform child marriage, and ensure that he [the District Collector] sends prohibitory orders to the parents of girls. If two-three such prohibitory orders reach every village, people will keep quiet. The orthodox will assume a subdued position the same way rats hide noiselessly in a home where the cat roams around. And the young children will have protection.[175]

Varalakshmamma also reminded women that they had a major role to play:

> Women have a major responsibility in eradicating these ignoble marriages. If women were aware of their own wellbeing, howsoever orthodox men may have been, could they have arranged the marriages of such small children, who played hiding behind the hem of the sarees [*pamita kongu*]

[173] Ibid., pp. 223–224.
[174] Ibid., p. 223.
[175] Ibid., p. 224.

of their mothers? Howsoever sharp the axe may be, can it fell a tree if it is not fixed to a wooden post?[176]

Dissatisfied with the Sarda Act in bringing about a substantial change in women's lives, Kadapa Ramasubbamma pointed out in 1939 that the Act had 'still not become very useful. Hence, it needed to be amended: all the child marriages conducted in violation of it be dissolved [and the defaulters sternly punished] to benefit the country.'[177] Deshiraju Bharati Devi, whose conviction it was that 'child marriages, which caused such a great harm, should be completely destroyed' and who believed that 'law was the only refuge to eliminate such things' because 'such evil practices did not completely die with mere preaching', while partially satisfied that 'the Sarda Act was useful to some extent for the development of women's education and girls' health', held that the colonial government was apathetic in the face of rampant violations. She remarked:

> Keeping quiet after making the Sarda Act is useless. The Sarda Act in execution at present is of no consequence. People have no fear of the Bill [Act]. If disallowed in Guntur, marriage can be conducted in Mathira [in the adjoining Nizam's State]. There is no fear of conducting child marriages once people cross the British boundaries. The British government is not punishing the violators. Unless the violators have any enemy, and s/he files a suit by incurring some financial loss, the culprit is not punished. Because of this, out of a hundred, not even ten cases are coming to light. Therefore, we should get all the existing provisions in the Sarda Act… [amended]. For this, the British government must take utmost interest. Just as the British government assigned to the village level employees the task of collecting census, it must order the village *munasab*s to enquire if any marriage is conducted in any home and ascertain the age of the brides and grooms and take necessary action. They alone know about the age of boys and girls because they have in their possession the records of the census. So, it is the duty of women to undertake an agitation and force the government into bringing about instant changes in this regard.[178]

Women thus treated the eradication of child marriages as 'their responsibility' and they ardently appealed to the public to remain vigilant, be sensitive

[176] Ibid.

[177] See Grihalakshmi Pratyeka Pratinidhi, 'Cuddapahlo Jarigina Andhra Rashtra Mahila Mahasabhalo Mahilamanula Gambhiroktulu', *Grihalakshmi*, January 1940, pp. 750–763.

[178] Deshiraju Bharati Devi, 'Abhivrudhdhi Kaavalenanna' (If At All We are to Make Any Progress), *Grihalakshmi*, October 1941, p. 434.

themselves and sensitise others in this regard. A number of civil society organisations were formed to ensure that the Sarda Act worked better, and women played very important roles in them. For example, Peddada Subbamma and Damerla Kamalaratnamma were elected vice-president and joint-secretary, respectively, of the Sarda Vigilance Society (*Sangha Samskaranabhivridhdhi Samiti*)[179] of the Godavari District.[180] Women like M. Subhadramma were on the executive committee of the *Sarda Shasana Paripaalana Sanghamu* (Society for the Implementation of the Sarda Act), Madras.[181]

After the Sarda Act came into force, all marriage advertisements regarding the requirement of grooms and brides, including widows for remarriage, invariably stated that they 'should be above 14-years-old.' Consider the two following advertisements, one before the passage of the Sarda Act, and after it.

Wanted Groom

A Vaishya groom, possessing the wealth of education, is wanted. The virgin is 11-years-old. [Interested people] should send letters to reach K. Chalapati Rao, Vijayanagaram.[182]

Wanted a Vaishya Widow

For marrying a 27-year-old handsome Vaishya young man, a Vaishya widow is required. She should be above 14 but below 20-years-of-age. Ornaments worth 2,000 will be provided. For further details, write to the following address.

Darishi Chenchaiah
Govindappanayani Street,
Madras.[183]

[179] A number of Sarda Committees were formed throughout Andhra to educate public opinion and also ensure that child marriages did not take place. The committees lodged complaints against the violators of the Act. A 'Sarda Act Propaganda Committee' was formed in Visakhapatnam District with K. Venkata Rao Pantulu, Joint Registrar, Visakhapatnam, as secretary. 'Its chief aim was to educate the public in the district on the benefits arising out of the "Sarda Act" and to induce them to educate the girls sufficiently, on right lines.' See *Bharatamata*, November 1929, p. 184.

[180] See 'Vivaha Visheshamulu' (News of Marriages), *Grihalakshmi*, December 1933, p. 841. Avasarala Rama Rao and Kavikondala Venkatrao were elected President and Joint-Secretary, respectively, of the Society.

[181] See 'Sarda Shasana Paripaalana Sanghamu, Madrasu', *Vasavi*, July 1932, p. 137.

[182] See 'Vivaha Prakatanalu' (Marriage Advertisements), *Vasavi*, May 1927.

[183] See 'Vaishya Vitantuvu Kaavalenu' (Wanted a Vaishya Widow), *Vasavi*, August 1930.

Intensifying the Campaign for Post-Puberty Marriages

Owing to the sustained campaign for post-pubertal marriage, the idea gradually gained ground and a few pioneers emerged amid intense orthodox opposition. The contemporary pro-reform journals gave wide publicity to the courageous actions of parents who kept their daughters unmarried even after they attained puberty. Reviewing the status of post-puberty marriages among the Vaishyas, one writer presented an interesting account of the same. Applauding the 'daring step' taken by the 'lion-like' Gontla Sriramulu Setty, an advocate from Kanigiri (Nellore District) who sent invitation cards requesting people to participate in the puberty-related function of his daughter, Satyavati Devi, he stated that it was 'a very bold step in several ways.' First, that he allowed his daughter to remain unmarried until she attained puberty; second, he courageously made a public declaration of the same; and third, organised a 10-day long celebration on the occasion. He reproduced the invitation card:

Invitation to the Great Celebration of Puberty[184]

To
Ma. Ra. Ra. Shri……

Sir;
I pray to you to make me feel honoured by taking part, along with your family, in the auspicious celebration of the first pubertal ceremony of my daughter, Chi. Sau. Satyavati Devi. The function will last for ten days starting from 12.11.1932.

Yours Sincerely,
(Sd.) Gontla Shriramulu Shetty, B.A., B.L.,
Advocate; Kanigiri.

Kanigiri
2.11.32.

With best complements from: Chimakurti Subbaraya Gupta, Police Sub-Inspector, Buchchireddy Palem; Chimakurti Venkata Subbaiah B.A.,; Darishi Rangaiah Setty B.A., B.L., Nellore; S. Krishnaiah Setty, Police Sub-Inspector, Tadivari Palle; Matla Harinarayana Shetty, B.A., B.L.,

*All the above will join the celebration along with their families.

---

[184]See 'Vaishyulalo Rajaswalanantara Vivahamulu' (Post-Pubertal Marriages among the Vaishyas), *Vasavi*, December 1932, pp. 352–353. He wrote that Kanigiri was a big village remotely located in Nellore District, where there were none among the Vaishyas, not even among the educated Brahmins, who concurred with the views of Sriramulu Shreshthi. Though none in the entire taluq had the courage to openly excommunicate him, they might secretly arrange such things by avoiding visiting his home.

The reporter was happy to note that 'at last, post-puberty marriages were taking root [even] in remote villages like Kanigiri.' He was confident that 'before 1940, post-puberty marriages would become a normal phenomenon among the Vaishyas.'[185]

It was not the English-educated and reform-minded alone who kept their daughters unmarried until the latter attained puberty. There were a few sensitive 'traditionalists' who took such measures. Addepalli Mamidaiah narrated the story of the courageous Gajjala Sriramamoorthy[186] who, despite being a traditionalist and not a social reformer with Western education, took the bold decision of not marrying off his daughter, Sushila, before she attained puberty. He successfully resisted the attempts of his 'rank [conservative and] traditionalist' relatives to disrupt his commitment. He organised a function inviting all his relatives when his daughter attained puberty.[187]

Women regularly campaigned for post-puberty marriages. They emphasised that girls must have a say in their marriage; their 'consent' was a must, and for this it was necessary for them to be older.[188] D. Anasuyamma

[185] Ibid.

[186] He lived in Buttayipeta in Bandar (Machilipatnam), and was a noted figure who worked as Honourary Secretary of the Andhra Bank for some time.

[187] Addepalli Mamidaiah, 'Rajaswalayaguvaraku Putrikanu Avivahitaganunchuta' (Keeping One's Daughter Unmarried Till She Attained Puberty), *Vasavi*, November 1931, pp. 272–273. While appreciating Gajjala Sriramamoorthy's courage and commitment, Mamidaiah made interesting remarks about pseudo-reformers, who maintained double standards. Mamidaiah wrote that despite delivering lectures in favour of post-puberty marriages and styling themselves as social reformers, many did not stick to their words till the end and failed in the test. They performed child marriages of their daughters on flimsy pretexts of obstructions by women and torturous relatives. Worse still, they conducted child marriages even after the passage of the Sarda Act. He also noted that though post-puberty marriages were not unknown to Vaishyas, they were earlier conducted in secret, obscuring the woman's status; Sriramamoorthy's actions were therefore remarkable.

[188] A number of reform-minded men supported this shift. Kavuluru Hanumantaraya Sharma said that though non-Brahmin communities practiced post-puberty marriages, their chastity remained intact. He questioned the validity of the Dharmashastras and said that they should be understood in their particular historical context. According to him, the consent of the girls was important in marriage and post-puberty marriages would help them make better choices because, by that age, they would have attained a certain level of mental maturity. Kavuluru Hanumantaraya Sharma, 'Rajaswalanantara Vivahamulu' (Post-Puberty Marriages), *Grihalakshmi*, December 1934, pp. 695–696. Also see, Dasu Madhava Rao, 'Rajaswala Vivahamulu' (Post-Puberty Marriages), *Andhra Patrika Samvatsaradi Sanchika*, April 1913, pp. 142–148. Valluri Suryanarayana Rao,

wrote that it was 'foolish' on the part of parents to get their daughters married off without the latter's 'consent'.[189] Kanuparti Varalakshmamma proposed not only adult marriages, but also insisted on the 'mutual consent' of the bride and the groom, believing that this would mitigate any domestic problems.[190] She also condemned the excessive parental interference and pressure in girls' marriage and desired that they be ended.[191]

Tunuguntla Venkata Subbamma, a staunch advocate of post-puberty marriage, reported about 14-year-old Annapoorna Devi, who had been studying in the Sharada Niketanam (an educational institution for girls; also called Sharada Ashramam) in Guntur for four years and preparing for the 'Sahiti' exam, and whose menses began on 3 December 1931. Venkata Subbamma was jubilant that the girl's parents signed an agreement with the Ashramam that they would allow their daughter to continue her studies with them even after the onset of puberty.[192] The girl's parents were true to their words: at the age of 16, after she completed her examination, she was married to 26-year-old Ranganatham Gupta, an educated man.[193]

Appealing to parents to admit their daughters in such ashramams, Venkata Subbamma wrote that they 'would be relieved of the burden of raising their daughters, and the farce of searching for grooms from very childhood.' Better the ashramam than to marry off the 'child-beasts [girls]' who were devoid of the 'sandal-scent of education' as soon as they turned 8 years old, that too by offering dowry. Instead, they could receive education for eight years and return home as 'Shiromani' once they turned 16. '[After that], if she was given in marriage to an educated and cultured young man, their family life would become holy as the couple developed love for each other and produced good children. Elders should think of such things.'[194]

'Rajaswalanantara Vivahamulu' (Post-Puberty Marriages), *Andhra Patrika Samvatsaradi Sanchika*, 1915, pp. 78–82.

[189] D. Anasuyamma, 'Patananiki Karanamu Veru' (The Reason for the Fall [of Women] is Different), *Grihalakshmi*, March 1938, pp. 31–32.

[190] Kanuparti Varalakshmamma, *Sharda Lekhalu*, November 1928, pp. 39–45.

[191] Ibid., pp. 39–48.

[192] Tunuguntla Venkata Subbamma, 'Sharada Niketanamunandu Vaishya Balika Rajaswalayaguta' (A Vaishya Girl Attains Puberty in the Sharada Niketanamu), *Vasavi*, February 1932, pp. 355–357.

[193] See Addepalli Mamidaiah, 'Rajaswala Vivahamu' (Post-pubertal Marriage), *Vasavi*, July 1933, pp. 131–135.

[194] Tunuguntla Venkata Subbamma, 'Sharada Niketanamunandu Vaishya Balika Rajaswalayaguta' (A Vaishya Girl Attains Puberty in the Sharada Niketanamu), *Vasavi*, February 1932, pp. 355–357.

Many women held 16 years as a marker of girls' adulthood and therefore the 'right marriageable age'. This view had been in existence right from the 1910s. For example, in an essay published in 1912, Kalagara Pichchamma had proposed raising the age of consent to 16 years for girls and 25 years for boys.[195] Similarly, in her essay published in the same year, Mosalikanti Ramabayamma held 16 years to be the 'right age' for girls to get married.[196] Women with adult marriages were treated as role models and spoken of in women's conferences. In fact, adult marriage captured women's imagination to the extent that it became a subject of women's literary production: take for example, the small play *Swayamvaramu* by Gudapati Lakshmi Narasamma. It was authored to celebrate the adult marriage of Achanta Rukminamma to Achanta Lakshmipati and to appreciate the reform orientation of Rukminamma's father, Srinivasa Rao.[197]

Women who advocated post-puberty marriages simply did not preach to others. They practised it in their personal lives. Balantrapu Sheshamma, editor of *Hindu Sundary* and secretary of the Shri Vidyartini Samajamu, kept her only daughter, Mahalakshmi Sundari (Mahalakshmi Sundaramma), unmarried until after she attained puberty: she was married on 20 March 1932 at the age of 18. Until then, she received education, passing several examinations such as the matriculation exam of the Benaras Hindu University. *Grihalakshmi* commented that 'the people of Andhra knew well the pro-reform stand of Balantrapu Sheshamma and it was established by her daughter's post-puberty marriage.' It appreciated Sheshamma for 'raising' her daughter to 'such an appreciable status'. It wished the girl 'success in life'.[198]

In a short story titled 'Sushilaa Rajaswalanantara Vivahamu' (Sushilaa's Post-Puberty Marriage), Maddula Damayanti Devi portrayed how traditional women gradually changed their minds in favour of adult marriage.[199] The story perceptively captured the anxieties of such mothers watching their daughters grow up, the mindset due to which they pressurised

---

[195] 'Balya Vivahamulavalana Kalugu Nashtamulu' (The Evil Effects of Child Marriages), *Hindu Sundary*, April 1912, p. 8.

[196] 'Rajaswalananatara Vivahamulu' (Post Puberty Marriages), *Hindu Sundary*, March 1912, p. 30.

[197] The book was advertised in the June 1913 issue of *Hindu Sundary*. To the subscribers of *Hindu Sundary*, it was given for 0.4 annas, and to others for 0.6 annas. However, I could not find the book in the various libraries I consulted.

[198] 'Shrimati Balantrapu Sheshammagari Sanghasamskaramu' (The Social Reform of Srimati Balantrapu Sheshamma), *Grihalakshmi*, May 1932, p. 279.

[199] *Grihalakshmi*, April 1934, pp. 120–123.

their husbands to arrange a match before puberty and the various fears that haunted them. Even the presence of the Sarda Act did not deter them from considering child marriage.

The story opened with Kalyani, wife of Ranga Rao, a rich man of the Vaishya caste, anxiously asking her husband to arrange the marriage of their 12-year-old daughter, Sushila. Ranga Rao, seated at the dining table, impatiently reminded her of the Sarda Act, which mandated that girls could not be married before they were 14. Pressurising her husband, the anxiety-ridden Kalyani said:

> In about a year or so, she [Sushila] will attain puberty. People in the world are like crows. They will excommunicate us from caste. We will be utterly humiliated because of that. Nobody will visit our home. Nobody will invite us to his/her home. ... So, please arrange a groom to marry off Sushila.[200]

Here, Ranga Rao became determined to change Kalyani's mind. No doubt voicing the author's opinion, Ranga Rao launched into a lecture detailing the various troubles the practice of child marriage caused:

> These days post-puberty marriages are held everywhere without any fear. Even Brahmins are conducting such marriages. Then, why should you worry? Why fear thinking that those people will boycott or these people will excommunicate? We must think whether such marriages [post-puberty marriages] are in accordance with our conscience or not. Women hold such superstitious beliefs and traditions because they are devoid of education. In their greed... they are giving their extremely innocent daughters in marriage to some old man or a second-marriage fellow. The girl will attain puberty at the age of 10. When she is 11-years-old, she is sent to in-laws' home. Alas! The uneducated girl does not know how to manage the home and how to serve her husband. It is impossible to describe the torments she suffers from day one at the hands of mother-in-law, if the latter is not a good person. Apart from this, there are the sisters-in-law to add to her travails. Then, look at the condition of her husband, with his wife on one side and mother on the other. Unable to take sides, he gets crushed between the two. In such a situation, who can tell how much the good-natured girl suffers being caught in the fire of grief? She will perish from protracted grief, thinking that she is undergoing such sufferings because she is not educated and is married off in childhood in a state of utter ignorance. Learning her difficulties, her parents repent thinking that they are responsible for all of her miseries. Because she becomes a mother while herself being a child, being unable to raise them and mend

[200] Ibid., p. 120.

> her home properly, [out of frustration] she will express her anger at the children. The condition of girls with child marriages is miserable in these ways. Have you understood, [my dear]!

Continuing his lecture, Ranga Rao said:

> Moreover, it is not needed to reiterate the poignant state of widowed girls. So, think well. Let us give higher education to our daughters and marry them to the boys of their liking after they cross fifteen years of age. You may well ask if problems do not arise if they are married in adulthood. But, now that they are grown up, educated and well aware of things, they will have the maturity to solve their problems. Even if they have to face problems, they will boldly bear with and face them. Because they will have choice marriages, they will not blame parents. So many such marriages [adult marriages] are taking place in the world today.

The wife was thoroughly reformed after this speech. Contrary to her apprehensions, when Sushila attained puberty, all invitees (*perantrandru*), except some two or three traditionalist women, visited her home wholeheartedly blessing Sushila. Sushila was finally married to a 21-year-old educated youth Sudarshan whose parents held a modern outlook. The author concluded that 'Kalyani was overjoyed for her daughter got a good and suitable husband. After Sushila's marriage, Kalyani started preaching among the village women to perform the marriages of their daughters only after they attained puberty [and were 14 years].'[201]

Velidanda Choodikudutamma's short story titled 'Samskarana Vivahamulu' (Reform Marriages) welcomed not only adult marriages but also inter-religious marriages.[202]

Though women continued to discuss the issue of child marriage during the 1940s and 1950s,[203] a few of them appear to have lost interest in discussing the issue anymore. One certain M. Varalakshmi (from Srikakulam), in her letter to the editor, opined that the debating clubs of the Andhra Mahila Sabha should conduct debates on 'more progressive [and important] issues [like women's right to property, etc.]' rather than on the 'routine' topics like child marriage and women's education.[204] This indicates two kinds of approaches to the issue. That a few women were losing interest shows that

---

[201] Ibid., p. 123.

[202] *Grihalakshmi*, September 1934, pp. 538–543.

[203] For example, see Samayamantri Rajyalakshmi, 'Katha Addamga Tirigindi' (The Story has Taken a Wrong Turn), *Andhra Mahila*, 19 February 1944, pp. 29–34.

[204] See 'Paathakula Lekhalu' (Letters to the Editor), *Andhra Mahila*, April 1947, p. 12.

they perhaps felt that the problem had been resolved. However, others felt the necessity of a continued discussion and saw legislation as only the end of the beginning of a long dharma yudhdha (war for a just cause).

Women Supporters of Child Marriage

While most women intellectuals, as we have seen earlier, treated the practice of child marriage as an *invention* made during medieval 'Islamic rule', a few of them stubbornly maintained that the practice had Hindu roots, being firmly rooted in Ancient Indian tradition. We now turn to their voice, as represented by Pulugurta Lakshmi Narasamamba.

Pulugurta Lakshmi Narasamamba, as mentioned earlier, a reputable scholar-activist, was rabidly opposed to widow remarriage[205] and preferred parent-arranged child marriages to consensual adult marriages.

Obsessed with inculcating the 'exquisite' virtue of pativratyam (conjugal fidelity)—'the source of India's uniqueness, greatness, honour and reputation in the comity of world nations'—among women, she emphasised that it was only the practice of child marriage that ensured the 'purity' of the same. She claimed that the social reformers, who mimicked the Western values, belittled Indian marriage practices and tried to graft Western values to India.[206]

Reacting to the views of reformers—who maintained that great women like Sita, Chandramati and Savitri could become pativratas because of their adult and choice-based marriages (*swayamvaram*), and that the present women could not achieve 'firm pativratyam' unless they followed their example—she argued that swayamvaram was approved only for royalty. She warned that 'we should not dare to desire that all women marry the swayamvara way, and ought not to say that, if they did not, their fidelity was at stake' (*nischala pativratyamu*). 'It was not the swayamvara marriages that made our country the fountain of pativratyamu', she stressed.[207] She sarcastically suggested the 'modern wise people' look to the difficulties

[205] Her stand on the question of widow remarriage is discussed in detail in the following chapter.

[206] Pulugurta Lakshmi Narasamamba, 'Pativratyamu' (Conjugal Fidelity), *Savithri*, July 1911, pp. 1–17, for this reference, pp. 3–4.

[207] Ibid., pp. 6–7.

suffered by that *Medipandu*-like Western country Great Britain,[208] the role model of the reformers because of its adult marriages (*proudha vivahamulu*). They were asked to listen to the victims of such marriages in the Western world.

To corroborate her stand that adult marriages were problematic, jeopardised the pativratya dharma of Indian women and that they had deprived Europeans of 'marital bliss', she quoted a scholar Frederick Pincard (*paaschatya panditudu*), who said that 'the absence of free system of marriage [*swechcha vivaha padhdhati*] in India saved Indian girls from the fickleness [*chapalyamu*] of [and the consequent difficulties faced by] English girls.' He was quoted as having opined that 'in India, the bride and the groom thought that Brahma [fate] tied them to each other and therefore they should continue to live together till the last.' 'Since childhood, they learnt to adjust to the future times [when they actually start living like husband and wife].' 'It was known to all that mutual understanding formed the basis of marital bliss...and child marriage developed such required understanding', he reasoned. Further, he said:

> These exquisite provisions have stood the test of centuries. Their praiseworthy status is revealed by their fruitfulness. All are unanimous about the fact that the Hindu family [*grihasthashramamu*] is a happy one. Howsoever mad the present social reformer may be, he/she will certainly not think that Hindu marriages are unhappy ones. This alone [domestic marital happiness] is an example to state that, that system is paragon, and those trying to disrupt it deserve condemnation.[209]

Lakshmi Narasamamba emphasised that 'even the civilised foreigners unequivocally agreed that the Hindu marriage practices alone presented higher ideal to the world.'[210]

Westernising reformers questioned the 'authority' of parents in arranging the marriage of their daughters when they were still very young: this they did because such a practice was treated as wrong in the West. If it was right for the West, it need not be so with Indians, Narasamamba argued. Again she brought Frederick Pincard, who was all praise of Indian parents' responsible nature, to her defense, quoting him:

---

[208] 'Medipandu' refers to the glamorous fig fruit, which bloomed from outside, but contained insects within.

[209] Ibid., pp. 7–8.

[210] Ibid., p. 9.

> In India, parents think it binding upon them to procure grooms for their daughters. To do this, the father is ready to spend all the wealth he has earned all his life. This is responsible for the Hindu marriage not being treated as an insignificant affair as is the case in the West. According to the Hindu system, it is obligatory that the guardian arranges a girl's marriage, facing any number of hardships and spending any amount of money....[211]

If Indian parents interfered too much in the marriage of their daughters, it was justified, Lakshmi Narasamamba wrote, since unlike the Western parents who used contraceptives to avoid childbirth and saw procreation as a means of 'carnal pleasure', Indian parents spiritualised the same: they prayed to God, offered *puja*s and observed *vrata*s and *nomu*s to beget children. Therefore, they could not afford to be irresponsible to avoid interference in their daughters' marriages.[212]

According to her, 'many, including the modernists [*nava naagarikulu*] and the completely civilised Westerners [*sampoorna naagarikulaina paaschatyulanekulu*] believed that only such marriages were noble that were conducted long before love dawned in the hearts of girls and thus protected their pativratyam by stabilising their minds and hearts.'[213] She stressed that 'today's people should understand that the system developed by our ancestors to marry off girls at appropriate time [*yukta kalamulone*] to safeguard the king of virtues called pativratyam, the root of Hindu country's glory and respect, was not without [relevance and] appreciation.'[214] She brought another English scholar, O. S. Fauler, to her support. Fauler is quoted to have written that

> If a suitable husband is arranged at the right time and her love is channelised towards the right path and allowed to [reach] fruition, not even one among ten will be dragged to the evil path. [In the Hindu marriage system], since a husband is already arranged by the time the need for marriage is felt [by the girl], such arrangement, by allowing [and ensuring her] love to be fully focused on the husband, makes it impossible

[211] Ibid. Frederick Pincard provided safe shelter to many who supported child marriage. Chivukula Appaiah Shastry and Shivapurapu Virabhadra Pakayaji, trenchant critics of the very idea of adult marriage of girls and staunch proponents of child marriage, quoted him at length to attack social reformers. See 'Rajaswala Vivaha Khandanamu' (Condemnation of Post-Puberty Marriages), *Abhinava Saraswati* 8 (7–9, July, August, September) 1916, pp. 97–120; for this reference, p. 112.

[212] Pulugurta Lakshmi Narasamamba, 'Pativratyamu' (Conjugal Fidelity), *Savithri*, July 1911, p. 10.

[213] Ibid.

[214] Ibid.

> for the [love-possessed girl] to take any evil path. If such arrangement is not made, i.e., if the girl is not married very young [*jinnanadu*], her love will flow in other [wrong] directions.... Except death, nothing can stop it [from flowing in wrong directions].[215]

Narasamamba appealed to all to observe that child marriage[216] was appreciable for it made 'our country' a greater center of *pativratyam* than other countries. She wondered 'if the reformers suggested [that] girls, whose marriages their parents arranged, [should] quit husbands and marry others of their liking, if they did not like their parent-arranged husbands.'[217]

Rayaprolu Shesha Somidevamma proved to be a wonderful intellectual heir to Narasamamba in furthering the project of occidental vilification during the Sarda Act controversy. In her inaugural address to a conference of the women's wing of the 'Andhra Desha Varnashrama Dharma Sabha' at Vijayawada,[218] Rayaprolu Shesha Somidevamma[219] spoke about the

[215]Ibid., pp. 10–11.

[216]What is remarkable to note is that, in this source, she rarely used the phrase '*baalya vivahamulu*' or '*atibaalya vivahamulu*', the phrases used by her contemporaries for 'child' or 'infant' marriage. The phrases she used—'*chinnanadu chesina vivahamulu*' or '*yukta kaalamulone vivahamulu*'—are rather unclear. She did not specify what the appropriate age, *yukta kaalamu*, would be. However, in the beginning of her essay, she used the phrase, '*nati baalyamunane baalikalaku vivahamu cheyuta*' (marrying off girls in their infancy), terming the same as 'unscientific'. Further, she found fault with the practice of marrying off girls to old men and infant boys. She stressed that 'unless such demerits were corrected, our country would not regain the past glorious state'. However, on the whole she supported prevailing Hindu marriage practices, including child marriage. She said that changes were required, but not in the way the modern reformers (*navina budhdhimantulu*) desired. She wanted development on 'nationalist lines', not the Western way. Ibid., pp. 3–5.

[217]Ibid., p. 11.

[218]The conference was held in November 1929, where more than 1,800 'traditionalist' women assembled. Women 'condemned' the Sarda Act and 'resolved to disobey it'. A *hartal* (agitation) was staged opposing the Act. The conference was presided over by Gudipudi Indumati Devi. See *Swadharma Prakashini*, 6 (7, December 1929), p. 24. Kanuparti Markandeya Sharma, editor of the conservative monthly, *Swadharma Prakashini*, was the secretary of the 'Andhra Desha Varnashrama Dharma Sabha'. Govu Ramachandra Rao was its joint secretary. The organisation launched a serious campaign against the Sarda Act holding it to be 'opposed to opinion of the majority'. See 'Prakatana' (Announcement) in ibid., pp. 4–5.

[219]As of now, all that we know about her is that she was the founder of the 'Durga Rishikula Vidyalayam' and authored two books, *Baalya Vivaha Chandrika* and *Satidharma Sangrahamu*.

'greatness' of child marriages and the 'evil effects' of girls' adult marriages.[220] Informing her female audience about the way the Sarda Act outraged women's dharma, she appealed for their support. Emphasising the indispensability of protecting women's marriage-related dharmas to ensure the purity of caste, varna and race, she said:

> Among all the dharmas, the dharma related to women deserves to be protected with great care and honour. It is emphasised that woman is the center of everything.... It is mandatory that *stridharma* is always to be protected. If women are spoilt, it leads to *varnasamkara* [mixing and contamination of varnas]; with this, Indian race will be destroyed. So, whether women or men, whatever they may do, they must ensure that, instead of getting destroyed, the Indian race regains its original glory. 'What has come to spoil women today', you may ask. Listen. Now the Sarda Act has come into existence. 'So, what is the harm?' you may ask. The Act prohibited the marriage of a girl below the age of 14; if you perform, you will be punished. In our country, girls generally attain puberty between 12 and 13 years-of-age. Post-puberty marriages are against the Dharmashastras; they cause us hell. Many have written about the way women are becoming licentious and pushing the entire society into troubles in those countries where post-puberty marriages are in vogue. Women of that age [14 years and above] may marry on their own a man of their liking or freely roam around discarding marriage itself. If we allow our girl to marry according to her choice, she [may]... marry a man of a different caste/varna. Or, she will not marry at all. In either way, *varnasamkara* and destruction of race are inevitable.

Vilifying Western women, she claimed that unmarried women in the West caused 'a state of deluge' to their countries. She observed that 'those demanding post-puberty marriages of women desired women's educational development, their independence and equal rights to men'. However, she went on, child marriage did not obstruct women's education for women were expected to receive an entirely different kind of education:

> I fail to understand how child marriage is an impediment to women's education. Because people are under the illusion that women's education means English education, and receiving that means passing the B.A., or M.A., they are talking so. But, if we understand that education really means reading the Puranas, etc. in the native languages and Sanskrit

[220] 'Andhra Desha Varnashrama Dharma Sabha Stree Shakha, Bezawada: Durga Rishikula Vidyalaya Sthapakuralagu Rayaprolu Shesha Somidevamma Garicheniyabadina Swagatopanyasamu', *Abhinava Saraswati*, June 1930, pp. 5–8.

and gaining the knowledge contained in them, I humbly convey to you that child marriages are not obstacles to such an education. Between 6 and 10-years-of-age, girls may be allowed to receive education from a male teacher. After that, she may be taught [at home] by her father and thereafter by her husband [if they so wished]. She should not be taught by some Apparao, Subbarao and Venkatrao [Tom, Dick and Harry]. Women's education should be such that it makes a woman a good homemaker [*sadgrihini*]. Therefore, women must be taught such subjects as the duties of a pativrata, domestic management, modesty, devotion to God [and husband], generosity, raising children and cattle rearing, etc. Such things are available in the knowledge contained in the native languages. [So, there is no need to learn English, a foreign language, which has the potential to unsex Indian women.]... Woman is dependent on man as per the rule of nature. The Dharmashastras teach that women's dependence on men is [the real dharma]. Only those in such a relationship are able to enjoy their lives.... Therefore, I request women that they should not conduct with independence and enjoy life themselves depending on men. Equality, which is not there in [God's] creation, does not come into existence merely because we wish it. Those desiring women's independence are establishing organisations for women the same way they are established for men. Because of this, instead of performing their due [*dharmic*] responsibilities, women are treading the wrong paths.... Home is the theater to the play of women's lives. Husband is the principal actor [*sutradhari*] and children the other actors. By performing her due roles in this play, a woman can derive the greatest pleasure [*bramhanandamu*]. Such sacred dharmas of women can be achieved by child marriage only. In the adult and choice based marriages, all these dharmas get contaminated [and lost permanently]. In our country, even among those castes, which are performing adult marriages of girls, they are not independently choosing their husbands.... But, today, if you allow girls to marry as per their choice, they can examine only the external characteristics, and not beyond that, and marry [some low born fellow]. Any adult girl will marry keeping in mind the man's physical features, age, wealth or education, without bothering about caste honour. This leads to contamination of varnas. Therefore, I appeal to you all to think of all these things and convey through our men [because we, the pativratas, should not do such things on our own] our strong opinion [objection] to the government that post-puberty marriages are harmful, that they are banned for the twice-born [*dwijulu*], and that to compel [us] to conduct such marriages is against our dharma. I pray that those who wish to know more about the dharmas of women may read my book, *Satidharma Sangrahamu*.

Given this support of child marriage, it is not surprising that conservative women petitioned the British government registering their objections to the Sarda Bill. The intensity of Andhra women's opposition to the Bill/Act can be easily gauged by the number of petitions they sent to the government during a week's time between 25 August 1929 to 2 September 1929.

Despite this, a majority of literate women, as evidenced by our sources, continued to oppose the practice and demanded a further increase in the age of consent for both girls and boys. Reflecting on the decision of an United Nations committee that met in Geneva, where it was resolved that all nations should make 15 years the minimum marriageable age of girls, an editorial in *Andhra Mahila* commented that though the proposal was 'acceptable', it was certainly not adequate because 'girls of 14 or 15 years-of-age would be in the twilight of childhood and adulthood'. Though the proposal made an advance over the age mandated by the Sarda Act, 'as per the changing times', the article sought a minimum age of 18 years and suggested that this should be legally enforced.[221] It was only in 1978 that the independent Indian government fixed 18 years as the minimum marriageable age for girls.[222]

However, despite the legal ban on and a sustained campaign against child marriage, the number of child marriages did not diminish; rather it increased. Table 3.6 demonstrates this tragic fact.

Conclusion

In this chapter, we have discussed how the problem of child marriage engaged the attention of women intellectuals in Andhra right from the start of the twentieth century. Apart from the progressive voices of women, we have heard the conservative voices as well. In the arguments of women against child marriage, both rational and religious aspects could be discerned. While almost all women intellectuals initially cited the Hindu

---

[221] See 'Kanyalaku Vivaha yogya Vayassu' (Suitable Age of Marriage for Girls), *Andhra Mahila*, May 1961, pp. 2–3.

[222] In 1949, 20 years after the Sarda Act, which had fixed 14 as the age of consent, the limit was revised to 15 years. The same age continued in the Hindu Marriage Act of 1955. For details, see Jaya Sagade, *Child Marriage in India: Socio-Legal and Human Rights Dimensions*, pp. 44 and 75. For a brilliant analysis of the politics involved in the 1978 amendment, see Geraldine Forbes, 'Women and Modernity: The Issue of Child Marriage in India', *Women's Studies International Quarterly* 2, 1979, pp. 407–419.

Table 3.5: Number of petitioners against the Sarda Bill from 25 August 1929 to 2 September 1929

District	Men	Women
Godavari	4543	1000
Krishna	2500	400
Guntur	3500	400
Nellore	900	200
Kurnool	1350	100
Bellary	1200	–
Cuddapah, Anantapur & Chittoor	500	–
Vishakhapatnam	500	–

Source: *Swadharma Prakashini*, Vol. 6, No. 7, December 1929, pp. 3–4.

Table 3.6: Child marriages of girls between the ages of 0–15 in the Rayalaseema districts, 1921–1961

District	1921	1931	1961
Cuddapah	13,573	15,651	25,324
Kurnool	17,547	23,591	27,317
Bellary	16,804	20,220	27,389
Anantapur	16,689	17,679	29,539
Chittoor	16,206	23,363	N.A.

Source: T. V. Manjulatha Devi, 'Child Marriages in Rayalaseema, 1920–1950', *Itihas* 16 (1, January–June) 1990, p. 172.

shastras, this later became less significant as women argued against the practice on rational basis and 'everyday experience'. They emphasised that child marriage was against nature, obstructed the education of women, spoiled their health and damaged the reputation of the nation. Child marriage stifled the natural growth of girls and caused 'civilisational shame'. Saving the mothers' health and that of the infants was emblematic of saving the nation's health, a rhetoric strategy that figured prominently in the later writings of women. They vividly described the problems faced by child wives and child mothers and the incompatibility that the practice caused between wives and their relatively older husbands, resulting in perennial domestic turmoil. Child marriage was thus the root problem behind the degeneration of 'Mother India'.

Along with campaigning for raising the age of consent, particularly for girls, women campaigned to reduce the age gap that existed between wives and husbands. They berated older men for marrying 'granddaughter-like' girls and demanded a ban on marriage of men over the age of 40 with young girls. As time progressed, women constantly demanded post-puberty marriages, emphasised 'choice' and 'consent' of girls and denouncing excessive parental interference in marriages. If delayed marriages enhanced the educational opportunities of girls, the presence of greater higher educational institutions ensured the postponement of marriages. As the issues of women's marriage and education were so closely interconnected, women demanded the establishment of women's higher educational institutions. With this realisation, several women activists themselves established schools for girls, and those who could not regularly campaigned in their favour. Women's organisations played a significant role in this regard.

Women who were opposed to child marriage argued that the practice was not there in the 'original religion' of the Hindus and that it was a latter day 'invention'. They found the need for such an 'invention' in 'villainous medieval Muslim Rule' and the bogey of the 'abducting Musalman'. This communal view was dominant in the writings of reformist women intellectuals. However, conservative women, who argued in favour of child marriage, consistently and stubbornly maintained that the practice had original Hindu roots and certainly not an invention made during the 'Muslim rule'.

The reformist women intellectuals also expressed their disagreements with male nationalist leaders who thought that social reform/woman's question could wait until the attainment of political freedom. Many of them did not think that allowing the foreign government to interfere in the 'internal' affairs of the Hindu home was undesirable; rather, they *welcomed* it as a *panacea* to their problems. We have established in this chapter that reformist women were strongly in favour of the British government's interference from the very start of the twentieth century. We have seen how women like Uppuluri Nagaratnamma extolled British rule.[223]

---

[223] According to her, it was 'more benevolent and beneficent' than the rule of the 'divine incarnations' like Rama, Sri Krishna and Yudhistara. Never before had Indians experienced and enjoyed such a 'just rule'. Uppuluri Nagaratnamma, 'Angleya Paripalanamuvalani Labhamulu' (Benefits of the British Rule), *Vivekavathi*, May 1912, pp. 234–237.

Naturally, they campaigned to ban child marriage through legislation and were overjoyed when the Sarda Act was passed, seeing a new dawn of hope in it. However, as they witnessed the Act being freely flouted by the orthodox sections, they criticised the British government for its 'indifference' in taking stringent action against the violaters, and campaigned for suitable amendments. Women's organisations played a commendable role in educating public opinion, lobbying with the British government and keeping the issue alive during the heyday of the national movement. The change that was effected by the Child Marriage Restraint Act was small but very significant. It was certainly much more than a symbolic victory to women.

The impression that one gets by a careful reading of the contemporary women's journals, particularly those edited by women, is that a majority of literate women were in favour of abolition of child marriage, with only a minuscule minority opposed to it. In the following chapter, the allied subject of widows and widow remarriage will be analysed.

4

Representing Widowhood

Tragedy, Defiance and the Conservative Backlash

> Raja Rammohun Roy got the [practice of] Sati banned. But, I feel that *sahagamana*, which kills you instantly, is better than suffering from the humiliation [of being a widow] all through the life.... In this society, which is full of evil practices, death is better than life.
>
> Prabhavati, a child widow,
> in Adurti Bhaskaramma's eponymous short story[1]

A devastating consequence of the practice of child marriage was the problem of early widowhood. As per the Census of 1911, there were 2,70,00,000 widows in India, of whom 250,000 were below the age of 14, and 14,000 were below the age of four.[2] Table 4.1 shows the number of widows aged 0–15 years in Madras Presidency, as per the Census of 1911. Further, the problem of early widowhood in the Telugu-speaking districts of Madras Presidency is amply demonstrated in Table 4.2.

Despite strenuous efforts made by early reformers in Andhra in the mid- to late-nineteenth century, opinion against widow marriages was still strong in the first half of the twentieth century. The problem of child widows was more acute in the coastal districts than in Rayalaseema. Among the coastal districts, Ganjam and Krishna witnessed a slight decline in the number of child widows between the years 1921–1931, whereas

---

[1] *Bharati*, August 1926. *Bharati* was a famous literary monthly journal. All translations are by me, unless specifically mentioned otherwise.

[2] See 'Aayachotla Jarigina Sangatulu: Hindu Deshamandali Vidhavalu' (Widows in India), *Vivekavathi*, July 1913, p. 319. The journal reported 433 widows under the age of one year in Bangalore city alone. The report concluded with a public appeal to 'remove our loving lasses from the terrible slavery of widowhood'. Equating widowhood with slavery is a telling sign of how the state of widows was viewed.

Table 4.1: Number of widows (0–15 years of age) in Madras Presidency, as per 1911 Census

Age Group	Number of Widows
0–1	859
1–2	1,039
2–3	1,886
3–4	3,732
4–5	8,180
5–10	78,407
10–15	2,27,367
Total	**3,21,470**

Source: 'Editorials: Some Startling Facts Concerning Child Widows', *Vivekavathi*, March 1915, p. 163.

Table 4.2: District-wise statistics of widows in the age group of 0–20 years

District	1891	1901	1911	1921	1931
Ganjam	6960	6429	10638	9130	7979
Visakhapatnam	7618	10137	11207	10794	12985
Godavari	8271	8677	6158	5428	11050
Krishna	5766	5613	7026	6270	3623
Nellore	3042	3382	2689	2908	3791
Cuddapah	2921	125	2103	2485	2420
Kurnool	1759	1780	1986	2284	2749
Anantapur	1396	1739	2238	2759	2614
Chittoor	–	–	2118	2334	3196
Guntur	–	–	4394	4445	6040
Bellary	1613	2078	2516	2774	2521
Madras City	–	657	763	562	837

Source: B. Kesava Narayana, 'Widow Marriage Movement in Andhra', *Itihas* 2 (1), January–June 1974, p. 161.

Visakhapatnam, Godavari and Guntur districts registered an increase. Within the Rayalaseema region, Cuddapah and Anantapur saw a marginal decline, while there was a slight increase in the number of child widows in the rest of the region.

Widows, regardless of age, were disallowed from remarrying and subjected to innumerable hardships. They were forced to undergo ritual tonsuring, barely allowed any food, treated as ill omens, routinely harassed and forced to shoulder domestic duties with little rest; in short, they were deprived of a proper human existence. The physical and psychological pressure was so great that a few died by suicide, several ran away from their homes,[3] and yet others formed illegitimate sexual relationships.[4] Sexual exploitation was another issue. Due to the pressure from stringent sexual prohibitions, widows would sometimes murder children who were illegitimate; this happened in cases of consensual relationships, as well as in cases of pregnancies resulting from rape.[5] Many silently suffered these forced ignominies. The widow remarriage movement, initiated by male social reformers like Veeresalingam, inspired many women. To register

[3] *Vivekavathi* published a news item about a widow who sought to escape the confines of her social status. A young Brahmin widow was interested in remarriage and ran away, seeking refuge in a 'Widow Home' run by Veeresalingam at Rajahmundry. Alleging theft, her father dragged her back home; however he was later arrested. A more detailed description of the case is available in Chapter 2, this volume. See *Vivekavathi*, November 1909, pp. 34–35. *Hindu Sundary* also reported on the ongoing case. See 'Vartamanamulu' (News), *Hindu Sundary*, August 1909, p. 30. Veeresalingam's autobiography mentions a number of widows who ran away from their natal homes for remarriage. See the section 'Recovering Widows' Agency' in this chapter.

[4] Illegitimate relationships were taboo and yet extremely common. Attitudes towards women's sexuality are reflected in the fact that the word '*munda*' in Telugu was a pejorative that could be used for both widows and sex workers. In his autobiography, Veeresalingam mentioned a 16-year-old young widow in Rajahmundry who, being barred from remarriage, became involved in an illicit relationship. What is remarkable is that her family members, despite opposing her wish to remarry, grudgingly approved of her relationship. See Kandukuri Veeresalingam, *Sweeya Charitramu*, Part 1, pp. 177–179. Veeresalingam alleged that celibate disciples of the religious head, Sri Shankaracharya, who feverishly opposed widow remarriage, maintained illicit sexual relations with widows. One such affair, between a disciple and a Brahmin widow, was exposed and Veeresalingam's students dragged them out onto the street. While narrating this episode, Veeresalingam pejoratively termed widows in such relationships as '*randa*' (a corruption of the Hindi slur *randi*, or prostitute). Ibid., p. 221. He also used 'munda' while deriding a relationship that his cook, a Brahmin man, was engaged in. Ibid., p. 233.

[5] A news item in the *Andhra Patrika* reported that a Brahmin widow of Chirala village in Guntur district (now in Bapatla district) delivered a baby, evidence of her 'secret prostitution'. The baby was killed and hidden in a pot. The police arrested the widow. See 'Vrittantamulu: Kula Pavitratakoraku Shishu Hatya' (News: Infant Murdered for Caste Purity), *Andhra Patrika*, 16 August 1914, p. 9.

their anger at the barbaric treatment of widows and to advocate remarriage, women made effective use of print media, particularly journals.

Women's journals covered the issue of widowhood in a variety of ways. Apart from publishing articles, speeches, poems, short stories, burlesques, short plays and novelettes by authors—both women and men—the journals published a variety of information about widows and widowhood. As we have seen, they regularly published statistical data about widows in India and the Madras Presidency, along with news about the establishment of rescue homes for widows across the country, photographs of widows who had emerged as public figures, and news of widow remarriages performed in various parts of the country. The editorials of these journals took a special interest in this issue.[6]

A careful reading of women's writings in these journals reveals that, despite the involvement of women like Kandukuri Rajyalakshmamma, in the initial phase (from the late-nineteenth century till about 1910), few writings or speeches openly advocated widow marriages. Most of them focused on describing the suffering of widows, evoking great sympathy for their miserable plight and appealing to the larger public to show mercy on them; very few displayed the courage to directly propose remarriage for widows. Drawing attention to the numerous encumbrances imposed on widows, they pleaded for humane treatment and freedom from restrictive norms. Women's writings highlighting the horrifying aspects of Hindu widowhood flooded women's journals of the period, usually published under titles designed to appeal to readers' emotions, such as 'Mana Hindu Vitantuvula Dusthiti' (Miserable Condition of Our Hindu Widows)[7] and 'Vitantuvula Mora' (Lamentation of Widows)[8].

We can broadly identify four streams of voices in the discourse on widows: (*a*) those who confined themselves to describing the atrocities inflicted on widows and demanded amelioration, but not remarriage; (*b*) those who advocated remarriage of child widows only, citing the sanction of Hindu scriptures; (*c*) those who advocated remarriage for both child and adult widows based on legal provisions, and argued that widows,

[6] We have already seen the way the individual women's journals covered and treated the issue in Chapter 2.

[7] Varanasi Kameshwari, 'Mana Hindu Vitantuvula Dusthiti' (Miserable Condition of Our Hindu Widows), *Hindu Sundary*, April 1905, pp. 1–5.

[8] Savitri, 'Vitantuvula Mora' (Lamentation of Widows), *Hindu Sundary*, August 1909, pp. 26–27.

too, had the right to a happy married life (including a right to sex); and (*d*) those which strongly objected to widow remarriage.

Descriptions of the Suffering of Widows

A rigorous sensitisation campaign laid bare the miserable life of widows, particularly child widows. For instance, the following song (*paata*) by 'A Woman' portrays the lamentation of a widow:

> Oh, mother! Oh, sister!
>
> So miserable on this earth
> My life has stood.
> Without my consent,
> I have fallen prey to widowhood.
>
> Oh, mother!
>
> With a knife so sharp,
> When my locks are shaved off,
> No showers of pity,
> Even from my own mother.
>
> Oh, mother!
>
> Shorn off attractive apparel,
> And given a coarse scrap of cloth,
> Alas!
> Why is fate so cruel?
>
> Oh, mother!
>
> Powdered down are
> Bangles and bracelets,
> Oh, dear!
> And, so terribly starved,
> The stomachs are.
>
> Oh, mother![9]

Another poem, authored by Uppuluri Nagaratnamma, who was herself widowed in childhood and remarried later, poignantly appealed to God:

> Listen, O Lord, to the grief of widows.
> Not to give an ear to our plight,
> Is it great on your part?

[9] 'Oka Stree' (pseudonym, meaning 'A Woman'), *Hindu Sundary*, December 1909, p. 31.

Married off to a man,
The moment we are born.
Hung around our necks the sacred ties,
Even before we opened our eyes.
When falls dead the husband such,
The elders subject us to troubles much.
Turned into ugly we, the beautiful,
Are ground under the tortures, so scornful.
With no fear of sinning,
Alas! They cause us so much suffering.

We deserve only one meal, they say,
And do not feed us properly, and the hunger is not away.
Finding faults and belittling,
Subject us to harshness, the cunning.

Treated as servants,
Rarely given just the tattered rags,
Assigned works of all sorts,
Alas! Never ending grief to women.[10]

Essays authored by women were more straightforward and openly critical. The genre was more effective in facilitating direct and lucid communication, allowing even amateurs to express themselves clearly. In the first two decades of the twentieth century, women's journals carried more essays than writings in other genres.

For many of these writers, death was preferable to the torturous existence of widowhood. Balantrapu Sheshamma likened the trouble 'our people' caused to young widows with 'putting furnaces in their laps'.[11] To Varanasi Kameshwari, the mere sight or mention of the state of widows caused sorrow. She questioned how the parents of widows, who cried over the death of their son-in-law, could bear to tell girls as young as five years that their husbands were dead.[12] 'Whose heart did not melt, if one thought of their situation?' asked an anonymous writer. In her view, 'even the hearts of the butchers, who killed living animals and sold their flesh, melted

[10] Uppuluri Nagaratnamma, 'Stree Punarvivahamulu' (Widow Remarriages), *Hindu Sundary*, October-November 1911, pp. 27–28.

[11] Balantrapu Sheshamma, 'Rajahmundry Prarthana Samajamuna Srimati Balantrapu Sheshammagarichchina Upanyasamu' (Balantrapu Sheshamma's Lecture delivered at the Prarthana Samaj in Rajahmundry), *Hindu Sundary*, December 1909, pp. 18–23; for this reference, p. 21.

[12] Varanasi Kameshwari, 'Mana Hindu Vitantuvula Dusthiti' (Miserable Condition of Our Hindu Widows), *Hindu Sundary*, April 1905, pp. 1–5; for this reference, p. 2.

looking at the trauma experienced by the widowed girls'.[13] According to Kashinathuni Ramabayamma, 'the unbearable grief of child widows in our country' would attract the 'sympathies of even the most hard-hearted'. Through customary practices of '*mundanamu*' (tonsuring), '*yeka bhuktamu*' (single meal) and '*amangalyamu*' (removal of the sacred marital knot), which exacerbated their suffering, widows were symbolically turned into 'living corpses' (*jeevachchavamu*).[14] She further said that

> it was impossible to describe the worst way enforced widowhood affected the widowed girls, society and the country. The Europeans looked down upon the Hindu race because of this evil practice. Unless their [widows'] lamentation [*ghosha*] was removed, [our] Hindu race would not [re]gain [the lost] reputation.[15]

An essay titled 'Hindu Vitantuvu' (Hindu Widow), credited simply to '*Oka Andhra Stree*' (An Andhra Woman), effectively stated that 'in the world, there was no other greater suffering than being a Hindu widow', and 'any number of pages could be filled writing about the atrocities perpetrated on her'.[16] In addition to emphasising the tonsuring of widows and denial of adequate food or basic comforts, she described other difficulties:

> The sufferings of Hindu widows are not of one kind. Is it not a matter of great worry that the beloved husband is dead?… They cannot join the auspicious occasions such as marriages. If the Hindu women chance to see their faces early in the morning, [they curse them] and do not come out…. Any number of pages can be filled writing about the troubles the widows are subjected to. Howsoever stone-hearted one may be, his/her heart melts like clarified butter, if s/he listens to the sufferings of widows…. We may strongly say that it is better that [the widows] die along with their husbands [by committing sati] than exist [in the world] as a Hindu widow.[17]

---

[13]'Kru. Pa.', 'Vitantuvula Durgati' (The Deplorable Condition of Widows), *Hindu Sundary*, May 1905, pp. 52–56. The comparison to a butcher clearly reflects a certain caste logic that would have been prevalent among the upper-caste readers and contributors of these journals.

[14]'Andhra Mahila Sabha: Sabhadhipurali Upanyasamu', *Hindu Sundary*, March 1913, pp. 23–40; for this reference, p. 36.

[15]Ibid., pp. 36–37.

[16]Oka Andhra Stree, 'Hindu Vitantuvu' (Hindu Widow), *Vivekavathi*, January 1914, pp. 108–109.

[17]Ibid., p. 108. She complained that while 'a few wise people' argued for remarriage, 'the superstitious and foolish Hindus', rather than accepting their advice, excommunicated them from their caste. She observed that among the 'lower castes', widows married

Women lambasted the ritual disfiguration of widows. In a scathing attack on the 'self-styled protectors of society and Arya Dharma', 'Kru. Pa.', the pseudonymous writer mentioned earlier, wrote:

> Which just-minded person can say that justice is being done to our widows?.... They are not allowed to grow their beautiful hair by applying jasmine oil, but lay them down to the razor of the barber. They are not allowed to apply the pleasing... vermilion mark [*kumkuma* bottu], but only the bottu of ash, which makes the face as dull and unattractive as the dead. Bangles are broken, bracelets are removed and the hands are made barren. Their bodies, which are as soft as the *shirisha* flowers, are mortified by the regular fasts. They ought to sleep on hard floor only and not enjoy any comforts. They are allowed to eat only once and remain hungry. They have to brood in a corner of the home, but not happily mix with others.... They are forced to remain isolated in a corner of the home, even on auspicious occasions [such as marriage] ... Though they are physically unfit [i.e., deprived of strength because of inadequate food and rest], they are used for cooking, drawing and carrying of water for domestic and ritual purposes. Alas! Alas! Even when the earth and the sky are reverberating that it is not good to treat these widows as worse than birds and animals, among those who have taken birth as humans, sympathies are a far cry.[18]

Furiously criticising the dietary restrictions imposed on widows, Varanasi Kameshwari wrote:

> Let us see what more sufferings we are causing to our widowed sisters. By mustering some courage, if they eat at night, why is there this much of censure and this amount of ridicule? Instead of food, if we eat flour for one night, the next morning we cannot move our hands and legs because of the weakness caused by hunger. [Then], just think of their poor souls, who remain without food from dusk to dawn all through their life.... [Y]ou are troubling in numerous ways, those, who are already drowned in the ocean of sorrow. They [widows] are like living and yet not living by the kind of feeding we are giving them. Though they are suffering from starvation, we are giving them floor only.... We are depriving them of the basic needs of human existence, which God has arranged for every human being. If somebody offered some food to them secretly, and we

---

again. She held parent-arranged child marriage responsible for such a state of affairs. She emphasised that unless such marriage practices were replaced by choice-based adult marriages, foolishness would never cease and the country could not make any progress.

[18]'Kru. Pa.', 'Vitantuvula Durgati' (The Deplorable Condition of Widows), *Hindu Sundary*, May 1905, pp. 52–56.

> have chanced to notice it, we are severely censuring it. We are becoming beasts by laughing at them.[19]

Women writers vehemently denounced the disfiguration of widows,[20] particularly forcible tonsuring. Kameshwari observed that parents of widows sought to tonsure their daughters at the age of 15 because they thought it was objectionable to receive water from a widow with an unshaven head. 'They mounted great atrocities to remove her hair given by God since her birth', she wrote. Kameshwari concluded that no matter how courageous they may be, widows developed a sense of disgust towards their own lives in the face of such trauma: they were forced to hate themselves.[21] Another writer, Savitri, compared the practice of tonsuring windows to 'slitting the throats of goats during the "*Gangamma jaatara*" [Gangamma fair].'[22]

Petitions/Mahajars to the Government against Forcible Tonsuring

The widespread condemnation of tonsuring as 'the most brutal crime' against widows sparked numerous calls for action. Terming it as a 'horrendous barbaric practice', Mosalikanti Ramabayamma, the editor of *Hindu Sundary*, launched a signature campaign to bolster her petition in 1904–1905. She prepared a petition addressing the British government (at both Presidency and national levels) as well as the Emperor, citing various *shastras* and smritis to support her argument. She urged the government

[19] Varanasi Kameshwari, 'Mana Hindu Vitantuvula Dusthiti' (Miserable Condition of Our Hindu Widows), *Hindu Sundary*, April 1905, pp. 4–5.

[20] However, there were many widows who voluntarily submitted to ritual disfiguration because of the strong cultural conditioning. Rayasam Venkata Sivudu wrote about his mother who 'volunteered' for the 'cruel act' despite his own opposition as well as his brothers'. *Atma Charitramu*, p. 341. But there were a few defiant widows like Tarigonda Venkamamba (1800–1866), who refused to get her hair shaved off. In defiance of convention, she continued to adorn her hair with flowers and wear her jewelry. For a few details, see Susie Tharu and K. Lalita, ed., *Women Writing in India*, vol. 1, pp. 122–125. For more details about her, see Utukuri Lakshmikantamma, *Andhra Kavayitrulu*, pp. 87–99. Also see Andra Sheshagiri Rao, *Andhra Vidushimanulu*, pp. 358–425.

[21] Varanasi Kameshwari, 'Mana Hindu Vitantuvula Dusthiti' (Miserable Condition of Our Hindu Widows), *Hindu Sundary*, April 1905, p. 2.

[22] Savitri, 'Vitantuvula Mora' (Lamentation of Widows), *Hindu Sundary*, August 1909, pp. 26–27.

to ban 'enforced tonsuring' and append the legislation to the Widow Remarriage Act of 1856. The petition argued that the decision to shave one's head should be left to widows themselves, rather than being forced upon them.[23]

It was in this context that Ramabayamma appealed to her readers for their cooperation by sending in their signatures. Meticulously referencing the shrutis and smritis, she stressed that Hindu scriptures such as the *Parashara Smriti* commanded widows to observe celibacy only, not their tonsuring:

> Vedas are the chief source of inspiration to the Brahmans. It is learnt that tonsuring of widows is nowhere mentioned in them. Scholars have agreed…that it is not mentioned in them. It is not mentioned in the *Manusmriti*, the first [and most important] of all the smritis. It is not sanctioned even by the *Parashara Smriti*, which is unanimously accepted by all Hindus as being the most important text in the Kali age. It is not mentioned in the *Vyasa Smriti*, authored by the great sage Vyasa. In such case, the shlokas attributed to sage Vyasa in Madana Ratnakaramu and Nirnaya Sindhuvu are just [cunningly] inserted at a later stage and they cannot be said to have been authored by Vyasa Muni. Had he authored them, could we not have found it in the Smriti authored by him![24]

Appealing particularly to men, she continued:

> O Aryan brothers, enriched by education and wisdom! Forced tonsuring of widows is [therefore] of recent creation only, and that it does not have the sanction of the shastras…. not tonsuring widows is not against the shastras. Brahmanhood [*Brahmanatvamu*] of the Brahmans will not be affected by that in any way…. Are not hair a [natural] embellishment acquired by birth? What amount of grief must have driven the otherwise [extremely timid], superstitious and frog-in-the-well like Hindu widows [*sic*], who are confined to the kitchen and hearths, to complain [against forcible tonsuring] in the law courts? Can any woman [really] dare [do

[23] Mosalikanti Ramabayamma first notified about the petition in the May 1904 issue of *Hindu Sundary* (p. 75). For the full text of the petition, see Mosalikanti Ramabai, 'Vitantu Shiromundanamunugoorchina Mahajaru' (Petition against the Tonsuring of Widows), *Hindu Sundary*, July 1904, pp. 146–153. See also 'Hindu Vitantuvula Shiromundanamu' (Tonsuring of Hindu Widows), *Hindu Sundary*, November 1905, pp. 198–201.

[24] Mosalikanti Ramabai, 'Vitantu Shiromundanamunugoorchina Mahajaru' (Petition against the Tonsuring of Widows), *Hindu Sundary*, July 1904, pp. 146–153; for this reference, p. 151.

> so]? Are we not noticing many complaints being registered in this regard, and many being tried?[25]

Appealing to women, she wrote:

> Jewel-like women of my country!… People are mistaking this horrible act to be a good tradition and forcibly shaving off the hair of even infant widows. A few Vaishya women are also under the illusion of treating this evil practice as a good tradition, and are shaving their heads. Alas! How unwise this is! Fearing people's taunts and the wrath of the religious heads, the Brahmin women are practising it…. like the saying, 'the jackal branded himself with spots just like a tiger', women of the other varnas, who do not have to observe this, are imitating them… The shastras have only instructed a widow to maintain celibacy after the death of her husband. A few have inserted a few shlokas in books such as Nirnaya Sindhuvu and Madana Ratnakaramu, and have been committing this [sinful] practice for a long time. But, if we observe the opinions of great *rishis*, and the makers of various shrutis, smritis and Puranas, it does not appear that they have agreed to tonsuring. Because the shrutis and smritis have only commanded the observance of celibacy, and tonsuring being nowhere mentioned, it becomes clearer that the opinion of our rishis is against tonsuring.… One may argue that widows may [secretly work as] prostitute[s], if their hair is there, and therefore, it is better shave their heads. But I humbly submit to my sisters that it is not the hair that engages in prostitution. Are we not observing many tonsured widows indulging in prostitution? Having or not having hair hardly matters to the un-virtuous widows.… Mothers! Because this practice is a great humiliation to the entire race of women, all of you–the wise–resolve and come forward to stop it.[26]

Mosalikanti Ramabayamma emphasised that 'as she understood well that the religious heads', who were all men, 'having enslaved themselves to the greed of money, would not agree to the eradication of this practice', she had decided to send a *mahajar* to the British government[27] that was 'all dharmas personified and very great'.[28] She was all praise of the colonial government for releasing (Hindu) women from the shackles of social evils. She insisted that 'had the British government, the great and all dharmas personified, not

---

[25] Ibid., pp. 151–152.

[26] Mosalikanti Ramabai, 'Vitantu Kesha Khandanamu' (Tonsuring Widows), *Hindu Sundary*, November 1905, pp. 210–214, for this reference, pp. 210–213.

[27] Ibid., p. 213.

[28] Mosalikanti Ramabai, 'Vitantu Shiromundanamunugoorchina Mahajaru' (Petition against the Tonsuring of Widows), *Hindu Sundary*, July 1904, p. 152.

eliminated such horrible practices [as sati] through legislation, no woman would have existed [in India] to send *mahajars*' such as hers.[29] She wrote further:

> Some may think that such matters have to be resolved by ourselves. This is, undoubtedly, a good argument. However, because our people lack in unity, uniform opinion, and the wisdom to distinguish as to what is good and what is bad, we [women] are forced to appeal to the British government through a *mahajar*. We have been requesting the government for making a law banning child marriage. The princely states of Mysore and Baroda have already made laws in this regard. There, there is a provision in the penal code making forcible tonsuring a punishable crime. [But], for various reasons, it is really becoming impossible to establish it [the crime]; this is because it is related to [a deep rooted] social practice.... There are several instances of girls, aged between 10–12 years, being forcibly tonsured. Unable to bear the humiliation, many commit suicide. Therefore, the present provision in the Penal Code is inadequate. It is my opinion that it should be modified, banning the tonsuring of widows below 30-years-old. Thereafter, it should be left to the widow to decide for herself. I appeal that the lovers of our country and race deeply think [how to] to stop the cruel act either by sending a *mahajar* or by mutual consultation....[30]

While a section of women simply wished that widows be treated humanely rather than subjecting them to harsh troubles, a few boldly proposed remarriage as a remedy to the sufferings of child widows from the very beginning of the twentieth century. While most of the female proponents of child widow remarriage argued based on the scriptural sanction for the same, some demanded remarriage of widows—child or adult—without bothering about the scriptural sanction or ban.

Child Widows Should Remarry: Beyond the Shastra-based Argument

After narrating the difficulties imposed on widows at length, Varanasi Kameshwari proposed remarriage to the child widows. She tried to convince women stating that 'it was learnt that the Dharmashastras approved of the remarriage of those who became widows before attaining puberty.' What

[29] Ibid.

[30] Mosalikanti Ramabai, 'Vitantu Kesha Khandanamu' (Tonsuring of Widows), *Hindu Sundary*, November 1905, pp. 210–214, for this reference, pp. 213–214.

was remarkable about her understanding of the issue was that she went beyond the shastric sanction to press for widow remarriage. 'Moreover, because it appealed to our mind that it [conducting remarriage] was a good thing, why to trouble such pitiable creatures [the child widows],' she asked. Advancing her argument further, she asked 'if it was not better that we applied our discretion, mustered courage to listen to the lamentation of such pitiable creatures and arranged the remarriage of those who desired it.'[31] She observed that because of the encouragement provided by Veeresalingam, a few widows had mustered courage to remarry and enjoy their lives. She was sad to note that 'our people' did not tolerate such women and were suspicious of them as well as anyone associated with them. Kameshwari appealed to readers to have tolerance for them.[32]

According to Varanasi Kameshwari, compared to parents of girls of other religions, the Hindu parents were extremely unkind to their daughters for the latter performed child marriages, and did not remarry their daughters, if they got widowed as a result of the mismatched marriages. Parents of girls of other religions did not perform child marriages. Even if they did, if a girl chanced to become a widow, they arranged her remarriage and brought her happiness back.[33] Castigating the opponents of widow remarriage, she sarcastically remarked that they had no courage to arrange the remarriages of widows, but had enormous courage to add on to the miseries of widows and inflict severe humiliation on them.[34]

About those young/adult widows who had experienced '*samsara sukhamu*' (an allusion to sexual pleasure) for some time, she assumed that 'they would develop aversion [*virakti*] to family-related pleasures'. She proposed that such widows be given education so that they read books on spirituality, followed the path of *bhakti* and attained *mukti* rather than turning them into ignorant domestic drudges. For child widows, she proposed both remarriage and education.[35] 'Jewel-like sisters! ... Let us remove the difficulties of such sisters in our families or among our friends by arranging remarriage of those, who are young and desire it [widow remarriage], and encourage those not interested in remarriage, to receive education,' she appealed.[36]

[31] Varanasi Kameshwari, 'Mana Hindu Vitantuvula Dusthiti' (Miserable Condition of Our Hindu Widows), *Hindu Sundary*, April 1905, p. 3.

[32] Ibid.

[33] Ibid., pp. 2–3.

[34] Ibid., pp. 1–2.

[35] Ibid., pp. 3–4.

[36] Ibid., p. 5.

In an essay, 'Vitantuvula Mora' (Lamentation of Widows), Savitri, perhaps a widow herself, poignantly appealed to parents, society, god and the river Krishna to show mercy on the grief-stricken widows and passionately argued for widow remarriage. Mixing rage with sarcasm in her essay, she exposed the complicity of 'unkind' parents, Hindu scriptures and society at large in stigmatising widowhood:

> O Indians! I think that you are not showing as much interest in our remarriages as you are showing in promoting your businesses. You must publish in journals in favour of the remarriages of our child widows, who are weak [*abala*]. By delivering lectures, you must campaign in villages and towns in our favour. We are so humbly requesting you because we are not capable [*sic*]. O great men! We are just asking for the remarriage of those widows who do not even know who their husbands were. Have we, like men, asked for five marriages, including one to the banana tree? Why do not you pity us? O unkind parents! You should get us remarried in case our husbands die in our childhood. If you cannot arrange our remarriage on the pretext that the Vedas do not agree or that it is against the shastras, then it is better you kill by poisoning rather than putting us to all sorts of troubles. Perhaps, all these Vedas, shastras and Puranas have taken birth only for us [to suffer]!... What to say about one's own parents? Are they not watching our difficulties with their own eyes? Alas! How to blame parents, whom we treat equal to God?... O lovers of our country! How can your country develop when thousands of girl widows are incessantly crying? Unable to bear the separation... [from their] husbands [and disallowed to remarry], a few girls are drowning in the wells and dying; a few are plunging into the ponds and dying; a few others are poisoning themselves and dying; a few more are running away from homes; and yet others are silently suffering at homes, covering their [shaven] heads. Is it just on your part to subject women, the weak, to sufferings like this? Watch the forthcoming Krishna *pushkarams*. Just as the throats of the goats are slit during the Gangamma *jaatara* (fair), our heads will be chopped off. Just see—who will come to our rescue? Whom to look to for help? O God! You are our last resort. You alone save us, please. O Krishnaveni [the river Krishna]! Why do you keep quiet when, in your very presence, we are subjected to such torments? At least you sympathise with us and take us to your bosom [*sic*].[37]

While most women advocates of widow remarriage based their arguments on scriptural sanction, some, like Uppuluri Nagaratnamma, emphasised

[37] Savitri, 'Vitantuvula Mora' (Lamentation of Widows), *Hindu Sundary*, August 1909, pp. 26–27.

that since widow remarriage was enshrined in law, any sanction or ban of the shastras was immaterial, and that mere commonsense and everyday experience was enough to judge in favour of widow remarriages.[38] A leading activist-intellectual of the period, Nagaratnamma[39] was widowed when she was only five years old and remarried at the age of 18. Outspoken about the trauma borne by widows and remarkably forthright in her critique, she brought the sexual needs of widows into existing discourse and openly discussed the issue of their sexual fulfilment. Her advocacy of widow remarriage was unequivocal and unwavering, and she was associated with many reformers of the period including Veeresalingam, at whose widow home she had resided at one point. Her writings and work established her as a remarkable, radical voice. She was enraged that many people, particularly women, still questioned whether the Hindu scriptures approved of widow remarriage and whether it was useful to the advancement of women and the country. In a 1911 piece, Nagaratnamma wrote:

> The matter that widows have to be remarried is safely concluded not only by the sanction of the shastras but also by our everyday experience and commonsense. Why because, among our Hindu Brahmin and Vaishya castes, girls are married off… at such an early age when they do not even understand what husband means. … [W]hile the woman is lamenting because of enforced widowhood, her ten-times-older mother with ten children, and sisters-in-law of her age, keep enjoying their lives by

[38] Uppuluri Nagaratnamma, 'Stree Punarvivahamulu' (Widow Remarriages), *Hindu Sundary*, October–November 1911, pp. 26–30.

[39] Though her father thought of getting her married again, he was scared of the conservative elements and passed away soon. Desiring remarriage, Nagaratnamma personally wrote to Veeresalingam about her decision. Thereafter, she joined the Widow Home at Guntur established by Unnava Lakshminarayana and his wife Lakshmibayamma and studied there for a year. On 17 July 1904, in Guntur, at the age of 18, she remarried the English-educated Uppuluri Venkata Subbarao of Kakinada. For her biographical details, see 'Uppuluri Nagaratnammagari Jivitam' (The Life of Uppuluri Nagaratnamma), *Hindu Sundary*, March 1913, pp. 9–11. Nagaratnamma played a significant role in the women's movement and regularly published in contemporary women's journals. Apart from the present essay, she published several other articles. For example, see 'Aikamatyamu' (Unity), *Vivekavathi*, July 1911, pp. 299–300; 'Angleya Paripalanamuvalani Labhamulu' (The Benefits of British Rule), *Vivekavathi*, May 1912, pp. 234–237; 'Andhra Mahila Mahasabha, Nidudavolu' (All Andhra Women's Conference, Nidudavolu), *Hindu Sundary*, May 1912, pp. 23–28. Compared to many other 'progressive' women of her times, Nagaratnamma proved to be 'more progressive' given her firm stand on the question of widow remarriage, and the inclusive nature of contemporary women's organisations.

> draping colourful sarees in various strange styles, by decorating their hair in different ways... [the women] indulge in romance with their husbands in the neighbouring rooms. Will not the child widow feel sad thinking that she has no such happiness? Even if she has not had such experience until then, will not she desire it at least by watching them? God created both men and women in the world to experience equal enjoyment. In this respect, man has no obstacles in marrying as per his wish and any number of times whether his wife is alive or dead. Can there be a greater sin than disallowing the child widow, who never tasted the joy of husband even a bit, to have even one husband, and subject her to so many troubles at home?[40]

Deriding opponents of widow remarriage who proposed celibacy, as well as women's organisations that were reluctant to take up the issue of widow remarriage,[41] Uppuluri Nagaratnamma reiterated that remarriage alone was the best solution to the problems of child widows and the various undesirable effects of their unchannelised sexuality. She emphasised that the expectation to 'control one's sexual urges' and faithfully observe celibacy was impossible to meet, given that even the great sages like Vishwamitra fell prey to the 'arrows of Manmatha', the diety of love. Elaborating on the importance of householder's life, which included sexual life, to child widows, Nagaratnamma said:

> Are we not seeing so many such hypocrites and depraved people [widows], who are feigning to be observing celibacy and easily committing [such heinous crimes as] feticide and infanticide, but [readily] condemning widow remarriage and ridiculing those widows, who married again? It is to remove such sinful acts, which are calamitous to the country, that the reformers are emphasising that widow remarriage is helpful for the progress of the country. For this, they got an Act passed by the

---

[40] Uppuluri Nagaratnamma, 'Stree Punarvivahamulu' (Widow Remarriages), *Hindu Sundary*, October–November 1911, pp. 26–30.

[41] Nagaratnamma established her own organisation named 'Kakinada Stree Samajamu' of which she was secretary, with Aavula Subbayamma as president. This was possibly due to her dissatisfaction with the working of the Shri Vidyarthini Samajamu at Kakinada, which did not support the entry of remarried women into its fold and restricted membership based on caste. Nagaratnamma, along with other post-bearers, announced that their organisation would not observe any discrimination based on varna, and allow all 'respectable' women as members. See 'Aayachotla Jarigina Sangatulu', *Vivekavathi*, August 1913, p. 350. See also 'Aayachotla Jarigina Sangatulu: Kakinada Stree Samajamu', *Vivekavathi*, June 1913, pp. 286–287. The January–February 1913 issue of the *Hindu Sundary* published Nagaratnamma's full size photograph.

> government. How can you still argue that widows must observe celibacy and that this alone ensures the progress of the world?... Then, what is that [that really achieves national development]? That is nothing but the householder life [*grihasthashrama*], the paragon of all the four ashramas, a means to gain salvation.... Rightly realising the significance of householder's life, though a few Brahmin widows are remarrying, the Vaishya widows are not seriously considering remarriage.... Not to speak about these rank traditionalists, is it possible even for Brahma, the creator, to compel the child widows to observe *brahmacharya vrata* until their death, if they are not remarried?... It is the opinion of the modern reformers that because marriage fulfils all their desires, it is the married women, who will have stable minds and, therefore, can concentrate on useful works. The unmarried ones go astray and get spoilt on both fronts because of unfulfilled physical desires. Moreover, our elders say that women's sexual urge is six times more than men's [*sic*]. Is not it an injustice that they provided for any number of marriages to men, whose sexual appetite is less, and only one marriage to women, who possess excessive sexuality?[42]... Therefore, may my sisters realise that widow remarriage alone is helpful to the country, not the hypocritical celibacy, and remove the child widows from enforced widowhood and work for the upliftment of the country! May they not fear the vampire of caste [and the axe of excommunication]![43]

Questioning Double Standards in Social Morality

Women sharply questioned the double standards maintained with regard to the treatment of widows and widowers and their remarriage. In a forceful essay,[44] Kuditipudi Atchamamba attacked this form of gender discrimination:

> A man gets ready to trap a new bride the very next day after the death of his wife. But, is there any other happiness for a wife, whose husband

[42] She strategically used this patriarchal sexist idea to turn it upside down. Many other women were caught in this net of strategic argument. However, their strategic use aside, these arguments also fell in with patriarchal notions about women's sexuality which had to be controlled or regulated. Thus, otherwise very logical women intellectuals of the early twentieth century were carelessly falling prey to unreason.

[43] Uppuluri Nagaratnamma, 'Andhra Mahila Mahasabha, Nidudavolu' (All Andhra Women's Conference, Nidudavolu), *Hindu Sundary*, May 1912, pp. 23–28.

[44] 'Vydhavyamu–Dharmashastralu' (Widowhood and the Dharmashastras), *Grihalakshmi*, February 1939, pp. 819–822.

> is dead, other than ending her life by observing starving fasts [*sic*] in the name of the dead husband?… Why should the wife alone experience the troubles and trauma after the death of her husband, which the husband does not experience after the death of his wife? Has the God descended on the earth and informed somebody that she should suffer like that? Can this be said to be anything else other than being the selfishness of men? Is a woman not born with blood and flesh and nerves and heart like a man? Or, is there something special in the creation of a man? Food, sleep… and sex are equally important not only for human beings but also for all animals in the world. This being the case, why cannot a woman enjoy them after the death of her husband?… Remarriage for child widows has been accepted only after a great movement; and even this [small change] does not have popular acceptance.… She [a widow] is disfigured immediately after the death of her husband.… Joy turns its back at the widows.… What is the relationship between her husband's death and her being disfigured? … Is it justice to destroy her completely? Even the *Manusmriti* does not approve such whole-scale destruction.

Atchamamba was careful to term the achievements of the social reform movement as 'limited', since they had not yet brought full happiness in the lives of women.[45] Being extraordinarily sensitive to their plight, she wondered why the 'whole world was against the race of women'.[46] Reflecting on attitudes of the period, she stated: 'Those with a heart could not tolerate the way women were tied by the chains of social customs and such things that were imposed on their heads'.[47] Elaborating on the unequal treatment given to women and the way their lives were controlled and destroyed, she said

> [The] conjugal relationship is the spring in which the new buds of life of women and men will sprout and fruition. That both should enjoy or suffer the fruit of life equally is in keeping with the principle of justice. But our social practice is just the opposite of this. It is full of discrimination and has squeezed women's lives with the sharp cuts of a butcher. It has smashed them into ashes. It has suffocated them by closing all the nine holes. With the wicked idea that women would break out of it and become independent, it has used the grand weapon of sin.[48]

[45] Ibid., p. 819.
[46] Ibid.
[47] Ibid., p. 820.
[48] Ibid.

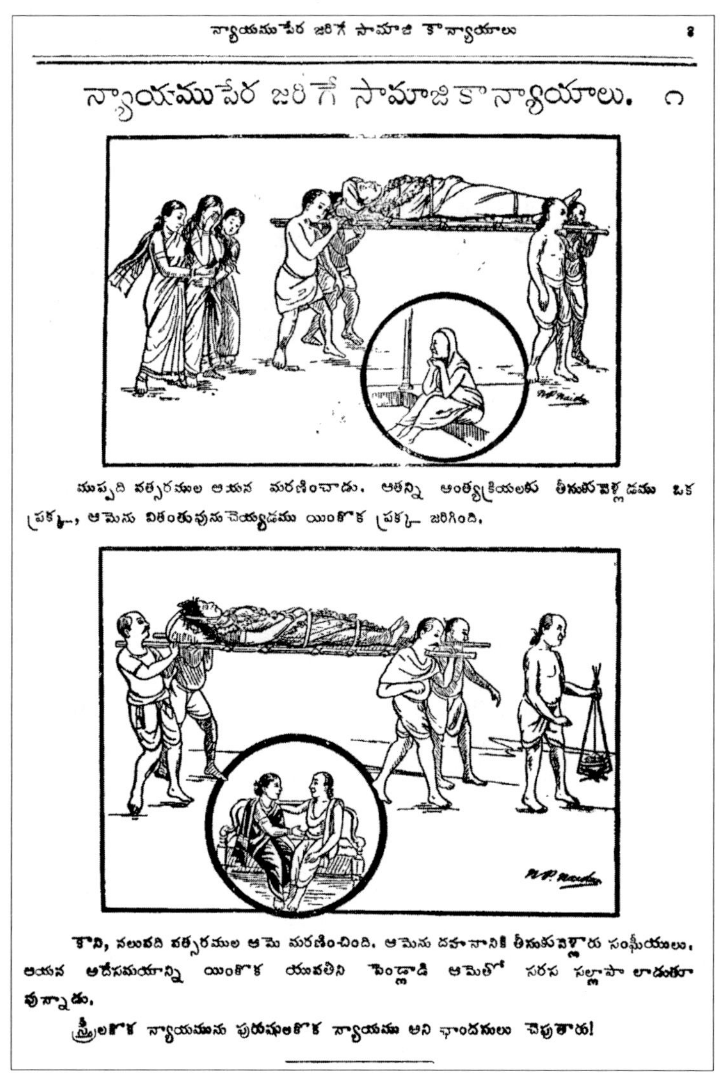

న్యాయముపేర జరిగే సామాజికాన్యాయాలు ౪

న్యాయముపేర జరిగే సామాజికాన్యాయాలు. ౧

ముప్పది వత్సరముల ఆయన మరణించాడు. ఆతన్ని అంత్యక్రియలకు తీసుకువెళ్లడము ఒక ప్రక్క, ఆమెను వితంతువును చెయ్యడము యింకొక ప్రక్క జరిగింది.

కాని, నలుబది వత్సరముల ఆమె మరణించింది. ఆమెను దహనానికి తీసుకువెళ్లారు సంఘీయులు. ఆయన ఆదేసమయాన్ని యింకొక యువతిని పెండ్లాడి ఆమెతో సరస సల్లాపాలాడుతూ వున్నాడు.

స్త్రీలకొక న్యాయమును పురుషులకొక న్యాయము అని ఛాందసులు చెపుతారు!

Image 4.1: Social injustice in the name of justice

Picture 1: A 30-year-old man dies. While his body is carried away, his wife is portrayed as a widow.

Picture 2: A 40-year-old woman dies. Her body is carried to the cremation grounds. Her widower marries another woman during the mourning period and is romancing her.

The conservatives maintain that justice is not equal to women and men!

Source: *Anandabodhini*, 1 June 1931.

Discussing the Dharmashastras in the context of widow remarriage, Kuditipudi Atchamamba said that 'while a few of them were liberal, the others were terrible'.[49] She continued: 'The difference between the contemporary conditions and the rules prescribed by the Dharmashastras was as big as the difference between an elephant and a mosquito. The time for forgetting the Dharmashastras and bothering about the reform regarding the question of widowhood should have come long time ago. But it has not come yet.'[50] She was extremely unhappy with the persistence of stigma against widows and widow remarriage and the slow pace of social reform. The most remarkable aspect of Kuditipudi Atchamamba was that she declared that the Dharmashastras were 'irrelevant' to contemporary society and that they were to be 'totally rejected'. However, she discussed them because they had a grip over the common people. Moulding public opinion against the Dharmashastras was the undercurrent of her essay.

A cartoon published in a contemporary journal brilliantly caricatured the double standards maintained in society with regard to widow and widower remarriage (see Image 4.1).

Widow Remarriage: Literary Representations by Women

Several women writers chose to centre widow remarriage in their literary writings. These texts reflect a conviction that widows, too, needed emotional and sexual fulfilment, in keeping with the motto of firebrand feminist Gudipati Venkata Chalam: 'Woman also has a body that needs exercise. She has a brain that needs knowledge. She has a heart that needs feelings/ experience.'[51]

V. Saraswati's eponymous short story, 'Sudha', portrayed the emotions, love and sexuality of a young widow.[52] The protagonist was a young and

[49] While the *Manusmriti* was 'liberal', prescriptive texts like *Nirnaya Sindhuvu* and *Dharma Sindhu* were most cruel. They prescribed the most difficult code of conduct. The author of *Dharma Sindhu* prescribed two things for widows—practicing ascetic widowhood or sahagamana. The widow who observed celibacy would get back her husband [perhaps in the next birth] and enjoy heaven. She should therefore 'protect her sexual character'. If it was violated, her husband would collapse from the heavens to *paatal* (a water-filled underwold). Even her parents and brothers would be deprived of heaven.

[50] Ibid., p. 822.

[51] Chalam, *Stree* (Hyderabad, 1979), p. 6.

[52] *Grihalakshmi*, May 1933, pp. 223–226.

beautiful 18-year-old widow who lived with her brother, Rama Rao, and her termagant sister-in-law, Janaki. Despite being English-educated, her brother lacked 'independent ideas' and was 'scared of society'. The author implied that it was because of social fear that he did not arrange her remarriage. Sudha and Rajagopalam—Janaki's brother—fell in love and became sexually intimate. The narrative makes it clear that Rajagopalam had a modern outlook on love, romance and the heterosexual relationship. Unaware that Sudha had become pregnant, he decided to get a job in order to be eligible to marry her. She was bereft when he left for Madras:

> She was leading her life like a living corpse. Though she was involved in domestic work during the day times, she always remembered Rajagopalam. Her pillow was drenched with her tears all through the nights. The fire of grief, which she kept in her heart, was released through her tears. Who can she share her grief with? Who was there to console her? She was deteriorating day by day like the moon which gradually deteriorated during the *Krishnapaksha*. She did not eat. She became so weak that she was unable to get up from the bed. Janaki started insinuating that she pretended ill health to avoid housework.[53]

The story took a tragic turn once Sudha's pregnancy was revealed in the household, leading to accusations that she was a 'prostitute' who had lured an innocent man, and similar abuse at the hands of the village. Unable to bear this abuse, Sudha committed suicide. Upon hearing the news, Rajagopalam lost interest in life and wandered like a *sanyasi*. Although the story ended in the lovers' doom, Sudha's suicide sparked a transformation in Sudha's brother—he joined a widow remarriage association and conducted five to six widow remarriages.

The clear suggestion of the author was that had Sudha been able to remarry, she would not have been compelled to engage in a clandestine affair, and the tragedy could have been averted. If the English-educted men like Sudha's brother had some courage, and performed remarriages, they would not have to repent the way Sudha's brother did.

Another short story, 'Pushkaramu Baala Vydhavyamunu Manpinadi',[54] by Pulavarti Kamalavati Devi, depicted the travails of Subbalakshmi, a

---

[53] Ibid., p. 225.

[54] 'Pushkaramu' is celebrated once in every twelve years at certain holy rivers like the Godavari and the Krishna. Normally, *Pushkarams*, where people from far-off places gather for a holy dip, was a nightmare for widows because they would be compelled to dress as per the dictates of widowhood, even on such auspicious occasions. A few of the widows used the occasion to remove themselves permanently from the trouble of

parentless child widow, at the hands of her brother and sister-in-law.[55] The protagonist was routinely exploited by her brother and sister-in-law, to the extent that even when the family visited the Godavari during *pushkaramu*, she was only brought along to 'cook for them' and 'provide other services'. She was not taken to see a 'swadeshi exhibition' at the festival, and was abused when she expressed a desire to watch the film 'Prahlada'. Driven to despair by abuse and neglect, Subbalakshmi attempted suicide by jumping into the overflowing Godavari. The passages describing her anguish illustrate the state of widows:

> What a murderous fate! There is no other hell in India than being a widow, you know! The Indian widow does not have the freedom even of a slave, you know! Because a slave is purchased, s/he is offered at least food and water because people think that otherwise s/he may die. Because the Indian widow is not purchased, people have no such fear. A man can get ready to marry any number of times after one wife is dead.... it seems that the sinner God has sanctioned me a long life. How-much-ever I think of tolerating [this abuse], my sister-in-law's tyrannical actions and accusations are multiplying and crossing tolerable limits. Brother is a weak-hearted scoundrel. Sister-in-law is a *brahmarakshasi* [great female demon]. At this moment, I see no other way than embracing death. The elders emphasise that suicide is a great sin. With that, one will be reborn as a *brahmarakshasi*, they say. How does it matter, if I become a *brahmarakshasi* to shun away this *brahmarakshasi*?[56]

Subbalakshmi was rescued by Mohun, Captain of a Scouts unit, a reform-minded man who wished to remove the difficulties faced by child widows. At the end of the story, Subbalakshmi and Mohun were married at the Veeresalingam Garden in the presence of thousands of reformers.

The story evocatively unravelled the traumatised mental universe of child widows, cruelties they faced at the hands of relatives and society in general, their slave-like dependence on unsympathetic family members,

---

widowhood: they committed suicide by drowning. The title and content of the story are unconventional. Here, Pushkaram is used by the author to remove widowhood, contrary to granting the figure of a widow. Where Pushkarams were normally (mis)used to completely disfigure the widows, the author overturned its normal usage and put it to a contrasting use i.e. erasing widowhood and granting Sumangalihood to a widow. Clearly, the author has trodden an unusually radical path.

[55]Pulavarti Kamalavati Devi, 'Pushkaramu Baala Vydhavyamunu Manpinadi' (Pushkaram Removed Child Widowhood), *Vasavi*, September 1932, pp. 194–198.

[56]Ibid., p. 195.

Image 4.2: Pulavarti Kamalavati Devi

Source: *Grihalakshmi*, October 1929.

the economic disadvantages to women due to gender differentiation, etc. The happy ending of the story, among other things, demonstrated women inellectuals' continued commitment to the cause of widow remarriage.

In Susarla Lakshmi Narasamamba's story titled 'Raja Pelli', a widowed mother arranged the remarriage of her widowed daughter without bothering about social censure.[57] Rajarajeshwari, a girl of about 14 years of age, lost her husband even before she entered the in-laws' home.[58] Despite his reservations about how society may react, her father resolved to arrange her remarriage. However, he died before his daughter could be remarried, leaving her 'drowned in the ocean of sorrow'. At this juncture, her now-widowed mother, remembering this promise, set about arranging the remarriage of her daughter. She sought their relatives' consent and received the support of three-fourths of them, following which the marriage was swiftly conducted. About the social acceptability to the remarriage, the author wrote:

> The marriage was held soon. Those who were given invitations and [even] those who were not given attended the marriage. Half of the relatives came. It was held in Bezawada.... The marriage was conducted very pleasantly. A few notable persons in the town also attended. Those who could not attend sent telegram messages blessing the couple. Srimati Dronamraju Lakshmibayamma[59] sent the following poems blessing the bride and the groom.... They were excommunicated in the village. What did it mean? The villagers threatened that they would not dine in their home. But the marriage party said, 'no problem; there is nothing that we will lose. We ourselves have boycotted you. All our relatives came to celebrate the marriage. They will come to our home. If you wish to come, you come; otherwise, do not come. We go by our own wish.' There was a hue and cry in the village. Some said that there was nothing wrong in the marriage. Some others said that it was one thousand times better than the horrible things [caused by widowhood] taking place in society, which they could not bear seeing. The traditionalists said that it was against the Dharmashastras. A few adament people, who were opposed to widow remarriage, threatened that they would not allow their sons to indulge in such things so far as they were alive, and, if they did, they would commit suicide. People said all kinds of things.... One day, a religious ritual was performed in Raja's natal home. All those who liked them enthusiastically participated. They dined there. Approaching the traditionalists, who sat on the *chaultry* and muttered [about the marriage], they asserted that no ill fate befell them.[60]

[57] *Grihalakshmi*, December 1933, pp. 797–798.

[58] It is remarkable that women authours ensured that characters who remarried in their stories were older than 14 years, keeping in mind the Sarda Act.

[59] It is significant that a woman who is known to have existed in real, Dronamraju Lakshmibayamma, is mentioned in this fictional account. This indicated the wider acceptance of widow remarriage among Andhra women.

[60] *Grihalakshmi*, December 1933, pp. 797–798.

The author's support for widow remarriage was clear. What was more significant was that, undaunted by social criticism, the widow's mother took the initiative in getting her daughter remarried.

In her short story,[61] Vatti Ammaji depicted the mother, Rajani, repenting for having given her 12-year-old daughter Vijaya in marriage to a wealthy old man who died soon and left Vijaya a widow. Vijaya's mother had rejected a match from her nephew, Mohun, an educated and handsome young man, because Mohun was not wealthy. One evening, while speaking to Mohun, the widowed Vijaya revealed her traumatic condition. Overhearing this, the mother had a dramatic change of heart and appealed for 'pardon', lamenting that 'she had committed such a horrible act'. Blaming 'dirty society' for her 'unwise' act, she remarked that social norms created such panic, 'as if a catastrophe [would] occur if a girl remained unmarried for two or three years after attaining puberty'. It was because of social fear and pressure that parents hastened to arrange child marriages without minding the suitability of grooms. The marriages of men who were already elderly were even more worrying: because of them, both the families underwent untold sufferings and the girls' whole lives were rendered useless. Having resolved that she would not be scared of 'dirty society anymore', the mother appealed to Mohun:

> Mohun! I have now understood the magnitude of the crime I committed. Please excuse me for having rejected you then and save my Vijaya [by accepting her now]. About society! It is very cruel! If I am scared of the society, my child's life will be ruined. I will not be scared of society anymore. I will arrange the remarriage of Vijaya!! I will arrange the marriage of Sujana [her other daughter] as per her wish. I will not object to my daughters' [wishes]. I will not be afraid of society.

Socially Alive, Sexually Dead: Nationalist Women's Resolution of the Widow Question

While remarriage was one solution that women offered to the widows, the other was to make them 'useful members of society and nation'. Kanuparti Varalakshmamma best represented this strand of thought.[62] In her reply to

[61] Vatti Ammaji, 'Sanghaniki Veriste!!' (If We are Scared of Society!!), *Andhra Mahila*, April 1949, pp. 43–44.

[62] This was also a popular subject of women's creative literature. For example, see P. Rukminibai's short story, 'Sundari', *Grihalakshmi*, October 1929.

a fictitious widowed friend 'Kalpalata', who had questioned 'what her fate would be', Varalakshmamma reassured her and suggested a different path:

> My dear sister! There is nothing wrong in your question. The very moment you are widowed, all of Hindu society views you unsympathetically. Your path appears to be filled with thorns in every direction.... With its rules and regulations, religion captures you. Society ties you with its chains. Tradition binds your legs making your movements difficult. Your parents-in-law get ready to cheat you. Your parents will never be satisfied by your domestic work. Your brothers treat you like a servant. The burden of maintaining strict celibacy, which is impossible even to those great sages who read different kinds of shastras and who maintained themselves by eating fruits in the wild forests, falls over your head. If you slip a bit from this, you will fall to the *paatal* [the underworld in Hindu cosmology]. Being surrounded by these many inevitable troubles, if you ask as to what your future will be, what wrong will be there in that? However, if you can come out of that great forest-like home; if you can break the chains of tradition a bit, and look at your motherland once, you will find a number of ways to make your life worthwhile and meaningful.[63]

Varalakshmamma wrote that Kalpalata was now 'removed from the coil of family life' (*samsara janjhatamu*) and advised her 'not to take over her head the evil burden of the families of both her brothers and sisters out of madness'. The moment her family was destroyed with the death of her husband, she belonged to the family of the universe and she was to treat the larger world as belonging to her own family and prepare to serve all its people. Now that she was a brahmacharini and a 'flower, whose fragrance was not tasted yet', she was to make morality and *dharma* her bodyguards, undertake the *vrata* (spiritual vow) of service and enter the field of action. For this, she was not to travel any distance, but just look at women in her own country and she would find a wide range of opportunities for productive work.[64]

Varalakshmamma offered a set of concrete suggestions. Kalpalata could try to educate illiterate women; train as a midwife or nurse, or become a doctor to contain infant and maternal mortality; facilitate the remarriage of child widows or encourage them into undertaking social service; encourage

---

[63] Kanuparti Varalakshmamma, *Sharada Lekhalu*, vol. 2, pp. 28–40. See Chapter 2 for a detailed description of this fictional correspondence. In the context of this particular exchange, Varalakshmamma wrote that her answer and the prescriptions therein applied to the 'lakhs of widows like her friend'.

[64] Kanuparti Varalakshmamma, *Sharada Lekhalu*, vol. 2, p. 30.

women's economic independence; the writer even suggested that she could help prevent suicides among women by working to resolve or mitigate domestic conflict with their husbands or mothers-in-law.[65] The list of social work avenues was exhaustive: sensitising 'unsympathetic' parents towards their daughters; reviving handicrafts traditions among women; dispelling the 'god of superstition'; raising civil and political consciousness among women; and, importantly, mustering support for the Sarda Act to save infants in the cradle from being married off.[66]

According to Varalakshmamma, widows had to follow these paths rather than resigning themselves to idle and empty spirituality.[67] As there were so many ways to make her life a worthy one, her friend need not lose hope. She warned that the same world of women, for whose sake she would undertake social service, would ridicule her actions, get angry, condemn and hate her. However, she was to tolerate them the same way a mother tolerated her child who bit her finger while she gave her medicine.[68] Varalakshmamma's prescriptions fall in line with Uma Chakravarti's observations on the nationalist approach to widowhood: The fact 'that widows could in a sense "sublimate" their sexuality, pre-figures Gandhi and was an important stand in the nationalist resolution of widowhood. The widows' energies here get channelised into serving the nation.'[69] Many nationalist women in Andhra accepted the 'sexual death of widows'[70], particularly adult widows.

The ideology that widows should become useful to society and the nation was internalised by many widows, who *opted* not for remarriage but social service to ensure that they led purposeful lives. Three prominent widows made remarkable contributions to social and political development in colonial Andhra/India: they were Madabhooshi Choodamma, Battula Kamakshamma and Duvvuri Subbamma.

Madabhooshi Choodamma (d. 14 February 1938), an activist-intellectual and women's organiser, was born in Karapa village near Kakinada.[71] She became a widow at just 16. Although she was widowed

---

[65] Ibid., pp. 31–33.

[66] Ibid., p. 33–36.

[67] Ibid., pp. 14–27.

[68] Ibid., pp. 36–40.

[69] Uma Chakravarti, *Rewriting History*, p. 250.

[70] I have taken this phrase from Uma Chakravarti's *Rewriting History*, p. 268.

[71] Much of the information furnished about her is from Balantrapu Sheshamma's obituary essay, 'Keerti Sheshuralyna Madabhooshi Choodammagaru' (Late Madabhooshi Choodamma), *Hindu Sundary*, February 1938.

during the heyday of the widow remarriage movement in Andhra and encouraged by her family elders to remarry, she *chose* to remain a widow because she 'firmly believed in leading a celibate life' as mandated within her caste.

A year after her husband's death, Choodamma relocated to Kakinada to help educate her brothers. There, she was introduced to Balantrapu Sheshamma and they quickly formed a close friendship, both emerging as important figures in the women's movement. An erudite scholar, Choodamma passed the formidable examinations conducted by the Vignana Chandrika Parishad and a similar body at Narasapur, winning a cash award of Rs. 116 and a gold medal. In 1920, she spent six months working as a Telugu teacher at Lady Wellington High School, Madras.

She was part of a group of women who revived the Shri Vidyarthini Samajamu, the most famous women's organisation in Kakinada, in the beginning of the twentieth century.[72] The Samajamu's achievements owe, in part, to the leadership provided by Madabhooshi Choodamma. After the organisation took over the management of *Hindu Sundary*, the first women-edited and an all-women-managed women's journal, Choodamma served as its editor for nearly a decade and spread the message of the women's movement in various parts of Andhra.[73] She authored a few works like *Shatakamu* (a canto) and a prose version of Atukuri Molla's *Ramayana*. She provided support to girls who wished to educate themselves but did not have the means to do so. For instance, she supported E. Venkataratnamma and Savitramma, who worked as nurses in King George Medical College at Visakhapatnam, and even got homes constructed for both of them. Her passion for scholarship was such that she started preparing for the Vidwan examination at the age of 60.[74]

Battula Kamakshamma, born in 1886 in Rajahmundry, was widowed at 13. She too chose to remain a widow throughout her life.[75] Undeterred

---

[72] Details of the organisation are given in Chapter 1, this volume.

[73] The journal's contribution to the women's movement is discussed in Chapter 2, this volume.

[74] *Hindu Sundary* published a few obituaries on her along with a photograph in the February 1938 issue.

[75] In her brief reminiscences, she wrote how the activists, both men and women, involved in the widow remarriage movement in Rajahmundry tried to convince her to remarry and how she resisted the same. She wrote that she was getting books from the library established by Nalam Krishna Rao. As the managers of the library found that she was more interested in the books authored by Veeresalingam, 'they sent books related to widow remarriage and tried to know her opinion about widow remarriage.' Scared that

Image 4.3: Battula Kamakshamma

Source: *Grihalakshmi*, November 1935.

by the hardships of widowhood, she turned her attention to education and public service, established institutions and rose to a position of prominence. With the help of Nalam Ramalingaiah, she established the

the list of books on widow remarriage issued against her name might 'generate doubts', she warned her domestic help to bring only those books she asked for and not any others. Once, Kotikalapudi Sitamma, a disciple of Veeresalingam, went to see her and told that she would like to introduce Kamakshamma to Veeresalingam. 'With her words, I felt that she was encouraging me for remarriage,' Kamakshamma wrote. See Srimati Battula Kamakshamma, 'Smrutlu, Anubhavamulu' (Reminiscences and Experiences) in Devulapalli Venkata Krishna Shastry, Telikicharla Venkata Ratnam and Avula Samba Siva Rao ed., *Yuga Purushudu Veeresalingam* (Hyderabad, n. d.), pp. 69–72.

Vaishya Sevasadanam at Rajahmundry in 1920, which in 1931 became the Andhra Yuvati Samskruta Kalashala (Andhra Women's Sanskrit College), with Kamakshamma as its principal. The college provided higher education to women. She was so passionately committed to the promotion of women's education that in 1935, when Nalam Ramalingaiah, founder and chief financier of the college, expressed his inability to sustain the college and wanted to close it down, she was instrumental in keeping it from closing.

An erudite scholar, Kamakshamma was fluent in English, Hindi and Telugu and passed reputed examinations such as the Vidwan and the Ubhayabhasha Praveena. She served as magistrate of the Honourary Bench, Rajahmundry, was a member of the Board of Studies, Academic Council and the Senate of the Andhra University, and was also a member of the Rajahmundry's municipality. She presided over the Arya Vaishya Mahila Sabha held at Guntur in 1924. Kamakshamma was also an executive committee member of the All-Andhra Women's Conference, an Andhra branch of the AIWC, since its inception in 1927 and presided over one of its annual conferences in 1936. She regularly attended AIWC's annual conferences as a delegate from Andhra. Given her scholarship, commitment to the women's cause, and activism, it was not surprising that she received numerous awards and was praised in a number of women's journals. *Vasavi*, a monthly journal published by a progressive section of the Vaishyas, featured her in the column '*Vaishya Vanita Ratnamulu*' (Jewels among Vaishya Women). Lanka Sundaram, a well-travelled writer, compared her with Florence Nightingale, Sylvia Pankhurst and Emmaline Booth. A volume titled *Sri Kamakshi Vijaya Sanchika* was published in her honour when she turned 60.[76]

Another important figure, in this context, is Duvvuri Subbamma (1880–1964),[77] whose husband passed away ten years after their marriage, leaving her behind as a childless young widow. Undaunted by these circumstances, she was able to transform her life by becoming an important woman activist in the freedom movement.

[76] For more details, see Solasa Bapaiah, Nalam Krishna Rao et al., ed., *Sri Kamakshi Vijaya Sanchika* (1947). For more on her life, see *Grihalakshmi*, January 1938, pp. 812–815.

[77] Unless especially mentioned, the information furnished below is from Volga et al., *Mahilavaranam*, pp. 46–47 and K. Janaki, *Role of Women in Freedom Struggle in Andhra Pradesh* (Hyderabad, 1999), pp. 46–48.

Image 4.4: Duvvuri Subbamma

Source: Volga et al, ed., *Mahilavaranam*, 2001.

Subbamma's political career began with her participation in the Non-Cooperation Movement, and she took active part in the Civil Disobedience and Quit India movements. As early as 1921, she demanded complete freedom for India at a political conference in Kakinada. An enthralling orator, she delivered hundreds of lecturers propagating the ideas of freedom and self-rule, even as her work incurred the wrath of the colonial government. Subbamma holds the distinction of being the first woman to be sentenced to one year of rigorous imprisonment—she was sentenced on 4 April 1922. She refused the government's offer to release her if she tendered an apology.[78] She was arrested again and detained in Vellore jail for participating in the Salt Satyagraha. Thus, arrests and jail sentences became an integral part of her life. She and her companions confronted and reprimanded the *lathi*-wielding police so severely that they were reportedly afraid of her. She agitated in jail for basic amenities and forced colonial authorities to improve prisoners' condition.[79]

[78] She had a grand reception after her release. A big procession was taken out and a public meeting with about 8,000 people was held, with Tanguturi Prakasham presenting the welcome address.

[79] For the way Subbamma spent her life in the Vellore jail and the way she troubled the colonial officials, see Sangam Lakshmibai, *Naa Jailu Gnapakalu*, p. 13–15.

Once she stepped out of jail, Subbamma poured her energies into the Khadi Movement. An organiser of the Ladies' Congress Committee formed in 1922, she directed the energies of the committee to the organisation of the use and production of khaddar and went from village to village with a bundle of khaddar on her shaven head. In 1924, she also started a nationalist school for widows, the Sanatana Stree Vidyalayam, Rajahmundry. Given her commitment to the nationalist cause, the people of her native Godavari District honoured her with the title *Deshabandhavi* (Benefactor of the Nation). An article in *The Hindu*, published after her release from the first jail sentence, termed her 'one of the self-sacrificing and most sincere of India's daughters'. Her fame spread so far and wide that the *Chand*, a women's periodical in Hindi, applauded her for her political action as 'a model for Indian women'.[80] Volga and others have rightly observed that 'for Duvvuri Subbamma, the [freedom] struggle was her life.'

Duvvuri Subbamma opposed widow remarriage. She wanted widows to receive education and, like her, serve the society and nation. For example, at the fifth Conference of the Andhra Rashtra Mahila Mahasabha, held on 21–22 November 1931 in Guntur, when a resolution on remarriage for child widows came up for discussion, Duvvuri Subbamma bitterly opposed it. She questioned as to why the guardians should help when the widows already decided to remarry. Further, she was alarmed to state that, if child widows were allowed to remarry, the adult/aged widows might wish it in future, which would 'taint sacred India'. The president of the conference, however, responded that the resolution did not say anything about the remarriages of adult widows.[81]

Social Attitudes in the late 1930s-1950s

The many social attitudes towards widows and widow remarriages during the late 1930s and 1940s can be understood by looking at the remarriage of Kondapalli Koteshwaramma to Kondapalli Sitaramaiah, both of the Reddy caste. Born in 1920 in Pamarru village, Krishna District, Koteshwaramma was a well-known public figure. Her political participation began when she donated gold ornaments to Mahatma Gandhi. As a child, she sang patriotic songs and later campaigned in favour of the Swadeshi movement and

[80] Francesca Orsini, *The Hindi Public Sphere, 1920–1940* (New Delhi, 2010 [2002]).

[81] See Kanuparti Varalakshmamma, 'Gunturu Mahilasabha Visheshamulu', *Grihalakshmi*, February 1932, pp. 1049–1055.

prohibition of alcohol consumption. Koteshwaramma's[82] autobiography, *Nirjana Varadhi*, offers a wealth of information about its circumstances.[83] She was unaware of her status as a child widow until a classmate made a scornful remark about it. Koteshwaramma then learnt from her grandmother that she had been married to her maternal uncle at four or five years of age and that her husband had died of tuberculosis some two years after their marriage.

Koteshwaramma's mother was deeply interested in getting her remarried and requested the reformer Tammareddy Ramaswamy for help. The autobiography details reactions of family members and fellow villagers:

> While my mother wanted me to be happy, my father was worried that our neighbours and others in the locality would pass remarks about my appearance and my marriage. They used to scare us saying that my fate could not be changed and that wearing flowers in my hair or vermilion on my forehead would bring bad luck to my brother. Thus, my father was worried that my remarriage could result in excommunication, and nobody would then offer their daughter's hand in marriage to my brother. He also had a lingering doubt that I would not get my first husband's property if I remarried. But my mother was serious about it and their arguments on this issue became routine. I was afraid that the issue of my remarriage would turn our home into hell.[84]

Koteshwaramma wrote that when her menses first appeared, none of her relatives arrived and there were no festivities, much to her mother's dismay. Feeling that she was an 'unfortunate' person, Koteshwaramma stopped wearing flowers and applying bottu, as did her mother. Her younger brother got 'a much better match' because his in-laws had an eye on the property she inherited from her dead husband. Amid more talks of remarriage, she wondered:

> Would our relatives come to *my* wedding? Won't I face the wrath of my brother's wife's family if I marry now? Won't we be excommunicated? Could I be happy in a marriage that would cause so many troubles for

[82] She authoured and published a number of works. See Volga et al., *Mahilavaranam*, p. 114–115. Also see her autobiography *Nirjana Varadhi*.

[83] Kondapalli Koteshwaramma, *Nirjana Varadhi* (Hyderabad, 2012). Interestingly, her autobiography begins with her observations on being a child widow. The autobiography has been translated into English as *The Sharp Knife of Memory*, trans. V. B. Sowmya (New Delhi, 2015).

[84] *The Sharp Knife of Memory*, pp. 4–5.

> my father and brother? I wanted to tell Ramaswamy that I did not want to hurt my father by marrying someone in this situation, but I could not muster the courage to say so.[85]

As the friends of Ramaswamy learnt of her prospective remarriage, they used to offer her flowers and bottu, which were forbidden for a widow. They told her that *karma* (fate) was merely a myth and that widows who had remarriage produced children and enjoyed their lives.[86] The local teachers' union resolved to support her remarriage. Gradually, her father also changed his mind and agreed to arrange her remarriage. Her father requested for a groom from the same caste to avoid further conflicts in the village.

Koteshwaramma described reactions to the match:

> We were Pamarru Reddys and Kondapalli Sitaramayya was a Jonnapadu Reddy. When the villagers came to know of our match, they objected because, normally, there was no intermarriage as the two Reddys saw themselves as belonging to different branches. According to them, widow remarriage was in itself unacceptable; on top of that, choosing someone from another Reddy community was just out of the question. They felt that it would bring disgrace to our village and threatened that they wouldn't let the wedding take place. My father was frightened. Everyone would notice if the wedding happened in the month of Sravana. So, it was decided that it should happen in the month of Ashada. Since it was impossible to perform the wedding ceremony in our village, the elders decided to perform it in Ventrapragada, a communist bastion where Chandra Rajeswara Rao lived. My father owned and operated two route buses. But instead of using them, we rented another bus and left for Ventrapragada. I was escorted by about twenty-five to thirty young men. The wedding venue was a big house owned by a friend. Sitaramayya and his parents came in a veiled bullock cart, like women in purdah hidden from the view of their fellow villagers. Chandra Rajeswara Rao's wife, Savitramma, dressed me as the bride. Communist comrades took on the role of elders and conducted the marriage.[87]

The next problem was where the couple would reside. A few elders held that it was better send them to Pamarru, the native place of the bride. However,

[85] Ibid., pp. 5–6.

[86] They informed her about a teacher named Ramabrahmam, who married a widow by name Ramatulasamma and that they got beautiful children. Not only this, they took her there over a feast and made her caress their children. The widow remarriage couple offered to her bangles and bottu, which were forbidden for a widow, as they knew that she was likely to get remarried and thus encouraged her.

[87] Ibid., pp. 7–8.

her aunt (*pina talli*, that is, her mother's younger sister) had just passed away, leaving her mother grief-stricken, with relatives claiming that the 'inauspicious' remarriage had caused the death. Therefore, the couple went to Jonnapadu. Later, her father arranged a grand wedding feast in Pamarru, in the face of hostility and ridicule:

> Some people in Pamarru attempted to excommunicate us. They prevented the washerman and barber from visiting our house. They also prevented members from my brother's wife's family from visiting. One day, a few friends came to see us and I was standing outside the house after seeing them off. One Acchamma, passing by, began swearing at me. I asked, 'Why do you scold me? What wrong have I done?' She slapped me and called me names for talking back. My mother saw this and shouted at her, attracting the attention of our neighbours. Acchamma walked away, still shouting. The teachers' and students' society members came to our house after hearing about this incident and assured us that they were with us. They promised to talk to Acchamma's family and teach her a lesson.... Akkayya Choudhary came to visit me and brought the news that people were criticising Sitaramayya, addressing him as 'the useless fellow who married a widow'. He consoled me, saying that his friends and he were thinking of ways to handle the situation.[88]

Koteshwaramma's second marriage brought her into the Communist Party, of which her husband was an active member. From 1939 to 1942, she busied herself in cyclostyling and circulating *Swatantra Bharati*, the underground journal of the Communist Party, and conducting cultural programmes in villages to create consciousness among the rural poor. She was part of the movement for the construction of the Krishna Canal. An accomplished singer who was known to use music to boost the morale of peasants, she was also a theatre artist, having acted in Gurajada Appa Rao's *Kanyasulkam* and staging plays to raise relief funds during the Bengal Famine. She went underground during the Telangana Peasant Movement and diligently carried out the responsibilities assigned to her by the Communist Party. After the Communist Party called off the armed struggle, she continued to work with women's organisations. As her marriage soon ran into trouble, she sought economic independence and studied in Durgabai Deshmukh's Andhra Mahila Sabha, later working in Kakinada Women's Polytechnic College to support herself.

The problems of widows engaged the attention of women intellectuals through the 1960s as well. Their criticism of social and religious institutions

[88] Ibid., pp. 9–10.

became sharper and the widows represented in their literature turned highly resistant to the established codes of conduct. The female characters even reminded the women's organisations of their responsibility for prompt and positive intervention on widows'/women's issues. S. Manorama Devi's[89] 'Goruchuttupy Rokati Potu'[90] ('Pestle-Blow on the Whitlow', that is, one serious problem over the other), a playlet with two scenes, portrayed such widows. Scene I of the playlet opened with the 20-year-old Ramani, who had recently lost her husband and was struck by deep grief, being pushed to prepare for her ritual disfiguration. Dispite her continuous resistance, the neighbourly widow, Venkayamma, pressurised for the ritual; Ramani's mother, although aggrieved, silently accepts the commands of the traditional Venkayamma. When urged on by her mother, Ramani poignantly pleaded that her mother should not 'sacrifice her to that useless and meaningless evil practice'. When her mother told her that 'everything is lost with the death of her husband', Ramani replied: 'Only the mangalasutra [sacred thread of marriage] is lost with the death of husband. It comes with him and it goes with him. That's all. Because the other things like the *pasupu kumkuma* [turmeric and vermilion mark], bangles and hair do not come with him, they need not go [be removed] with him.' Questioned by Venkayamma 'if there should not be a difference between a widow and a *muttaiduva* (a woman with a living husband)', a shocked Ramani sharply questioned the double standards in social morality concerning widows and widowers.[91]

> Why should there be differences in social traditions concerning widows and widowers? Is it a crime on the part of a woman to have lost her husband? You are punishing the innocent. Disfiguring her [a widow] is one mistake. Imposing social boycott is the second mistake. Abusing her as 'munda' is the third mistake. Rather than healing the wound, you are

[89]S. Manorama Devi established the Mahila Sanghamu (Women's Organisation), Gudiwada, in 1945. In 1949, she became the Secretary of the Krishna District Women's Association. S. Manorama Devi, et al., ed., *Mahila Sanghamu: Gudivada–Bhavana Prarambhotsava Sanchika*, 28 April 1966, other details, n. a., pp. 1–5.

[90]Ibid., pp. 63–70.

[91]When her mother tells Ramani that men in society uttered bad words about her and that her maternal uncle could not bear to hear those words, Ramani questioned if her maternal uncle did not comb his hair, did not try to bring 'the new aunt' after the death of his wife. To her mother's reply that he was a man and that his act was justified, Ramani persuades her mother saying that 'one should not discriminate between women and men and thereby humiliate women. The ornaments [hair] that came with birth would have to go only with death, and not in between, [i.e. with the death of husband].'

> aggravating it and, above all, sprinkiling chilly powder on it [i.e. adding insult to injury].

When an aghast Venkayamma declared that she had never seen 'such strange and extreme things during their times', Ramani replied that 'if they had used their wisdom in their generation, the troubles would have been avoided for our [Ramani's] generation. The butcherism [*kasayitanam*] would not have continued in society.' When her mother tried to convince that 'God has done injustice' to Ramani, she chided her mother 'not to impose the wrongs done by society on the mouthless and voiceless God.' Various people, including relatives who came to perform the ritual disfiguration of Ramani, forced her to remove the mangalasutram. But when they demanded that she remove her bangles, bottu and have the head shaved, she scornfully replied that she would not and escaped to the local women's organisation for help, where she was a member, leading into Scene 2.

Ramani, standing in for the author, attacked the casual attitude of the women's organisations towards the problems of women and demanded their prompt and positive intervention. What is most important about S. Manorama Devi's understanding is that, like present-day feminists, she recognises that the supposedly 'private' family affairs are very much a matter for the 'public'. Advised by Sharada, the president of the organisation, to remarry if she so wishes, Ramani stated that she 'did not go to them for that purpose and that she does not want it. All that she needs is the freedom to lead her life as per her wish with her two children.' When Sarala, the Vice-President, remarked that disfiguration of widows was 'common' (*mamulega*), an angered Ramani questioned her audacity to downplay the issue. When the President advised her not to blame the women's organisations and questioned 'what rights they have got to interfere in her [Ramani's] family matters', Ramani minced no words:

> You do not have [the right to interfere]! Dear Lawyer, you do not really have [the right?] To say so tarnishes not only your presidential post but also your legal profession. Listen. You know about my husband's death. But did any one of you turn up [to see me]? No, you did not. Perhaps you did not have time. Caught in the struggle between life and death, I myself sent information requesting protection [from the planned disfiguration]. My letter reached you. Did it not! … Yes, you got it. I expected that you would remove the pestle-blow on my whitlow.… [But you failed.] Save the unfortunate like me from the atrocities of society. You have got the right. It is your duty also. Sitting in this building, you cannot do anything. [So, come out in to the society for field-based social action]. Had Raja

> Rammohun Roy sit in his palace, that ghastly evil of *sahagamana* could not have been removed. Had the great man Kandukuri [Veeresalingam] sat in his library, the flame of the grief of widowhood could not have been extinguished. You know well what they did. You also tread that path. Come, get ready.

The conservatives, who were determined to disfigure her, pursued her to the women's organisation. When her mother tells the president and the vice-president that they followed her because they were afraid that 'she might commit suicide by plunging into some well', Ramani confidently states that 'she was not that cowardly' and that 'they do not have to have that fear' and urges them to 'leave her' to live as per her wishes. When her mother threatens Ramani that her father would come to take her back to home, Ramani says that 'she is over 20-years-old and, therefore, a major' and 'he has no right to atrocise her [*sic*]'. As the pressure increases that Ramani should return home, which she rejects, the president of the organisation requests the police for help and the conservative mob flees. The organisation takes over the responsibility of Ramani and her two children. 'Our women's organisation takes care of her and such organisations are there for such purposes only,' the office-bearers state in the story, reminding women's organisations of their responsibility.

The Problem of Sadhava Vydhavyamu

There was another kind of 'widowhood': '*sadhava vydhavyamu*', that is, experiencing the condition of widowhood even while the husband was alive. This was the problem of abandoned wives who were caught in the peculiar situation of being a *sadhava* and a *vidhava* simultaneously. Barring their appearance, with marks such as the tali (marriage thread), bottu (vermilion mark), bangles, hair over the head and draping colourful sarees, they generally experienced all the ignominies, particularly sexual deprivation, forced upon a vidhava. Such women were pejoratively termed '*mogudu vidichina munda*' (a 'widow' abandoned by her husband). Women intellectuals vividly narrated the sufferings borne by such women and campaigned for their remarriage.

A letter by a woman named Sitamma, published in *Telugu Zenana* as far back as 1903, brought to light the travails of an abandoned wife. She narrated the troubles of her friend 'Sushila' (a pseudonym), who was maltreated and subsequently abandoned by her husband.[92] The writer and Sushila were both married in the same year; Sushila's husband was in the service of the British government. Though she was 'extremely beautiful', he engaged in extramarital affairs, driving her out of the home and abandoning her. Sitamma lamented that 'Sushila's virtues and beauty became like the 'moonlight showered on [a] forest' (*adavigachina vennela*), and that she was forced into 'sadhava vydhavyamu'. She could not understand how the British government allowed such a characterless and vile person to continue in office, and how the neighbouring elderly approved of his irresponsible behaviour. Lamenting whether it was not possible for the wise to eradicate the grief of 'sadhava vydhavyamu', she urged the editor of *Telugu Zenana* to publish the remedies suggested in this regard by the 'wise' for the sake of women. The letter is significant because it represented one of the earliest campaigns in support of abandoned wives, and against the extramarital affairs and 'licentiousness' of men.

In her short story titled 'Idi Ashastriyama?' (Is This Against the Dharmashastras?), Peddada Kameshwaramma advocated the remarriage of abandoned wives.[93] Bhanumati, the protagonist in the story, was abandoned by her husband, leaving her in near-destitute condition. The 'crow-like neighbours' questioned her about her husband, causing her great embarrassment and agony. One day, her brother, Gopal Rao, informed her that he got the 'written consent' of her husband that, if she wished, she could remarry and persuaded her to marry again. Shocked at this advice, Bhanumati replied:

> Brother! What are you saying? How can I, a Hindu woman, remarry? For the Hindu woman, birth is only once, marriage is only once and death is only once in a lifetime. I am born in the Hindu race which is famous in the world for its women's conjugal fidelity. Will not my marrying again go against the injunctions of the Dharmashastras?[94]

To this, the brother said:

> Sister! You are in a state of ignorance. New ideas are not occurring to our women and men because they are not properly educated. Let the Dharmashastras be in their place. They are not written by God, you know! Human beings authored them as per the changing times. They are for

[92] Sitamma (probable pseudonym), 'Sadhava Vydhavyam' (An Unhappy Marriage: A Letter; translation as in original), *Telugu Zenana*, July 1903, pp. 35–37.

[93] *Grihalakshmi*, December 1929, pp. 808–810.

[94] Ibid., p. 809.

> humans and not vice versa. Even then, where are people who have read them well and understood their spirit in the right way? Which shastra can justify your miserable state? When the husband has rejected [you] saying that 'I do not need this wife' in an unjust manner, and that too for no reason; according to which shastra does the remarriage of such a woman become a taboo? Therefore, there is nothing like transgressing the dharma in this. You do not hesitate and do not be afraid of and marry any one of my friends and enjoy your life.[95]

Questioned by Bhanumati whether people would not criticise her for marrying again, through her brother, the author said that 'it was impossible for anyone to please all' and that 'she had a right to a happy life in the world'. Further, she said that 'being self-centric always, men would not try hard to remove the sufferings of women. The shastras were biased in favour of them [men] and therefore they did not know any suffering.' Bhanumati was persuaded that 'if she agreed to and had a remarriage, she would be serving as a role model to the crores of Indian women who also suffered like her.' Bhanumati was thus convinced and exercised her 'right to a happy life' by marrying a young man.[96]

Tenneti Venkata Ratnavali reviled men who abandoned their wives, 'whom they had married with fire as the witness', for being 'cruel-hearted'. She condemned them as 'traitors of society' and pointed out double standards in how men and women were treated. The 'cruel tigers called husbands' were neither ashamed of nor afraid of society. But, it was not easy for a woman. 'She could neither laugh nor jump. Even tucking flowers in her hair was treated wrong [and watched with suspicion]. Howsoever obedient and virtuous she might have been, people would not allow her peace of mind because of her wicked husband.' 'Such women, who desired remarriage,' Ratnavali emphasised, 'should have the opportunity to do so'.[97]

Women's Organisations and the Widow Question

Although women's organisations discussed the problems of widows, in the beginning almost all of them hesitated to discuss the issue of widow remarriage. For example, among the various issues listed to be discussed

[95] Ibid., pp. 809–810.

[96] Ibid., p. 810.

[97] Tenneti Venkata Ratnavali, 'Stree Swatantryamu' (Women's Independence), *Grihalakshmi*, May 1941, pp. 191–192.

at the second All-Andhra Women's Conference held on 28–29 April 1911 in Kakinada, widow remarriage was not included; instead, it included a topic on 'how widows could be made useful'. This attests the reservations of women's organisations on the issue of widow remarriage.[98] At the third All-Andhra Women's Conference (23–24 May 1912 at Nidudavolu), women discussed whether widow remarriages were helpful to the development of women's education, what was essential for the progress of the nation—widow remarriages or celibacy and duty.[99] Though the fourth All-Andhra Women's Conference (1913) included many progressive issues on the agenda of discussions, the question of widow remarriage was conspicuous by its absence, indicating the prevalence of orthodox opinion against widow remarriages in the initial women's conferences.[100] At the seventh Arya Vaishya Mahila Mahasabha held on 14 July 1928 at Vayalpadu, women resolved that 'to enable widows to receive education and thereby serve the society, it was essential to send them to women's educational institutions to train them as teachers, doctors and preachers.' Though the conference did not oppose widow remarriage, it did not resolve in its favour either. The attitude of making widows 'useful' members of society was predominant.[101]

However, in the 1920s and later, the initial hesitation of women's organisations began to fade and they discussed and resolved in favour of widow remarriages in women's conferences. For instance, in the fifth conference of the Andhra Rashtra Mahila Mahasabha, held on 21–22 November 1931, Guntur, women resolved that guardians should get the child widows remarried, if the latter wished so. The resolution was passed almost unanimously despite some objection.[102] Individual women's organisations like the Sharada Niketanamu[103] and Saubhagya Niketanamu[104] not only provided shelter to widows but also campaigned for widow remarriage and conducted a number of widow remarriages.

Despite this progress, the conservative section of women vehemently denounced the very idea of widow remarriage. In the following section, we

---

[98] 'Andhra Mahila Mahasabha, Kakinada', *Savithri*, March 1911, pp. 1–8.

[99] 'Andhra Mahila Sabha, Nidudavolu', *Hindu Sundary*, April 1912, pp. 22–25.

[100] 'Andhra Mahila Sabha', *Hindu Sundary*, January-February 1913, pp. 22–24.

[101] *Vasavi*, August 1928, p. 203.

[102] Kanuparti Varalakshmamma, 'Gunturu Mahilasabha Visheshamulu', *Grihalakshmi*, February 1932, pp. 1049–1055.

[103] Details of the organisation are provided in Chapter 1.

[104] For details, see *Grihalakshmi*, June 1935, pp. 338–339.

listen to the voices of conservative women, who rose against the tides of the widow remarriage movement.

The Conservative Backlash

Controversy surrounding the question of widow remarriage is not new. We already know that rival camps—pro and anti-widow remarriage groups represented by Kandukuri Veeresalingam and Kokkonda Venkataratnam and others—had bitterly fought over the issue. However, that debate was an *all-male* affair.[105] However, the issue of widow remarriage was also extremely contested among women reformers and caused a rift in women's organisations.

As the widow remarriage movement was marching ahead, including with the support of several women, there were a section of conservative women, who bitterly opposed the widow remarriage movement and attacked social reformers for advocating the same. As discussed in Chapters 1 and 2, Pulugurta Lakshmi Narasamamba led the anti–widow remarriage faction. She strongly felt that by advocating and performing widow remarriages, the reformers were foolishly abandoning the world-renowned pativratyam (conjugal fidelity) of Hindu women. Citing the British government's census data, which established that women outnumbered men, she questioned what would happen to unmarried girls if widows and 'those married girls' (*satantuvulu*) who refused to live with their parent-arranged husbands, started taking up new husbands.[106] She scornfully claimed that 'the reformers, who stated that enforcing celibacy on the widows was cruel, will, perhaps, impose the same on virgin girls.'[107]

Finding fault with the reformers' questioning as to how the widowers remarried disallowing the same to the widows, she wondered:

[105] Vedam Venkataraya Shastry (1853–1929), Dasu Sriramulu (1846–1908), Kashibhatta Brahmaiah Shastry (1863–1940) were a few among the many remarkable personalities, who opposed widow remarriages. For details, see V. Ramakrishna, *Social Reform in Andhra*, pp. 116–118. For the views of Brahmaiah Shastry on the reformist stand on widowhood and widow remarriage, see Vakulabharanam Rajagopal, 'Anti-reform discourse in Andhra: Cultural Nationalism that failed' in Michael Bergunder, Heiko Frese and Ulrike Schroder, ed., *Ritual, Caste, and Religion in Colonial South India* (Delhi, 2011), p. 323.

[106] Pulugurta Lakshmi Narasamamba, 'Pativratyamu' (Conjugal Fidelity), *Savithri*, July 1911, p. 12.

[107] Ibid.

> Ohoho! What adventurous words! Like the popular saying, 'asked why somebody is climbing the Toddy tree, he replied, for cutting grass for the calf', how unhesitatingly they are speaking! They are saying that if our [widowed] women, too, remarried, there is nothing wrong in it because a few Aryan [Hindu] religious men and a few Brahmo religious men are remarrying. Are you observing how elegant and ethical their sermon is! Just because some are indulging in corrupt practices, which are to be condemned by one and all in the world, how can the same be agreeable to all? Is this what the word reform means?... What does reform mean—correcting errors or, spoiling the society by erring in ever-newer ways?... Is not it that because of the presence of such [wicked and] selfish people alone that our mother country–the land of knowledge [and morality]–is broken into pieces and is severely ruined![108]

She criticised male reformers for pretending to understand the problems of widows. Questioning the argument that widows found it difficult to strictly observe celibacy, she quoted a north Indian woman, Vidyavati Devi:

> The widows of India do not desire remarriage. They desire life's fulfilment by gaining knowledge of morality and dharma and freedom from worldly attachments instead. Therefore, by establishing suitable ashrams and educational institutions, we must make them masters in such matters as the science of morality and dharma. In social reform conferences, people are hailing a man as a great reformer, if he married a widow. O Aryans! What kind of social reform have you brought through widow remarriages? You are trying to push women also into the same pit in which you have already fallen. Is this social reform? No. Nobody, except the wicked and the lustful [*dhoortulunu, kamukulunu*] will endorse such an act. Thinking that their vices will be treated as virtues, men are marrying several times and are telling that widow remarriages have the sanction of the shastras.... O Aryans! Why do you corrupt caste honour by undertaking such an act banned by the Vedas? Why do you spoil the pativratyam of women? Will women, who are deprived of the education of *dharmagnana* and are drowned in darkness, keep themselves away from deeds of *adharma* with widow remarriage alone? ... One can see with opened eyes the abominable and horrible acts being committed by people in the European continent, where widow remarriage is permitted. Why are you importing evil practices into India?[109]

Hailing Vidyavati Devi's views as 'truths' and 'efficacious', Narasamamba brushed aside the objections of the reformers as 'baseless' and commented

[108] Ibid. pp. 12–13

[109] Ibid., pp. 13–16.

that 'they were not needed to succumb to their [reformers'] sermons', which were like 'childish talk'.[110] Interestingly, Vidyavati Devi's essay had been reproduced, in full, in the *Hindu Sundary* over a year before Narasamamba quoted it approvingly. The proprietor of *Hindu Sundary* had reproduced it, thinking that 'it would be better if women published a rejoinder to the essay than men'.[111] That *Hindu Sundary* rejected Vidyavati Devi's views was clear.

Conservative women's determined opposition to the widow marriage movement can further be demonstrated best by a controversy that engulfed the women's organisation, the Shri Vidyarthini Samajamu at Kakinada.[112] The year was 1911. As we have already mentioned, under the leadership of Pulugurta Lakshmi Narasamamba, the organisation conducted the second Andhra Mahila Mahasabha (or, All-Andhra Women's Conference) on 28–29 April 1911 at Kakinada in combination with the annual function of the Samajamu, which was held on 30. On this occasion, differences emerged between Narasamamba, the president of the Samajamu, and its secretaries—Balantrapu Sheshamma and Damerla Sitamma—leading to a protracted and fiery controversy that lasted for over a year. Consequently, the organisation got divided.

Controversy raged on the issue of the presence of a remarried woman (*punarvivahita*)[113] in the second Andhra Mahila Mahasabha, and on the question whether the *punarvivahitalu* (widows, who remarried) could be invited there. It culminated in an argument about whether they could be treated as 'kulanganas' (respectable/chaste women). The group led by Narasamamba maintained that widows who remarried were not to be

---

[110] Ibid., pp. 15 and 3. She sadly noted that the reformers alleged the crime of suicide on widows, who were extremely devoted to their husbands, when they committed Sati. Ibid., p. 13. Replying to the reformist contention that customs and traditions were to be modified according to changing times and spaces, she said that though it was true, certain 'permanent dharmas (*shashvata dharmamulu*) would never change.' 'To our country and to us, our pativratya dharma would never change,' she emphasised.

[111] Her essay was originally published in English in the *Gurukul Samachar*, published from Haridwar. It was reproduced in translation in the *Andhra Kesari*, and *Hindu Sundary* borrowed it from the latter. See 'Stree Punarvivahamulu' (Widow Remarriages), *Hindu Sundary*, February–March 1910, pp. 44–47.

[112] Details of the organisation are given in the section on women's organisations in Chapter 1.

[113] Unfortunately, our sources did not mention her name. However, we may guess that she was Uppuluri Nagaratnamma, who started the rival organisation, the Kakinada Stree Samajamu. Her remarks also strongly suggest this. See her essay 'Andhra Mahila Mahasabha, Nidudavolu' (All Andhra Women's Conference, Nidudavolu), *Hindu Sundary*, May 1912, pp. 23–28.

treated as 'kulanganas'. This difference of opinion resulted in the expulsion of the secretaries from the Shri Vidyarthini Samajamu. With this, the debate intensified and each of the two groups claimed legitimacy over the organisation presenting interesting arguments.

The conservative group of women[114] accused the secretaries of 'transgressing the rules and regulations of the organisation'. They complained that the secretaries 'dared' bring the 'punarvivahitalu' to the weekly meetings of the organisation, particularly to its annual function, and also the second Andhra Mahila Mahasabha, which was 'against the norms of the organisation'. They had thereby 'caused displeasure not only among the members of the organisation but also among the women of the town [Kakinada].' They further complained that the secretaries did not stop there; they 'continued to bring the remarried women even after the annual function of the organisation' was over. As a result, they complained, 'many women stopped attending the regular meetings of the Samajamu leading to its deterioration.'

The 'progressive group', headed by the 'expelled' secretaries, presented an altogether different story.[115] The 'expelled' secretaries wrote that the writings of Narasamamba and the 'newly nominated E.C. members' (whose note appeared in the 7 July 1911 issue of the *Krishna Patrika*, p. 9.) regarding the organisation were not only 'strange' but also 'very saddening'. They maintained that the charge that they 'transgressed the rules and regulations of the organisation' was a baseless allegation. 'Had it been so, the [other] members themselves would have removed us', they pointed out. According

---

[114]Narasamamba led the group. The other members were: Bhavaraju Mahalakshmamma, Kashibhatta Sooramma, Uppuluri Sundaramma, Chintalapudi Sitadevamma, and Manyam Venkata Subbamma. See, 'Shri Vidyarthini Samajamu', *Savithri*, July 1911, pp. 3–5. Manyam Venkata Subbamma deserves to be specially mentioned for one of her writings created a fascinating controversy about five years before the eruption of the present controversy. Kandukuri Veeresalingam was involved in this controversy. Narasamamba supported Subbamma and bitterly attacked Veeresalingam. For details on the verbal duel between Manyam Subbamma and Veeresalingam, see the section on *Savithri* in Chapter 2.

[115]See 'Shri Vidyarthini Samajamu, Kakinada', *Hindu Sundary*, July 1911, pp. 4–8. The group had more than 10 members. They were: Madabhooshi Choodamma, Duggirala Ramanamma, Pemmaraju Lakshmidevamma, Mamidanna Kameshwaramma, Attota Sheshamma, Attili Subbamma, Burra Venkata Subbamma, Malladi Lakshmidevamma, Maddali Rajyalakshmamma, Goteti Lakshmikantamma and Kallepalle Venkata Ramanamma apart from Balantrapu Sheshamma and Damerla Sitamma, the 'expelled' secretaries. Ibid., p. 6.

to them, Narasamamba herself had deserted the organisation; this indicated who actually went against the norms of the organisation. They complained that Narasamamba did not attend any meeting of the organisation after the Andhra Mahila Mahasabha despite repeated requests. 'This made it very clear as to how concerned she was about the development of the organisation [and of women]', they remarked sarcastically.[116]

According to the progressive group of women, a letter signed by 13 members was sent to Narasamamba on 1 July 1911, requesting her to convene the Executive Committee meeting. She neither replied nor made herself present. Instead, invitation cards printed in her name reached them at about 1 pm on 2 July 1911: the cards contained the information that 'the venue of the organisation was shifted to Jagannathapuram' [Narasamamba's residence] on the ground that the meetings at the earlier venue were 'conducted in violation of the norms of the organisation'. The invitation explicitly stated that 'widows who remarried would not be admitted into the organisation' (*punarvivahitalindunjerchukonbadaru*). 'With this', the 'progressive' women said, 'they came to a conclusion that she [Narasamamba] was not going to attend the proposed meeting'. Therefore, they conducted a meeting on 2 July 1911, which was presided over by Duggirala Ramanamma. They decided to replace Narasamamba with Kallepalle Venkata Ramanamma[117] as the president. Damerla Sitamma and Balntrapu Sheshamma were elected as secretaries for a period of one year.

The above narrative makes it clear that contending viewpoints of women on the widow question led to the division of an important women's organisation. A pitched war of words was waged on the issue that had sparked the controversy, with several interlocutors. Though there were many who

---

[116]Complaining further, they said that Narasamamba never discussed the matter of shifting the venue and the library with the members of the organisation. 'The president did not have the right to take a unilateral decision either to remove the secretaries or to change the venue of the organisation without the consent of the members', they stressed. Aghast at her act, they said that 'they could not understand as to who gave her the right to do what she did'.

[117]Venkata Ramanamma was an intellectual activist, who played a prominent role in the women's movement in colonial Andhra. She was one among those who saved and successfully ran the Shri Vidyarthini Samajamu serving as its president for six consecutive years, during 1911–1916. In that capacity, she took a leading role in convening the conferences of the Andhra Mahila Mahasabha. She was instrumental in the revival of the *Hindu Sundary*: she edited it for some time. A prolific writer, she published widely on women's issues in the contemporary journals. She had also edited the women's monthly, *Andhra Lakshmi*.

questioned Narasamamba, owing to constraints of space, we discuss only a few, who flayed Narasamamba. She, in turn, pulled no punches.

The *Andhra Patrika*[118] commented that the naming of the state level women's conference—Andhra Mahila Mahasabha—was not justified given Narasamamba's stand on the issue of widows who remarried. It said that 'going by its name, one would assume that the Mahasabha was open to all Andhra women, where they could go and also deliver lectures'. But Narasamamba objected to the entry of remarried women and Andhra Christians (as well as Muslim women, although the article did not explicitly mention this). Therefore, its name should not have been as it was. Rather, the *Andhra Patrika* quipped, it should have been named *Punarvivahitastree Nishedha Andhra Brahmana Stree Sabha* (an Andhra Brahmin Women's Conference, where remarried women and women of other castes and communities were unwelcome).[119]

Many others raised objections to the phrase '*jaaturvarnyamulaloni kulanganalu*' ('the respectable women of the four varnas'), which appeared in the invitation letters of the Andhra Mahila Mahasabha.[120] The invitation letters[121] specified that '[only] all Andhra kulangana women belonging to the four varnas' were welcome to attend the conference. Now the debate shifted to arguing as to who could be called 'kulanganas' and whether the punarvivahita women could fall in that category. Narasamamba was of the view that the term 'kulangana' did not include the punarvivahitas, and issued rejoinders to build her case.[122]

[118] It began publication on 9 September 1908 from Bombay, founded by Kashinathuni Nageshwara Rao. Initially, it was a weekly; later, a daily was also started with the same name. From 1 April 1914, the place of publication shifted to Madras. The paper was started with the profit that Nageshwara Rao made by selling his famous pain balm, Amritanjan. The *Andhra Patrika* supported the cause of social reform as well as the freedom movement. For an in-depth study of the *Andhra Patrika*, see C. V. Raja Gopala Rao, *Andhra Patrika Charitra* (History of the *Andhra Patrika*) (Hyderabad, 2004).

[119] Pulugurta Lakshmi Narasamamba, 'Andhra Mahila Mahasabha', *Savithri*, June 1911, pp. 3–4.

[120] Ibid., pp. 5–6.

[121] Narasamamba notified the proposed Mahila Mahasabha in the *Savithri*, extending a warm welcome to 'the dear kulangana sisters belonging to the four varnas'. Also, it was notified that 'special arrangements would be made according to caste and sub-caste considerations and preferences, if the same was informed to her in advance'. See 'Andhra Mahila Mahasabha–Kakinada', *Savithri*, March 1911, pp. 1–8; 'Andhra Mahila Mahasabha-Ahvaana Patrika', *Savithri*, April 1911, pp. 1–2.

[122] The characteristic feature of Narasamamba's writings/rejoinders was that they were very lengthy, running into nineteen pages! For example, see her essay 'Andhra

Berating the editor of the *Andhra Patrika*, she said that such a criticism only exposed the 'jealousy in the minds of our highly scholarly brothers'. She wondered that she could not understand as to how a conference that was attended by Brahmin, Vaishya and Shudra women could be termed a 'Brahmin's Women's Conference'. Countering the charge that she did not invite Christian [and Muslim] women, she said that 'Andhras meant only the Hindus living in the Andhra/Telugu country, and not the others like Christians [and Muslims]'. An annoyed Narasamamba argued that if the name 'Andhra Mahila Mahasabha' was not justified, the name of 'Andhra Patrika' also came under scrutiny.[123] She continued that 'Andhra Patrika' deserved to be named '*angleyabhashasamskara sankalita sanghasamskarapriyamrutanjana patrika*' ('A beloved paper published with the profit of a pain balm, claiming to be mixed in nectar, and, having been influenced by English language and culture, is striving for social reform').[124]

She dwelt at length on the issue of 'kulanganas'. It was her conviction that widows, who remarried, could not come under the category of '*kulanganalu*'. She said that the pro-widow remarriage reformers cited the example of Damayanti's second 'swayamvara' to defend their point. Citing the same sources, she pointed out that 'even if the shastras did not ban widow remarriage, they certainly did not treat it without contempt'. It was also her contention that the shastras agreed to the remarriage only of the

---

Mahila Mahasabha', *Savithri*, June 1911, pp. 2–20. See also 'Kulanganalu', *Savithri*, October 1911, pp. 1–9; 'Pativratyamu' (Fidelity), *Savithri*, July 1911, pp. 1–9. Her writings are captivating for they are studded with stunning logic, exhibit her scholarship of the various shastras, full of wit and humour, embellished with proverbs which added special effect to the content, and were highly polemical.

[123]She built on a stunning parapet of logic to justify her arguments. Attacking the editor of the *Andhra Patrika*, she asked: 'How does the paper deserve its name? Is it because it is published in the Andhra region? Is it because it is published by the Andhras? Is it because it is published in Andhra [Telugu] language? Or, is it because it is published for the Andhras?' Herself answering these questions, she tried to prove that the name—Andhra Patrika—was mismatched. She said that since the Patrika was published from Bombay i.e. outside Andhra region, the naming was inappropriate. A Brahmin published the Patrika. The Brahmins, according to her, were not Andhras and the Shudras were the real Andhras. Since a Brahmin published the Patrika, the name did not match. Since three-fourths of the vocabulary the Patrika employed was Sanskrit, and that it had a large number of Urdu and English words, the name did not suit. Since the Patrika was not exclusively meant for Andhra, its name was not justified. See 'Andhra Mahila Mahasabha', *Savithri*, June 1911, p. 5.

[124]Pulugurta Lakshmi Narasamamba, 'Andhra Mahila Mahasabha', *Savithri*, June 1911, pp. 3–5.

'ordinary women', not kulanganas. Citing a quotation from the *Manusmriti* that was used by pro–widow remarriage activists, she argued that the text did not approve of the remarriage of a *saadhvi* (chaste woman). According to her, 'different shastras expressed different views concerning the issue: they contained both good and bad things, and all the things present in them could not be treated as good'! Therefore, 'even if the shastras sanctioned remarriage of widows, it could/should not be practised by the kulanganas'. She went as far as to claim that remarriage amounted to 'prostitution'. According to her, the shastras reverberated that 'a kulangana had only one husband, whether dead or alive: his status of being a husband did not disappear with his death.'[125]

Terming pro-remarriage reformers as 'experts in creating nuisance', she derisively claimed that 'if the *sadhvimani*s [jewels among chaste women] like Sita, Savitri, Damayanti, Chandramati, Shakuntala, Ahalyabai, etc., who brought glory and purity to 'our Hindu *deshamu*', were to come to Kakinada, the pro-widow remarriage men would blame even them, saying that the women beat their husbands on their backs'.[126]

Contesting the allegation that she could not bear even the sight of widows or those who remarried, Narsamamba termed these claims '*kallabolli paluku*' (a wild lie). She admitted that she had invited only the kulanganas to the conference, excluding remarried women. She claimed that this was in view of the 'educational advancement' of other members: '*sumangali*' women did not like the presence of the 'punarvivahitalu' in their gatherings. 'If a widow, who remarried, ever chanced to come, the sumangali women were aghast, looked at each other's face, got agitated thinking that attempts were being made to defile them by joining them with the punarvivahitas. A few of them abruptly left the venue thinking that they should not have gone there, and decided never to return.' Further, Narasamamba stated that the apprehension that 'women's organisations were established for conducting widow remarriages, and also for mixing us [the 'sumangalis'] with them [punarvivahitalu] was widely prevalent among women'.

Countering the writings of Narasamamba, Burra Buchchi Bangaramma wrote in the *Krishna Patrika* (25 August 1911, p. 4)[127] that 'one could not

[125] Ibid., pp. 5–11.

[126] Ibid., p. 12.

[127] Cited in Pulugurta Lakshmi Narasamamba's 'Kulanganalu' (Respectable Women), *Savithri*, October 1911, p. 1. Uppuluri Nagaratnamma quoted Bangaramma's piece in her essay 'Stree Punarvivahamulu' (Widow Remarriages), *Hindu Sundary*, October–

be called a *kulata* (an adulteress/fallen woman; opposite of kulangana) how many ever times one married'. Bangaramma further wrote that 'it was undesirable to have contempt for a woman, who did not have only one husband.' Narasamamba held this to be downright outrageous. She lamented that 'bad times had fallen on the virtuous land, the Aryavarta'. For her, 'it was a matter of great sorrow for women themselves held such strange views [*viparita dharmamulu*] which were bound to uproot the pativratya dharma of fellow women.' For Narasamamba, this was unacceptable: 'if we went by the words of Bangaramma, even the prostitutes would have to be treated as kulanganas.'[128]

Enraged by the reformist stand, Narasamamba sternly warned the pro-widow remarriage dectractors:

> O pro-widow remarriage brothers and sisters! Do not try to cheat the world for the purpose of establishing your prodigious dharmas. Do not bring ill-fame to the word reform by drowning those, who do not agree with your views, in the mire of blame, and by pouring your rebuking scholarship on them! ... Blaming is not the way of doing any good thing. Following ones duties and also allowing the others to follow their duties alone would bring good to the world.[129]

A particularly harsh critic of Narasamamba was Kotikalapudi Sitamma, a writer, teacher and Veeresalingam's biographer.[130] Sitamma remarked that 'though she [Narasamamba] established herself as a scholar, she failed to recognise the changes taking place in society, and struggled hard to perpetuate the blindly-practised traditional evils.'[131] She stressed that Narasamamba 'tried to hide her own faults: her behaviour brought ill fame

---

November 1911, pp. 30–31. Replying to Narasamamba, Bangaramma said that even if a few shastras opposed widow remarriages, one needed to ignore that. According to her, such Dharmashastras were framed keeping in view the needs of society and were not fixed in stone. Since the government had legalised widow remarriage, they should be performed. Given the need for marriage, a punarvivahita, according to Bangaramma, was definitely a kulangana. Ibid., p. 31.

[128] Pulugurta Lakshmi Narasamamba, 'Kulanganalu', pp. 1–2.

[129] Ibid., p. 9.

[130] For a detailed account of Sitamma's life and work, see V. Ramakrishna, *Social Reform in Andhra*, p. 101. See also Utukuri Lakshmikanthamma, *Andhra Kavayitrulu*, pp. 101–105.

[131] Kotikalapudi Sitamma, 'Andhra Mahila Mahasabha Karyadarshinigaragu, Srimati Pulugurta Lakshmi Narasamambagarikoka Vinnapamu' (An Appeal to Smt. Pulugurta Lakshminarasamamba, the Secretary of the Andhra Mahila Mahasabha), *Hindu Sundary*, August 1911, pp. 1–6.

to the entire women folk about which one was to be ashamed.'[132] Sitamma argued that people did not independently assume that the term 'kulangana' excluded the punarvivahitas. It was only Narasamamba's known disapproval that drove others to exclude remarried widows. To substantiate her stand, Sitamma reminded Narasamamba of her speech delivered at Bandar (Machilipatnam), where the latter had opposed widow remarriage.[133] Sitamma ridiculed the speech as arrogant and called her a 'foolish woman' (*alpagna*) who 'did and could not have any adverse effect' on the widow remarriage movement'. She advised Narasamamba 'not to indulge in giving futile replies anymore' and 'behave wisely'.[134]

Several others criticised Narasamamba, including the editor of the journal *Deshamata*,[135] Sattiraju Shyamalamba,[136] Bangaramma,[137] and Madabhooshi Choodamma. Amidst this barrage of criticism, an anonymous writer 'Hitavadi' (a pseudonym, meaning 'well-wisher') argued on her behalf, but was quickly countered by Madabhooshi Choodamma.[138] As the debate stretched on, Sattiraju Sitaramaiah, the founder of *Hindu Sundary*, intervened and suggested that they should 'end the debate and work for the improvement of women's education in the way each group deemed fit'.[139] After the controversy ended, the Shri Vidyarthini Samajamu was taken over by the 'progressive' section of women, and it prospered under their leadership to survive beyond the 1960s.

---

[132] Ibid.

[133] Ibid.

[134] Ibid.

[135] It appeared in the 09 September 1911 issue. Cited in Pulugurta Lakshmi Narasamamba, 'Kulanganalu', pp. 3–7.

[136] Her views were published in the September 1911 issue of the *Krishna Patrika*. Cited in ibid., p. 9.

[137] Bangaramma published an article titled 'Kulanganalevaru?' (Who are the Kulanganas?) in the 25 August 1911 (p. 4) issue of the *Krishna Patrika*. Cited in ibid., pp. 1–2. Excerpts were reproduced by Uppuluri Nagaratnamma in her essay 'Stree Punarvivahamulu' (Widow Remarriages), *Hindu Sundary*, October-November 1911, pp. 30–31. With the pseudonym 'Kulangana', somebody published an article in the 8 September 1911 issue of the *Krishna Patrika*. Cited in Pulugurta Lakshmi Narasamamba's 'Kulanganalu', p. 9.

[138] An article appeared in the name of 'Hitavadi' in the 16 August 1911 issue of the *Andhra Prakashika* (see p. 6). Madabhooshi Choodamma refuted the claims of the 'Hitavadi'. See 'Shri Vidyarthini Samajamu', *Hindu Sundary*, October-November 1911, pp. 31–38.

[139] *Hindu Sundary*, October–November 1911, p. 38.

The controversy attests the deeply divided opinion among women on the issue of widow remarriage. It demonstrates that not all educated women were in favour of remarriage, and a few were in fact bitterly opposed to it. Further, it reveals that while remarriage could resolve some of the problems faced by widow, it also led to social censure and a fall in status. Women who remarried were treated contemptuously and stigmatised. Accused of tarnishing the chaste image of 'Hindu Aryan' women, they were treated as *kulatas*, denied any respect, and deemed unworthy of interaction. The punarvivahitas had to silently suffer from the want of social acceptance and respect. In a nutshell, the controversy confirms the widespread prejudice against a punarvivahita. However, the defeat of the 'conservative' group in the hands of the 'progressive' section of women, who were supported by many, indicates that the wind was blowing in favour of widow remarriage.[140]

Objects of Reform or Agents of Social Change? Recovering Widows' Agency

It is quite common for studies on the widow remarriage movement to valourise male social reformers, who were presented as having taken enormous pains by swimming against the currents of rabid conservatism—which, no doubt, they did. They 'reformed' the miserable conditions of widows and thus 'uplifted' them. In such renderings, the widows become mute objects of reform. This overshadows the admirable and stunning initiative of widows themselves, exhibiting enormous courage to change their conditions. Without their readiness, the widow remarriage movement could not have registered the success it did.[141]

It is crucial to establish widows as active agents who sculpted their own destiny. We see several instances of widows taking interest in the widow remarriage movement and exhibiting great courage by consenting to remarry, often against the wishes of family elders and their communities, and

[140]It is important to note that all this happened when Veeresalingam was alive, towards the end of his life (he passed away in 1919). But it appears that he did not respond to this. Given the fact that he had encountered Narasamamba about five years before the eruption of the controversy, his silence presents a great puzzle.

[141]Very few studies on social reform in Andhra pay attention to women's, particularly widows', contribution to and perspective on the widow remarriage movement. For example, see V. Ramakrishna, *Social Reform*. B. Kesava Narayana, 'Widow Marriage Movement in Andhra', *Itihas*, pp. 147–164.

secretly running away from their homes. Several mothers and grandmothers of widowed girls took pains to ensure that their daughters/granddaughters were relieved of the torment of enforced widowhood. The wives of male social reformers, along with many other women including widows, enriched the movement through their contributions. By demonstrating a willingness to remarry, courage to withstand familial pressures and a strong desire to escape the oppressive conditions forced upon them, widows seriously and sincerely sought to change the social script. While a few married, others were content with sexual relationships with men of their liking. A few others, who decided to remain celibate, established schools and shelter homes.

The vigorous widow remarriage campaign, according to Veersalingam, 'sprouted the hope of happiness in the hearts of virgin widows.'[142] However, at the same time, it alarmed the conservative families, sparking deep-rooted fears of caste corruption in their hearts. Veeresalingam presented the interesting story of an assertive widow who rebelled against prescriptions. According to Veeresalingam, a 16-year-old 'virgin' widow, cousin of an orthodox Vaidiki Brahmin, lived with him in Rajahmundry. Other than the lack of the bottu, she lived a normal life like that of a sumangali woman (*suvasini*), wearing normal sarees, jackets and jewels, etc. Alarmed by the stir caused by the widow remarriage campaign, her family members hastened to give her the markers of widowhood, that is, giving widows' clothes and tonsuring her head, etc. When her cousin offered to her the coarse white cloth meant for widows, she sarcastically told him to give them to his wife. Aghast at this unanticipated reply, he questioned how clothes meant for widows could be given to his wife, a *muttaiduva* (a married woman with a living husband). To this she boldly replied: 'Elder brother! Do not be angry. How are these clothes useful to me for I am planning to become a *muttaiduva* like your wife?' Her unconventional reaction left her family members and the larger community dumbstruck. She sent shockwaves by her boldly stated decision—an independent decision she took for and by herself—to remarry.[143]

[142] Veeresalingam, *Sweeya Charitramu*, Part 1, p. 177.

[143] She could not marry as per her wish due to family interferece. However, she did not surrender to be disfigured either. Finally, a compromise was arrived at: the family allowed her to pursue sexual relations with anybody she liked, but not remarriage. Thus, they successfully deterred her from the thought of remarriage. On this, Veeresalingam observed that 'being traditionalists, our people could approve of immoral and secret prostitution, but not remarriage which, they thought, was against tradition.' Citing the popular saying that 'marriage is not required if sexual needs are fulfilled' (*ranku saagina*

A man named Vummettala Venkatapati Rao of the Vaishnava Madhva sect wrote to Veeresalingam on 24 June 1882, requesting him to arrange for the remarriage of his 16-year-old daughter, Shanagavarapu Lakshmibayammma. He mentioned that 'she particularly desired to [re]marry.'[144] Another by the name Peddibhatla Yagnanna wanted to get his widowed sister remarried. However, both the men backed out because of social pressure and fear. However, the girls were not disheartened. As they were educated, they wrote to Veeresalingam (they, in fact, had begun correspondence with him much before the father and the brother approached him)[145] expressing their willingness for remarriage. Therefore, Veeresalingam, 'leaving aside their guardians… decided to complete the task by maintaining correspondence with the girls themselves'.[146] While one widow lived in Peddapuram, the other lived in Kakinada. Veeresalingam decided to execute the plan through his friends and admirers living in those places: Gummadidala Manoharam Pantulu (Peddapuram), a police inspector, and Tanjavuri Venkata Chalapati Rao.

It is necessary to recount how the widow from Peddapuram escaped to Rajahmundry. The woman, in fact, guided Veeresalingam and his friends on how this could happen. The first two attempts were thwarted as the girl's parents sensed something suspicious and remained vigilant. The carelessness of Veeresalingam's messengers also contributed to the failure of the mission.[147] However, without getting disheartened, she continued the correspondence until finally, she escaped. Veeresalingam vividly described the way the girl managed to escape.

> In that cloudy and rainy dark late night of *Amavasya* (no-moon night), as her mother was attending her father, who was suffering from headache, on the pretext of urinating, the girl came out into the street and told our man [Munisamy, who was resting on a raised platform attached to her home pretending to be a passerby] about her willingness to go with him [escape]. Instantaneously, he took the girl along with him and started [for

pendliyakkaraledanu sameta), he scornfully commented further that 'the unfortunate one was still continuing in the caste without facing excommunication and, by continuing her bad practice, she was sanctifying her caste' (*kulamunu paavanamu cheyuchunnadi*). Kandukuri Veeresalingam, *Sweeya Charitramu*, Part 1, pp. 177–179.

[144] Ibid., p. 237.

[145] There were a number of such educated widows, who wrote to Veeresalingam 'requesting him to save them from the perennial misery of widowhood.' Ibid., p. 179.

[146] Ibid., p. 237.

[147] Ibid., p. 243.

> Rajahmundry]. After travelling some distance, he dressed her in men's clothes, and in the short-cut route he had fixed in the morning, drenching in rain in that thick darkness, running for some distance, and lifting the girl [over his shoulders] for some distance, covering about twenty miles by the time it was dawn, hiring a cart there, he brought her home the next day early morning.[148]

As the family members could not find her, they were convinced that she had run away for (re)marriage. Alleging that she had fled stealing jewellery, they lodged a complaint with the police and got an arrest warrant issued that very night.[149] Her parents complained that Veeresalingam and his friends 'kidnapped' a minor girl, and lodged an FIR. Veeresalingam described that 'having reached his home, despite the bride's mother and other relatives cried, shouted, threatened and persuaded her to win her back, all their varied efforts could not succeed. Having got disappointed, they had to return.'[150] So strong was her determination to relieve herself of the oppressed existence! Finally, the marriage was conducted on 22 October 1882. Sitamma and Tadurti Rama Rao were the bride and groom, respectively.

Driven by the desire for remarriage, another child widow by name Sheshamma from Kakinada cleverly gave the slip to her family members, made her way to Rajahmundry and married. On a fine early morning, she met Tanjavuri Chalapati Rao, a follower of Veeresalingam who lived opposite her home, and presented to him a strategy of her escape. She found a convenient escape route amid a marriage procession that was to pass through her lane. She informed Chalapati Rao that she would get an opportunity to escape during the procession. Accordingly, it was planned and a palanquin arranged. Chalapati Rao shrewdly took her brother and maternal uncles to a magic show much ahead of the scheduled time of display. As the marriage procession passed by her home at about 10 pm with the dance of the *veshya* women providing a distraction, she escaped from home. The family, including the mother and a maternal uncle, did make their way to Veeresalingam's home. 'Crying, the girl's mother tried to convince her to return home, but the determined girl relentlessly refused,' wrote Veeresalingam. She married Pulavarti Sheshaiah on 3 January 1883.[151]

---

[148] Ibid., pp. 246–247.

[149] Ibid., p. 247.

[150] Ibid., pp. 249–250.

[151] For a graphic description of the entire episode, see ibid., pp. 255–258.

Veeresalingam appointed Sampara Venkanna on a monthly salary of Rs. 8 for the purpose of searching for widows and convincing their parents to remarry their daughters. However, quite ironically, Venkanna never bothered to arrange the remarriage of his own 18-years-old widowed daughter by name Sooramma. She ran away from her father's home and requested Veeresalingam to provide her *pati bhiksha*. She married Gopalam, who worked in the printing press of Veeresalingam.[152]

Another widow by name Venkamma was taken to Rajahmundry by her mother and elder brother to get her head tonsured on the banks of the river Godavari on the occasion of *pushkaralu*. One night before the fated day, the girl escaped and reached Veeresalingam's house seeking shelter and remarriage. Though her previous husband had been a school teacher, she was ready to marry anybody, regardless of wealth or education. Her marriage was fixed with 23-year-old Chebolu Venkaiah and held on 13 March 1883. Venkaiah worked as a cook in the home of a lawyer.[153]

The 19th widow remarriage performed by Veeresalingam, on 6 November 1892 between Manuri Purushottam Pantulu and Sitamma, was really an amazing one. Sitamma was a 16-year-old widow. Though her father wanted to arrange her remarriage, he could not because he was scared of social pressure. She expressed to the wife of Sattiraju Mrityunjaya Rao her desire to remarry and promised to run away from home as and when a groom was arranged. Informed by Mrityunjaya Rao about this, Veeresalingam arranged a groom and a date was fixed.[154] The bride had to reach Veeresalingam's home on the fixed date, but could not make her own way there, and arranging for his men to accompany her would raise suspicions. Therefore, a strategy was prepared. She was instructed to follow Kameshwara Rao, brother of Mrityunjaya Rao. The signal was to watch for a house whose steps Kameshwara Rao climbed up and down. She neatly executed the instructions and slipped past her mother and older sister. Once they realised that she had escaped, her relatives raided Veeresalingam's home and tried to disrupt and halt the marriage proceedings. Veeresalingam's students boldly confronted them and barred their entry.

As the bride was seated on the wedding dais, her elder sister lunged at her, fiercely trying to pull her away and tearing her bridal saree. On

[152] Ibid., pp. 260–261.

[153] Ibid., pp. 261–263.

[154] Well in time for the wedding, he arranged several meetings of the prospective bride and groom at the residence of Mrityunjaya Rao. After some consultation, both of them agreed to marry.

Veeresalingam's instructions, his students firmly caught the sister by the arms and legs and threw her out on a sand mound. Having failed to intrude and stop the marriage, the men lodged a complaint against Veeresalingam alleging that he had kidnapped the minor girl who was under the guardianship of her father. Interestingly, her father did not come to argue with Veeresalingam. (He perhaps was not opposed to her remarriage; he did not complain to the police himself either.) But Veeresalingam proved with the help of a doctor that the girl was 16-years-old and therefore a major.[155]

The desire for remarriage was so strong among a few widows that, having learnt of widow marriages being performed at Rajahmundry through the media, they escaped from their homes and reached Rajahmundry, travelling long distances and exhibiting stunning courage. One such woman, Sitamma, the 'heroine' of the twentieth widow remarriage, strenuously covered a few hundred miles all alone. Her hair-raising adventure was recorded by Veeresalingam:

> The child widow... Sitamma reached Rajamahendravaram [Rajahmundry] all the way from Aska village in Ganjam District. In those days, there were no railways [between Aska and Rajahmundry]. Those who wanted to travel had to go by bullock carts. She is said to have heard of widow remarriages being performed at Rajahmundry as her brother read out the news in a newspaper! Moreover, it is learnt that his brother procured my books and was reading them! It is not unnatural for child widows, who hear the news of widow remarriages, to desire that they, too, should enjoy the happiness of marital bliss.... Such people [widows] submerge the desire in their hearts because of social fear. However, this little girl, during a conversation with her sister-in-law (*vadina*), slipped her tongue stating, 'Child widows are getting married in Rajamahedravaram.' Instantly, her *vadina* is said to have chided her, 'you should not utter such [evil things] like that; [it is] wrong.' Having learnt of her heart, the little one never again uttered the word marriage before her. [But] she, along with another girl, who also had lost her husband during childhood, thought over it, decided to go to Rajamahendravaram, secretly left the village, and reached Vijayanagaram. [Tired of the cumbersome journey] and having lost heart, the second one could not proceed further. [But] as the hope of future happiness propelled her, this little one moved ahead without stepping back, meeting travel expenses by selling away the jewelry she was carrying in a box, hiring a bullock cart for some distance, and covering some more distance on foot. Thus, having undertaken a continuous and [tedious] journey, she landed herself in our home and fulfilled her desire. Is it not

[155] Ibid., part 2, pp. 92–98.

laudatory that such a little orphan girl started off all alone, and without money in hand, crossed districts, travelling hundreds of miles! She and Somanatha Rao married on 28 June 1893.[156]

Initiatives Taken by the Mothers of Widows

As we already noted, moved by the misery of their daughters, several mothers of widowed girls showed great interest in getting their daughters remarried. While a few of them encouraged their daughters to flee from homes and secretly arranged for their escape, others abetted their deceptions in order to fulfil their daughters' mission and ambition. What is remarkable is that the very first widow remarriage among the upper castes in nineteenth century Andhra owed as much to the conviction of a woman—in this case, the mother of the widow—as it did to reformers. That Seetamma—the mother—was instrumental in getting the secret escape of her daughter to reach Veeresalingam could be best attested by a letter written to him by Brahmasri Darbha Brahmanandam,[157] who had informed Veeresalingam of the availability of a 12-year-old Brahmin child widow for remarriage, promising to convince her mother to secretly send her daughter away, if Veeresalingam could send his 'trust-worthy' men to Repudi, the place of the girl, to take her away. On 5 November 1881, Brahmanandam wrote to Veeresalingam:

> Your letters have reached me in time. As the mother of the young widow has left her village and gone to see her relatives, I could not talk to her and send you a reply earlier than this. I have just now talked to her. She promised to send her daughter to you as soon as you send your people here to fetch her [the widow] there. Please send trust-worthy, upright and firm-minded people to escort the girl there. They should keep the thing a profound secret. If they are hypocrites, they are sure to frustrate our object. Please see that they really uphold our cause. Nobody here should know the purpose for which they come here till the marriage actually takes place. Seetamma [mother of the girl widow] wants you to send not more than two people for the purpose. She also thinks that our efforts may, at the end, again prove a total failure. She has also agreed to give you her written permission for the marriage. Let your people come here

[156] Ibid., pp. 98–99.

[157] A friend of Veeresalingam, and an admirer of the widow remarriage movement, he worked as Deputy Tehsildar of Tiruvuru in Krishna District.

> as travellers with a note from you and meet me without giving the least smell [*sic*] of the matter to anybody here. They can go to Repudi, the girl's village, even from this place. I told Seetamma not to leave her village till your men come and take her daughter away. Please send your people at your earliest convenience.[158]

As Brahmanandam had to leave for another place on official duty, he wrote to Veeresalingam 'to tell his people not to be disappointed by his absence but to go to Repudi and talk to the mother of the girl and take her [the girl] away.'[159] It was only with great difficulty that the messengers could escape with the girl. It was possible only with the conviction of the mother and the courage of the girl. Otherwise, who would send their child with strangers and, that too, unknown men? How much the mother must have convinced and given confidence to her daughter to run away from home and that too at midnight![160] The marriage was performed on 11 December 1881. Gavaramma and Gogulapati Sriramulu were the bride and the groom, respectively, of this first widow remarriage in colonial Andhra.[161]

Veeresalingam wrote in his *Sweeya Charitramu* that, on the fourth day after the first widow remarriage was performed, a woman came to Veeresalingam along with her 12-year-old widowed daughter and lied that her husband had sent her there to get their daughter remarried.[162] The marriage was performed.[163] Thus, in the very first two widow remarriages, mothers' role was legendary; they were instrumental in arranging brides for the widow remarriage movement. But for their interest, support, boldness and active involvement, the movement could have remained only in the

---

[158] Kandukuri Veeresalingam, *Sweeya Charitramu*, part 1, pp. 183–184.

[159] Ibid., p. 185.

[160] Veeresalingam observed that the widow's family was rich and reputable. He further remarked that 'only the mother was interested, and none else in her relations.' Ibid., p. 186.

[161] For a graphic description of the way the first widow remarriage was conducted, see ibid., pp. 187–190. In this whole episode, while Veeresalingam appreciated Sriramulu's courageous action as 'praiseworthy' (ibid., p. 188). He did not acknowledge the courage exhibited by the widow to escape from her home.

[162] In reality, her husband did not know about this plan. That was why the anti-widow marriage group instigated him to file a suit against Veeresalingam and his friends. Having learnt of the truth from the mother and her sister, Veeresalingam and his friends somehow managed to convince the girl's father. Ibid., p. 203.

[163] Ibid., p. 201. This was the second recorded widow remarriage among upper castes in nineteenth century Andhra. Ratnamma and Racharla Ramachandra Rao were the bride and groom, respectively.

speeches and booklets of male social reformers, that is, in the air. Women's involvement brought the 'movement' on to the ground.

Another mother, a Vaishya and herself a widow, came to Veeresalingam along with her 10-year-old widowed daughter, Ramalakshmamma, requesting remarriage of her daughter. The girl was married to 20-year-old Boda Sriramulu on 11 April 1883. It was the first widow remarriage among the Vaishyas.[164] Likewise, there were several other mothers and a few grandmothers who were eager to support the movement.[165] Veeresalingam's grandmother, who did not approve of his involvement in the widow remarriage movement initially and had left his home out of rage, gradually began to appreciate his activities and 'started arguing with those who were abusing him.'[166] We have already seen the voluminous interest shown by Kondapalli Koteshwaramma's mother in getting the former remarried.

The foregoing discussion makes it clearer that there was *radicalism* in widows' remarrying: this was certainly a rebellious act against the oppressive cultural practices in Hindu society. The assertion of the sexual rights of widows was a severe blow to patriarchal ideology.

Women's Direct Action in the Widow Marriage Movement

Apart from sensitising the larger public about widow remarriage through their writings and speeches, women were also involved in actually performing widow marriages, running shelter homes and schools for widows and

[164] Ibid., p. 264.

[165] An unnamed lady, whose brother had just passed away, promised to bring the mother of her brother's widow. This widow's sister, too, had been widowed. They were aged 12 and 10, respectively. The mother of the widows reached Madras as Veeresalingam and his friends had decided to perform a few marriages there. However, only the older one's (Kopamma) marriage could be performed because the mother declined to give her younger daughter in marriage to Prakasha Rao, the selected groom. The marriage was performed on 8 June 1883. For more details, see ibid., pp. 265–271. An old widow belonging to Vaidiki sect came to Veeresalingam from Tatipaka requesting for remarriage of her 13-year-old parentless widowed granddaughter. Having travelled a long distance along with the appointed Pulavarti Sheshaiah, they secretly reached Rajahmundry. She was married to Kodandaramaiah, who belonged to a different Brahmin sect. This was the first inter-sect marriage. Ibid., pp. 272–273. Until this marriage, all the widow marriages were intra-sect and intra-caste marriages.

[166] Kandukuri Veeresalingam, *Sweeya Charitramu*, Part 1, pp. 204–205.

training them for an independent living. Kandukuri Rajyalakshmamma, wife of Veeresalingam, is one example of this.

Rajyalakshmamma (1851–1910)[167] was the foremost woman social reformer in Andhra. Without her active involvement and unwavering support, the widow remarriage movement initiated by her husband could never have achieved the success it did. She remained deeply involved in the movement, braving enormous pressure from relatives and even ostracism and social boycott. Apart from arranging for the celebration of widow marriages performed in Rajahmundry, generally at her home, she accompanied her husband to far-off places to perform such marriages. Her house was a ray of hope to distressed widows. Showering 'motherly affection' on them, she provided the much needed solace, confidence and courage. She readily welcomed any widow who went to the rescue home even in the absence of Veeresalingam.[168]

She taught unlettered widows[169] and gently corrected those who continued to tread the 'wrong paths'.[170] Attending to the needs of the widows was a greater priority for her than her personal engagements.[171] Conservative backlash against the widow remarriage movement was so threatening that, fearing the axe of excommunication, domestic aides ran away from the homes of the pro-widow remarriage households, resulting in an increased burden on the women of such families. When the domestic aides—cooks and water carriers, etc.—deserted Rajyalakshmamma's home, she herself walked a long distance to the Godavari to fetch water and also

[167] Her original name was Bapamma. As she lost her mother during childhood, she was raised by her childless maternal uncle, Venneti Venkataratnam and his wife Lachchamamba. Her maternal uncle sent her to the local school, where she received some education and learnt by heart works such as *Rukmini Kalyanamu*. She married Veeresalingam at the age of eight (Veeresalingam was then 12). The marriage was consummated (*punassandhanamu*) when she was 12. The present name was given to her by Veeresalingam's mother after marriage. Kandukuri Veeresalingam, *Sweeya Charitramu*, Part 2, pp. 424–425.

[168] Ibid., pp. 428–430.

[169] Ibid., p. 428.

[170] Ibid., pp. 428–429.

[171] Once, hardly she had started from her home for visiting the newly constructed Town Hall along with her friends, when a widow from Aska (Ganjam District, now in Odisha) reached there in an extremely bad shape. Without any fuss, she asked her friends to wait for some time, took the widow inside, gave her a bath and offered good clothes. As there was no food at her home, she brought some from the neighbours and fed the tired widow. After providing her comfort, she left for the Town Hall. Ibid., pp. 429–430.

cooked herself.[172] She patiently suffered the 'insulting remarks' people (mostly women) made at such places.[173]

Rajyalakshmamma started the 'Patita Yuvati Rakshanashala' (Rescue Home for the Fallen Young Women/Widows) and worked to improve the lives of 'fallen' women, mostly widows. As mentioned in Chapter 1, she helped seven such women.[174] She also had one such pregnant Brahmin widow admitted to the local maternity hospital to facilitate a safe delivery. When she found out that the widow wanted to leave the infant at the hospital, she rushed there, brought the baby home and raised it: the girl baby was named Premavati. As the domestic aide refused to clean the clothes of the baby, she herself washed them and carefully looked after the baby.[175] By virtue of her activism, she was a source of such a great strength to Veeresalingam that, after her death, he became 'utterly helpless'.[176]

Was Rajyalakshmamma a mere 'shadow' (*chhaya*) of her husband? Was her involvement a mere reflection of her husband's? Veeresalingam's writings establish Rajyalakshmamma's *own interest* in matters concerning social reform, which is also a pointer to the *independent interest* women had in issues of social change and women's progress: Rajyalakshmamma 'was involved in the widow marriage movement not just because he was involved in it; she actually evinced great interest in removing the difficulties of the orphan girls [widows].'[177] This was equally true of several other women reformers.

Unnava Lakshmibayamma (1882–1956),[178] wife of the prominent social reform and nationalist leader Unnava Lakshminarayana, made

---

[172] Kandukuri Veeresalingam, *Sweeya Charitramu*, Part 1, p. 263.

[173] Kandukuri Veeresalingam, *Sweeya Charitramu*, Part 2, p. 434.

[174] Ibid., p. 431.

[175] Ibid., pp. 431–432.

[176] The feeling of his helplessness was so acute and poignant that he titled the fourth chapter (dealing with the years 1910–1913) of the second volume of his autobiography as 'Asahaya Dasha' (Phase of Helplessness). After her demise, Veeresalingam's physical as well as mental health and his social mission experienced a steady deterioration.

[177] Ibid., p. 428. Also see ibid., Part 1, pp. 263–264.

[178] Apart from social reform, the ongoing freedom movement of the country engaged her attention. Plunging into it during the Non-Cooperation Movement, she participated in boycotting foreign goods, etc. When her husband was arrested for leading the No-Tax Campaign of Palnadu in 1921, she is reported to have said to him, seeking his permission at the railway station, where she reached with Congress flag and a garland, that 'the white man had punished only half of his body with imprisonment. The other half of it was outside and she would carry on the struggle.' Kanuparti Varalakshmamma, *Unnava Dampatulu*, pp. 32–33. For her involvement in the freedom struggle, she was

significant contributions to the widow remarriage movement, devotedly helping her husband in establishing the 'Widow Remarriage Centre' in Guntur, in 1902. Born to Nadimpalli Sitaramaiah and Lakshmidevamma (Arvela Niyogi Brahmins) in Aminabad village in Guntur District, she was married to Unnava Lakshminarayana at the age of 10. The biographer of the couple informed that 'she rejected the matches brought by her father and insisted on marrying Lakshminarayana', and thus 'exercised her will and freedom in choosing her partner'. When her husband, a close follower of Veeresalingam, was excommunicated for performing the first ever widow remarriage in conservative Guntur, she was at her natal home and expecting to soon deliver their child. Her parents threatened Lakshminarayana that they would not send his wife to him if he did not undergo penance and rejoin the caste, and detained Lakshmibayamma. However, in spite of parental pressure, she joined him and encouraged him to continue his project of reform.[179] She accompanied him to several places to take part in widow remarriage celebrations. When Lakshminarayana left for the University of Dublin for higher studies, where he stayed for two years, she cared for her child all alone in Guntur as her relatives refused to accept her into their homes.[180] Invited by Veeresalingam to look after the Widow Home in Rajahmundry, the couple lived there for some time, served the institution and returned to Guntur in 1908.[181] Several widows lived with her in her home.

Lakshmibayamma is remembered more for the establishment of the famous women's institution, the 'Sharada Niketanamu', which served as a multi-purpose project–as a school, a shelter home for widows, and also an orphanage for the destitute children. Apart from educating widows and girls, and thus enabling them to make careers, the organisation performed as many as 30 widow remarriages. Several students of the Sharada Niketanamu became very successful. The best example is Sangam

---

arrested thrice. Ibid., p. 43. She was so committed to the cause of India's freedom and principled in personal life that when she was awarded the prestigious Grihalakshmi Swarna Kankanam, she told K. N. Kesari that she had vowed not to wear gold ornaments during the freedom struggle, and would accept the honour only if she was not asked to wear it. Respecting her conviction, Kesari did so. Ibid., pp. 48–49.

179 Excommunication was such an extremely excruciating experience that Kanuparti Varalakshmamma remarked that 'people were not so much scared of a tiger [*puli*] as they were of excommunication [*veli*].' Kanuparti Varalakshmamma, *Unnava Dampatulu*, p. 19.

180 Ibid., pp. 16–39.

181 K. Janaki, *Role of Women in Freedom Struggle in Andhra Pradesh*, pp. 50–51.

Lakshmibayamma (1911–1979) who, though born in Telangana region and widowed at the age of 10, received education at Sharada Niketanam, and achieved several public positions of eminence.[182] This was possible because of the Sharada Niketanamu and Lakshmibayamma, who steered it effectively. Lakshmibayamma was so sensitive and conscious of women's identity, self-respect and dignity that she once abruptly walked out of a literary conference, stating that it was an insult to women for the (male) speaker to have made his speech without mentioning a single female scholar. She is said to have questioned him angrily: 'What kind of a lecture is this? You have not mentioned the name of any woman [scholarly figure]! Are there no scholars among the Telugu women? Are there no poets? Are there no musicians? Are there no artists? The world of Andhra women is [intellectually] not so barren [as you men think]. How can this be a comprehensive conference of the Telugus, when we do not utter a single word about women, who are half of the Telugu population?'[183]

Darishi Annapoornamma,[184] the first wife of Darishi Chenchaiah, proved to be to him in the 1920s what Rajyalakshmamma had been to Veeresalingam in the previous four decades. She courageously stood by her husband until her death, in 1931, in all his adventurous activities, and most significantly in the widow remarriage movement.[185] Like Rajyalakshmamma,

[182]She served as a warden in the Narayanaguda Girls' High School (Hyderabad) and as a Telugu teacher in the Kachiguda Government Training College. She took part in the Salt Satyagraha and was imprisoned in the Vellore jail. Her experiences in the Vellore jail are compiled into a book. See Sangam Lakshmibai, *Naa Jailu Gnapakalu—Anubhavalu* (My Experiences in the Jail and Reminiscences), collected by Neti Sita Devi (Hyderabad, 1980). She also took part in the Telangana Struggle. In independent India, she achieved several public positions of eminence such as Member of the Legislative Assembly, Deputy Minister of Education (1954–56) and Member of Parliament (1957–1971). Inspired by the example of Lakshmibayamma, her mentor, she established the Indira Seva Sadanamu in 1952, which served not only as a shelter home for the destitute girls but also as a High School and a Vocational Training Centre for girls. In 1980, about 700 girls were enrolled in it. For details, see ibid. Also see Volga et al., *Mahilavaranam*, pp. 88–89.

[183]Kanuparti Varalakshmamma, *Unnava Dampatulu*, pp. 45–46. Given this sharp condemnation of male indifference to acknowledge the contribution of women to arts and letters, it is no wonder that today's Telugu feminists have aptly termed her to be 'an early feminist of Andhra'. Volga et al., *Mahilavaranam*, pp. 48–49.

[184]For a detailed discussion, see Chapter 1, this volume. Here, we provide details of her engagement with the widow remarriage movement only.

[185]Chenchaiah was excommunicated by the Vaishya caste six times because of his involvement in the widow remarriage movement. She patiently bore the psychological

who accompanied Veeresalingam to various places to perform widow remarriages, Annapoornamma accompanied Chenchaiah to several places, despite having young children to care for.[186] Wherever she lived, whether in Guntur or Vijayawada or Madras, she happily accommodated several widows in her home. She, along with her husband, performed 18 marriages in different castes—many of them among the Vaishyas—often performing the role of *kanyadata* (bride-giver).[187] Along with her friend Turlapati Rajeshwaramma,[188] she founded the *Vitantu Sharanalayamu* (Rescue Home for Widows and Abandoned Children) in Vijayawada in 1927/1928.[189] Soon, many pregnant women/widows reached there, safely delivered their babies, and left their infants if they could not care for them.[190]

Annapoornamma held the view that 'remarriage alone did not solve the problems of widows: if widows had to surmount their difficulties, they needed education'. She encouraged as many as 12 widows and a few

---

pressure of the same without complaining. Darishi Chenchaiah, *Nenoo – Naa Desham*, p. 204. At times, she had to face stone-pelting (*raalla varsham*; 'rain of stones') by orthodox disrupters while performing widow marriages. Darishi Chenchaiah (Compiled), *Marapurani Annapoorna*, p. 219.

186 Darishi Chenchaiah, *Nenoo – Naa Desham*, p. 227.

187 As parents of widows whose remarriages were arranged were afraid to come forward, normally, the reformist couple acted as kanyadatas.

188 For details, see 'Turlapati Rajeshwaramma' in Darishi Chenchaiah, *Naa Divya Smrutulu*, pp. 84–93.

189 This was a result of a horrible scene they witnessed on the banks of the Rivus Canal in Vijayawada while out on a morning walk. They saw two abandoned infants being pierced and eaten up by crows. They went back home weeping, and after consulting their husbands, they immediately started the organisation by making an announcement in the *Andhra Patrika*. Darishi Chenchaiah, *Nenoo – Naa Desham*, pp. 233–235. Also see 'Turlapati Rajeshwaramma' in Darishi Chenchaiah, *Naa Divya Smrutulu*, pp. 88–89.

190 While Rajeshwaramma herself adopted a girl, several childless couple came forward to adopt the babies. Chenchaiah wrote that there were about 60 such babies in Vijayawada alone. Darishi Chenchaiah, *Nenoo – Naa Desham*, pp. 235–236. Women medical practitioners were also important contributors to the cause in Vijayawada and Madras. Dr Ranganayakamma (1898—1940) readily came forward to help in Vijayawada. Ibid., p. 235. For more details on her, see Volga et al., *Mahilavaranam*, pp. 58–59. As it became difficult to maintain secrecy of the widows in the rescue home in Vijayawada, some of them were sent to Madras for shelter in the rescue homes there. Here, Subhadramma (who married Chenchaiah after the death of Annapoornamma) took care of such widows, along with one Ms Peters, who attended pregnant widows in deliveries and other maternal needs, and admitted those who desired education in her school. Darishi Chenchaiah, *Naa Divya Smrutulu*, pp. 91–92.

abandoned women to attend schools, and arranged stipends for them.[191] Significantly, one of them went on to become a medical doctor.[192] It is tragic but perhaps unsurprising that Annapoornamma died at the young age of 25—her hectic public life had resulted in the deterioration of her health. She died of heart attack in Madras just four days after she returned from Bandar, where she had been to perform a widow remarriage. It is not at all an exaggeration that she laid down her life for the cause of social change in Madras Presidency.[193]

Reflecting on her contribution to social reform movement, Chenchaiah wrote that 'whatever amount of hard work men put, they could not succeed in women's movements without the help of their wives.'[194] Further, he wrote about his wife that 'she was enthusiastic about women's movements'. 'In fact', he stated, 'she married me in the hope of practicing social reform.'[195] 'If I could achieve such a big task with this much of courage, it was with my wife Annapoornadevi's help only', he recalled gratefully.[196] It is extremely saddening that such an important woman activist-intellectual has been completely forgotten by social historians in the Andhra region.

Atyam Satyavati Devi and her husband, Atyam Narasimha Moorthy (an MA holder from New York) established the 'Stree Punarvivaha Sahayaka Sanghamu'[197] (Widow Remarriage Association) at Narasapur (West Godavari District). Satyavati Devi served as its President. The Sanghamu was actively involved in the widow marriage movement over the

---

[191] Darishi Chenchaiah, *Marapurani Annapoorna*, pp. 220–221. Darishi Chenchaiah, *Nenoo - Naa Desham*, pp. 237–240. See also Darishi Chenchaiah, *Naa Divya Smrutulu*, pp. 92–93.

[192] Darishi Chenchaiah, *Nenoo - Naa Desham*, p. 238.

[193] Many contemporaries paid glowing tribute to her. T. Venkateshwara Rao, a barrister from Vijayawada, rightly observed that 'she lived a life of usefulness and died like a heroine'. See Darishi Chenchaiah, *Marapurani Annapoorna*, p. 47. Shikharam Kotishwara Gupta, a prominent social reform leader of the Vaishyas, bemoaned that 'she was very young. A life of usefulness and public life was nipped in the bud.' Ibid., p. 70. Seetharamanjaneyulu from Guntur stated that 'they [Vaishyas] saw in her a leaderess [*sic*] to womanhood—not to their community alone, but to the whole of India.' Ibid., p. 88.

[194] Darishi Chenchaiah, *Nenoo - Naa Desham*, p. 233.

[195] Ibid., p. 231.

[196] Darishi Chenchaiah, *Marapurani Annapoorna*, p. 235.

[197] Renamed as 'Andhra Rashtra Stree Punarvivaha Sahayaka Sanghamu', it was registered on 10 December 1938. See 'Andhra Rashtra Stree Punarvivaha Sahayaka Sanghamu', *Vasavi*, January 1939, p. 328.

1930s and 1940s.[198] Under the supervision of Satyavati Devi, several widow remarriages were conducted for couples from different castes such as Brahmin, Vaishya, Telaga, etc. across Andhra.[199] The *Vasavi* appreciated the couple for their contribution to the social reform movement[200] and specially featured Satyavati Devi under the column, 'Vaishya Vanita Ratnamulu' ('Jewels among the Vaishya Women').[201]

Andallamma, also addressed as Lady Venkata Subbarao, and her husband Sir Mutta Venkata Subbarao established the 'Stree Seva Sadanamu' (Home for Serving Women) in Madras, in 1925. Andallamma managed the institution in the capacity of both Secretary and Superintendent for about forty years. Though it was started for the purpose of educating women, soon it had to perform multiple functions such as a shelter home for the destitute women, particularly widows and a center for performing widow marriages. Starting with a handful of girls and women, soon the number of residents went beyond a thousand.[202] The Sadanamu ran a school, an industrial training center, a hostel, and a special hostel for the working women. Apart from widow marriages, the Sadanamu conducted inter-varna marriages also. Darishi Chenchaiah observed that 'it developed into an institution, which tried to solve every problem concerning women.'[203]

---

[198] For example, see 'Brahmana Vadhuvu, Varudu Kavalenu' (Brahmin Bride and Groom Required), *Vasavi*, 1 October 1938, p. 233.

[199] For the marriages conducted under her supervision, see *Vasavi*, March 1939, p. 392. See also *Vasavi*, January 1939, pp. 331–332. The organisation faced criminal cases for conducting widow remarriages. For instance, when a Brahmin widow Vishalakshmamma (aged 18) of Tanuku reached the organisation desiring remarriage, her father (Dhulipala Satya Suryanarayana Siddhanti) filed a criminal suit against the secretaries and tried to get them jailed. The sub-divisional magistrate dismissed the case. The widow was married on 9 February 1938. For details, see 'Stree Punarvivaha Sahayaka Sanghamu, Narasapuramu', *Vasavi*, April 1938, p. 32.

[200] See 'Atyam Dampatula Samskaranabhilasha' (The Atyam Couple's Enthusiasm for Social Reform), *Vasavi*, April 1938, p. 32. In his *Nenoo – Naa Desham*, Darishi Chenchaiah, though did not mention her name, commended the work the association had been doing. See p. 215.

[201] She served in the capacities such as Honourary Magistrate, a member of the Narasapur District Board, and made multidimensional contributions to society. See 'Vaishya Vanitaratnamulu', *Vasavi*, July 1938, p. 127.

[202] Darishi Chenchaiah, *Naa Divya Smrutulu*, pp. 70–71.

[203] Ibid., p. 73.

Image 4.5: Atyam Satyavati Devi

Source: *Grihalakshmi*, January 1936.

Widows and girls in need of support were sent there for shelter and training from different parts of Andhra also.[204]

The miserable fate of 'fallen women' (*patitalu*) moved Andallamma so deeply that she allowed such women to reside in her house. However, in keeping with the paternalistic attitudes towards women who were seen

[204] Darishi Chenchaiah sent several girls/women there for help. Darishi Chenchaiah, *Nenoo - Naa Desham*, pp. 237 and 239. For his critical remarks on the class bias maintained in the Sadanamu, see ibid., pp. 257–258.

as social deviants, she did not admit them in the Sadanamu or the hostel, deeming it to be inappropriate. She arranged the marriages of several of them in order to 'bring them on the right track'.[205] Featuring her under the column, 'Vaishya Vanita Ratnamulu', the *Vasavi* commended her contribution to social reform, and informed us about her oratory skills in English, and the award of 'Kaiser-e-Hind' ('*Kesari Hindu*') bestowed upon her by the British government.[206]

Srimati Manchikanti Venkataratnamma established the 'Saubhagya Niketanamu' at Prejarupeta in Kakinada to provide shelter to widows and arrange remarriages. In an appeal published in *Grihalakshmi*, she wrote that the organistion would render all possible help in arranging the remarriages of girls of the 'respectable families', who lost their husbands before attaining puberty and those adult widows whose marriages were not consummated. Parents and guardians of widowed girls/women were urged to 'pity the destitutes' and get them remarried. Those who were afraid of relatives and society could send their daughters/sisters to the 'Saubhagya Niketanamu' where they would be educated and trained in handicraft industries until their remarriages were arranged. The prospective grooms were welcomed either to write to them or to meet in person to know the details of prospective brides. She promised 'secrecy' with regard to the correspondence between the prospective brides and grooms.[207]

The 'Sevashramamu', a society for conducting child-widow remarriages, was established in Uppada, Godavari District, on 16 February 1932. Gampala Padmanabham was its founder. The organisation provided shelter to widows and conducted three child widow remarriages from June to December 1933. In the same year, it published five pamphlets advocating widow remarriages. The organisation appointed 'campaigners' for widow remarriage who worked 'even in villages'. However, the organisation faced stiff resistance, with the orthodoxy, resorting to picketing and excommunication. Sevashramamu's secretaries wrote that though there were many child widows, their marriages could not take place because they were uneducated and wanted to marry within their caste or sect. Such organisations, not surprisingly, fell short of financial resources. By 1933, while the organisation received Rs. 201.2, the expenditure incurred was Rs. 492.8, leaving it with a debt of Rs. 169.7. *Grihalakshmi* appealed that

---

[205] For more details, see 'Mutta Venkata Subbarao' in Darishi Chenchaiah, *Naa Divya Smrutulu*, pp. 65–77.

[206] *Vasavi*, July 1938, p. 127.

[207] 'Saubhagya Niketanamu', *Grihalakshmi*, June 1935, pp. 338–339.

Table 4.3: Widow remarriages performed by the widow home at Tenali

Date of Marriage	Name of the Bride	Name of the Groom
2.11.1932	Mahalakshmamma	P. Sitrama Venkata Ramayya
1.10.1933	Venkata Subbamma	T. Ramayya
18.4.1934	Sukanya	K. Satyamurti
1.8.1936	Hanumayamma	B. Sheshayya Pantulu
19.9.1937	Venkata Subbamma	M. Venkata Subbarao
24.9.1937	Satya Jnanaprasunamba	D. Venkata Krishnayya
22.10.1937	Ranganayakamma	R. Lakshminarasimha Rao

Source: B. Kesava Narayana, 'Widow Marriage Movement in Andhra', *Itihas* 2 (1, January–June), 1974, p. 163.

unless the admirers of social reform relinquished their indifference and generously made donations, such a great movement would extinguish.[208]

S. Rajamma Devi of Madras was the honourary superintendent of the Akhila Bharata Vitantu Vivaha Sahaya Sanghamu (All India Widow Remarriage Association) established on 1 July 1938 at Secunderabad.[209] Women-managed educational institutions such as the Vaishya Seva Sadanamu and Andhra Yuvati Samskruta Kalashala in Rajahmundry, Vaishya Yuvati Vidyalayamu and Sharada Niketanamu at Guntur provided educational opportunities and careers to widows. And widows enriched such institutions through a range of contributions.

Srimati Munupalle Ramakotamma was the guardian (*samrakshakuralu*) of a Widow Home at Tenali. A child widow, she had herself taken shelter there and in 1930 married M. V. Sheshagiri Rao, the secretary of the Home. By June 1934, the home had conducted 10 widow remarriages. It was

[208]'Vivaha Samskarana Sangha Nivedika (Sevashramamu, Uppada)', *Grihalakshmi*, November 1933, pp. 756–757.

[209]This was generally known as 'Secunderabad Vitantu Sharanalayam'. It was started by S. Narayanacharyulu F. R. E. S., the editor of *Vishwakarma*. He wrote that he had been campaigning for widow remarriages for many years through writing and public speaking. Having married a widow to set an example for others, by July 1938, he had conducted 10 widow marriages. There were generally at least 10 widows in the *sharanalayamu* at any given time. For more details, see 'Akhila Bharata Vitantu Vivaha Sahaya Sanghamu', *Vasavi*, July 1938, pp. 133–134. Also see 'Secunderabadu Vitantu Sharanalayam', *Vasavi*, 1 November 1938, p. 261.

considered second only to Veeresalingam's widow home in Rajahmundry.[210] A table recording the marriages conducted by the home was published in the journal *Itihas* (see Table 4.3). Another important figure was the wife of Karivarada Rama Rao Pantulu, Diwan of the zamindaris of Nandigam, Saluru and Tarla. Although she remained unnamed in available sources, *Grihalakshmi* noted her compassion and generosity. Interestingly, the journal commented that 'despite her being a Sanatanist [traditionalist/ conservative] who visited a number of temples and dipped in a number of holy rivers, she agreed to perform child-widow remarriages'. An educated woman who had learnt English, she carried out various forms of social work, like getting a well dug and a *koneru* (tank) built to help locals.[211]

The Vanguard of the Widow Remarriage Movement in Andhra

The various studies on the widow remarriage movement, by and large, focus on the leaders of the movement, who are generally men, be it Ishvarchandra Vidyasagar or Kandukuri Veeresalingam. Occasionally, women leaders like Kandukuri Rajyalakshmamma do figure. However, we rarely come across the names of the couples at the centre of the movement. Apart from the unavailability of adequate materials, this lacuna is a result of an obsession with 'great' men, and occasionally 'great' women, who 'made' and 'led' the movement. The cumulative effect is that the *real* heroines and heroes—the women and men who sought such marriages through the movement—are largely ignored. Notwithstanding the 'greatness' of activists who made and led the movement, the widowed women who became ready for remarriage and the men whom they married deserve recognition. The couples who came forward for remarriage *really* made the reform possible and brought it about on the ground.

In the following table, we will find the names of these heroines and heroes of the widow remarriage movement in colonial Andhra. Till serial number 59, the table draws from 'Madhurakavi' Nalam Krishna Rao's *Vitantu Vivaha Charitra (1904 Sam. Varaku)* (History of Widow Remarriages till

[210] See 'Tenali Vidhava Vivaha Sahayaka Sanghamu', *Grihalakshmi*, June 1934, pp. 344–345.

[211] See *Grihalakshmi*, October 1934. The journal also published a photograph of the woman. It is really regrettable that we do not know the name of such an important woman activist.

1904),[212] with some necessary editing and the addition of a 'Venue' column. I have correlated/compared the information from this source with the information provided by Veeresalaingam in his autobiography, and the necessary corrections in dates are indicated in brackets. The rest of the information has been collected from various contemporary journals and newspapers. Wherever information about the age of the bride and the groom at the time of remarriage was available, I have listed the same in parenthesis. Please note that this is not, by any means, an exhaustive list: archival sources often discuss widow remarriage without offering details about the people who were thus married. The 'venue' column will provide a sense of the geographical spread of the movement.

Additionally, it is necessary to highlight one facet of how widow remarriages were reported in periodicals. From the 1920s onwards, women's journals like *Grihalakshmi* and caste journals such as *Vasavi* began publishing the photographs of such couples prominently. For example, the December 1927 issue of *Vasavi* published a photograph of Rukminamma and Puram Rangaiah Setty; the March 1928 issue of *Vasavi* featured a photograph of Kanaka Durgamba and Narasapalli Chennappa Setty; the December 1933 issue of *Grihalakshmi* published the photograph of Kamala Devi and Iska Chenchaiah (in addition to Kamala Devi being a widow, theirs was an intercaste marriage). Similarly, in its August 1940 issue, *Grihalakshmi* carried the photograph of a widow named Rajupalem Lakshmamma who had remarried Radhakrishna Moorthy: this was an inter-sect marriage as she was a Vaidiki and her husband was a Niyogi. In this way, we find a large number of photographs of couples where the woman had remarried post widowhood, which must have encouraged many others to emulate their example.

Conclusion

The problem of early and enforced widowhood was acute in the Telugu-speaking districts of the Madras Presidency. Brahmin and Vaishya women were the chief victims of the practice. Veeresalingam pioneered the widow remarriage movement in Andhra, registering the first success on 11 December 1881. Although women like Kandukuri Rajyalakshmamma were deeply involved in the widow remarriage movement from its very inception,

[212] Rajahmundry, 1950 (preserved in Gautami Library, Rajahmundry).

most Andhra women intellectuals did not publicly propose remarriage for widows through writing and public speaking. Progressive women's writings in the first decade of the twentieth century strictly confined themselves to a poignant description of the miserable conditions of widows, especially focussing on the multiple atrocities perpetrated on them.

By the beginning of the 1910s, there was a visible change in the register used by women to address the issue. They began to openly advocate widow remarriage. However, this was initially limited to a discussion of child widows and sexually inexperienced ones only and later expanded to include widows of all age groups, including those with children. Remarkably, women who had themselves remarried (punarvivahitalu) started campaigning for widow remarriage through their writings and public speaking in this period. They were radically different from male social reformers in their articulation of women's choice, sexuality and the need to look beyond scriptural sanction. Women also introduced a new concept—'sadhava vydhavyamu', i.e. experiencing nearly the conditions of widowhood. This referred to the problem of abandoned women. What is striking is that women campaigned for the remarriage of such women and demanded punishment for their 'merciless' husbands who abandoned them.

Women questioned the double standards maintained in social morality concerning widows and widowers and openly and strongly advocated widow remarriage. They even began to question Hindu religious scriptures from the late 1920s onwards. Women intellectuals wrote on widow remarriage in their creative literature, allowing them to recreate the terrified and mutilated life of widows in a more beautiful way. Women continued to write on the question of widow remarriage throughout the heyday of the nationalist movement and beyond. This indicates that nationalism could not push the issues of feminism back and that the widow question, despite making some appreciable headway, was far from resolved.

However, nationalist women like Duvvuri Subbamma and Battula Kamakshamma *chose* to remain widows, the former even opposing widow remarriage. Instead of remarriage, they offered social and national service to widowed women. This argument sought to persuade young widows that there was available a vast field of social and national service, which included programmes for women's development and into which they should channel their energies. Some of these women established schools and colleges for girls, rescue homes for widows and destitute women and encouraged them to participate in the freedom movement.

Women intellectuals were not content with mere writing and public speaking: they maintained that *deeds* were more important. Therefore, many of them actively participated in the widow remarriage movement, acted as kanyadatas and took part in the marriage processions. They also provided encouragement and shelter to the remarried woman and her husband and, most importantly, established homes for widows.

What is most significant to note is that widows, in our discussion, emerged as *agents* of change for themselves as well as society in general: many of them simply refused to remain mere *objects* of reform or see themselves as 'victims'. Several mothers and grandmothers of widowed girls took pains to ensure that the young widows in their care, whether daughter or granddaughter, were relieved of the torment of enforced widowhood. While a few were happily remarried, others were content with intimate relations beyond marriage. Widows' act of remarrying was *radical*: a form of rebellion against orthodox and oppressive cultural practices, and an assertion of the right to family life, which included the right to sexual life. This dealt a severe blow to patriarchal ideology.

The foregoing discussion, however, should not mislead us into thinking that all educated women in the region were in favour of widow remarriage. There were highly scholarly women activists who despised the very idea and bitterly opposed the widow remarriage movement. According to this conservative section, widow remarriage tarnished Indian women's pativratyam. For them, Hindu women married only once and remarriage amounted to 'prostitution', which they saw as reprehensible. They emphasised that widows who remarried would not be accorded the status of kulanganas. Further, they argued that widow remarriage proved an obstacle in the way of women's educational advancement and deprived as-yet-unmarried girls from finding matches, since the pool of marriageable women now increased to accommodate widows. The punarvivahitas, that is, widows who remarried, often suffered for want of social acceptance and respect. The infamous Shri Vidyarthini Samajamu controversy confirms the widespread prejudice against widows and widow remarriage in the period, even as the ultimate victory of the progressive faction suggests that times were changing.

While the prejudices against widows continued and stigma aginst them persists till date—manifesting in a variety of obnoxious ways—what is striking about the views expressed in women's journals is the range of rational and nuanced arguments put forth by those who fought against the system. In the next chapter, we shall take up other issues that were prominent and evoked similar passionate responses from women intellectuals.

Table 4.4: Widow remarriages performed in colonial Andhra from 11 December 1881 to 10 February 1939

S. No.	Name of the Bride	Name of the Groom	Caste/Sect	Date	Venue
1	Gavaramma	Gogulapati Sriramulu (22)	Brahmin/Niyogi	11.12.1881	Rajahmundry
2	Ratnamma (12)	Racharla Ramachandra Rao	Brahmin/Niyogi	15.12.1881	Rajahmundry
3	Sitamma	Taduri Rama Rao	Brahmin/Madhva	22.10.1882	Rajahmundry
4	Sheshamma	Pulavarti Sheshaiah	Brahmin/Vaidiki	03.01.1883	Rajahmundry
5	Sooramma (18)	Munjuluri Gopalamu (20)	Brahmin/Niyogi	30.01.1883	Rajahmundry
6	Venkamma (17)	Chebolu Venkaiah (23)	Brahmin/Vaidiki	13.03.1883	Rajahmundry
7	Ramalakshmamma (10)	Bodaa Sriramulu (20)	Vaishya	17.04.1883 (According to Veeresalingam, the date is 11)	Rajahmundry
8	Kopamma (12)	Tanuku Chalapati Rao	Brahmin/Niyogi	08.06.1883	
9	Ratnamma	Saladi Ramaiah	Vaishya	18.08.1883	
10	Subbamma (13)	Nallagonda Kodanda Ramaiah	Brahmin/Yagnavalki	05.01.1884	
11	Poornamma (According to Veeresalingam, her name is Valluri Punnamma)	Kommaraju Gopalamu	Brahmin/Niyogi	07.07.1884 (According to Veeresalingam, the date is 6)	
12	N.A. (15)	Chittooru Subba Rao	Brahmin/Niyogi	12.02.1885	Bellary (Rayalaseema region)
13	N. A. (12)	Jataprolu Rama Rao	Brahmin/Niyogi	12.02.1885	Bellary (Rayalaseema region)

(Contd) ...

Table 4.4 (Contd)

S. No.	Name of the Bride	Name of the Groom	Caste/Sect	Date	Venue
14	Vishveshwaramma	Tumukuru Rama Rao	Brahmin/Madhva	18.07.1885	
15	Narasamma	Pataneni Venkaiah	Karanakamma	20.12.1885	
16	Mangamma	Nallagonda Kodanda Ramaiah	Brahmin/Yagnavalki	17.10.1888	
17	Kameshwaramma	Pataneni Venkaiah	Karanakamma	02.02.1889	
18	Ammanna	Grandhi Venkata Reddy	Vaishya	21.03.1889 (According to Veeresalingam, the date is 29)	
19	Lakshamma	Tanuku Narasimham	Brahmin/Niyogi	25.09.1892	
20	Sitamma (16)	Kunooru Purushottam	Brahmin/Madhva	06.11.1892	
21	Narasamma	Gani Subba Rao	Brahmin/Madhva	18.09.1893	
22	Sitamma	Aadipudi Somanatha Rao	Brahmin/Niyogi	28.06.1893	
23	Abhiramamma	H. Baji Rao	Brahmin	18.11.1894	
24	Tulashamma	Dronamraju Sheshagiri Rao	Brahmin/Madhva	09.08.1895	
25	Ranganayaki	Kopalli Sheshagiri Rao	Brahmin/Madhva	30.06.1896	
26	Paarvatamma	Naallacheruvu Krishna Rao	Brahmin/Madhva	08.10.1896	
27	Varalakshmi	Tumukuru Rama Rao	Brahmin/Madhva	01.01.1897	
28	Paarvatamma	Pullaabhatla Gavaraiah	Brahmin/Vaidiki	16.10.1897	
29	Sannamma	Kommaraju Gopalamu	Brahmin/Niyogi	23.10.1897	

(Contd) …

Table 4.4 (Contd)

S. No.	Name of the Bride	Name of the Groom	Caste/Sect	Date	Venue
30	Sheshamma	Nandula Gopalaswamy	Brahmin/Vaidiki	27.08.1898	
31	Ratnamma	Pataneni Venkaiah	Karanakamma	27.09.1898	
32	Bangaramma	Aadipudi Gopala Sharma	Brahmin/Niyogi	26.01.1899	
33	Mahalakshmamma (over 20 years)	Nyapati Sheshagiri Rao (over 40 years)	Brahmin/Madhva	26.02.1900	Gajapatinagaram
34	Chittemma	Gopalakrishnaiah	Brahmin/Vaidiki	1900	
35	Sitamma	Lingala Virabhadraiah	Brahmin/Niyogi	28.10.1900	
36	Lakshmibai	Mahadeva Modaliyar	Vellala	05.11.1900	
37	Mahalakshmi	Ogirala Lakshminarayana	Brahmin/Niyogi	22.01.1901	
38	Kausalya	Pullabhatla Gavaraiah	Brahmin/Vaidiki	31.12.1901	
39	Chiranjivamma	Kokaa Subba Rao Naidu	Adi Velama	03.01.1901	Madras
40	Chittemma	Manjuluri Gopalam	Brahmin/Niyogi	12.05.1901	
41	Chokkamma	Sheshaiahngaar	Vaishnava	11.07.1902	
42	Ramanamma	Paranandi Ramachandra Rao	Brahmin/Vaidiki	13.09.1902	
43	Venkata Ramanamma	Betapudi Jogi Suryaprakasha Rao	Brahmin/Niyogi	11.10.1902	Guntur
44	Venkatalakshmamma	Turumella Venkata Subba Rao	Brahmin/Niyogi (*inter-sect marriage*)	24.10.1902 (the date may be 14)	Rajahmundry

(Contd) …

Table 4.4 (Contd)

S. No.	Name of the Bride	Name of the Groom	Caste/Sect	Date	Venue
45	Sitaramamma	Bhattiprolu Sharabhaiah	Brahmin/Niyogi	19.11.1902	
46	Kamakshamma	Bhandaru Dandapani (brother-in-law of Bhandaru Atchamamba)	Brahmin/Niyogi	1902	
47	Sheshamma	Dheram Venkateshwara Rao	Brahmin/Vaidiki	26.12.1902	
48	Annapoorna	Kotturti Namashshivaya	Vishwakarma	14.02.1903	
49	Varalakshmi	C. N. Srinivasachari	Vaishnava	12.03.1903	
50	Sitaramamma	Uppuluri Subba Rao	Brahmin/Niyogi	26.06.1903	
51	Sitaramamma	Kasturi Subba Rao	Brahmin/Niyogi	16.07.1903	
52	Venkubai	Pasumarti Krishnamoorthy	Brahmin/Niyogi	30.09.1903	
53	Ratnamma	Putrevu Subba Rao	Brahmin/Niyogi	01.04.1904	
54	Nagaratnamma	Uppuluri Subba Rao	Brahmin/Niyogi	17.07.1904	
55	Hanumayamma	Adharapurapu Sanjiva Rao	Brahmin/Madhva	14.08.1904	
56	Hanumayamma	Bandlamudi Venkata Rao	Brahmin/Vaidiki	10.11.1904	
57	Ranganayaki	Mellachervu Tandava Krishnaiah	Brahmin/Vaidiki	25.12.1904	
58	Krishnammal	Venkata Varadayyangaar	Vaishnava	31.07.1892	
59	N. A.	Chittooru Subba Rao	Brahman	31.07.1887	

(Contd) ...

Table 4.4 (Contd)

S. No.	Name of the Bride	Name of the Groom	Caste/Sect	Date	Venue
60	N. A. (Daughter of Attaluri Srishailapati)	Nagabhooshanacharyulu	Vishwabrahmin	08. 2.1912	Attota; Tenali Taluq[213]
61	Rukminamma (16); first married at 6 years; widowed at 6 years	Pachchipulusu Kannaiah Setty	Vaishya	22.12.1926	Guntur[214]
62	Rukminamma (16)	Puram Rangaiah Setty (30)	Vaishya	17.11.1927	Eluru[215]
63	Kanaka Durgamba; first married (8); widowed before puberty (12)	Narasapalli Chennappa Setty	Vaishya	03.2.1928	Bellary[216] (Rayalaseema region)
64	Varalakshmamma (16)	Rangaiah Setty (25)	Vaishya	19.8.1928	Madanapalli[217] (Rayalaseema region)
65	Gudivada Mahalakshmamma	Reddy Ramaiah	Vaishya	04.12.1928	Bezawada[218]

[213] Oka Sanghikudu, 'Vrittantamulu–Oka Vaarta' (A News), *Prabodhini*, February 1912, pp. 25–26.

[214] 'Vaartalu—Vitantu Vivahamu' (News—Widow Remarriage), *Vasavi*, December 1926, p. 45. For a detailed description of the marriage proceedings, see 'Arya Vaishya Sangha Samskarana Sabha: Kanya Vitantu Vivahamu' (The Arya Vaishya Social Reform Society: Marriage of a Virgin Widow), *Vasavi*, January 1927, pp. 33–34.

[215] 'Arya Vaishya Yuvati Parinayamu (Arya Vaishya Sangha Samskarana Sabhavaru Jaripinadi)', *Vasavi*, December 1927, pp. 401–405.

[216] 'Vitantu Kanya Vivahamu' (Marriage of a Virgin Widow), *Vasavi*, March 1928, p. 525.

[217] 'Arya Vaishya Vitantu Kanyaa Vivahamu' (Marriage of an Arya Vaishya Virgin Widow), *Vasavi*, September 1928, pp. 254–257.

[218] 'Vaishya Vitantu Vivahamulu' (Vaishya Widow Remarriages), *Vasavi*, January 1930, p. 368.

(Contd) …

Table 4.4 (Contd)

S. No.	Name of the Bride	Name of the Groom	Caste/Sect	Date	Venue
66	Janakamma	Atyam Sriramulu	Vaishya	07.4.1929	Eluru[219]
67	Ramulamma (14)	Shingapu Damodaram (27)	Vaishya	25.9.1929	Secunderabad[220]
68	Gavaramma (16)	Pachchipulusu Satyanarayana (28)	Vaishya	November 1929	Vishakhapatnam[221]
69	Narayanamma	Sanka Vishwanatham Shreshthi	Vaishya	18.11.1929	Eluru[222]
70	Kanakaratnam (12)	Rama Rao (20)	Vaishya	19.12.1929	Visakhapatnam[223]
71	N.A. (22)	Paluru Chinna Thimmaiah Setty (35)	Vaishya	28.12.1931	Madras[224]
72	Gunna Mahalakshmi	Major M. R. Gandhi M.B.C.M., IMS	Vaishya	05.6.1932	Madras[225]
73	Kamalamma	Sriramulu	Vaishya	05.6.1932	Madras[226]

[219] Javvaji Apparao Gupta, 'Vitantoodwahamu' (Widow Marriage), *Vasavi*, May 1929, pp. 51–53.
[220] 'Vaishya Baala Vitantu Vivahamulu' (Child Widow Marriages among the Vaishyas), *Vasavi*, December 1929, pp. 320–322.
[221] Ibid., pp. 319–322.
[222] 'Vaishya Vitantu Vivahamulu' (Remarriages of Vaishya Widows), *Vasavi*, January 1930, p. 368.
[223] 'Vaishya Bala Vitantu Vivahamu' (Remarriage of a Vaishya Child Widow), *Vasavi*, February 1930, pp. 379–380.
[224] 'Vidhava Vivaha Sahayaka Sabha, Madarasu' (Widow Remarriage Society, Madras), *Vasavi*, January 1932, p. 344.
[225] 'Yukta Dampatyamu' (Compatible Conjugality), *Vasavi*, July 1932, p. 141.
[226] Ibid.

(Contd) ...

Table 4.4 (Contd)

S. No.	Name of the Bride	Name of the Groom	Caste/Sect	Date	Venue
74	Subbamma	Kamaiah	Vaishya	05.6.1932	Madras[227]
75	Shyamala (18)	Karamsetty Venkatarangaiah Setty	Vaishya	23.6.1932	Possibly Madras[228]
76	Ramalakshmamma (18) (daughter of Sri Ramaiah, who belonged to Gollapalle village in Badvel Taluq of Kadapa district in Rayalaseema region of A.P.)	Subbaiah (son of Tallam Subbaiah, who belonged to Vempalli village in Kadapa district in Rayalaseema region in A.P.)	Vaishya	07.7.1932	Madras[229]
77	Satyavati Devi	Bollisetty	Vaishya	27.7.1933	Chirala[230]
78	Parvati Vardhanamma	Chimakurti Subbaraya Gupta	Vaishya	14.9.1933	Madras[231]
79	Lakshmamma	S. Venkatramaiah	Vaishya	14.9.1933	Madras[232]
80	Venkata Subbamma (14)	Tadikamalla Venkaiah (22)	Vaishya	01.10.1933	Tenali[233]

[227] Ibid.

[228] Ibid.

[229] 'Vartalu: Arya Vaishya Vitantu Vivahamu' (News: An Arya Vaishya Widow Remarriage), *Vasavi*, August 1932, pp. 182–183.

[230] 'Vartalu: Baala Vitantoodwahamu' (News: Child Widow's Remarraiage), *Vasavi*, November 1933, p. 278.

[231] 'Chennapurilo Vaishya Vitantoodwahamulu: Vidhava Vivaha Sahayaka Sabhavari Yajamanyamuna Jaruguta', *Vasavi*, November 1933, pp. 257–258.

[232] Ibid.

[233] 'Vartalu: Baala Vitantoodwahamu' (News: Child Widow's Remarriage), *Vasavi*, November 1933, p. 278.

(Contd) ...

Table 4.4 (Contd)

S. No.	Name of the Bride	Name of the Groom	Caste/Sect	Date	Venue
81	Ramatulasamma	Ramabrahmam B.A.,	–	25.01.1934	Eluru[234]
82	Sundaramma	Boyina Venkatappaiah	Vaishya	N.A. (may be January or February 1934)	Narasannapeta (Ganjam Dist., Odisha)[235]
83	Lakshmamma (22)	K. Subbaiah	Balija (first widow remarriage among the Balijas, a Shudra caste)	25.3.1934	Nellore[236]
84	Subbamma	Chinaswamy Setty	Vaishya	30.10.1935	Kavali[237] (Nellore District)
85	Manchiraju (16)	Buchchiraju (23)	Vaishya	08.11.1935	Koyyalagudem[238]
86	Mutyam (15)	Maturi Panchakshari (22)	Vaishya	08.11.1935	Koyyalagudem[239]
87	Vishalakshmamma (18)	Tativarti Venkata Narayana (28)	Brahmin	09.2.1938	(?) Narasapuram[240]

[234] 'Vivaha Vishayamulu' (Matters related to Marriages), *Grihalakshmi*, March 1934, p. 73.

[235] Ibid.

[236] 'Vartalu–Visheshamulu', *Grihalakshmi*, May 1934, p. 239. The news item says that 'more than one hundred women and men attended the marriage and blessed the couple'.

[237] 'Vaishya Vitantu Vivahamulu' (Vaishya Widow Remarriages), *Vasavi*, December 1935, p. 297–298.

[238] Ibid.

[239] Ibid.

[240] 'Stree Punarvivaha Sahayaka Sanghamu, Narasapuramu', *Vasavi*, April 1938, p. 32.

(Contd) ...

Table 4.4 (Contd)

S. No.	Name of the Bride	Name of the Groom	Caste/Sect	Date	Venue
88	Kamala Devi	Putteti Subrahmanyacharyulu	Vishwabrahmin	20.2.1938	Madras[241]
89	Somavalli	Pandiri Satyanandamu	–	16.3.1938	Rajahmundry[242]
90	Sitamahalakshmamma	Perumalla Krishnamoorthy	–	22.3.1938	Gangaparru[243]
91	Manikyamma	Srinivasa Setty	Vaishya	06.3.1938	Salem (T. N.)[244]
92	Enikepalli Rangamma	Pola Krishnaiah	Vaishya	30.9.1938	Secunderabad[245]
93	Pankajamma	Lingamallu Gopala Rao	Vaishya	13.10.1938	Madras[246]
94	Kotiratnam	Devarasetty Gurunatham	Vaishya	26.10.1938	–[247]
95	Gnanaprasoonamba	Venkata Suryanarayana Moorthy	Vaishya	02.2.1939	Vetapalem[248]
96	Rajaratnamu	Palakurti Rangarao	Vaishya	10.2.1939	Mandavalli (East Godavari)[249]

[241] *Vasavi*, April 1938, p. 32.

[242] 'Atyam Dampatula Samskaranabhilasha', *Vasavi*, April 1938, p. 32.

[243] Ibid.

[244] 'Arya Vaishya Stree Punarvivahaka Sanghamu, Salem', *Vasavi*, April 1938, p. 32.

[245] 'Vaishya Vitantu Vivahamulu' (Vaishya Widow Remarriages'), *Vasavi*, 1 November 1938, p. 260.

[246] Ibid.

[247] Ibid.

[248] 'Vaishya Sanghamu: Vaishya Vitantu Vivahamulu' (Vaishya Society: Vaishya Widow Remarraiges), *Vasavi*, March 1939, p. 392.

[249] Ibid.

(Contd) ...

Table 4.4 (Contd)

S. No.	Name of the Bride	Name of the Groom	Caste/Sect	Date	Venue
97	Lakshmidevamma (14)	Rajashri Chilla Narayanaswamy Setty (30)	Vaishya	N.A. may be October or November 1935	Gudipalle (Mysore State)[250]
98	Mahalakshmamma	P. Sitarama Venkata Ramayya	-	2.11.1932	
99	Venkatasubbamma	T. Ramayya	-	1.10.1933	
100	Sukanya	K. Satyamurti	-	18.4.1934	
101	Hanumayamma	B. Sheshayya Pantulu	-	1.8.1936	
102	Venkatasubbamma	M. Venkata Subarao	-	19.9.1937	
103	Satyagnana Prasunamba	D. Venkata Krishnayya	-	24.9.1937	
104	Ranganayakamma	R. Lakshminarasimha Rao	-	24.9.1937[251]	

[250] 'Vaishya Vitantu Vivahamulu' (Vaishya Widow Remarriages), *Vasavi*, December 1935, pp. 297–298.

[251] From serial number 98 to 104, the information is from B. Kesava Narayana, 'Widow Marriage Movement in Andhra,' *Itihas* 2 (1, January–June), 1974, p. 163.

5

Equality or Patriarchal Benevolence?

Education and Domestic Training

> She [Rajyalakshmamma] disliked indolence. She always involved herself in some useful work, did not waste time even a bit and thus made use of it for good things. She had unparalleled skill in home management and cooking. Though she was generous in feeding others, she did not like wasting even a single penny. Ever since she got up very early in the morning, she looked after the domestic chores without any rest and, in between, if she found some time, she spent writing or reading something. Among all her duties, she treated it [as] her primary responsibility to look after me the same way one looked after an infant. Whatever the good things I undertook, she always helped me and followed me like my shadow in everything and thus in every respect became eligible to be called a *sahadharmacharini*.... [Thus] ever since she joined me when she was thirteen years old, both of us developed mutual love and began to hold the same opinion. Given the kind of deep love she had for me, she developed immense faith in me, treated being in my company, for good or bad, [as] her universe, and following me in all things, just as a larva metamorphoses into a butterfly, she metamorphosed to become like me. That is why whichever adventurous deed I undertook, she neither stepped back nor pulled me back and, following like my shadow, encouraged me to march ahead.[1]

This was how Veeresalingam described the qualities of Rajyalakshmamma, making clear his overwhelming satisfaction and pride at having got her as his wife. Rajyalakshmamma represented the *ideal wife*, a companionate figure that was aspirational for most

[1] Kandukuri Veeresalingam, *Sweeya Charitramu*, Part 2 (Rajahmundry, 1936 [1911]), pp. 435–436, 425–426.

English-educated or Western-influenced young men of the nineteenth and early-twentieth century Andhra.

Image 5.1: 'Ideal Couple': Kandukuri Veeresalingam and his wife Rajyalakshmamma

Source: Devulapalli Venkata Krishna Sastri, Telikicherla Venkata Ratnam and Aavula Sambasiva Rao, ed., *Yugapurushudu Veeresalingam* (Shri Kandukuri Veeresalingam Smarakotsavamula Sangham, Hyderabad, n. d.).

The impact of British colonial culture was clearly felt in almost all arenas of Indian (and more specifically, Andhra) life, especially the domestic sphere, ranging from the physical arrangement of the home and domestic paraphernalia in general to the man–woman relationship in particular. Westernising reformers wanted to remodel their domestic life on the lines of the British—their colonial masters.[2]

[2]At least a few reformers displayed signs of this influence. For instance, Rayasam Venkata Sivudu (see Chapter 2), one of the prominent social reformers of Andhra, was so deeply impressed by the domestic life of the British that he translated 'with certain necessary modifications' a domestic manual authored by E. M. M. Hood (formerly Rids Dale), headmistress of the Maharani Girls' School, Mysore. The English original, titled

The Disorderly Hindu Home: Indian Reformers' Critique

Indian Male Reformist Critique of the Hindu Home

Indian reformers imbibed the colonial critique of the Hindu home, which was seen as symbolising the 'backwardness' of Indian civilisation. They criticised its 'unhealthy' construction, organisation and maintenance. Scholar and seasoned reformer Tekumalla Rajagopala Rao (1876–1938)[3] offered searing criticism of the Hindu home,[4] reiterating in *19va Shatabdapu Hindu Sangha Samskara Charitramu* (History of Hindu Social Reform in the 19th Century)[5] that the Hindu home was full of darkness, smoke, dirt, dust, disorderliness and infested with insects. In contrast, European homes, he argued, were beautiful in shape, the various household articles arranged in an attractive way and the clothes and bodies of the Europeans were clean and hygienic. 'Because of these qualities, our people [Indians] respected them, despite their being *mlechchas* [impure].' Rajagopala Rao concluded

---

English Home-Life, was translated as *Englishuvari Samsara Padhdhatulu*. It was first serialised in *Telugu Zenana* over 1900–1901 and later published as a book. Dealing with a range of issues related to English domestic life, Sivudu placed Indian domestic life in a comparative framework and suggested that 'there was much to learn' from the English example.

[3]For information on T. Rajagopala Rao, a committed reformer and close associate of Veeresalingam, see Koganti Durga Mallikarjuna Rao, 'Kee. She. (Late) Tekumalla Rajagopala Rao Shatajayanti', *Andhra Prabha* (daily newspaper), 18 January 1976 and Tekumalla Kameswara Rao, *Naa Vaangmaya Mitrulu*, pp. 119–123. Rao edited *Satya Samvardhani*, a monthly journal devoted to religious and social reform and later opened an English monthly *South Indian Research* as well as a publishing house. He established a religious reform organisation for students, Hindumata Bala Samajamu, in Vijayawada and even 'risked his life' to organise a 'major' social reform conference in Vijayawada, presided by Mahadev Govinda Ranade.

[4]T. Rajagopala Rao, 'Hindu Grihamulu' (Hindu Homes), *Telugu Zenana*, April 1902, pp. 305–309. The Hindu home was the theme of many others' literary production. C. H. Virabhadra Rao authored a play, *Hindu Grihamu* (Hindu Home) in 1898, and another work, *Hindu Samsari* (Hindu Householder) in 1898. Nandiraju Chalapati Rao authored a burlesque titled *Hindu Grihamanu Hindu Sanghika Prahasanamulu* (*A Social Burlesque Called the Hindu Home*). See Kashinathuni Nageswara Rao, *Andhra Vangmaya Suchika: Mudritamudrita Granthamula Pattika* (Hyderabad, 1993/1994 [1929]), pp. 243–245.

[5]The book was published in 1900. See ibid., p. 245.

that 'while the European homes improved your health and increased life expectancy, the Hindu homes destroyed life'.[6]

Despite these criticisms, Rajagopala Rao was fully aware of the practical limitations of Hindus:

> Because the Hindus are not as rich as the Europeans, they cannot model their homes on the fashion of the Europeans. We cannot live lonely [*sic*] in desolated and expansive places like them. Our capacity will not allow us to decorate our homes with large almirahs, tables and chairs. However, it is not impossible for us to keep our homes hygienic.[7]

He identified three important defects in Hindu homes: *first*, they were dark, *second*, they were 'filthy', and *third*, household items were placed so haphazardly that the house 'looked like a forest'.

Rajagopala Rao reasoned that it was not possible for all Indians to construct new homes, though the rich were welcome to do so. He advised that the poor must have windows in their homes to allow light and air to pass. It was because they were dark and unventilated, as some opined, that dangerous diseases like plague broke out in the Bombay Presidency. Ants, cockroaches, scorpions, centipedes and even cobras lived in these homes, and their residents often became weak, caught disease and died early. Unhealthy gases and vapours that entered such homes, or animals like rats that died there, could not be easily removed. Rao reminded readers that all over the world, people compared darkness with sin and light with virtue, and therefore suggested that even those who were not wealthy should arrange for windows without resenting the expenditure. His advice was particularly aimed at his female readers (*naa sodarimanulu*, that is, 'my sisters'), who were told to repair their homes to protect their own and their husbands' health.

The contrast between European and Hindu homes was all too visible even from a distance. While the former were clean, whitewashed and gleaming, the latter had stained walls and were patched and pasted with dung:

> Look here, the wife got up early in the morning and is mixing dung with water and sprinkling it [in front of her home]. In the process, drops of the dung-mixed water fell on the wall, giving it a colour. Lime removes all stenches. It is perhaps because of this that the housewife is laying *muggulu*[8]

[6] T. Rajagopala Rao, 'Hindu Grihamulu', *Telugu Zenana*, April 1902, p. 305.

[7] Ibid.

[8] A pattern or diagram, drawn with lines of flour or coloured powder.

> on the floor applied with dung paste! What is that happening that side? Her daughter-in-law has lit lamps with cardamom oil and is wiping her oil-stained hands on the wall. She is somewhat better! Some women wipe their dirty hands to their clothes. What is this black colour on the wall of this home? Is it really colour! No. The wall darkened because of the black smoke released by kerosene-lit lamps placed near the wall. The sediment… spread all over the wall as she tried to remove it with broomstick. After a long time, the householder purchased a table and a chair, recently. Though it has been only one month, its glaze is lost. How will it be glazed when the housewife does not wipe the dust regularly! The householder is not an intelligent fellow. Recently, I saw him wiping the ink that spilled over the table and chair. At times, he roams all over the town barefoot, returns home with dust-stained feet and places the [dirty] feet on them…. What a pity! Our Jogaiah's home is full of cobwebs hanging. The smoke from the kitchen spread all over the home to turn the cobwebs into soot. Alas! Why blame Jogaiah? [We have to blame his wife for not clearing them]. Did not a scorpion from the cobweb fall on the back of my daughter and bite her the day before yesterday? That little girl cried inconsolably for two days. [My wife has to be blamed for this.] Even if the most dangerous devils are hiding in the thatching of our home, one cannot see them![9]

Anxious about this state of affairs, he advocated a slew of measures to make the Hindu home clean, attractive, hygienic and 'civilised':

> All have to get their homes whitewashed at least twice a year. You should not wipe your hands to the walls. Why say a thousand things, you should never place your hands on the walls. Except in times of troubles, we must get the thatches of our homes dusted and walls cleaned twice a month. Just like we wipe the silt in our homes daily, we must clean each and every article daily…. The dust that falls from above [on household items] apart, because of dirty habits, our people tread [on] them, wipe wet and oil-stained hands on them. Thus, they are applying a new colour—the Hindu colour [*Hindu varnamu*]—to them. The practice of using kerosene-lit lamps is increasing in our homes day by day. When they are lit, they release great amount of smoke, which is hazardous both to the beauty of the home and the health of its inmates. Other varieties of kerosene lamps are available in the market today. They do not release any smoke, give more light than the ones in use and consume less oil. They are very advantageous both in terms of money and health. Before I conclude, I have to say something about the cooking hearth. Given our current practices, great difficulties are involved in matters concerning cooking.

[9] Ibid., pp. 307–308.

> But, at the same time, we cannot become *anacharulamu* [one who abandons established tradition]. It is better use iron-made hearths called Stoves. Brahmins can use them for cooking for children. The Shudras can use them always. You will be relieved of the trouble of blowing them with breath. If you use kerosene stoves, you do not even have to make fire. Because they do not release smoke, articles used for cooking will not be spoilt. The cook [*vantakatte*] will not have to be scorched sitting before the burning hearth [lit with firewood]. It is not expensive than the usual firewood-lit hearth. Even the cooking vessels will not get so much stained. Their cost is also less.[10]

Fictional Representation of the 'Orderly' Hindu Home

In fiction penned by reformers who held such views, one finds a romantic vision of the home. For instance, Kandukuri Veeresalingam's novel, *Rajasekhara Charitramu*,[11] features an elaborate description of the protagonist Rajasekhara's home:

> Among the houses of the period, that of Rajsekhara was considered very handsome. On each side of the street-door was an extensive *pial*.[12] Between these pials lay the walk that led within. At the end of this walk was the lion-portal, or front-door. Near the threshold there was picturesquely carved on each doorpost a lion crouching on the head of an elephant.... Adjoining the ends of this porch were two rooms; and on the south side was a line of double doors in the wall, which, when opened, admitted the cool mountain breeze to fan the perspiring company [of visitors]. Beyond these doors extended a veranda; and beyond that again a tiny area which was a feast for the eyes with many varieties of flowering plants. Within, on the three walls of the porch just mentioned, large pictures were hung on nails at the height of a man.... On the west side of the well, built apart from the house, were two hutches for storing rice in the husk.... Were we to pass this door, we would stand in Rajasekhara's bedchamber.... The bed itself was draped with mosquito curtains and fringe, while between the posts were lacquered wooden salvers and caskets.... The walls of the room were whitened with lime.... Opposite the bedstead, along the south wall,

[10] Ibid., pp. 308–309. The reference to caste draws on the idea that Brahmins, especially adult men, were only supposed to eat food cooked using firewood; such prohibitions were not observed among oppressed caste groups.

[11] Veeresalingam mentioned in his *Sweeya Charitramu* that the description of the home of Rajasekharudu, the protagonist of the novel, was, by and large, that of his own home. *Sweeya Charitramu*, Part 1, p. 7.

[12] A long, raised veranda-like seat of earth or brickwork.

> *kavadi*-boxes were arranged in a row on the lower shelf. In these boxes were kept common, everyday clothes, and Rajasekhara's Sanskrit books written on Bengal paper in the Nagari character. Against the western wall of this room stood a huge chest secured with a strong lock. In the small lock-boxes which this chest contained were kept the family jewels, valuables, cloths for use on feast-days, and cash.... At a little distance to the left of this again, a jasmine vine crept upon a trellis; and, although not then in bloom (that being the wrong season), charmed the sight with a wealth of green shoots. In the porch adjoining Rajasekhara's bedroom, a parrot's cage was suspended from a beam.... At a little distance further in the same paddock a *tulasi* plant, just beyond perennial jasmine plants, and close to these a creeping vine trained upon a broadleaved rosebay tree ... Here, too arranged in rows along the wall, were marigolds and lilies lovingly tended by Rukmini and her sister. Within the kitchen area, which joined hard to the south side of the west room, plantain trees feasted the eyes with their wealth of green foliage.[13]

Women Reformers' Visions of the Hindu Home

In 1940, Vempati Sharada Devi wrote in a domestic manual[14] that 'howsoever small the house may be, it should have proper windows to allow air and light to pass. The kitchen must have large windows to allow the smoke to go out freely.' It was also necessary to ensure proper drainage, and to have a separate kitchen, dining hall, bedroom and verandah. A well or tap in the backyard would be an added comfort for women. She also stated that the

[13] The *Rajasekhara Charitramu* (pub. 1878) was translated into English by J. Robert Hutchinson as *Fortune's Wheel: A Tale of Hindu Domestic Life* and published from London in 1887. The quote is from the translation, pp. 26–32.

[14] Vempati Sharada Devi, *Stree Hitabodhini: Grihatantra Paathamulu* (Sermons to Women: Lessons on Domestic-craft) (Gottipadu, 1940). The book was priced 0.4 annas for members of the Sahitya Kutiramu and 0.6 annas for others. What is significant about the book is that, unlike other domestic/instructional manuals that were typically in the form of poetry, this text was written in prose and that too in a simple and lucid style. Another important aspect was that it was sponsored by men. Varanasi Venkateshwarlu, editor of the publications of Sahitya Kutiramu, noted in his 'Editorial' that 'the book would be of immense use to women in organising their homes in an attractive way for the duties to be performed by the housewives from dawn to dusk were represented, like a mirror, in it'. With 61 pages and 24 chapters, the book discussed a variety of issues such as daily ablutions, habit of coffee, health and hygiene, food habits, the way of arranging kitchenware, hair oils, tooth powder, sewing and embroidery work, method of preparing soaps, child rearing, cares to be taken by pregnant women, girls and their schools and conjugal relations, etc. Some aspects of the book are discussed in the following pages.

size of the house should be in proportion to the number of family members, and that a smaller house was better since it would not require as much effort to maintain.[15]

Sharada Devi was of the opinion that if women were intelligent, they would organise the home in an attractive way. She emphasised that 'there should be a place for everything and everything should be in its place', ensuring that the kitchen, bedroom, and dining hall were populated with the appropriate items and decor. It was better to hang the pictures of gods, national leaders and family members on the walls. Nude imagery, in contrast, was highly undesirable in family homes (*samsarika grihamulu*).[16]

The manual also discussed the need to keep the house clean, carry out regular repairs, and whitewash the home. Sharada Devi provided a host of practical suggestions: for instance, lime was an insect repellant, and if mixed with a bit of indigo, it would keep our eyes cool. As light entering the rooms increased, the home would acquire a new beauty. Used water was to be properly drained lest it begins to stink, become host to harmful bacteria and cause disease. Wooden fixtures were to be polished with a mix of colours and varnish annually to beautify the home and get rid of pests.[17]

In the section on 'Domestic Articles and the Method of Organising Them', she wrote:

> The cooking utensils [kitchenware] must be kept in the kitchen itself. After using them, they should be cleaned and kept in the same place where they have to be. A wooden plank with holes made in it should be nailed to the wall and articles like spoons and *atlakadas* should be inserted in the holes. You can easily take them when needed rather than searching in the entire home. It is good to keep every article in a specific place. Otherwise, one may have to search for hours together [even] for a needle. One may not find it finally. The pickle pots, salt containers, cooking utensils, eating plates and bowls and firewood, etc. have to be placed in the kitchen itself.... There should be two ropes separately to dry the washed clothes and to place the used ones. The clothes-to-be-washed should not be thrown in a haphazard way all over the home. Because of this, the home not only turns into a *chaki revu* [a place where the washerwo/men wash clothes] but also gets spoilt by collecting dirt on the floor. There should be wooden hangers [nailed to the wall] for women and men separately to hang their clothes

[15] Ibid., p. 49.
[16] Ibid.
[17] Ibid., p. 50.

... There should be separate *vuttis*[18] to store buttermilk, curd, ghee, jaggery and sugar. It will be very good, if they are ant-resistant *vutti*s ... There should be *almirah*s and lofts [*ataka*] in the home, [just like] in the kitchen. We can keep the articles that we do not use regularly in/on them. If you do it this way... the home does not appear narrow; rather it appears spacious. [Therefore] it will be comfortable to have lofts, etc. even if the home is small. Tin containers are good to store rice ... By all means, it should not be stored in gunny bags because rats will bite the bags and eat the rice.... Therefore, fit well the cap of the tin box containing rice. It is important to store various grams, chilly-powder and tamarind powder in tin boxes.... It is important to have mats in the home, even if there are chairs. After using, the mats should be rolled and placed atop. As it is dusk, you need to light lamps.... There should be a lantern in the kitchen.... There should be suspended iron-bar-hooks [*vanke*] to hang the lanterns.... You need to be very careful while cleaning the lanterns.... If you are careful, you can reduce expenditure. While lighting the hearth, some [women] bend the lantern to allow the kerosene oil to drain into the hearth. At times, more than the required amount of kerosene drains and gets wasted. Those with this habit must stop [instantly]. After dinner, you must hang the lantern to the *vanke*, put it off and go to bed.... Those who heat up *ghee* on the lanterns should carefully clean up the dregs.... After using the *kattipita*s[19] and sickles, they should be kept in the designated place [and certainly not in people's way].... After using, the match box should be kept away from the reach of children.... After combing hair, you should clear the comb off hair and dust. The bunch of removed hair should not be kept at home, but carefully thrown outside.... While combing [the hair of] children, proper care should be taken that the uncapped oil-bottle does not roll on the floor. There must be at least one mirror in every home. The elders say that a home without a mirror and a woman is nothing but a forest. After using, it should be hanged on the same hook.... As far as possible, one must have a cot, a thin mattress and a pillow. If the means permit, one may have blankets and costly mattresses.... Cots must be removed to a specific place soon after getting up from sleep.... If you have a wall clock or an alarm clock, they should be kept in a specific place and keyed at the right time. Only one must do the keying.... Broomsticks, sandals and dirt-removing clothes should be kept away from the sight of others. If they are placed at any place as one pleased, it will be disgusting. Each article we use should be kept neat and clean. Each article in the home must be cleaned and

[18] A fibrous network sling in which pots, etc. are suspended from the beams of the house.

[19] A large knife standing slantwise in a block of wood upon which vegetables are sliced.

placed in the right place.... There is no use, if we are clean and the articles we use are not. Women must importantly observe this [*sic*].[20]

The Man-Woman Relationship and a Happy Home

It was not just in the matter of the physical arrangement of the home that English-educated men wanted reform. The relationships between and among the residents were also to be scrutinised and transformed, with a particular focus on the conjugal relationship. Influenced by colonial culture, this milieu desired romantic love and longed for companionate marriages. However, given the wider context—girls were generally forced to remain uneducated and married off extremely young—women could not match the expectations of their modern, romantically ambitious and often much older husbands, leading to increasing frustration among these men in both social and familial terms. Faced with the threat of thwarted dreams and the 'sapping' of marital bliss because of their unlettered and 'uncultured' 'child wives', and also 'in response to the changing demands of life under British rule, English-educated and/or Western-influenced Indian men increasingly saw the reform of women's social conditions—most particularly women's literacy and education—as the key to both India's progress and their own'.[21] The colonial context compelled them to thoroughly restructure their personal as well as family life: 'in their homes, they wanted system, order, efficiency, and hygiene; in their wives, literacy, education, companionate marriage, and love'.[22]

To be more specific, this new class of Western-educated men wanted to replace the existing 'master–slave relationship' between husband and wife with a model of companionship. They wished for their wives became their friends, helpmates and soulmates. They craved for a romantic relationship where spouses would address each other by name;[23] where they, like an

[20] Ibid., pp. 19–29.

[21] Judith E. Walsh, *Domesticity in Colonial India: What Women Learned When Men Gave Them Advice* (New Delhi, 2004), p. 21.

[22] Ibid., p. 87.

[23] K. N. Kesari, founder of *Grihalakshmi* (see Chapter 2, this volume), was disappointed when his first wife, Kanakamma, objected to his habit of addressing her by name. He explained that 'in Madras, the Komati [Vaishya caste] men used to address their wives as "*evaraadaa*". A few addressed with the symbolic names such as "*Ose*", "*Osee*", "*Ekkadunnavu*", "*Aan*", "*Uun*", etc. A few wise people say '*Emammoyi*' or "*Amma*". When the wives addressed their husbands, they used honorifics such as "*Settigaru*", "*Ayyaru*",

English couple, could walk side-by-side in the evenings;[24] where they could attend public meetings or social reform conferences[25] and watched dramas/theatre together. Wives should be equipped to receive and entertain guests in their absence.[26] Along with these romantic aspirations, men also

---

"*Pantulu*", "*Emandi*", "*Nayudu*", "*Modaliyaru*", etc. If asked the names of their husbands, a few wives respond that her husband's name is the same as the husband's name of the neighbouring Krishnavenamma. I do not know how the tradition of not uttering husbands' names has come into existence. Our people seem not to have understood the meaning of the marriage-day ritual when husband and wife utter each other's names. It was intended to address each other by names from then on. A few husbands are addressing their wives by names; but no wife is addressing her husband by name. A few educated women write the names of their husbands on a piece of paper, when asked about their husbands' names. But, [unlike the Telugus] the Tamils seem to be not so particular about this.'

See *Naa Chinnanati Muchchatlu* (Madras, 1953), pp. 42–43.

[24] Rayasam Venkata Sivudu was very fond of going for evening walks along with his 16-year-old wife Rayasam Ratnamma. When he lived in Vijayawada (in the year 1893), he demanded that his wife join him for these walks. But she would refuse, resulting in quarrels between them. Sivudu remarked that Hindu society treated evening walks by spouses to be an 'adventurous deed'. Hindu women enjoyed such freedom in big cities like Chennapuri (Madras), but not in small towns like Bezawada (Vijayawada). It attracted the 'crude remarks of neighbourly women'. Rayasam Venkata Sivudu, *Atma Charitramu*, p. 233. While in Madras, Veeresalingam would go to the beach and public garden along with his wife, Rajyalakshmamma, 'every evening'. He did not walk, but rode 'a big horse-drawn cart'. He remarked that, in Madras, he enjoyed more comforts and respect. Moving with his wife was definitely a part of those 'comforts'. Kandukuri Veeresalingam, *Sweeya Charitramu*, part 2, p. 136.

[25] The desire to attend public meetings or social reform conferences along with wives was so strong among the English-educated young men that Dasu Sriramulu, an ardent advocate of social reform, took his wife (her name was not mentioned) to the Godavari District Social Conference held on 9 June 1897, the first ever public meeting attended by colonial Andhra women, 'though her menses [had] appeared just the previous day.' Despite being 'threatened by his elder brothers of severing all ties with him', Sattiraju Kameshwara Rao reached the venue along with his wife. For details, see Kandukuri Veeresalingam, *Sweeya Charitramu*, part 2, pp. 86–87. Rayasam Venkata Sivudu attended along with his wife Rayasam Ratnamma, despite objections raised by his mother. Veeresalingam too attended with his wife Rajyalakshmamma. See Rayasam Venkata Sivudu, *Atma Charitramu*, pp. 293–294.

[26] K. Narasimham appreciated Darishi Chenchaiah for his first wife, Darishi Annapoornamma, possessed this quality. In his condolence message to Chenchaiah after the demise of Annapoornamma, K. Narasimham recalled that 'she was a very good lady. Once, when I had been to your home in your absence, she received me well and very kindly.' The letter was dated 1 December 1931. See Darishi Chenchaiah, *Marapurani Annapoorna*, p. 55.

wanted their wives to be well-trained in practical matters such as household management. More importantly, wives were expected to be meticulous in financial management and book-keeping; they were to be frugal, and not attracted to luxury. Another attractive quality was the knowledge of music. Women were to be loving, caring and devoted to their husbands and sincere in their concern for their in-laws. Thus, the Westernising male social reformers advanced a model of what I term *beneficial domesticity*, which primarily benefitted men even as it offered some improvements for women.

Educating Women to Turn Home to Heaven

It was these demands of colonial modernity that pushed male social reformers to feverishly advocate women's education and raise their voice against the maltreatment of women. Most prominently, they attempted to mould women into successful managers of the home. The social location of many of these men—as petty employees in the colonial machinery—also created a need for their wives to be diligently trained in household management, with a special emphasis on domestic financial management. Therefore, themes such as household management, health and hygiene, the separation of spheres (the 'private' realm for women, and the 'public' realm for men), personal conduct of women both within and outside the family, devotion to husband and need to uphold pativrata dharma, music, embroidery and beautification were staples in the columns of women's journals. Both men and women contributed to writings in this vein, though the pioneers were men. By laying emphasis on 'womanly' virtues/duties/knowledge and instructing women in such matters, the journals reinforced essentialist notions of women and their place in family and society.

Veeresalingam wrote that, 'if men want their homes to be a heaven on earth, rather than a big wild forest, they should educate their wives and, with the help of the lamp of education, they should remove the darkness of ignorance and ensure that those serpents and tigers called un-virtuousness and evil traditions did not find shelter in their hearts.'[27] Education was a 'lamp', which dispelled the darkness of un-modernism. In his autobiography, he clearly stated the reasons for starting *Sathihitha Bodhini* exclusively for women:

> I am deeply interested in women's education and advancement. Deeply worried looking at their dismal position, I always thought that it will never be possible for men to progress, if women are kept in such degraded

[27] Kandukuri Veeresalingam, *Sweeya Charitramu*, part 2, p. 35.

> conditions. Making women educated, learned and wise is inevitable for men, if the latter are to progress.... As I felt that there are no good books for women in Telugu, I thought of filling a gap, to the extent my abilities permit me, and started in 1883 a journal for women in Telugu with the name Sathihitha Bodhini.[28]

Concerted efforts at casting women in men's mould began with the journal. Veeresalingam was of the view that 'the burden of managing the home was of women, not men. If women were educated, they would perform the task carefully/well. Since women were not well-versed with it, the burden fell on men who, having already been overburdened with outside work, performed it with vexation.'[29] *Sathihitha Bodhini* accordingly published several items *instructing* women in the art of household management and their personal conduct. The reformer firmly believed that 'it was impossible for men to develop if women were kept in a degraded position. If men were to progress, they needed to upgrade the position of women by giving them education; and together they could make progress a possibility.'[30] He continued: 'If men alone made progress keeping women in slavery, they could not really progress; rather it was inevitable that they would [fail and] fall.'[31] As he 'found' that there were 'no good books in the Telugu language for the use of women', apart from publishing *Sathihitha Bodhini*, he authored and published several works keeping in view the '[special] need' of women,[32] many of which were first serialised in the journal. This included the *Patnihita Suchani* (Advice to Housewives, published in 1896) which dealt with menstruation, pregnancy, childbirth, and child-rearing), *Deharogyadharma Bodhini* (1889) on women's physiology and health, *Satyavati Charitramu* and *Chandramati Charitramu* (1884), histories of Satyavati and Chandramati, the Puranic pativratas; *Satya Sanjivani* (1887) on morality, particularly the consequences of 'telling lies', as well as another book on morality in 1893, *Nitikatha Manjari*; and *Uttama Stree Charitramu*, an illustrated volume of 80 pages on 'Noble Women' such as Joan of Arc, Lady Jane Grey, Mary Carpenter, Elizabeth Fry, etc. (including one essay

---

[28] Ibid., pp. 203–204.

[29] Kandukuri Veeresalingam, 'Stree Vidya' (Women's Education) in Akkiraju Ramapati Rao ed., *Veeresalingam Rachanalu*, pp. 143–150. See also Kandukuri Veeresalingam, 'Bharyabhartala Aikamatyamu' (Unity/Compatibility between Wife and Husband) in ibid., pp. 196–198.

[30] Kandukuri Veeresalingam, *Sweeya Charitramu*, pp. 203–204.

[31] Ibid.

[32] Ibid., pp. 204–214.

each on the 'Noble Mother' or *Uttama Mata* and the 'illuminator of women's morality', or *Stri Niti Deepika*).[33]

Training Women in Scientific Griha Nirvahakatvamu

The *Telugu Zenana* enthusiastically pursued the task of tailoring women to fit the aspirations of men. It emphasised the 'need' for women to master the art of domestic management. Therefore, the theme of *griha nirvahakatvamu* (home management) occupied a dominant place in the journal, to the extent that there was not even one issue without a piece related to it. Venkata Sivudu was so relentless on this subject that he authored a book titled *Griha Nirvahakatvamu*. Begun in August 1895, it was first serialised in *Telugu Zenana* and eventually took the shape of a book.[34] It was so popular that 300 copies of the first edition sold out soon after publication, encouraging him to publish a revised edition.[35]

As *Telugu Zenana* saw the home and the hearth as women's 'natural' place, articles and stories stressed that it was 'essential' for women to be alert to the affairs of the home and 'master' the intricate details of household management, insisting on system, order, efficiency, cleanliness, hygiene, etc., to be ensured in homes. The journal clearly put forth the patriarchal sexual division of labour, consigning women to the domestic sphere, their 'natural' arena of activity, and one where they had to excel. Stressing that housekeeping was *the* primary responsibility of women, one contributor, V. Narayana Moorthy, reiterated that 'setting the house right was the duty of women, not men'. According to him, a woman who was good at household management effectively ran her family and scrupulously maintained the house with minimal wastage, resulting in a happy home; in contrast, a woman who was poor at the skill, or did not know it at all, was doomed to fail miserably in her family life, creating misery for her husband and becoming a 'laughing stock of her neighbours [*sic*]'.

Holding women to be the embodiment of 'patience', which men 'naturally lacked', Moorthy stressed that women were more 'befitting' and 'well qualified' to manage the household. If men were made to perform

[33] Ibid. pp. 204–214, 249, and p. 414 in Part 1. See also V. Ramakrishna, 'Women's Journals in Andhra during the Nineteenth Century', pp. 81–82; Akkiraju Ramapati Rao, *Veeresalingam Pantulu: Samagra Parisheelana* (Hyderabad, 1972), pp. 204–205.

[34] Rayasam Venkata Sivudu, *Atma Charitramu*, pp. 263–264.

[35] Ibid., p. 335. Even the second edition of the book was sold well, making Venkata Sivudu 'extremely happy' about it. Ibid., p. 362.

both professional and household duties, one was sure to be spoilt. Houses managed by men were typically 'disgusting like the poultry farm', since for men household management was 'more difficult than agriculture'. Apart from 'skill', it demanded 'more patience'. The clear suggestion was that the sexual division of labour was necessary because women were patience personified![36]

Practical Dimensions of Women's Training

Apart from the view that women were 'naturally' suited to the home and the hearth, the authors in the journal saw a practical dimension to the 'need' for women to master these skills. Girls and young women were to be prepared for their future career as 'wives', and as they were bound to take on the responsibility of running their marital home sooner or later, they needed to be 'properly trained in the art of domestic management', so as not to be ostracised by demanding mothers-in-law. Hence, women were exhorted to learn the intricacies of household management since childhood in order to ease them into their future career of wifehood.[37]

Women writers also reflected on this issue. Kanuparti Varalakshmamma's fictitious autobiography *Premalata–Sweeya Charitramu* (Autobiography of Premalata), which we have discussed earlier, is one example. This account is remarkable for it shed light not only on the patriarchal power relations within the family, but also for its unabashed critique of such dynamics. After dwelling at length on how young wives were maltreated by mothers-in-law and husbands, the text appealed for humane treatment of daughters-in-law. Curiously, she earnestly appealed to parents to train their daughters well in the art of domestic management so that 'they would not face the same murderous difficulties she had to suffer at the in-laws' place.'[38] Establishing cordial relationships between mothers-in-law and daughters-in-law and sisters-in-law was a serious concern of women writers. Therefore,

---

[36] V. Narayana Moorthy, 'Griha Nirvahakatvamu' (Management of the House; translation as in original), *Telugu Zenana*, December 1902, pp. 161–164.

[37] Ibid. Nalam Krishna Rao compared mothers-in-law to a 'crocodile', who tormented the young daughters-in-law. He reminded men that it was their responsibility to save their young wives from the 'knife cuts' they received at the hands of the mother-in-law. *Streelayedala Manamugavinchu Pancha Mahapatakamulu* (The Five Great Sins We Commit against Women) (Rajamahendravaramu, 1912), p. 9.

[38] Kanuparti Varalakshmamma, *Premalata–Sweeya Charitramu* (Autobiography of Premalata), *Anasuya*, July–August, pp. 13–29 & September–October 1919, pp. 9–30.

contemporary women's journals were flooded with writings on this issue. It was so serious an issue that one 'Manini' (pseudonym) ranked freedom from the domination of mothers-in-law and sisters-in-law to be greater than freedom from male domination: 'We should free ourselves from the domination of women first, before we relieve ourselves from the domination of men.'[39]

Training Women in Financial Management

'Stree Hitabhilashi' (a pseudonym which translates to 'well-wisher of women'; the writer was certainly a man) wrote in *Telugu Zenana* that management of the home did not mean only cooking and other domestic work, but also the crucial tasks of financial management, book-keeping and running the family along the principles of health and hygiene. According to him, 'men performed better than women in such matters as financial management, and women needed to learn them from men'. To substantiate his point, he narrated a story which he claimed to have witnessed. The story portrayed women as being extremely poor at financial management, whose 'unmindful spending' on not so necessary things as jewelry landed their families in deep troubles.[40] Hence, women were given lessons in accounts keeping and financial management.

A short story also published in *Telugu Zenana* compared the family lives of two women—one who had mastered the skill of household management including financial management, and the other who was ignorant of it. The first one's life was aglow with care and warmth for the children—everybody

---

[39] Manini, 'Adu Biddalu' (Sisters-in-law), *Grihalakshmi*, October 1930, p. 650.

[40] The story was about Ramaiah, a government employee who was careful with his salary, and his 'not so educated' wife Sitamma who demanded unwise spending on jewellery. Failing to understand that her husband sought to save money, she complained to neighbours that he was miserly. One fine evening, Ramaiah handed over his whole salary to Sitamma and asked her to manage the house. She spent the money so unmindfully that it was exhausted within ten days. Alarmed, she borrowed from the neighbours. This continued the following month as well, till one afternoon when Ramaiah returned home and found his wife crying. Consoling her, he explained that her lack of knowledge in domestic management was the cause of all difficulties and let her in on 'secrets of household management'. Thus, women were treated as mindless spendthrifts who often troubled their husbands for jewellery and caused misery to hard working and careful husbands and themselves. See Stree Hitabhilashi, 'Ramudu–Sita: Griha Nirvahakamunu Bodhinchunoka Katha' (Rama and Sita: A Story on the Management of the House, translation as in original), *Telugu Zenana*, January 1903, pp. 217–223.

was always cheerful, the entire family was healthy, children were disciplined and the family was as fresh and lively as a 'perennial river'. But the latter's family life was 'highly disordered' like a 'wild forest': she was often irritated, screamed, cursed and beat children, the latter always cried and wallowed; children saw a '*pratyaksha rakshasi*' (living demon) in their mother. All in all, it evoked the popular saying, '*samsara sagaram dukhkham*' (the ocean of family life is woeful).[41]

Cooking to be Done on 'Scientific' and 'Economic' Principles

Cooking, which constituted an important component of household management, was seen as an 'instinctive quality' of women. Hence, both rich and the poor women were tasked with mastering the skill: while rich women did not need to cook themselves, they needed to be able 'to supervise the work of the maidservants.' Moreover, 'howsoever rich a woman was', she 'naturally felt like feeding her nears and dears at least occasionally'. For the common woman, there was no escape from cooking.[42] Since cooking constituted the vital aspect of domestic management, the general consensus was to include it as a 'compulsory subject' in the curriculum of girls' schools. As school lessons were 'not sufficient' to master the art of cooking, parents (that is, mothers) were to train daughters at home. Rayasam Venkaiah, citing a periodical to support his claim, commented that 'it was not wrong to state that there were not many Hindu women who were skillful in the art of cooking'. He also cited a Health Department officer's statement that unhygienic cooking caused disease and the death of many Indians.[43]

'If there were two persons in the home, and the food cooked could be had by four, much would be wasted. Everybody was to observe this carefully,' Vempati Sharada Devi cautioned. Cooking was to follow economic principles and avoid wastage, as over consumption and carelessness were

[41] See 'Sita–Savithri: Griha Nirvahakatvamunu gurinchina yoka Paathamu' (Sita and Savitri: A Lesson on Household Management, translation as in original), *Telugu Zenana*, April and May 1905, pp. 318–322.

[42] R. Venkayya, 'Griha Nirvahakatvamu' (Hints on Domestic Economy, translation as in original), *Telugu Zenana*, March 1903, pp. 273–277. However, men were also reminded of their duties in household management. They were to go to the market to purchase vegetables and other essential provisions and had to know their quality and prices lest they be cheated. Men were to purchase them personally and not send servants for their own 'satisfaction'.

[43] R. V. (Rayasam Venkaiah), 'Griha Nirvahakatvamu' (Hints on the Management of the House, translation as in original), *Telugu Zenana*, April 1903, pp. 289–291.

seen to contribute to poverty. Except in rare cases, costly vegetables were not to be purchased.[44] Sharada Devi also stipulated that women must ensure punctuality in cooking and meals, else men's jobs would be in trouble.[45] Praising the general practice in many families of women eating only after their husbands, she conceded that eating together could be a 'pleasure' if only the husband and the wife were at home. However, she criticised the popular practice of eating the husband's leftover in the same leaf platter: 'This is a foolish act. Some say that it is a symbol of devotion to husband [*pati bhakti*]. But this is false. Because of this, women contract their husbands' diseases....'[46]

'Scientific cooking' was given such importance that many cookbooks were published during this period. Sattiraju Sitaramaiah, the founder of *Hindu Sundary*, authored *Vantalakka*.[47] In a pictorial illustration, a young girl is shown reading the book as the mother keenly listens. An advertisement for the book in *Hindu Sundary* claimed that women of the Telugu country were not skilled in the art of cooking.[48] 'Each village and each home must possess the book. When one does not get the idea [as to what to cook], they can just look at the book and they will find a number of items. The book purchased by spending 0.4 annas will do much better than a *brahmanakka* [a female Brahmin cook] hired for 4 rupees a month,' the advertisement stated.

Bhandaru Atchamamba also authored a book on cooking, and she was praised by her contemporaries for her extensive knowledge of cooking diverse cuisine.[49] During the 1930s and 1940s, women's journals such as the *Grihalakshmi* conducted a special column on cooking. In the column, 'Paka Kala' (The Art of Cooking), *Grihalakshmi* regularly included various methods of food preparation, drawing on the enthusiastic contributions of

[44] Vempati Sharada Devi, *Stree Hitabodhini*, pp. 13–17.

[45] Ibid., p. 31.

[46] Ibid., pp. 29–30.

[47] Sattiraju Sitaramaiah, *Sweeya Charitra*, p. 73.

[48] However, the advertisement continued, women wished to acquire techniques relevant to a variety of cuisines. Some learnt from women of other South Indian states. However, as they did not cook them regularly, they forgot these different methods. With this in mind, the book was prepared with the help of a number of women: along with Andhra cuisine, foods and a variety of chutneys from Mathura, Rameshwaram, Kashi, Prayaga, Allahabad and Mysore were included in the book. See *Hindu Sundary*, January–February 1913.

[49] In his obituary, Veeresalingam appreciated her expertise at cooking and the wide knowledge she acquired in this regard. See *Telugu Zenana*, February 1905, pp. 225–229.

women readers and writers. The column indirectly stressed that cooking was women's 'duty', and suggested that they should master the 'art'.

'Suguname Bhushanamu': Virtue as the 'Real Jewels' for Women

Women's desire for jewellery was systematically denounced and discouraged. Instead of demanding gold and silver ornaments, which enhanced women's 'physical beauty only', women were asked to inculcate virtuous behaviour for 'virtues were the real ornaments to women'.[50] Good conduct was projected as 'the invaluable ornament'.[51] '*Sadvartanamu*' (good conduct), which brought 'reputation' and ensured a person's place in posterity, was seen as the 'most invaluable embellishment' to the character of a woman, and was held to be more 'essential' for women than men.[52] Women were sternly told that their spending on 'not so necessary things as jewellery' landed their husbands and families in trouble[53] and they were advised to 'treat it to be ignoble to trouble their husbands for jewellery'.[54] It is not surprising, then, that *Vivekavathi*, a Christian missionary women's journal, should print the Biblical maxim, 'a virtuous woman was more precious than a pearl' (*Gunavatiyayina Stree Mutyamukante Namoolyamynadi*), below the masthead in every issue.

Vempati Sharada Devi wrote that 'there should be a limit to women's craving for jewellery', keeping in mind the husband's income, family savings, property, etc. 'It was unjust on their part to torment husbands for jewellery.' However, men should provide jewellery as and when they could. Unlike early domestic manuals, which reserved all blame for women, Sharda Devi

[50] G. A. Ramamoorthy, 'Nagalu' (Jewellery), *Andhra Patrika Ugadi Sanchika*, 1917. The poet persuaded women that jewellery made of gold and silver was 'menial' compare to 'eternal' jewels such as education, virtuous behaviour, including the 'tiny jewel called *pati bhakti*' (devotion to husband). While jewellery enhanced women's physical beauty, their husbands were sure to incur debts.

[51] Damerla Sundaramma, 'Sadvartanamu' (Good Conduct), *Savithri*, October 1904, p. 5.

[52] See 'Stree Niti Deepika', *Savithri*, August 1904. See also 'Stree Niti Ratnavali', *Savithri*, October 1904.

[53] See Stree Hitabhilashi, 'Ramudu-Sita: Griha Nirvahakamunu Bodhinchunoka Katha' (Rama and Sita: A Story on the Management of the House, translation as in original), *Telugu Zenana*, January 1903, pp. 217–223.

[54] See 'Stree Dharmamulu' (Duties of Women), *Savithri*, April 1904.

found fault with men for incurring debts for providing jewellery during their daughters' marriages.[55]

Sharda Devi added a nationalist dimension to embroidery, a craft typically taken up by women. She observed that women normally used 'foreign thread' and advocated that they begin using swadeshi thread instead. She also discussed how useful sewing could be in reducing household expenditure. Women could make clothes for children, *banyans*, table-mats, bed-sheets and curtains themselves. Although this involved more labour and was expensive, she wrote that women were 'enthusiastic' to take up this work. 'Women who practised sewing would be benefitted more.'[56] She encouraged women to avoid using foreign-made cloth and choose homemade cloth instead. Reminding women of Gandhi's belief that 'India would be relieved of poverty, if every home had a spinning wheel', she said that if women used homemade cloth, rather than investing on imported foreign cloth, Indian wealth would no longer be drained by foreign countries.[57]

Learning Music to Reinvigorate the Tired Husband's Soul

Knowledge of music was an essential quality of the ideal housewife (*grihalakshmi*). It allowed the conjugal couple, particularly the husband, to forget the hard realities of life, and relax. Music provided solace amid various difficulties and the tumult of colonial rule. According to an article published in *Telugu Zenana* and *Sathihitha Bodhini*, women who were skilled in music—both vocal and instrumental—provided 'new enthusiasm to their husbands, who returned home tired after a day's hard work outside [*sic*]'. 'Well-dressed, and with a pleasing face,' if the wife melodiously sang a song, 'the husband's tired soul got reinvigorated'. (Otherwise, it was implied, there was every possibility that the tired man's soul may seek solace in the lap of a sex worker!) A woman who could sing lullabies would be able to calm crying children and help them fall asleep. 'It [knowledge of music] enhanced her prestige in the neighbourhood for the neighbouring women approached her requesting for a song, and also to learn music from her.

[55] Vempati Sharada Devi, *Stree Hitabodhini*, pp. 52–53. She advised against extravaganza in marriages. 'Spending hundreds and thousands [of rupees] in marriages, etc. would prove to be traumatic even for those with moderate means. For the rich, anything was okay,' she observed. Ibid., p. 52.

[56] Ibid., pp. 35–36.

[57] Ibid., pp. 31–32.

She brought splendor to [auspicious] occasions such as marriage by her musical performance.' Music was useful even for spiritual purposes: 'it was better praying [to] God in songs/hymns rather than words.' (Perhaps god understood poetry better than prose!) In a nutshell, 'with the knowledge of music, women earned the appreciation and love of husbands; caused joy to parents and relatives; brought flavor to family, caste, and lineage, and made them proud; earned them the respect and love of other women; and they personally overcame grief and enjoyed life.' Hence, girls were told to receive lessons in music and parents encouraged to make the required arrangements.[58]

Writing in 1940, Vempati Sharada Devi felt that a greater knowledge of fine arts would 'enhance women's honour'. This knowledge would help them 'please their husbands' and also 'overcome their own tiresomeness caused by domestic work'. She encouraged women to learn the fine arts like music, painting, dance (*bharata natyamu*) and poetry. Women were to avoid 'immoral dances shown in cinemas'; however, practice of bharata natyam was welcome. It provided them 'physical exercise' and enabled them to keep their husbands happy and 'ensured' that the latter maintained good sexual conduct. 'Therefore, if women were skillful in fine arts, they gained honour and reputation.'[59]

'No God Other than the Husband': Instruction in Pati Bhakti

The journals emphasised women's absolute devotion and unquestioning subordination to their husbands specifically, and men in general. Their agenda was to establish the husband's centrality in a woman's life. A piece published in *Telugu Zenana* in verse form best demonstrated this. Some choice excerpts include:

> Always adore husband, and never answer him back; if you did, you had no salvation [for] there was no other God for a wife other than the husband.
>
> Never eat and sleep before your husband eats and sleeps; if you treat him to be your God, people treat you as a pativrata.

that is, a woman who is devoted to her husband, maintaining conjugal fidelity. Other verses similarly proclaimed:

---

[58] K. R. S., 'Sangeetamu' (Music), *Telugu Zenana & Sathihitha Bodhini*, December 1904, pp. 161–167.

[59] Vempati Sharada Devi, *Stree Hitabodhini*, pp. 41–42.

> O soft-bodied being [*komalangi*]! [You must] never feel dissatisfaction and ridicule [your] husband even if he is a lame, insane and an imbecile person [*sic*].
>
> Never even think of other man, howsoever rich he is, and [instantly] forget him. A woman becomes sinful the moment she develops thoughts of love for another man, and all the virtues are lost immediately and permanently. Hence, control your thoughts.
>
> Arrange the home in such a way to give pleasure to your husband. It is essential that neatly dressed, you wait for him; never ever be at the neighbours' door when it is time for his arrival.
>
> Do not quarrel with him for jewelry for there is no better ornament than your virtues; be contented with whatever you have.
>
> Do not administer any [magical or ayurvedic] drugs in the desire to bring him under your control [for] there is no other better drug than your virtues.[60]

In *Savithri*, the second women-edited journal, men/husbands enjoyed an exalted status. The journal was obsessed with inculcating morality and pativratya dharma (conjugal fidelity) among women. Hence, it published a number of pieces emphasising mortality and pativratya as the quintessence of *sati* dharma, mostly in verse. It is noteworthy that most of these writings were by men.[61] However, this was a favourite theme of women writers also.[62] Several writings in *Savithri* seemed calculated to terrify women into

---

[60] Kannepalli Suryamu, 'Pati Bhakti' (Devotion to Husband), *Telugu Zenana*, October 1903, pp. 112–115. *Marulu mandulu* or ayurvedic powders were sold with claims that they would redirect the attention of married men from the natal home to their wives. These dubious preparations had reportedly resulted in many deaths.

[61] A number of men wrote independent books of instruction for women. We are already aware of Veeresalingam's works. Among the lesser-known examples are works by Malladi Suryanarayana Sastri, Telugu pandit in the Board High School at Amalapuram, who authored *Stree Dharma Bodhini* (Kakinada, 1904). Similarly, Mangu Venkata Ranganatha Rao authored *Stree Niti Sangrahamu* in 1914 (Kakinada). Journals published 'instructional materials for women' during the 1930s. For instance, see Manmahopadhyaya Bramhasri Kalluri Venkatarama Sastry, 'Stree Niti Ratnavali', *Bharati*, October 1930, pp. 644–646. This verse was originally written in April 1905. The author requested the heads of various journals 'useful to women' to publish it as he had written it 'for the benefit of women' in a lucid style and in the manner of a mother's advice to a daughter.

[62] Women like Pulugurta Lakshmi Narasamamba, the editor of *Savithri*, authored the *Mahilakalabodhini*, Hevalambi year (English month not given), Madras. Chebrolu Saraswati Devi's *Pativrata Shatakamu* was published in 1931.

unquestioningly submitting to male authority, and specifically to that of their husbands.

All these writings had a single-point agenda of casting women in the mould of the pativratas by inculcating in them morality, good conduct, devotion to husband, submission and self-sacrifice. 'Pativratyamu' was propagated as 'the paragon quality of a woman', which ensured her 'wellbeing in life here and hereafter'.[63] They stressed that 'all wishes of a woman who observed pativratyam would be fulfilled'. But how did one prove herself a pativrata? This was possible only through ensuring complete subordination to the husband! Women were threatened that their life without a husband was 'like a steamer boat without an anchor.'[64] One verse said: 'She [woman] should serve husband like a *dasi* (servant), assist him like a counsellor, feed him sumptuously [like a mother], provide him comforts, abstain from giving him pain, and bear the burden of family like *Panchali*', that is, Draupadi, the polyandrous wife of the Pandavas, heroes of the epic *Mahabharata*.[65]

Another verse instructed: 'Attend to the problems of your husband first; do not believe the words of even your nearest ones if they inform you about your husband's sexual promiscuity, do not question him, do not blame him, do not curse him even in your heart, if you get angry with him'.[66] 'God will bless you in the proportion of your devotion to your husband; treat it to be ignoble to trouble your husband for jewellery; treat him like God however terrible he is', instructed another verse.[67] Yet another verse stated that 'salvation was possible only through devotion and complete subordination to husband'—the self-effacing women would be the first to attain salvation! It suggested:

> Do not reveal your problems to your husband when he returns home tired; [first] give him water to clean his feet, allow him to rest and press his feet, and provide comfort; do not question [your] husband even if he scolds [and brutally beats] you. Only those women attain *mukti* who have [unquestioned] *bhakti* towards their husbands; always pray to him wholeheartedly'.[68]

---

[63] Pulugurta Lakshmi Narasamamba, 'Pativratyamu' (Fidelity), *Savithri*, July 1911, p. 2.

[64] 'Niti Padamulu' (Verses on Morality), *Savithri*, January 1904.

[65] 'Sati Dharmamulu' (Duties of a Chaste Woman), *Savithri*, January 1904.

[66] 'Sati Dharmamulu' (Duties of a Chaste Woman), *Savithri*, February 1904.

[67] 'Stree Dharmamulu' (Duties of a Chaste Woman), *Savithri*, April 1904.

[68] 'Stree Niti Ratnavali' (A String of Jewels on Women's Morality), *Savithri*, October 1904.

Another verse emphasised that 'it was the duty of women to serve men [like a slave].'[69] '*Sadvartanamu*' (good conduct), which brought 'reputation' and was said to ensure the soul's immortality, was seen as the 'most invaluable embellishment' to the character of a woman, and was held to be 'essential' for women than men. 'Bad conduct of a woman caused more harm than [that of] a man', one verse suggested, 'for the latter brought ill-fame to his parents only. But the former tarnished the reputation of both parents and parents-in-law.' To prevent such a situation, *Savithri* provided certain guidelines to women about how they should conduct themselves both within and outside the home, focused on one's conduct with parents-in-law, brothers and sisters-in-law, neighbours, relatives, etc.[70]

Education for Enlightened Subordination

Male social reformers advocated women's education for it was potentially an instrument to instil the desired qualities in women. The *Sathihitha Bodhini* stressed the indispensability of pativratyam for women and appealed to them to inculcate and protect it themselves. It held that only education could ensure and enhance conjugal fidelity among women. Elaborating on the instrumentality of education, the journal's June 1883 issue stated that

> men had been trying hard since ancient times to guard the pativratyam of women [but could not succeed]. Women's chastity could not be protected through the vigilance and supervision of men. It was possible only through the character women themselves acquired and assiduously built by receiving education, and not by the force men employed.[71]

That Veeresalingam published the histories of ancient pativratas like Satyavati and Chandramati to establish them as role models for women is already noted. Modern women were expected to read such histories and fashion themselves along the lines of these pativratas, to the delight of their husbands.

On the 'benefits' of women's education, an article published in the *Telugu Zenana* argued:

> If girls are educated, they gain knowledge and become morally sound; it would [eventually] be useful for their children. They will not remain

[69] 'Stree Niti Deepika' (Illuminator of Women's Morality), *Savithri*, August 1904.
[70] Ibid. See also 'Stree Niti Ratnavali'.
[71] Cited in Potturi Venkateswara Rao, *Andhra Jaati Akshara Sampada*, pp. 107–108.

> the mere slaves of husbands; they become their friends. They learn pativrata *dharma* by themselves, and become humble companions of their husbands.[72]

It was emphasised that 'only when women became educated like men, and moulded themselves according to the designs of men, that the reform efforts would become fruitful without causing much strain [to men!].'[73]

As women were to be prepared for their future careers as wives and mothers, they needed to be properly 'instructed' in household management, and the qualities of a pativrata. Education sharpened their skills in domestic management, and inculcated/enhanced virtues in them. An article published in the 1906 issue of *Telugu Zenana* stated:

> If we observe the performance of the uneducated women in household management, we will appreciate the idea of educating them in domestic science. Though they may fare well in this by virtue of experience, if proper knowledge/education is added to it, they will perform in a much better way. Since they have insufficient knowledge [of domestic science], there are certain defects in their performance. However, with proper education, they will be corrected. A woman, who has the experience of cooking since childhood, can comfortably feed her husband and children. However, if she has the scientific knowledge of cooking, and physiology and health, she will not only cook new varieties, but also keep in mind the weather and physiological conditions while cooking, and thus will protect the health of her nears and dears, and will be appreciated by them. Hence, our women need education to perform their household tasks in an efficient manner.[74]

Educated women proved to be good mothers. Explaining the importance of education in turning women as good nurturing mothers, the very first issue of *Sathihitha Bodhini* stated that 'if a mother was uneducated… she spoilt her children. If she was educated, she took all necessary care in training them at home and thus made them learned and wise.'[75] It published an

[72] Y. Ganganna, who was a teacher in Kakinada, authored it. See 'Iddaru Balikala Sambhashana' (A Dialogue between Two Girls, translation as in original), *Telugu Zenana*, February 1899, pp. 250–252.

[73] R. Krishnamurthi, 'Stree Vidyayokka Prasthuta Sthiti (The Present State of Female Education, translation as in original), *Telugu Zenana*, January 1901, pp. 214–216.

[74] See 'Streela Grihakrityamulu' (Home Duties of Women, translation as in original), *Telugu Zenana*, August 1906, pp. 201–207.

[75] Cited in Potturi Venkateswara Rao, *Andhra Jaati Akshara Sampada*, p. 107.

interesting story that demonstrated the efficacy of educated mothers and claimed that such women would be rewarded. In the story, a king went to supervise a village school. When he had tested the children there, a 'young boy' gave 'good answers' to all his questions. The surprised king asked the teachers whether they had taken a 'special interest' in teaching the child. Replying in the negative, the teachers explained that since his mother was educated, she taught him at home. This was why the child, despite being the youngest, excelled among his classmates. The delighted king gave a present to the child and sent a diamond ornament to his mother.[76]

Therefore, there was a need for girls' schools to include household management in their curriculum, with the aim of eventually turning in the girls to pativratas. The existing curriculum was found to be 'lacking' in this regard. One article observed that the 'incomplete education' that girls were generally made to receive was responsible for their lack of domestic management skills.[77] Hence, it advocated the kind of curriculum found in Belgium, which was seen as the 'most comprehensive course' in girls' schools.[78]

Women's Education Ensures Companionate Conjugality

Women's education was essential to ensure compatibility between spouses. If the husband was educated and the wife was not, it resulted in conjugal incompatibility, culminating in the breakdown of marriage itself. For example, the conjugal life of the very first widow remarriage couple—Gogulapati Sriramulu and Gavaramma—in Andhra[79] did not go smoothly because the husband was educated and the wife was not. Eventually, the

[76] Ibid.

[77] Since girls were not allowed to attend schools for a long time (child marriage was a reason), it was difficult to impart full-fledged instruction in such things as household management and physiology.

[78] It detailed the curriculum followed in the girls' schools in Belgium, which was designed to make women successful *gruhinis*. To mention a few: tailoring, washing clothes, pressing, cooking, maintenance of health and hygiene, managing the hearth, serving food, gardening, personal hygiene, physiology and domesticating poultry. Girls would be trained in successive stages. In the end, it suggested that if Indian girls were to achieve mastery in household management, Belgian type of schools should be started in India and that the government as well as Indians should consider this possibility.

[79] The marriage took place on 11 December 1881.

marriage broke down irretrievably. Veeresalingam analysed the reasons for this:

> The groom, who is trained by me, is brought up in a town, English educated and civilised in modern manners. The bride was brought up in a village, lived amid the village folk, devoid of the scent of education, and is like a beast. Because of this, their opinions did not match in every matter, causing disunity and quarrels. Meanwhile, the mother of the bride, who sided with her, tried to make the son-in-law their slave. As a result, the situation got aggravated reaching a breaking point of the family. I thought that, being married to an educated man, the couple will lead a happy life. But when he planned something, God planned another. Had I married off this girl to an [uneducated, and therefore] uncultured fellow, who approached me for marriage, their life could have been happier.[80]

Educated husbands and uneducated wives did not make a really happy conjugal couple. The 'civilised' husband could not adjust with the 'beast-like' wife; and the beast-like girl, who grew up in villages amid the uncultured village folk, failed to understand and appreciate the sense of culture, civilisation and modernity that her educated husband brought with him. Their tastes and attitudes varied so greatly that such a pairing often resulted in unhappy endings. Therefore, girls needed to be educated so that they understood, appreciated and eventually adjusted to the attitudes of their husbands.

If both the husband and the wife were educated, they got along well with each other. Such men, who had educated wives, were thought to be fortunate and appreciated. *Grihalakshmi*, a male-edited women's journal, celebrated such a bonding by publishing the photograph of newlyweds Mrs Naraharisetty Nagamani and Mr Sheshagiri Rao. Informing readers that Nagamani was the author of a book *Shakuntala*, *Grihalakshmi* jubilantly declared that 'poets getting poetesses as wives was nothing but the fruit of the virtuous lives they led in their previous birth.'[81]

---

[80] Kandukuri Veeresalingam, *Sweeya Charitramu*, part 1, pp. 250–251; see also pp. 387–388.

[81] *Grihalakshmi*, September 1934.

Image 5.2: Newly wedded couple: Naraharisetty Nagamani and Sheshagiri Rao

Source: *Grihalakshmi*, September 1934.

Private Needs and Public Deeds

Why did the issue of women's reformed domesticity occupy such an important place in the women's journals edited by men? Why were reform-oriented men so keen on instructing women in such matters? As we have already observed in the beginning, their personal dissatisfactions with their 'uncouth' young wives also emerged as an important factor behind their advocacy of social reform, particularly women's education. Influenced by

Western culture, they wanted to remodel their domestic life on the lines of their colonial masters, the British. But this was no easy feat: they needed the active 'support' and participation of women. If women did not cooperate, their ideals and aspirations would never be realised. As the 'wide gap' between the 'civilised' husband, who desired his wife to be a 'helpmate' in his endeavours, and the 'uncivilised' wife potentially frustrated their social as well as personal ambitions, they wanted to cast women in a mould suited to them. Let us explain this with examples from the personal lives of Rayasam Venkata Sivudu and K. N. Kesari, who strove for social reform, and as a part of it, published (and also edited) the women's journals–*Telugu Zenana* and *Grihalakshmi*–respectively.

'Intiloni Poru Intintagaadayaa' (Domestic Conflict is Infinite): Rayasam Venkata Sivudu's Domestic Life

Rayasam Venkata Sivudu (1870–1954), editor and publisher of *Telugu Zenana*, provides the best example of this situation. A passionate advocate of social reform right from his youth, he quite unequivocally expressed his utter dissatisfaction with his wife who, being uneducated initially,[82] could not provide him the expected enlightened company. At various places in his autobiography, he vented his annoyance at his 'uncooperative' wife. In 1893, they were 23 and 16 years of age, respectively. He regretted that 'their minds did not at all meet'. On 2 June 1893, he received his monthly salary of Rs. 70. His wife insisted on purchasing kitchenware, but due to his other responsibilities, Sivudu could not allow this, resulting in the eruption of 'conflict' between wife and husband. He lamented that 'his wife charged him with miserliness'.[83] Other matters also contributed to their domestic conflicts. He became angry with her if the food she prepared was 'tasteless'; if she did not read the lessons and write and did not carefully follow his teaching as per his 'orders';[84] and if she indulged in 'superstitious' practices

[82] Later on, she transformed herself according to his wishes and 'made him happy'. She attended several widow remarriages with her husband. Venkata Sivudu mentioned one such marriage in Guntur, at the residence of Devaguptapu Sheshachalapati Rao in the year 1909. *Atma Charitramu*, p. 483. In his short story 'Sarada', he strikingly depicted his wife's transformation into an educated and cultured being. See 'Sarada', *Telugu Zenana*, April (pp. 301–313) and May (pp. 333–335) 1901. See also *Atma Charitramu*, pp. 150–151.

[83] Rayasam Venkata Sivudu, *Atma Charitramu*, pp. 232–233.

[84] Ibid., pp. 235–236.

such as having a holy dip in the Krishna on the occasion of Shivaratri,[85] etc. He 'ordered her to learn English and stop indulging in traditional and superstitious practices. But as she was unable to manage the home affairs all alone, his tutoring appeared to her to be thorny.'[86] He described his wife's condition with a proverb: 'sport to the cat and death to the rat' (*pilliki selagatamu, yelukaku branasankatamanunattuga*),[87] and that of his with a saying of Vemana (a popular medieval Telugu poet) that 'domestic conflict is infinite' (*Intiloni poru intintagaadayaa*).[88]

There was a 'wide gap' in their thinking, tastes and attitudes, resulting in quarrels and domestic turmoil. Venkata Sivudu discussed this at length in his autobiography. The title of one chapter—'Kotta Kodalu–Klishta Paristhitulu' (Difficulties Caused by Young Wife)—speaks volumes of the magnitude of his maladjustment with his wife, and his eventual frustration.[89] The chapter was devoted to narrating his difficulties in living with an 'uneducated' and 'superstitious' wife within the joint family system. So overwhelming was his frustration that, at another point in his book, he came down heavily on 'uneducated' and 'uncultured wives.'[90]

---

[85] Ibid., pp. 312–313. Rayasam Ratnamma went to the river Krishna for a holy dip. This was quite unacceptable to him. In retaliation, that afternoon he ate on a porcelain plate. Ratnamma refused to eat that day because of her being ritually 'polluted'. An enraged Sivudu shouted at her and cajoled her into eating her dinner. As the festival day passed in their home with his shouting and her crying, his brother humorously called it 'chippala Shivaratri'. Ibid., p. 313. A Brahmo, Venkata Sivudu had a strong disliking for Hinduism and idolatry. On 5 September 1893, on the request of his maternal uncle, he took the latter to the Durga temple in Vijayawada, but 'his hands could not rise to pray to that idol'. His uncle got annoyed at his indiscipline. 'I somehow got out of the temple without paying even a penny either to the Goddess or the priest,' he jubilantly noted. Ibid., p. 242.

[86] Ibid., p. 312.

[87] Ibid., p. 236.

[88] Ibid., p. 313.

[89] Ibid., pp. 146–151.

[90] Venkata Sivudu admired companionate couples. He deeply admired Dhanwada Anantam (headmaster of the Mission High School in Vijayawada, where Venkata Sivudu was also employed) and his second wife Soubhagyavati, a native Christian couple. According to him, 'their mutual love was praiseworthy' and that 'he never saw Anantam getting annoyed with his wife, and she being dissatisfied with him.' Their companionate conjugal life (*anukula dampatyamu*) was an 'ideal' for him. The 'Dhanwada couple' used to offer tips to the Venkata Sivudu couple on domestic happiness. Venkata Sivudu held them to be so 'praiseworthy' that he devoted nearly four pages in his autobiography to narrate their family life. See 'Dhanwada Dampatulu' in ibid., pp. 236–239.

In a semi-autobiographical essay titled '*Satiyuta Sangha Samskari*' (A Reformer with [an Uneducated] Wife), Venkata Sivudu vividly described the difficulties faced by an ambitious 'reformer' in the face of his 'uneducated and old-fashioned wife'. He urged readers to treat the narrative as his personal experience. The 'reformer' was wise, highly educated, well-mannered and rational. He possessed exceptional potential, held a modern outlook and was 'full of virtues'. His 'unlettered, superstitious and irrational wife', who grew up like a 'wild beast', however, preferred to wander in the 'wilderness' of ignorance and superstition. She therefore could not appreciate the 'noble ideals' of her 'reformer' husband. 'The wide gulf between the educated husband and the unlettered wife' caused escalating tension in the family, rendering 'all the energies' of the reformer 'useless'. Venkata Sivudu lamented for such a noble man 'fell into the hands' of such a 'wild beast', who 'destroyed his ideals, which were as dear to him as his own life was'. [91]

Expanding on the theme, Sivudu wrote that educated men alone could not be blamed for their failure in solving the social problems of Indian society. Women were also to blame, though to a smaller degree. His rationale was that since 'women had been deprived of education for centuries together', they suffered from backwardness and were not in a position to cooperate with men. The bottom line of his argument was that women's cooperation was a must, if men were to succeed in redeeming Indian society. Since 'a wife was [and needed to be] her husband's *ardhangi*[*ni*]'[92]and *sahadharmacharini* (a companion in life's dharmas/duties), 'she should stand by' and 'offer help to her husband, whose life mission was social reform'.[93] Without education, she was sure to fail to realise the 'worth' of her educated and reform-minded husband, thereby failing to 'appreciate his social actions', and consequently causing him deep frustration. To avoid this, young women/wives needed to be 'carefully tutored'. But the joint family set-up, the epicentre of conservatism, was not conducive to this. Therefore, he advocated 'breaking away from the joint family', which also symbolised old patriarchy, and the 'establishment of a nuclear family', which allowed 'open and uninterrupted interaction between the wife and husband'. 'The Hindu ideal of pativrata dharma, which gave husband dictatorial authority over the wife, should be

[91] *Atma Charitramu*, pp. 367–369.

[92] The idea that the wife is one half of her husband.

[93] Ibid., p. 150.

put to use to accomplish the task,' he stressed.[94] This certainly clarifies why Venkata Sivudu chose to publish *Telugu Zenana*.

'Samsara Sagaram Dukhkham' (The Ocean of Family Life is Woeful): K. N. Kesari with His 'Simpleton' Wife

Such maladjustment seems to have been experienced by a substantial section of English-educated/Western-influenced and reform-minded men. For example, K. N. Kesari, one of the leading figures in the reform movement during the post-Veeresalingam era and editor-publisher of *Grihalakshmi*,[95] explored such a dynamic in great detail in his autobiography, *Naa Chinnanati Muchchatlu*.[96] Kesari married twice and lived in Madras. Reflecting on his first wife Kanakamma's 'failure' in domestic management, he described her as 'very innocent and a simpleton.' Comparing their domestic life with that of their neighbours, an Iyer family, he felt that his conjugal life paled before theirs. Though Mr Iyer and he had the same monthly income (Rs. 20 a month), Iyer saved some money, whereas he could not. This was because Mrs Iyer carefully managed her home, whereas his 'careless' wife 'unmindfully' spent money and 'always fell short of [basic necessities such as] *sarees*'. Being unmindful of her husband's income, she made too many donations to Brahmins. Since she 'lacked in the skill of [properly] cooking, there was always plenty left over', which 'the maid servant and her children ate'. Thus, the unskilled wife allowed wastage, leaving her husband worried.

She was such a 'simpleton' that 'once she had pasted [together] a broken [piece of] jewellery [a gold *jada billa*, worn in the braid] and kept it outside the home for drying up, and forgot [*sic*]'; naturally, somebody stole it! Was it not difficult for the low-income husband to purchase a new one for her? Apart from being 'careless' and a 'simpleton', she had no knowledge of music, unlike her Iyer counterpart, who often melodiously sang the Thyagaraja *kriti*s 'while working in the kitchen or grinding chutney'. His 'old fashioned wife' held the view that 'housewives should not and did not sing', implying that only courtesans or *devadasi*s could do so, and 'simply disliked music'. Kesari, however, was very fond of music, and enjoyed listening to the songs of Mrs Iyer. When he 'advised his wife to learn the good habits from

[94] Ibid., pp. 72–74.

[95] See Chapter 2 of the present volume.

[96] Madras, 1953. The following discussion is based on Chapter 7, 'Toli Kapurapu Muchchatlu' (Tidings on Family Life with the First Wife) in his autobiography, pp. 30–45.

Mangalamba [that is, Mrs Iyer]', a tearful Kanakamma replied that 'there was nothing to learn from the poor lady who sold old *saree*s and firewood to run her home'. His 'superstitious' wife hesitated to take his name before others. 'She was of the opinion that husband and wife should not address each other by their names. So, she objected to his [habit of] addressing [her] by her name as Kanakamma'.

Kesari admired the expertise of Mangalamba in household management. He described it thus:

> **Life and Habits of Mr. and Mrs. Iyer:**
>
> The Tamil housewife kept her kitchen neatly. She swept and wiped the floor and made it shining. She cleaned the vessels and kept them in an *almirah*. It was nice to look at her kitchen.... She never wasted firewood and used only very little quantity. They were very careful about food also and there were no leftovers. They used well water for bathing and boiled water for drinking. They cooked only once a day and, as they were free in the evenings, visited the nearby Chenna Kesava temple along with their children. His monthly salary was Rs. 20/-. He put Rs. 5/- in the savings bank and gave the rest to his wife. She managed her household expenses with this and, out of this, saved Rs. 20/- per annum. She sold old firewood and old clothes and sarees and, in exchange, got glasses and tumblers. With her savings of Rs. 20/- and other small savings, she bought 'Kornad' saree for Deepavali.... She wore this always while going to the temple, on festival occasions as well as working in the kitchen and while sleeping. She washed it daily and it always looked new. She had some old ones also and had no shortage of sarees. She never slept in the afternoons. She passed her time stitching, reading or making *appalam*s. When her baby cried, she used to put her to sleep by singing lullabies. She sang devotional songs of Thyagaraja and Purandaradasa, which I used to hear. Mangalamba took her bath daily in the morning and dressed neatly. She was neat and had good habits.... Iyer now and then called his wife Mangalam for one thing or the other and they spent their spare time playing cards.[97]

This was in contrast to his wife Kanakamma's domestic management:

> **My Wife's Housekeeping:**
>
> I shall [now] narrate my wife managing household duties. She used to wipe her kitchen with water mixed with cow dung. So, one had to be careful while stepping into the kitchen.... She stored firewood in the kitchen and, on one side of it, the kitchen utensils and other things....

[97] Ibid.

> She kept all kinds of old vessels in the kitchen. She would keep firewood burning and then go for a bath. By the time she returned, the whole house would be filled with so much smoke that it was difficult to see anything.... Curries, pickles and chutneys were essential every day. At night also, buttermilk, *gongoora* and other pickles were served. On Fridays, she made some tiffin as *naivedyam*. On Saturdays, she made some *palaharam*s for Lord Venkateswara. She observed *vratam* and never gave me any of these things to eat, saying that she would not be observing the *vratam* properly, if she did so. We used ghee for curries and it was costly. My salary was not even sufficient to buy ghee. In those days, its cost was Rs. 1-4-0 per *visse*.... She engaged a maidservant to wash her clothes. The servant maid was careless and the sarees were torn in no time. My wife used to wear silk sarees for wedding functions. She would wipe her hands full of ghee in that saree and would fling it in a corner after reaching home. With the saree smelling of ghee, rats would make a hundred holes in that. After that, she would give it to the servants.... So, being careless, she was always short of sarees.... She did not have a knack for cooking. There was always plenty left over and the maidservant and her children ate them.... She was not good at stitching or making *appalam*s. So, in the afternoons, she slept. While working in the kitchen or grinding chutney, she used to sing old songs, which her mother had taught her. She hated the Tamil lady singing Thyagaraja krithis and would say that housewives should not sing.... She used to give as gifts to a Brahmin, dal and potatoes to get rid of *graha*s [evil forces].... She was of the opinion that husband and wife should not address each other by their names. So, she was against my addressing her as Kanakamma.... My wife was of a timid nature. When cats made noises during the nights, she would say thieves were coming. When tree branches moved due to [a] breeze, she would say that some evil spirits were doing that. In the morning, she would worship to please that evil spirit. *Mantravadi*s [experts in magical charms] used to come and tie talisman. She had many talismans around her neck.[98]

Concluding that there was a 'vast difference between Tamil and Telugu housewives', he exclaimed, 'this was how the Telugu housewife was'. It was hard to believe how he had been able to meet his family expenses with such a small income' sharing life with an 'unskillful', 'careless', 'superstitious' and 'foolish' wife.[99] Hence, he shouldered the burden of civilising such 'unwise' and uncivilised women by publishing a journal for them.

---

[98] Ibid.

[99] There was no dearth of 'foolish' women in the world, Kesari felt. At another place, he condemned a 'foolish mother' who, being ignorant of children's health, 'poured sizzling water over the head of her daughter to kill the lice in her hair. She had been doing

'Ille Swargamu': 'Blessed' Kaleswara Rao's Life with a 'Cooperative' Wife

Apart from Veeresalingam, there were a few other 'lucky' men who enjoyed the blissful company of their 'considerate', 'cooperative' and 'companionate' wives. Ayyadevara Kaleswara Rao, a prominent leader of social reform movement in the post-Veeresalingam period and also a veteran nationalist leader who occupied various political positions of eminence in independent India/Andhra, was one among them. He married in 1894. At the time of their marriage, he was 14 years old and his wife, Subbamma (her name was changed to Durgamba after marriage) was 10. In his autobiography, he described his wife's 'cooperation' in his varied public activism:

> [After the death of my mother] my wife Durgamba took over the responsibility of our home. In terms of efficiency, spirituality and treatment of the guests, she followed in the footsteps of my mother and ensured our family honour well. She happily got the food cooked for the many guests that I invited [without informing her in advance]. She cooked herself if the domestic help was not available.... She encouraged me in all the good activities. She made my life very peaceful and comfortable.... When I had decided to practice reforms such as widow remarriage, dining with the post-puberty marriage couples and accommodating the Harijans at home, etc. in my home itself, she completely conducted according to my wishes without any hesitation. Convincing her was very easy for me.... Though she worships *Ammavaru* [Kanaka Durgamma, worshipped in idol form], she used to recite the monotheistic Brahmo hymns and the devotional Bhakta Chintamani poems. She used to read the *Bhagavatam*. Because of the blessings of God, such a noble *saadhvimani* [jewel-like virtuous woman] became my *dharma patni* [dutiful wife].... My wife, my elder sister and my younger sister—all three of them got habituated to dining with the widow remarriage couples, couples of the post-puberty marriages and those who returned from foreign countries, if they were Brahmins.... But, later, as I invite and dine with not only the non-Brahmins but also with the *Mala*s and *Madiga*s, Muslims, Christians and foreign nationals at my home, my wife and my sisters are helping me [with their cooperation]. Once, a Sanskrit student of Japanese nationality lived in our home for a week and dined with us. Ms Tennent, an American

---

that for the past many days. No wonder, the daughter was reduced to a lunatic.' 'What a nice remedy to kill bugs and lice! I was also born in the same country, you know!' he remarked sarcastically. 'Toli Kapurapu Muchchatlu' (Tidings on Family Life with the First Wife), in his autobiography, *Naa Chinnanati Muchchatlu*, pp. 30–45.

> woman lived in our home and dined with me. As I dined in the homes of people of different castes and religions, removed the sacred thread, and stopped observing the death related rituals, my wife and my sister did not object at all.[100]

The examples we have furnished above confirm the observations made by Judith E. Walsh (in the context of Bengali domestic manuals in the late nineteenth century):

> The motivations of these men were not entirely, or perhaps not at all, altruistic. Although men might speak and write of women's emancipation and greater freedom in this period [late nineteenth and early twentieth centuries], a central point of new patriarchy's reforms was... to create women whose morality, conduct, attitudes, and ideas would be more appropriately adjusted to their husbands' needs in British ruled India.[101]

This can be further corroborated by K. N. Kesari's annoyance at women who, at a later stage, that is, from the 1930s on, began to question and severely condemn male domination and double standards. His frustration increased as a section of women appeared to be slipping out of the clutches of the new patriarchs. Perturbed by the pointed attacks on men and male domination, the irked editor was prompted to warn that 'women should avoid the mindless condemnation of men, be friendly with them, and work for the improvement of women by taking men into confidence'.[102] At another place, he reminded women of the 'natural' differences that existed between women and men and the responsibility of women in performing their respective 'duties'. They were warned not to ape 'western values and culture' and 'demand' unnatural 'rights'.[103]

Such stern warning and emotional blackmail only indicated that the new patriarchs did not want to lose control over women. They did not at all like women developing wings to fly away from the wider cage created by 'new patriarchy'. The irony was that a section of women successfully made use of the spaces created by reformist patriarchs and broke the iron bars of the cage in their mental plane. It is paradoxical that the textual space of

---

[100] Ayyadevara Kaleswara Rao, *Navyandhramu*: *Naa Jeevita Katha*, pp. 21 & 158–160.

[101] Judith E. Walsh, *Domesticity in Colonial India* (New Delhi, 2004), p. 110.

[102] See 'Sampadakiyamu: Vudyamabhivruddhiki Ninda Yeduruchukka' (Editorial: Accusing [Men] is an Obstacle to the Advancement of the Women's Movement), *Grihalakshmi*, March 1938, pp. 70–71.

[103] See 'Sampadakiyamu' (Editorial), *Grihalakshmi*, January 1939, pp. 809–810.

women's journals like *Grihalakshmi*, run by the liberal patriarch Kesari, was used by women to craft the tools for breaking out of the iron cage.

As this discussion demonstrates, by visualising women primarily as housewives and mothers, by emphasising women's place and role at home, and by systematically informing and exhorting them to master the intricacies of household management, women's journals edited by men neatly put forth the patriarchal sexual division of labour. The journals feverishly advocated women's education, not to make them independent individuals who, with the aid of education, would realise their potential for self-fulfilment, but to encourage them to mould themselves according to the designs of men, assuming the incarnation of companionate wives who would offer enlightened company to their Western-influenced husbands.

Thus, women's journals, particularly those edited by men during the late-nineteenth and early-twentieth centuries, attempted to scrupulously sculpt a 'new woman', the sophisticated *Grihalakshmi*. The new woman, being educated, successfully removes herself from her previous condition where like a 'wild beast' she 'wandered in the wilderness of ignorance', causing embarrassment and frustration to her colonially modern and 'cultured' husband. By fashioning herself on the lines of the husband's designs and aspirations, she not only offers him the desired enlightened company at home, but also appreciates his social ventures, and aids him in all his social actions. By offering her fullest cooperation in such matters, she makes her husband's tasks at home and in society easy. As a skilful manager of the home, she turns it into a 'sweet home'.

By editing and publishing women's journals, mainly before the 1920s, male social reformers in Andhra meticulously performed the job of reducing women to mere 'shadows' of their husbands. With the help of women's journals, they firmly implanted the 'new patriarchy'. This new patriarchy, despite offering women relative freedom, represented a wider cage. Reform-oriented new patriarchs desired to lock women in the widened cage, and keep the keys safely in their coat pockets.

Women's Early Responses to Male Reformers' Prescriptions

In these circumstances, how did women respond to the new patriarchal prescriptions of men? Did all of them accept all these ideas silently? Or were there some who held a different view? Initially, women seem to have accepted these views, but gradually they began to question and even reject such prescriptions.

Bhandaru Atchamamba (1874–1905), the leading woman activist-intellectual from the 1890s to the beginning of the twentieth century, echoed the perspective of the male social reformers. Her short stories[104] best represent the way women intellectuals in the early decades of the twentieth century *positively* responded to the prescriptions of male social reformers concerning the image of ideal woman/wife. Through her stories, she propagated modern reformist ideas about the conjugal relationship and the qualities of a companionate wife. The stories aimed to inculcate among women the virtues discussed earlier in this chapter: prudence, frugality, industriousness and avoiding indolence at all costs; devotion to one's husband and supporting him even in the most difficult circumstances; gently correcting husbands if they were found to be treading dishonest paths such as corruption; ensuring proper childcare and household hygiene, etc. Atchamamba's short story, 'Gunavatiyagu Stree' begins by defining one aspect of the ideal woman:

> It is not a big thing [for a woman] to run the home well, if her husband is rich. But, if he is poor, it is very difficult to somehow run the home with whatever little is available at hand and keep him happy without causing trouble.... a woman [*sati*] who learns to manage her home prudently is called a virtuous woman[*gunavati*]....[105]

To illustrate this aspect of ideal womanhood, Atchamamba retold a story from Dandin's *Dashakumara Charitam*.

---

[104]The first woman short story writer in Telugu, she authored 11 short stories, as per the available records. Recently, some of them have been compiled and published in the form of a book. See Sangisetty Srinivas ed., *Bhandaru Atchamamba Toli Telugu Kathalu* (Hyderabad, 2010). Srinivas mistakenly attributed the authorship of the story titled 'Janakamma' to Atchamamba. The first two stories of Atchamamba were discovered by Shaik Mahaboob Basha. See 'Achcha'myna Maro Rendu Toli Kathalu' (Two Earlier Telugu Short Stories), *Andhra Jyothy*, 19 August 2013. A feminist scholar has recently compiled some of the speeches and essays of Atchamamba. See Kondaveeti Satyavati, *Bhandaru Atchamamba Sachcharitra* (Hyderabad, 2012).

[105]*Telugu Zenana*, May 1901, pp. 344–346. In English, the title is translated as 'A Prudent House-Wife'. It was the tradition in those days to give the English translations of the titles.

Image 5.3: Bhandaru Atchamamba

Source: *Hindu Sundary*, September–October 1903.

Shaktikumarudu, the son of a rich merchant in Kanchipuram, wanted to marry a 'prudent' girl who could provide him sumptuous food with merely a handful of paddy, and no other provisions. Only one girl came forward to meet his challenge. She husked the paddy for fine rice and asked her mother to sell the husk to a blacksmith. With this money, she purchased dried firewood and earthen pots. Gently pounding the rice to make rice-powder, she boiled the rice and kept aside the starch. Using firewood to make coal, she sold the coal and used the money to buy curd, tamarind, chilly, salt and vegetables. Along with the rice-powder already on hand, she used this stock to make a curry and two chutneys, and the starch to prepare soup.[106] Shaktikumarudu ate the gently served food with immense

[106] It is very interesting that first she offers him soup and serves food later. I wonder if soup culture (i.e., consuming soup before food) is Indian. This must certainly have been

gratification. Satisfied with her skillfulness at household management, he married her. However, he put her to further tests, conducting himself badly, treating his wife with cruelty, and even bringing home a 'prostitute'. Despite her anguish, the woman did not even hint at her unhappiness and continued to treat him 'like God', and the 'prostitute' as a 'sister'. Because of her 'kindness', the domestic help faithfully followed her orders. Convinced with all these things, the husband left the entire burden of managing the home to her and enjoyed his life fully.

In 'Prema Parikshanamu'[107] (The Test of Love; translation as in original), the husband, a petty employee, wanted to test his wife's love for him as well as her patience and courage. He lied to her that he lost his job and even the bank where they had some deposits had folded. Pretending that he was extremely aggrieved, he reminded her of how pompously they had celebrated the previous year's Deepavali—he had bought her a costly Benaras saree, which he would not be able to do this year. He also expressed concern about their daily meals and household upkeep without servants. Although the wife was alarmed by this news, she mustered her courage and told him not to worry much and spoil his health. She suggested that he should sell her gold ornaments for sustenance while searching for a new job. She dismissed the domestic help and undertook housework herself. When the husband expressed regret for her difficult situation, she confidently stated,

> I can easily handle any amount of difficult work myself. It is Draupadi's love for her husbands that made her [happily accept] any number of troubles you know. If we are affectionate to each other and run our home carefully, what can this Goddess of poverty do to us?

The husband finally reveals the truth, stating that he knew his wife was virtuous but still wanted to test her. 'I am overjoyed that I have got such a wife. It is not an exaggeration to say that, if everyone in the world gets such a virtuous wife, heaven will be here [on earth itself],' he wishes. Thus, Atchamamba's central message through this story is that women should not lose heart even in the worst of circumstances and should stand by their husbands.

Women's 'craving' for luxurious items such as silk sarees and jewellery and the 'humiliating' consequences of 'borrowing' such things from others

---

a result of British food habits. However, the poor had soup (*ganji*) because they could not afford proper food.

[107] *Telugu Zenana*, July 1898, pp. 193–198.

is the theme of 'Yeruvala Sommu Baruvula Chetu' (Story of a Golden Nose-Ring).[108] The wife in the story, Janakamma, loved luxuries and extravagance and was a braggart. Her disgust for housework demonstrated her 'indolence'. Unmindful of her husband Rammoorthy's income, she made too many demands. 'Though her husband is a very good person', the narrator tells us, she always complained against him. So demanding was she that she told her husband to buy only the prized Benaras saree, and nothing less, 'whatever may be its cost'. She demanded a nose-ring telling him to borrow some 50–60 rupees.

Janakamma borrowed a nose-ring and leg-chains from a neighbour in order to participate in a function. Her 'false pride' was satisfied by the praise she garnered and she was overjoyed. However, on returning home she found that the nose-ring was missing. The owner demanded that she pay its cost, a sum of Rs. 300. The other women abused her carelessness, causing public humiliation. Her husband had to take up additional work to pay off the debt. Janakamma was thus forced to confront the consequences of living beyond her means and began to repent. This incident fuelled a transformation: she began to do housework herself and stopped coveting luxuries. One fine day, she luckily found the nose-ring in a corner of her house, enabling the couple to free themselves of their loan. The story thus ended on a happy note:

> From then on, Janakamma abandons all her previous bad qualities and starts conducting well as per the wishes of her husband. Carefully using the money Rammoorthy earned by hard work and avoiding all possible wastage, she saves at least 300 rupees by every Sankranti festival.... Because of Janakamma's heartening home management... they soon became rich.... But [our] Janakamma never forgot the borrowed nose-ring![109]

---

[108] Literally, it means 'borrowing brings humiliation'. *Telugu Zenana*, September 1898, pp. 89–96. Writing in 1940, the woman writer of a domestic manual observed that 'women borrowed jewels from others to attend functions such as marriage. By chance, if they lost the ornaments, it would not only cause great monetary loss but also bring humiliation. Not only that; even if the borrower returned them, the lender might say that they were not returned. Or, the borrower might argue that she returned them, even if she never did. Therefore, not just borrowing, even lending of ornaments was not good. They cause quarrels.' Vempati Sharada Devi, *Stree Hitabodhini*, pp. 52–53.

[109] Another story, 'Bharyabhartala Samvadamu: Nagalanugoorchi' (Dialogue between Wife and Husband on Jewellery), discourages women's craving for jewellery. In the story, the not-so-wealthy but intelligent husband persuades his wife not to covet jewellery beyond their means. He instead points to the 'God-given ornaments' of 'obedience, gentleness, modesty, virtuosity, serenity [and simplicity], truthfulness,

Venkatamma, the protagonist in Atchamamba's 'Beeda Kutumbamu' (Poor Household), was diametrically opposed to Janakamma.[110] The widowed Venkatamma worked hard 'day and night', husking paddy and grinding wheat while also raising her six children. Wherever she went for work, she would confine herself only to her assigned tasks and consciously avoid idle chatter and gossip. She raised her children in such a disciplined way that they never asked others for alms, aid or food, nor were they ever unclean. She sewed their clothes herself and her daughter washed them. Atchamamba's friend was 'amazed at the way Venkatamma brought up her children'. Being educated, she read some good books when she found the time and supervised her children's studies. As a result, her sons became highly accomplished and her daughter was married to an affluent family. The story presented a widowed woman's spirit of liveliness and uprightness.

In 'Dhana Trayodashi'[111], the protagonist Vijayalakshmi reformed her husband, Venkataratnam, a petty clerk earning Rs. 10 a month, after he trod the wrong path by stealing a hundred rupees in his employer's home. She refused to accept it and pressurised him to return the 'theft money' (*donga sommu*), questioning the need for it when neither she nor their children ever asked for clothes and luxuries. Even as she felt duty-bound to correct him, Vijaylakshmi was mindful of her role: 'Though she gets extremely angry her eyes turning red, she does not forget that he is her husband and it is inappropriate on her part to shout at and abuse him'. She always eagerly awaited her husband's return from the office, received him with a smile, and reassured him that she did not need anything beyond his love.

In another short story, 'Bharya Bhartala Samvadamu: Stree Vidya'[112] (A Dialogue between Husband and Wife on Women's Education), the

---

compassion, helpfulness, etc.' that are already in her possession. The beauty brought by gold ornaments, the story emphasised, is only temporary. But the beauty one acquires through the ornaments of virtues is everlasting. The Puranic pativrata Savitri's legacy persists not because of her gold ornaments, but rather the 'jewels' of virtue she possessed. The husband asserts that 'no language has the vocabulary to describe those decorated with the ornaments of virtues. If our country's women stop craving for these illusionary [gold] ornaments at least now and strive to acquire the ornaments of virtues, there is no doubt that our country will outshine all other countries in the world.' See *Hindu Sundary*, August 1903, pp. 6–11.

[110] *Savithri,* 1 (2 and 3), February 1904. Atchamamba retold the 'real story of a virtuous woman' narrated to her by her friend [Sattiraju Shyamalamba].

[111] *Hindu Sundary* 1, 8 November 1902, pp. 1–19. Dhana Trayodashi is the Telugu version of the festival Dhanteras. The story takes place in Bombay city.

[112] *Hindu Sundary*, December 1902, pp. 1–10.

husband persuaded his uneducated wife to receive education. The husband contended that the wife 'cannot fulfill her duty completely, if she remains uneducated'. The educated woman maintains household accounts by herself, allowing her husband proper rest after a day's hard work. She could read her husband's letters when he was away from home—only then could the husband freely reveal his heart's feelings for her. Were she uneducated, he could not do so because she would have them read by others, revealing the romance-filled secrets of his heart, and causing him embarrassment and shame! Moreover, if a mother was educated and virtuous, her children would follow suit: even the training provided by ten teachers could not match the training a mother provides her children.

Having thus been tutored in the 'advantages of women's education,' the wife dramatically assured her husband:

> *My Lord*! Do I disobey your order? If you want me to receive education, I will start right from tomorrow. Even if I remain uneducated [and] stupid, [still] I strongly feel that I have no other God other than the husband, and that it is my most important duty to obey his order. I do not fear, even if my grandmother gets angry, and the neighbours ridicule and laugh at me. Obeying your order, I will educate myself, and please you.[113] (Emphasis mine.)

Many women thought in the same way. Valiveti Balatripura Sundaramma stated in a lecture at the women's conference (*zenana sabha*) at Rajam in 1903:

---

[113] *Hindu Sundary*, December 1902, pp. 6–7. However, in 'Dampatula Prathama Kalaham' (The First Dispute of a Wife, translation as in original), another story, the obstinate wife [*kachche pilla*] is persuaded by her grandmother to unquestioningly submit to her modern, educated husband. The husband asks her to accompany him for a play, along with his colleagues and their wives. The stubborn wife refuses to join him. When he tells her that the money spent on tickets would be wasted, she questions if he asked her before purchasing the tickets and scornfully says that 'it is not possible for her to join him for she has to go to some other place.' Further, she says that 'it is not possible for her to fulfill [all] his desires because she is not his slave to conduct according to his wishes.' The husband is enraged and leaves the house, while the wife too leaves for her grandmother's home. Lalita (the wife) narrates the matter to her grandmother who, in turn, narrates her own sad story that because of such obstinacy she had displayed, her husband left her forever. Struck with a fear of repeating this history, Lalita apologises to her husband, assuring him that she will never repeat 'such a crime' and 'falls at his feet'. 'From that day onward, as Lalita has changed her mindset, never again such a dispute took place between them and they lived happily. With this, their first dispute became the last.' *Hindu Sundary*, June 1902.

> The duties of men and women are clearly laid down in the world. The educated women can discharge their duties easily and in a better manner than the uneducated ones. By undertaking the domestic responsibilities with alertness, they save men from taking pains [in the domestic domain]. They will raise their children well. They will come to know children's needs and fulfill them, and will correct the defects in them. They will be able to read some spiritual books and can distinguish between *paap* [sin] and *punya* [virtue]. They shed their bad habits/qualities and turn good.... For all the above reasons, women need education.[114]

Emphasising the importance of education to women, Achanta Rukminamma wrote that 'what the art of sculpture was to stones, education was to human mind. Education would bloom human mind and help realise its energies'.[115] Citing Carlyle, the English poet who reportedly said that 'people without education were like a human being without hands and legs' and that 'depriving men and women of the advantages of education was like chopping off their hands and pulling out their eyes', she said that 'our learned scholars [Indians] have also said that "one without education was a strange animal"'. But 'it was extremely saddening that despite knowing well the benefits of education, our men made women illiterate and superstitious'. Reflecting on the 'present status of women's education', she observed that, despite being in the contact of the Europeans for more than one century, women's education in India could not 'go beyond the initial stage'.[116] Indian Christians showed 'great enthusiasm for education', she wrote, and 'gave higher examinations... competing with men equally'. Native Christian women became doctors, nurses, etc. Rukminamma exhorted her readers: 'Just look at them. Though they are very few in number, they are removing the difficulties of many people' simply by virtue of their education.[117] However, she still proposed role-based education for girls:

---

[114] *Hindu Sundary*, July 1903, pp. 17–19.

[115] Achanta Rukminamma, 'Stree Vidya, Vivahamunaku Tagina Vayassu (Suitable Age for Women's Education and Marriage), *Hindu Sundary*, February 1912, pp. 20–25.

[116] Ibid., p. 21.

[117] 'You must have heard of the wife of Dr. S. Satyanathan [Kamala Sattianadhan], who is the editor of *Indian Ladies' Magazine*. You must have heard of Mrs. Krishnamma, wife of Mr. Hensman. Both of them have given M.A. Exams. The people of the entire Madras Presidency [*sic*], particularly the Telugus, should be proud of them', she stressed. She urged Hindu women to compete with Christian women by receiving education: 'We have among us [Hindus] Brahmin girls and girls of reputable families, who are not only equal to them [native Christian women], but are rather more intelligent than them. Why cannot they aspire for attaining higher education? I am afraid that, if our

> Education does not mean memorisation of [a few] books: this is equally true for both men and women. While girls are in schools, certainly they should be taught domestic management and child-rearing. They should be provided training in morality. There should be a provision for physical exercises to make the bodies strong. Some say that, if given education, girls will spend wasting time reading bad stories and Puranas and will not undertake household work. I do not agree with that view. My opinion is that they read during the leisure time and will carry out housework as well. Sometimes, when they get too restless, reading books will help them gain peace of mind. With such reading, they will perform housework much better than before.... [Therefore], I am emphasising that educated women will be more suitable to shoulder the burden of family than the uneducated ones.[118]

Even when women talked about the need for 'higher education' to women, they actually meant not the attainment of bachelor's degrees, but the perfect mastery of the art of domestic management. Kallepalle Venkata Ramanamma's article, 'Streela Vunnata Vidya' (Higher Education of Women), amply attests this. She wrote:

> Since there are a few bachelor degree holders among women, it is generally assumed that women's higher education implies obtaining a bachelor degree. This opinion hinders our progress... Earning money like men is not the task of women. Their duty is to manage the household affairs. Therefore, women need education in the subjects like natural science, morality, primary health, cooking, childrearing, stitching, music and the histories of the Pativratas, which suits [and will be helpful in] their work. Women need to have the capacity to study and comprehend these subjects. If they are well versed in these subjects, they will/ should be considered to be highly educated. Even the graduates cannot match them.[119]

---

country's women remain like this without receiving education, our *Bharatakhandamu* [India] will never develop. Is not it true that the future greatness of the country rests on our children? How can they turn wise, if the mothers, who are supposed to educate their children, remain foolish'. Ibid.

[118] Ibid., pp. 23–24.

[119] Kallepalle Venkata Ramanamma, 'Streela Vunnata Vidya' (Higher Education of Women), *Savithri*, October, November and December 1911, pp. 15–19. For similar views, see also K. Kanakamma, 'Streela Vunnata Vidya' (Higher Education of Women), *Savithri*, 1911, pp. 1–7; Pulugurta Lakshmi Narasamamaba, 'Streela Vunnata Vidya' (Higher Education of Women), *Hindu Sundary*, May 1903, pp. 5–15.

Such a view persisted through the 1920s–1940s. Delivering a lecture at the All-Andhra Women's Conference (also referred to as the Andhra Rashtra Mahila Mahasabha) held at Bejawada in 1929, Turlapati Rajeshwaramma said:

> Women do not need all those elements of education which men need. Men learn to earn a living; women should learn just for the sake of knowledge. Women generally do not need jobs. Therefore, they need only that kind of education which inculcates in them morality, patriotism, devotion to God and husband and prepares them as good mothers, better housewives and Veeramatas [mothers of brave men].[120]

N. Rajyalakshmamma felt that women needed such an education which enabled them to perform their domestic 'responsibilities' with enhanced skills. In her words:

> Women need education to skillfully manage the household affairs—to keep the home clean and attractive, and to look after the health of the family members, especially children. They should be taught financial management, respecting husband, parents-in-law and friends.... Women do not need education for earning a livelihood. This is the duty of husbands/ men.... If a husband does not allow his wife to take up a job [requiring her going outside the home], he should not be treated as selfish.... Can the husband look after the home, if a wife takes up a job outside the home? Certainly, he cannot.... [Then] what will happen to children, who cry for milk? If both husband and wife take up jobs outside, who will look after the children?[121]

Women's Assertions

However, a careful examination of women's writings in journals such as *Hindu Sundary*, *Grihalakshmi* and *Andhra Mahila* which were also edited by women reveals that a substantial section had begun to question the new patriarchal prescriptions by the end of the 1910s. This, however, is not to suggest that such writings were totally absent before that, though

---

[120] Turlapati Rajeshwaramma, 'Andhra Mahila Sabha–Bejawarda', *Grihalakshmi*, 1929, p. 902.

[121] N. Rajyalakshmamma, 'Streelaketti Vidya Avasaramu?' (What Kind of Education Do Women Need?), *Grihalakshmi*, August 1930, pp. 430–431. For similar views, see also Atluri Sitalakshmamma, 'Sanatana Dharmamu: Stree-Purusha Hakkulu' (Rights of Women and Men in the Sanatana Dharma), *Grihalakshmi*, 1933, p. 216.

they were fewer. Women's questioning ranged from demands for equality of opportunity in education, to their assertion that they were not weak, but possessed physical as well as intellectual strength equal to that of men; they rejected the sanctity of Hindu scriptures and launched a scathing attack on male domination in both family and society.

Women Reject a Separate Curriculum

As we have observed, a number of women intellectuals consented to receiving gender-segregated education. However, there were many others who opposed role-based education and the idea of a separate curriculum for women and men, and stressed that there should be no restrictions in matters concerning education. Women intellectuals put forth such ideas from the very beginning of the twentieth century.

Unnava Lakshmibayamma, the celebrated educationist, social reformer and freedom fighter, took serious issue with men for speaking against women's higher education. Referring to a meeting held on 27 October 1903 at Mission College, Guntur, where men spoke against higher educational opportunities for women, she chided them for being narrow-minded, asking them to look to the examples of Pandita Ramabai, Raghumabai Kelkar, Bhandaru Atchamamba, Kotikalapudi Sitamma, Peddibhotla Venkata Subbamma and others, who had attained higher education and become famous. She warned men not to be 'narrow-minded'. If they continued to hold such views, it would be 'dangerous' to the advancement of India. She stressed that women had the right to higher education and they should acquire higher degrees like the BA.[122]

Over the 1930s and 1940s, the demand for higher education for women grew rapidly, stressing on women's 'choice'. Women intellectuals like Nandagiri Indira Devi emphasised that women needed education for self-fulfilment, as a means to their economic independence and to ensure their individuality. It was their conviction that women must receive any branch of knowledge as per their choice. Admonishing the proponents of a separate curriculum for women, Nandagiri Indira Devi wrote:

> Nobody has the authority to compel either women or men to receive a particular kind of education.... Women and men can receive education according to their choice and objective. If a girl is interested in joining the

[122] Unnava Lakshmibayamma, 'Stree Vidya' (Women's Education), *Hindu Sundary*, November 1903, pp. 14–16.

> army by receiving the relevant education, she should not be forced away from doing it. In the same way, if a boy wants to learn cooking, he should have the opportunity to do so.[123]

Similarly, 'Satya' (a pseudonym) wrote in *Andhra Mahila* that 'education was the birth right of women as well as men. For the progress of the nation, both should be educated. Women should have equal right to men in terms of receiving education.' She emphasised the importance of the same curriculum for both women and men:

> Women need the same curriculum as men.... Women can excel in all professions such as medicine, engineering, and teaching and they can become scientists even. Therefore, there should be an opportunity and the environment to allow women to realise their right to receive education in any branch of knowledge [as per their choice].[124]

'Stree Abala Kaadu': Women are Not Physically Weak

The twentieth century brought with it a new self-confidence and positive self-concept among educated Andhra women. The publication of Bhandaru Atchamamba's *Abala Sachcharitra Ratnamala*[125] (History of Noble Women) in 1901 is a watershed moment.[126] The book's significance lies not only in its contents, but also the aims with which it was written. The author outlined her objectives thus:

[123] Nandagiri Indira Devi, 'Vanitaloka Samskaranamu' (Reforming the World of Women), *Grihalakshmi*, 1938, p. 908.

[124] 'Satya' (pseudonym), 'Streela Pradhana Samasyalu: Vidya' (The Main Problems Faced by Women: Education), *Andhra Mahila*, April 1946, pp. 11–12.

[125] The book contains the brief history of women heroes like the Queens Durgavati, Chand Bibi and Lakshmibai of Jhansi, and modern women like Anandibai Joshee. She put admirable effort to collect information from Marathi and Hindi, etc. She understood the power of history so well to say that a message communicated through historical examples (*nijamyna charitra*) would leave more impact and was, therefore, more fruitful than the mere sermonising texts (*upadesha grandhamulu*) and fiction (*kalpana kathalu*).

[126] This was also the time when Andhra women began to organise themselves and publish women's journals. We have already learnt that the first women's organisation, the Aska Stree Samajamu, was established in September 1902. The first All-Andhra women's conference was held in 1910. Thus the first decade of the twentieth century was extremely significant in terms of women's rising consciousness and accelerating movement. Women began editing the first women's journal *Hindu Sundary* in December 1903 and the second women-edited journal, *Savithri*, in January 1904.

1. Some people [claim] that women are weak, foolish and unwise and are home to all bad qualities. My first objective is to prove that all these attributes imposed upon women are false and that there were women who were extremely courageous and valorous, extraordinarily educated scholars, exceptional administrators, patriots, repositories of all virtues, and such women are found even in the present. Apart from this, I would like to establish that women instinctively move in the direction of virtuosity and not the wicked way.
2. Some great men [*mahanubhavulu*] emphasise that, if women are educated and given freedom and independence, they will be spoilt, disrespect and humiliate their husbands and destroy family peace. My second objective is to prove with examples that these allegations are baseless and that women's education can help remove evils than contribute to them and that women's education and freedom are very helpful to our nation than being harmful and that women's education is indispensable.
3. My third objective is writing a book which will provide useful entertainment combined with a message to the women in Andhra. It is known to all that message communicated through real history will be more fruitful than the mere sermonising texts and fiction. Therefore, through the real histories of these women, I want to communicate with my Andhra sisters on issues such as pativratya, love for the country/patriotism and women's education.[127]

This indicates the emerging level of confidence of at least some women of Andhra. Almost all the women intellectuals in Andhra refused to accept the idea of their being '*abala*'; they consistently argued that they were '*sabala*' both physically and intellectually. They condemned the patriarchal idea that women were 'inferior' to men. This contestation was so important that the question of women's being abala or otherwise formed the topic of essay writing competitions for women. In 1930, the Progressive Union at Nellore conducted an essay-writing competition to women on the topic 'Stree Abala Kaadu' (Woman Is Not Weak). Kanuparti Varalakshmamma's essay was adjudged best out of a total of 12 submissions and awarded the 'Kesari

[127] See 'Upodghatamu' (Introduction) in the book. It is pertinent to make an important observation here. Though she vehemently refuted the patriarchal idea that women were 'weak', her book's title begins with the word 'abala'. Literally, the title of the book may be translated as *The Good Histories of the Weak*! In Telugu, 'abala' was/is synonymous with woman. The time for questioning patriarchal vocabularies was yet to come. At times, women put the idea of 'abala' to a strategic use to tilt the argument in women's favour and to their advantage.

Gold Medal'. The *Grihalakshmi* published all the essays in order of merit. While Varalakshmamma's essay was published in full, important excerpts were published from other women's essays.[128] All of them were united in rejecting the idea that women were weak and inferior to men. They confidently stated that women were not only equal to men but also superior to them in some respects. They based their arguments on the grounds of medical science, biological constitution of women, reproductive capacities, the work of women scientists, innovators and professionals, census reports, women's domestic work and other forms of labour, etc.

In her first-prize essay, which comprehensively refuted the argument that women were physically and intellectually weaker than men, Kanuparti Varalakshmamma drew from a number of figures, from ancient times to the present.[129] She wrote that in India, woman had always been considered an 'offshoot of *Shakti*, which meant power'. Questioning how an offshoot of *Shakti* could be called *abala*, she argued that women possessed a special power, 'the soul force, which was unmatched'.[130] She cited the records of women waging wars in Puranic scriptures as well as historical times. Women like Gargi, Mythreyi, Sulabha and Sarasavani of the Vedic period proved that women were intellectually powerful. Likewise, the Buddhist period offered examples like Kashisundari, Malini and Sanghamitra. Rajput women further proved women's physical and mental strength. Even during the Muslim period, when women were forced into purdah, denied education and lost freedom, women like Nur Jahan exhibited their skill in statecraft, establishing that women could rule empires.

In the modern period, when India did not require waging of wars, women like Tarabai Shando and Rukmabai demonstrated their physical strength in circuses. The various higher examinations women passed, the

[128] See 'Doctor K. N. Kesarigari Bangarupataka Bahumanamunandina Vyasamu: "Stree Abala Kaadu"', *Grihalakshmi*, April 1930, pp. 132–140. This was the essay by Kanuparti Varalakshmamma. The other participants were (in order of merit): Shikharam Kamalamba, Siripi Atchamamba, Puriti Sooryanarayanamma, B. Lakshminarasamma, Kamaraju Mythreyi, Achanta Satyavatamma (*Grihalakshmi*, May 1930, pp. 202–209), Krishnaveni Bhishagratna, Akkaraju Sitaramamma, Sooraparaju Rukminamma, G. Veeramma, and Addanki Anasuya Devi (*Grihalakshmi*, June 1930, pp. 295–300). It is interesting to remark that all of them were '*srimatis*', that is, married women.

[129] See Kanuparti Varalakshmamma, 'Stree Abala Kaadu', *Grihalakshmi*, April 1930, pp. 132–140.

[130] She recounted the stories of Puranic pativratas who entered heaven while still alive, stopped the sun from rising, turned the *trimurthis* into children, fought the god of death and brought their husband's life back.

great institutions they managed, the wonderful activities they undertook, the amazing lectures they delivered and the higher positions they held all pointed to their strength. Varalakshmamma was confident that the various laws made in favour of women would further enhance their capacities in multiple dimensions. If that was the case, how was it that women came to be known as abala? Varalakshmamma blamed 'men's selfishness' for this misconception, since 'it [men's selfishness] always tried to suppress women's personality.' She noted that there was a 'steady deterioration in the status of women from time to time':

> ...in every age, women's natural powers and wisdom were suppressed by the Shastric injunctions, religious rites, social customs and traditions, the institution of family and the denial of education. As a result, the principle of equality between women and men was lost, giving way to the principle of ruler and the ruled and master and slave. Because of such intolerable restrictions imposed on women, they gradually became objects of men's luxury and turned into inanimate beings. When such insurmountable restrictions had been blockading women's development, what wonder was there if women's hearts [and minds] turned weak? However, even in such constricting situations, whenever they got opportunities, women proved no inferior to men in terms of the power of mind, speech and body. Nobody could completely erase women's power despite imposing such constraints.... Even though women were systematically kept away from taking part in the great works concerning society and nation by way of imposing various restrictions, women still had infinite work to perform in the home.... Is it possible that a woman who has these many burdens of domestic works over her head be abala? Do we not know that God placed the difficulties of pregnancy and associated problems on women![131]

Varalakshmamma felt that such notions did the 'greatest possible harm' to the 'race of women.' It was on this basis that men held a scornful attitude towards women, assuming that they could not do anything; women developed a negative self-concept that they were abala and therefore they could do nothing. She further observed that this problem was unique to India and not an issue in the West where such ideas had been long erased. There, women proved equal to men in all respects and, in some respects, had even established their superiority. Therefore men like Henry Ford, the millionaire, opined that 'if women were wise, they could become a great

---

[131] Ibid.

force and it was his belief that, with the blessings of women, a new energy would take place in the world'.[132]

She emphasised that the peculiar conditions of India required that it soon realise the harm caused by casting women as abala:

> Today's needs of India [sic] also require recognising the harmful effects of terming women [as] abala. Women's help is essential to India, which wants to achieve all round development. Without the help of women, no religion can expand; no social system can be corrected; no reform can be practised and propagated; no ruined empire can be resuscitated and no dependent country can achieve independence. Therefore, if Indian women do not recognise their power and still continue to hold the notion of their being 'abalas', it will be detrimental to the progress of the country. Only when women make use of their powers of mind, speech and physique for the development of the country, any country can progress faster. However, it is the duty of men to awaken the dormant power hidden in women. If this all-influential power [of women] gets kindled, its result will be extraordinary. If provided with opportunities, women's power can build nations; manage statecraft; wage wars; produce scientific knowledge; compose poems and patronise arts and letters; deliver speeches; and produce the brave hearts, scholars, patriots and literary figures. Ah! Is there anything which is beyond the capacity of women? ... [Tell me] are such women abalas? No.[133]

To G. Veeramma, the very notion of women being weak appeared 'so strange' that it was really 'one of the wonders of the world', that is, it defied all logic. She sardonically remarked that 'some great fellow' (*mahapurushudu*) had branded women to be weak at their very birth and thereafter the idea crept into everything (except, of course, in performing housework)—the Puranas, poetry, modern art forms and all such writings. 'There were none who questioned this wrong proposition,' she noted with some sadness.[134] According to Shikharam Kamalamba, if women appeared weak in the present, it was not because they were 'weak by nature's principle' for God created both women and men equally. It was the historically imposed restrictions on women that rendered them weak.[135]

[132] She quoted Henry Ford from his piece on conjugality published in the *Krishna Patrika*.

[133] Ibid., pp. 139–140.

[134] G. Veeramma, 'Stree Abala Kaadu', *Grihalakshmi*, June 1930, p. 299.

[135] Shikharam Kamalamba, 'Stree Abala Kaadu', *Grihalakshmi*, May 1930, pp. 202–204, for this reference, p. 202.

Kamaraju Mythreyi suggested that the reproductive role of women was indirectly a cause of their subjection to men. She speculated in an attempt to uncover the historical roots of women's subordination:

> When they became weak [during pregnancy], men maintained them. It turned into a tradition that women confined themselves to the home looking after the household work and men pursuing the outside work. From then on, gradually, women surrendered to men to reach the present state.[136]

According to Krishnaveni Bhishagratna, the supposed weakness of women was not because of their sex but because of the process of gendering. Her understanding of the difference between sex and gender is very close to contemporary understandings that distinguish between biological and socio-cultural constructs.[137]

Women cited medical science to substantiate their argument that women were equal to men in terms of physical strength. Shikharam Kamalamba wrote that girls had better immunity than boys, and therefore did not fall sick as frequently and grew up faster.[138] According to Krishnaveni Bhishagratna, women had superior powers of 'resistance' to hardships such as famines. She cited the census reports of 1921, which remarked that 'famine mortality fell more heavily on men than on women, the latter sex apparently being constitutionally more able to resist the hardships which economic stringency brings' to substantiate the claim.[139] Women's reproductive abilities were also proof as they endured the highest of difficulties, 'risking their own lives' during labour.[140] Siripi Achchamamba recalled the English saying that 'the hand that rocks the cradle rules the world' and confidently stated that 'therefore, woman was not weak'. Women produced the strongest

---

[136]Kamaraju Mythreyi, 'Stree Abala Kaadu', *Grihalakshmi*, May 1930, pp. 206–208; for this reference, p. 207.

[137]Krishnaveni Bhishagratna, 'Stree Abala Kaadu', *Grihalakshmi*, June 1930, pp. 295–297; for this reference, p. 296.

[138]Shikharam Kamalamba, 'Stree Abala Kaadu', *Grihalakshmi*, May 1930, pp. 202–204; for this reference, pp. 202–203.

[139]Krishnaveni Bhishagratna, 'Stree Abala Kaadu', *Grihalakshmi*, June 1930, pp. 295–297; for this reference, pp. 295–296. She furnished a table which showed the number of deaths of women per every 1000 deaths of men. In all the places represented—Bengal, Bihar and Orissa, Bombay, Burma, Central Provinces, Madras, Punjab and North-West Frontier Provinces—women's deaths were lower than those of men. For Madras Presidency, it was 977. For the table, see p. 296.

[140]Kamaraju Mythreyi, 'Stree Abala Kaadu', *Grihalakshmi*, May 1930, pp. 206–208; for this reference, p. 206.

men—emperors, valorous soldiers, great poets, founders of religions, and artists, etc. 'If all women were weak, where did the strong men come from?' she questioned. Was it appropriate to call the mothers of talented men, as well as the *veera maata*s (mothers of bravehearts), weak?[141]

Women's strength was also established in terms of the strenuous domestic responsibilities they successfully performed on a regular basis. Shikharam Kamalamba wrote that girls were barely past the stage of childhood when they got married and began performing domestic tasks, which included pounding, husking, grinding, drawing and carrying of water, etc. 'Would it have been possible for women to perform such [difficult] tasks, if they were not strong?' Even cooking and serving food involved crouching and then straightening up uncountable times. She also referred to the common scene of rural women carrying two to three waterpots on their heads as they hoisted a child by the armpit, even when pregnant.[142] Kamalamba also described a 15-year-old girl who easily took off a rice-cooking bowl weighing 10 *ser*s (roughly 15 kilograms) from the hearth.[143] All these instances, according to her, established that women were physically strong. She further said that 'had women been weak, the race of women in India would by then have extinguished because 50 per cent of India was filled with child-mothers'.[144]

Women used an awareness of Puranic stories as well as real-life facts to make their arguments. Kamaraju Mythreyi and Achanta Satyavatamma recounted the story of Sita who, while playing, easily lifted the bow of Shiva (*Shiva chapamu*), which all other kings failed to lift barring Lord Rama.[145]

---

[141] Siripi Achchamamba, 'Stree Abala Kaadu', *Grihalakshmi*, May 1930, pp. 204–205. She mentioned Shivaji—his mother was instrumental in turning him into a 'braveheart' by narrating the stories of brave men to him from an early age.

[142] By narrating such things, middle-class women pressed lower-class women into the service of their arguments, though they conveniently appeared to be speaking for *all* women. Here, the lower-class women's strength gets converted into the strength of middle class women. This may be taken as an indication of gender identity cutting across classes, regions, nations and languages. The examples of *other* women—who did not belong to their caste/region/language and nationality—they used, speaks positively in this direction.

[143] Shikharam Kamalamba, 'Stree Abala Kaadu', *Grihalakshmi*, May 1930, pp. 202–204; for this reference, pp. 202–203.

[144] Ibid., p. 203.

[145] While the former told the story in some detail, the latter made a cursory remark. It appears that the story was in wide circulation among women. Kamaraju Mythreyi, 'Stree Abala Kaadu', *Grihalakshmi*, May 1930, pp. 206–208; for this reference, p. 207.

Shikharam Kamalamba wrote that girls' or women's performance in sports and games like running, swimming and weightlifting rivalled that of boys or men. She even mentioned one girl who outshone boys in a swimming competition held in Bangalore.[146] Kamaraju Mythreyi similarly mentioned a woman from 'some European country' who secured the first prize for swimming the English Channel. She also wrote about Tarabai Shando, a female weightlifter 'who exhibited physical strength' equal to that of the male bodybuilders like Kodi Ramamoorthy.[147] Krishnaveni Bhishagratna mentioned a number of non-Indian women, who were reputed to be as strong as men or even stronger:

> The Iyashi women of Nigeria are stronger than their men. Their physical structure is more exquisite than their men's physiques. Californian women's physical energy is superior to that of their men. The Arab, Syrian, Kandhaharan and Afghan women have physical fitness equal to that of their men. The Tibetan women are superior to their men. You may have heard a number of times that the Bhutanese women carry their men during travel. We may provide any number of such examples from many other countries. So, finally, what is the conclusion? It is not possible to say that one has less physical strength and the other more. Difference in sex does not mean the existence of difference in physical strength. Even if there is difference, it is the result of circumstances [gendering], not because of the sex.[148]

'Stree Abala Kaadu': Women's Intellect is Not Inferior

As with the physical strength debate, women rejected the misogynist idea that women were intellectually weak or inferior to men. Krishnaveni Bhishagratna quoted Robert Kingman, a cognitive scientist (*medha shastra praveenudu*), who proposed that the size and weight of the brain would be equal for women and men of the same height and weight; he also wrote that the number of neurons was equal for both sexes.[149] Women scientists

---

Achanta Satyavatamma, 'Stree Abala Kaadu', *Grihalakshmi*, May 1930, pp. 208–209; for this reference, p. 208.

[146] The girl's name is not mentioned. However, this establishes women's growing awareness and networks.

[147] Kamaraju Mythreyi, 'Stree Abala Kaadu', *Grihalakshmi*, May 1930, pp. 206–208; for this reference, p. 207.

[148] Krishnaveni Bhishagratna, 'Stree Abala Kaadu', *Grihalakshmi*, June 1930, pp. 295–297, for this reference, p. 296.

[149] Ibid., p. 295.

and innovators were frequently cited. Krishnaveni Bhishagratna wrote that long before Simpson, a woman (who went unnamed) had already invented chloroform, but was shot dead by the Church and State on the pretext that 'she went against the will of God'. Bhishagratna also mentioned Madam Curie, who discovered radium.[150] Puriti Sooryanarayanammal wrote that 'women were also equally skilful to men in terms of scientific research. Like men, they would also invent new things'.[151] Appreciating Madam Curie's research potential, she termed Curie 'a brave Western woman' (*paaschatya veera vanita*) who had, 'with enormous hard work… invented the "Radium" [*sic*] and announced it to the scientific world. The research skill she exhibited then was very laudable.' Referring to other scientists like Hertha Ayrton, a British mathematician, she wrote that

> a number of women like them contributed to human knowledge, welfare and development of [their] countries. The world media greatly praised the American women for inventing new machinery by undertaking scientific research. It was a living example that women, who were treated as abala, acquired scientific knowledge and contributed to national development.[152]

Women argued that acquiring education and entry into modern professions was itself proof of their intellectual capabilities. For example, B. Lakshminarasamma argued that calling women 'abala' was blatantly 'unjust':

> Do not we see today many young women receiving education like men? Are not such educated women, who acquired equal capacities like men, entering into various professions? If that is the case, why should we call women weak? Is not it unjust to say so? It is not at all appropriate to call women inferior in terms of education, when they are not inferior to men in such matters. Are not women clearing the higher examinations? Are they not becoming school inspectors and teachers in the education department and working for the development of boys and girls? Are they not excelling in politics and businesses? Are they not showing their capabilities in such matters? What kind of weakness women are showing in these things? Or, is it a casual thing to call women abala?[153]

Shikharam Kamalamba wrote that girls possessed 'superior comprehension abilities' than boys and therefore understood things 'faster'. 'As they got

[150] Ibid., p. 297.
[151] Puriti Sooryanarayanammal, 'Stree Abala Kaadu', *Grihalakshmi*, May 1930, p. 205.
[152] Ibid.
[153] B. Lakshminarasamma, 'Stree Abala Kaadu', *Grihalakshmi*, May 1930, p. 206.

the opportunities, they received education equal to men', she reasoned. That a number of illiterate women remembered a number of songs, etc., also established that women's mental faculties were not inferior to men. Women's skill in managing the home was also a marker of their cognitive potential. Kamalamba argued that the home was like a 'small kingdom' where the women were unilaterally discharging the duties of finance, health, defense, home and education ministers. 'If women were intellectually weak/ inferior, how could they discharge all these duties [simultaneously and successfully]?'[154] She quoted the *sloka*, '*Buddhischapi chaturgunah*', which meant that women were four times wiser than men.[155] Kamaraju Mythreyi also advanced the domestic-work-ability argument to prove that women were mentally stronger than men.[156]

Women were extremely angry with men for not recognising their worth and for failing to provide opportunities to realise their potential. All of them unequivocally emphasised that, if provided with proper opportunities, they would prove equal to men in every respect. Akkaraju Seetaramamma penned a sharp critique:

> A few selfish men who are not recognising women's power are under the illusion that women are created to be the slaves of men, and therefore they are not giving them freedom to participate in movements and are doing great harm to the country. What is man able to do without the help of women? Can he swim through [the ocean of] family without her helping hand? Why talk of a thousand things? It is enough if we observe one thing.... Like men, they are able to perform well even in politics in these times when the status of education of women is abysmally low. Were they to have educational and other opportunities equal to men, does one even need to ask about the amount of help they would render to men?[157]

Grihalakshmi published the photograph of Annie Besant to establish that women were not weak. The comment it published alongside her photograph is interesting.

---

[154] Shikharam Kamalamba, 'Stree Abala Kaadu', *Grihalakshmi*, May 1930, pp. 202–204; for this reference, pp. 203–204.

[155] Ibid., p. 204.

[156] Kamaraju Mythreyi, 'Stree Abala Kaadu', *Grihalakshmi*, May 1930, pp. 206–208; for this reference, p. 206.

[157] Akkaraju Seetaramamma, 'Stree Abala Kaadu', *Grihalakshmi*, June 1930, p. 298. She cited the example of Maganti Annapoorna Devi to establish the fact that women could selflessly serve the nation even by scarifying their lives. What they needed were proper opportunities.

> To establish that woman is not weak, she [Annie Besant] provides the best example in the modern times. She is an old woman of 80 years. If she decides to undertake any daunting task, she completes it at any cost. Her dedication to work is untiring. Her name has become a household name in India. Those who observe her life history certainly agree that woman cannot be addressed with the synonym, abala.[158]

Apart from these women, there were a number of others who tirelessly argued that women were not inferior to men. A contributor who signed as K. M. remarked in 1937 that 'if we observed the world with a judicious view and not with bad logic, the indescribable greatness of women would become evident' and 'their capacity was extremely praise-worthy.'[159] Women proved their worth in terms of administration, valour, social and national service, industry, scholarship and spirituality, etc. 'Woman was the basis of everything' and 'she was all capable,' she asserted. She provided a number of examples to corroborate her stand.[160] Her essay argued:

> We are witnessing a few men airing narrow-minded views rather than appreciating the many women elected to the Imperial Legislative Assembly. Mother India's wish is that she achieve higher status with her children—women and men—developing equally. Among the children, one may be jealous of the other. But the mother treats all of them equally. It is not that the world does not know about the greatness of women from the very ancient times. It is not for the first time that women are participating in politics. Despite their being 'sabala', they were considered 'abala' because of their wealth of humility. Though the following things

[158] *Grihalakshmi*, April 1930. This also establishes the stand of the journal on the issue. The very fact that the topic of the essay-writing competition is in the affirmative ('Stree Abala Kaadu', i.e., Woman is not Weak/Inferior) is another indication of the journal's stance.

[159] K. M., 'Streeyabalaya?' (Is Woman Weak/Inferior?), *Grihalakshmi*, May 1937, pp. 196–199.

[160] To demonstrate women's administrative abilities, she cited the examples of queens like Ahalyabai, Durgabai, Tarabai, Rudrama Devi and Victoria. She was all praise of the last. For valour, she cited the examples of Joan of Arc, wife of Khadga Tikkana, the Rani of Jhansi and the Rajput queens. For social and national service, the examples of Florence Nightingale, Sarojini Devi, Muthulakshmi Reddy, Achanta Rukminamma and 'a number of Congress women' were cited. For scholarship, names of Molla and Kanchanapalli Kanakamba were mentioned. It is very clear that Indian women intellectuals drew inspiration from both indigenous and foreign sources even during the heyday of Indian national movement.

> are not unknown to the world of readers, I believe that it is not wrong and unnecessary to reiterate them.[161]

The first and second place winners of an essay-writing competition on the topic 'Is Equality between Women and Men Desirable or Harmful?', Mydavolu Padmavati and Vedula Meenakshi, unequivocally emphasised that women needed absolute equality with men in all respects and that there was nothing that women could not do what men did.[162] According to Padmavati, 'granting freedom to women was a precondition to India's attainment of Swaraj'. She was highly critical of men's 'hatred' for women and stated that they had 'injected [an] inferiority complex' in women. 'Will those [men] who rode on us so far like to grant us [women] freedom?' she asked, suggesting that 'it was an illusion to expect that men would ever help women'. She reasoned that 'women themselves must work for women's freedom. Women themselves must work to correct their [dismal] conditions'. In every respect, whether education, employment, politics and civil rights, or any other issue, women were to enjoy equality. She was confident that women would not forsake their domestic responsibilities if they enjoyed such equality and freedom.

The editor of *Grihalakshmi* sharply reacted to the views of both authors. Their demand for absolute equality of women to men appeared to him so 'unnatural' that K. N. Kesari published an editorial on 'limitations' in the essays. He wanted to inform the readers about perspectives that the prize-winning essays had apparently 'failed to' discuss! Emphasising that 'nature' imposed certain 'limitations' on women, he concluded that while demanding equality, women needed to keep in mind such biological differences and limitations and abstain from making such 'unnatural' arguments. For example, women could not do all the jobs that men did: they were more suited to professions like teaching and nursing, which were soft and according to the 'nature' of women. Men, who were 'innately strong', could perform 'hard tasks' better, but certainly not 'soft' jobs like nursing. Therefore, naturally, there would and should be difference in the kind of education required for women and men. Given the importance of the views expressed in the essays of women intellectuals and the reaction of the male editor, I have translated them fully and placed in the Appendices to this

[161] Ibid., p. 196.

[162] 'Stree Purusha Samanatvamavashyakama, Yendeni Yanarthadayakama?' (Is Equality Between Women and Men Desirable or Harmful?), *Grihalakshmi*, November 1936, pp. 661–673. For Mydavolu Padmavati, pp. 661–666; For Vedula Meenakshi, pp. 667–673.

volume.[163] While the two women's views represented a radical women's consciousness, the reaction of the editor represents the limited liberalism of male reformers and nationalists, who continued to hold patriarchal views and wanted women to parrot their views. They were so greatly disturbed that they chastised and threatened women against making 'unnatural' demands that would lead to 'unwanted troubles'.[164]

Equality Should be the Basis of Conjugality

At a time when male intellectuals like Chalam were envisioning new forms of the man–woman relationship, women's life beyond the family and even advocating sexual liberation, the majority of women intellectuals firmly upheld domestic life as essential. What they wanted was not a dissolution of the family, but reorganising and reordering of the same. They wished domestic relations to be based on democratic principles: there should be equality between woman/wife and man/husband and husbands shun their patriarchal attitudes. Together, they should make a happy home. For this, women offered certain suggestions to be observed by husbands and wives.

In the beginning, however, it was men who tutored women on the issue of domestic management, including the conjugal relationship. Women welcomed and appreciated this for they expected an improvement in their circumstances. They also took part in the discussions on women's domestic responsibilities. However, they did not blindly accept men's prescriptions. From the 1920s onward, women began to assert that men too must shoulder some domestic responsibilities: some women were gentle in broaching the subject, while others sharply critiqued husbands. Conjugal happiness could be ensured only when both shared responsibility at the home. Ravi Narasamma, a married woman writing for *Grihalakshmi*, offered 13 points in this regard:

Thirteen Points for a Happy Home:

1. They should not have mad/useless imagination about man-woman relationship and hold wise ideas. This means that they should realise that the chief purpose of marriage is begetting healthy children.

[163] See Appendices 2–4.

[164] 'Stree Purusha Samanatvamavashyakama? Yendeni Yanarthadayakama?' (Is Equality Between Women and Men Desirable or Harmful?), Editorial, *Grihalakshmi*, December 1936, pp. 731–735.

2. They should take all necessary care to ensure that their love for each other does not decrease. They should tolerate each other's faults/limitations.
3. They should not think that it is enough if they have love for each other in their hearts, and [should] exhibit the same in their external behaviour.
4. They should avoid counting each other's faults and discuss them openly and resolve.
5. Be it in the manner of dressing up or speaking, they should keep their spouses happy.
6. Without dictating that one should do this and should not do that, they should conduct [themselves] in an amicable way.
7. They should not cultivate closeness with other men and women who may have been their friends.
8. Husband and wife should save some money from their income.
9. They should avoid discriminatory feelings that one is superior and the other inferior.
10. Each should trust the other completely and should never give space to distrust.
11. As far as possible, they should not allow relatives to stay with them for a long time.
12. There should not be any gap between husband and wife with regard to savings and expenditure.
13. Husband and wife should always discuss good things. [165]

The theme of 'hints for a happy conjugal life' continued to have a very strong presence in women's writings even in the 1950s. Tayi Venkata Subbamma juxtaposed the duties of husband and wife:

Duties of a Husband:

1. A husband must respect his wife and love her the same way a man respects a woman before marriage.
2. He should bring flowers for her now and then. He should give her gifts on occasions such as birth day and marriage day without forgetting.
3. The husband should give his wife sudden pleasant surprises by offering gifts and exhibiting respectfulness.
4. Husband should never count the faults of [his] wife in front of others.

[165] Ravi Narasamma, 'Bharyaabhartalu Santoshamugaanundutaku Gamanichavalasina Vishayamulu' (Points to be Observed by Wives and Husbands to be Happy), *Grihalakshmi*, February 1934, p. 1020.

5. Apart from the money intended for domestic use, he should give her money for her personal use and allow her to make use of it the way she likes.
6. He should understand his wife's mental condition and cooperate with her to enable her to come out of feelings such as annoyance, tiresomeness and loss of courage.
7. He should spend at least half of his leisure time with her.
8. He should never compare his wife's domestic and other capabilities with those of his sisters' and mother's in a belittling way.
9. Husband should take interest in his wife's social and psychological life and in the books she reads, and discuss the matters with her.
10. He should never hurt her with jealous words. He should provide her the opportunity to continue her friendships and relationship with her friends and relations she likes.
11. The husband should always be watchful of situations that provide him a chance to appreciate her.
12. He should express thankfulness whenever she did some work for him such as washing clothes, mending shirt buttons, etc.[166]

Duties of a Wife:

1. You should give him full freedom to pursue his profession and other avocations. You should not find faults with his friends, acquaintances and about his comings and goings to and from home [that is, do not question his late arrivals to home, etc.].
2. You should keep your home clean and beautiful to the extent possible. With decorative objects such as portraits, curtains and *muggulu*, you should make it appear beautiful and attractive.
3. You should not cook the same food items regularly and keep changing them. Otherwise, it will cause sickness.
4. Evince some interest in your husband's business/job. This will help you discuss your issues with him and [you can] offer him with your help.
5. In case your husband faces financial hardships, you should never be discouraged and should be bold. You should not count your husband's faults in case there are lapses on his part. You should never compare him with other rich people and [should instead] try to be considerate. This will help you. If you do like this, your husband's respect and love for you will multiply.

---

[166] Tayi Venkata Subbamma, 'Bharyabhartalu Cheyavalasina Vidhulu' (Duties of Wives and Husbands), *Grihalakshmi*, June 1950, pp. 363–364.

6. You should always try hard and have lots of patience to conduct well with his parents, [brothers] and sisters. Conduct with them with love and affection.
7. Choose the fashions and patterns of your dresses and other things keeping in mind the liking and disliking of your husband. This gives him pleasure.
8. Do not allow differences to creep in [regarding] petty matters. Make patience and satisfaction the cardinal principles of your life. This will prove auspicious and beneficial to you.
9. Try to take part in your husband's leisure time activities.
10. Try to understand the new ideas and information available through the new books and newspapers. This helps you participate in your husband's intellectual as well as emotional life.

For both husbands and wives, she wrote that 'they could follow these things one by one and experience the results themselves'. She also laid down a set of shared responsibilities:

1. Never grumble.
2. Do not discard each other's words in a scornful/belittling way.
3. Do not find faults.
4. Appreciate wholeheartedly.
5. Show respect even in small things.
6. Observe only the respectful social traditions.
7. Read at least one book on sexual life. Do not treat it to be wrong.

Radical Departures: Women's Critique of Society, Religion and Men

While the preceding section captures 'soft' stances on changing conjugal relations, other women intellectuals took a different approach. Chimakurti Satyavati Devi, for example, was very sharp and forthright. In a forceful essay, she bitterly attacked the world for reserving all 'sermons' for women alone and sparing men.[167] Deeply 'aggrieved' at the state of affairs, she wrote an article detailing what men's responsibilities should be. Satyavati Devi emphasised that men must observe *patnivrata* (devotion to wife) rather than simply expecting pativratya from women.

---

[167] Chimakurti Satyavati Devi, 'Bhartala Kartavyamu' (Duties of Husbands), *Vasavi*, February 1935, pp. 350–352.

Men Must Observe Patnivrata

Chimakurti Satyavati Devi observed that everywhere one found and heard, including in women's conferences, men and women delivering 'sermons' to women on the issues of devotion to husband and pativratyam. From the ordinarily educated ones, who could compose some poems, to the established scholars, all wrote on this issue, producing works such as *Manini Shatakamu*, *Sudati Suniti Shatakamu*, *Stree Niti Dipika*, *Kanta Suguna Dipika*, *Stree Hithabodhini* and *Kanta*, which she knew. 'There may have been many others, which I have not come across,' she commented. Her biting sarcasm is palpable: '[All] these virtuous poets descended to deliver sermons to women the same way the *Bramhastra* [the deadly Puranic weapon used as a last resort to smash one's worst enemy] was fired at a sparrow.'[168]

Image 5.4: Chimakurti Satyavati Devi

Source: *Grihalakshmi*, April 1930.

[168]This is a paraphrased presentation of a poem perhaps authored by Satyavati Devi herself. Ibid., p. 350.

This was quite 'unjust' and unfair. Satyavati Devi contended that Indian women had always been famous as pativratas. Such women who venerated their husbands as gods and served them with absolute love and devotion, even though the latter were wicked, were present even in the present. At least a few knew quite well that there were several such women who lost their happiness and life itself because of wicked husbands. It was really sad that, despite knowing this, people continued to find fault with women and delivered sermons on the importance of pativratyam. Such efforts, according to her, were misplaced. Correction must be made where it was required. 'Though women were virtuous and sound in pativratyam, all of it got wasted because of the foolishness of men. Such women's devotion to their husbands became useless, like a scent poured onto ashes.' It was better men themselves turned virtuous and set an example to women rather than delivering a hundred sermons to them. 'Patnivrata (devotion to wife) should be to a man what pativratya is to women,' she emphasised. 'Would not the wife be virtuous, if her husband was virtuous!' she exclaimed. 'If the husband was virtuous, there would be no reason for others to teach the wife the lessons in pativratyam,' she observed confidently. Reminding men that they needed to be patnivratas was certainly a radical, novel proposition and that diverged completely from dominant ideas about wife-husband relationships then in circulation. It reflects Satyavati Devi's distinct intellectual and political position.

Further, Satyavati Devi stressed that 'only the virtuous husband could be treated as equal to God, not the wicked one.' There was no use in teaching women to treat wicked husbands as gods. 'The journey of family life could not be a happy one, unless both husband and wife were mutually affectionate, virtuous and equal.'[169] If they were unequal, the cart of family life would be unbalanced like one yoked to an ox and a horse. Thus, she established equality of women and men as the basis of conjugal bliss. Rejecting the dictum to accord god-like status even to a wicked husband, and instead telling a wicked husband that he was wicked, is a clear and sharp departure from the early conduct books intended for women.[170]

Satyavati Devi's writings used irony to great effect. She suggested that it was perhaps because men were convinced that god would not appear to

---

[169] Ibid., p. 351.

[170] A verse in the *Savithri* read as follows: 'God will bless you in proportion of your devotion to your husband. Treat it to be ignoble to trouble your husband for jewellery. Treat him like god however bad he is.' See 'Stree Dharmamulu' (Duties of Women), April 1904.

women—the uneducated and weak—that they designed the 'easy' way of pativratyam for women: in the pativrata model, husband is god and wife a devotee. Men deserved great salutations, she remarked, for devising such an easy method for the salvation of women. She said that she had a doubt as to how women could uphold the pativratya dharma and worship husbands as gods given the fact that immoral, characterless and wicked husbands were found all around. It was the duty of men to put women, even if they were unwise, on the right path with kind words. Rather than doing this, if they treated wives like a parrot in the clutches of a cat, the question of ensuring *sati* dharma and this worldly happiness would never arise.

Further, she appealed for 'impartial judgement', questioning how one could run family life smoothly with a wicked husband, when swimming that ocean of family life filled with mutual affection and compatible conjugality itself was becoming extremely difficult. Was it not impossible for women, the weak and the ignorant, to lead life on a virtuous path when men, the 'superiors',[171] themselves were treading the un-virtuous paths? She warned men that if they did not correct themselves and continued counting the faults of women, the less knowledgeable, they could not possibly expect the nation to prosper. Finally, she stressed that 'in her opinion, it was men's conduct that required significant correction rather than women's.'[172] She suggested that men should 'see the truth. Think from the angle of justice. Stop counting others' [women's] faults. Self-introspect, correct themselves and uplift the nation.'[173] She thus linked men's responsibility towards women to the interests of the nation. If men improved themselves and conducted well with women, it meant that they also fulfilled their responsibilities towards the nation. Nation's uplift was impossible to achieve, if men failed to fulfil their obligations towards women.

Identifying Men as Their Oppressors

In an issue of *Grihalakshmi* published in 1929, V. Saraswati wrote that 'Indian men or, for that matter, all men in the world were selfish'. According to her, 'men were solely responsible for the superstitions present in women. Just

[171] She was using this argument of 'men's superiority' to subvert the idea itself. It is certainly put to a strategic use. We have already seen in the preceding pages as to how women refuted the patriarchal idea that women were weak physically and intellectually.

[172] Ibid., p. 352.

[173] Ibid.

as the Brahmins suppressed the non-Brahmins, men suppressed women.'[174] We find such views being expressed by many women from the 1920s onward. Cherukuru Nagabhooshanamma wrote that 'men created stories [myths], moralities and dharmas, subjugated women and acquired rights over them; they treated women as their cattle and chattel'.[175] She suggested that 'women should not blindly follow whatever their husbands asked of them. They were not to meekly bear the torture of husbands. Realising that they were independent, they needed to come out of the shell of pativratya.' She wanted women to be educated for the educated women 'realised that they were individuals, did not follow others mindlessly, and acted according to their conscience.'[176] In a radical departure from discourse of the time, she found the practice of women taking on their husband's name to be 'negative and derogatory to women's dignity and individuality'. She wrote: 'This is worldwide slavery in the name of modern culture. To a woman with an individuality of her own, there is no greater humiliation than this. Women should become famous not by their husbands' names, but by their own strength, effort and capacity.'[177]

Men Had Failed the Women's Movement

Women's consciousness underwent such a tremendous transformation that they began to identify men's 'double standards' and 'opportunism' as the reason for the 'failure' of the social reform movement. A section of women lost faith in the efforts of the male social reformers, whose activities failed to effect any substantial change in women's lives. They urged women to take up the cause themselves, rather than depending on men. At the Godavari District Women's Conference, held on 23 September 1933, Sarangu Sita Devi delivered a speech in which she said:

> Educated men, who are interested in the development of the country, have been delivering lectures in favour of widow marriages, and in

[174] V. Saraswati, 'Srimati Vidyasundari Benguluru Nagaratnamu gariki V. Saraswati garu', *Grihalakshmi,* December 1929, pp. 917–919.

[175] Cherukuru Nagabhooshanamma, 'Inkennallu Manakee Banisatvamu?' (Women's Slavery: How Long Must It Last?), *Grihalakshmi,* October 1941, pp. 448–451, for this reference, p. 449.

[176] Cherukuru Nagabhooshanamma, 'Mana Patananiki Maname Karanamu' (We Alone are Responsible for Our Fall), *Grihalakshmi,* 1938, pp. 686–689.

[177] Cherukuru Nagabhooshanamma, 'Inkennallu Manakee Banisatvamu?', *Grihalakshmi,* October 1941, p. 450.

opposition to child marriages for a long time now! But no substantial change has taken place. It is because the same men who delivered lectures are reluctant when it comes to actual practice.... Though the reform movement has been in existence since the time of Raja Ram Mohan Roy, it has not succeeded because it is in the hands of men. These men have simply delivered lectures from the platform and got some two to three acts passed. That's all! [What we must remember is that] the social evils do not die out with the passage of a few acts. The reform movement cannot succeed, and be sustained, until and unless women, assisted by some good, strong-willed men, take up the task in to their hands. Hence, I appeal to you [women] to shoulder the burden of social reform and bring about [real] changes in our society.[178]

Condemning and Discarding Hindu Scriptures

Just as women challenged scriptural arguments about widow remarriage and the age of consent for girls, they posed serious questions about gender biases in Hindu religious texts and the Puranic heroes. These writers did not consider these texts sacrosanct and repudiated them for sanctioning a derogatory and subordinate status to women. Dharmavaram Lakshmi Devi was of the view that the 'Dharmashastras were not completely acceptable, and it was not possible for women to lead their lives [in the present] according to them'.

Women had to carve out new ways of living independently of the Dharmashastras by cultivating a rational mind. Unlike most of her contemporaries, she was highly critical of Rama and Krishna, the epic heroes of the Hindus, and condemned them for being unjust to women like Sita and Draupadi in the epics. She accused various Hindu religious texts of according a subordinate status to women.[179] Kanuparti Varalakshmamma too recognised the instrumentality of the Dharmashastras and the other Hindu religious texts in ensuring the subordinate status of women, and suggested that they had destroyed women's natural capacities and intellect, thus perpetuating asymmetrical gender relations.[180] V. Saraswati, a trenchant critic of the Hindu sacred texts, concurred with these views.

[178]See 'Mahila Sabhalu' (Women's Conferences), *Grihalakshmi,* November 1933, p. 755.

[179]Dharmavaram Lakshmi Devi, 'Sharadaku Pratyuttaramu', *Grihalakshmi*, October 1929, pp. 651–656.

[180]Kanuparti Varalakshmamma, 'Stree Abala Kaadu' (Woman Is Not Weak and Inferior), *Grihalakshmi,* April 1930, pp. 132–140.

'Hindu scriptures were biased against women because they were authored by men', she wrote. 'If they had been written by women, certainly their nature would have been different.' Contesting the authenticity of the Vedas, Dharmashastras and Puranas, she wrote that 'we [women] had nothing to do with the Vedas, shastras and the Puranas. We should be bothered about our present condition... Let there be anything in the Vedas, women did not have high place in Hindu society'.[181] Women understood that 'men created stories, moralities, and dharmas; subjugated women and thus acquired rights over them'.[182] Women were sad for 'women accepted whatever men wrote, especially that they considered the Vedas, which were written by men, as divinely ordained guiding principles for ever'.[183]

Image 5.5: Dharmavaram Lakshmi Devi

Source: *Grihalakshmi*, October 1929.

[181] V. Saraswati, 'Srimati Vidyasundari Benguluru Nagaratnamu gariki V. Saraswati garu', *Grihalakshmi*, December 1929, pp. 917–919.

[182] Cherukuru Nagabhooshanamma, 'Inkennallu Manakee Banisatvamu?' (Women's Slavery: How Long Must It Last?), *Grihalakshmi*, October 1941, p. 449.

[183] V. Saraswati, 'Srimati Vidyasundari Benguluru Nagaratnamu gariki V. Saraswati garu', *Grihalakshmi*, December 1929, p. 917.

In an essay titled 'Stree Swatantryamu' (Women's Independence), V. Saraswati criticised Hindu religious texts, epics, texts on morality, and men's attitudes and conduct. Most surprisingly, she linked men's loss of independence to the British with the loss of women's independence to men. In a remarkably crisp essay, she proposed that women's independence from men's domination was a precondition to men's independence from colonial domination. She suggested that god would also not cooperate with men if they did not mend their ways and improve their conduct towards women.

> Today, everywhere in our country, great efforts are being made to achieve independence [from the British]. However, they are not successful. What is the reason? ...Women, who occupy fifty percent of the Indian race, are enslaved to men. Men who are living with enslaved women cannot come out of slavery and become independent, you know! Whenever the issue of women's independence is discussed, the scholars [*shastravidulu*] start making tall claims that a number of rights are granted to women in the Hindu scriptures [*Hindu Dharmashastramu*]. But upon close scrutiny, I have come to the conclusion that it is the same Hindu Dharmashastras which caused the slavery of Indian women. As per the *Manusmriti*, woman does not have any right over her own body all through her life. Father in childhood, husband in the adulthood and son in the old age protect her. Are not women and men a part of the same class [species] of humans! Of them, one has no freedom over its own body! And the other class [of men] wants freedom for the country! What an incompatible and absurd statement! The Indian man is a damn selfish fellow. He codified in bulky books how woman has to conduct [herself] with him....[184] howsoever useless that fellow may be, woman has to be his *paada daasi* [slave at the feet] and adore him like a God. Now, you see [what he has said] about the way a man has to conduct with a woman....[185] It is said that a man can abandon his wife for the most trivial flaw, no matter even if she is a mother of ten children. It is said that even if he is a useless funeral bier [wretch], the woman ought never to leave him. Further, it is said that she should believe that her ultimate salvation is with him alone. How unjust? Indian literature is spoilt with the books authored by men wherein it is written that the husband is God and the wife has to adore him howsoever wicked he is and if she does, she attains heavens and if she does not, she lands in perennial hell. In the name of Puranic recitation, the reciter—a man—narrated [stories] from these books to the innocent Indian women every day [and thus indoctrinated them].... If man wishes to regain the

[184] Here, she mentioned a poem from the *Mahabharata*.

[185] Here, she mentioned a poem from the *Neeti Shastramu*.

> lost glory and attain independence [from colonial domination], he should grant independence to woman first. If he does so, God will grant him independence. If he does not, God will not grant him independence. This is certain.[186]

Questioning Women's Confinement to the Domestic Domain

Given this progressive change in the consciousness of a section of women, it was not surprising that they questioned the patriarchal division of labour. For example, Achanta Satyavatamma challenged this idea in her writings. Her story 'Saraswati–Pushpavati' condemned the patriarchal culture that confined women to the domestic domain alone, as well as the discrimination meted out to them. Objecting to the notion that childcare was women's duty alone, she complained:

> our people [Indian nationalists] oppose discrimination [by the British] against the Blacks [that is, Indians]. [But] how are they allowing it against women? Women alone are undertaking the responsibility of child rearing, which is supposed to be shared by both men and women. Why should women remain at home always?'[187]

Demanding men's participation in domestic activities, she broke the patriarchal gendering of roles. When she questioned why women had to remain at home, she was, in fact, visualising the expansion of women's place beyond children and the kitchen.

Salaries for Housewives?

Having perceived the significance and value of their domestic labour, women appealed for its recognition. An anonymous 'lady' observed that educated women who did not take up jobs, and who remained at home to look after the domestic chores, should 'demand pay from their husbands'. She wrote this to dissuade educated women from taking up jobs outside the home. Though her suggestion was confined only to educated women, it

---

[186] V. Saraswati, 'Stree Swatantryamu' (Women's Independence), *Grihalakshmi*, October 1929, pp. 616–617.

[187] Achanta Satyavatamma, 'Saraswati–Pushpavati', *Grihalakshmi*, February 1935, p. 882.

was still important because it stressed the need for recognising and valuing domestic labour.[188]

However, Yallapragada Sitakumari[189] challenged this view. She saw men's 'conspiracy' behind the advancement of such arguments. According to her, as women received higher education and began taking up jobs, men got alarmed. Men feared that, if women earned their livelihood by taking up jobs outside the home, they no longer remained the subordinates [slaves] of men. This put men in an awkward position. Therefore, men argued that, if women took up jobs and went outside the home, there would be no one to look after the home and 'chaos would prevail'. She sarcastically remarked that that was why women, though educated and employable, were asked to remain at home and 'beg' for salaries from husbands! She brought out the contradictions in the argument by asking, 'who would give salaries to widowed, single or separated women?', if they remained at home, and did not take up jobs to earn their livelihood.[190]

Yallapragada Sitakumari also found another 'big problem' in this argument. She wrote that an employee could change a job and take up another if needed. She asked whether it was possible for women to change husbands, if they did not like them. She said that wives would have to compromise, even if the salary offered by husbands was petty or if she was not treated well. Problems would arise between wife and husband with regard to spending money for domestic necessities. In her view, what was desired for women was not a salary from their husbands, but mutual understanding and respect between wife and husband to run the family smoothly. She judged that 'giving salaries to wives would perpetuate women's slavery by denying them the opportunity to take up jobs outside, earn their livelihood and thus retain their freedom and dignity.'[191]

---

[188] 'Oka Sodari', 'Gruhineetvaniki Jeetala?' (Salaries for Housewives?), *Grihalakshmi*, December 1936, pp. 741–743.

[189] For the life and works of Sitakumari, see Ankaraju Vidyarani and Muktevi Bharati, *Yallapragada Sitakumari Jeevita Visheshalu*, Kotamraju Shashibala and Yallapragada Ashokavardhan, Hyderabad, n. d.

[190] Yallapragada Sitakumari, 'Bharyalaku Jeetala!! Ichchevaaru Bhartala!!' (Salaries for Housewives!! And Husbands Give Them!!), *Grihalakshmi*, c. February 1932, pp. 931–934.

[191] Ibid. The argument of 'salary to wives' appears to have generated much discussion. The editor made it clear that it was not either his or the writer's (of the earlier article, 'Gruhineetvaniki Jeetaala?') intention to perpetuate women's slavery. To avoid confusion and make things clear to readers, he republished some of the passages from the earlier article. It was mentioned that the argument of 'salary to wives' was first raised by one

It is significant to note that the idea of 'salaries to housewives' reappeared in Indian public debates some 80 years after Andhra women discussed the issue. In September 2012, the Ministry of Women and Child Development (WCD), Government of India, came up with the proposal of making it mandatory for men to offer salaries (later clarified as 'honorarium') to their wives. Newspapers publicised the issue with captions like 'Government considering salary for housewives from husbands'[192] and 'Homemakers likely to get monthly salary from husbands soon.'[193]

WCD Minister Krishna Tirath reportedly said that 'the idea, mooted by some NGOs, would also be discussed in a meeting to be held with ministers of different states.'[194] The minister also stated that in their responses to a government survey, most housewives replied that they did nothing, clearly suggesting that these women did not realise that their work at home was also a worthwhile activity that contributed to national development. Therefore, the government felt that a 'mechanism' could be 'devised to quantify and calculate the value of work' the housewives do for their families, which, the minister hoped, would 'give a more socially empowered identity' to such women. The minister rightly identified women's domestic work as an 'economic activity' that had been devalued. Allocating 'a portion of husband's income' as the 'wife's share' would compensate women, ensure better food and education of children, and also improve the 'overall quality of standard of living' of a particular 'household.'[195]

The ostensibly progressive proposal received a wide range of responses from women and men. One such response came from Maya John, an activist and researcher based in Delhi University, who analysed the issue in some detail and criticised 'the sheer hollowness of such proposed legislation' which was '*informed by a poor understanding of economics surrounding household work and women's labour in general*' (italics in original).[196] It is important to note that *colonial* Yallapragada Sitakumari's understanding of the issue is very close to the understanding of a *contemporary*, metropolitan woman activist. Sitakumari's question about whether a wife could leave her

---

certain P. N. Mehili in the *Bombay Chronicle*. Reflecting on that, 'Oka Bharta' [pseudonym that means 'A Husband'] wrote in the *Yugavani* that the scheme of offering salaries to wives was good.

[192] *The Times of India*, 11 September 2012.

[193] *The Times of India*, 9 September 2012.

[194] Ibid.

[195] Ibid.

[196] Maya John, 'A Salary Plan that Changes Nothing', *The Hindu*, 1 October 2012.

husband, the way an employee may look for a better employer, signals a radical sensibility that moves beyond its time. Like Maya John, Sitakumari also raised the issue of widows, and further raised the issue of single and separated women also. With great foresight, Sitakumari identified any such proposal as a 'conspiracy of men'.

Problematising the Kitchen and Children

In her short story 'Vanta Yevaru Cheyyali?' (Who Should Cook?), S. Sarojini Devi raised an interesting question as to who should cook—men or women. Kantam, the central character, being an educated and affluent woman, did not know how to cook, which was normally expected of a woman in a traditional patriarchal society. Rama Rao, her unemployed husband, who married her despite his parent's opposition, broke out of the joint family. Kantam's father asked him to employ a maidservant as his daughter did not cook, but Rama Rao could not afford to do so. Now the author asked the question: 'who should cook?' The story ended abruptly with no clear answer. Yet the question is important because in a patriarchal society, woman's reluctance to perform her 'normal duty' itself is of great significance.[197]

Women complained against domestic drudgery and wished to liberate themselves from its 'formidable clutches'. Focusing on the 'oppressive' nature of the kitchen, a contributor, Satya, criticised the way tradition has turned women into the 'slaves of kitchen'. According to her, it was 'unpaid work', a kind of *vetti* (bonded labour):

> Cooking regularly makes women fatigued. But she has no other way. Whether she likes it or not, she has to spend her whole life in the kitchen. She is prepared for this since her childhood.... She has become slave of the kitchen.... The society has already decided her profession.... However knowledgeable a woman—particularly a middle-class woman—is, she does not find time for other activities as she is forced to spend most of her time in the kitchen. She cannot decide her profession; [society and] the elderly have already decided it for her.... [But] a man decides his profession. His work is time bound [and is paid]. He can use his leisure time according to his wishes. But a woman is denied the right to decide for herself, and the profession forced upon her is infinite.... This is an unpaid job, *vetti*, which brings not even gratitude. In the garb of sweetness in family life, she is bound to it. When everyone is flattering that it [cooking]

[197] *Grihalakshmi*, April 1934, pp. 136–138.

> is a great quality the *Gruhini* has to uphold, she is scared to dissent, and is thus compromising.[198]

Satya problematised motherhood also. She saw it as a 'problem' in the way of women's self-fulfilment:

> Motherhood is great. [But] the result of reproductive services rendered by a woman is her confinement to [the] home. Children belong to both mother and father. But the mother alone is forced to bring up children. Nine months in childbearing, two to three months in recovering health after delivery, and another two years in child-rearing. Again the cycle of bearing and rearing follows. Thus a significant portion of a woman's life is spent with children.... Man works outside. There is a time limit for it; he may work for six to seven hours a day. He makes use of the rest of his time according to his wish. But a woman's work of child-rearing has no time limit. That is there throughout the day [and night as well]. She is forced to look after them always. Hence, she does not find time to go anywhere.... It is a reality in the middle and lower middle class families that women are wearied with child-rearing. It is also a reality that women are losing their freedom because of children.[199]

Women's Liberation First, National Liberation Next

Komarraju Atchamamba,[200] writing in 1937, urged women to challenge and overthrow male domination; she emphasised that women's liberation

---

[198] Satya, 'Streela Pradhana Samasyalu: Vanta' (Main Problems of Women: Cooking), *Andhra Mahila*, February 1946, pp. 11–12. Just compare Satya's views with that of Maya John's. Maya John wrote, 'First, as a society we must learn to accept that there is sheer drudgery involved in day-to-day household work. The fact that such work is performed by a woman for her husband and other family members in the name of "care" and "nurturing" cannot be used to conceal that this is a thankless job which the majority of women feel burdened.... [W]e cannot write off the helplessness with which the average woman walks towards her kitchen hearth, every day without fail. Here, there is no retirement age, no holiday, and definitely, no concept of overtime.' How striking is the resonance between Satya's views and those of an activist writing in 2012!

[199] Satya, 'Streela Pradhana Samasyalu: Biddalu' (Main Problems of Women: Children), *Andhra Mahila*, January 1946, pp. 11–12.

[200] A medical doctor specialising in gynaecology and obstetrics, Atchamamba was involved in India's freedom struggle. She set up a hospital for volunteers who fell unconscious under police *lathis*. Having acquired her RCP and LIM degrees from Dublin Medical College, she set up a practice in Vijayawada. Her services as a doctor to the women of Krishna District were noteworthy. She conducted a course at the Women's Training Camp held in 1946 in Vijayawada on delivery, childcare, anatomy,

from the clutches of male domination was much more important than the political liberation of the country from foreign domination. In other words, women's liberation must precede the national liberation. According to her, women needed 'unrestrained freedom' to completely unfold their potential:

> Now we [women] are of a low status. Marrying and producing children have become our major duties and responsibilities! We have no other alternative than depend on others [men]. We have become puppets in the hands of men, and are being used by them as commodities and articles. Various traditions have been haunting us since our childhood, and are obstructing us towards enjoying equal rights to men. The various laws of marriage, adoption, succession, and the right to property are against us. Many among us feel that it is our fortune to have a husband, who offers us limited freedom at his will. This thinking is nothing but a result of centuries of slavery and subjugation. In fact, we need equal rights to men in all respects—social, economic and political—to retain our individuality, and enjoy unrestrained freedom. What we must do is to look at the women of France, Russia, etc., and realise the significance of our freedom and individuality. Before demanding the freedom of our country, we should free ourselves [from male domination]. Until then, we and our country will have no future.[201]

Conclusion: Thorny Feminist Critics and the Liberal Patriarchs

Thus, women questioned patriarchal prescriptions with such candour that they sometimes sparked alarm. As we have disussed, K. N. Kesari

---

healthcare and the condition of women in society. Her book on delivery and childcare, *Prasuti-Shishuposhana*, was the first of its kind in Andhra. She became a member of the Communist Party in 1940 and contested elections from the Eluru assembly constituency in 1946; later she joined the Congress and was elected as MP for Vijaywada. Her marriage with long-time friend Vajhala Venkatarama Shastri, defying Hindu rituals, was a cause for consternation in those times. She worked extensively on the Dowry Prohibition Act as an MP, was secretary of the All India Rural Women's Association, and served as President of the Vijayawada Medical Association. See Volga et al., *Mahilavaranam*, p. 75.

[201] Komarraju Atchamamba, 'Neti Rajakeeyalu-Streelu' (Today's Politics and Women), *Grihalakshmi*, June 1937, p. 295. There were many other women who expressed similar views. See Darishi Subhadramma, 'Bharata Streela Prastuta Sthiti' (The Present Condition of Indian Women), *Grihalakshmi*, May 1938, p. 146.

warned women to avoid 'mindless condemnation of men'.[202] Komarraju Atchamamba delivered a speech that he found particularly incendiary. She was reported to have said that 'like beasts, men mercilessly inflicted violence on women, and being selfish, they kept women in a degraded condition'. Kesari shot back through his journal *Grihalakshmi*:

> Ever since man realised that neither he nor his race [Indians] could advance without elevating women on par with him, he had been striving to better their conditions. He showed women the path of their development. From then on, and until this moment, both women and men are working for the progress of women. This is nothing new to women. Hence, women can progress with the aid of men. If they think that men's help is not necessary, they may work independently. They know it very well that in this enterprise accusing men is absolutely unnecessary!... How are women benefited by accusing men?[203]

Elsewhere, he reiterated his views on gender roles:

> Women and men shall enjoy different rights according to time and space. Just as there are physiological and mental differences between them, differences are bound to be there in terms of their behaviour, the rights they enjoy, and the duties they perform.... If they do not perform their respective roles, the symmetry of the universe will be disturbed, and it will become topsy-turvy. Given their physical structure, it is the duty of men to work hard. Women's duty is to preserve the fruit of men's hard work by using it in the right way. The home is a kingdom. Woman is its queen. It is the duty of man [the king] to acquire the things needed to maintain the kingdom. Woman ensures that the kingdom runs smoothly without any troubles.... Women naturally perform the domestic activities well. If they deny performing them, how can men [who are naturally disqualified!] perform? ... Aping the meaningless Western values and culture, if we demand [unnatural] rights, society will not progress, rather it will be destroyed.[204]

Such warnings and persuasions from the male editor only serve to highlight the radical consciousness women had begun to exhibit, and the growing alarm of men—particularly the 'reforming' new patriarchs. It indicates how

---

[202] See 'Sampadakiyamu: Vudyamabhivruddhiki Ninda Yeduruchukka' (Editorial: Accusing [Men] is an Obstacle to the Advancement of the Women's Movement), *Grihalakshmi*, March 1938, pp. 70–71.

[203] Ibid.

[204] See 'Sampadakiyamu' (Editorial), *Grihalakshmi*, January 1939, pp. 809–810.

far men thought women 'should' go and makes evident that a section of women had certainly transgressed this lakshmana rekha.

But what is remarkable to note is the paradoxical situation the journals were caught in. On the one hand, women's journals such as *Grihalakshmi* asked women to submit to the new patriarchy. On the other hand, by accommodating women's radical voices, they were allowing women to question this very attitude. If, by publishing women's journals, the new patriarchs sought to fit women into a structure acceptable/useful to them, a substantial section of women began to make use of that same space to dismantle the structure, questioning and rejecting the new patriarchal prescriptions as witnessed during the 1930s, 1940s and 1950s.

Conclusion

One of the chief means through which British colonialism sought to establish its moral superiority over the 'natives' and thus 'govern' and 'civilise' them was by pointing at the low position of native women. Indian women, particularly among upper-caste Hindus, suffered greatly due to the prevalence of social norms and practices such as the denial of education to girls and women, child marriage, enforced widowhood and also the existence of *sati*. As the status of women was seen to indicate the status of a civilisation, the dismal position of women fuelled a deep-rooted sense of inferiority among the Indian male intelligentsia. The colonial critique of Hindu culture forced them to introspect, and since the status of Hindu women was the most serious criticism leveled by colonial rulers, they sought to offer a corrective by 'uplifting' women. Thus, women became the focus of the social reform movements in colonial India. Right from the second half of the eighteenth century, reformers began to advocate for women's education and establishing schools, raising their voices against sati, child marriage and enforced widowhood.

Apart from the need for a native cultural defense, there was a strong personal dimension to the reform movement initiated by men. Influenced by British culture, particularly in terms of conjugality and family life, this emerging class of men harboured a desire for romantic love and companionate wives. Thus, they wanted educated wives who would offer them enlightened company and aid in their personal as well as social activities. However, given the context wherein girls generally did not receive education and were married off early, women were 'uncultured' and could not match the expectations of their husbands. Faced with the possible collapse of their dreams of marital bliss, men undertook the project of 'reforming' women.

As part of a pan-India phenomenon, male social reformers and intellectuals in Andhra began to address the woman's question from about the mid-nineteenth century. Reform ideas that pre-dated Veeresalingam coalesced into a concrete movement under his leadership. In the beginning, women remained the mere 'receivers' of reform. However, from the beginning of the twentieth century, they emerged as the 'initiators' of social reform as well. Women realised that they could not afford to rely exclusively on men's benevolence for ameliorating their conditions, and this pushed them into the field of activism, leading to the formation of a number of women's organisations throughout colonial Andhra. Begun in 1902, the process of establishment of women's organisations continued throughout the first half of the twentieth century. With this, women gained access to the public sphere, though in a limited way, to discuss secular issues concerning women. Women's desire for an expanded public space resulted in the formation of the Andhra Mahila Mahasabha in 1910. This broadened the scope of their public operations and accelerated the growth of the women's movement. With the formation of the Andhra Rashtra Mahila Mahasabha, the Andhra branch of the All India Women's Conference, in 1927, Andhra women integrated their movement with the pan-India women's movement.

Through the space provided by women's organisations, women continued the project of social reform with great vigour. Women social reformers and intellectuals firmly upheld the relevance of the woman's question even as the nationalist movement gathered momentum. The impression one gets by looking at women's organisations' varied activities is that, rather than fade away, social reform reached its peak during the first half of the twentieth century. Women reformers and intellectuals stubbornly refused to allow their issues to be submerged under the tide of nationalism. Moreover, a number of non-Brahmin caste associations pressed for social reform and their women's wings were deeply involved in social reform activities. We have also seen how women like Gadicharla Ramabai, editor of the *Soundaryavalli*, expressed dissatisfaction, as early as 1918, with the nationalist suggestion that the woman's question could wait until the achievement of political freedom.

Print culture was pressed into the service of social reform. From writing and publishing pamphlets to small tracts and books, and journals, reformers made extensive use of this burgeoning culture in their bid to spread reform consciousness in society. Almost all social reformers set up journals to propagate their ideas. The medium of print was thus a powerful instrument in the making, consolidation and acceleration of the social reform movement in colonial Andhra. As women constituted the focus of the reform agenda, many of these new journals were meant exclusively for women.

The social reform movement initiated by men had a positive impact on women. The new class of literate women readily recognised the need to be agents rather than mere 'objects' of reform. In their war against patriarchal cultural norms, they wielded words as their weapons, with women's journalism emerging as a direct result of their 'action-oriented outlook'. Not surprisingly, the twentieth century in Andhra saw the proliferation of women's journals edited and managed by women.

However, the first two women's journals were started and edited by men, Veeresalingam being the pioneer. Both journals were prone to sermonising and almost all their contributors were men. Women-edited journals—beginning with *Hindu Sundary* in December 1903—were more *positive* in terms of developing a positive self-concept among women. If the male edited journals held women to be 'ignorant', 'quarrelsome' and 'gossiping', women-edited women's journals, by and large, tried to understand the causes of these perceived behaviours. What was in need of reform was not *woman per se* but the *larger society and patriarchal culture* that made women what they were. The most significant aspect of the women-edited women's journals was that most of the contributors were women. Importantly, they clearly felt the continued relevance of their journals. That was why, as we have seen, if one women's journal ceased publication, a new one was born. It is amazing that journals like the *Hindu Sundary* managed to sustain themselves, amid severe financial constraints and social apathy, for over half a century. This speaks volumes of the commitment and perseverance of women activist-intellectuals to their movement.

The women-edited journals provided an expansive textual territory where they could move freely and speak their minds in public. Through their columns, women discussed various issues that concerned them and launched a serious and systematic campaign against such social problems. If the early examples like *Hindu Sundary* and *Anasuya* exhibited considerable ambivalence in their approach to women's issues and wanted women to be reformed within the boundaries of a liberal patriarchy, later journals gradually effected a paradigmatic change, redrawing the contours of women's public life and asserting women's individuality and independence. The early journals focused on limited issues such as women's education, child marriage, condition of widows and women's reformed domesticity. Later journals like *Grihalakshmi* and *Andhra Mahila*, on the other hand, expanded the concerns of women. They discussed their freedom and independence and amelioration of legal restrictions, demanded civil and political rights as well as political representation, condemned male chauvinism and domination and envisioned a society with gender equality and gender justice. With a continued discussion of women's issues, the journals moulded public opinion and transformed women's consciousness. More importantly, they sustained interest in women's issues in the face of the other struggles such as the Indian national movement.

However, not all women's journals were in favour of social reform. We have seen how *Savithri* bitterly opposed the very idea of widow remarriage and attacked social reformers, both women and men, who advocated in its favour. Although *Vivekavathi*, a Christian missionary women's journal, advocated social reform including widow remarriage, it had a strong Christian bias. Hindu women, in its telling, needed to be 'saved'. Therefore, it not only advocated loyalty to the British Crown but also subtly encouraged conversion to Christianity as a panacea to the problems of Hindu women.

Women's journals allowed for the creation of a shared identity based on gender and thereby keep the woman's question alive throughout the heyday of the national movement. Home to the varied thoughts and social work of women in colonial Andhra, the journals established their presence as intellectuals, activists and agents of their own destiny. But for these journals, women writers may not have found a collective space to express their minds and hearts. As Kotikalapudi Sitamma rightly observed, they served as 'ambassadors' taking the message of one woman intellectual to the other and vice versa. Significantly, as noted by women intellectuals of the time, these journals turned a number of women into accomplished writers, while beginners received training in the art of writing. The 'discovery' of fellow women intellectuals through the journals further emboldened them and encouraged many a woman to correspond with other 'sisters' without any hesitation. Thus, women's print media helped the emergence of an intellectual-activist female constituency in colonial Andhra.

Women-edited journals offer tremendous insights into the minds of a cross-section of the 'second sex' in early twentieth-century Andhra. The pages of the journals unveil how women spoke for themselves and for others, grappled with the wide gap between their aspirations and unfavourable ground realities and fought against internalised patriarchal mindsets as well as the larger patriarchal world that condemned them to 'slavery' and misery. They spread before us the map of women's changing consciousness and the agenda they set for themselves and for the larger nation. With the direct or indirect support of women's organisations, women's journals formed the backbone of the women's movement in colonial Andhra.[1] This platform enabled women to effectively combat the dehumanising effect of regressive social practices.

As discussed in Chapter 3, the problem of child marriage drew the attention of women intellectuals—both progressive and conservative—in Andhra right from the beginning of the twentieth century. In their arguments against child marriage, women deployed both religious and rational arguments, with the issue of scriptural sanction gradually losing importance as more and more women invoked medical science, rationality and 'everyday experience'. They emphasised that child marriage was against nature, destroyed girls' educational opportunities, ruined their heath and damaged the reputation of the nation. In sum, child marriage stifled the 'natural growth' of girls and caused civilisational shame. Saving the health of mothers and their infants was emblematic of saving the nation's health, activists emphasised. In women's later writings, we see repeated articulations that 'Mother India' needed healthy, strong and educated mothers who produced robust children. They vividly described the problems faced by 'child wives' (*baala bhaaryalu*) and 'child mothers' (*baala maatalu*) as well as the problems of 'incompatibility' (*ananukulata*) and 'forced conjugality' (*nirbandha dampatyamu*) experienced by child wives with relatively older husbands, which resulted in perennial 'domestic turmoil' (*grihachchidramu*). Women treated child marriage as the 'mother problem', that is, a fundamental issue that birthed many other problems that cumulatively led to the degeneration of Mother India.

Along with campaigning for raising the age of consent for both sexes (but especially girls), women intellectuals insisted on reducing the age gap between wives and husbands. As we have discussed, they berated older men for marrying 'granddaughter-like' girls and demanded a ban on marriages between men older than 40 and young girls. As time progressed, women consistently demanded post-puberty marriages, emphasising the 'choice' and 'consent' of girls and denouncing excessive 'parental interference'. If delayed marriages enhanced the educational opportunities of girls, the converse was also true: the presence of higher educational institutions ensured later marriages. As the issues of women's marriage and education were so closely interconnected, women demanded the proliferation of women's higher

[1]It may be a surprise to learn that the Andhra region does not have as many women's journals post-independence compared to colonial times.

educational institutions. As Gade Chudikudutamma observed, merely increasing the age of consent would be no use without also establishing such institutions. Several women activists themselves established schools for girls, and those who could not regularly campaigned in favour of them. Women's organisations played a significant role in this regard for many of them established girls' schools.

Women intellectuals who opposed child marriage argued that the practice was not there in the 'original' practice of Hinduism and in fact a later 'invention'. They found a convenient rationale for such an 'invention' in 'villainous medieval Muslim Rule' and the figure of the 'abducting *Musalman*'. This communal interpretation of 'Muslim Rule' as responsible for the 'present day degeneration of Hindu women' was dominant in the writings of reformist women intellectuals. Interestingly, however, conservative women who supported child marriage consistently and stubbornly maintained that the practice had 'original Hindu' roots and denied that it had any connection to 'Muslim rule'.

Not only did reformist women challenge the (male) nationalist claim that the woman's question could wait till after independence, some of them *welcomed* the foreign government's interference in the 'internal affairs' of the Hindu home. They saw it as a *panacea* to their problems. Women like Uppuluri Nagaratnamma expressed great faith in the colonial government's potential for achieving women's liberation from the evil traditions, referring to British rule as 'benevolent', 'beneficent' and 'soothing' (*Britishuvari challani palana*). They held legislation in high esteem because of its power to effect greater positive changes compared to 'mere preaching' about women's issues. When the 'internal' matters could not be resolved from within, as Mosalikanti Ramabayamma emphasised, external intervention was indispensable.

Naturally, they campaigned for banning the practice of child marriage through legislation and were overjoyed when the Sarda Act was passed in 1929. However, as they saw the Act being freely flouted by the orthodox sections, they criticised the British government for its 'indifference' in taking 'stringent action' against violators and campaigned for amendments to address loopholes. They believed that the passage of the Sarda Act was just the end of the beginning of their fight against child marriage and continued the propaganda work with renewed enthusiasm. The women's organisations played a commendable role in educating public opinion, lobbying with government and keeping the issue alive during the zenith of the Indian national movement. The change that was effected by the Child

Marriage Restraint Act was small but very significant. It was not merely a 'symbolic victory' to women.

Conservative women intellectuals like Pulugurta Lakshmi Narasamamba, who campaigned in favour of child marriage, saw it as the quintessence of Hindu women's pativratya dharma. As we have discussed, their arguments were rooted in a fear of 'varnasamkara', contamination of caste and varna, if young girls' sexuality was left unchecked. They condemned Indian reformers who blindly 'aped' Western values and, contrary to women reformers, emphasised the authority of parents in decisions regarding marriage. Such arguments thoroughly vilified and maligned Western women, warning their readers of great suffering and 'dharma *bhanga*' (destruction of dharma) if Western practices were adopted. Not surprisingly, therefore, many of them petitioned the British government to revoke the Sarda Act.

Despite this conservative backlash, the picture that emerges by a careful reading of the contemporary journals, particularly those edited by women, is that a majority of the literate women were in favour of the abolition of child marriage, with only a minuscule minority opposed to it. In women's journals, voices that demanded the abolition of the practice of child marriage were dominant.

Andhra women intellectuals discussed the problem of early and enforced widowhood. Women of the Brahmin and Vaishya castes were the chief victims of the practice, though Shudra castes like the Vishwa Brahmins and Kammas also disallowed their widows from remarrying. Despite the heartening fact that activists like Kandukuri Rajyalakshmamma were deeply involved in the widow remarriage movement from its very inception, Andhra women intellectuals as a whole did not publicly advocate widow remarriage through writing and public speaking in the first decade of the twentieth century. They strictly confined themselves to poignant descriptions of the miserable conditions of widows, especially focussing on the 'multiple atrocities' they had to bear. They vividly described the dehumanisation of widows, from routinised humiliation to abject starvation, to the 'horrendous' and 'barbaric' disfiguration of widows especially through the act of tonsuring their heads. The humiliation heaped on widows as well as restrictions on their freedom were so 'unbearable' and acute that a number of widows preferred death through either *sahagamana*, that is, sati, or suicide. Blaming 'unkind' parents for lacking any sensitivity towards the plight of their daughters, women intellectuals criticised the stigma associated with widowhood and petitioned the colonial government against practices like ritual tonsuring of widows. The faith of women like Mosalikanti

Ramabayamma (editor of *Hindu Sundary*) in the British government was so immense that they praised the British government for releasing Hindu women from the 'shackles of social evil'. One may recall Ramabayamma's emotionally charged appreciation of the colonial government: 'had the British government, the great and all dharmas personified, not eliminated such horrible practices [as sati] through legislation, no woman would have existed [in India] to send *mahajars*', such as hers.

By the 1910s, one could clearly perceive a change in women intellectuals' writings and public speaking. They were now willing to openly demand widow remarriage—initially restricting themselves to child widows and those deemed sexually inexperienced, and later including widows of all age groups, including those with children. Remarried women (punarvivahitalu) began to campaign for widow remarriage themselves at this point, through writings and public speaking. The best example is provided by Uppuluri Nagaratnamma, a child widow who had a remarriage. Paying explicit attention to the sexual needs of widows, activist-intellectual women like Nagaratnamma emphasised that because widow remarriage was legalised through an Act, one need not bother about any sanction or ban in the shastras, and that 'mere commonsense and everyday experience' was enough to judge in favour of widow remarriage. With such arguments, she and other women intellectuals like Kuditipudi Achchamamba marked a radical new approach that challenged the limited social change advocated by reformist men. Interestingly, women introduced a new concept by coining a new term *sadhava vydhavyamu*, that is, experiencing nearly the conditions of widowhood. This was the problem of abandoned women as discussed in a woman's letter to the editor of *Telugu Zenana* as far back as 1903. What is striking is that women campaigned for the remarriage of such women and demanded punishment for their 'merciless' husbands who abandoned them. Most significantly, they demanded that the British government punish such men, who were its employees.

Women intellectuals questioned the skewed sense of social morality that mandated discrimination against widows even as widowers were free to remarry. The questioning of double standards and the Hindu religious scriptures was sharpened over the late 1920s and beyond. As we have seen, Kuditipudi Achchamamba declared that the Dharmashastras were 'irrelevant to contemporary society' and that they were to be totally discarded. Women intellectuals supported widow remarriage through their literary output, from poetry and essays to short stories, novels and plays. Women's pursuit of feminist issues even after independence demonstrates both, their refusal to back down, and the persistence of problems despite remarkable progress.

However, nationalist women like Duvvuri Subbamma and Battula Kamakshamma *chose* to remain widows and the former even opposed widow remarriage. Instead of remarriage, they offered 'social and national service' as a proper solution to the problems of widows and thereby treated them as sexually inert beings. Kanuparti Varalakshmamma, despite being a proponent of widow remarriages, suggested to widows that there was no need for them to 'despair' because there was a vast field called 'social and national service', which included programmes for women's development, open for the widows to channelise their energies. Rather than indulging in 'cheap gossip' and 'empty spiritualism' (*shushka vedantamu*), they were to live a 'life of purpose' and turn themselves into socially and politically 'useful' beings. As they were 'relieved of the shackles of family life', they were to concentrate on the 'higher ideal of national service'. In other words, widows were to be sexually dead, but socially alive and active. Such widows like Duvvuri Subbamma and Battula Kamakshamma established schools and colleges for girls, rescue homes for widows and the destitute women and made outstanding contributions to the freedom movement of the country.

Women intellectuals were not content with mere writing and public speaking: they always wrote and said that words were not enough and that *deeds* were more important. Therefore, many of them actively participated in the widow remarriage movement. From Kandukuri Rajyalakshmamma, Unnava Lakshmibayamma, Darisi Annapoornamma, Atyam Satyavati Devi, Munupalle Ramakotamma, Manchikanti Venkataratnamma, Rajamma Devi to Andallamma (Lady Venkata Subba Rao), women activists were deeply involved in the widow remarriage movement. Attending widow remarriages and participating in the wedding processions, acting as kanyadatas of widows at widow remarriages, providing encouragement and shelter to the remarried couples and, most importantly, establishing and running widows' homes were only a few of the *deeds* that such activist-intellectual women undertook throughout the period of our study. Some of them held the widow remarriage movement dearer than their own lives. In fact, Darisi Annapoornamma's untimely death can probably be attributed to her hectic involvement in the movement: it was no accident that she died of heart attack just four days after she returned from Bandar (Machilipatnam), where she had performed a widow remarriage. This intense involvement stemmed from the feminist recognition that, as Sarangu Sitadevi emphasised, the reform movement/women's movement could not succeed, or sustain itself, until and unless women themselves took up the cause of social and cultural change.

We have also seen how widows emerged as *agents* of individual and social change. The desire among these women to remove themselves from the oppressive trappings of widowhood was so strong that, exhibiting incredible zeal and courage, they secretly ran away from homes, often travelling all alone for as much as thousand kilometres (as Sitamma did from Ganjam in Odisha to Rajahmundry). They provided roadmaps to male reformers about the way to take them away from their homes, and later refused to be persuaded by their parents and other family members to leave the shelters they found. By remarrying, often against the wishes of family elders and their communities, the widows sculpted their own destiny and enriched the widow remarriage movement. Several mothers and grandmothers of widowed girls took pains to ensure that their daughters or granddaughters were relieved of the torment of enforced widowhood. By expressing willingness to remarry (which in itself questioned patriarchal structures), exhibiting the courage to withstand the pressure of family and society and their strong desire to come out of the oppressive conditions forced upon them, widows seriously and sincerely tried to wrest control over their own fate. There was *radicalism* in the widows' act of remarrying. Moreover, some were content with sexual liaisons with men of their liking, outside the institution of marriage. With this, they rebelled against the orthodox and oppressive cultural practices. They asserted their right to family life, which included the right to sexual life, and this was a severe jolt to the circumscribing patriarchal ideology.

It is no surprise that some conservative women despised the very idea of remarriage for widows, with Narasamamba leading the charge once again. The conservative position was that widow remarriage tarnished Indian women's pativratyam (conjugal fidelity), for which India had been famous 'all through the time and all over the globe'. Branding remarried women as disrespectable, they made the circuitous claim that widow remarriage would hinder women's educational advancement: they argued that young women would have to compete with widows to find grooms, reducing their opportunities for a good match! Widow remarriage was so deeply contentious that the prominent organisation Shri Vidyarthini Samajamu was split in two camps on the subject and a highly public, protracted controversy ensued for over a year.

The controversy attested to deeply divided opinions among women intellectual-activists on the issue of widow remarriage and the place of widows in society. Further, it revealed that though remarriage removed a few of the immediate difficulties faced by widows, their social status declined considerably. They were treated contemptuously and were largely unwelcome in society. Their very association, let alone close company, was to be avoided, the conservative women held. Blamed for 'tarnishing' the chaste image of the 'Hindu Aryan women', they were treated as *kulata*s (prostitutes) and denied any respect. The punarvivahitas, that is, widows who remarried, had to silently suffer from the want of social acceptance and respect. In short, the controversy confirmed the widespread prejudice against the punarvivahitas. However, the ignominious defeat of the 'conservative' group led by Pulugurta Lakshmi Narasamamba at the hands of the 'progressive' section of women, who were supported by many—both women and men—indicated a new social undercurrent supporting widow remarriage and social change. But the prejudices against widows continued, and the stigma persists till date, manifesting itself in a variety of obnoxious ways.

We have discussed domestic ideology as it emerged in late-nineteenth- and early-twentieth-century Andhra, and the multiple perspectives on women's education. We have seen how Indian intellectuals, both women and men, particularly the latter, responded to British colonial critique of the native domestic arrangements—material as well as human. Men being the first to have been exposed to colonial culture, it was they who first desired a thorough reordering of their domestic domain, particularly demanding changes in the way women ran the family, conducted themselves with their husbands and other members of the family, etc. Men demanded that women learn the 'art' and 'science' of domestic management (*griha nirvahakatvamu*), received education and provided enlightened company to their husbands and better training to their children. They saw the home as a microcosm of the nation. As the 'disorderly' Hindu home, which indicated the 'backwardness' of Indian civilisation, came under heavy attack by the colonisers, 'native' intellectuals rushed to alter it. Civilising the home, according to them, was a precondition to civilising the nation and this alone could combat the colonial critique. It must be carefully noted that, though British domesticity provided them with a model, they did not want to copy it as it was, but rather made modifications to suit Indian conditions.

In the model of *beneficial domesticity* put forth by the male social reformers and intellectuals, a new woman took birth, who was educated, industrious, disciplined, frugal, scientific and rational, kind-hearted, virtuous, uncomplaining and, in brief, 'civilised'. In other words, she was a perfect *grihalakshmi* (goddess of the home). She was no more a symbol of his civilisational shame, but a source of pride. She was a *sahadharmacharini*, perfect companion in discharging life's duties, and *uttama maata*, noble mother, in the imagination of Veeresalingam, Rayasam Venkata Sivudu and other male reformers and intellectuals. She was expected to be 'ideal' in all the roles she needed to perform—ideal wife, ideal mother, ideal daughter-in-law, ideal sister-in-law, and ideal neighbour and, finally, an ideal woman. Thus, reformist men overburdened her with all their grand expectations. She was allowed the liberty to move in and out so far as she could meet their demands. They, thus, redrew the lakshmana rekha originally drawn in the repressive regime of 'old patriarchy' and redefined women's freedom to suit men's needs.

In the beginning, that is, last decade of the nineteenth century and the first two decades of the twentieth century, women intellectuals like Bhandaru Atchamamba positively responded to the *demands* of liberal patriarchs since liberal patriarchy offered them relative freedom unavailable in the structures of 'old patriarchy'. However, as they strategically made use of this new freedom and gained a voice, they began questioning men's domination within family and society, discrimination against women, and demanded equality with men in all aspects of life. They questioned patriarchal culture and structures, including religious injunctions and institutions that stifled their natural growth, and demanded radical changes in society based on gender equality and gender justice. They asserted that they were in no way inferior to men, whether physically or intellectually, and provided a number of examples from history and the contemporary world to corroborate their stand. It was not women alone who had duties to be performed and morals to be observed. Men, too, needed to be 'virtuous' and 'faithful to their wives': they had to be patnivratas, the same way women were asked to be pativratas.

The increasing levels of gender consciousness among women made them identify men as their 'suppressors' and the principal cause of their 'backwardness'. This sharpened understanding of men's role in women's subjection resulted in their declaration that 'men [had] failed the women's movement'. Women intellectuals emphasised that because men would not 'sincerely' work for women's development, women themselves were required to come forward to 'lead the women's movement'. They demanded that all kinds of discriminations must end. Further, they pointed out that it was 'unjust' on the part of Indian male nationalists that they complained about British discrimination against Indians, but took men's discrimination against women for granted. The feminist consciousness of at least some of the women like Komarraju Atchamamba was so radical that they prioritised the women's movement over the Indian national movement. Their feminist understanding led them to question women's confinement to the domestic domain, complain against domestic drudgery, problematise the kitchen and children, debunk the proposal of salaries for housewives and demand a larger canvas for women's mobility and work.

This unexpected challenge alarmed the new liberal male patriarch. We have discussed the writings of K. N. Kesari, founder and editor of *Grihalakshmi*, which amounted to a chastisement of women activists who dared cross the *lakshmana rekha* established by reformist men. This fear of the erosion of masculine power was reflected in appeals to women's 'natural duties', their duty to uphold 'family peace' and 'Indian culture' instead of 'aping Western values', and their role in 'children's wellbeing'. This power tussle, and the frequent recourse to women's 'natural place', continues to this day.

While the liberal patriarchs proposed the model of beneficial domesticity, and though women initially accepted because they saw an advantage in it, very soon, they realised that the model benefitted men most. Therefore, they put forward a new model: what may be termed as *egalitarian domesticity*. This was manifest in women intellectuals' demand that 'equality should be the basis of conjugal relations' and that the domestic work be shared by both women and men. Women's recognition of the fact that 'their lives and careers had been already decided much before their birth' (*meekante mundu mee jeevitalu yerpaddayi*) was significant in itself. And it is a heartening fact that feminist intellectuals in colonial Andhra decided to rewrite their destiny.[2]

Women intellectuals identified education as an instrument that would empower them to rewrite their pre-determined life-paths. They demanded such an education which allowed them to realise their fullest potential as full human beings in society. They refused to be confined to the domestic domain and demanded an expanded public space. They firmly believed that

[2]See Gurajada's letter (dated 21 May 1909) to Ongolu Muni Subramanyam Pantulu in Setty Eswara Rao, ed., *Gurajada Rachanalu: Jabulu-Jawabulu, Dinacharyalu*, p. 8.

'half of the sky' as well as half of the earth was theirs and that they needed to capture it.

We have attempted to retrieve the powerful voices of this array of women that have somehow been otherwise lost, even though many of the issues they had raised as well as debates that had ensued continue to this day.

Appendix 1

Women's Journals

S. No.	Name of the Journal	Period of Publication	Editor(s)	Place(s) of Publication	Publisher	Rate of Subscription	Circulation	Frequency
1.	**Sathihitha Bodhini**	**1883–1904/1905** Break between 1885–1888; Merged with the *Telugu Zenana* in September 1904	Kandukuri Veeresalingam	Rajahmundry	Kandukuri Veeresalingam	Annual: Rs. 2 Half-yearly: Re. 1 Single copy: 0.4 annas	–	Monthly
2.	**Maharani**	**1889–1892**	M. Krishnamachariar	–	–	–	–	Monthly

(Contd)

S. No.	Name of the Journal	Period of Publication	Editor(s)	Place(s) of Publication	Publisher	Rate of Subscription	Circulation	Frequency
3.	**Telugu Zenana**	**July 1893–1907** Started in July1893 Break for 6 months in the second half of 1905; Revived in January 1906	Founder-editor Malladi Venkata Ratnam; later (from June or July 1894) owned and edited by Rayasam Venkata Sivudu; Joint Editors: in 1902 Venkata Ramaiah; in 1904–05 Kandukuri Veeresalingam	Initially from Guntur; Later from Madras, Bezawada and Rajahmundry	Initially Malladi Venkata Ratnam; Later Rayasam Venkata Sivudu	Annual: Re.1 till 1900; Increased for some time to Rs. 2, but reverted to Re. 1 from September 1904	300	Monthly
4.	**Stree Hitha Bodhini**	**1893**	Rapaka Kaustubham	Kakinada	–	Circulated free of cost	N.A.	Monthly
5.	**Balika**	Started **March 1896**	Sangitarao Baupiraju	Chicacole (Srikakulam)	Sangitarao Baupiraju and K. V. Narasiah Naidu	Annual: 2.5 annas	N.A.	Monthly

(Contd)

S. No.	Name of the Journal	Period of Publication	Editor(s)	Place(s) of Publication	Publisher	Rate of Subscription	Circulation	Frequency
6.	**Hindu Sundary** (first women-edited journal)	**(1902–beyond 1960)** Started in April 1902; discontinued between January 1908–May 1909; Revived in June 1909; discontinued again during the 1920s Revived a second time in the 1940s	Founder: Sattiraju Sitaramaiah; December 1903—May 1913: Mosalikanti Ramabayamma and Vempali Shantabayamma; From June 1913: Madabhooshi Choodamma and Kallepalle Venkata Ramanamma; During the 1940s: Balantrapu Sheshamma	Initially from Eluru; From Kanteru in April/May 1905; and finally from Kakinada (June 1913 onward)	Initially: Sattiraju Sitaramaiah; From March 1913, *Shri Vidyarthini Samajamu*	Initially: Annual: Re. 1; After revival in June 1909: Annual: Rs. 2 Half-yearly: Rs. 1. 40 Single copy: 0.4 paisa	800 by 1904, two years after its inception	Monthly
7.	**Griha-lakshmi**	**1903**	Nandiraju Chalapati Rao	Eluru	Raja Mantripragada Bhujanga Rao	–	–	Monthly

(Contd)

S. No.	Name of the Journal	Period of Publication	Editor(s)	Place(s) of Publication	Publisher	Rate of Subscription	Circulation	Frequency
8	**Savithri**	**1904–1917** Break from 1907 to possibly July 1910	Pulugurta Lakshmi Narasamamba	Cocanada (Kakinada)	Pulugurta Venkata Ratnam	Annual: Re. 1 Single copy: 2 paisa	1,500	Monthly
9	**Vivekavathi**	**1909–beyond 1934**	First editor: Ms McLaurin Second editor: Ms Archibald M. A., (October 1910–18 August 1913) Third editor: Mrs McCauley Fourth editor: Mrs M. A. Shreenivassa B.A., L.T., (during the last years of publication)	Madras	Christian Literature Society; managed by a 15- member Vivekavathi Committee	Annual: 12 annas; Single copy: 1 anna	1,500 (by October 1913)	Monthly
10.	**Sundari**	**1909**	B. Narayana	Komari Palem (Godavari District)	–	–	–	Monthly
11.	**Streela-koraku Vartamana-mulu**	**January 1898–beyond 1916**	Ms E. S. Mc Cauley	Guntur	–	–	–	Monthly

(Contd)

Appendix I (Contd)

S. No.	Name of the Journal	Period of Publication	Editor(s)	Place(s) of Publication	Publisher	Rate of Subscription	Circulation	Frequency
12.	**Anasuya**	**July 1917–1924**	Vinjamuri Venkata Ratnamma	Cocanada (Kakinada)	Vinjamuri Venkata Lakshmi Narasimham	Annual: Rs. 1. 50; Single copy: 3 annas	–	Monthly
13.	**Stri Dharma** (Multi-lingual: in English, Tamil, Hindi and Telugu)	**January 1918–August 1936**	Margaret Cousins, Muthulakshmi Reddy Malati Patwardhan (Telugu section editor)	Madras	Women's Indian Association (WIA)	For WIA members: Rs. 4. For Indians: Rs. 4; for foreigners: 7 shillings. Single issue: 5 annas	–	Monthly
14	**Bala Bharati**	**1918**	Duvvuri Jagannatha Sharma	Kakinada	–	–	–	Monthly
15	**Soundar-yavalli**	Started in **July 1918**	Gadicharla Ramabai	Madras	–	Annual: Rs. 3	–	Monthly
16	**Andhra Lakshmi**	**December 1921–1924**	Kallepalle Venkata Ramanamma	Barampuram (Ganjam Distt.; now in Odisha)	Kallepalle Shivaramaiah	Annual: Rs. 2 Single copy: 4 annas	–	Monthly
17	**Hindu Yuvati**	**1923**	Yamini Poorna Tilakamma	Madras	–	–	–	Fortnightly
18	**Bharata Mahila**	**1925**	U. Sundaramma	Anantapuram (Rayalaseema)	–	–	–	Monthly

(Contd)

S. No.	Name of the Journal	Period of Publication	Editor(s)	Place(s) of Publication	Publisher	Rate of Subscription	Circulation	Frequency
19	**Griha-lakshmi**	**1928–beyond 1960** Started on 1 March 1928; Break between: 1942–1947	K. N. Kesari (till his death in 1953); C. C. Punnaiah subsequently became Acting Editor	Madras	K. N. Kesari; after his death, Kesari Kutiram Pvt. Ltd.	Annual: Rs. 3 Half-yearly: Rs. 1. 80. Single copy: 0.4.0 annas Rates changed during 1950s Annual: Rs. 4.80 Half-yearly: Rs. 2. 80 Single copy: 6 annas	2,000 (in 1940)	Monthly
20	**Yashoda**	During **1930s**	T. K. Yashoda Devi	Rajahmundry	–	–	–	Twice a week
21	**Vishwa Gnani**	–	Yamini Poorna Tilakamma	Madras	–	–	–	–
22	**Shri Sharada Niketanamu**	**c. July 1937**	Three women were on the Editorial Board. They were: Unnava Lakshmi-bayamma, Vidwan Ma-jumdar Savitri Devi and Pasupuleti Lalita Devi	Guntur	Sharada Niketanamu	Annual: Re. 1	–	Monthly

(Contd)

S. No.	Name of the Journal	Period of Publication	Editor(s)	Place(s) of Publication	Publisher	Rate of Subscription	Circulation	Frequency
23	**Andhra Mahila**	**1944–beyond 1960** Started on 15 May 1944	Founder Editor: Durgabai Deshmukh. Associate Editor: M. Vishweshwara Rao; Assistant and Co-editors before 1950: Achyutuni Girija (1945-1946), K. Sugunamani (1947), and Mamidipudi Vaidehi (1948). Editors: Channaghantamma (since June 1953); Lakshmi Raghuram (for eight months); Adurti Bhaskaramma (since July 1955); Lakshmi Raghuram (since 1959); Ramalakshmi Arudra (Joint editor)	Madras	Andhra Mahila Sabha Durgabai Deshmukh	Initially: 8 annas; since 15 July 1944: 4 annas; Annual: Rs. 5 Half-yearly: Rs. 2. 80. Since May 1951: Annual: Rs. 6 Single copy: 0.8.0 annas	–	Started as fortnightly; became a monthly in January 1946

(Contd)

Appendix I (Contd)

S. No.	Name of the Journal	Period of Publication	Editor(s)	Place(s) of Publication	Publisher	Rate of Subscription	Circulation	Frequency
24	**Soubhagya**	**1945**	–	Madras	Women Welfare Officer, Government of Madras; later Andhra State Women Welfare Officer	–	–	Monthly
25	**Andhra Vanita**	Started in **March/April 1948**. Congress government banned the publication after just two issues were out.	Darishi Subhadramma	Vijayawada	Andhra Rashtra Mahila Sangham (Organisation of the Communist Women of Andhra)	N.A.	N.A.	Monthly
26	**Vanita Vihar**	**Early 1949**	Three editors: Satyavati Devi, Rajyalakshmi and Mahalakshmi	Rajahmundry	N.A.	N.A.	N.A.	Unsure, possibly monthly
27	**Vanita**	**April–December 1956**	Abburi Chaya Devi	Hyderabad	Andhra Yuvati Mandali	Annual: Rs. 3	N.A.	Monthly
28	**Narilokam**	**c. 1956**	K. Rangamma Reddy	Vijayawada	–	–	–	Monthly

Appendix 2

Is Equality between Women and Men Desirable or Harmful?[1]

Mydavolu Padmavati Devi

The status of women reflects the status of a country. It is because of women that a country either attains glory or slips down to the bottom. The respect enjoyed by women in a country is the respect given to it. The good fortune of women in a country reflects the good fortune of the country. The respect women enjoy indicates the respect a nation enjoys. Needless to say, a nation in which half of its people are suppressed, cannot develop. Where women constitute half of the nation, the backwardness of women turns out to be the backwardness of the nation. A nation attains eligibility for Swaraj only when it attains gender equality. Independence of countries like Japan, Turkey and Russia was possible only because they have achieved equality between women and men. A nation can never attain salvation as long as men, in [their] selfishness, restrict and captivate women [even though they] are equal to men in number.

If our country has to attain Swaraj, the first step should be granting freedom to women. Women have to develop a personality of their own. Woman is not the property of man. Man should treat her as a separate entity.

Earlier, men greatly respected women for they thought that women were sensitive and destined by God to be comfortable and safe at home.... It was the tradition of our country that earning money was the part of men and meaningful utilisation of the same was that of women. But, as time passed, the queenship [*raanitvamu*] once enjoyed by women disappeared and she became the property of men and then their slave.

[1]'Stree Purusha Samanatvamavashyakama, Yendeni Yanarthadayakama?' *Grihalakshmi*, November 1936, pp. 661–666. This essay was awarded first prize.

The condition of women in our country now is very deplorable. The reason for it is nothing but the violence inflicted on women by men and society. The community of men not only hates the community of women but has also injected an inferiority complex [in them] and is ruling [over] them by force.

Being selfish, man confines woman to the home and treats her as the slave of the kitchen and the bedroom. He uses her as a luxury item. Society accepts man marrying and abandoning any number of women and resorting to highly immoral deeds. The scriptures also support him. But if any woman loses her chastity, society excommunicates her, rendering her helpless, and subjects her to disgrace and disgust. How can a woman become immoral without a man? Isn't it? But society would never dare punish that great man, it cannot even try to do so. Moreover, it compliments by praising him [as] 'Male, the King' [*moga maharaju*] and also says metaphorically 'the bee shall weigh down as many flowers as it can' [*yenni poovulan vraladu teti*].

What an injustice! It is enough if one just takes birth as man to rule over woman, to harass them and even to exchange [one for another] as one changes cloaks. He can marry one thousand women, but a woman does not have the right to separate from a husband who is a drunkard and who scolds and beats [her] and subjects her to enormous grief.

The scriptures say, 'Na Stree Swaatantryamarhati', or woman does not deserve independence. This is the celestial sword with which men have kept women in captivity all these years.

Being selfish, men always thought of their own knowledge, comfort and welfare and suppressed women all these years by creating rules and scriptures, and declared them not worthy of anything. The suppression was possible because scriptures were written by men. And man alone symbolises society!

Why are women treated as inferior? Are women not part of the human race? Alas! They are not inanimate beings, you know! They are also human beings, you know! God created women on par with men by giving them similar hands and legs, physical and intellectual strength, and the ability to distinguish between good and bad. Yes, He had created both of them as equals. Not only equal: in some ways, women are more than equal. The same great Manu who said that women do not deserve freedom, himself had said that women are four times more intelligent than men. How can it be justifiable to say that women do not need freedom, when they possess intellect and emotions in equal measure? Is it not the selfishness of men to suppress women, who are in no way inferior in terms of intellectual abilities?

Is it not the selfishness of men that has kept women inferior, helpless and captive? Devoid of opportunities, women's abilities are kept in the dark. Otherwise, women are in no way inferior to men.

According to the scriptures, woman is a thing, not an individual. Woman must develop a personality of her own. If woman has to develop a personality and if she has to enjoy freedom equal to man, she must have equal opportunities and rights in the field of education, civil rights and membership in legislatures. The innate abilities of women have not been utilised till now because adequate opportunities are not provided to them.

Women should overcome cowardice and get rid of the demon called fear in them, leap beyond the domestic domain to be considered equal to men and be honoured like them.

Women alone should fight for their freedom. They alone should solve their problems and set their conditions right. We alone should secure what we need. The problems of women are better known to women themselves. Therefore, the responsibility of reforming the society also rests with women. It is [a] false [notion] that men ever help women. Those who bore down on us all these years, will they ever willingly grant freedom to us now? Will the same men who were reluctant to allow women any freedoms [at all], now bind their own hands [by giving up their power]? If they really [were to] grant freedom the moment we ask, not only we but the nation also would have got it by now. If we sit idly and say we need equality, it will never come. Men will never give [it to us]. Hence, women alone should achieve freedom and power. How can we formulate laws [to this effect]? It will be possible only when women enter the legislature. It is not enough if one or two women enter the house, but they should enter in equal or greater numbers than men. Only then will laws that help women be promulgated. Even though a few men who fight for the rights of women are present in legislature, they are overpowered by women-haters who are in large numbers, and who are hell-bent on defeating laws beneficial to women. Women's rights are achieved only when women representatives are greater in number. Making laws alone is not enough. They should be put into practice. Laws not observed or followed are as good as laws not promulgated. Women must take the lead in implementing laws. When women implement them, things impossible become possible and, when they do not, things possible also become impossible. Therefore, the responsibility of reforming the society rests with women.

One needs money not to depend on others. If women have to be economically independent, they should enjoy an equal right to property.

Right to property is equal to one crore other rights. Equality and freedom cannot be achieved without wealth. Where is the place to freedom, if one cannot separate and live alone when disputes arise between [wife and husband]? So, to be independent, one needs to earn money. Look at people of the labouring class in India. The women among them work along with men and earn money. They enjoy much better freedom than women belonging to the wealthy classes.

According to scriptures, the livelihood of a woman rests in marriage. Since women do not have a share in the property of their parents, the husband has become the one and only source of livelihood for them. Parents educate their sons, but it is rare that they educate their daughters. Hence, to earn money, women have the option of cooking or carrying water, but no other alternative. Therefore, if parents give a share in their property to daughters also, they can keep it like principle fund, receive education and lead an independent life.

According to Hindu and Islamic scriptures, women have very few rights and those scant rights are also offered to them only by benevolent men.

Daughters are also carried in the womb for nine months, like sons, by their mothers. Daughters and sons share equally the blood and strength of their mothers when they are carried. But when it comes to property, it goes in its entirety to sons. Daughters do not get so much as a piece of a broomstick. Daughters cannot even claim the spoiled betel nut from their natal homes. So it is from in-laws' home. When a woman dies, the jewellery on her body goes to her husband only. But property of the husband never goes to the wife. If it is earned by his father, it goes to his brothers or cousins. If it is earned by the husband himself, it goes to whoever he wishes. But there is no provision that it should go to his wife. The condition is slightly better if a woman has a son. Brothers-in-law would give her a share. Otherwise, she has to lead a life of helplessness and degradation. She has a right to nothing other than the atrocities she suffers at the in-laws' house. Therefore, it is indispensable that women should have a right to property equal to men.

Women need education. Without education, no one can do anything. Woman should shoulder the responsibility of facing the social, economic and political predicaments of society. Women should learn all that is learnt by men, to argue with them, enter all professions men are engaged in and emerge equal to them. Hence, women must be treated as equal in all respects and be honoured, and opportunities should be provided to enter all the institutions and offices. Today, women are not entitled to sit for apex exams like the Indian Civil Service, Engineering and Agriculture. Such obstacles must be removed to ensure that women enter all such professions.

Earlier, in India, both women and men were permitted to remain bachelors or spinsters. But, now, women cannot remain single, but a man can. Some of the women might not be willing to marry. For such women, is not marriage a confinement? Therefore, women should have the right to remain a spinster all through their life.

A widower is eligible for remarriage, but not a widow. Woman also should have the right to remarry when she loses her husband. Remarriages would help growth in population and there are no evils involved in it. It is quite well-known that not all widows desire remarriage. Then, is not the denial of the right to remarry an infliction of violence on those widows who want to marry?

Woman must have the right to divorce. Many are afraid of giving women such a right under the false pretext that women would keep changing husbands and resort to living a life of pleasure and immorality. In India, the relationship between wife and husband is not something related to pleasure and lust only. It is not a rotten fruit that falls down from tree with a mere touch. If it is really so, in special circumstances, would not breaking the bond be much better than continuing it?

Women would not misuse this right. There may be one in a crore amongst them who takes recourse to it. Even in such a case, women going for divorce cannot be misuse but rather, a justifiable [step]. Are women killing their husbands who insure wives' lives? No. Isn't it? Similar would be the case with the right to divorce also. One should not say no to the Divorce Act thinking that innocent young girls will misuse it and thereby suffer troubles. Will anyone stop learning to swim because one may get drowned when stepping into water? Divorce Act is essential even though it may be useful to a very small number of women. Why should we be scared of it? Will any wife demand divorce from a husband who loves and is faithful to her? What happens if a provision for divorce is included in law? Why don't the husbands conduct with their wives in such ways that women would not put it to use at all? Hence, all that is said above is essential to relieve women from bondage.

Women who secure all the above rights will be gaining equality and freedom. Then women will have the freedom to lead their lives as per their tastes and preferences. There will not be any kind of force operating on them. Those who want to remain unmarried and wish to take up jobs will have the freedom to do so, and those who want to be housewives shall flourish as goddesses of homes.

Therefore, women's total equality with men will not corrupt society. The nation will progress when both men and women enter all professions without any hesitation or difference. There is no doom that shall befall the nation.

Equality will relieve women from bondage and helplessness and lead to national progress and thereby to Swaraj. Therefore, equality is essential and not deleterious in any case.

Anyway, I made it clear earlier itself that mere acquisition of equality through law shall not help much unless it is put into practice. Putting it into practice is all-important. Practising equality or exercising rights means revolting against old customs and traditions and the deeply internalised ideas of slavery. Men have been revolting against their slavery for a long time. But they have not been able to win independence because women are not joining them in the revolt.

Women do not relinquish their natural duties of the household with the acquisition of equality. It is not good for the educated and propertied women to give up their household duties. Some of them are really under the impression that it would be degrading to them to perform household duties. So they entrust the duties of caring for their children and husbands to maids and servants and, thereby, turn their heavenly homes into hell. That is why misconceptions about women's equality are rampant everywhere.

If women and men share all professions equally, no damage would be caused to women's household activity.

Appendix 3

Is Equality between Women and Men Desirable or Harmful?[1]

Vedula Meenakshi Devi

> If scriptures are taught like [they are to] men, they learn;
> If trained in archery, they kill soldiers of enemies;
> If enthroned, with all enthusiasm they rule the world;
> Is there any knowledge that women cannot learn, if they are taught with love?

In India there is no independence, not even for men. The Indian nation is striving hard to regain the independence it once enjoyed. If women are permitted to join in their endeavour, will not men gain a double benefit?...

What is equality? Something that is good for men cannot be bad for women simply by virtue of difference between the sexes. It is like this. If [a] potato pudding gives strength to men, it will be the same for women also. Men and women are equal in physical and mental abilities. Some may doubt [this, saying] that we do not have women like men with strong bodies and high intellect. We neither have such opportunities nor [managed to] create them for ourselves to grow like men.... The physical and mental features of men and women are the same. So it is not unnatural for the women to have similar wants as those of men.

However, a few thoughts of those who negate equality are to be discussed before the question where equality should exist is answered.

---

[1] 'Stree Purusha Samanatvamavashyakama, Yendeni Yanarthadayakama?' *Grihalakshmi*, November 1936, pp. 667–673. This essay was awarded second prize.

Who says no to equality? Normally, it is men. Even men do not have independence in India.… Women in India today are more or less 'slaves'. Men try to control us. So, some think that we have become slaves of slaves. However, I do not mean that all men are like that. Some of them are liberal. I salute them. Among men, some forget without fail, and even the best of them sometimes need to be reminded, that 'women also have mind and heart and that they have good and bad in them'. Hence, under such circumstances, women need the strength of equal status to put men on the right path.

Many men argue that women do not deserve equality. Why? Let us critically examine some of the reasons put forth by them. They say that inequality is natural. They also argue that it is so since a long time. But it is found in Vedic literature that men and women enjoyed equal rights. Men and women are two wheels of the chariot called family. Of the two, each wheel has equal responsibility. When asked why inequality is natural, they only say that it has been like that through the ages. This only means that men have been telling the same [story] all through the ages. They felt that inequality is natural. It appeared like that to the male perception. Men never found anything that restricted their freedom [to be] natural. Did they find the loss of political independence natural? Did they find absence of freedom of speech natural? No. Women's not having equality [similarly] does not appear to be natural. But will they agree?

Men say, 'Women accept their incompetence. It is natural that women do not want mastership. They accept men as their superiors and masters'. Who accepted it? It may be recalled that articles written by our sisters and published in *Grihalakshmi* are proving that 'women are not weak'. Women may not ask for mastership, but they definitely not [accept] slavery! They are asking for equality.

It is men who do not desire women's equality. Some women keep quiet fearing that their men may get annoyed or because of the respect they have for them. If so, the question may arise as to why women are tolerating this [position of] inferiority. Bearing the ailment is not for pleasure but because as it has become inevitable without a way out. Women may be thinking out of ignorance that the ailment itself is natural.

There is another argument. Some men say that, if women are given independence, they will not care for household responsibilities and will not even produce children. Is it because women are subordinated to men that family life and growth of population is sustained? Do you [mean to] say that women do not have [any] longing for children and family? Desire for children is as natural to women as it is to men; maybe more so in women than in men. Hence, these greater activities will not be stopped because of the equal status of women. For argument's sake, if a woman is really unwilling to perform these activities and not bothered about society, why should man alone bother?

History reveals that there was once equality between men and women. Bhavabhuthi's *Uttara Ramacharitra* demonstrates the equality existing in the field of education through [its depiction of] Athreyi studying along with male students. *Malati Madhaveeyam* narrates the female hermit Kamandaki's discussion with male hermits on scriptures. According to the *Rigveda*, there were some female conjurers [*mantra drashta*]. A learned woman called Vaagambhruni taught theology. During the age of the *Yajurveda* and *Atharvaveda*, women did participate in debates on scriptures. Mythreyi, wife of Yagnavalkya, is the best example of this.

It is clear that asking for equality is not asking for superiority. The point, however, is that women having aspirations is as natural as men having them.

Let us discuss equality of women in the political arena. The political arena includes electing a government that we need and equal positions to men in people's government as well as a commitment to perform national service.

Government has the right over women the same way it has on men. All laws passed by government apply to women as they apply to men. If such a government is elected by men only, they will not have any concern for the rights of women. Some may argue that now there is concern for women's rights. But when it is not legalised, who can assure us that it will continue to do so? Because men do not want to allow equal rights, they are not giving us the right to vote. The right to vote will help us in protecting our other natural rights. Some may harbour the doubts that since women are ignorant of elections, they may misuse the right to vote. What is happening when men are misusing it? If we are educated and properly trained, like men, we can also judiciously exercise our right to vote. Do we stop giving [people] food [altogether] on the argument that it will be unhealthy [if someone receives] unlimited and imbalanced food?

If women are elected to the legislative bodies in equal number, they can take part in the making of laws and discuss their merits and demerits with regard to women, because women constitute half of the population that has to face the repercussions of these laws. Mrs Achanta Rukminamma is a member of Madras Legislative Council. Has she not been showing her abilities in the deliberations of the Council? This is a matter of the present. If one wants examples from history, one can cite many. There were great women like Queen Victoria, Queen Elizabeth and Queen Durgavati, who were all rulers [and all of them proved their political mettle]. There were chief advisors like Nurjahan. There were innumerable warrior women and mothers of warriors in history.

We women are asking for equality to serve the nation. Mr Rajendra Prasad already appreciated the services rendered by women to the Indian National Congress. Can anyone deny equality to women on looking at the service rendered by Mrs Sarojini Naidu, Durgabayamma [Durgabai Deshmukh] and many other women from the Telugu districts, and the Kshatriya women of Bhimavaram Taluk during the recent Salt Satyagraha movement launched by Mahatma [Gandhi]? If anybody wants many more examples, we can provide them.

Some are under the impression that women will not have the necessary qualities of impartiality and toughness in politics for they are naturally kind and partial. No doubt that the political arena is such that there is no place for kindness or sensitivity. However, there are examples of women who successfully proved to be tough in political matters: Draupadi, and the wife of Khadga Tikkana, who inspired their husbands to go to battle field; and of course [Lakshmibai, the queen of] Jhansi, who by herself slaughtered enemies in the battlefield.

Let us examine economic equality. Economic equality includes the opportunity to earn money without any restrictions, by working in areas which have got social approval, a provision to enjoy the properties of ancestors and the liberty to spend money freely earned by oneself. Such economic needs are equal for men and women.

It is the right of men to earn money for their livelihood. If he wants to deny the same right to women, he means that he wants to keep women dependent on himself and society forever. Employment is not a sin or [considered] wrong for men. Then why should it be so for women alone? Maybe the fear of unemployment? Was there employment to all men when women were not in competition? Women are not responsible for the problem of unemployment. There are different reasons for the unemployment of men and women.

It is learnt that during the Great War, when men in those countries involved in war went to [the] war [front], it was women who took up the charge and performed the duties of clerks, radio operators and also in medical works and post offices successfully.

Women in India have entered the legal profession recently. Everybody knows that there is ample number of capable women performing in the medical profession. There is no need to talk about women in the teaching profession. The abilities of women in the above are appreciable. Are there any deficits in them that aid arguments opposing women's equality? If at all there are some deficits, it may be because of lack of training. Are all men in all professions really capable?

Men enjoy the property of their ancestors. Because the laws are made by men, to keep us under their control, they have not allowed the right to inheritance to women. They say, 'Men, by working hard and facing all the hardships, are giving you a comfortable and happy life'. But only prisoners do not have to labour. There will be no happiness where there is no labour. What women need is self-respect and freedom. Self-respect shall be acquired by self-confidence. Self-confidence could be gained by possessing wealth. This will be possible when women are given a share in their fathers' property.

Equality is achieved when equal conditions prevail. We need the right to earn and inherit property so as not to allow men to see us as their dependents and therefore cheap. Families where mutual respect and love between wife and husband exist shall alone flourish. Friendships are of such a nature. It shall be the source of happiness to men finding friendly qualities in wife and similarly women finding the characteristics of a companion in her husband. Isn't it? It means that happiness exists in 'equal status'.

I need to say one thing. A question may arise: do all women have the ability to earn? It may be impudent to question: are all men really able to earn? Amongst women, those who can earn may be allowed to do it. That is all. So, if men have to respect the race of women, it is essential that the latter has economic equality.

Now, I shall discuss social equality between men and women. At the outset, I will touch upon the issue of marriage, followed by relationship between men and women in matters of family and society, and, finally, the behavioural aspects of the two.

Acceptance of each other is essential in running the family smoothly. Men have the right to marry women of their choice. [But women do not have any say in their marriages.] Parents are the ones that express acceptance on behalf of women. One cannot say that parents do not care for the well-being of their daughters. But can we say that, maybe because of poverty or ignorance, they are selling or giving away their daughters to most undeserving men? Child marriages are to be eradicated if consent of women is to be considered in their marriage. Do not ask what you will do if a woman opts for the wrong husband. Trouble invited by oneself is like an ailment invited by taking unlimited and imbalanced food. In such a marriage, there is no scope for blaming or getting angry with others. Would not a woman try for a match that is suitable to her tastes and desires? All marriages opted for by women will not fail.

There will be comfort in a family when equal rights are enjoyed by men and women. Why are we asking for equality? It is because social responsibilities will be successfully performed when they are felt as theirs. We will be mentally comfortable when there are equal rights in family matters. But there is one thing to be accepted. A husband who is greater in age, will be greater in experience also. Normally, husband holds the decision-making part [of the work], leaving the execution to the wife. I do not say that our equality is at stake because of it. When a decision is taken, it can be followed, if it is positive. Or, it can be rejected, when it is not.... I would request to ensure that the chariot of family depends on both wheels....

I have established that equality between men and women is not harmful while discussing various things. What is asked for is equality, not superiority. We are saying that we need responsibilities equal to men. It does not mean that we are discarding natural duties like child bearing and rearing, and duties entrusted by society like household management. We will manage all those aspects ourselves. What we are asking for is equality in social, economic and political aspects.

Such equality is not at all deleterious. There are the advantages [we have discussed]. There is a strong misconception among men that the race of women survives only because of them. There is nothing we lose because of this. But men are belittling the race of women. That is not good to us or to society.... Men are wasting the abilities of half of the population by not providing them equality. It is good that we also serve the nation by attaining equality.

It will be proper and very important to the womenfolk to realise that equality between men and women in all respects is essential and that it will lead the world towards welfare and prosperity. Our race of women must work for this.

Appendix 4

Is Equality between Women and Men Desirable or Harmful?[1]

– Editorial

These days, when women are struggling for equality with men in all respects, it was thought that it would be useful to readers if a gold medal is presented to the writer who writes the best essay on the topic 'Is equality between women and men desirable or harmful?', and the same was announced in the Dussehra issue of 1935. Subsequently, amongst the essays we received, the essays by Mrs Mydavolu Padmavati Devi and Mrs Vedula Meenakshi Devi have been considered best and they were published in the previous issue.

Both these fellow sisters have emphasised that equality between men and women is very essential in all aspects of life and that there is nothing harmful in it. But, there are a few problems involved in their propositions [before we] totally accept them. Hence, we intend to discuss those aspects in which equality would be deleterious and that were not discussed by them at length.

Those who preach equality between women and men are arguing very strongly that women should enjoy all those rights enjoyed by men, and that there should be no obstacles left in the way of women to undertake all the activities performed by men. But what we have to consider is whether it is really possible and whether life becomes comfortable with that.

The writings on this issue shall not be understood well unless an illusion that has existed among men and women for quite a long time is driven away.

[1]'Stree Purusha Samanatvamavashyakama? Yendeni Yanarthadayakama?' *Grihalakshmi*, December 1936, pp. 731–735.

Women enjoyed greater respect in the past. However, this gradually reduced, maybe in accordance with changing times, or maybe men wanted to execute their suzerainty; or maybe [it is] due to their mere selfishness, [that] they may have relegated women to their present, dismal status. But now there are men who repent for what they did to women and [who have] wholeheartedly started working for the betterment of women. In spite of their strenuous efforts, there are some women who could not be reformed. However, there are some women, who do not care for truth and untruth, justice and injustice, and are holding the strange opinion that men always feared granting independence to women. And thus whatever men do, and how much ever they write, these women consider it important to condemn them.... So it would be better that both of them purge themselves of their partial attitudes and find out a way for social development and conduct accordingly. We hope that the various aspects discussed here under shall be taken impartially by our brothers and sisters.

When one speaks or writes about the independence of women and their rights, one should always bear in mind the majority of the women and not consider the opinions and difficulties of one or two. It cannot be acceptable to take the examples of one or two women who, under special circumstances, had to lead a life of freedom. It is because development of the society is to be judged by the development of the majority, not of one or two individuals.

God did not create men and women unequal. He did not create one as the superior and the other as inferior; one as the master and the other as slave; one as independent and the other as dependent. But He created a difference in the domains of work they perform and the life they lead. Women are not only the source of creation but they are instrumental in sustaining it. That is why it is inevitable for them to perform the duties of motherhood and childcare. The physiological and the biological nature of women is created to suit these functions. Men have been created to protect women when the latter undergo these circumstances. Therefore, when one discusses the equality of men and women, one should always keep in mind the respective naturally formulated characteristics of each of them.

The condition of today's Indian woman demands improvement. It is good to try to eradicate all those customs that come in the way of women's welfare in the name of religion and society. The political, religious and economic issues involved in it have been well discussed by our writer sisters. It would be mere rumination to discuss them again.

But it will be of no use to fight for women's participation in all those activities that men perform. Let us see a few of them as examples. Today's system of education is not useful even to men. It is squeezing their money and energy, making them unfit for any employment and thereby throwing them into perdition. There can be no doubt that such a system of education will definitely harm women. But this does not mean that women should not receive education. The education that women need is different from that of men. One should acquire knowledge of a kind suitable to them. What is the use of women learning all that is learnt by men?

Men have enough natural stamina to work hard physically. Nature never creates any obstacles to them. That is why they deserve such an education. Women going for that sort of education would imply that they are leaving their natural responsibilities. You may question: what happens if they leave those responsibilities? One may say that both can earn money. Whatever is said, it is not advantageous to stop doing natural duties. On top of that, it will cause trouble.

Let us see another example. Though there is good number of educated men, why women alone are appointed as nurses? Is it not because they attend patients with the required patience, kindness and sympathy? Even if they try, can men act in that way? If men really say that they can also do such jobs and demand for equal opportunities in nursing, how ridiculous and foolish would it be?

Not only nursing—men, though they are skilled, can they learn child-rearing? Is it not true that men fall behind women in terms of household management, the art of cooking and fine arts? However great one may be, will he appoint a man or a female nurse to care for a baby? Why is it so? Because caring for an infant is not natural characteristic of men. It is known to all that no one excels with pretend characteristics! So, think well how far it is beneficial to women to take up, in the name of equality, all the professions that men do?

There is one more hurdle to women taking up employment. Though women possess the required energy, knowledge and patience to do a job, physiological and biological factors necessitate them to take rest for a certain period every month. Keeping the health aspect in mind, our ancestors have formulated certain regulations to be observed during that period. It is not strange to state that the violation of such regulations lead to ill health and suffering. The fate of those women who disregard them is witnessed by us. Such regulations cannot be observed in employment. Moreover, women need an inevitable interval during pregnancy and the post-natal period. It goes without saying that employment cannot be continued uninterrupted under such conditions.

This is an aspect that applies to all. It is not my opinion that women should not do any job, however profitable it may be and however precarious her circumstances may be. It is not my intention that they remain at home. They can take up work, if it is not deleterious and is helpful to them. They can be more successful than men, especially in professions like medicine and teaching at elementary level. Their services may be much more useful when aspects such as household management are to be taught to girls. Hence, it would be a misadventure to say that all professions shall be useful and profitable to all.

Some argue that in the Western countries, men and women are treated equally and that women of those countries are entering all the professions like men, and that a similar situation must prevail in India. But our educated fellow sisters should know that the Western sisters are carrying out the household responsibilities better than our Indian sisters and that they desire their natural jobs more than other jobs. However, [what is most important is that] we cannot imitate them in all respects. Therefore, please stop aping Western values and behave like Indian women.

Appendix 5

Slavery of Women, How Long Must it Last?[1]

Cherukuru Nagabhushanamma

> Our race of women cannot develop unless woman has a personality of her own, herself is aware of the value of independence and the degradation in slavery and, finally, the recognition of herself as a human being, and the strong aspiration for achieving all those rights that men have.[2]

It is evident to all those who have eyes that Indian women are deprived of all rights. Devoid of independence and subjugated to men, they are leading a life of slavery. Additionally, they are devoid of education and knowledge and are subjected to lots of difficulties and odds.

Injustice done by Men

The entirety of Hindu literature, from the various Dharmashastras to the Puranas and the *Itihasa*s and even the *Sumati* and *Bhaskara Sataka*s, has been proclaiming that after the Vedic age men have been suppressing women and that the latter are mean and slavish. This idea has been digested in the blood of both men and women for a very long time. It is very sad to observe that not only men but even women are unaware that they are deprived of a conscience of their own, independent thinking and an independent personality. Today's Indian women not only do not have the economic, social and other rights, but also do not feel their absence. They are in such a thoughtless and deplorable condition that, ignorant of their

[1] 'Inkennallu Manakee Banisatvamu?' *Grihalakshmi*, October 1941, pp. 448–451.

[2] This part was given as blurb.

plight, they think, 'what else women would have in this world'. It is because of such an abjectly internalised slavery that their confidence is reduced to its lowest ebb. They walk in twisting steps before men. They do not have enough courage to go to meetings and sit where there are men. Even if they go and sit, they get perplexed as if they have made a big mistake. Why such [turmoil]? They are [reduced to] such a low status that even if they are dying out of hunger, they would think it wrong to have food before their husbands eat. It is disgraceful to women that they do not take up independent decisions even in smaller issues, if not in bigger ones. So, when women do not have freedom even in petty issues, one can say without hesitation that women do not have a personality at all. Throughout the ages, men have successfully kept women in their hands by creating deceitful rules, regulations and moralities, deprived them of rights and powers and turned them to be their tools and cattle in their backyard. They have used women as slaves and have been exploiting them.

Lack of Education among Women

Educated women in our country, including those who only have basic literacy, are just two per cent. In such a situation, what wonder is there that women are unable to understand their state of slavery? It is for this reason that women are not able to treat the beatings, scolding and humiliation inflicted by their husbands as wrong. Rather, they are habituated to believe that [silently withstanding] such things is a marker of their virtue, the characteristic features of chaste women, noble pativratas. Women think that following the path of their husbands and not deviating from it is their ultimate virtue. Nothing shall be more foolish and ignominious than this. If women are not thinking of setting it right, it is because they are not educated.

If women really are sufficiently intelligent, why do they spend extravagantly on saris or jewellery and indulge in pompous displays without any understanding of their income? Why do they waste their time on useless talk and extravaganza? They do not know what is needed and what is missing from their homes and spend money on unnecessary things. This is the case with wealthy women. A similar attitude prevails among poor families as well. If any male reformers try to reform certain superstitions and improper customs, these women come in the way and say that ancient customs cannot be repudiated and insist that there is a need to host five-day marriage festivities for their sons or daughters, that an orchestra must be arranged, that the ritual of trimming the nails of toes is to be performed and that gods and demons must be satisfied through proper offerings. They do not care for good or bad, profit or loss in many such household activities. It is the ignorant women that are largely responsible for large number of deep-rooted superstitions existing in our country.

Women in Other Countries

Since in countries like Italy, Germany, England, France, Russia, America and Japan, more than eighty or ninety per cent or sometimes even hundred per cent of women are educated, and are living with a consciousness of themselves as human beings, they have acquired equal rights to men and leading a life of comfort and happiness. They are working in higher ranks in the army, police, factories, courts and schools and in all other departments. Unlike Hindu women (except the rural and labouring women) who lost their individuality and who eat if men provide food or sit crying when not provided food, they have not lost their individuality, have acquired all rights and now fulfilling all their aspirations. They have not become useless animals like Indian women who observe 'Ghoshaa' [seclusion] and do not step out of their homes fearing that they may be seen by men. Like our women, who shiver like sheep finding a tiger in front of it, those women are never afraid to see their men. They never entertain the ideas of man being god; that he is everything and that he is superior to women. Such things are never borne in the minds of those women.

Slavery

As the days went by, the enslavement of women, including of the educated has increased. They have reached such a state of degradation that they cannot appear publicly without attaching the names of their husbands to their own. This is a bad practice in the guise of culture and has spread all over the world, firmly establishing the enslavement of women. It can be seen quite often in the meetings where women are introduced as 'Mrs so and so'. This is most disgraceful. This does not sound bad to those being addressed that way because they are habituated to being addressed so. Normally, men's names are prominent all over society as they are educated and involved in public activities. This is a custom evolved to popularise the names of such men's wives, who have [themselves] not done anything great. There will be no greater [form of] degradation than this for a woman who has individuality and who knows the value of independence. Women should be known through their own capabilities and commitment to work and the greater tasks they achieve, not by the name and fame of their husbands. The condition of women is similar to those people of lower castes, who are suppressed and habituated to be scolded and beaten up by the people of upper castes and yet think that it is natural and according to their fate. The reason I am writing on this aspect in such a strong voice is that our race of women cannot develop unless woman has a personality of her own, is herself aware of the value of independence and degradation in slavery and, finally, the recognition of herself as a human being, and the strong aspiration for achieving all those rights that men have.

It does not mean that women with all the freedom and liberty should revolt against their husbands without listening to them, regardless of good or bad [things] they say. My good intention is that women should get rid of this [state of] abject slavery, become independent and lead a life of comfort and happiness through mutual cooperation and respect with men.

Resolution

Educated people should find the path for any reform or development to take place in the world. Common people will follow them. This is the case all over the world and also throughout human history, especially in societies where development is still evolving. So, if women's problems are to be solved by women themselves, the responsibility of laying the path falls on educated women only. Hence, as suggested above, one should stop using the pair names and start using their names solely. For this, there is no need to carry on prolonged discussions and pass Acts the same way the Sarda Act was passed. And there will be no opposition to this. This is a small issue which is in our own hands. There is a need to pass a resolution to that effect not only in women's organisations at Taluk, District and State levels but also in the meetings of the All India Women's Conference. Then it will be relevant to the whole of India. In accordance with the resolution, we may suggest that editors and owners of newspapers and journals not publish [women under] pair names and they will change their earlier methods. No difficulty whatsoever is involved in it to anyone.

Rajahmundry is the venue to the All India Women's Conference scheduled next December. I have decided to propose a resolution against the use of pair names in it. I believe my fellow sisters would accept and support it.

True independence is not achieved unless women have rights in matters of property, marriage and divorce equal to men. The reason for all these problems faced by women is that daughters do not have an equal share of their fathers' property as with sons. Economic rights shall solve all other problems. If we remain silent on all these issues, our enslavement shall last forever. To a certain extent, both men and women have awakened. But many more rights are to be achieved for which we will have to lead stringent agitations. Nothing is achieved without pressure. So, all my sisters should strive hard to eradicate our enslavement and prove ourselves as human beings. I believe that they struggle to the best of their abilities to keep their self-respect standing high.

Appendix 6

'Let Women also Survive'[1]

Nanduri Kameshwari

When women get into trams, men who are seated look here and there and stand up, offering them their seat. This will be the case in trains and even in cinema theatres. Maybe the intention of men is for others to note that they are following the rule of 'women first' without any deviation.

This sort of respect given to women is not new. This has been the case throughout the centuries. On closer observation, it appears to be a big conspiracy [*pedda kutra*] hatched by men. They appear to be treating women with all respect, but in reality are snatching away all their rights. They need not spare their seats for us in trams and thereby need not show sympathy, treating us as weak and helpless.

Women have been fighting for their rights for hundreds of years. Women in Britain have fought remarkable battles to secure their rights. During the same period, similar women's movements have emerged in countries like France. Consequently, women secured the right to vote.

Okay, the right to vote was granted. But what has been achieved? Nothing! I cast my vote in the municipal elections quite a few years ago. It was thrilling to have the contestants knocking at the doors even at midnight and asking us, 'Please cast your vote in favour of me'. But what did they do in return for voting them to power?

But there is one fact to be reckoned with. Those respectable men whose hands got burnt a little in the process of removing the rust, have fought in favour of women in legislatures. A Bill was passed in the Sindh Province

[1] 'Streelanukooda Bratakanivvandi', *Andhra Mahila*, 1 December 1944, pp. 16–17.

restricting the dowry to be offered.[2] Since daughters do not have a share in father's property, all that they get from him is this much only.

They rejected the Divorce Act saying that it would be a blemish on [the sanctity of] Indian wifehood. Then how come men marrying many wives one after the other is [not an issue]? Perhaps, it is a *respectable* and even a *noble* act!

What we demand and are demanding is only one thing—to treat us as human beings, grant us equal status in society and provide equal opportunities and rights in areas like employment and business.

I have observed a few people pronouncing, 'We have given freedom to women. There is no inequality between men and women. Skill of execution is all that matters.' But I strongly contest this. This is a pretext made by men to keep women suppressed forever.

How come all the jobs with bigger responsibilities and powers and with huge salaries go to men and jobs like nurses, telephone operators and stenographers to us? Should we be satisfied with this much only?

Why cannot we do bigger jobs? Look at those countries involved in the [Second World] War where, while men are involved in warfare, women are taking up all the jobs and professions in which men were involved. When they are successfully handling all the difficult works hitherto done by men, to say that women are not efficient is a kind of madness, and maybe foolishness.

Allegations of Men

'You women are weak, innocent, not capable of decision-making and are highly emotional. You are volatile, can only do smaller works leisurely talking to each other, but not the important work,' are some of the imputations made by men against us.

It is true that we are *abala*. But do we need to carry heavy loads on our shoulders or turn big machines? Do we need expertise in boxing, fighting and fencing or do the hired labour to perform our duties?

Oh! I am reminded of something when I say hired labour. Are not women of our country working in mines? In Russia, are not women digging trenches and working in armour factories?

---

[2] She was referring to the Sindh Deti Leti Act, 1939, which was aimed at restricting the practice of dowry. It set the limits for dowry demands and prescribed penalties for non-compliance.

I will never accept that women are by nature less intelligent than men. Intelligence is mainly the result of education, training and the opportunities available.

It is alleged that we cannot make decisions. If decision-making can only be done by men, why do they go bankrupt in businesses, despite being educated? Why, like frogs in the well, do they grieve in ignorance?

You say that we women are fickle. What do you mean by that? Is it because we look meek and slight? Is it because [you think] we float like moonlight, casting naughty smiles at you?

If yes, it is because you want us to be like that. It is because you say that if we do not look like the delightful moonlight, your hearts and souls and lives shall suffer in darkness. You say that if our faces are soaked in sorrow, your hearts will turn like skies without clouds.

Shall I tell you my opinion? Men are scared of women who are capable of independent thinking and ready for riveting dialogue.

I am not saying this out of anger. All that I have said is only [in order] to ask for equality. Hardly for a minute can men remain without women and women without men.

Ensure that all the natural rights deserved by women are available to them. Then, women shall carry out all their responsibilities in making the world a place for comfortable and happy life. 'Let women also survive' is the slogan that I am handing over to my fellow sisters.

Bibliography

Primary Sources

1. Journals (Telugu)

A. Women's Journals

Anasuya. 1917–1924. Sri Gautami Prantiya Grandhalayam, Rajahmundry; hereafter GLR.

Andhra Lakshmi. 1921–1924. Andhra Pradesh State Archives, Hyderabad; hereafter APSAH.

Andhra Mahila. 1944–1961. GLR and Sri Krishnadevaraya Andhra Bhasha Nilayam, Hyderabad; hereafter SKDABNH.

Balika. 1896–1897. Press Academy of Andhra Pradesh Archives; hereafter PAAPA.

Bharata Mata. Annual Number, April 1912. GLR.

Grihalakshmi. 1928–1961. GLR, SKDABNH and Saraswata Niketanamu, Vetapalem, Prakasham District, Andhra Pradesh; hereafter SNV.

Hindu Sundary. 1902–1945. GLR; SKDABNH; SNV.

Maharani. 1889–1892. PAAPA.

Sathihitha Bodhini. 1883–1904/1905. PAAPA.

Savithri. 1904–1917. GLR.

Soubhagya. 1955–1956. PAAPA.

Soundaryavalli. 1918–1919. SKDABNH.

Streelakoraku Vartamanamulu. 1914–1916. PAAPA.

Stri Dharma. Telugu section, 1924–1927. PAAPA.

Telugu Zenana. 1893–1907. GLR.

Vanita. April–December 1956. Collected from Abburi Chaya Devi, editor of *Vanita*, from her residence in Hyderabad, January 2012.

Vanita Vihar. 1950. PAAPA.

Vivekavathi. 1909–1934. GLR; Ram Mohan Library, Vijayawada; hereafter RMLV.

B. Other Journals and Newspapers

Abhinava Saraswati. 1906–1945. PAAPA.
Ananda Bodhini. 1930–1933. PAAPA.
Ananda Vahini. 1930. PAAPA.
Andhra Patrika. 1947–1960. PAAPA.
Andhra Patrika Samvatsaradi Sanchika. 1912–1965. PAAPA and Sundaraiah Vignana Kendram, Hyderabad; hereafter SVKH.
Arya Prakashika. 1929. PAAPA.
Arya Tilaka. 1915–1916. PAAPA.
Aryamata Bodhini. 1913–1914. PAAPA.
Aurogyam. 1913. PAAPA.
Bharata Dharma. 1928–1948. PAAPA.
Bharati. 1924–1960. PAAPA and SVKH.
Golakonda Patrika. 1927–1960. PAAPA.
Hindujana Samskarini. 1886–1912. PAAPA.
Prabodhini. 1907–1915. GLR.
Sathya Samvarthani. 1892–1901. GLR.
Sri Vivekavardhani. 1879. PAAPA.
Swadharma Prakashini. 1907–1931. PAAPA.
Telugu Swatantra. 1948–1957. PAAPA.
Telugu Talli. 1937. PAAPA.
Vasavi. 1926–1940. GLR.
Vaishya. 1929. PAAPA.

2. Autobiographies

A. Autobiographies of Women in Telugu

Kanakamma, Ponaka. 2011. *Kanaka Pushya Raagam: Ponaka Kanakamma Sweeya Charitra*, ed. Kalidasu Purushottam. Bengaluru: Sunayana Creations.

Koteshwaramma, Kondapalli. 2012. *Nirjana Vaaradhi*. Hyderabad: Hyderabad Book Trust.

Lakshmikantamma, Utukuri. 1993. *Sahiti Rudrama*. Bapatla: self-published.

Lakshmibai, Sangam. 1980. *Naa Jailu Gnapakalu—Anubhavalu* (My Jail Experiences and Reminiscences), comp. Neti Seetadevi. Hyderabad: Andhra Pradesh Swatantrya Porata Charitra Sankalana Sangham, Government of Andhra Pradesh.

Paripurna, Namburi. 2017. *Velugu Darulalo ...: Namburi Paripurna Sweeya Charitra*. Hyderabad: Aalambana Prachuranalu.

Saraswathi, Gora. 1992. *Gorato Naa Jeevitam* (My Life with Gora [Goparaju Ramachandra Rao]). Vijayawada: Nasthika Kendram.

Satyavati, Edidamu. 2005 [1934]. *Atmacaritamu*. Hyderabad: Asmita Resource Centre for Women.

Sitadevi, Goparaju. 1998. *Janani, Janma Bhoomischa ... Goparaju Sitadevi Sweeya Charitra (50 samvatsarala Mahila Udyama Anubhavalu-Gnapakalu)*. Vijayawada: Sanghamitra Prachuranalu.

Subbamma, Malladi. 1991. *Paativratyamnundi Feminismdaka* (From Pativratyam to Feminism). Hyderabad: Malladi Subbamma Trust.

Swarajyam, Mallu. 2019. *Na Gonte Tupaki Toota: Mallu Swarajyam Atma Katha*. Hyderabad: Hyderabad Book Trust.

B. Autobiographies of Men in Telugu

Chalam, G. V. 1999 [1986]. *Chalam. (1972)*. Vijayawada: Aruna Publishing House.

Chenchaiah, Darishi. 1985 [1952]. *Nenoo-Naa Desham*. Vijayawada: Jayanti Publications.

Dharma Rao, Tapi. 1979. *Raloo-Rappaloo*. Vijayawada: Vishalandhra Publishing House.

Kaleswara Rao, Ayyadevara. 2006 [1959]. *Navyandhramu-Naa Jeevita Katha*. Hyderabad: Telugu Samiti.

Kesari, K. N. 1953. *Naa Chinnanati Muchchatlu*. Madras: Vavilla Press.

Lakshmi Narasimhamu, Chilakamarti. 2007. *Sweeya Charitramu*. Hyderabad: Prachee Publications.

Laxmana Rao, Wuppala. 2015 [1983]. *Bathuku Pusthakam*. Vijayawada: Sahiti Mitrulu.

Pattabhi Rama Rao, Parakala. 2012. *Samasamaja Saadhana Samaramlo: Parakala Pattabhi Rama Rao Sweeya Charitra*. Vijayawada: Sanghamitra Prachuranalu.

Prakasham, Tanguturi. 2006 [1946]. *Naa Jivita Yatra*. Hyderabad: Telugu Samiti.

Ramachandra, Tirumala. 2004. *Hampi Nunchi Harappa Daka*, ed. Akkiraju Ramapati Rao. Hyderabad: Ajo-Vibho-Kandalam Prachuranalu.

Sitaramaiah, Sattiraju. 2002. *Sweeya Charitra*. Eluru.

Subramanya Sastri, Sripada. 1999. *Anubhavaloo-Gnapakaloonu*. Hyderabad: Vishalandhra Publishing House.

Venkatappaiah, Konda. 1966. *Sweeya Charitra*. Hyderabad: Dakshina Bharata Hindi Prachara Sabha.

Venkata Ranga Reddy, Konda. 2010 [1967]. *Sweeya Charitra*. Hyderabad: Vignana Sarovara Prachuranalu.

Venkatarangaiya, Mamidipudi. 1981. *Maarutunna Samajam: Naa Gnaapakalu*. Machilipatnam: Telugu Vidyarthi Prachuranalu.

Venkata Sivudu, Rayasam. 1933. *Atma Charitramu*. Madras: Andhra Patrika Press.

Virabhadra Rao, Madala. 1998. *Naa Katha*. Hyderabad.

Veeresalingam, Kandukuri. 1936. *Sweeya Charitramu (1911)*. Rajahmundry: Rajan Electic Press.

3. Speeches Delivered at Reform Conferences and Reports of Caste Associations

Andhrajana Sanghamu-Kalyani. Prathama Dwitiya Varshika Nivedika, 1928–1930. (The First and Second Annual Reports of the Andhrajana Sanghamu-Kalyani, 1928–1930). n. d. Tadipatri: Deshabandhu Mudranalayamu. GLR.

Arya Vaishya Mahasabha, 1915–1916 (Report of the Arya Vaishya Mahasabha, 1915–1916). n. d. Madras: Hoe & Co. Printers. GLR.

Arya Vaishya Mahasabha, 1916–1918 (Report of the Arya Vaishya Mahasabha, 1916–1918). n. d. Madras: Hoe & Co. Printers. GLR.

Arya Vaishya Samajamu Vidya Shakha, Bezawada, Kaarya Nivedanamu: 1915va Samvatsaramu April Antamuvaraku (Report of the Education Wing of the Arya-Vaishya Samajamu, Bezawada, till April 1915). n. d. Bezawada: Manjari Press. GLR.

Arya Vaishya Yuvakula Sahiti Sanghamu Prathama Varshika Charitra (History of the First Year of the Arya Vaishya Young Men's Literary Association). n. d. GLR.

Ati Balya Vivahamu (A Lecture on Early Marriage), other details, n. a. GLR.

Krishna-Guntur Mandala Vishwabrahmana Prathama Mahajana Sabha Vivaranamu: Mukhyamagunupanyasamulu, Sandesha Padyamulu (Report of the First Krishna-Guntur Districts' Vishwa Brahmins' Conference: Important Speeches, Message-giving Poems). n. d. Duggirala: Duggirala Ram Subrahmanyam, Prabodhini Press. GLR.

Krishna Rao, K. R. V. n. d. *Sangha Durachara Samskarana Samajamunu, Daaniyuddeshamulunu* (Social Reform Association and Its Objectives). GLR.

Krishna Rao, Nalam. n. d. *Sangha Samskarana Pratikakshuniki Bratyuttaramu* (A Reply to an Anti-Reformer). Speech delivered at the Town Hall, Rajahmundry. GLR.

Padunalugava Niyogi Mahajana Sabha: Ahvanasanghagrasanadhipatyupanyasamu (Fourteenth Niyogi Mahajana Sabha: Speech of the President of the Reception Committee). n. d. GLR.

Padunaidava Niyogi Mahajana Sabha, Amalapuramu: Sabhadhyakshulagu Kashinathuni Nageshwara Rao gari Sambodhanamu (Fifteenth Niyogi Mahajana Sabha, Amalapuram: Address of Kashinathuni Nageshwara Rao, the Chairperson). n. d. Madras: Andhra Patrika Press. GLR.

Prakasa Row, D. V. S. n. d. *Hinu Vivaha Vyayamulanugurinchi* (On Hindu Marriage Expenses). GLR.

Prathama Arya Vaishya Yuvajana Mahasabha Charya Nivedika (Report of the First Arya Vaishya Youth Conference). 1926. Madras: Phoenix Press. GLR.

Report of the Fifth Kamma Mahajana Sabha. 1916. Gudiwada, 25 April. GLR.

Sangha Samskaranopanyasamu (A Lecture on Social Reform). 1920. Chennapuri. GLR.

Singamma, T., *Nari Ratnamulu*. n. d. Speech delivered at the first anniversary of the Brundavana Stree Samajamu. GLR.

Stree Punarvivahamu Ashastriyamanu Vishayamai Madarasu Thiruvallikkeni Sri Uttaradi Mathamulo Jarigina Prasangamu (Lecture delivered at the Madaras Thiruvallikkeni Sri Uttaradi Matham establishing that Widow Remarriage is against the Shastras). 1884. Madras: Empress of India Press. GLR.

Upanyasa Manjari. 1910. Speeches by women at the first conference of the Andhra Mahila Mahasabha, Guntur. Compiled and published by Pulugurta Venkata Ratnam. Kakinada: Savithri Mudraksharashala. GLR.

Upanyasa Manjari. 1912. Speeches delivered at the second conference of the Andhra Mahila Mahasabha, Kakinada, 1911. Compiled and published by Pulugurta Venkata Ratnam. Kakinada: Savithri Mudraksharashala. GLR.

11va Andhra Mahajana Sabha, Chennapuri, Gadde Rangaiah Nayuni Ahvanasanghadhyakshopanyasamu (Speech of Gadde Rangaiah Nayudu, President of the Reception Committe, at the Eleventh Andhra Mahajana Sabha, 20 October 1924). n. d. Madras: Andhra Patrika Press. GLR.

4. Books (Telugu)

A. Authoured, Edited and/or Compiled by Women

Atchamamba, Bhandaru. 1901. *Abala Sachcharitra Ratnamala*. Madras: publisher n. a.

Atchamamba, Komarraju. 1968 [1959]. *Prasuti—Shishu Poshana*. Vijayawada: Premchand Publications.

Krishnakumari, Nayani et al., ed. n. d. *Andhra Rachayitrula Prathama Maha Sabha Sanchika, Gunturu, May 1966*. Hyderabad: Andhra Pradesh Sahitya Academy.

Lakshmi Narasamamba, Pulugurta. *Mahilakalabodhini*. Hevalambi year (Gregorian date n. a.) Madras: Vyjayanti Press. GLR.

Manorama Devi, S. et al., ed. n. d. *Mahila Sanghamu: Gudivada–Bhavana Prarambhotsava Sanchika, 28 April 1966*, other details, n. a. PAAPA.

Saraswati Devi, Chebrolu. 1931. *Pativrata Shatakamu*. Nujiveedu. GLR.

Satyavati Devi, Rachamalla, ed. 1943. *Lakshmanaraya Vardhanti Sanchika*. Secundarabad: Telugu Talli Office. Courtesy of Kurra Jitendra Babu, Hyderabad.

Sharada Devi, Vempati. 1940. *Stree Hitabodhini: Grihatantra Paathamulu* (Sermons to Women: Lessons on Domestic-Craft). Gottipadu: Sahitya Kutiramu. SNV.

Sitadevi, Vasireddy and Kumari Panda Shamantakamani, ed. n. d. *Andhra Rachayitrula Saptama Mahasabha Sanchika, Vijayawada, February 1975*. Hyderabad: Andhra Pradesh Sahitya Academy. PAAPA.

Sridevi, P. 2001 [1958]. *Kalateeta Vyaktulu*. Hyderabad: Vishalandhra Publishing House.

Srinivasan, Parvati. 1948. *Matrutvamu-Shishu Samrakshana*, trans. Sita Devi Chellam, other details, n.a.

Varalakshmamma, Kanuparti. 1934. *Sharada Lekhalu*. Madras: publisher n. a.

B. Authoured, Edited and/or Compiled by Men

Appa Rao, Gurajada. 1984 [1910]. *Kathanikalu*, ed. Setty Eswara Rao. Hyderabad: Vishalandhra Publishing House.

——. 1986 [1897]. *Kanyasulkam*, ed. Setty Eshwara Rao. Hyderabad: Vishalandhra Publishing House.

——. 2000. *Jabulu-Javabulu, Dinacharyalu* (Letters, Correspondence and Diaries), ed. Setty Eswara Rao. Hyderabad: Vishalandhra Publishing House.

Brindavana Nagara Vaishyulu. 1934. *Vaishya Vidya Bhanoodayamu*. Tenali: Bharati Mudraksharashala. GLR.

Bapanaiah, Solaka, Nalam Krishna Rao, et al. n. d. *Sri Kamakshi Vijaya Sanchika*. Madras: Shashti Poorti Sammana Sangha Prachuranamu. GLR.

Bapinidu, Maganti, ed. n. d. *Annapoorna Devi Lekhalu*, other details n. a. SNV.

Brahmayya Sastri, Kasibhatta. 1911. *Upanyasapayonidhi*, ed. Nandiraju Chalapati Rao. Eluru: Manjuvani Mudraksharashala.

Chalam, G. V. 1997 [1925]. 'Vitantuvu', in *Yavanavvanam*. Vijayawada: Aruna Publishing House.

——. 1999 [1925]. *Stree*. Hyderabad: Sweet Home Publications.

——. 1993 [1935]. *Biddala Shikshana*. Vijayawada: Aruna Publishing House.

——. 1996. *Musings*. Vijayawada: Aruna Publishing House.

Chenchaiah, Darishi. 1958. *Meeroo - Nenoo (Kathala Samputi)*. Vijayawada: Navodaya Publishers.

——. 1961. *Naa Divya Smrutulu*. Vijayawada: Adarsha Grandhamandali.

——. comp. and ed. *Marapurani Annapoorna*, other details n. a. GLR.

Gopalakrishna, Pennepalli et al., ed. 2012. *Gurujaadalu: Mahakavi Appa Rao Samagra Rachanalu*. Hyderabad: Manasu Foundation.

Gurunadham, J. 1911. *Veeresalingam, the Founder of Telugu Public Life*. Rajahmundry.

Kotishwara Gupta, Shikharam. 1925. *Balya Vivaha Khandanamu*. Ongole: P. V. R. H. S. Press. GLR.

Krishna Rao, Nalam. 1912. *Streelayedala Manamu gavinchu Pancha Mahapatakamulu* (The Five Great Sins We Commit against Women). Rajamahendravaramu: Sri Manorama Brown Industrial Mission Press. GLR.

——. n. d. *Vitantu Vivaha Charitra (1904 Sam. varaku)*. Rajamahendravaramu: Hitakarini Samajamu. GLR.

Lakshmi Narayana, K., comp. and ed. 2006–2007. *Streela Kathalu*, vols. I–V. Anantapuram: Rama Publications.

Lakshmi Narasimha Rao, Panuganti. 2006. *Saakshi*. Vijayawada: Abhinandana Publishers. (The essays were originally published in the *Andhra Patrika* during 1913–1920.)

Murthy, Vivina, ed. 2015. *Diddubatalu: Diddubatuku Mundu Kathalu 92*. Illinois, USA: Telugu Association of North America Publications.

Nageswara Rao, Kashinathuni. 1993/1994 [1929]. *Andhra Vangmaya Suchika: Mudritamudrita Granthamula Pattika*. Hyderabad: Prachi Publications.

Narayana Rao, Kallakoori. 1999 [1921]. *Vara Vikrayamu*. Vijayawada: Jayanthi Publications.

Purushottam, Jathavallabhula. 1936. *Vimarshakagresara Kasibhatta Bramhaiah Sastry gari Jeevita Charitram*. Kakinada: Kakinada Mudraksharashala.

Ramapati Rao, Akkiraju, ed. 1987 [1970]. *Veeresalingam Dairylu, Lekhalu, Jeevita Charitra*. Hyderabad: Vishalandhra Publishing House.

Shivaramachandra Rao, Kovvali and Narayana Rao. 1910. *Puratana Hindu Streela Younnatyamu* (Greatness of Ancient Hindu Women). Tanuku: Soudamini Mudraksharashala. GLR.

Sri Krishna Dasudu (pseudonym). 1920. *Sangha Samskaranopanyasamu*. Chennapuri: Ananda Mudranalayamu.

Srinivas, Sangisetti, ed. 2010. *Bhandaru Atchamamba Toli Telugu Kathalu*. Hyderabad: Kavile Telangana Research and Referral Centre.

Veeraswamaiah, Enugula. 1992 [1838]. *Kashiyatra Charitra*. Hyderabad: Telugu University.

Venkatachalapati Rao, Atchyutuni. n. d. *Balya Vivaha Tatva Saramu*, other details, n. a. GLR.

Venkata Ranganatha Rao, Mangu. 1914. *Stree Niti Sangrahamu*. Kakinada: Sri Venkateswara Vidyasagara Press. GLR.

Venkata Sivudu, Rayasam. 1925. *Englishuvari Samsara Padhdhatulu*. Bezawada: Venkataram and Co. Sri Ramachandra Granthalayamu, Poduru, West Godavari District; hereafter SRGPWGD.

Venkata Subbaraya Gupta, Grandhi. 1922. *Sri Aatmuri Lakshminarasimha Somayaji: Jeevita Charitramu, Upanyasamulu*. Bezawada: Andhra Grandhlaya Mudraksharashala. RMLV.

Venkatramaiah, Bulusu. 1938. *Sharada Chattamanedi Balya Vivaha Nirodhana Chattamu*. Rajahmundry.

Viraiah, Daruvuri, ed. 1987. *Acharya Ranga Rachanalu*. Gunturu: Acharya Ranga 88va Janmadinotsava Ahvanasangham Prachurana.

Viresalingam, K. 1887. *Fortune's Wheel: A Tale of Hindu Domestic Life*, tr. J. Robert Hutchinson. London.

5. Books (English)

Apparao, Gurajada. 2011. *Girls for Sale (Kanyasulkam): A Play from Colonial India*, trans. Velcheru Narayana Rao. New Delhi: Penguin.

Chalam. 1986 [1925]. *Man and Woman (Excluding the Aspect of Love)*. Madanapalli: Wake-Up.

Deshmukh, Durgabai. 1980a. *Chintaman and I*. Hyderabad: Allied Publishers.

____. 1980b. *The Stone that Speaketh*, 2 vols. Hyderabad: Andhra Mahila Sabha.

Muthulakshmi Reddy, S. 1965. *Autobiography of Dr. (Mrs.) S. Muthulakshmi Reddy: A Pioneer Woman Legislator*. M. L. J. Press.

Nikambe, Shevantibai. 2004. *Ratnabai: A High-Caste Child-Wife*, ed. Chandani Lokuge. New Delhi: Oxford University Press.

Ramabai Sarasvati, Pundita. 1984 [1888]. *The High Caste Hindu Woman*. New Delhi: Inter-India Publications.

Ray, Renuka. 2005. *My Reminiscences: Social Development during the Gandhian Era and After*. Kolkata: Stree.

Satthianadhan, Krupabai. 1998. *Kamala: The Story of a Hindu Child–Wife*, ed. Chandani Lokuge. New Delhi: Oxford University Press.

Sen, Haimabati. 2011. *'Because I am a Woman': A Child Widow's Memoirs from Colonial India*, ed. Geraldine Forbes and Tapan Raychaudhuri. New Delhi: Chronicle Books.

Tilak, Lakshmibai. 1998 [1950]. *I Follow After: An Autobiography*, trans. E. Josephine Inkster. New Delhi: Oxford University Press.

Vidyasagar, Ishvarchandra. 2012. *Hindu Widow Remarriage*, trans. Brain A. Hatcher. Ranikhet: Permanent Black.

Secondary Sources

1. Books (English)

Agnes, Flavia. 2012. [1999]. *Law and Gender Inequality: The Politics of Women's Rights in India*. New Delhi: Oxford University Press.

Altekar, A. S. 1959 [1938]. *The Position of Women in Hindu Civilization*. Delhi: Motilal Banarsidas Publishers.

Anagol, Padma. 2007. *The Emergence of Feminism in India, 1850–1920*. Hampshire, England: Ashgate.

Anantha Raman, Sita. 1996. *Getting Girls to School: Social Reform in the Tamil Districts, 1870–1930*. Kolkata: Stree.

Anderson, Benedict. 1983. *Imagined Communities: Reflections on the Origin and Spread of Nationalism*. London: Verso.

Anderson, Linda. 2007 [1988] *Autobiography*. London and New York: Routledge.

Anjaneyulu, D. n. d. *The Philosophy of a Social Reformer: Focus on Veeresalingam and His Pioneering Work, Text of Kandukuri Veeresalingam Memorial Lecture delivered on 16.4.1979, the 131st Birth Anniversary of Sri Veeresalingam at the Chennapuri Andhra Maha Sabha, Madras*. Hyderabad: International Telugu Institute.

Bandyopadhyay, Sekhar. 2004. *Caste, Culture and Hegemony: Social Domination in Colonial Bengal*. New Delhi: Sage Publications.

Banerjee, M. Swapna. 2004. *Men, Women, and Domestics: Articulating Middle-Class Identity in Colonial Bengal*. New Delhi: Oxford University Press.

Basu, Aparna and Bharati Ray. 2003 [1990]. *Women's Struggle: A History of the All India Women's Conference, 1927–2002*. New Delhi: Manohar.

Basu, Aparna and Anup Taneja, ed. 2002. *Breaking Out of Invisibility: Women in Indian History*. New Delhi: ICHR and Northern Book Centre.

Benstock, Shari. 1988. *The Private Self: Theory and Practice of Women's Autobiographical Writings*. Chapel Hill: University of North Carolina Press.

Bhargava, Rajul, ed. 2010. *Gender Issues: Attestations and Contestations*. Jaipur: Rawat Publications.

Bhattacharya, Sabyasachi et al., ed. 2001. *The Development of Women's Education in India: A Collection of Documents, 1850–1920*. New Delhi: Kanishka Publishers.

Bjorkert, Suruchi Thapar. 2005. *Women in the Indian National Movement: Unseen Faces and Unheard Voices, 1930–42*. New Delhi: Sage Publications.

Blackburn, Stuart. 2006 [2003]. *Print, Folklore, and Nationalism in Colonial South India*. Ranikhet: Permanent Black.

Blackburn, Stuart and Vasudha Dalmia, ed. 2004. *India's Literary History: Essays on the Nineteenth Century*. Ranikhet: Permanent Black.

Borthwick, Meredith. 1984. *Changing Role of Women in Bengal, 1849–1905*. Princeton: Princeton University Press.

Brockway, Nora. 1949. *A Larger Way for Women: Aspects of Christian Education for Girls in South India, 1712–1948*. Madras.

Chakravarti, Uma. 1998. *Re-Writing History: The Life and Times of Pandita Ramabai*. Delhi: Kali for Women.

Chakravarti, Uma and Preeti Gill, ed. 2001. *Shadow Lives: Writings on Widowhood*. New Delhi: Kali for Women.

Chakravartty, Renu. 2011 [1980]. *Communists in Indian Women's Movement*. New Delhi: People's Publishing House.

Chanana, Karuna, ed. 1988. *Socialisation, Education and Women: Explorations in Gender Identity*. New Delhi: Orient Longman.

Chanda, Ipshita and Jayeeta Bagchi, ed. 2014. *Shaping the Discourse: Women's Writings in Bengali Periodicals, 1865–1947*. Kolkata: Stree.

Chandra, Bipan. 1984. *Communalism in Modern India*. New Delhi: Vikas Publishing House.

Chandra, Sudhir. 1998. *Enslaved Daughters: Colonialism, Law and Women's Rights.* New Delhi: Oxford University Press.

Chartier, Roger. 1987. *The Cultural Uses of Print in Early Modern France*, trans. Lydia G. Cochrane. Princeton: Princeton University Press.

____. ed. 1989 [1987]. *The Culture of Print: Power and the Uses of Print in Early Modern Europe*, trans. Lydia G. Cochrane. New Jersey: Princeton University Press.

Chatterjee, Indrani. 2004. *Unfamiliar Relations: Family and History in South Asia.* Ranikhet: Permanent Black.

Chatterjee, Partha. 2001 [1993]. *The Nation and Its Fragments: Colonial and Postcolonial Histories.* New Delhi: Oxford University Press.

Chaudhuri, Maitrayee. 2011. *The Indian Women's Movement: Reform and Revival.* New Delhi: Palm Leaf Publications.

Chaudhuri, Nupur and Margaret Strobel, ed. 1992. *Western Women and Imperialism: Complicity and Resistance.* Bloomington and Indianapolis: Indiana University Press.

Chaudhuri, Supriya and Sajni Mukherji, ed. 2004 [2002]. *Literature and Gender: Essays for Jasodhara Bagchi.* New Delhi: Orient Longman.

Chowdhury, Indira. 1998. *The Frail Hero and Virile History: Gender and the Politics of Culture in Colonial Bengal.* New Delhi: Oxford University Press.

Dalmia, Vasudha. 2015. *Hindu Pasts: Women, Religion, Histories.* Ranikhet: Permanent Black.

Devika, J, trans. and ed. 2005. *Her-Self: Gender and Early Writings of Malayalee Women, 1898–1938.* Kolkata: Stree.

____. 2007. *En-gendering Individuals: The Language of Re-forming in Early Twentieth Century Keralam.* Hyderabad: Orient Longman.

Downs, Laura Lee. 2004. *Writing Gender History.* London: Hodder Arnold.

Eisenstein, Elizabeth L. 1979. *The Printing Press as an Agent of Change: Communications and Cultural Transformations in Early-Modern Europe*, 2 vols. New York: Cambridge University Press.

____. 1983. *The Printing Revolution in Early Modern Europe.* Cambridge: Cambridge University Press.

Engels, F. 1948. *The Origin of the Family, Private Property and the State.* Moscow: Progress Publishers.

Febvre, Lucien and Henri-Jean Martin. 1976 [1958]. *The Coming of the Book: The Impact of Printing, 1450–1800*, trans. David Gerard. London: Verso.

Felton, Monika. 2003. *A Child Widow's Story.* New Delhi: Katha.

Fisch, Jorg. 2005. *Immolating Women: A Global History of Widow Burning from Ancient Times to the Present*, trans. Rekha Kamath Rajan. Ranikhet: Permanent Black.

Forbes, Geraldine. 1998. *Women in Modern India.* New Delhi: Cambridge University Press.

Forbes, Geraldine. 2005. *Women in Colonial India: Essays on Politics, Medicine, and Historiography*. Delhi: Chronicle Books.

Fuller, C. J. and Haripriya Narasimhan. 2015 [2014]. *Tamil Brahmans: The Making of a Middle-Class Caste*. New Delhi: Social Science Press.

Fuller, Marcus. 1900. *The Wrongs of Indian Womanhood*. New Delhi: Inter–India Publications.

Ganesan, S. 1992. *The Indian Publishing Industry: An Analytical Study with special Reference to Publishing in Regional Languages*. New Delhi: Sterling.

Ghosh, Anindita. 2006. *Power in Print: Popular Publishing and the Politics of Language and Culture in a Colonial Society, 1778–1905*. New Delhi: Oxford University Press.

_____. ed. 2007. *Behind the Veil: Resistance, Women, and the Everyday in Colonial South Asia*. Ranikhet: Permanent Black.

Gupta, Abhijit and Swapan Chakravorty, ed. 2004. *Print Areas: Book History in India*. Ranikhet: Permanent Black.

Gupta, Charu, ed. 2012. *Gendering Colonial India: Reforms, Print, Caste and Communalism*. New Delhi: Orient BlackSwan.

Gupta, Sarmistha Dutta. 2010. *Identities and Histories: Women's Writings and Politics in Bengal*. Kolkata: Stree.

Heimsath, Charles H. 1964. *Indian Nationalism and Hindu Social Reform*. Princeton: Princeton University Press.

Jayawardena, Kumari. 1995. *The White Woman's Other Burden: Western Women and South Asia during British Rule*. New York and London: Routledge.

Jones, Kenneth W. 1999 [1994]. *Socio-religious Reform Movements in British India: The New Cambridge History of India*. New Delhi: Cambridge University Press.

Kannabiran, Kalpana and Vasanth Kannabiran. 2003. *Muvalur Ramamirthammal's Web of Deceit: Devadasi Reform in Colonial India*. New Delhi: Kali for Women.

Karlekar, Malavika. 1991. *Voices from Within: Early Personal Narratives of Bengali Women*. New Delhi: Oxford University Press.

_____. 2005. *Revisioning the Past: A History of Early Photography in Bengal, 1875–1915*. New Delhi: Oxford University Press.

_____. ed. 2006. *Visualising Indian Women, 1875–1947*. New Delhi: Oxford University Press.

Kesavan, B. S. 1985. *History of Printing and Publishing in India: A Study of Cultural Reawakening, Vol. I. South Indian Origin and its Efflorescence in Bengal*. New Delhi: National Book Trust.

_____. 1986. *The Book in India: A Compilation*. New Delhi: National Book Trust.

Kesavanarayana, B. 1976. *Political and Social Factors in Andhra: 1900–1956*. Vijayawada: Navodya Publishers.

Kleinberg, S. Jay, ed. 1992 [1988]. *Retrieving Women's History: Changing Perceptions of the Role of Women in Politics and Society*. Oxford: Berg Publishers.

Kosambi, Meera. 2007. *Crossing Thresholds: Feminist Essays in Social History*. Ranikhet: Permanent Black.

——. 2008. *Feminist Vision or 'Treason Against Men'? Kashibai Kanitkar and the Engendering of Marathi Literature*. Ranikhet: Permanent Black.

Krishna, G., et. al. 1987. *Journalism in Andhra Pradesh: A Brief Survey*. Hyderabad: Hyderabad Union of Journalists.

Krishnamurthy, J, ed. 1989. *Women in Colonial India: Essays on Survival, Work and the State*. New Delhi: Oxford University Press.

Kumar, Radha. 1998 [1993]. *The History of Doing: An Illustrated Account of Movements for Women's Rights and Feminism in India, 1800–1990*. New Delhi: Kali for Women.

Lal, Ruby. 2013. *Coming of Age in Nineteenth-Century India: The Girl-Child and the Art of Playfulness*. New Delhi: Cambridge University Press.

Leonard, John Greenfield. 1991. *Kandukuri Viresalingam (1848–1919): A Biography of an Indian Social Reformer*. Hyderabad: Telugu University.

Lerner, Gerda. 1979. *The Majority Finds its Past: Placing Women in History*. New York: Oxford University Press.

Majumdar, Rochona. 2009. *Marriage and Modernity: Family Values in Colonial Bengal*. New Delhi: Oxford University Press.

Mangamma, J. 1975. *Book Printing in India with Special Reference to the Contribution of European Scholars to Telugu (1746–1857)*. Nellore: Bangorey Books.

Mehta, Shirin. 2009. *Women and Social Change*. Jaipur: Rawat Publications.

Menon, Visalakshi. 2003. *Indian Women and Nationalism: The U.P. Story*. New Delhi: Shakti Books.

Mill, J. S. 1869. *The Subjection of Women*. New York: Dover Publications, INC.

Minault, Gail ed. 1981. *The Extended Family: Women and Political Participation in India and Pakistan*. New Delhi: Chanakya Publications.

Mohan, Kamlesh. 2007. *Towards Gender History: Images, Identities and Roles of North Indian Women*. New Delhi: Aakar Books.

Mohanty, Sachidananda, ed. 2005. *Early Women's Writings in Orissa, 1898–1950: A Lost Tradition*. New Delhi: Sage Publications.

Moitra, Mohit. 1969. *A History of Indian Journalism*. Kolkata: National Book Company.

Murshid, Gulam. 1983. *Reluctant Debutante: Response of Bengali Women to Modernization, 1849–1905*. Rajshahi: Sahitya Samsad, Rajshahi University Press.

Nair, Janaki. 2000 [1996]. *Women and Law in Colonial India: A Social History*. New Delhi: Kali for Women.

Nanda, B. R., ed. 1990 [1976]. *Indian Women: From Purdah to Modernity*. New Delhi: Radiant Publishers.

Narasimha Rao, V. V. L. 1993. *Chilakamarti Lakshmi Narasimham*. New Delhi: Sahitya Akademi.

Naregal, Veena. 2001. *Language Politics, Elites, and the Public Sphere: Western India under Colonialism*. Ranikhet: Permanent Black.

Narla, V. R. 1968. *Veereshalingam*. New Delhi: Sahitya Akademi.

_____. 1979. *Gurajada*. New Delhi: Sahitya Akademi.

Natarajan, S. 1959. *A Century of Social Reform in India*. Bombay: Asia Publishing House.

Nijhawan, Shobna. 2012. *Women and Girls in the Hindi Public Sphere: Periodical Literature in Colonial North India*. New Delhi: Oxford University Press.

Nurulla, S. and J. P. Naik. 1964. *A Students' History of Education in India: 1800–1965*. New Delhi: Macmillan.

O'Hanlon, Rosalind. 1994. *A Comparison between Women and Men: Tarabai Shinde and the Critique of Gender Relations in Colonial India*. New Delhi: Oxford University Press.

Orsini, Francesca. 2010 [2002]. *The Hindi Public Sphere, 1920–1940: Language and Literature in the Age of Nationalism*. New Delhi: Oxford University Press.

Padma, A. 2001. *Women in Medieval Times: 11th to 14th Centuries A.D. With Special Reference to Andhradesa*. Hyderabad: self-published.

Panikkar, K. N. 1995. *Culture, Ideology, Hegemony*. New Delhi: Tulika Books.

Powell, A. Arvil and Siobhan Lambert-Hurley, ed., *Rhetoric and Reality: Gender and the Colonial Experience in South Asia*. New Delhi: Oxford University Press.

Ramakrishna, V. 1983. *Social Reform in Andhra (1848–1919)*. New Delhi: Vikas Publications.

Ramakrishna, Vakulabharanam and K. H. S. S. Sundar. 2007. *Legacy and Continuity: Social Reforms in Andhra Pradesh (1850–2000)*. Varni: Samskar.

Ramaswamy, Vijaya, ed. 2003. *Re-searching Indian Women*. New Delhi: Manohar.

Rao, Parimala V., ed. 2014. *New Perspectives in the History of Indian Education*. New Delhi: Orient BlackSwan.

Rao, P. R. 1997 [1993]. *History of Modern Andhra (Revised & Enlarged Edition)*. New Delhi: Sterling Publishers Private Limited.

Rao, Ranga, ed. 1995. *Classic Telugu Short Stories*. New Delhi: Penguin Books.

Ray, Bharati. 2012 [2002]. *Early Feminists of Colonial India: Sarala Devi Chaudhurani and Rokeya Sakhawat Hossain*. New Delhi: Oxford University Press.

_____. ed. 2001 [1995]. *From the Seams of History: Essays on Indian Women*. New Delhi: Oxford University Press.

Ray, Rajat Kanta, ed. 1995. *Mind, Body and Society: Life and Mentality in Colonial Bengal*. New Delhi: Oxford University Press.

Regani, Sarojini. 1998 [1972]. *Highlights of the Freedom Movement in Andhra Pradesh*. Hyderabad: The Ministry of Cultural Affairs, Government of Andhra Pradesh.

Roy, Anupama. 2005. *Gendered Citizenship: Historical and Conceptual Explorations*. Hyderabad: Orient Longman.

Russo, Ann and Cheris Kramarae, ed. 1991. *The Radical Women's Press of the 1850s*. New York and London: Routledge.

Sadasivan, D. 1974. *The Growth of Public Opinion in the Madras Presidency (1858–1909)*. Madras: University of Madras.

Sagade, Jaya. 2012 [2005]. *Child Marriage in India: Socio-legal and Human Rights Dimensions*, New Delhi: Oxford University Press.

Sangari, Kumkum and Sudesh Vaid, ed. 1985. *Women and Culture*. Bombay: SNDT Women's University.

———. ed. 1989. *Recasting Women: Essays in Colonial History*. New Delhi: Kali for Women.

Sarkar, Sumit and Tanika Sarkar, ed. 2007. *Women and Social Reform in India*, 2 vols. Ranikhet: Permanent Black.

Sarkar, Sumit. 1975. *Bibliographical Survey of Social Reform Movements in the 18th and 19th Centuries*. New Delhi: ICHR.

Sarkar, Tanika. 2001. *Hindu Wife, Hindu Nation: Community, Religion and Cultural Nationalism*. Ranikhet: Permanent Black.

———. 2009. *Rebels, Wives, Saints: Designing Selves and Nations in Colonial Times*. Ranikhet: Permanent Black.

Sen, Amiya P., ed. 2006 [2003]. *Social and Religious Reform: The Hindus of British India*. New Delhi: Oxford University Press.

Sen, Indrani. 2008. *Woman and Empire: Representations in the Writings of British India (1858–1900)*. Hyderabad: Orient Longman.

———. ed. 2008. *Memsahibs' Writings: Colonial Narratives on Indian Women*. Hyderabad: Orient Longman.

Shanta, V. 2012. *Muthulakshmi Reddy—A Legend unto Herself*. Occasional Publication 44. New Delhi: India International Centre.

Sharma, Kumud and C. P. Sujaya, ed. 2012. *Towards Equality Report of the Committee on the Status of Women in India*, general editor Vina Mazumdar. New Delhi: Pearson.

Sharma, Radha Krishna. 1981. *Nationalism, Social Reform and Indian Women*. New Delhi: Janaki Prakashan.

Sharma, S. P. 1996. *The Press: Socio-Political Awakening*, New Delhi: Mohit Publications.

Shevelow, Kathryn. 1989. *Women and Print Culture*. London: Routledge and Kegan Paul.

Sinha, Chitra. 2012. *Debating Patriarchy: The Hindu Code Bill Controversy in India (1941–1956)*. New Delhi: Oxford University Press.

Sinha, Mrinalini. 2006. *Specters of Mother India: The Global Restructuring of an Empire*. New Delhi: Zubaan.

Sogani, Rajul. 2002. *The Hindu Widow in Indian Literature*. New Delhi: Oxford University Press.

Soma Reddy, R., M. Radhakrishna Sarma and A. Satyanarayana. 1999. *Social Evils in Andhra Desa (17th and 18th Centuries, A.D.)*. Seminar Proceedings, Department of History, Osmania University. Hyderabad.

Southard, Barbara. 1995. *The Women's Movement and Colonial Politics in Bengal: The Quest for Political Rights, Education and Social Reform Legislation, 1921–1936*. New Delhi: Manohar.

Spongberg, Mary. 2002. *Writing Women's History since the Renaissance*. Palgrave and Macmillan.

Sreekumar, Sharmila. 2009. *Scripting Lives: Narratives of 'Dominant Women' in Kerala*. Hyderabad: Orient BlackSwan.

Sreenivas, Mytheli. 2009. *Wives, Widows and Concubines: The Conjugal Family Ideal in Colonial India*. Hyderabad: Orient BlackSwan.

Stree Shakti Sanghatana. 1986. *We Were Making History: The Life Stories of Women in Telangana People's Struggle*. New Delhi: Kali for Women.

Subbamma, Malladi. 1994. *Women and Social Reform*. Hyderabad: Book Links Corporation.

Subramanyam, K. 1984. *The Press and the National Movement in South India: Andhra, 1900–1932*. Madras: New Era Publications.

Sudarshanam, R. S. 2000. *G. V. Chalam*. New Delhi: Sahitya Akademi.

Taneja, Anup. 2005. *Gandhi, Women, and the National Movement, 1920–1947*. New Delhi: Har-Anand Publications.

Tharu, Susie and K. Lalitha, ed. 1994. *Women Writing in India: 600 B.C. to the Early Twentieth Century*. USA: Pandora.

Thirumali, Inukonda. 2005. *Marriage, Love and Caste: Perceptions on Telugu Women During the Colonial Period*. New Delhi: Promilla & Co.

Thorner, Alice and Maithreyi Krishnaraj, ed. 2000. *Ideals, Images and Real Lives: Women in Literature and History*. Hyderabad: Orient Longman.

Uberoi, Patricia, ed. 1996. *Social Reform, Sexuality and the State*. New Delhi: Sage Publications.

Vaikuntham, Y. 1982. *Education and Social Change in South India: Andhra, 1885–1920*. Madras: New Era Publications.

_____. 2004. *Studies in Socio-Cultural and Political History: Modern Andhra*. Hyderabad: self-published.

Varadachari, G. S., et al., ed. 2011. *Our Legends of the Fourth Estate: Telugu Stalwarts and Foot Soldiers of Journalism—Then and Now*. Hyderabad: Veteran Journalists' Association.

Venkatachalapathy, A. R. 2012. *The Province of the Book: Scholars, Scribes and Scribblers in Colonial Tamilnadu*. Ranikhet: Permanent Black.

Viswanathan, Gauri. 2009. *Masks of Conquest: Literary Study and British Rule in India*. New Delhi: Oxford University Press.

Vittal Rao, Y. 1968. *Education and Learning in Andhra under the East India Company*. Secunderabad: Vidyaranya Swamy.

Watt, Carey A. and Michael Mann, ed. 2012 [2011]. *Civilising Missions in Colonial and Postcolonial South Asia*. New Delhi: Anthem Press.

Walsh, Judith E. 2004. *Domesticity in Colonial India: What Women Learned When Men Gave Them Advice*. New Delhi: Oxford University Press.

Washbrook, D. A. 1976. *The Emergence of Provincial Politics: Madras Presidency (1870–1920)*. Cambridge: Cambridge University Press.

Yenadi Raju, P. 1994. *Evolution of Indian Nationalism (Rayalaseema), 1858–1920*, Bombay: M. N. M. Associates.

———. 2003. *Rayalaseema During Colonial Times: A Study in Indian Nationalism*. New Delhi: Northern Book Centre.

Zuckerman, Mary Ellen. 1998. *A History of Popular Women's Magazines in the United States, 1792–1995*. Westport, Connecticut and London: Greenwood Press.

2. Articles and Book Chapters (English)

Anagol, Padma. 2002. 'The Emergence of Female Criminal in India: Infanticide and Survival under the Raj'. *History Workshop Journal* no. 53 (Spring): 73–93.

———. 2008. 'Agency, Periodisation and Change in the Gender and Women's History of Colonial India'. *Gender & History* 20 (3): 603–627.

———. 2010. 'Feminist Inheritances and Foremothers: The Beginnings of Feminism in Modern India'. *Women's History Review* 19 (4): 523–546.

Anandhi, S. 1991. 'Women's Question in the Dravidian Movement c. 1925–1948'. *Social Scientist* 19 (5/6): 24–41.

———. 1991. 'Representing Devadasis: "Dasigal Mosavalai" as a Radical Text'. *Economic and Political Weekly* 26 (11/12): 739–746.

Arudra. 1968. 'Beginnings of Telugu Journalism'. In *Studies in the History of Telugu Journalism*, ed. K. R. Sheshagiri Rao. New Delhi: Narla Venkateshwara Rao Shashtyabdipurti Committee.

Bagchi, Jasodhara. 1990. 'Representing Nationalism: Ideology of Motherhood in Colonial Bengal'. *Economic and Political Weekly* 25 (42/43: WS65–WS71).

———. 1993. 'Socialising the Girl Child in Colonial Bengal'. *Economic and Political Weekly* 28 (41): 2214–2219.

Bandyopadhyay, Sibaji. 1994. 'Producing and Re-Producing the New Women: A Note on the Prefix "Re"'. *Social Scientist* 22 (1/2): 30–39.

Bannerji, Himani. 1991. 'Fashioning a Self: Educational Proposals for and by Women in Popular Magazines in Colonial Bengal'. *Economic and Political Weekly* 26 (43): WS50–WS62.

———. 2000. 'Project of Hegemony: Towards a Critique of Subaltern Studies' "Resolution of the Women's Question"'. *Economic and Political Weekly* 35 (11): 902–920.

Benei, Veronique. 2002. 'Missing Indigenous Bodies: Educational Enterprise and Victorian Morality in Mid-19th Century Bombay Presidency'. *Economic and Political Weekly* 37 (17): 1647–1654.

Berry, Kim. 2003. 'Lakshmi and the Scientific Housewife: A Transnational Account of Indian Women's Development and Production of an Indian Modernity'. *Economic and Political Weekly* 38 (11): 1055–1068.

Blunt, Alison. 1999. 'Imperial Geographies of Home: British Domesticity in India, 1886–1925'. *Transactions of the Institute of British Geographers* 24 (4): 421–440.

Chakrabarthy, Dipesh. 1993. 'The Difference – Deferral of (A) Colonial Modernity: Public Debates on Domesticity in British Bengal'. *History Workshop Journal* 36 (1): 1–34.

Chakravarti, Uma. 2001. 'The Women's Movement in South Asia: Everyday Challenges'. In *Looking Back: India in the Twentieth Century*, ed. N. N. Vohra and Sabyasachi Bhattacharya. New Delhi: National Book Trust.

Chanda, Sita P. 1991. 'Birthing Terrible Beauties: Feminisms and "Women's Magazines"'. *Economic and Political Weekly* 26 (43): WS67–WS70.

Dawar, Jagadish Lal. 1987. 'Feminism and Femininity: Women in Premchand's Fiction'. *Studies in History* 3 (1): 121–136.

Desai, A. R. 1985. 'Women's Movement in India: An Assessment'. *Economic and Political Weekly* 20 (23): 992–995.

Devika, J. 2005. 'The Aesthetic Woman: Re-forming Female Bodies and Minds in Early Twentieth-Century Keralam'. *Modern Asian Studies* 39 (2): 461–287.

Forbes, H. Geraldine. 1979. 'Women and Modernity: The Issue of Child Marriage in India', *Women's Studies International Quarterly*, Vol. 2.

_____. 1986. 'In Search of a 'Pure Heathen': Missionary Women in Nineteenth Century India'. *Economic and Political Weekly* 21 (17): WS2–WS8.

_____. 2000. 'Women's Movements in India: Traditional Symbols and New Roles'. In *Social Movements in India*, ed. M. S. A. Rao. New Delhi: Manohar Publishers.

Fuller, C. J. and Haripriya Narasimhan. 2013. 'Marriage, Education, and Employment among Tamil Brahman Women in South India, 1891–2010'. *Modern Asian Studies* 47 (1): 53–84.

Ghosh, Anindita. 2003. 'An Uncertain "Coming of the Book": Early Print Cultures in Colonial India'. *Book History* 6: 23–55.

Girija, S. 1996. 'Smt. Bharati Devi Ranga – A Profile'. *Proceedings of the Andhra Pradesh History Congress*, hereafter *PAPHC*.

_____. 1997. 'Desabandhavi Duvvuri Subbamma – A Dedicated Freedom Fighter'. *PAPHC*.

Gupta, Charu. 1991. 'Portrayal of Women in Premchand's Stories: A Critique', *Social Scientist* 19 (5–6): 88–113.

Hancock, Mary. 2004. 'Home Science and the Nationalisation of Domesticity in Colonial India'. *Modern Asian Studies* 35 (4): 871–903.

Hari Krishna, S. 1994. 'Revivalistic Journals of Andhra, 1872–1920'. *PAPHC*.

Heimsath, Charles H. 1962. 'The Origin and Enactment of the Indian Age of Consent Bill, 1891'. *The Journal of Asian Studies* 21 (4): 491–504.

Inna Reddy, S. 1993. 'Non-Brahmin Movement in Andhra, 1916–1939'. *Itihas* 18.

———. 1994. 'Women's Issues: The Reform and Legacy, 1920–1947'. *PAPHC*.

Jayalakshmi, T. 1996. 'Salt Satyagraha Movement (1930–31): The Women Freedom Fighters of Guntur District (A.P.)'. *PAPHC*.

Kakar, Sudhir. 1989. 'Gandhi and Women'. In *Intimate Relations: Exploring Indian Sexuality*: 85–128. New Delhi: Penguin Books.

Kameswari, Jandhyala and Rekha Pandey. 1987. 'Why Women's History?'. *PAPHC*.

Kapur, Jyotsna. 1990. 'Putting Herself into the Picture: Women's Accounts of the Social Reform Campaign in Maharashtra, Mid Nineteenth to early Twentieth Centuries'. *Manushi*, no. 56: 28–37.

Karlekar, Malavika. 1986. 'Kadambini and the *Bhadralok*: Early Debates over Women's Education in Bengal'. *Economic and Political Weekly* 21 (17): WS25–WS31.

Kesava Narayana, B. 1975. 'Widow Marriage Movement in Andhra'. *Itihas* 2 (1).

Kishwar, Madhu. 1986. 'Arya Samaj and Women's Education: Kanya Mahavidyalaya, Jalandhar'. *Economic and Political Weekly* 21 (17): WS9–WS13+WS15–WS24.

Kosambi, Meera. 1988. 'Women, Emancipation and Equality: Pandita Ramabai's Contribution to Women's Cause'. *Economic and Political Weekly* 23 (44): WS38–WS49.

———. 2001. 'Realities and Reflections: Personal Narratives of two Women from Nineteenth-Century Maharashtra'. In *From Myths to Markets: Essays on Gender*, ed. Kumkum Sangari and Uma Chakravarti. Shimla: Indian Institue of Advanced Studies.

———. 2014. 'Gender and the Freedom Struggle in Maharashtra: Contextualising Prema Kantak's Novel *Agniyan* (1942)'. In *Rethinking Western India: The Changing Contexts of Culture, Society and Religion*, ed. Dušan Deák and Daniel Jasper. New Delhi: Orient BlackSwan.

Kumar, Nita. 1991. 'Widows, Education and Social Change in Twentieth Century Banaras'. *Economic and Political Weekly* 26 (17): WS19–WS25.

Lakshmi, I. 2005. 'Contexualising Women Writing in Telugu: Readings into Molla Ramayanamu and Other Works of Women in Medieval Times'. Presidential Address. *PAPHC*.

Leonard, Karen. 1979. 'Women in India: Some Recent Perspectives', *Pacific Affairs* 52 (1): 95–107.

Mahaboob Basha, S. 2004. 'Challenges to Patriarchy in Colonial Andhra: A Study of Women's Writings (1928–1942)'. In *South India: Regions, Cultures and Sagas*, ed. Inukonda Thirumali. New Delhi: Bibliomatrix.

———. 2008. 'Against the Tides of Reform: Conservative Women's Journals in Colonial Andhra—The Story of *Savitri*, 1904–1912'. *Proceedings of the Indian History Congress* 68 (part 1): 1001–1020.

Majumdar, Rochona. 2003. 'History of Women's Rights: A Non-Historicist Reading'. *Economic and Political Weekly* 38 (22): 2130–2134.

Mani, Lata. 1986. 'Production of an Official Discourse on "Sati" in Early Nineteenth Century Bengal'. *Economic and Political Weekly* 21 (17):WS32–WS40.

Manjulatha Devi, T. V. 1990. 'Child Marriages in Rayalaseema, 1920–1950'. *Itihas* 16 (1). Hyderabad: A.P. State Archives.

Minault, Gail. 1998. 'Urdu Women's Magazines in the Early Twentieth Century'. *Manushi*, no. 48 (September–October): 2–8.

Mohan, Kamlesh. 2005. 'A Juster India for Women: The Thought and Work of Pandita Ramabai and Rameshwari Nehru'. In *India–Studies in the History of an Idea*, ed. Irfan Habib. New Delhi: Munshiram Manoharlal Publishers.

Mohanty, Sachidananda. 2004. 'Female Identity and Conduct Book Tradition in Orissa: The Virtuous Woman in the Ideal Home'. *Economic and Political Weekly* 39 (4): 333–336.

_____. 2007. 'Advice to Housewives: "Conduct Book" Tradition in Orissa'. In *Recent Studies on Indian Women*, ed. Kamal K. Mishra and Janet Lowry Huber. Jaipur: Rawat Publications.

Murali, Atlury. 1987. 'Perspectives on Women's Liberation: Andhra in the Nineteenth and Early Twentieth Centuries'. *Studies in History* 3 (1): 97–120.

Nair, Janaki. 2008. 'The Troubled Relationship of Feminism and History', *Economic and Political Weekly* 43 (43): 57–65.

_____. 2012. 'The Licit in the Modern: Protecting the Child Wife'. In *Mysore Modern: Rethinking the Region under Princely Rule*. New Delhi: Orient BlackSwan.

Orsini, Francesca. 1999. 'Domesticity and Beyond: Hindi Women's Journals in the Early Twentieth Century'. *South Asia Research* 19 (2): 137–160.

Pande, Ishita. 2013. 'Sorting Boys and Men: Unlawful Intercourse, Boy-Protection, and the Child Marriage Restraint Act in Colonial India'. *The Journal of the History of Childhood and Youth* 6 (2): 332–358.

Panikkar, K. N. 1987. 'Introduction'. *Studies in History* 3 (1): 1–8.

Rajagopal, Vakulabharanam. 1987. 'Social and Religious Ideas of Raghupati Venkata Ratnam'. *PAPHC.*

_____. 2003. 'The Rhetorical Strategy of an Autobiography: Reading Satyavati's *Atmacaritamu*'. *The Indian Economic and Social History Review* 40 (4): 377–402.

_____. 2005. 'Fashioning Modernity in Telugu: Viresalingam and His Interventionist Strategy'. *Studies in History* 21 (1): 45–77.

_____. 2011. 'Anti-reform discourse in Andhra: Cultural Nationalism that Failed'. In *Ritual, Caste, and Religion in Colonial South India*, ed. Michael Bergunder, Heiko Frese and Ulrike Schroder. New Delhi: Primus Books.

Ramakrishna, V. 1978. 'Origins of Prarthana Samaj in Andhra'. *PAPHC.*

_____. 1984. 'Kakinada Literary Association–A Study in the Stirrings of Early Political Consciousness in Modern Andhra'. *PAPHC.*

_____. 1987. 'Bibliographical Survey of Women and Social Reform in Andhra During the 19th Century'. *PAPHC.*

Ramakrishna, V. 1991. 'Women's Journals in Andhra During the Nineteenth Century'. *Social Scientist* 19 (5/6): 80–87.

——. 1993a. 'Reform Literature: Gurajada's Kanyasulkam'. *PAPHC.*

——. 1993b. 'Literary and Theatre Movements in Colonial Andhra: Struggle for Left Ideological Legitimacy'. *Social Scientist* 21 (1/2): 69–85.

——. 1994. 'Literature and Social Consciousness: Examination of a Lesser Known Telugu Monograph of the Early 19th Century'. *PAPHC.*

——. 1995. 'Construction of Colonial Culture and Ideology'. Presidential Address: Modern India, *PIHC.*

——. 1996. 'Colonial Culture in Andhra: Democratization of Language and Literary Genres'. *Social Science Probings* 13 (March–December, special issue on Culture).

Ramalakshmi, P. 1993. 'Women's Organisations', *PAPHC.*

——. 1994. 'Contribution of Women to Andhra Brahmo Samaj', *PAPHC.*

——. 1998. 'Venkata Ratnam Naidu and the Nautch Question'. *PAPHC.*

——. 1999. 'Reflections of Feminist Historiography in Telugu Works'. *PAPHC.*

——. 2000. 'Women Leadership in Social Reform Movement in Andhra'. *PAPHC.*

——. 2001. 'Dissent, Protest and Movement Against Patriarchy: Women's Writings in Modern Andhra'. Presidential Address, *PAPHC.*

Ramusack N. Barbara. 'Women's Organisations and Social Change: The Age-of-Marriage Issue in India'. In *Women and World Change: Equity Issues in Development*, ed. Naomi Black and Ann Baker, pp. 198–216. London: Sage Publications.

Rao, Parimala V. 2002. 'Educating Women – How and How Much: Women in the Concept of Tilak's Swaraj'. In *Education of the Disprivileged: Nineteenth and Twentieth Century India*, ed. Sabyasachi Bhattacharya. Hyderabad: Orient Longman.

——. 2010. 'Educated Women as Rakmabais and Ramabais'. In *Foundations of Tilak's Nationalism: Discrimination, Education and Hindutva.* New Delhi: Orient BlackSwan.

Ray, Bharati. 1991. 'Women of Bengal: Transformation in Ideas and Ideals 1900–1947'. *Social Scientist* 19 (5/6): 3–23.

——. 1995. 'The Freedom Movement and Feminist Consciousness in Bengal, 1905–1929'. In *From the Seams of History: Essays on Indian Women*, ed. Bharati Ray: 174–218. New Delhi: Oxford University Press.

Sarkar, Tanika. 2001. 'A Book of Her Own. A Life of Her Own: Autobiography of a Ninetenth-Century Woman'. In *From Myths to Markets: Essays on Gender*, ed. Kumkum Sangari and Uma Chakravarti. Shimla: IIAS.

Sen, Krishna. 2004. 'Lessons in Self-Fashioning: "Bamabodhini Patrika" and the Education of Women in Colonial Bengal'. *Victorian Periodicals Review* 37 (2): 176–191.

Sen, Samita. 2002. 'A Father's Duty: State, Patriarchy and Women's Education'. In *Education of the Disprivileged: Nineteenth and Twentieth Century India*, ed. Sabyasachi Bhattacharya. Hyderabad: Orient Longman.

Shukla, Sonal. 1991. 'Cultivating Minds: 19th Century Gujarati Women's Journals'. *Economic and Political Weekly* 26 (43): WS63–66.

Sunitha, Busireddy. 1990. 'Education of Women in Colonial Andhra (1800–1920)'. *PAPHC*.

Swaminathan, Padmini. 2001. 'Women's Education in the Madras Presidency: Issues of Class and Patriarchy'. *From Myths to Markets: Essays on Gender*, ed. Kumkum Sangari and Uma Chakravarti. Shimla: IIAS.

Swaroopa Rani. R. 1990. 'The Emergence of Women Associations in Hyderabad City (During Late 19th and Early 20th Century)'. *PAPHC*.

Talwar, Vir Bharat. 1989. 'Feminist Consciousness in Women's Journals in Hindi 1910–1920'. In *Recasting Women: Essays in Colonial History*, ed. Kumkum Sangari and Sudesh Vaid. New Delhi: Kali for Women.

Tambe, Ashwini. 2000. 'Review: Colluding Patriarchies: The Colonial Reform of Sexual Relations in India'. *Feminist Studies* 26 (3): 586–600.

Thakkar, Usha. 1997. 'Puppets on the Periphery: Women and Social Reform in 19th Century Gujarati Society'. *Economic and Political Weekly* 32 (1/2): 46–52.

Tusan, Michelle Elizabeth. 2003. 'Writing *Stri Dharma*: International Feminism, Nationalist Politics, and Women's Press Advocacy in Late Colonial India'. *Women's History Review* 12 (4): 623–649.

Vasantha Lakshmi, V. 1987. 'Women's Magazines'. In *Journalism in Andhra Pradesh: A Brief Survey*, ed. G. Krishna, et al. Hyderabad: Hyderabad Union of Journalists.

Venkataramaiah, A. 1995. 'Duvvuri Subbamma, 1887-1964', *PAPHC*.

Venkateswara Rao, G. 1995. 'Social Movements in Nellore District (A. P.)'. *PAPHC*.

Vindhya, U. 1998. 'Comrades in Arms: Sexuality and Identity in the Contemporary Revolutionary Movement in Andhra Pradesh and the Legacy of Chalam'. In *A Question of Silence*, ed. Mary John and Janaki Nair. New Delhi: Kali for Women.

———. 2000. 'Of Autonomy and Desire: The Legacy of Chalam's Writings'. *Indian Journal of Gender Studies* 7 (1): 17–31.

Wolf, Gita. 1991. 'Construction of Gender Identity: Women in Popular Tamil magazines'. *Economic and Political Weekly* 26 (43): WS71–WS73.

3. Books (Telugu):

Andhra Mahila Samajam. 1972. *Andhra Mahila Samajam, Barampuram (Ganjam), Vajrotsava Sanchika—72 (Diamond Jubilee Souvenir of Andhra Mahila Samajam, Barampuram)*. Brahmapuram: Andhra Mahila Samajam.

Appa Row, M. R. 1966. *Brahma Rishi Venkata Ratnam Naidu*. Hyderabad: Department of Cultural Affairs, Government of Andhra Pradesh.

Anandabhaskar, Rapolu. 1988. *Journalism Charitra-Vyavastha*. Hyderabad: Udyama Publications.

Bangorey, ed. 1973. *Brown Jabulu: Telugu Journalism Charitra*. Nellore.

Bhanumati, Sanka. 1966. *Kanuparti Varalakshmamma (1896–1996)*, centenary volume. Hyderabad.

Bomma Reddi, V. R. 2002. *Communist Patrikalu: Charitra—Vikasam*. Vijayawada: published by Visweswara Rao.

Brown, C. P. 2003 [1829]. *Verses of Vemana in the Telugu Original with English Version*. New Delhi and Chennai: Asian Educational Services.

Chaya Devi, Abburi. 2002. *20va Shatabdamlo Telugu Rachayitrula Rachanalu*, compiled edition. New Delhi: Sahitya Akademi.

Devadanam Raju, Datla. 2007. *Yanam Charitra*. Yanam: Shirisha Prachuranalu.

Janakibala, Indraganti. 2009. *'Margadarsi' Durgabai Deshmukh (1909–1981)*. Hyderabad: C. P. Brown Academy.

Jitendra Babu, K., ed. 2007. *Telanganalo Chaitanyam Ragilinchina Nizam Rashtrandhra Mahasabhalu*, 2 vols. Munagala: Sahiti Sadan Prachuranalu.

Kameswara Rao, Tekumalla. 1996. *Naa Vaangmaya Mitrulu: Aadhunika Andhra Rachayitala Jeevita Charitralu, Rekha Chitralu*. Hyderabad: Vishalandhra Publishing House.

Kannabiran, Kalpana, et al. 1995. *Sarihaddululeni Sandhyalu—Feminist Rajakeeyalu, Karyacharana, Prashnalu*. Hyderabad: Swecha Prachuranalu.

Kotishwaramma, V. 1999. *Bharata Desham—Mahila Udyamam*. Vijayawada.

_____. 2001. *Bharata Swatantra Samaram—Andhra Mahilala Mahojvala Patra*. Vijayawada.

Krishnakumari, Davuluri. 2011. *Stree Dipika: Vaangmaya Vyasa Sankalanam*. Vijayanagaram: N. K. Publications.

Krishnanandam, T. S. 1976. *Lakshmi Raghuram Jeevana Sravanti*. Hyderabad: Sanghamitra Publications.

Krishna Rao, Vasireddy. 1989. *Mahilabhyudayodyama Vangmaya Parichayam*. Hanmakonda: Charan Publications.

Lakshmana Reddy, V. 1985. *Telugu Journalism: Avatarana—Vikasam*. Vijayawada: Gopichand Publications.

Lakshmikantamma, Utukuri. n. d. *Andhra Kavayitrulu*, other details, n. a.

Lakshmikantam Shreshthi, P. 2001. *Mahasamskarta Shri Aatmuri Lakshminarasimha Somayaji Jeevita Charitra*. Machilipatnam: Shri Aatmuri Lakshminarasimha Somayaji Vaishya Samajam.

Lakshminarayana, Penugonda, ed. 2013. *Gunturu Kathalu*. Guntur: Andhra Pradesh Abhyudaya Rachayitala Sangham, Guntur District Unit.

Lalita, Vakulabharanam and Vakulabharanam Ramakrishna. 2010. *Durgabai Deshmukh*. New Delhi: National Book Trust.

Nithyananda Rao, Veludanda. 1987. *Viswavidyalayallo Telugu Parisodhana*. Hyderabad.

Olga, et al. 2007. *Saamaanyula Saahasam: Andhradesha Charitra Nirmanamlo Streelu*. Hyderabad: Asmita Resource Centre for Women.

Padamavati, Dantu. 1989. *Aspashta Pratibimbalu: Telugulo Streela Patrikalu—Oka Parisheelana* (1883–1947). Self-published.

Pattabhi Rama Rao, P., ed. 2000. *Stree Vimukti Udyamam: Nadu-Nedu-Repu*. Hyderabad: Andhra Pradesh Mahila Samakhya.

Prabhavati, Vasa. 2003. *Bharata Swatantryodyamamlo Telugu Mahilala Paatra*. Hyderabad: Vasa Prachuranalu.

Purushottam, Boddupalli, et. al. 1997. *Doctor Lakshmi Kantamma Samsmruti*. Bapatla: Smaraka Samiti Prachurana.

Purushottam, Kalidasu. 2007. *Englishu Journalisamlo Toli Telugu Velugu Dampuru Narasaiah*. Nellore: Society for Social Change.

Radhakrishna, Budaraju. 2004. *Komarraju Venkata Lakshmana Rao*. New Delhi: Sahitya Akademi.

Raja Gopala Rao, C. V. 2004. *Andhra Patrika Charitra*. Hyderabad: Andhra Pradesh Press Academy.

Rajani, N. 2007. *Tolitaram Telugu Katha Rachayitalu: Stree Samasyala Chitrana*. Hyderabad.

Rajyalakshmi, Polapragada. 2000. *Kanuparti Varalakshmamma*. New Delhi: Sahitya Akademi.

Ramachandra, Tirumala. 1975. *Marapuraani Maneeshi: Maneeshi Vatamsula Lekhini Chitralu*. Secunderabad: Yuvabharati Sahiti Samskrutika Samstha.

———. 1992 [1989]. *Telugu Patrikala Sahitya Seva*. Hyderabad: Vishalandhra Publishing House.

Ramakrishna, Vakulabharanam and Vakulabharanam Lalitha. 2010. *Brahmarshi Raghupathi Venkataratnam Naidu*. Hyderabad: Emesco Books.

Ramakrishna, Vakulabharanam. 2008a. *Kandukuri Veeresalingam*. New Delhi: National Book Trust.

———. 2008b. *Charitra, Samskruti: Vyasavali*. Hyderabad: Vishalandhra Publishing House.

Ramalakshmi, Arudra. 1987. *Durgabai Deshmukh*. New Delhi and Hyderabad: National Book Trust and Telugu Academy.

Ramalakshmi, K. 2009. *Mahilasphoorti: Durgabai*. Hyderabad: Stree Shakti Prachuranalu.

Ramana, K. S. 1987. *Chalam Musings—Vimarshanatmaka Parisheelana*. Hyderabad: Shreevalli Publications.

Ramana Reddy, K. V. 2012 [1969]. *Mahodayam: Jaatiya Punarujjivanamlo Gurajada Sthanam*. Vijayawada: K. V. R. Sharadamba Smaraka Committee.

Ramanuja Rao, Devulapalli. 2003 [1991]. *Telugu Seemalo Samskrutika Punarujjeevanamu*. Hyderabad: Vishalandhra Publishing House.

Ramanuja Rao, Devulapalli, et al., ed. 1983. *Telugulo Parishodhana: Sameeksha Vyasa Sankalanam*. Hyderabad: Andhra Pradesh Sahitya Academy.

Ramanuja Rao, Devulapalli, comp. 1976. *Telugu Vytalikulu: Upanyasala Samputamu*, vol. 1. Hyderabad: Andhra Pradesh Sahitya Academy.

——. 1977. *Telugu Vytalikulu: Upanyasala Samputamu*, vol. 2. Hyderabad: Andhra Pradesh Sahitya Academy.

Ramapati Rao, Akkiraju, 1978. *Komarraju Venkata Lakshmana Rao*. Vijayawada: Vishalandhra Publishing House.

——. 1972. *Vireshalingam Pantulu: Samagra Parishilana*. Hyderabad: self-published.

——. ed. 1986. *Vireshalingam Rachanalu: Upanyasalu, Vyasalu, Jivita Charitralu*, vol. 5. Hyderabad: Vishalandhra Publishing House.

——. ed. 1993 [1985]. *Vireshalingam Rachanalu: Navalalu*, vol. 3. Hyderabad: Vishalandhra Publishing House.

Ramarao, Chekuri. 2001. *Sahitya Mahilavaranam: Vyasala Sankalanam*. Hyderabad: Swechcha Prachuranalu.

Ranganathacharyulu, K. K. 2008. *Tolinati Telugu Kathanikalu–Modatinunchi 1930 varaku: Telugu Kathanikala Parisheelana*. Hyderabad: Dr. Madabhooshi Rangacharya Smaraka Sangham.

——. ed. 1984. *Noorella Telugunadu*. Hyderabad: Andhra Saraswata Parishattu.

Rao, Bhargavi. 2000. *Noorella Panta: Rachayitrula Katha Sankalanam*. Bengaluru: Prism Books Pvt. Ltd.

Ravi Krishna, Modugula, ed. 2014. *Swaabhimaana Pratheeka Vidyaasundhari Bengulooru Nagaratnamma Jeevitham, Konni Rachanalu*. Guntur: Samskruthi.

Saraswati Devi, Illindala. 1975. *Bharata Nari: Nadoo–Nedoo*. Secunderabad: Yuvabharathi.

Satyavati, Kondaveeti. 2012. *Bhandaru Atchamamba Sachcharitra*. Hyderabad: Hyderabad Book Trust.

Sheshagiri Rao, Andra. 1995. *Andhra Vidusheemanulu*. Visakhapatnam: self-published.

Shyamala, Gogu, ed. 2003. *Nallapoddu—Dalitha Streela Sahityam, 1921–2002*. Hyderabad: Hyderabad Book Trust.

Sita Devi, Neti. 1997. *Durgabai Deshmukh*. Hyderabad: Andhra Mahila Sabha.

Sridevi, S. 1967. *Stree Vidya: Konni Amshamula Parisheelanamu*. Hyderabad: Government of Andhra Pradesh.

Srikanth, Subbaiah V., et al., ed. 1972. *Kaviraju Smaraka Sanchika*. Madras: Kaviraju Vardhanti Utsava Committee.

Srimati Sarojini Naidu Jeevita Charitra. 1952. Madras: V. Ramaswamy Sastrulu & Sons, Vavilla Press.

Srinivasa Murthy G. Bala. 2004. *Telangana Patrikalu*. Hyderabad: Rachana Journalism Kalashala.

Srinivas, Sangisetti. 2003. *Shabnavees: Telangana Patrikaranga Charitra (1886–1956)*. Hyderabad: Kavile Telangana Research and Referral Centre.

Sriramamurthy, Koduri, et al. 2009. *Telugu Kathanika, 1925–1980: Parisheelana*. Hyderabad: Dr. Madabhooshi Rangacharya Smaraka Sangham.

Subbamma, Malladi. 1992. *Swatantranantara Streela Chaitanyam–Bhavisyaddarshanam*. Hyderabad: Stree Vimochana Shikshana Kendram.

____. 1993. *Streelu, Sahityam, Samskarana Viplavam*. Hyderabad: Stree Vimochana Shikshana Kendram.

Subbaramaiah, Muvvala. 2015. *Telugu Prachurana Rangam*. Vijayawada: Jayanthi Publications.

Sujata Reddy, Mudiganti, comp. 2002. *Telangana Tolitaram Kathalu*. Hyderabad: Rohanam Publications.

Sumitra Devi, G. 1998. *Grihalakshmi Swarnakankana Grahitalaina Kavayitrulu—Vari Kavyalu*. Hyderabad.

Sundaram, K. 2005 [1982]. *Aadhunika Andhradesha Charitra*. Hyderabad: Andhra Pradesh State Archives.

Suryakumari, Pakanati. 2006. *Kalaprapurna Utukuri Lakshmikantamma Jeevitam—Sahityam*. Guntur: self-published.

Varadachari, G. S., et al., ed. 2011. *Mana Patrikeya Velugulu: Telugu Patrikaranga Vytalikulu, Kirtisheshulu, Pramukhulu*. Hyderabad: Veteran Journalists' Association.

Varalakshmamma, Kanuparti. 1963. *Unnava Dampatulu*. Vijayawada: Sri Goda Grandhamala.

Veerabhadra Rao, Madala. 2005 [1982]. *Andhrodyama Charitra*. Hyderabad: Andhra Pradesh State Archives.

Velugu Sahiti Samskrutika Samstha. 1992. *Noorella Kanyasulkam (1892–1992)*. Vizianagaram.

Venkata Krishna Sastri, Devulapalli, Telikicherla Venkata Ratnam and Aavula Sambasiva Rao, ed. n. d. *Yugapurushudu Veeresalingam*. Hyderabad: Shri Kandukuri Veeresalingam Smarakotsavamula Sangham.

Venkatarangaiah, Mamidipudi and N. Innaiah. 1972. *Andhralo Swatantrya Samaramu*. Hyderabad: Samskrutika Vyavaharika Shakha, Andhra Pradesh Prabhutvamu.

Venkata Rao, Bodepudi, ed. n. d. *Srimati Tripuraneni Sadhuvamma Shashtipoorti Sammana Sanchika*. Sattenapalli: Sadhuvamma Shashtipoorti Sammana Sanghamu.

Venkata Rao, Nidudavolu. 1977 [1954]. *Andhra Vachana Vangmayamu*. Hyderabad: N. S. Sundareshwara Rao.

Venkateswara Rao, Potturi. 2003 [2000]. *Naati Patrikala Meti Viluvalu*. Hyderabad: Rachana Journalism Kalashala.

____. 2004. *Andhra Jaati Akshara Sampada: Telugu Patrikalu*. Hyderabad: Andhra Pradesh Press Academy.

Venugopal, Nagasuri and Samala Ramesh Babu, ed. 2014. *Cheragani Sphoorthi Taapi Dharmarao: Vishleshanala Samaharam*. Vijayawada: Tapi Dharmarao Vedika.

Vidmahe, Katyayani, comp. 2009. *Telugunata Mahilala Udyamam: Vimarshanatmaka Anchana*. New Delhi: Sahitya Akademi.

Vidmahe, Katyayani, ed. 2003. *20va Shatabdi Rajakeeyardhika Parinamalu: Telugulo Streela Sahityam*. Warangal: University Arts and Science College, Kakatiya University.

———. 1998. *Sampradaya Sahityam–Streevada Drukpatham*. Warangal: Stree Janabhyudaya Adhyayana Samstha.

Vidyarani, Ankaraju and Muktevi Bharati. n. d. *Yallapragada Sitakumari Jeevita Visheshalu*. Hyderabad: Kotamraju Shashibala and Yallapragada Ashokavardhan.

Vijayalakshmi, Kanuparti. 1991. *Bramha Samaja Sahityam: Oka Parisheelana*. Mandapeta: Sidhdhartha Publications.

Virachari, V. 1993. *Telugunata Samskrutika Punarujjivanodyamalu: Kavulu–Rachayitalu*. Kashipur, Mahboob Nagar district, Andhra Pradesh: Jana Jivana Prachuranalu.

Viraiah, Daruvuri and Bandlamudi Subba Rao. 1987. *Aacharya Ranga: 88va Janmadina Pratyeka Sanchika*. Guntur: Kisan Publications.

Viraiah, Daruvuri. 1992. *Bharata Mata Muddu Bidda Bharatidevi Ranga*. Guntur: Kisan Publications.

Vishweshwara Rao, Namala. 2003. *Telugu Journalism Charitra*, 2 vols. Hyderabad: Progressive Communications.

Volga, et al. 2001. *Mahilavaranam*. Secundarabad: Asmita Resource Centre for Women.

4. Articles and Book Chapters (Telugu)

Brahmaiah Shastri, Kashibhatta. 1920. 'Puratanandhra Varta Patrikalu'. *Andhra Patrika* (annual issue), 12 May.

Chayadevi, Abburi. 2011. 'Swatantryodyama Kalamlo Streela Samasyalu, Sahityam'. *Streevada Patrika Bhumika*, August.

Kalpana, Rentala. 2003–2004. '"Nishshabdam" py Yuddhaniki Nalugu Konalu'. *Streevada Patrika Bhumika*, November–February.

Mahaboob Basha, S. 2008. 'Valasandhralo Streela Sanghalu: Vivadaspada 'Shri Vidyarthini Samaja Katha'. *Veekshanam* (January, February, March, April and May issues). Hyderabad.

———. 2013a. '"Achcha" myna Maro Rendu Toli Kathalu'. *Andhra Jyothy*, 19 August.

———. 2013b. 'Labhyamyna Bhandaru Atchamamba "Toli" Kathalu'. *Streevada Patrika Bhumika* 9 (12, October).

———. 2013c. 'Bhandaru Atchamamba Katha Vastuvulu: Charitraka Sandarbham'. *Prajasahiti* 37 (4), November.

———. 2013d. 'Andhralo Toli Mahila Samajam'. *Veekshanam* 11 (12, December).

Malati, Nidadavolu. 2004. 'Aanati Streela Rachanalu'. *Andhra Jyothy*, 20 September.

Nalini Reddy, D. 1991. 'Telangana Rachayitrulu'. In *Hyderabadu—Nalugu Shatabdala Sahitya Viksam*, ed. S. V. Rama Rao. Hyderabad: Telugu Academy.

Nirmala, Kondepudi. 2003–2004. 'Streela Sampadakiyamlo Nadichina Patrikalu, Labhinchina Vivaralu'. *Streevada Patrika Bhumika*, November–February.

Padmavati, Dantu. 1998. 'Telugulo Streela Patrikalu-Samskartala Drukpatham (1883–1920)'. Anakapalle: *PAPHC*.

Radhakrishna Rao, Kommana. 2002. 'Sharada Lekhalu'. In *Shata Vasanta Sahiti Manjiralu*, ed. Prayaga Vedavati and Nagasuri Venugopal. Vijayawada: Andhra Pradesh Grandhalaya Sangham.

Raju, K. 1996. 'Sripada Subrahmanya Shastri Sahityam—Streela Samasyalu'. *PAPHC*.

Ramadevi, M. 1988. 'Sangha Samskaranodyamamu—Gunturu Sri Sharada Niketamu'. *PAPHC*.

Ramakrishna, V. 1992. 'Kanyashulkamlo Samskarana Bhavalu'. In *Noorella Kanyashulkam (1892–1992)*, special edition. Vijayanagaram: Velugu.

Ramakrishna, Vakulabharanam. 2002. 'Nenoo–Naa Desham'. In *Shata Vasanta Sahiti Manjiralu*, ed. Prayaga Vedavati and Nagasuri Venugopal. Vijayawada: Andhra Pradesh Grandhalaya Sangham.

Satyavati, Kondaveeti. 2003–2004. 'Toli Telugu Katha Rachayitri Bhandaru Atchamamba'. *Streevada Patrika Bhumika*, November–February.

Satyavati, Vemula. 2008. 'Durgabai Deshmukh'. *Streevada Patrika Bhumika*, April.

Shivaramakrishna Rao, Kodali. 1926. 'Andhra Varta Patrikalu: Andhra Deshamunaku Galiginchina Yabhivruddhi'. *Andhra Patrika*, 15 March.

Srinivasa Rao, Mylavarapu. 2002. 'Vara Vikrayamu'. In *Shata Vasanta Sahiti Manjiralu*, ed. Prayaga Vedavati and Nagasuri Venugopal. Vijayawada: Andhra Pradesh Grandhalaya Sangham.

Sundar, K. H. S. S. 1993. '19va Shatabdapu Dakshina Bharata Patrika Rangam: Andhrula Seva'. *Itihas* 19 (2, January–December).

Venkateshwarulu, Varanasi. n. d. 'Tarikonda Venkamamba'. In *Andhra Ratnamulu*. Narasarao Peta: Bhavani Book Publishers.

Vidmahe, Katyayani. 1995. 'Pitruswamya Mayajalampy Samaram'. *India Today* (annual literary issue).

———. 2003–2004. 'Streela Upanyasalu'. *Streevada Patrika Bhumika*, Novermber–February.

Vidmahe, Katyayani and Tota Jyothirani. 2009. 'Streela Sweeya Charitralu—Laingika Rajakeeyalu'. *Chinuku, 4va Vaarshika Pratyeka Sanchika*, April.

Vidmahe, Katyayani and Kandala Shobharani. 2008. 'Swatantryaniki Poorvam Telugu Kavayitrulu'. *Streevada Patrika Bhumika*, July.

Yakaiah, N. 2011. 'Telugu Patrika Rangamlo Streelu'. *Veekshanam*, June.

5. Unpublished MPhil/PhD Dissertations

Anandhi, S. 1992. 'Middle Class Women in Colonial Tamilnadu, 1920–1947: Gender Relations and the Problem of Consciousness'. PhD thesis submitted to Jawaharlal Nehru University, New Delhi.

Hari Krishna, S. 1991. 'Contribution of Telugu Journalism to Social Reform in Andhra, 1874–1920'. MPhil dissertation submitted to the University of Hyderabad.

Inna Reddy, S. 1992. 'Social Reform Trends in Andhra'. MPhil dissertation submitted to the University of Hyderabad.

———. 1998. 'Social Reform Movements in Andhra (1920–1947)'. PhD thesis submitted to the University of Hyderabad.

Mahaboob Basha, S. 2002. 'Perspectives on Women's Liberation in Colonial Andhra: A Study of the Women's Journal *Gruhalakshmi*, 1928–1942'. MPhil dissertation submitted to Jawaharlal Nehru University, New Delhi.

Manjulatha Devi, T. V. 1980. 'Educational Progress of Rayalaseema with special Reference to Cuddapah District, 1858–1920'. MPhil dissertation submitted to Sri Venkateswara University, Tirupati.

———. 1994. 'History of the Growth of Education in Rayalaseema, 1920–1950'. PhD thesis submitted to Sri Venkateswara University, Tirupati.

Sambasiva Reddy, G. 2002. 'Growth of Press and Nationalism under the British Raj (Cuddapah District)'. PhD thesis submitted to Sri Venkateswara University, Tirupati.

Somashekhar, G. 1993. 'The Role of Telugu Press in the Indian Freedom Movement'. PhD thesis submitted to Sri Venkateswara University, Tirupati.

Sudarshan Reddy, G. 1986. 'Caste Associations and Social Change in Andhra, 1900–1925'. MPhil dissertation submitted to Osmania University, Hyderabad.

Sundar, K. H. S. S. 1994. 'Origins and Growth of Political Consciousness in Andhra during the Nineteenth Century'. PhD thesis submitted to the University of Hyderabad.

Sunitareddy, Busireddy. 1989. 'Education of Women in Colonial Andhra, 1857–1947'. MPhil dissertation submitted to the University of Hyderabad, 1989.

Index